Criminology

Criminology: Explaining Crime and Its Context, Ninth Edition, is a highly acclaimed textbook offering a broad perspective on criminological theory. It provides students of criminology and sociology with a thorough exposure to a range of theories, contrasting their logic and assumptions, but also highlighting efforts to integrate and blend these frameworks. In this ninth edition, the authors have incorporated new directions that have gained traction in the field, while remaining faithful to their criminological heritage.

Several key notions are woven throughout, drawing connections between theoretical perspectives and offering concrete examples and discussing the policy implications of theory. Students are immersed in the substance of each theory or perspective, and given practical examples to help them grasp the importance of theory in responding to crime and deviance. Among the themes in this work are the relativity of crime (its changing definition) with abundant examples, historical roots of criminology and the lessons they have provided, and the strength and challenges of applying the scientific method. The authors do not shy away from the controversies surrounding each theoretical perspective as they present its strengths. This revision offers enhanced coverage of biosocial theories of crime, more global examples, and a new chapter on youth violence, improving on the most comprehensive and balanced theory text available for undergraduates.

Stephen E. Brown is a Professor of Criminology and Criminal Justice, and Department Head at Western Carolina University. He received his Ph.D. in Criminal Justice and Criminology from the University of Maryland in 1979. He went through the professorial ranks at East Tennessee State University, serving as Department Chair for 11 years, and left as Professor Emeritus in 2008. Brown has published articles in a number of journals, including *Criminology, Journal of Criminal Justice, Journal of Criminal Justice Education, Criminal Justice Review, Youth and Society,* and *Social Science Quarterly.* His areas of research interest have been broad, covering topics such as family violence, deterrence, delinquency, and application of statistics within criminology. He has served as a Trustee on the board of the Academy of Criminal Justice Sciences, and as editor of the American Society of Criminology's *The Criminologist.* He is currently working with several colleagues in assessing pedagogical challenges in teaching social science statistics.

Finn-Aage Esbensen is E. Desmond Lee Professor of Youth Crime and Violence, and Chairperson of the Department of Criminology and Criminal Justice at the University of Missouri, St. Louis. His previous faculty positions were at Western Carolina University (1982–86) and the University of Nebraska at Omaha (1992–2001). In addition to these academic appointments, he has held research positions at the following institutions: the Center for Criminal Justice at Harvard Law School (1974); Catholic University (1976–7); the Behavioral Research Institute, Boulder, Colorado (1980–1); and the Institute of Behavioral Science, University of Colorado (1987–92). He received his BA and MA from Tufts University and his Ph.D. from the University of Colorado. He is the author of more than 100 articles and chapters examining, among other topics, youth gangs and violence, methodological issues, and victimization. He is a Fellow of the American Society of Criminology (2014) and the Western Society of Criminology (2002). He is also the recipient of the Gerhard O.W. Mueller Award from the Academy of Criminal Justice Sciences and the Paul Tappan and President's Awards from the Western Society of Criminology. From 1998 through 2001, he served as Editor of *Justice Quarterly*.

Gilbert Geis, Professor Emeritus in the Department of Criminology, Law, and Society at the University of California, Irvine, died November 10, 2012, at age 87. Geis received his doctorate at the University of Wisconsin, Madison, and was a faculty member at the University of Oklahoma and California State University, Los Angeles, before joining the University of California, Irvine faculty in 1971, where he played a significant role in establishing the School of Social Ecology and the Department of Criminology, Law, and Society. Geis had the honor of being a member of Lyndon Johnson's President's Commission on Crime, and was a former president of the American Society of Criminology and recipient of its Edwin H. Sutherland Award for outstanding research. He was the recipient of awards by the Association of Certified Fraud Examiners, the Western Society of Criminology, the American Justice Institute, and the National Organization for Victim Assistance. The National White-Collar Crime Research Consortium named its distinguished scholar award in his honor. Geis was a giant in criminology research and education with more than 500 articles and book chapters and 28 books to his name.

Titles of Related Interest from Routledge and Anderson

Victimology, 7th Edition
William G. Doerner and Steven P. Lab

Criminological Theory: Assessing Philosophical Assumptions
Anthony Walsh

Understanding White-Collar Crime: An Opportunity Perspective, 2nd Edition
Michael L. Benson and Sally S. Simpson

Organized Crime: From the Mob to Transnational Organized Crime, 7th Edition
Jay S. Albanese

Biker Gangs and Transnational Organized Crime, 2nd Edition
Thomas Barker

Crime, Violence, and Global Warming
John P. Crank and Linda S. Jacoby

Marital Separation and Lethal Domestic Violence
Desmond Ellis, Noreen Stuckless, and Carrie Smith

Family Violence and Criminal Justice: A Life-course Approach, 3rd Edition
Brian P. Payne and Randy R. Gainey

Youth Justice: Ideas, Policy, Practice, 3rd Edition
Roger Smith

Offending Girls: Young Women and Youth Justice
Gilly Sharpe

Corporate Crime Under Attack: The Fight to Criminalize Business Violence, 2nd Edition
Francis T. Cullen, Gray Cavender, William J. Maakestad, and Michael L. Benson

Criminology Theory: Selected Classic Readings, 2nd Edition
Frank P. Williams III and Marilyn D. McShane

The Psychology of Criminal Conduct, 5th Edition
D.A. Andrews and James Bonta

Criminology

Explaining Crime and Its Context

Ninth Edition

Stephen E. Brown
Finn-Aage Esbensen
Gilbert Geis

Routledge
Taylor & Francis Group

NEW YORK AND LONDON

First published 2015
by Routledge
711 Third Avenue, New York, NY 10017

and by Routledge
2 Park Square, Milton Park, Abingdon, Oxon, OX14 4RN

Routledge is an imprint of the Taylor & Francis Group, an informa business

Library of Congress Cataloging-in-Publication Data
Brown, Stephen Eugene
  Criminology : explaining crime and its context / by Stephen Brown,
Finn-Aage Esbensen, Gilbert Geis. — Ninth edition.
    pages cm
  Includes bibliographical references and index.
  1. Criminology.   I. Esbensen, Finn-Aage.   II. Geis, Gilbert.   III. Title.
  HV6025.B76 2015
  364—dc23
  2014049568

ISBN: 978-1-138-91559-6 (hbk)
ISBN: 978-0-323-35648-0 (pbk)
ISBN: 978-0-323-35739-5 (ebk)

Typeset in Giovanni, Stone Sans, and Helvetica
by Apex CoVantage, LLC

Printed and bound in the United States of America by Sheridan Books, Inc. (a Sheridan Group Company).

In memory of our mentor and friend, Gil Geis

Contents

CHAPTER 7   **Social Structure Theories of Crime**   **257**

CHAPTER 8   **Social Process Theories of Crime**   **299**

CHAPTER 9   Social Reaction Theories of Crime   353

CHAPTER 14   Youth Violence   549

Preface

At the core of criminology lies the challenge of explaining crime and deviance. Theory is the staple that should shape all criminological inquiry and thinking, and has guided this text from its inception. In fact, its origins lie in our early career frustration with the scarcity of criminology texts that focused both on theoretical foundations and presented them in a fashion palatable to undergraduates. It was the desire to fill that void that originally set this text project in motion in the mid-1980s. While a plethora of texts has since emerged examining criminology from a narrower theoretical framework and others offering broad but superficial coverage, we have continued to focus on in-depth presentation of a wide range of theoretical perspectives.

Particularly rewarding has been witnessing the evolution of criminological theory to the diverse and integrated range at the criminological forefront in 2015. The advancement in criminological theory that has unfolded across the life of nine editions of this work is simply remarkable. In this vein, the ninth edition is thoroughly updated to reflect ongoing developments. It is our goal to prepare students to expect continuing theoretical evolution and to equip them with the analytical tools to understand and appreciate those shifts.

ORGANIZING THEMES OF THIS BOOK

Criminology: Explaining Crime and Its Context, ninth edition, is organized around the following premises. It is our belief that application of these themes will both help students to understand criminology and equip them to think like criminologists going forward.

⇒ **Theory provides the anchor for introducing criminology.**
   While six of 14 chapters comprise the heart of this book and are devoted exclusively to presenting theories of crime, the opening chapters offer a lens through which theories should be viewed by providing a paradigmatic framework and examining the tripartite relationship between crime, law, and criminal justice. The closing unit of the book then applies theory to

a wide range of criminal and delinquent behaviors. Completely new to this edition is Chapter 14, devoted to the topics of youth bullying, school violence, and gangs. Other new topics in the closing chapters include serial and mass murderers.

⇒ **Pruning theoretical perspectives to a "nutshell" undercuts that mission.**
While theory can be daunting to students, tempting us to seek simplification, we are convinced that "watered down" theory contributes little and may reinforce any negative predispositions. The approach of this text is to steer students gently through a detailed coverage of each, including the context in which ideas emerged, their critical concepts, relationship to other theories, and policy implications. We propose that the first thing a student of criminology must appreciate is the complexity of crime and deviance, followed by a careful examination of a myriad of theories.

⇒ **The theoretical foundation built for the student needs breadth as well as depth.**
A myriad of theories indeed. From its inception we have designed this text to expose students to a wide range of perspectives, pointing out both common ground and disagreements. This breadth, combined with the depth of theory coverage, results in a lengthy book. While some instructors will elect to skip certain chapters to allot more time to others, the theoretical menu is quite diverse.

⇒ **Linkage of theoretical positions should be more "and" than "or." That is, students should recognize that theories tend to be more complementary than competing.**
While Chapter 10 is specifically devoted to theoretical integration and life-course criminology, both connections and distinctions between theories are emphasized throughout. Addressing biosocial explanations of crime, Chapter 6 provides a particularly poignant exercise in contrasting the old "nature *or* nurture" debate with a contemporary "nature *and* nurture" framework. Crime typologies offered in the last unit also illustrate how different theories may fit various subtypes of offenders.

⇒ **Application of theories serves as a valuable tool for comprehension.**
Although all six theory-laden chapters are interlaced with applied examples and analogies, the final four specifically apply various theories to a wide range of offenses. An array of highlights, features, tables, and figures is liberally inserted throughout the chapters to assist in application. As with the breadth of this work, the need for these applied chapters and features will vary with the student audience, a calculation that instructors can make in the design of their course.

⇒ **Scrutinizing the social and historical contexts from which theoretical perspectives emanated enhances both understanding and application.**
Presentation of every theory includes discussion of its origins and, in some cases, ebb and flow of popularity. Highlighting such contexts will

equip students to assess more realistically the wide-ranging homage to scorn attributed to various perspectives across time and place. Discussion of the context of major paradigm shifts is an especially important part of this contextualization.

⇒ **The concept of relativity of crime provides a contextual pillar for the explanation of crime and deviance.**

A large portion of Chapter 2 introduces the concept of relativity of crime. Detailed application to illegal drugs, alcohol, rape, humor, and other lively topics assists in inculcating the concept. It is then often deployed in other chapters, particularly in review of crimes without victims and victims without crime in Chapter 13.

⇒ **Theories of crime are largely generated through application of the scientific method.**

The opening chapter discusses "criminology as science" and Chapters 3 and 4 delineate the crime data collection process within the realm of criminology. With this foundation in place, theory testing efforts are reviewed throughout.

⇒ **Cross-cultural examples broaden discussion of theoretical strength and application.**

We have been pleased at the number of intercontinental adoptions that this book has had, opening doors to a more international criminology. It has been translated into Korean, a country where both the Korean and English versions are used at numerous universities. It has a long history of use in Africa and Europe as well; yet the cross-cultural examples spread throughout are especially valuable for American students. The adage that we live in a shrinking world is especially applicable to understanding crime and its context. We hope that our efforts contribute both to better understanding and explaining crime and to global awareness.

Study Aids Incorporated

Each chapter includes the following features to guide study. Instructors may choose to guide students in their use of these, depending upon course goals and testing format.

→ Broad learning objectives are offered at the beginning of each chapter.

LEARNING OBJECTIVES

After reading Chapter 1, you should be able to:

■ Discuss criteria for assessing the harmfulness of crime.

■ Develop a definition of criminology that reflects major issues within the field.

■ Explain ideology as it relates to the field of criminology.

■ Contrast competing definitions of crime.

■ Outline and compare five different paradigms within criminology.

■ Discuss the meaning and controversies surrounding criminology and policy.

■ Critically assess the role of the media in understanding the causes of crime.

→ Key terms and concepts are identified in bold colored print and listed
at the end of each chapter.

KEY TERMS AND CONCEPTS	
Assault and BatteryBattered-Child Syndrome	Manslaughter
	Mass Murderers
Battered Women	Money Laundering
Collective Efficacy	Premeditation
Cycle of Violence	Relative Deprivation
Extortion	Serial Killers
Felony-Murder	Street Code
Homicide	Subculture of Violence
Lifetime Murder Risk	Terrorism
Malice Aforethought	Victim Precipitation

→ Key criminologists are also listed at the end
of each chapter.

KEY CRIMINOLOGISTS	
John Braithwaite	Lyn Lofland
Mary Owen Cameron	Edwin H. Sutherland
Donald Cressey	Thorstein Veblen
Gilbert Geis	Richard T. Wright
John Lofland	

→ Practice discussion questions appear at
the end of each chapter.

DISCUSSION QUESTIONS

1. Identify key assumptions underlying strain, control, and learning theories.
2. List and describe the three factors necessary for establishing causality.
3. What are the benefits of policies that are based upon the criminal career paradigm? What are some barriers to effectively implementing policies that are based upon the criminal career paradigm?
4. How does the population heterogeneity perspective explain stability in behavior? How does the state dependence perspective explain stability in antisocial behavior?
5. Moffitt and Sampson and Laub's theories are similar in many ways, but differ in other important ways. According to Moffitt and Sampson and Laub, what would be the origins of life-course offending? According to both theories, what process(es) would promote stability in antisocial behavior? According to both theories, is it likely that life-course–persistent offenders will desist from crime? What factors drive desistance in both theories?
6. How does Sampson and Laub's theory fit within the state dependence perspective? How does Moffitt's theory apply to the population heterogeneity perspective? How does Moffitt's theory apply to the state dependence perspective?
7. Following the life-course and developmental perspective, when might antisocial behavior emerge?
8. Identify key turning points discovered by developmental criminologists.

Ancillaries for Students and Instructors

The ninth edition of *Criminology: Explaining Crime and Its Context* is accompanied by the following resources to aid instructors in planning their course and
students in learning the material. Instructors can selectively use these ancillaries
to guide students in accordance with course goals and design.

- *Instructor's Lesson Plan*
  Each chapter comes with an instructor's lesson plan that contains key terms and concepts, critical thinking questions, class discussion points and a list of key criminologists mentioned throughout the chapter.
- *Chapter PowerPoint Slides*
  Each chapter comes with detailed PowerPoint slides to guide the instructor and students seamlessly through the chapter.
- *Instructor's Test Bank*
  Each chapter comes with an instructor's test bank that includes 15 multiple-choice questions and ten true/false questions.
- *Online Student Self-Assessment Questions*
  Each chapter come with five multiple-choice questions and five true/false questions students can access to gauge their comprehension of the material.
- *Online Student Flashcards*
  Each chapter comes with a complete set of online flashcards that contain the key terms and concepts and their definitions.

Acknowledgments

No textbook is ever completed without the support, guidance, and encouragement of many. Over the evolution of this work, we have benefited from critical and insightful discussions with many students and colleagues. Of note during preparation of the ninth edition, Kyle Burgason, Iowa State University, prepared the ancillaries. Stephen Hesselbirg and Sydney Hurt, both graduate assistants at WCU, lent valuable aid to literature review and manuscript preparation. The following colleagues at the University of Missouri, St. Louis, provided a variety of helpful comments and encouragement: Bob Bursik, Michael Campbell, Stephanie DiPietro, David Klinger, Janet Lauritsen, Rick Rosenfeld, Lee Slocum, T. J. Taylor, Stephanie Wiley, and Richard Wright. Thanks also to Saundra Trujillo, graduate assistant at UMSL, for her help.

Working with our editor, Ellen Boyne, has been most helpful for keeping us focused on the best directions to improve the ninth edition of this work. Likewise, Pamela Chester and Mickey Braswell, also part of the Anderson/Routledge team, have provided valuable direction in the project.

PART 1

Foundations for Criminology

The opening unit of this text provides a framework for studying criminology and a foundation for the units to follow. Criminology is an expansive interdisciplinary field. Nevertheless, there are some central notions that have shaped the evolution of the criminological enterprise, and these issues are examined in Chapters 1–4. By consensus, although not unanimity, contemporary criminology is the scientific study of crime and especially its causes. But across time, understanding of both crime and how it should be scrutinized have shifted dramatically. Those changes alone are critical; thus, a generous dose of history is incorporated in *Criminology: Explaining Crime and Its Context*. Indeed, one of the premises of this text is that appreciating history is paramount in understanding where we are and where we may go. Knowing the history of the discipline of criminology, as well as major societal shifts, gives us the "big picture" needed to "connect the dots" in attempting to understand the complexities of explaining crime.

The central thesis, or *raison d'etre*, for criminology is to explain why crime occurs, which is a process of theorizing. While many criminologists do more than develop and/or test theories of crime, it is those explanations that provide the foundation for all other criminological endeavors. Predicting criminality and policy development should logically be rooted in some explanatory framework. This text examines a number of frameworks for explaining crime and, therefore, is suggestive of many strategies for addressing it.

In defining crime and criminology, these initial chapters draw attention to the *relativity of crime*. What is considered a crime varies by time, place, and who is doing the defining. Examination of crime in the context of diverse cultures from around the world illustrates, perhaps most vividly, the importance of the concept of relativity in understanding crime and deviance. In that sense criminology is inherently cross-cultural. While the focus within the book is more on U.S. criminological thought, material from a range of cultures is included to bolster a broader understanding of crime, deviance, and social control. It turns out that the relativity of crime is a fruitful concept for understanding the continual redefinition of crime within our own cultures.

The impact of *ideology* on explanations of crime and on crime policy is another nagging problem for criminologists and a cornerstone of this book. A conscious effort has been made to highlight the role of ideology by presenting a wide range of explanations of crime rooted in five dominant paradigms, as well as emerging perspectives on crime. The intent is to offer a balanced perspective on the field of criminology. While many criminology texts are rooted in a single paradigm, theory, or ideological perspective, *Criminology: Explaining Crime and Its Context* represents a conscious effort to present an eclectic range of thought produced by many thoughtful criminologists. While space limitations (and the time constraints of what can be covered in an academic semester) prevent inclusion of the full array of criminological ideas, a quite sizable sampling of efforts that have garnered notable criminological respect follows.

As a largely scientific endeavor, criminology is heavily reliant upon measuring social concepts and collecting data on human behavior. Chapters in this opening unit describe some fundamental criminological tools for these tasks, as well as presenting descriptive data on crime and delinquency. A basic understanding of legal traditions, presented in this unit as well, will round out the toolbox for use in the remainder of the text. In sum, this unit provides a foundation in law and crime/delinquency measurement and an understanding of ideology, the relativity of crime, and paradigms that underlie theories explaining crime. The units to follow delve into the causes of crime and examine a number of crime types.

Crime and Criminology

LEARNING OBJECTIVES

After reading Chapter 1, you should be able to:

- Discuss criteria for assessing the harmfulness of crime.
- Develop a definition of criminology that reflects major issues within the field.
- Explain ideology as it relates to the field of criminology.
- Contrast competing definitions of crime.
- Outline and compare five different paradigms within criminology.
- Discuss the meaning and controversies surrounding criminology and policy.
- Critically assess the role of the media in understanding the causes of crime.

Crime and criminals capture the attention of nearly everyone. The public fascination with these matters has not escaped the news and entertainment media. From the tragic killing spree at Sandy Hook Elementary School in 2012; the bombing of the 2013 Boston marathon; the hundreds of billions of dollars lost to cybercrime annually; and on to the racially charged shooting of Michael Brown in Ferguson, Missouri, the curiosity is continuous. Sometimes people romanticize criminals so that outlaws like Robin Hood and Jesse James become folk heroes. Other criminals, or alleged offenders, are demonized and become outlets for anger, fear, and other emotions. In other scenarios, those claiming to be victims are vilified, or angry debate ensues over who is the "criminal" and who the victim.

At the heart of this fascination with crime-related issues lie some intriguing questions: Why do people commit these crimes? How should we respond? Why are some behaviors considered crimes and not others? We might exclaim about some outrageous but legally permissible act: "There oughta be a law!" While the public is intrigued, criminologists address these issues in a more systematic manner. One definition of a **criminologist** is "one who studies crime, criminals, and criminal behavior. One who attempts to determine the causes of crime" (Rush & Torres, 1998:52). But what is **crime** and how serious are different forms of it? Consider each of these brief scenarios, and rank-order them from most to least serious. After doing so, consider your rationale for the rank you gave each, and then compare your rankings to those of several classmates. Are they different? If so, how and why?

- George points a .38 caliber revolver at the cashier in a liquor store, and yells, "Put all the money in the bag!"
- Karen and Mary smoke marijuana a couple of evenings a week in their college dormitory room while listening to CDs. They laugh a lot.
- Executives hide the fact that their corporation is losing large sums of money. They pay themselves huge bonuses, while encouraging employees to invest more. Ultimately, the corporation declares bankruptcy, resulting in thousands of employees losing their jobs and retirement benefits.
- Two young men, aged 14 and 15, holding American citizenship and from families long subscribing to the Islamic faith, are detected participating in electronic communication with jihadists located in foreign countries. The FBI arrests them at a U.S. international airport where they are boarding a plane to a Middle Eastern country. There is clear evidence that their intent was to join the Islamic State of Iraq and Syria (ISIS).
- A group of automobile executives discusses a faulty brake system in one of their car models. They knew that the brake system could contribute to a number of accidents that could bring serious disabilities and loss of lives. They conclude that they will not recall the vehicles because it is more profitable not to do so, based on the number of lawsuits that their company can expect to lose versus the cost of the recall. Over the next year, 14 people die in crashes that are attributed to faulty brakes.
- "Snake" and "Slim" take great pride in their tough personas. They like to fight and feel this earns them respect or neighborhood "rep." They equally value degrading people whom they regard as different. In living out these psychological needs they frequently consume large volumes of alcohol and seek out young men whom they believe to be gay as targets for physical assaults. One Saturday night their savage beating of a college student, while screaming sexual orientation epithets, results in hospitalization of a young man with three cracked ribs, a broken nose, and multiple abrasions.
- Abby is a teenager with a two-year-old son. She lives with Manley, her 22-year-old boyfriend, who burns her son with cigarettes and urinates on the burned flesh. She has seen him do this several times, but has never

reported it to the authorities because, she says, she loves Manley. After the injuries were reported by a teacher, authorities had the boy examined by a physician who reported that several of the scars on his arms and legs were permanent, but that he was otherwise in good health.

- Jake is a third-year police officer. He has heard that a local gang member, Frederic "Big" Johnston, has raped several young girls in his neighborhood. There has never been physical evidence to support these rumors and no one living in the neighborhood has ever complained to police. Jake, however, feels that after three years of police work he has a good read of street toughs. He finds "Big" alone in an alley one night, gives him a severe beating with his nightstick, and expresses to him in extremely vulgar language what he plans to subject Big to if he hears more rumors of his sexual victimization of young girls.

- Dr. Hippocrates likes to buy a new Mercedes each year, and prefers to pay cash. When the new model appears on the market, he finds that he is short of cash. He tells the parents of each child brought to him that month with a sore throat that a tonsillectomy is necessary. He performs seven such operations at a charge of $4,500 each.

- Sharon is a 23-year-old in her second year as a high school science teacher. She begins meeting Jim, a 14-year old freshman, after school to have sex in her apartment.

- Jay is a 22-year-old college student who is quite savvy on the Internet. He spends a lot of time meeting high-school girls online and "sexting" with them. This leads to several rendezvous involving sexual activity with girls 13 to 16 years old.

- Coach Smith has led the football team of Valley Junior High to four championships. He routinely takes his players on picnics, to movies, and other wholesome bonding activities. One evening the janitor observes Coach Smith fondling one of his players in the shower.

Let's consider your ranking of the "seriousness" of the above scenarios. Which did you find most and least serious? Why? Which offenders should be sentenced to serve time in prison? Which should not? This exercise should raise a number of questions. First, in order to rank the seriousness of the behaviors, this term must be operationally defined. Most typically, crime or wrongdoing will be defined in terms of harm rendered. How do we determine what behaviors are most harmful? Comparing your views with those of others, you may find a lot of disagreement. Harm is a construct that often is in the eyes of the beholder. Rarely, however, is harmfulness the exclusive criterion for assessing misconduct. Other values are usually injected. For example, there are classes of people such as children, the elderly, and disabled, to whom extra protection is extended under the law. What groups from these scenarios arguably merit special or extended protection? Why?

Second, note that there is wide variation in how the criminal justice system would respond to the scenarios. Not all are crimes in all jurisdictions, nor will there be criminal justice intervention in all of the portrayed acts even where the behaviors are criminalized. Others on the list are likely to be aggressively pursued by the criminal justice system, but still may not be thought of by you as matters that should be the business of criminal law. In other words, you will likely conclude that these scenarios include examples of both excluded harms and overcriminalized behaviors. These scenarios represent both sides of the **relativity of crime** (or law), a major thesis in this book. Stated succinctly, all of us do not agree on what ought to be treated as crime and what should not. Our perceptions of wrongdoing will vary along lines of gender, religion, race, social class, sexual orientation, region of residence, and many other characteristics. Ultimately, however, moral assessments of behavior will shape our response, resulting in some being treated as crimes while other behaviors are not. The general public, special interest groups, and criminal justice personnel will have varying degrees of influence in this process of designating certain behaviors as criminal.

Third, offenses in the scenarios may reflect characteristics with which you or other students empathize. Conversely, others may seem to you obnoxious or revolting behaviors. Should all who bring harm to others be held equally accountable or should the offender's circumstances and characteristics be taken into account? Does it matter if the offender is rich or poor, healthy or unhealthy, or has led an easy or deprived life? That is, should we only consider the act (crime) or should we also consider characteristics of the offender in ranking seriousness? Table 1.1 summarizes some of the questions raised in assessing crime seriousness.

Dealing with the "crime" of a society is a trying task. On the one hand, an important philosophical question is whether the criminal law largely reflects the collective interests of members of society, what criminologists call a **consensus** model, or more the interests of the elite. Criminologists apply the **conflict** label to elite dominance. Either way, public opinion can play an important role. According to the consensus model, citizen values will inform the law, while the conflict model suggests manipulation of public opinion by politicians and the media. A concern among criminologists is that the complexity of the crime problem is often not appreciated by politicians, the media, or the general public. The gap between criminological research and public policy is explored later in this chapter.

TABLE 1.1 Common Criteria for Assessing Crime Seriousness	
Harm inflicted:	What is the objective level of harm caused by the behavior?
Status of victim:	Does the victim merit special protection by the law?
Moral judgments:	What and whose moral judgments will influence the criminalization of behaviors and activation of the criminal justice process?
Offender characteristics:	What is the role of the background and circumstances of offenders?

Who looks like a criminal to you?

CRIMINOLOGY AS SCIENCE

As illustrated in the preceding section, "crime" is a relative phenomenon, conveying different thoughts and meanings to different people. Thus, criminology is not a field readily reducible to a concise definition. A starting point, however, is Edwin Sutherland's classic delineation of the tripartite boundaries of **criminology** as "the study of the processes of making laws, breaking laws, and reacting towards the breaking of laws" (Sutherland & Cressey, 1974:3). Such a broad definition, however, has the disadvantage of being unmanageable in a single text. Studying reactions to *law breaking* is essentially what has emerged in recent decades as the realm of "criminal justice," and there is some debate regarding whether criminology and criminal justice are distinct. It appears, however, that the debate in some sense is being resolved in favor of Sutherland and Cressey's (1974) broader definition. In fact, "criminology is now most commonly housed in departments along with criminal justice . . . signaling that there is a difference between the two fields of study while, at the same time, recognizing their important connection" (Triplett & Turner, 2010: 27). But for the purposes of this text, the focus is on what Sutherland and Cressey (1974) identified as "breaking laws," but appreciating the link of this issue to both making laws and reacting to the breaking of laws. They are intricately intertwined, but the focus here is on explanations for the breaking of laws.

Two essential components of a science are its theoretical and its methodological branches. **Theory** represents an effort to explain or make sense of the world, thus revolving around the "why" of crime, criminalization, and similar concerns. **Methodology** refers to the techniques or methods that criminologists use as they attempt to determine the "whys" of crime (see Chapter 3). Theory and methods are integrally related in the **scientific method** of studying crime. Theories are developed to explain observed facts, while observations are undertaken to test theories. But some of those committed to a scientific criminology object to an "empirical scientism" that they believe has elevated methodology above theory, contributing to what they see as the demise of the criminological imagination (Williams, 1984). The coverage within this book of an array of recent efforts to explain crime suggests much vitality in terms of criminological theorizing. Despite dominance of the scientific view, some criminologists advocate a broader base including, for example, a humanistic approach to understanding crime. This more expansive conception of how to seek knowledge is championed within a critical criminology that focuses on how the power elite define crime to suit themselves. Defining criminology as the scientific study of the causes of crime, however, dominates the field and provides a fundamental reference point for this book.

IDEOLOGY AND CRIMINOLOGY

Ideology refers to a set of beliefs or values that all of us develop, usually unconsciously, about the way that the world is or ought to be. Ideologies reflect religious, political, social, and moral positions. The resulting views serve as guiding biases in all manner of social relations. An ideology ". . . serves the interests of one segment of a society more than all other segments . . ." (Curra, 2000:6). The benefits may accrue to one gender, a particular ethnic group, a certain religion, a political group, and so forth. It is within this larger framework shaping political and religious ideology that a bias regarding our view of crime and criminals emerges. It is not that ideology per se is a bad thing. To the contrary, it is vital, and inevitable, that we be bound by a set of beliefs. We should, however, strive to recognize what those values are. Moreover, we should be willing to carefully assess them, and, above all, strive to prevent replacement of rational thinking with ideological loyalties.

How is ideology formed?

CREDIT:
©iStockphoto.com/
Courtney Navey.

Political ideology may be conceptualized as falling on a continuum, ranging from left-wing (politically liberal) to right-wing (politically conservative). Each position on the continuum is associated with values that have dramatic implications for defining and responding to the crime problem. Current debate reflects relatively clear ideological lines regarding crime issues. Mark Ramirez (2013) equates the conservative or right-wing end of the ideological criminological continuum with "punitive criminal justice policies" designed to "punish, incapacitate or increase the transaction costs of crime" (332). At the other end of the ideological spread, liberals or left-wing actors favor "rehabilitation in prisons and drug treatment programs" (332). Table 1.2 contrasts a sampling of conservative and liberal views. For criminologists, the division is largely between various "control" (see Chapter 8) and deterrence (see Chapter 5) theories typically embraced on the right and social structure/support theories (see Chapter 7) preferred by those on the left. The broad strategy of the former is to seek ways to exert control over offenders, while the structuralist/support theorists identify ways to provide more adequate opportunities for those whose environments press them toward crime. As Frank Cullen and his colleagues (Cullen et al., 1999:189) explain it, the popularized control perspective "requires doing something to a person rather than for a person. Control theories thus can easily be tilted in a repressive direction." Conservatives, however, begin with the assumption that the offender is flawed or morally defective. They call for placing more people in prison for longer periods of time, while more liberal-leaning criminologists advocate enhancing social supports for those most at risk for delinquent or criminal behavior.

Religious views comprise another important part of this ideological underpinning, permeating many views regarding crime. Criminologists, however, have given scant attention to religion and religiosity in explaining crime. On the one hand, Frank Cullen (2012) argues that this could be due to pivotal work of Travis Hirschi (1969) and Hirschi and Rodney Stark (1969) failing to

TABLE 1.2 Conservative versus Progressive/Liberal Crime Ideology	
Conservative	**Progressive**
■ Advocate broad use of death penalty	■ Oppose use of death penalty
■ Favor low age of criminal responsibility for juveniles	■ Favor higher age of criminal responsibility for juveniles
■ Favor high levels of incarceration for drug users	■ Favor minimal levels of incarceration for drug users
■ Favor mandatory and minimum prison sentences for many crimes	■ Generally opposed to mandatory and minimum prison sentences
■ Favor long prison sentences for many types of crime and criminals	■ Favor reserving long prison sentences for selected crimes and criminals
■ Favor use of criminal laws to control vices	■ Generally oppose the use of criminal laws to control vices
■ Favor harsh prison conditions	■ Favor humane and comfortable prison conditions

find support for the religion–delinquency hypothesis and subsequent exclusion of religion from Hirschi's influential control theory (see Chapter 8). On the other hand, Cullen (2012) candidly depicts criminology as a staunchly secular humanist discipline with little ideological predisposition to entertain spiritual factors in the explanation of crime, while acknowledging that such inattention may have been premature.

Brian Johnson and Sung Joon Jang (2012) recently made an excellent argument that removing the ideological blinders preventing careful empirical scrutiny of crime and religion variables is overdue. They argue that on both the micro and macro levels, religion and religiosity variables hold strong potential to help explain crime, both directly and through a host of widely accepted theoretical frameworks reviewed in this text (e.g., learning theory, control theory, self-control, and strain theory). They observe that while Hirschi and Stark's (1969) "hellfire" study failed to unearth evidence that religion plays a significant role in preventing deviance, recent studies have been quite supportive. Cullen (2012: 154) agrees that the control premise of "the Hellfire approach got the research agenda on religion and crime off on the wrong foot."

Because bias, or close-mindedness, often permeates ideology, advocates of both conservative and liberal-based crime policies typically cling to a singular view. Ling Ren, Jihong Zhao, and Nicholas Lovrich (2006) contrasted the two ends of the ideological spectrum and went on to empirically assess the success of crime reduction programs rooted in both. To the chagrin of ideologues, they found that increased expenditure on police activity (consistent with conservative ideology) and on community development (congruent with liberal premises) both were associated with lower rates of violent crime. They recommended "that an effective public policy on crime control should combine the merits of both the conservative and the liberal perspectives on crime" (2006:28). Because ideological bias so permeates competing criminological paradigms, few are likely to heed their advice (Williams & Robinson, 2004). The stalemate in addressing the crime problem is much like that of Democrats, Republicans, and Tea Party Republicans in refusing to compromise in facing a plethora of other social, economic, and public safety issues. Ideological inflexibility results in lost opportunities to address many problems, including criminal behavior. Unfortunately, Walter Miller's (1973:142) assertion over four decades ago that "[I]deology is the permanent hidden agenda of criminal justice" continues to ring true.

For illustrative purposes, let us briefly examine a couple of ideological matters and their implications for understanding criminal behavior. Conceptualization of gender roles is an example of an ideological domain with which everyone must come to grips. How one does so will be heavily influenced by other ideological input such as religious indoctrination. Islamic fundamentalist states have restricted all manner of women's lives by criminalizing all but a narrow range of modes of dress, traversing public space without a male escort, or driving an automobile to name only a few. Taliban terrorists attempted to murder Malala Yousufzai, a 15-year-old Pakistani girl, for advocating female rights to a basic education. In the United States religious leaders subscribing to Christian fundamentalism and politicians parroting their positions call for recriminalization (Chapter 2 further examines this as an example of relativity of crime) of most or all forms of abortion as well as other matters falling within the realm of women's reproductive capacities. Likewise, Americans such as Eric Rodolph and Paul Hill carried out murders as part of their ideological campaigns to recriminalize abortion. As we see with all brands of terrorism, many mainstream figures sympathize with the causes of extremists and terrorists. In this instance, some fundamentalist Christians and conservative politicians deploy the same rhetoric as terrorists, labeling those who facilitate abortions as murderers, Nazis, and the like (Filipovic, 2013). This observation blends nicely with learning theories and particularly learning values that neutralize norms (these theories are reviewed in Chapter 8), thus enabling criminal behaviors.

Another belief directly tied to religious and other social indoctrination is how human nature is fundamentally regarded. Whether we view humankind as more selfish or altruistic will, in turn, render us more or less receptive to competing explanations for crime. This will become evident in our discussion of criminological paradigms later in this chapter. How we view human nature, along with other ideological biases, will greatly influence receptivity to various theories of crime. Shedding ideological blinders, supported by the research of Ren et al. (2006), opens the door to objective inquiry and evidence. As discussed in the last section, this is critical to the application of the scientific method that is at the heart of criminological research.

Ideological bias is socially constructed, particularly at a young age. Lisa Kort-Butler (2012) has looked at how views of human nature as they relate to crime causation are conveyed in superhero comic books. She found that the dominant ideology surrounding crime, as they depicted it, suggests that "criminals are *different* from law-abiding people" and that they "are rational and therefore culpable actors" (576). Conversely, she noted that scant attention was paid to "the social conditions or power relationships that are the root causes of crime" (579). While youthful learning experiences may be especially powerful in shaping views, socialization into various ideological slants to explain crime permeates our social experiences, often fostering ideological bias, simplicity, and rigidity. Let us turn to the role of the media in that process.

MEDIA AND CRIMINOLOGY

The media helps shape public understanding of crime (Britto & Noga-Styron, 2014), which results in widespread *mis*understanding of what is best defined as criminal behavior, the causes of that behavior, and how to best respond. Both more and higher-profile coverage extend to sensational crimes (Lin & Phillips, 2014). In addition, reporting patterns have become more blatantly ideological in recent years. The result is a misinformed citizenry, shallow public discourse about the crime problem, and ultimately poor public policy. At the root of skewed media coverage of crime, Lin and Phillips (2014) assert, are (1) its need to secure high ratings in order to reap greater advertising profits and (2) its reliance on criminal justice agencies in portraying crime. Combined with the motivation to feed or cater to ideological extremes, public comprehension of crime and its causes has become increasingly shallow. As this text emphasizes, the causes of crime (and consequently, prevention and control) are extraordinarily complex matters. The *context* of crime cannot be ignored if we are to gain causal understanding. Context alerts us to a set of variables predictive of criminal behavior. That is the logic underlying the title of this text: *Criminology: Explaining Crime and Its Context.*

Media simplicity fundamentally undermines any effort to comprehend crime and deviance intelligently and sensibly. In an analysis of crime segments aired on each of the three 24-hour cable news networks (MSNBC, Fox, and CNN) during a three-month period, Natasha Frost and Nickie Phillips (2011) found that 83 percent of the "experts" interviewed did not offer any commentary regarding causation. Of the few who did, most comments contributed no more than individual pathological slurs, "such as 'sick wacko, and crazy' . . . [that offer] guests an easy way out allowing them to avoid any serious consideration of the motivation for crime" (p. 99). Only 4 percent of the purported "experts" were criminologists who professionally study crime, and the few of them failed to contribute significantly more causal analysis. To make matters worse, Frost and Phillips (2011) "found evidence of anti-intellectualism as various guests scoffed at the notion of addressing root causes of criminal behavior, suggesting instead quick fixes through increasing crime control." They concluded that this "may be part of a larger cultural pattern seen over the past decade including attacks on issues from evolution and global warming to scientific inquiry itself" (p. 107).

The extensive coverage the media gives to atypical cases only serves to undermine public policy. In the time period (Summer, 2006) studied by Frost and Phillips, more than 90 percent of cases reported were street, sex, or terrorist offenses, compared with a mere 1.7 percent for white-collar crimes (but see the associated costs in Chapter 12) and an astonishingly miniscule 1.1 percent for drug-related crimes (for which more than half a million American citizens are currently imprisoned). In short, they found that sensational and atypical criminal events dominated the news cycle. Similarly, many crimes are extended high-profile coverage because they play well to particular ideological agendas. A review of the crime news on any given day will reveal ideological bias. For example, on October 28, 2014, Fox News was headlining a Mexican illegal immigrant's shooting of California deputies, which paired well with their ongoing call for strong border control and deportation of undocumented workers. In contrast, on that same day MSNBC made no mention of this offense in its profiling of crimes. It did, however, provide coverage of a Santa Fe County, NM, shootout between two deputies during a drinking spree, which resulted in one of their deaths. MSNBC also included coverage of a Texas police officer accused of offering a female driver waiver of a citation in return for his smelling and licking her feet. Both of these incidents are rare and sensational but coincide with left-wing MSNBC interest in emphasizing shortcomings within our justice system. Indeed, all three cases confirm that ideology reigns in the crime news industry.

In sum, ideological rigidity undermines both defining and responding to crime. The changing definition, or relativity of crime, examined in detail in Chapter 2, is driven primarily by ideology. Relativity of crime and ideological positions are inexorably intertwined. Ideological leanings impact not only our understanding of the causes of crime and response to it, but even our definition of it. Crime cannot be defined independently of some ideological framework, and consequently, any definition favors some groups over others.

Sheriff Robert Garcia speaks during a news conference in Santa Fe, New Mexico, in response to the October 2014 shooting of a Santa Fe County deputy by a fellow deputy at a Las Cruces hotel.

CREDIT: AP Photo/*The Santa Fe New Mexican*, Clyde Mueller.

THE "CRIME" IN CRIMINOLOGY

Defining criminology only as "the scientific study of crime" leaves unanswered a pivotal question, "What is crime?" Definitions of crime offered by criminologists vary widely along a continuum. Representative of the narrower end of this definitional continuum is Paul Tappan's highly **legalistic definition**:

> Crime is an intentional act in violation of the criminal law (statutory and case law), committed without defense or excuse, and penalized by the state as a felony or misdemeanor. In studying the offender there can be no presumption that . . . persons are criminals unless they also are held guilty beyond a reasonable doubt of a particular offense (1947:100).

This perspective reduces the subject matter of criminology to a subset of those actions or inactions proscribed by criminal law, consisting of only those behaviors successfully processed by the criminal justice system. It excludes behavior that is not criminalized, detected, or reported to law enforcement authorities and successfully prosecuted. All contemporary criminologists view this as an exceedingly restrictive definition. Criminology has rejected such a rigid legalistic definition of its province of study. Edwin H. Sutherland, widely regarded as the dean of American criminology during its formative years, introduced the concept of white-collar crime, which substantially broadened the boundaries of the field. Articulating a modified legalistic definition, Sutherland maintained:

> The essential characteristic of crime is that it is behavior which is prohibited by the State as an injury to the State and against which the State may react, at least as a last resort, by punishment. The two abstract criteria generally regarded by legal scholars as necessary elements in a definition of crime are legal description of an act as socially harmful and legal provision of a penalty for the act (1949:31).

Sutherland noted, however, that "[a]n unlawful act is not defined as criminal by the fact that it is punished, but by the fact that it is punishable" (1949:35), and thereby challenged Tappan's notion that study must be restricted to convicted offenders. He argued that white-collar crime meets such a legalistic definition because it is punishable (by fines, injunctions, etc.), even though less punitive and stigmatizing processes have been developed to soften the consequences of illegal behaviors by powerful persons. Sutherland maintained that white-collar crimes were real crimes, both in the behavioral and the legalistic sense, but that they were being diverted into a distinct category of behavior by legislative fiat that provided for "differential implementation of the law" (1949:42). Sutherland thereby expanded the realm of criminology to focus on the law in action.

Representative of the next position on the continuum, and pushing toward a broader definition of criminology, are the works of Hermann Mannheim and those of Thorsten Sellin. Mannheim (1965) firmly rejected the value of law in delineating criminological boundaries, identifying all antisocial behavior as the subject matter. Similarly, defining criminology as the study of violations of conduct norms, only a subset of which are embodied in the criminal law at any given place and time, Sellin concluded:

> The unqualified acceptance of the legal definitions of the basic units or elements of criminological inquiry violates a fundamental criterion of science. The scientist must have freedom to define his own terms, based on the intrinsic character of his material and designating properties in those materials which are assumed to be universal (1938:21).

Such definitions are defended, in part, because they are not biased in favor of the legal status quo. More legalistic criminologists maintain, however, that state definitions of the crime problem may be objectively studied, while broader definitions tend to reduce criminology to the study of deviant behavior, with each criminologist individually judging which acts merit attention.

The broadest criminological conceptualization of crime emanates from the critical camp of criminologists. Similar labels applied to this perspective are **new criminology** and **radical criminology**. From this perspective, crime and deviance are also considered synonymous. This approach broadens criminological theory, however, by contending that political and economic forces play the key role in generating crime and deviance. These factors, termed the "political economy of crime," are said to form the backdrop for both the crime problem and the structure of reactions to it. What behaviors are subject to criminalization and decriminalization are believed to be contingent on the power structure of society.

"New" criminologists find the more restrictive definitions of the criminological domain shortsighted because they depoliticize criminology. Materialism, forced production, division of labor, and other features of capitalism are said to create a political and economic environment that necessitates criminalization of deviance. This, it is argued, should be the focus of criminological study. Sutherland's examination of white-collar crime, for example, "was informed hardly at all by an examination of the ways in which white-collar infractions were (and are) functional to industrial-capitalist societies. . . ." (Taylor et al., 1973:273–74). Rather, Sutherland focused on the disparities of law in action, contending that white-collar crime was "real crime," that is, a violation of the legal code. In contrast, new criminologists have asserted:

> A criminology which is not normatively committed to the abolition of inequalities of wealth and power, and in particular of inequalities in property and life-chances, is inevitably bound to fall into correctionalism [reforms failing to address underlying problems]. And all correctionalism is irreducibly bound up with the identification of deviance with pathology. A fully social theory of deviance must, by

its nature, break entirely with correctionalism . . . because . . . the causes of crime must be intimately bound up with the form assumed by the social arrangements of the time. Crime is ever and always that behavior seen to be problematic within the framework of those social arrangements: for crime to be abolished, then, those social arrangements themselves must also be subject to fundamental social change (Taylor et al., 1973:281–2).

Herman Schwendinger and Julia Schwendinger (1975) are representative of this view of the boundaries of the crime problem. They maintain that the definitional premises of criminologists such as Sutherland, and even Sellin, overlooked social injuries induced by the elite who control the state. Although Sellin broadened criminological parameters to envelop violation of legal and extralegal conduct norms, his assumption that "no conduct norm without a sanction can be imagined" (1938:34) left unquestioned the social injuries perpetrated by political and economic elites who are able to dictate the structure of established institutions. Thus, the usual definition of the terms of criminological inquiry may leave many issues of harmful social conduct unexamined. Economic "violence" denying work, living quarters, decent wages, child care, and health care are excluded from criminological inquiry except under this radical perspective. Schwendinger and Schwendinger (1975) offered an alternative humanistic definition of crime founded upon the notion of human rights.

Redefinition of crime on the basis of human rights requires explication of the content of such rights, who violates them, how, and why. Human rights, Schwendinger and Schwendinger declared, are "the fundamental prerequisites for well-being, including food, shelter, clothing, medical services, challenging work and recreational experiences, as well as security from predatory individuals or repressive and imperialistic social elites" (Schwendinger & Schwendinger, 1975:133–4). Both individuals and institutions may infringe upon these rights. Many behaviors widely prohibited by criminal law are subsumed under this definition, while many human rights violations typically excluded from the criminal law also are embraced. Primary among the latter in Schwendinger and Schwendinger's view, and for them of far greater magnitude than most social harms addressed by criminal codes, are racism, sexism, imperialism, and poverty. By analogy, they asked:

> Isn't it time to raise serious questions about the assumptions underlying the definition of the field of criminology, when a man who steals a paltry sum can be called a criminal while agents of the State can, with impunity, legally reward men who destroy food so that price levels can be maintained whilst a sizable portion of the population suffers from malnutrition? (1975:137)

Commenting on U.S. military conflicts, William Chambliss (2004:242–43) contended:

In all my work with counterintelligence in Korea I learned how U.S. soldiers murdered and raped Korean civilians during the war . . . today in Iraq we see the same or worse crimes being committed against Iraqi prisoners, citizens and suspected terrorists . . . the fact is that these are crimes of the state and should be high on the list of crimes to be researched and explained by criminologists.

Criminologists such as the Schwendingers and Chambliss argue that the discipline should cease serving as defenders of state institutions that are often criminal (by the human rights definition) and instead ought to become guardians of human rights.

Definitional parameters of criminology, it can be seen, reveal sharp contrasts that have dramatic implications for what criminologists do and do not study. Table 1.3 reviews the continuum of definitions that have been discussed. This text examines a range of issues, consistent with these diverse definitional approaches, with particular emphasis on matters consistent with the modified legalistic and normative definitions.

PARADIGMS IN CRIMINOLOGY

What is done in criminology is determined not only by the definition of crime, but by the theoretical orientation or "school of thought" that is followed. There are a number of competing theoretical perspectives, sometimes termed **paradigms**, within criminology. Paradigms, a term introduced to the sciences by Thomas Kuhn (1970), are difficult to define briefly but surely are much broader than a singular theory. Rather, they provide a general orientation to explaining and understanding a phenomenon (crime in our case). They incorporate an array of assumptions about how knowledge is generated, subsuming both methodological and theoretical premises. One concern is that the paradigm that criminologists identify with tends to reflect particular ideological biases (Chaires & Stitt, 1994), returning us to the issue of scientific objectivity. The vagueness of conceptualizing paradigms, combined with ideological undertones, results in a state of affairs wherein criminological thinking is populated by multiple paradigms. In fact, an exhaustive listing of criminological paradigms is not possible. That said, five major paradigms have dominated thinking about crime and provide an organizational framework for this book: (1) rational choice, (2) positivism, (3) interactionism, (4) critical criminology, and (5) theoretical integration. Chapters in Part II are devoted to theories affiliated with each of these paradigms. Just keep in mind that this is only intended as a very general conceptual scheme for identifying differences between theoretical perspectives.

Although largely neglected in American criminology for several generations, the **rational choice** paradigm has provided the basis for much criminological inquiry in recent decades. The deterrence doctrine (examined in detail in Chapter 5) has served as its focal point. The legitimacy of criminal law, from this perspective, is a given, with the issue only being how to dissuade people from

TABLE 1.3 Continuum of Crime Definitions

Definitional Approach

	Legalistic	Modified Legalistic	Normative		New	
	Tappan	Sutherland	Sellin	Mannheim	Taylor, Walton & Young	Schwendingers
Representative(s) of the approach						
Definition of crime	Judicially determined violation of criminal law	Socially harmful act with provision for penalty by the state	Violations of conduct norms	Antisocial behavior	Political and economic production of deviance	Violations of human rights
Preferred focus of criminology	Adjudicated criminals	White-collar offenders and reactions to them	Variety of norm violations and reactions to them	Variety of behaviors judged antisocial and reactions to them	Political and economic factors that shape state responses to deviance	Imperialism, racism, sexism, and poverty

violating it. That goal is achievable because, it is assumed, people are rational and able to make decisions regarding their own behavior. The question is how to structure and administer sanctions for outlawed behavior.

The *positivistic* paradigm, or **positivism**, dominated American criminology for most of the twentieth century. It assumes that forces beyond the control of individuals, rather than rational decisions, determine criminal behavior. Suppose you attend a party at which someone covertly drops acid (LSD) in the punch and you do some really bizarre things after consuming it. The force that determined your deviant behavior (i.e., ingestion of the laced punch) was beyond your control. You did not "choose" to do those strange things, though someone might argue that your actions reflected a "choice." Although legal responsibility for conduct is a separate matter, the positive criminologist is seeking causal explanations. Causal forces, for positivists, may originate with biogenic sources (see Chapter 6), criminogenic social structures (see Chapter 7), or deficient social processes, such as poor family interaction (see Chapter 8). All positivistic theories are founded on the assumption that crime is generated by forces that are largely beyond the realm of individual choice. They also accept the criminal label as nonproblematic, asking only what caused the behavior and not why the behavior is criminalized. Many theories rooted in the positivistic paradigm empathize with offenders, maintaining that social, biological, or other pathologies are responsible for their conduct. The premise that the conduct itself is criminal, however, is uncritically accepted.

The *interactionist* paradigm (explained in Chapter 9), or **interactionism**, revolving around the actions and reactions of persons and groups, may focus on any deviant or criminal behavior, but has particularly provided the theoretical framework for study of victimless crimes (see Chapter 13). Criminologists subscribing to this paradigm tend to analyze state definitions of crime and the operation of social control agencies such as the police. State definitions of crime are received with skepticism because at the heart of the perspective is the belief that no acts are inherently deviant. Instead, it is thought that acts become deviant only because the reactions of others so label them. Social control agencies are particularly likely to enhance negative labeling of behaviors that otherwise might be dismissed as only mildly deviant, rather than as criminal. These labels may then be incorporated as part of the self-concept of the labeled person, leading to additional (secondary) deviance. Labeling thus generates a self-fulfilling prophecy that propels its subject into a spiral of deviance. Chapter 9 examines labeling theory.

Critical criminology, including new, radical, and Marxist perspectives, is a paradigm that provides a broad definition of the crime problem. It goes further than the interactionist paradigm by rejecting state definitions of crime, asking why relatively powerless wrongdoers are so much more subject to criminalization than are powerful ones. Its focus includes the full range of deviance, with particular attention accorded crimes of the powerful. This paradigm is examined in Chapter 9.

Integration rests on the belief that optimal explanations of crime can be derived from combinations of two or more theoretical perspectives rather than by exclusive use of a single one. Integration does not imply any particular definitional orientation to crime. Integrationists argue that singular theoretical models have stagnated, but that integration holds potential for a paradigmatic revolution (Swigert, 1989). Advocacy for combining theories rests on an assumption that the many competing theories "merely reflect differences in focus or emphasis rather than fundamentally opposed views of the world" (Hirschi, 1989:39). Critics maintain that integration will yield "theoretical mush" by so diluting the characteristics and assumptions of independent theories that their individual explanatory powers will be reduced (Akers, 1989). Some criminologists also object that integration of distinct theories fails to generate new theoretical insight, much less a new paradigm. Specific integrated theories of crime are discussed in Chapter 10, but the approach has become so widespread that it is characteristic of many theoretical perspectives that have earned their own place in theoretical nomenclature. Life-course criminology (reviewed in Chapter 10), for example, has become so popular and is such a broad perspective that some criminologists refer to it as a paradigm. Frank Cullen (2011:310) went so far as to suggest that it "should become the organizing framework for the study of crime causation." Professor Cullen was arguing that, indeed, it is time for life-course criminology to emerge as the central paradigm of the discipline. No doubt, this perspective is growing dramatically as a shaping force in theorizing about and researching delinquent and criminal behavior.

Table 1.4 summarizes the five primary paradigms that provide the perspectives from which explanations of crime are sought. Each is explored in some detail in the chapters specified in the right-hand column. As with definitional diversity, each paradigm or perspective contributes to our understanding of crime, and each serves as a point of departure for many significant contributions to contemporary ideas about criminal behavior.

CRIMINOLOGY AND PUBLIC POLICY

Criminologists for many decades were inclined to view the field as pure social scientific pursuit of truth. There was a healthy criminological skepticism that seeking to answer policy questions threatened to compromise and corrupt the field. The fear was that efforts to inform policy would invite ideological bias. Herbert A. Bloch and Gilbert Geis, for example, described criminology "as a field oriented to the understanding of criminal behavior . . . and not necessarily as a pursuit dedicated to the reduction of crime" (1962:12). The renowned Edwin Sutherland (Sutherland & Cressey, 1974) clearly viewed policy matters as secondary to theoretical explanations for criminal behavior. In recent years, however, the tides have shifted in a direction of closer linkage between the work of criminologists and policy development.

Todd Clear's (2010) presidential address to the American Society of Criminology (ASC) praised the emergence of "evidence-based" criminological endeavors and urged that we take advantage of that shift. In 2013, the dean of

TABLE 1.4 Paradigmatic Framework for Examining Crime

Paradigm	Explanation for Crime	Crime Focus	View of Criminalization	Reference Chapters
Rational Choice	Individuals are able to make rational, calculating choices regarding behavior. Criminal choices are made when advantageous.	Any criminalized behavior.	State definitions of crime are unchallenged.	5
Positivism	Many distinct pathological conditions may be the genesis of criminal behavior.	Any deviant or criminal behavior, but most often those traditionally perceived as relatively serious.	State definitions of crime tend to be uncritically accepted.	6–8
Interactionism	Reactions of persons and groups to particular behaviors result in some being labeled criminal.	Victimless crimes.	State definitions of and reactions to crime are critically analyzed.	9, 13
Critical	Power elite define crimes and operate agencies of social control in their own interest, preserving their position in society.	Crimes of the state and powerful individuals.	State definitions of crime are rejected.	9
Integration	Crime can best be explained by combining two or more theoretical perspectives.	Varies with theories incorporated.	Varies with theories incorporated.	10

Florida State University's storied College of Criminology and Criminal Justice, Thomas Blomberg, edited a special issue of *Criminology and Public Policy* "to address the criminological question of how best to advance criminal justice policy and practice" (Blomberg et al., 2013:572). While Blomberg and his colleagues acknowledged that some disagreement remains among criminologists regarding the prudence of drawing policy inference from research that fails to establish causality, they concluded that drawing from the "best available" scientific evidence is sufficient. Blomberg and many others see this as the direction of criminology. Progressive practitioners have also been discussing how policy-making might become better informed by research. In a 2010 speech, Glenn Schmitt, Director of Research and Data at the United States Sentencing Commission, outlined how researchers and policymakers might better interact. He echoed the stance of many contemporary criminologists in concluding "it is at the intersection with policy-making that the research community has its opportunity to have its work used to make people's lives better" (Schmitt, 2013:309).

The ASC has experienced its own controversy regarding official policy stances. To date, the organization has endorsed only two specific policy positions. The first, pronounced in 1989, was to oppose capital punishment. One of the authors of this text (Brown) was editing the *The Criminologist* at the time and received a strident letter from Ernest van den Haag, a staunch proponent of capital punishment, resigning his membership in protest. Indeed, it is difficult for an organization comprised of thousands of criminologists to take specific policy stances because "the fundamental knowledge base in our field is much thinner than we would like" (Blumstein, 2009:3). In 2007, ASC adopted its second specific policy position: the view that UCR data should not be employed in ranking the safety of American cities. Although this position is less controversial, several ASC leaders have argued that the organization should avoid specific policy positions. Akiva Liberman (2009) contends that the organization should limit its advocacy to the process of testing policies through application of scientific experiments or what he calls "evidence-generating policies." Carter Hay (2009) similarly suggests that crime control policy should be routinely informed by theoretically driven program evaluations and longitudinal (across time) data. Alfred Blumstein (2009:4) suggests that the organization should limit "its advocacy role to those policies that accrue to the benefit of the field rather than to endorse public policies" and both Todd Clear (2009) and Gary LaFree and Katharine Huffman (2009) maintain that theory and research should be driving ongoing inquiry. Clear adds (2009:5) that these efforts should be "free from expectation that it necessarily bases its agenda on whatever program priorities exist in the justice's [Department of Justice] current program initiatives, or whatever program interest excites the field at the moment."

ASC official policy endorsements notwithstanding, it is clear that criminologists are increasingly injecting their research into public policy debate. Virtually all criminologists now agree that our knowledge and expertise have not contributed to policy as they should. As with any other field reliant upon scientific advances, this will require greater investments. A sad example, however, is that dental research is funded at a level eight times higher than all research on crime and justice matters combined (Blumstein, 2009). We will have to do much better than that if we are to understand and ultimately reduce the crime problem in the United States. Undoubtedly, similar neglect plagues crime control research in other parts of the world. It will be necessary to shed the ideological blinders that frequently drive crime and justice policies and draw upon the scientific knowledge base of criminology, restricted as it may be, if we are to more effectively contend with matters of crime and social control. Sadly, as the schism between the political parties in addressing all manner of public policy reflects, this will not be easy. Even in his optimism regarding a new era of policy input from the criminological ranks, Todd Clear concluded his 2009 presidential address noting, "Undeniably, the policy world is complicated—too often sullied by the hard edge of politics and ideology. The prerogatives of politics will color any policy action undertaken in the field of justice" (2010:20). Or as Blomberg et al. (2013:582) concluded, narrowing "the confrontation between political ideology and best available research knowledge will not be easily accomplished."

SUMMARY

Table 1.5 summarizes key themes of this chapter. Crime is a subject of great interest to people. Many firmly believe that they understand the causes of crime and what ought to be done about it. Yet despite some surface agreement (consensus) about the ranking of crimes by "seriousness," more careful research reveals many differences (conflict) in public views on crime issues. Perhaps neither of the polar arguments about what underlies criminal law, conflict or consensus, is entirely accurate. Moreover, views of crime shift dramatically across time and space. Crime, in other words, is a relative phenomenon. The shifts themselves are largely driven by ideology, often injecting biases that lead to emotional exploitation of the public by politicians and the media.

Depending upon their ideological leanings, criminologists vary considerably in the methods they employ, what they see as the goal(s) of criminology, what constitutes "crime," and the paradigm or theoretical perspective that guides their work. While most criminologists view the field through a social science lens, calling for empirical testing of theories, some advocate qualitative approaches, arguing that observing statistical patterns may miss the human, or even spiritual, element of crime. More mainstream criminologists counter that the discipline must be able to predict conditions that will lead to crime and that denial of the importance of that predictive power is a reflection of ideological bias. They ask, what is criminology to do if not explain what conditions will lead to crime? While this text includes discussions of works

TABLE 1.5 Fundamental Issues in Criminology

Issue	Description
Ideology	Basic beliefs or values, usually formed early in life, and through which people filter information
Relativity of crime	The variation in conception of what behavior is criminal from one time, place, or context to another
Paradigm	A general framework or orientation, including some basic assumptions, on which theories are based
Scientific method	An approach to the study of phenomena that incorporates both theory and observation
Consensus	A belief that the law reflects the interest of most people in society more or less evenly
Conflict	A belief that the law disproportionately reflects the interest of a powerful minority within society

from a variety of methodological perspectives, it reflects the dominance of the scientific approach.

Most criminologists think that their work should lead to insight regarding the causes of crime and hopefully have implications for crime prevention. Some heavily emphasize the importance of crime etiology, while others place more concern on practical implications for crime prevention. The trend in recent years, however, has been to seek a stronger tie between the scientific studies of criminologists and public policy.

Four conceptual definitions of crime for setting the parameters of criminology were reviewed in this chapter. Conceptions of crime fall along a continuum from relatively narrow to quite broad. One of the major themes of *Criminology: Explaining Crime and Its Context* is the relativity of crime, as is emphasized in the "normative" definition.

This book is organized around five paradigms for explaining crime: free will or rational choice, positivism, interactionism, the critical perspective, and integration. It is very important that you develop an ability to contrast these theoretical orientations in terms of how they tend to define crime, how they explain it, and their policy implications.

You should also consider what type of crime might best be explained by each theoretical approach. An effort has been made to present the various paradigms in a way that will broaden your thinking about the causes of crime and, most importantly, will impress upon you the complexity of criminological matters. As one of the authors routinely notes in his course syllabus, "the only erroneous understanding of crime is that it is a simple issue. Our hope is to sensitize you to the complexities of the problem so that as professionals in the field, and/or informed citizens, you will never fall prey to the 'dumb and dumber' approach of contemporary politicians in your understanding of criminal behavior."

Some other themes of this book should be clear from reading the introductory chapter. First, there is a conscious intent to take full account of the impact of ideology upon our definition and understanding of crime. Criminological works are always colored by the ideological biases of the times, as will be seen in many of the theories discussed in chapters ahead. At times racism, sexism, and other biases have crept, or oftentimes jumped, into the accounts offered for crime. Closely related to this is the relativity of crime that provides a central thesis in this work. What is construed as criminal varies widely across space and time. For that reason, examples are drawn from cultures around the world, and crimes are discussed in historical context. Crime can be better understood by considering diverse social contexts. Technological changes are rapidly shrinking the globe, and these changes must be incorporated in the criminological enterprise. Emphasis is also placed on the assumptions underlying theories and their policy implications. The policy impact of criminology, or lack thereof, has received much attention in recent years. Finally, media depictions of crime are critiqued. As you enter the world of criminology, it is urged that media simplicity and sensationalism be left in the coffee shop.

KEY TERMS AND CONCEPTS

Conflict	Methodology
Consensus	New Criminology
Crime	Paradigms
Criminologist	Positivism
Criminology	Radical Criminology
Critical Criminology	Rational Choice
Ideology	Relativity of Crime
Integration	Scientific Method
Interactionism	Theory
Legalistic Definition (of Crime)	

KEY CRIMINOLOGISTS

Hermann Mannheim	Thorsten Sellin
Herman Schwendinger	Edwin Sutherland
Julia Schwendinger	Paul Tappan

DISCUSSION QUESTIONS

1. Define relativity of crime and provide three to five examples.
2. What renders criminology a science? What is the relationship between the essential components of science?
3. List and define four different definitions of crime.
4. What is a paradigm? How do paradigms impact definitions of crime and how it is explained?
5. Which criminological paradigm can you most identify with? Why?
6. How has the media prepared you for this class? How will you adapt?
7. Now that you have read the introductory chapter of *Criminology: Explaining Crime and Its Context*, how does the overview of the field contrast with your perceptions before entering the class?

REFERENCES

Akers, R. L. (1989). A social behaviorist's perspective on integration of theories of crime and deviance. In S. E. Messner, M. D. Krohn, & A. E. Liska (Eds.), *Theoretical integration in the study of deviance and crime* (pp. 23–36). Albany, NY: State University of New York Press.

Bloch, H. A. & Geis, G. (1962). *Man, crime, and society.* New York, NY: Random House.

Blomberg, T. G., Mestre, J., & Mann, K. (2013). Criminology, causality, and public policy: Seeking causality in a world of contingency. *Criminology & Public Policy, 12,* 571–86.

Blumstein, A. (2009). What role should ASC take in policy advocacy? *The Criminologist, 34,* 1–4.

Britto, S. & Noga-Styron, K. E. (2014). Media consumption and support for capital punishment. *Criminal Justice Review, 39,* 81–100.

Chaires, R. H. & Stitt, B. G. (1994). Paradigmatic concerns in criminal justice. *Journal of Crime and Justice, 17,* 1–23.

Chambliss, W. (2004). On the symbiosis between criminal law and criminal behavior. *Criminology, 42,* 241–51.

Clear, T. (2009). ASC's policy efforts. *The Criminologist, 34,* 1–5.

Clear, T. (2010). Policy and evidence: The challenge of the American Society of Criminology: 2009 presidential address to the American Society of Criminology. *Criminology, 48,* 1–25.

Cullen, F. T. (2011). Beyond adolescence-limited criminology: Choosing our future—The American Society of Criminology 2010 Sutherland address. *Criminology, 49,* 287–330.

Cullen, F. T. (2012). Toward a criminology of religion: Comment on Johnson and Jang. In R. Rosenfeld, K. Quinet, & C. Garcia (Eds.), *Contemporary issues in criminological theory and research: The role of institutions* (p. 154). Belmont, CA: Wadsworth.

Cullen, F. T., Wright, J. P., & Chamlin, M. B. (1999). Social support and social reform: A progressive crime control agenda. *Crime & Delinquency, 45,* 188–207.

Curra, J. (2000). *The relativity of crime.* Thousand Oaks, CA: Sage.

Filipovic, J. (2013). *How the right plays with murder: The antiabortion movement's cycle of violence.* www.salon.com/2013/09/10

Frost, N. T. & Phillips, N. D. (2011). Talking heads: Crime reporting on cable news. *Justice Quarterly, 28,* 87–112.

Hay, C. (2009). Examining the key causes of crime in terms of their potential responsiveness to policy manipulation. *The Criminologist, 34,* 5–8.

Hirschi, T. (1969). *Causes of delinquency.* Berkeley, CA: University of California Press.

Hirschi, T. (1989). Exploring alternatives to integrated theory. In S. E. Messner, M. D. Krohn, & A. E. Liska (Eds.), *Theoretical integration in the study of deviance and crime* (p. 39). Albany, NY: State University of New York Press.

Hirschi, T. & Stark, R. (1969). Hellfire and delinquency. *Social Problems, 17,* 204–13.

Johnson, B. R. & Jang, S. J. (2012). Crime and religion: Assessing the role of the faith factor. In R. Rosenfeld, K. Quinet, & C. Garcia (Eds.), *Contemporary issues in criminological theory and research: The role of institutions* (pp. 117–49). Belmont, CA: Wadsworth.

Kort-Butler, L. A. (2012). Rotten, vile, and depraved! Depictions of criminality in superhero cartoons. *Deviant Behavior, 33,* 566–81.

Kuhn, T. S. (1970). *The structure of scientific revolutions* (2nd ed.). Chicago: University of Chicago Press.

LaFree, G. & Huffman, K. (2009). The ASC goes to Washington: How and why now? *The Criminologist, 34,* 1–4.

Liberman, A. M. (2009). Advocating evidence—Generating policies: A role for the ASC. *The Criminologist, 34,* 1–5.

Lin, J. & Phillips, S. (2014). Media coverage of capital murder: Exceptions sustain the rule. *Justice Quarterly, 31*, 934–59.

Mannheim, H. (1965). *Comparative criminology.* Boston, MA: Houghton Mifflin.

Miller, W. B. (1973). Ideology and criminal justice policy: Some current issues. *Journal of Criminal Law and Criminology, 64*, 141–62.

Ramirez, M. D. (2013). Punitive sentiment. *Criminology, 51*, 329–64.

Reiman, J. H. (1990). *The rich get richer and the poor get prison* (3rd ed.). New York, NY: Macmillan Publishing Company.

Ren, L., Zhao, J., & Lovrich, N. P. (2006). *Liberal vs. conservative public policies on crime: What was the comparative track record in the 1990s?* Paper presented at the Annual Meeting of the Academy of Criminal Justice Sciences (p. 28). Baltimore, MD.

Rush, G. E. & Torres, S. (1998). *The encyclopedic dictionary of criminology.* Incline Village, NV: Copperhouse Publishing.

Schmitt, G. R. (2013). The intersection of social science research and federal policy-making: Is anyone listening? *Justice Quarterly, 30*, 304–9.

Schwendinger, H. & Schwendinger, J. (1975). Defenders of order or guardians of human rights? In I. Taylor, P. Walton, & J. Young (Eds.), *Critical criminology* (pp. 133–7). Boston, MA: Routledge and Kegan Paul.

Sellin, T. (1938). *Culture conflict and crime.* New York, NY: Social Science Research Council.

Sutherland, E. H. (1949). *White collar crime.* New York, NY: Dryden.

Sutherland, E. H. & Cressey, D. R. (1974). *Criminology* (9th ed.). Philadelphia, PA: J.B. Lippincott.

Swigert, V. L. (1989). The discipline as data: Resolving the theoretical crisis in criminology. In S. E. Messner, M. D. Krohn, & A. E. Liska (Eds.), *Theoretical integration in the study of deviance and crime* (pp. 129–35). Albany, NY: State University of New York Press.

Tappan, P. W. (1947). Who is the criminal? *American Sociological Review, 12*, 96–102.

Taylor, I., Walton, P., & Young, J. (1973). *The new criminology: For a social theory of deviance.* New York, NY: Harper Colophon Books.

Triplett, R. A. & Turner, E. M. (2010). Where is criminology? The institutional placement of criminology within sociology and criminal justice. *Criminal Justice Review, 35*, 5–31.

Williams, E. J. & Robinson, M. (2004). Ideology and criminal justice: Suggestions for a pedagogical model. *Journal of Criminal Justice Education, 15*, 373–92.

Williams, F. P. III (1984). The demise of the criminological imagination: a critique of recent criminology. *Justice Quarterly, 1*, 91–106.

The Relativity of Law and Crime

LEARNING OBJECTIVES

After reading Chapter 2, you should be able to:

- Discuss the relativity of law across time and space.
- Delineate differences between conflict and consensus explanations of the origin of law.
- Describe key differences between criminal, civil, and administrative law.
- Describe the four distinct goals of the American criminal justice system.

Just as our understanding of crime and deviance are relative, changing across time and space, so is the content of criminal law. Criminalization of behaviors is a political process and, therefore, the content of criminal codes varies. This chapter establishes a criminological framework by examining the concept of criminal law and its creation. It will become clear that criminal law, and thus official recognition of "crime" and "criminals," is entirely relative to time and space.

THE CONCEPT OF LAW

Law provides the baseline for formal social control. From a **consensus** perspective, law is thought to contribute to fair and orderly functioning within complex societies. From a **conflict** vantage point, law serves to preserve existing power relationships. Whichever perspective one subscribes to, law is a large, substantive mass that can be subdivided into criminal, civil, and administrative components. Each is designed to control behavior, but there are important differences among them.

Crimes may be acts of commission (i.e., a prohibited act such as rape or intentional marketing of unsafe products) or acts of omission (i.e., failure to perform a required act such as filing an income tax return or providing proper care to a child in one's custody). Under **criminal law** there is no crime unless the conduct prohibited or required is enunciated in the federal or state criminal code in clear and precise language. The code must also specify sanctions that may be applied as a consequence of violations. **Felonies** are the most serious offenses, punishable by execution or by imprisonment for one year or more. **Misdemeanors** may be subject to incarceration in jail for a period up to 11 months and 29 days. The least serious category of crimes are violations (sometimes called infractions or offenses), punishable by relatively small fines.

Every crime consists of specific elements that must be proved beyond a reasonable doubt to support a conviction. The *actus reus*, or "guilty act," is the physical element in a crime. It is comprised of conduct that is prohibited or of failure to act in a manner required by the criminal law. The *mens rea*, or "guilty mind," is the mental element of crime, generally termed intent. Intent ordinarily is an essential element of crime, although in some cases it may be inferred or there may be strict liability. A common example of the latter is statutory rape. The law forbids sexual intercourse with a person under a specified age, typically 18, whether or not the relationship is consensual. Table 2.1 presents common law definitions of several major felonies.

These descriptors of criminal law do not apply to **civil law** violations (torts). The heart of the distinction between criminal and civil law involves a difference of purpose. Civil law makes no provision for penal sanctions, although it can mandate compensation. Likewise, civil law does not require the same degree of specificity as criminal law. Civil law may even be retroactive, a situation constitutionally forbidden in criminal law. Most distinctively, criminal law in theory addresses wrongs that injure society at large, while civil law violations are legal wrongs against individuals. The following two scenarios are illustrative:

1. An acquaintance asks to borrow your car. You agree to loan it after she assures you that it will be properly maintained. She then drives it a long distance, severely damaging the engine as a consequence of failure to add oil. The repairs cost you $500.
2. An acquaintance asks to borrow your car, but you decline to loan it. She takes the car without your permission, driving it a long distance and severely damaging the engine as a consequence of failure to add oil. The repairs cost you $500.

In both cases you have suffered and you could likely recover your $500 expense through a civil suit for damages, at least if the offender is solvent. Such a civil proceeding would place you (Smith), the injured party or plaintiff, against the offending party or defendant (Jones). The case would be designated Smith versus Jones, or in the usual form of *Smith v. Jones*. In the second scenario, the state could also prosecute Jones for violating a criminal statute

TABLE 2.1 Common Law Definition and Elements of Major Crimes

Crime	Definition	Elements
Murder	Unlawful killing of a human being by another human being with malice aforethought	1. Unlawful killing 2. a human being 3. by another human being 4. with malice aforethought
Rape	The act of having unlawful carnal knowledge by a man of a woman, forcibly and against her will	1. Unlawful 2. carnal knowledge (or sexual intercourse) 3. by force or fear, and 4. without the consent or against the will of the female
Robbery	Felonious taking of money or goods of value with intent to steal from the person of another, or in his presence, against his will, by violence or putting him in fear	1. Trespass 2. taking 3. carrying away 4. personal property 5. property of another 6. with intent to steal 7. from the person or presence of another 8. by violence or intimidation
Assault	Unlawful offer or attempt to injure another, with apparent present ability to effectuate the attempt under circumstances creating a fear of imminent peril	1. An attempt or offer 2. with force and violence, injury to another 3. with apparent present or immediate ability
Battery	Unlawful touching of the person of another by the aggressor or by some substance put in motion by him	1. Unlawful 2. application of force 3. to the person of another
Kidnapping	Forcibly detaining another against his or her will to unlawfully obtain ransom, or lawfully restraining another and forcibly moving the person imprisoned to another place	1. Detaining another 2. by force 3. without his or her consent 4. without legal cause, and 5. moving him or her to another place or to unlawfully obtain ransom
Arson	Willful and malicious burning of the dwelling house or outbuilding within its curtilage	1. Burning 2. a dwelling house (or outbuilding within its curtilage) 3. house must belong to or be occupied by another person, and 4. burning must be done or caused maliciously
Burglary	Breaking and entering the dwelling house of another in the nighttime with the intent to commit a felony therein	1. A breaking 2. and entry 3. a dwelling house 4. of another 5. in the nighttime 6. with intent to commit a felony therein

Source: Adapted from Pollock, J.M. (2013). *Criminal Law* (10th ed.). Boston: Anderson/Elsevier.

prohibiting auto theft. This criminal court proceeding would be titled The State versus Jones (*State v. Jones* or *People v. Jones*) and would be distinct from your civil action.

Although a single act may involve both criminal and civil liability, the legal actions emanate from different kinds of harm. A wronged individual may sue for damages based on the notion that the state, through civil law, will serve as the arbiter of personal disputes in order to see that they are resolved in a fair manner. Criminal proceedings, however, rest on the premise that the accused has violated the rights of the community at large and has failed to meet a social obligation of all residents. In this sense, a criminal wrong is an injury to society.

The highly publicized O.J. Simpson case of the 1990s illustrates the dual liability, criminal and civil, that a person may face. In 1995, Simpson was acquitted of criminal homicide charges resulting from the stabbing deaths of his ex-wife Nicole Brown Simpson and her friend Ronald Goldman. In a subsequent civil case, however, Simpson was ordered to pay $25 million for the wrongful deaths. Similarly, in 2001, Robert Blake, the star of the 1970s *Baretta* television show, was acquitted of murdering his wife, Bonnie Bakley, but ordered to pay $30 million in a wrongful death suit. Such an outcome is confusing to many who want to conclude that the "facts" are known; the person is guilty or innocent. What cases like those of Simpson and Blake turn on, at least in part, is the standard of evidence required. A criminal conviction requires "proof beyond a reasonable doubt," while a civil judgment requires a "preponderance of evidence." The difference is substantial. To think of it in numerical terms, the weight of evidence that needs to be established for civil versus criminal liability is on the order of 50.1 as compared to 99 + percent. Other evidentiary standards vary as well. Intent is generally required in criminal, but not in civil, proceedings. Protection against self-incrimination operates in criminal proceedings, but a person may be compelled to testify in civil cases. And, as the Simpson case highlighted, the potential sanctions differ considerably. Criminal law sanctions include fines, probation, incarceration, and (in 38 states, the Federal system, and the military) capital punishment. Civil remedies, however, are limited to financially compensating or otherwise providing relief for the plaintiff. Such distinctions between types of law are summarized in Table 2.2.

Moreover, a person who is a victim of crime is, at least in principle, obligated to cooperate with the state's prosecution of the offender. Reference to victims "not prosecuting" a crime reflects a common misconception of criminal law. Actually, if a victim is unwilling to provide evidence, the state will likely drop the case. This was not done in the 1993 Detroit case of Darlene Kincer, who pleaded with the judge to drop a charge of assault with intent to murder filed against her boyfriend who, according to witnesses, dragged her with his van, resulting in the loss of an arm, a leg, and her unborn baby. The victim protested that the charges were keeping her and the assailant from patching up their relationship and that her 16-year-old

TABLE 2.2 Summary Dimensions of the Branches of Law

	Criminal	Civil	Administrative
Victim/complainant	State (society at large)	Individual	State (society at large)
Legality	No crime without specific law	May be broad or retroactive	May be broad or retroactive
Sanction	Fine, incarceration, probation, execution	Payment to the wronged individual	Civil fines, injunctions, closure, seizure, license revocation, criminal action
Conviction/ Judgment Standard	Proof beyond a reasonable doubt	Preponderance of evidence	Administrative determination (or proof beyond a reasonable doubt in criminal actions)
Intent	Required	Not required	Not required

daughter testified against the man only because she did not want a man in her mother's life (*Johnson City Press*, 1993). In this extreme case the judge acted consistent with the theory of criminal law that the assaultive behavior was a wrong against society.

Suppose that your campus is plagued by a serial rapist whose *modus operandi* (crime method) invariably entails taking women on two dates, both involving no more than tasteful entertainment and pleasant conversation. On the third date, there is forced sex in the offender's apartment. Each victim may have grounds for civil action to seek compensation for emotional trauma and physical harm. The state has an interest in prosecuting the offender to punish him for his action and to avert harm to additional persons. The rapist, like a drunk driver or a thief, is seen as posing a threat to social order. The police officers' and prosecutors' complaint that many rape victims "won't prosecute" illustrates the discrepancy between the law in books and the law in action.

Administrative law combines elements of criminal and civil law. It is based on the delegation of rule-making authority from a legislative body to a regulatory agency. Regulatory agencies have legislative (rule-making), executive (enforcement), and judicial (sanctioning) authority within the boundaries of the powers delegated to them. Civil fines, injunctions, and license suspensions may be administratively imposed or criminal proceedings initiated for violating rules of regulatory agencies. Administrative law emerged only about a century ago, but has grown enormously owing to the perceived need to control business, professional, and corporate activities. There are hundreds of regulatory agencies in the United States, including the Federal Trade Commission, the Securities and Exchange Commission, the Food and Drug Administration, the Internal Revenue Service, and the Environmental Protection Agency.

CONFLICT OR CONSENSUS?

Criminologists seeking to comprehend the forces underlying creation of criminal law largely subscribe to one of two general orientations, although many also favor a blend of the two. The consensus perspective portrays criminal law as a product of social needs and values, while from the conflict tradition, law is seen as the embodiment of the interests of powerful groups. Each tradition includes variations, but the two major themes may be contrasted in terms of their underlying assumptions.

The consensus perspective maintains that criminal law develops and operates in the interest of society at large. Rules and laws are viewed as serving the needs of a majority of the society. The law is deemed to formalize the norms and mores of the community. Emile Durkheim (1893/1933; 1895/1958), an early proponent of this view, conceived of crime as functional to society. Crime, he argued, delineates the boundaries of acceptable behavior and solidifies society in support of those boundaries. Consider, for example, the widespread social condemnation of use of illicit drugs. From the uncompromising messages of school programs such as DARE to the imprisonment of thousands of persons in U.S. prisons and jails, a strong statement is registered that the use of certain types of drugs crosses the boundaries of acceptable behavior. The consensus paradigm focuses on explaining behavior violating normative boundaries and, Durkheim argued, concludes that if no violations occur, society will find it necessary to create new rules so that the boundaries of behavior will be clear.

From the conflict orientation, criminal law is seen as operating in the interest of a wealthy and powerful elite whose desires often conflict with those of members of less privileged groups. Only behaviors contrary to the interests of those elite are criminalized or, at least, are enforced by the law in action. The poor and powerless bear the brunt of legal sanctions, while the elite remain untouched, despite their perpetration of acts harmful to others. Criminologists adopting a conflict perspective focus on explanations of the content of legal codes, that is, on why certain behaviors are made illegal, while others that are equally or more harmful go unattended. Thus the conflict theorist would contend that the heavy criminalization of drugs in the United States does not so much set broad social boundaries as it limits availability of mind-altering substances to certain classes of people. Those with sufficient resources may avoid law violation by turning to legalized drugs administered through the medical establishment. Moreover, even when violations occur in the upper classes, they are less likely to be processed within the criminal justice system.

Evidence may be marshaled in support of both consensus and conflict perspectives. There is a very strong agreement among virtually all people that acts such as murder and rape (or at least some forms of taking human lives and sexual exploitation) are abhorrent and ought to be severely sanctioned by criminal codes. On the other hand, most people also believe that crimes committed by the elite are treated differently by both the legal codes and in the manner by which they are enforced. This is reflected by the person on the street who reacts to outrageous elite conduct by exclaiming that "rich people can get away with anything!"

Chapters 7 and 8 examine social structure and social process theories of crime that are rooted in a consensual view of society. Consensual theories undergird efforts at social control and provide the basis for tactics to try to keep people within the bounds of "acceptable" behavior. Chapter 9 considers social reaction theories derived from the conflict orientation and explicates the content and the administration of the criminal law in terms of these ideas.

THE RELATIVITY OF CRIME

It should be clear from the introductory chapter that the placement of behaviors along a continuum of social desirability is a vague, perhaps even arbitrary, process. Assessments of any given behavior may vary dramatically across time and space. As John Curra (2000:2) explains it, no human behavior "will be universally judged as improper by all people in all societies . . . at all times." What is defined as laudable behavior at one time may be labeled criminal at another. Behaviors deemed bold or courageous in one place may be regarded as criminal at another. Reactions to behavior often shift more subtly. For example, an act seen as laudable at one time or place may come to be seen as conforming, but not especially admirable, at another. Figure 2.1 illustrates a continuum of the social desirability of behavior, highlighting the most extreme shifts. Movement in and out of the "criminal" end of the continuum is what criminologists refer to as the **relativity of crime**. In an emotional debate over initiating a state lottery to fund education, a Tennessee state Senator unwittingly recognized this principle of law when he quipped, "A few years ago we put people in prison for doing what the state's about to do" (*Johnson City Press*, 2003).

Box 2.1 summarizes news reports of "criminal" behavior that has been harshly dealt with in Islamic countries. These offenses, and Islamic justice responses to them, highlight the crime definition gap between cultures. Consider some examples that can be applied. In Iraq, prior to the 2003 American

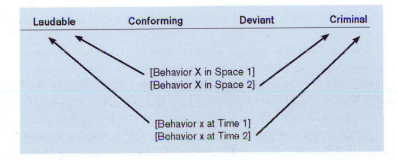

FIGURE 2.1
Continuum of the relative social desirability of behavior.

BOX 2.1 RELATIVITY OF LAW ACROSS SPACE: ISLAMIC VERSUS WESTERN CONCEPTIONS OF LAW

- A 1999 report of the execution of an Afghan woman for killing her husband in a domestic dispute detailed the public stoning before thousands of citizens in a stadium. The crowd included many women with their children. Following the execution there were widespread shouts of "God is great!"

- A Nigerian couple was sentenced to death by stoning for "having sex outside of marriage" (*Johnson City Press*, 2002b).

- Reporting another Nigerian stoning sentence for adultery, a 2002 AP report (*Johnson City Press*, 2002c) noted that the rash of such sentences by the Islamic courts represented a struggle between northern, predominantly Muslim states and the predominantly Christian southern states. In this case, the female offender gave birth more than nine months after a divorce. The

court delayed her execution until 2004 to allow time for her to nurse her baby.

- In an article titled "Driving While Female," the *New York Times* (Dowd, 2002) reported on 47 Saudi women who defied the law by driving cars in Riyadh, the capital of Saudi Arabia. Islamic clerics responded to the violation by labeling the women "whores" and "harlots." They lost their jobs and passports, experienced death threats, and had to agree to never speak of their short-lived act of protest. When a Saudi man serving on the King's Consultive Council again raised the issue in 2005, he was soundly repudiated.

- Iran tortured and hanged two 16-year-olds and an 18-year-old boy for having gay sex on July 19, 2005. It is estimated that more than 4,000 Iranians have been executed for homosexual behavior since clerical rule was established in 1979.

invasion and the fall of the Saddam Hussein regime, it was a serious crime to disfigure statues or paintings honoring the Iraqi leader. On the day Baghdad fell, however, such behavior was fostered by the authority of the new occupying American forces and widely perpetrated by crowds of citizens. Similarly, the "Boston Tea Party" was a serious criminal transgression, but soon became a nationally revered act of defiance of "unfair" law. As a general rule, revolutionaries are criminals unless or until their cause wins. George Washington, Fidel Castro, Mao Tse Tung, and Vladimir Lenin—all were largely viewed in their respective countries as heroes but, had their revolutionary efforts failed, they likely would have been executed as criminals.

Relativity Across Time

Legal codes vary across time, perhaps because the interests of the elite or powerful change or perhaps because societal consensus alters. Conduct at one time in violation of legal codes may later be decriminalized and, conversely, behavior deemed acceptable later may be criminalized. Until the U.S. Supreme Court's decision in *Roe v. Wade* (1973), abortion was illegal except in a few American jurisdictions where it was permitted if the life of the pregnant woman was in jeopardy. Since 2000, however, The Center for Disease Control and Prevention (CDC) in Atlanta has reported a little more than 800,000 legal abortions annually (CDC, 2008). Abortion law in Mexico, a predominantly Catholic country, remained in an essentially pre–*Roe v. Wade* status until 2007. Even then, the right to a first-trimester abortion was extended to women only in the Federal District of Mexico City, not in the individual states. Moreover, reform of the federal abortion laws generated a conservative backlash of "right to life" legislation in 16 of 27 states and led to increases in prosecution of women acquiring abortions (Becker & Olavarrieta, 2013). Highlight 2.1 presents a dreadful example of one American state's position on "right to life" versus "right to die."

As a sample of other changes in laws, tobacco products were freely smoked in virtually all public settings in the United States until recent years, but all states now restrict public smoking by statute. Even tobacco-producing states like Tennessee and North Carolina have passed legislation broadly prohibiting smoking in restaurants and other public places. Suicide was once against the law; now the debate centers upon physician-assisted suicide, which is legal in Oregon, but a felony in Michigan. Racial segregation used to carry the force of law in the southern United States, but now discriminatory actions constitute crimes. What used to be considered only "jokes" may now be construed legally as sexual harassment or creating a hostile environment. Even the beating of women by their spouses used to be

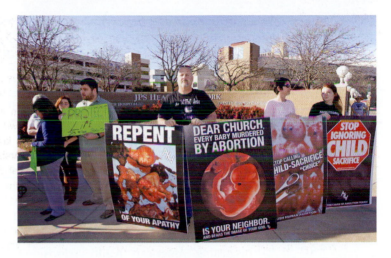

Anti-abortion demonstrators protest during a memorial at John Peter Smith Hospital in January 2014 after life support was removed from the pregnant and brain-dead Marlise Muñoz.

CREDIT:
AP Photo/*Star-Telegram*, Ron Jenkins.

HIGHLIGHT 2.1   RIGHT TO LIFE AND RIGHT TO DIE: A CASE IN RELATIVITY OF LAW

Marlise Muñoz, a 33-year-old paramedic, suffered a loss of oxygen due to a blood clot in her lungs, which left her brain-dead. But because she was 14-weeks pregnant and had lived in the state of Texas, one of 12 that has criminalized removal of life support from a pregnant woman, the family was forced to leave her body on respirators for more than two months until a court finally ruled that the law did not apply to a legally dead woman. Because of the oxygen deprivation and gestation in a brain-dead body, the fetus had major abnormalities, including heart problems and enough distortion of the lower body that sex could not be determined. Court proceedings had been attended by dozens of pro-life activists who expressed a view that the unborn fetus "was executed by judicial tyranny" and that the family had not done the right thing. The husband felt that people were "using my wife . . . as a political argument." Her father said, "I get angry with the state. What business did they have delving into these areas? Why are they practicing medicine up in Austin?"

Understanding the relativity of law clarifies that legislators, in fact, are continually delving into every aspect of people's lives. It is a matter of how just those interventions are perceived. In this case, the husband and parents of Marlise Muñoz felt that the state took away their loved one's right to die with dignity, but some moral entrepreneurs felt that no one had the right to withdraw any life-support measures. Which right do you believe takes precedence?

Sources: http://www.slate.com/blogs/xx_factor/2014/01/06/marlise_munoz_pregnant_brain_dead_woman_forced_to_stay_on_life_support_in.html

http://www.nytimes.com/2014/01/15/us/suing-to-end-life-support-for-woman-and-fetus.html?_r = 0

https://www.lifesitenews.com/news/marlise-munoz-removed-from-life-support-baby-executed-by-judicial-tyranny-p "acceptable" behavior within some U.S. state legal codes, providing that the man did not use a stick larger than the diameter of his thumb for the task. Things change so much, as John Curra (2000:14) notes in his excellent work, *The Relativity of Deviance*, that "change is the only real constant." The relativity of crime is the ongoing story of criminal law. The American experience with substance abuse (illegal drugs, alcohol, and tobacco), sodomy, and rape are reviewed below as examples of changes in the law across time.

Substance Abuse

Cultures generally have rules and customs regarding the ingestion of substances into the human body. Consensus across cultures regarding what is acceptable "food" is far from complete. Mere mention of epicurean delicacies from other cultures often elicits groans and perhaps pale countenances. Does the thought of sitting down to a plate of snail, dog, termites, or chicken feet sound delightful, or disgusting? American "reality" television shows bank on the notion that eating substances not culturally defined as foods will be so shocking as to attract viewers.

Aside from cultural perceptions, we are objectively impacted by the substances that we introduce into our bodies. Nutritionists assert, "we are what we eat." If we eat excessively, we can become obese. If we do not eat enough or do not have sufficient balance in our diet, we may become emaciated. If we consume too much caffeine we may display excessive nervousness. Garlic may leave unpleasant breath or a diet of beans may lead to excessive gas.

Persons who flagrantly violate eating norms come to be defined as deviants. Ingesting the wrong substances can dramatically impact how we are seen. Imagine the public reaction in his or her homeland to the Hindu sitting down to a beef steak dinner, the Jewish person devouring a pork sandwich, the vegetarian reaction to their potatoes being fried in animal fat, or the college students discovered by campus police sharing marijuana-sprinkled brownies in their dorm. What we put in our body may be considered deviant by others, and even prohibited by criminal law. Here, we consider drugs, alcohol, and tobacco.

Drugs

Students of criminology, as well as the average citizen, are often unaware that criminalization of drugs is a twentieth-century American creation. Earlier, what we now construe as "drugs" were not dealt with differently than the vast array of other substances that arguably hold some potential for damaging (or enhancing) health. What we now think of as "hard drugs" were once readily available as medicines and even food additives. Coca-Cola once lived up to the advertisement jingle dubbing it the "real thing" by including cocaine as a stimulating ingredient, later replaced by caffeine (Drug Policy Alliance, 2002a). Our contemporary view of drugs was launched when Congress passed the **Harrison Act** in 1914, effectively criminalizing the sale and possession of opiates. Legislation criminalizing marijuana was in place in 16 states by 1930, and in all states by 1937, when the Federal government passed the **Marijuana Tax Act** (Galliher & Walker, 1977), which, oddly, did not make it illegal to possess marijuana, but did make it an offense not to have paid the exorbitant tax placed on the drug.

The past more than 40 years have witnessed a "drug war" based on the idea that law enforcement should aggressively seek to eliminate specified drugs. Consequently, the number of arrests for drug offenses has skyrocketed to 1,663,582 in 2009, nearly half (858,408) for marijuana, and contributing to an overall prison population of 2,424,279, all at an annual cost of more than $51,000,000,000 (Drug Policy Alliance, 2011). In addition to saving more than $50 billion annually in expenses, decriminalization of marijuana could generate scores of billions of dollars by facilitating taxation of the drug, something that would make sense in terms of budgetary policy. According to Erich Goode (2001), the "war on drugs" represents an immense gap between an objective body of knowledge about drugs and a socially constructed image of the problem. As Craig Reinarman (2000:148) expresses it, drug scares "are a form of **moral panic** ideologically constructed" to assign blame for other social problems. Not unique to drugs, moral panics have been identified as responses to concerns as diverse as witchcraft, communism, child abuse, and alcohol. One of the primary tactics to create a moral panic is a campaign of misinformation. The infamous 1930s film, *Reefer Madness*, exemplifies this in the anti-marijuana campaign, depicting the drug as causing violent behavior. Politicians of that era openly attacked marijuana as a highly addictive drug, a distortion that has not yet fully subsided. The ideologically driven campaign of information distortion continues today. In a 1997 summary of the scientific evidence regarding effects of the substance, Lynn Zimmer and John Morgan identify some 20 common marijuana myths, summarized in Highlight 2.2.

One of the most common claims, at least by those with an ideological predisposition favoring the continued criminalization of marijuana, is that it is a **gateway drug** or "stepping stone" that leads to later use of "hard" drugs. While this is a complex issue, a *causal* link between the use of marijuana and other drugs has not been demonstrated (Morral et al., 2002; Zimmer & Morgan, 1997). On the one hand, those who do use marijuana are far more likely to go on to use other drugs, but in a complex statistical review of the evidence Andrew Morral and his colleagues (2002) noted that use of both is likely explained by the same risk factors. One's genetic makeup and the neighborhood a person lives in, for example, are strong predictors of a wide range of law-violating behaviors, including use of both marijuana and hard drugs. This text reviews many possible causal processes or theories to explain this. Most people who use marijuana never go on to use other illegal drugs and there are no physiological factors that would lead them to do so. The observation that most hard drug users tried marijuana first is, at least in part, an artifact of the widespread popularity of marijuana and relative rarity of other drugs. Most people consume applesauce before trying caviar, but apples are not said to create a "gateway to caviar." And most sex offenders

Our contemporary view of drugs was launched when Congress passed the Harrison Act in 1914, effectively criminalizing the sale and possession of opiates.

CREDIT:
©iStockphoto.com/Jerry Koch.

HIGHLIGHT 2.2 MYTHS, MORAL PANIC, AND MARIJUANA

Myth	Fact
Science has proven that marijuana is harmful to health.	Evidence leads to a conclusion that, while marijuana use may pose some risk, it does not appear to be great.
Marijuana has no medical benefit.	It has been found effective for treatments associated with glaucoma, cancer, and AIDS.
Marijuana is addictive.	No physical dependence is associated with it.
Marijuana causes people to go on to harder drugs.	There is no causal link between use of marijuana and other drugs.
Marijuana use is extensive because the laws do not sufficiently punish.	Sanctions have dramatically increased in recent years with widespread punishments, including arrests, prison, fines, and probation.
Marijuana causes brain damage.	No human studies have ever supported this claim.
Marijuana drains users of motivation.	While very heavy use of any substance is associated with low achievement, no greater impact has been found with marijuana than with other substances.
Marijuana use impairs memory.	Use of marijuana leads to short-term memory loss as part of the "high." There is, however, no evidence of long-term memory loss.
Marijuana use can lead to mental illness.	Marijuana use does not cause permanent or long-term psychological effects, but can produce psychological effects under its influence.
Marijuana causes aggression and crime.	Marijuana decreases aggression and is not statistically associated with crime, other than the crime of using it.
Marijuana has a widespread effect on sex hormones.	Marijuana may have some impact on fertility.
Marijuana causes birth defects.	There is no consistent evidence of differences between children with and without prenatal marijuana exposure.
Marijuana impairs the immune system.	While there is no evidence of general immune system impairment, findings with tobacco warrant examination of the effects upon persons with compromised immune systems.
Marijuana is more harmful to the lungs than tobacco.	Marijuana smoke does contain carcinogens, but users, on average, consume much smaller quantities.
THC remains in the body and can alter behavior.	THC does remain in fat cells for several weeks, which makes it easy to detect in urine samples. However, it disappears from brain cells within hours of use.
Marijuana causes automobile accidents.	While some doses of marijuana reduce motor skills, the effect is far less than alcohol. Moreover, marijuana tends to result in more cautious behavior, while alcohol is more likely to generate aggressive behavior.
Marijuana is stronger now than it used to be.	Potency appears not to have significantly changed over time.
Marijuana use can be prevented.	The success of American drug prevention programs is very limited.

Adapted from Zimmer, L., & Morgan, J. (1997). *Marijuana myths, marijuana facts: A review of the scientific evidence.* New York, NY: Lindesmith Center.

probably engage in some nonoffensive touching of others prior to their assaultive behavior. All are examples of correlation, but not causality. Marijuana is simply the most widely used illegal drug and, consequently, virtually always precedes use of other drugs. Those with especially high risk factors for drug use will go on to hard drugs, so it is likely that the best policy practices will address those propensities rather than a presumed "gateway."

The history of marijuana and how it is perceived in the United States provides a remarkable example of relativity of law. Its use has moved from acceptable, or at least tolerated, behavior in the early 1900s to a serious crime by mid-century, only to become less stigmatized in the 1960s and 1970s as middle-class college students took up the habit, followed by still another harsh reversal of the pendulum in the 1980s and early 1990s, and finally movement (again) toward decriminalization. As of 2015 there are 23 states that have legalized marijuana in some form, including four for recreational purposes. Washington, D.C. residents voted to legalize the substance and Congressional bids to intervene failed. Law in action surrounding marijuana possession is also shifting. The New York City Police Department, for example, has replaced arrests with a citation policy for individuals found with no more than 25 grams of the substance. In sum, use of marijuana, like many behaviors, has moved about rather dramatically on the continuum of social/legal acceptability for the past three-quarters of a century.

A drug category that has more recently moved quickly in the criminalized direction is anabolic steroids. From the American pastime sport of baseball's Barry Bonds and Olympic track star Marion Jones's prison sentences to positive steroid testing of Tour de France winners Floyd Landis and Alberto Contodor, steroids and other performance-enhancing drugs appear to have become both pervasively used and aggressively sanctioned, although currently widely condemned as dangerous tools of "cheaters." A study by Peter Kraska and his colleagues (2010) of steroids in the bodybuilding world suggests that this represents another "moral panic" in the "war on drugs." Tracing the history of these drugs, they observe that they have not been criminalized in many other countries, but were made so in the United States with passage of the Anabolic Steroid Control Act of 1990, broadened to a longer list of substances under the Anabolic Steroids Act of 2004. The "war on steroids" has reached its height as "law enforcement officials have recently gone from taking a very passive role in the enforcement of steroid laws to more aggressive efforts" (p. 163). The unfolding of all of this led them to conclude, "more so than even previous drug wars, drawing legal lines around society's pursuit of bodily perfection through [other] drugs will likely result in a mishmash of moral inconsistencies and political hypocrisy" (p. 183).

Alcohol

Increasingly viewed as a "drug" in recent years, "alcohol poisoning kills more people every year than all illegal drugs combined"(Drug Policy Alliance, 2002b). More people are also killed in alcohol-related automobile "accidents" each year than the total recorded in the Uniform Crime Reports as "murders." Alcohol is heavily implicated in a large portion of officially recognized murders. Marvin Wolfgang's (1958) groundbreaking homicide study found that alcohol was present in the offender and/or victim in nearly two-thirds of Philadelphia homicide cases, a finding which has largely held true at different times and places. Alcohol also takes a huge toll in nonvehicular accidents and illnesses. It can be a physically addictive substance and has afflicted millions.

Alcohol has produced death, injury, and illness on such a massive scale that it dwarfs the illegal drug problem. Yet the issue is far too complex to simply support the conclusion that "there oughta be a law" prohibiting alcohol. We had such a law in the form of **Prohibition**, mandated by the **Eighteenth Amendment** to the U.S. Constitution (1920 until 1933) and it was a dramatic failure by most measures. Just because something is objectively harmful does not mean that it will be criminalized, nor because something causes little or no harm can it be assumed that it will be legal (Goode, 2001). The relativity of crime/law is, to some degree, a function of other social forces that shape the law. Alcohol is a legal, albeit regulated, substance, and Prohibition ended because its use was considered acceptable to a large, and powerful, segment of the population. The experiment in prohibition, in fact, is most often explained in conflict terms. It was largely supported by a politically dominant rural, Protestant, native-born constituency and opposed by a growing urban, Catholic, foreign-born population. Legal prohibition is far more effective in homogeneous societies. Nonetheless, the U.S. prohibition effort did hold some marginal deterrent effect (see Chapter 5). It succeeded in reducing the overall consumption of alcohol. Its failure lay more in **unintended consequences**, such as increasing consumption of distilled spirits relative to less potent beer and providing organized crime with the classic marketing situation of a commodity in high demand, but legally prohibited.

Of course, many college students are quick to argue that prohibition remains in effect for millions of young Americans. According to the International Center for Alcohol policies, the United States is one of 11 countries worldwide that define 21 as the legal drinking age, along with Egypt, Fiji, Guam, Indonesia, India (in some states), Palau, Pakistan, Sri Lanka, Solomon Islands, and Tonga. Five countries have an overall legal ban on alcohol (Brunei, Libya, Qatar, United Arab Emirates, and Yemen). Within the United States there is a patchwork of laws further illustrating relativity in regard to criminalization of alcohol consumption. Attorney J. Tom Morgan (Morgan & Parker,

How did the American experiment in Prohibition (the Eighteenth Amendment) work out?

CREDIT:
©iStockphoto.com/
IGphotography.

2010; Morgan, 2013) addresses these for the states of North Carolina and Georgia, pointing out some peculiar variations. An underage person may legally be served alcohol by their parents in Georgia, but not in North Carolina. Texas allows underage consumption within parental sight. In North Carolina, a person under 21 who consumes *any* alcohol and drives a motor vehicle is guilty of DUI. In short, the crime of alcohol consumption continues to vary across both space and time. For a number of years, most college and university chancellors have opposed this inequitable criminalization, but the conversation has shifted of late with attention to campus rapes. There is no question that a substantial portion of rape victimizations involve alcohol consumption by both victims and offenders. There is widespread concern that alcohol undermines decision-making more for persons under the age of 25 than for those over that age, an observation supported by the biology of brain development.

Despite the scope of problems associated with abuse and the dramatic failure of prohibition, the topic should not be left without pointing to related contemporary trends and misinformation. Alcohol consumption has been increasingly condemned in recent years within certain contexts. There has been a substantial crackdown on drunk driving (see Chapter 5) with harsher punishments and lowered blood alcohol content levels, the raising of the legal drinking age, and greater restrictions placed on where alcohol can be consumed. These legal changes appear to have influenced social norms as well. The designated driver, for example, is a far more common role now than in years past. Likewise, the college-sanctioned "beer bust" has become a rarity, and the faculty member who meets with graduate seminars at off-campus pubs is much more likely to be seen as deviant and to accrue legal liability. In short, a moral panic, albeit on a lesser scale than witnessed by marijuana use, has proliferated. One symptom of this has been an overexplanation of crime by attributing unequivocal causal power to alcohol. Many commentators allude to the extraordinarily high rates of alcohol problems in the history of convicted felons and conclude that alcohol causes crime. Causality, however, as reviewed in Chapter 3, is complex. While correlation is a necessary component of causation, it is not sufficient to demonstrate causality. While the correlation is so strong that there is no question that alcohol plays an important role in crime causation, one cannot ignore the widespread use of alcohol entirely independent of crime or the fact that alcohol is merely one of a series of problems that plague most convicted felons.

Tobacco

Within the United States there has been a shift from nearly entirely unregulated public consumption of tobacco, widespread advertising, general availability to youths, and media depictions as glamorous, to the opposite of substantial regulation of public smoking, limits placed upon advertisement, prohibition of tobacco sales to minors, and frequent unfavorable depictions of smoking. Gone are the days when the tobacco industry could openly depict smoking as a healthy habit. Advertising phrases such as "to keep a slender figure," for

Gone are the days when the tobacco industry could openly depict smoking as a healthy habit. Here a 1929 ad for Lucky Strike cigarettes says "Light a Lucky, and you'll never miss sweets that make you fat . . . Reach for a Lucky instead of a sweet."

CREDIT:
Copyright Bettmann/Corbis/AP Images.

"healthy nerves," "a flow of energy," "relief from fatigue," and "better digestion" were deployed by the tobacco industry (Blum, 1980) prior to widespread dissemination of knowledge of the harm to smokers and involuntary smokers subjected to second-hand smoke. Nor are tobacco companies of the twenty-first century likely to repeat statements from the pre-1980 era, exposing their intent to "hook" young generations on nicotine, as Highlight 2.3 illustrates.

Tobacco companies finally had to acknowledge publicly that tobacco is a harmful drug, dramatically reshape their rhetoric, and agree to pay a $246 billion settlement to help compensate the states for the health damages caused by the commodity they market. Philip Morris Company, the largest tobacco marketer, conceded in 1999 that its product both causes cancer and is addictive. In 2000, however, the Clinton administration encountered a major setback to regulation of tobacco with a 5-to-4 Supreme Court ruling that the Federal Drug Administration (FDA) lacked authority to do so. Ironically, the FDA has been granted authority to regulate only "safe" drugs, but has concluded that tobacco is an unsafe drug. Thus, the Supreme Court reasoned in *FDA v. Brown & Williamson Tobacco Corp.* (2000) that the FDA would have no choice but to declare tobacco illegal. As that raises the tumultuous political question of criminalization, the Court concluded, "If they cannot be used safely for any therapeutic purpose, and yet they cannot be banned, they simply do not fit" within FDA parameters. The industry has experienced a precipitous decline in smoking prevalence, from 42.4 percent of the American population in 1965 to 24.7 percent in 1995 (Dreyfuss, 1999). However, what used to be acceptable within the United States remains so in many less-developed parts of the world. The American tobacco industry continues many of its old marketing practices outside of the United States where such acts remain legal. Vietnam's Ministry of Health reported that at as recently as 1998, at the Hanoi Tet festival, Philip Morris Tobacco Company provided "a large tent with Marlboro horses to ride

HIGHLIGHT 2.3 TOBACCO COMPANY STRATEGIES FOR HOOKING KIDS

One of the most obvious ways to deliver additional nicotine in a low-tar cigarette is to add nicotine from an outside source. . . . The problem is one of finding a source of the additional nicotine, and determining how to apply it.

To ensure increased and longer term growth for CAMEL FILTER, the brand must increase its share penetration among the 14–24 age group. . . . Maintenance of the smoking habit demands that smokers receive an "adequate" dose of nicotine (Blum, 1980).

Some children are so active (hyperkinetic) that they are unable to sit quietly in school and concentrate on what is being taught. We have already collaborated with a local school system in identifying some such children presently in the third grade. . . . It would be good to show that smoking is an advantage to at least one subgroup of the population. http://www.health.state.ok.us/program/tobac/doclinks.html

on for children, and young, nicely dressed cowboy girls offered single cigarettes free of charge to young boys" (Dreyfuss, 1999). A statement by Essential Action, an anti-tobacco organization, and some 30 women's, girls', and public health organizations noted, "The tobacco industry is aggressively targeting women and girls in developing countries with seductive advertising that blatantly exploits ideas of independence, power, emancipation, and slimness. . . . The launching of Virginia Slims in Hong Kong at a time when less than 2% of Hong Kong women under the age of 40 smoke exemplifies industry attempts to create a market"(Intl-tobacco, 2000). The report noted the bestowing of gift packs for Taiwanese women containing Virginia Slim Light cigarettes and lighters, the use of female pop stars to advertise the products, the low awareness of the hazards of smoking in these international "growth markets," and the wide array of cigarette advertising in these countries. Consequently, rates of female smoking, especially in developing countries, are increasing dramatically, as are the projections of premature smoking-related deaths. The tobacco industry's history of targeting youths, women, and the Third World as "growth markets" can be traced back more than 30 years (Brown, 1982), but has increased as domestic sales have declined. It is the relativity of law that both causes and allows this. As tobacco has been increasingly defined as a harmful and addictive drug, shifting legal and extralegal responses have reduced conventional domestic markets, resulting in increased industry efforts to pursue nonconventional and less regulated nondomestic markets. While the health impacts of smoking remain the same, social and legal responses have changed significantly.

Sodomy

Much of the debate regarding criminalization and decriminalization involves activities that, when criminalized, are frequently called **victimless crimes**, owing to the absence of a complaining victim (see Chapter 13). Sodomy is a salient example of this variety of crime, and it has been especially conspicuous with the focus on homosexuality. A U.S. Supreme Court decision, *Bowers v. Hardwick* (1986), upheld a Georgia sodomy statute as it applied to homosexuals. That statute declared, "A person commits the offense of **sodomy** when he performs or submits to any sexual act involving the sex organs of one person and the mouth or anus of another. . . ." (Georgia Code Annotated, 1984). The law provided for 1 to 20 years of imprisonment.

A Tennessee case was prosecuted shortly after the *Bowers* decision, but based on sodomy interpretations under common law, and thus applying to all persons. Clearly, however, it was rarely being enforced and then only against homosexuals. The incident, occurring on a college campus, involved police investigation of a parked car during late hours, revealing that it was occupied by two men, one of whom was not wearing pants. Both men were arrested and charged with "crimes against nature," interpreted at the time as any form of oral or anal sex. The prosecuting District Attorney General noted in regard to the gay community, "It's high time the gay community realizes it [homosexuality] is not simply an alternate lifestyle—it is a crime." He said he was "concerned about it [homosexuality] in

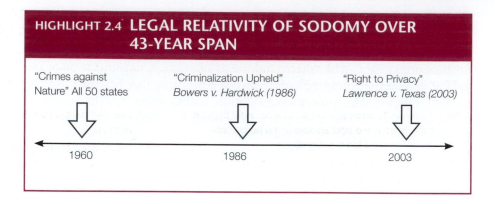

HIGHLIGHT 2.4 LEGAL RELATIVITY OF SODOMY OVER 43-YEAR SPAN

"Crimes against Nature" All 50 states

"Criminalization Upheld"
Bowers v. Hardwick (1986)

"Right to Privacy"
Lawrence v. Texas (2003)

1960   1986   2003

this community. In light of the apparent ease of which I have observed many of these people to engage in homosexual encounters . . . they are endangering everyone by spreading AIDS" (*Johnson City Press*, 1987:3). The two men received five-year sentences, the legal minimum for sodomy or "crimes against nature." The *Bowers* case was overturned in Georgia in 1998, while Tennessee replaced its common law approach with a "Homosexual Acts" provision in the state criminal code in 1989. That legislation was overturned in *Campbell v. Sundquist* (1996).

While in 1960 sodomy was criminalized in all 50 states, the United States Supreme Court took note in *Lawrence v. Texas* (2003) that the number had dwindled to 13 (four, including Texas, were for homosexual sodomy only) and used this as part of their rationale in stating that the *Bowers* decision was wrong. With same-sex marriages now legal in the majority of states, the move away from criminalizing consensual sex acts is abundantly clear. Highlight 2.4 depicts how relativity (across time) shifted sodomy from a criminal act in all 50 states to a constitutionally protected privacy right in a little over 40 years.

Rape

Many consider rape as a clear example of consensus—a crime so objectionable that it was a capital (death penalty) crime in America until 1977 when that penalty for rape was invalidated by *Coker v. Georgia* (1977). Yet what constitutes a rape varies widely across time and space. Over a 60-year period (1945–2005), no less than 119 countries expanded their definition of rape (Frank et al., 2009). Under English common law rape required forcible and nonconsensual penetration of a woman's vagina by the penis of a man not her husband. It was legally impossible both for a man to rape his wife and for a man to be a victim of rape. Clearly, however, there have always been both husbands who brutally forced their wives to engage in sexual acts against their will and men who were sexually violated against their will. Such seemingly common sense observations (by today's vantage) played a role in the wholesale reconstruction of American rape laws over the past quarter century. The changes, illustrating the relativity of rape, fell into three broad categories: marital rape, reconceptualization as gender neutral, and altering definitions of force and consent.

HIGHLIGHT 2.5 *STATE V. DOMINY*: SPOUSAL RAPE CONTINGENT ON DOG

The Tennessee State Supreme Court has offered some interpretation of that state's "Limited spousal exclusion" for the crime of rape. Section 39–13–507 of the Tennessee Code Annotated reads:

(a) A person does not commit an offense under this part if the victim is the legal spouse of the perpetrator except as provided in subsections

(b) (1) "Spousal Rape" means the unlawful sexual penetration of one spouse by the other where:

(A) The defendant is armed with a weapon or any article used or fashioned in such a manner to lead the victim to reasonably believe it to be a weapon;

(B) The defendant causes serious bodily injury to the victim; or

(C) The spouses are living apart and one (1) of them has filed for separate maintenance or divorce.

Under common law, women were viewed as property and marriage as a contract that entitled the husband to sexual services of the wife. This influence on the definition of rape persisted until the 1970s. Not until 1976 did the first state redefine forced sexual intercourse with a woman by her husband as rape and the definition of spousal rape remains quite diverse (Hasday, 2000). The case of *State v. Dominy* (1997) in Highlight 2.5 illustrates how bizarrely the legal rationale seems to have evolved in some states, although the spousal exclusion in Tennessee has since been eliminated. Antigua and Barbuda similarly abandoned spousal exclusion from the crime of rape in 1995 (Frank et al., 2009).

The facts of the case, originally presented in *State v. Dominy* (1997), were as follows:

Terry Allen Dominy of Hamilton County, Tennessee, asked his wife to have sexual intercourse with their dog. She refused his demand and he bound her hands and feet with duct tape. He then prompted the dog to have sex with his wife by manipulating its penis to arousal and placing it in his wife's vagina. The wife said that Dominy had been drinking and smoking dope. She testified that the assault lasted some 10–15 minutes with the defendant watching and laughing. He then had intercourse with her himself. He was convicted of aggravated rape and sentenced to three 25-year prison terms.

On appeal Dominy claimed a marital exemption for rape, and the Tennessee Court of Criminal Appeals agreed, overturning his conviction. The Tennessee State Supreme Court reversed once again, however, concluding that because the 68-pound German Shepherd had snapped at the woman, this constituted the "weapon" necessary under subsection (b)(1)(A) under the Limited Spousal Exclusion. In still another appeal to the state Supreme Court in 2001, the court declared that since Dominy had not originally been charged with spousal rape, even though the prosecutor was well aware that he was married to the victim, the state had forfeited its right to prosecute for that offense. Dominy was set free (*State v. Dominy*, 2001).

By substituting the penetration of any sexual orifice by any object for the common law penile–vaginal penetration, rape in recent years has been more broadly defined in two senses. First, it now encompasses a wider range of sexual violations. Secondly, it facilitated transition to a gender-neutral crime. Rape in the United States now recognizes victimized males and female offenders, crimes that previously were legal impossibilities. South Africa serves as another example of a country that expanded the definition of rape in this manner, doing so in 1998, as Zimbabwe did in 2001 (Frank et al., 2009). Consequently, one form of "new" rape, examined below, that has emerged in the public eye involves young male victims and adult female rapists. Such behavior is not new, but was accorded little attention and largely viewed quite differently a couple of decades ago.

The force/consent element of rape also has changed in a number of ways in recent years. One of them is the evolution of statutory rape laws. This offense holds the perpetrator criminally liable even if the sexual activity is purely consensual, indeed, even if the two parties assert deep and abiding love for one another. The legal concept is to protect the victim based upon the logic that they are incapable of formulating reasoned consent due to their young age. Until the 1970s statutory rape could only be committed by a male upon a female and the male offender could be the same age, or younger, than the female victim. Beginning in 1971, however, statutory rape laws began incorporating 2 to 6 year age spans between a younger victim and an older offender, as well as redefining the offense as gender neutral (Cocca, 2002a). Tracing the political process that produced age-spanned statutory rape legislation, Carolyn Cocca (2002a) found that conservatives, church groups, and anti-abortion activists campaigned against them out of fear that the exemption of similar-aged persons from rape liability would license teens for sexual activity. As a result of these political debates different definitions of statutory rape prevailed from state to state, with the age of consent varying from 14 to 18, although most have redefined the crime as gender neutral and incorporated some age span.

Another study undertaken by Cocca (2002b) suggests that the concept of a moral panic can be applied to a recent trend for states to toughen statutory rape laws to combat teen pregnancies. She contended that while the purported rationale is to protect young girls from older predatory men and to reduce public assistance to unwed mothers, the data belie these goals, revealing that only 8 percent of the fathers of pregnant teens could potentially be subject to prosecution for statutory rape. This is because nearly two-thirds of the child-bearing teens are old enough for consensual sex (18 or 19), and many of the 15-to 17-year-olds were impregnated by boys of the same age and some are legally married. Thus the real goal arguably is to redefine teen sex in terms that facilitate control of a morally objectionable behavior. Consequently, the recent legislative trend has been cast in a light of predatory men victimizing teenage females. The result is statutory rape laws congruent with a conservative agenda of:

> . . . targeting of the poor, pregnant teen and her equally poor and immoral impregnator: few would stand up to defend non-marital adolescent sexuality and pregnancy; the target populations are disempowered by their gender, age, class, race and/or ethnicity . . . (Cocca, 2002b:66).

Moral outrage regarding sexual liaisons between adolescent males and adult women also fueled the revisions of statutory rape laws. Reviewing the history of California's 1993 legislation, Cocca (2002a) recounted a 1992 case of a 40-year-old woman having sex with eight 14- to 16-year-old boys, generating outrage that she was not eligible for a statutory rape charge. This was followed the next year with publicity surrounding a high school football coach who pressed one of his players into sexual activity with his wife an estimated 1,000 times, conduct again not falling within the bounds of statutory rape as then defined. Later in 1993 California passed legislation that provided both broadened and toughened statutory rape parameters, including jail time even for sexual partners within the three-year span of a person under 16 years of age and a gender-neutral provision. Similar legal changes in the state of Washington set the stage for the internationally known case of Mary Kay Letourneau that illustrates a number of issues bound up in the relativity of law.

At the time of her statutory rape case in 1997, Mary Kay Letourneau was 34 years old, and her victim, Vili Fualaau, was 12. At the time Letourneau was a sixth-grade teacher and Fualaau her student. Letourneau had known him since she was his second-grade teacher. She was widely regarded as a model teacher and he as an artistically talented student who she continued to tutor over the next four years. Letourneau was married and the mother of four children, ages 3 to 12, when Fualaau was assigned to her sixth-grade class. As in her work role, she had an excellent reputation as a mother. But important in the eyes of many commentators, Letourneau was struggling with several problems at that time. She and her husband had filed for bankruptcy, openly acknowledged marital strife, and she had suffered a miscarriage. Most significantly, her father, to whom she was very close, succumbed to cancer. Such stresses are sometimes considered sufficient to account for deviant behaviors through "strain" explanations (see Chapter 7). Letourneau was also, however, diagnosed with bipolar disorder, a mental illness based upon a chemical imbalance in the brain that is strongly associated with bizarre and irrational behaviors. The diagnosing physician identified classic signs of this mental disorder that she displayed as mania, hypersexuality, and high risk-taking behavior. Letourneau was prescribed Depakote (divalproex sodium), a milder drug than the lithium that was, at that time, more traditionally used to treat bipolar disorder. And again, she displayed a classic sign of the disease in her later refusal to take the medication and her denial of the disorder. But is it more in order to seek an explanation of her deviance or to consider why the state of Washington chose to brand Letourneau a child rapist? Analysis of this event pits positivism (e.g., strain and mental illness) against interactionism (e.g., labeling).

The concept of relativity is particularly appreciated from the interactionist paradigm. Consider how events unfolded and decide which you find to be the most important question. The young Fualaau was large and exceptionally mature for his age, described by his mother as "an old soul trapped in a young body" (Cloud, 1998:3). He pursued Letourneau sexually, bragged to friends that he would have sex with her, and even placed a $20 bet that he would. That bet was won shortly after the school year ended, and just before Fualaau's thirteenth birthday. The sexual relationship continued until February, 1997, when Letourneau was arrested in the principal's office of her school as a consequence of anonymous charges leveled by one of her husband's relatives. To add to the shock of the case, Letourneau was pregnant with the boy's child, who was born in May, 1997. Letourneau was convicted of second-degree child rape and sentenced to 7½ years in prison, with all but 2½ months suspended in lieu of her agreement to continue medication for her bipolar disorder and to have no unsupervised contact with minors. Shortly after her release, however, she violated both agreements, again becoming pregnant by Fualaau. She was returned to prison in February, 1998, and completed her original 7½-year sentence in 2005. The two were married later that year in a lavish wedding.

Letourneau saw herself as a victim of the relativity of law. In her earlier words, "When the relationship started, it seemed natural. What didn't seem natural was that there was a law forbidding such a natural thing" (Alexander, 1997:1). As Fualaau then looked at it, "It's unfair. I want Mary to be with me and the kids" (*People Weekly*, 1998:1). While on tour to publicize a book (*One Crime, Love*) released by the couple, Fualaau said that Letourneau was "a victim at the same time they say she's a criminal" (Associated Press, 1998). With her prison time behind her, Letourneau and her husband, Fualaau, are now raising their two daughters. As Greg Olson, author of one of the books about her commented, she has always had a personal need to "prove to the world that this is a love story and not a crime story." Relativity of crime is indeed poignant.

In a 2004 case of striking similarity, 27-year-old Tennessee teacher, Pamela Rogers Turner, was charged with 13 counts of statutory rape of a 13-year-old male student. As in the Letourneau case, the relationship was revealed by an anonymous tip. Turner also was able to initially avoid prison time through a plea bargain that sent her to jail for six months and agreeing to have no further contact with her victim. Within two months of her release, however, she was twice arrested and charged with violating her probation by contacting the boy, placing her at risk, like Letourneau, of having to serve a seven-year prison sentence.

In 2005 still another statutory rape case involving a strikingly attractive 23-year-old Florida female teacher and a 14-year-old male student caught national attention. Debra Lafave pleaded guilty in one county to lesser charges and agreed to three years of house arrest. Charges were dropped in another county because the parents of the boy did not want him to have to testify. Lafave, like Letourneau, was diagnosed with bipolar disorder (see Chapter 6) and stated that she felt the mental disorder "had a lot to do with" her behavior (Fox News, March 22, 2006).

Major procedural changes in prosecuting rape have been incorporated in what are called **rape shield laws**. Historically, criminal procedure for the crime of rape was heavily biased against female victims in order to minimize the likelihood of false rape accusations against men. Under common law women were required to physically resist, quickly report the crime, and to face hostile questioning in court. These views were evident in the legal and procedural requirements of rape cases until addressed in the rape reform era that began in the 1970s. Rape reform was encouraged, in part, by the widespread view that victims of rape were twice victimized, once by the rapist, and again in court proceedings. The rape victim could expect to be accused of consenting to sex with the rapist, to be disparaged by defense claims of a pattern of immoral behavior, and to be embarrassed by revelation of irrel-

Debra Lafave, convicted of sexual relations with a teen student in 2005, speaks to reporters at the Tampa Criminal Courthouse in 2009 after a court hearing in which she asked a judge to approve unsupervised contact with the children of family and friends. In 2012, a judge ordered Lafave back on probation.

CREDIT:
AP Photo/*Tampa Tribune*, Jay Nolan.

evant sexual history. Rape shield laws imposed substantial limits on the ability of the defense to introduce information or pursue a line of questioning about the history and character of the alleged victim, swinging the procedural balance in the direction of the victim's interests. The 2003–4 Kobe Bryant case, however, was viewed by many as a major erosion of rape shield laws. The victim eventually decided that she would not testify and charges were dropped, but not before a lot of derogatory information about her was made public by the defense team and allowed by the judge.

The term **post-penetration rape** was introduced in 1991 (McLellan, 1991) and gained appreciable legal precedent in the recent California *In re John Z.* (2003) case. Post-penetration rape occurs when a woman has given her consent to engage in sexual intercourse, but then withdraws the consent during the sex act, and the male partner refuses to immediately withdraw from the activity. While *In re John Z.* concluded that a rape has taken place whenever consent is withdrawn during sexual intercourse, but the male participant continues, it has been objected that this redefinition is counterproductive. Some legal theorists have argued that rather than a "rape," this should be designated as some other form of sexual assault, as "calling the two scenarios 'rape' confounds the definition of the crime. Moreover, doing so demeans the victims of traditional rape" (Fradella & Brown, 2005:13). Others argue that a rape is a rape is a rape. From the vantage of relativity of crime neither is correct. A rape, or any other crime, is whatever those with the political influence to define it declare at any given time and place.

Relativity Across Space

Just as the law is not fixed across time, it varies from one location to another. What is defined as crime may differ dramatically from one country to another or between locations within a specific country. Differences in norms and laws often lead to cross-cultural conflicts. The "ugly American" image may be largely a consequence of an affluent population traveling widely within other cultures, while remaining ignorant of their norms. In some instances, the conflict may be rooted less in ignorance than in **ethnocentrism** (believing that the customs and values of one's own culture are superior to those of others). In some instances, the norm violations will be regarded not only as insulting, but as criminal behavior.

Since the terrorist hijacking and subsequent suicide airline crashes into the World Trade Center on September 11, 2001, attention has focused on the conflict between Islamic extremists and Western culture. This is the highest profile, contemporary example of the relativity of law across cultures. Those who perpetrate such attacks are labeled "terrorists" in the West, are loathed, and more vigorously pursued than any other type of "criminals." It was labeling them as outlaw terrorist-sponsoring regimes that provided American justification for the invasions of Afghanistan and Iraq. Yet, those same "criminals" are widely regarded as martyrs within Islamic cultures.

The clash between Islamic and Western conceptions of law extends far beyond terrorism and military issues. What is regarded as criminal under fundamentalist Islamic law is often shocking from a Western perspective. The plight of two American aid workers, thinly disguised missionaries, serving in Afghanistan at the time of the September 11 attacks, is illustrative. Dayna Curry and Heather Mercer were arrested by Taliban authorities for being in a private home and preaching Christianity, charges punishable by death under Afghani law at that time. Missionaries were not allowed in the country, so the two women had entered under the auspices of an "aid" organization. However, they had in their possession Bibles, a film about Jesus, a book titled *Sharing Your Faith with a Muslim*, and a paper that documented the frequency of a Christian broadcasting station. Preaching Christianity is a serious crime in most Islamic countries, although often overlooked by the law in action.

In the aftermath of the 2010 Haiti earthquake, 10 American missionaries from an Idaho church found themselves facing kidnapping charges for attempting to move 33 children across the border, to the Dominican Republic. Child trafficking is a pervasive problem in Haiti; a single count of kidnapping carries a possible prison sentence of five to 15 years.

Even matters seemingly as innocuous as humor fall within the confines of relativity of crime. What is laughed about in one culture may constitute deviant or criminal words in another. Political figures, for example, traditionally provide fodder for American humor. Whether crude sexual innuendos about former President Bill Clinton or derogatory "Bushisms" belittling President George W. Bush, such caustic commentary is characteristic of American culture. Other cultures, however, view such words as deviant or criminal. Thai culture, for example, regards derogatory humor directed at King Bhumibol Adulyadej as not just disrespectful but criminal. The owner of a Thai-themed Philadelphia lounge was dismayed that her advertisement, incorporating a photo touched up to present the elderly Adulyadej as a hip and funky figure, led to numerous diplomatic protests by the Thai government (*Johnson City Press*, 2002a).

The world witnessed even more serious cultural clashes of humor in 2006. The publication of a series of cartoons in a Danish newspaper sparked diplomatic retaliation, huge demonstrations throughout the Muslim world, boycotts of Danish products, burning of Danish embassies, and loss of lives as demonstrations turned violent. Under Islam, any representations of Muhammad are prohibited. The Danish caricatures depicted the Prophet in such unflattering poses as wearing a bomb on his turban and admonishing suicide bombers to stop because the supply of virgins was exhausted. Humor of this sort is viewed as blasphemous by Muslims and is therefore prohibited under Islamic law. One Pakistani cleric announced a bounty in excess of a million dollars for killing the cartoonists who have since been extended security protection by their government.

For their part, most Danes were caught in an unusual quandary. Denmark has long had a reputation as a tolerant country, but also one that places a premium on freedom of expression. They were unaccustomed to seeing their flag burned, being targeted by boycotts, and held in disdain by other cultures. Yet the conflict pitted religious tolerance against freedom of expression. The Danish editor, Flemming Rose, who released the cartoons, made the case for the latter in this way:

> I think it's problematic when a religion tries to impose its taboos and values on the larger society. When they ask me not to run those cartoons, they are not asking for my respect. They're asking for my submission. . . . To me, those cartoons are saying that some individuals have hijacked, kidnapped and taken hostage the religion of Islam to commit terrorism" (Fleishman, 2006:2).

Humor, like all other matters, is relative. What is a laughing matter in one culture may be criminal in another. In short, as we study crime, we must avoid the simplistic thinking that a crime is a crime is a crime. What is a crime depends on where one is, when one is there, and what interest groups have sufficient power to incorporate their ideologies into the law.

Two glaring examples of crime and humor transpired just as this ninth edition of the book was going to press. First was a massive cyberattack on Sony Pictures Entertainment. The suspicion was that the attack came from North Korea, motivated by their objection to the forthcoming release of a comedy, *The Interview*, which included an assassination plot against North Korean dictator Kim Jong Un. North Korean spokespersons, while condemning the spoof as "terrorism" and an "act of war" denied any involvement, although some evidence suggested otherwise. The cyber attackers posted on the Web movies not yet released, revealed personal identifying data on many who had worked at Sony, shared many embarrassing internal company and private emails, and generated costs in the tens of millions of dollars. Threats were also leveled at Sony employees and their families. The climax of the incident came when threats of terrorist attacks on moviegoers led theaters, and ultimately Sony, to cancel the Christmas Day, 2014 release of the film. Within days, however, negative public reaction to this momentous infringement on the American value of free expression compelled its release to private theaters and then to Netflix. So in the end, a quite mediocre film (53 percent Rotten Tomatoes score) was extended far more attention than merited by its cinematic value. So anything, even comedies that most Americans would describe as "silly," can be dubbed "criminal" or incite serious criminal acts. That is, comedy is sometimes no laughing matter to those who view it as something that *should be* criminal and who are willing to use that humor as justification to commit crimes.

An even more ghastly recent clash of humor and crime was seen in the terrorist attack on the offices of *Charlie Hebdo*, a French satirical magazine, in Paris. The publication had printed several cartoonish depictions of Muhammad responding negatively to radical Islamic ideas. Two Islamic terrorists wielding assault rifles responded to this satire by forcing their way into the magazine's offices, where they murdered 11 staff members. Exiting the building, the assassins, who were later hunted down by French police and killed in shoot-outs, were heard shouting in Arabic "We have avenged the Prophet Muhammad" and "God is great." World leaders quickly assembled in Paris to display support for the French and millions demonstrated in memory of the slain satirists. Much of the world was shaken by the deadly clash between religion and both humor and free speech. The rights to free speech and even distasteful humor are valued so highly as to be seen as principles worth dying for in many societies. In others, they are seen as so deviant or criminal as to be worth killing for.

THE CRIMINAL JUSTICE SYSTEM

To understand crime and criminals, it is essential to know something of the **criminal justice system**, the process whereby the law is used to officially label people as criminals. We have already seen that not all conduct harmful to society is designated criminal, nor can everything prohibited or required by law be justified under the notions of safety and harm to society. There is no law in most states against failing to help a drowning person, for instance, although this might be easily done. However, it is illegal to gamble at work on a football game—although not in Las Vegas. It is generally legal for a 19-year-old to have a string of sultry love affairs, but not to drink a beer. Crime is relative in the eyes of the beholder and to who has the power to define particular behaviors as crimes. Moreover, the criminal law is applied differentially. Only a very small portion of crimes lead to official action. Typically, a 19-year-old may drink alcoholic beverages with older friends without drawing the ire of the juvenile/criminal justice systems, but on occasion such behavior may be dealt with very severely due to campaigns by moral entrepreneurs or the lodging of a complaint by someone holding a grudge against one of the persons in the drinking group. Understanding discrepancies between law in books and law in action helps explain the criminal justice process.

There are important interdependencies between criminal justice and criminology. The focus of criminology is on explaining crime, while criminal justice is more concerned with societal, and particularly official, reactions to crime and criminals. Criminology, consequently, tends to be more theoretical and to include explanations that do not have immediate, or at least not readily adoptable, policy implications. Criminal justice is often more descriptive and is more likely to suggest courses of action for criminal justice practitioners. But the distinction is a matter of emphases, not mutual exclusivity, and many students of crime use these disciplinary labels interchangeably. Academic labels aside, a thorough familiarity with criminal justice is essential to understanding and explaining crime. Conversely, official reactions to crime and offenders cannot be improved without sound theoretical premises.

The most common way to organize knowledge of criminal justice is to do so in reference to its three broad components: police, courts, and corrections (Bernard & Engel, 2001). That approach is taken here, with each component being viewed in terms of four specific goals of criminal justice: (1) deterrence, (2) incapacitation, (3) rehabilitation, and (4) retribution.

Goals of Criminal Justice

Criminal justice is intended to link practice with broader social goals that, in turn, are associated with certain values and assumptions. Some goals are more sensitive to the interests of society; others are more attuned to individual needs. The popularity of each goal varies with the social priorities and elite interests of the time. Generally, as noted above, criminal justice theory explicitly recognizes four formal goals: deterrence, incapacitation, rehabilitation, and retribution. Each involves specific policies, although a particular practice in criminal justice may accommodate two or more distinct goals (Table 2.3).

Deterrence (examined at length in Chapter 5) uses punitive sanctions to dissuade persons from committing criminal offenses in the future. The sanctions can be administered either to "teach a lesson" to the convicted offender (**special deterrence**) or to serve as an example to others of the perils of criminality

TABLE 2.3 The Goals of Criminal Justice

Goal	Definition
Deterrence	Prevention of crime by instilling a fear of punishment in potential offenders
Incapacitation	Prevention of crime by physically eliminating capacity for crime, usually through imprisonment
Rehabilitation	Preventing additional criminal acts by offenders through elimination of their motives to offend
Retribution	Punishment of offenders because they deserve it as a consequence of their law violations

(**general deterrence**). Deterrence theory and policy revolve around modes of punishment delivery, and focus particular attention on police, prosecutorial, and judicial operations. Deterrence, then, has the pragmatic goal of preventing crime by scaring offenders or potential offenders with the threat or application of punitive sanctions. This goal has been increasingly emphasized since the 1970s.

Incapacitation seeks to reduce or to eliminate the capacity of offenders to commit additional crimes. Capital punishment is the only conclusive means of incapacitating offenders. In the past, criminal transgressors were exiled, in part for incapacitative purposes. The English transported offenders first to America and later to Australia. This measure obviously affected only the capacity to commit offenses in England, not in the locales to which the offenders were sent. Futurists speak of kindred incapacitative schemes that rely on fantastic technology, such as the crystal prisms utilized to exile condemned villains in the motion picture *Superman* saga or the penal space colonies depicted in the motion picture *Star Trek* adventures. Other advocates of incapacitation promote surgical stratagems such as lobotomies and castration, but evidence suggests that such awful incapacitative schemes are not foolproof. Reviewing studies of castrated Danish sex offenders, for instance, Robert Martinson observed of their recidivism that it was "not, interestingly enough, a rate of zero; where there's a will, apparently there's a way" (1974:36).

Imprisonment is the primary criminal justice practice designed to achieve incapacitative goals. There is common sense in the notion that persons imprisoned will be kept from criminal activity. Clearly, however, incarceration is not a completely incapacitative measure because imprisoned offenders may victimize institutional staff and other inmates and, on occasion, escape. A larger concern is whether imprisoned offenders "make up for lost time" by committing crime at a higher rate or of a more serious nature following release than would have been the case had they not been institutionalized. If so, the net incapacitative effect could diminish to zero or even to a negative value. The goal of incapacitation has contributed to increased recourse to prisons in recent years, particularly for offenders labeled "career criminals."

Rehabilitation is designed to change offenders by removing the motivation to engage in criminal behavior. The assumption behind rehabilitation is that behavior can be modified by altering attitudes, values, skills, or constitutional features that cause criminal behavior. Based on a medical model, rehabilitation assumes that appropriate treatments may be prescribed according to the nature of the offender's defect. Rehabilitation may mandate treatment modes as diverse as job training, psychotherapy, and methadone maintenance for heroin addicts.

The goal of rehabilitation dominated the administration of justice from the beginning of the twentieth century until the emergence of an anti-rehabilitation movement in the early 1970s. Rehabilitation was based on optimism that it could lower recidivism rates. At the same time, rehabilitation was considered a compassionate and benevolent response to offenders. In the early 1970s, however, skepticism began to fester, based on disbelief that rehabilitation works, discomfort with the inequities that accompany individualized decision making necessitated by the medical model, and doubt about the accuracy of predictive restraint (e.g., parole) decisions. Rehabilitation and associated policies and procedures (such as probation and parole) in the administration of justice have been de-emphasized in recent years. The issue of the earlier promise of rehabilitation, however, is far from resolved (e.g., Andrews et al., 1990a,b; Cullen, 2005 Logan & Gaes, 1993).

Deterrence, incapacitation, and rehabilitation are all utilitarian goals of criminal justice; the assumption is that they can prevent crime. **Retribution** is based solely on moral reprobation or outrage at criminal misconduct. It involves the punishment of past wrongdoing in order to achieve a moral balance. Retributivists contend that crime, a violation of the rights of others, requires imposition of a penalty that will remove the advantage gained by the offender and restore social equilibrium. Punishment, then, is morally required.

The punishment must also be proportionate to the harm caused or risked, although mercy can be extended once it is acknowledged that the punishment is deserved. Retributivists argue that their position leaves the human dignity of the offender intact. We punish animals to train them, but humans are punished because they deserve it. As with deterrence, human rationality is presumed. In contrast, rehabilitation assumes that the individual is defective. Most important, retributivists assert that their position provides the only justification for punishment. In recent years retribution, sometimes called **just deserts**, has become widely supported as the major goal of criminal justice. Research by Harold Grasmick and his colleagues has identified support of retributive rationale for punishment partially as a function of fundamentalist religious beliefs (Grasmick et al., 1992). The Old Testament reference to "eye for an eye, and a tooth for a tooth" on three occasions underlies this belief.

In reinstating capital punishment in *Gregg v. Georgia* (1976) after a four-year court-decreed moratorium, the U.S. Supreme Court explicitly acknowledged retribution as a valid punishment goal. This, however, is a moral question and "no empirical research can tell us if the argument is 'correct' or 'incorrect.' Empirical studies can neither answer the question of what specific criminals (or noncriminals) 'deserve,' nor settle debates over other moral issues surrounding capital punishment" (Radelet & Akers, 1996:1). Deterrence and incapacitation, on the other hand, are goals that can be empirically assessed in relation to capital punishment.

These aims of criminal justice can be complementary. Andrew von Hirsch (1976) argued that just deserts alone might justify a system of punishment, but that the other aims, especially deterrence, are useful supplementary crime control strategies. Similarly, David Fogel (1975), in advocating a retribution-based "justice model" for corrections, acknowledged a role for rehabilitative services, so long as the offenders are volunteers. James Q. Wilson and Richard Herrnstein (1985) saw some virtue in diversity of criminal justice goals and approvingly discussed the merits of retribution along with the usefulness of incapacitation and deterrence.

Incongruities often arise among these goals, however. When should societal interest in deterrence or incapacitation take priority over just deserts? When should the rehabilitative needs of offenders take precedence over protection of society through deterrent or incapacitative measures? Jack Henry Abbott had been in prison some 20 years when he so impressed Norman Mailer with his literary talent that Mailer befriended him and advocated his parole, based largely on a rehabilitative rationale. Before Abbott's release, Mailer wrote these words in his preface to Abbott's book depicting his prison experience:

> It is certainly time for him to get out. There is a point past which any prisoner can get nothing more from prison, not even the preservation of his will, and Abbott, I think, has reached these years. Whereas, if he gets out, we may have a new writer of the largest stature among us . . . (Abbott, 1981:xviii).

Abbott was paroled, and days later murdered a young man working in a restaurant with whom Abbott had a trivial disagreement. Before his release, Abbott had said of freedom:

> I have the right, at least, to walk free at some time in my life even if the odds are by now overwhelming that I may not be as other men (Abbott, 1981:198).

Did Abbott have that right? Or did society and his murder victim have the right to be protected from him? And what of those who are suffering in prison, but would use freedom in a socially acceptable and productive manner? This is the crux of the dilemma in selecting goals for criminal justice. It is not an easy task, and clarity of goals must precede sound policy.

By examining the provisions of legal codes for every state correctional department, Velmer Burton, Gregory Dunaway, and Renee Kopache (1993) depicted the status of formal criminal justice goals. They found that the majority of states have legislatively endorsed more than one goal. Rehabilitation remained the most common goal despite a conservative "get-tough" attitude toward crime that was taking hold at that time. The most recent legislative pronouncements, however, were nonrehabilitative. Incapacitation (custody/control) was the second most frequently legislated goal, followed by retribution (punishment/discipline), and deterrence.

Which of these goals is just? According to those who fully appreciate the relativity of crime, a measure of injustice is inevitable. Take the Letourneau/Fualaau affair, for example. If one accepts the premise that Letourneau's actions victimized Fualaau and that she poses a threat to other children, then her 7.5 years in prison might be justified on grounds of any of these goals. One could argue that she is getting "what she deserves" (retribution), that other children are being protected (deterrence and/or incapacitation), or that she is very sick and needs help (rehabilitation) and should be in a facility equipped to counsel and medicate her. If we do not accept the premise that Fualaau was her victim, even if we find her actions offensive, then the logic of intervening disintegrates. She may be the victim, and the state, the real criminal entity. Philosophical questions aside, what the criminal justice system is supposed to pursue ideally is not necessarily what it pursues in practice, a matter the next section explores.

The Administration of Justice

Justice is administered in America by a "system" made up of police, courts, and corrections, generally referred to as the criminal justice system. Study of criminal justice as a system or process has increased dramatically in recent decades and this system (or process) is intricately linked to criminology. For social reaction theories drawn from the interactionist paradigm these processes are critical. Such understandings of criminal behavior deeply incorporate the actions of criminal justice officials, along with other societal components, in explaining how criminal careers unfold. Likewise, the actions of criminal justice officials are an intricate part of rational choice explanations of criminal behavior. If the formal justice system fails to deliver the necessary criterion for deterrence, for example, the theoretical premise collapses due to an operational failure. The theory could be correct but the mode of delivery is faulty. In short, the connection between criminological explanations of criminal behavior and the operations of the criminal justice system is critical. Echoing Edwin Sutherland's tripartite definition of criminology, some would contend that operation of the criminal justice system is merely subsumed within the criminological domain. While this text is focused on the body of theory or explanations for criminal behavior, further study of criminal justice as a system or process will provide a deeper understanding of the causes of crime.

SUMMARY

Both the content and origins of criminal law are important to the criminologist. Whether it is a product of consensus, meeting the needs of larger society, or whether it serves the interests of the elite in conflict with others, is a widely debated issue. It is clear, however, that crime is relative. The content of legal codes varies dramatically across time, as does the law in action. The conceptualization of behaviors as diverse as substance abuse, sodomy, and rape illustrate the problem.

Private wrongs are addressed by civil law, while public wrongs are the subject of criminal law. Criminal procedure is substantially more restrictive because so much is usually at stake. A criminal statute may prohibit the commission of acts (e.g., robbery, rape, and murder) or may require acts and penalize their omission (e.g., filing income tax returns). Such offenses are classified as felonies, misdemeanors, or violations in terms of their perceived seriousness and the range of potential punishments.

Justice is administered by a criminal justice system that is charged with pursuing some combination of deterrence, incapacitation, rehabilitation, and retribution. The system is comprised of police, courts, and corrections agencies. In practice each exercises a great deal of discretion that introduces additional complexities in efforts to understand crime and criminals. Many criminological perspectives require careful scrutiny of activities within the criminal justice system. To many, studying systems of justice is part of the larger criminological enterprise.

KEY TERMS AND CONCEPTS

Actus Reus

Administrative Law

Charlie Hebdo

Civil Law

Conflict

Consensus

Criminal Justice System

Criminal Law

Deterrence

Eighteenth Amendment

Ethnocentrism

Felonies

Gateway Drug

General Deterrence

Harrison Act (1914)

Incapacitation

The Interview

Just Deserts

Marijuana Tax Act (1937)

Mens Rea

Misdemeanors

Moral Panic

Post-penetration Rape

Prohibition

Rape Shield Laws

Rehabilitation

Relativity of Crime

Retribution

Sodomy

Special Deterrence

Unintended Consequences (of Prohibition)

Victimless Crimes

KEY CRIMINOLOGISTS

John Curra

Emile Durkheim

CASES

Bowers v. Hardwick, 478 U.S. 186 (1986)

Campbell v. Sundquist, 926 S.W. 2d 250 (1996)

Coker v. Georgia, 433 U.S. 485 (1977)

FDA v. Brown & Williamson Tobacco Corp., 529 U.S. 120 (2000)

Gregg v. Georgia, 428 U.S. 153 (1976)

In re John Z., 29 Cal. 4th 756, 128 Cal. Rptr. 2d 783, 60 P.3d 183 (2003)

Lawrence v. Texas, 539 U.S. 558 (2003)

Roe v. Wade, 410 U.S. 113 (1973)

State v. Dominy, No. 01 C01–9512-CC-00404 (Tenn. 1997)

State v. Dominy, 67 S.W.3d 822 (Tenn. 2001)

DISCUSSION QUESTIONS

1. Discuss three examples of relativity of law across time.
2. Discuss three examples of relativity of law across space.
3. List and discuss at least three critical events in the U.S. criminalization of drugs.
4. Outline the factors that must be present for a crime to have occurred.
5. Contrast both sides of the "gateway drug" debate. Is the concept useful or misguided?
6. List and summarize at least five U.S. Supreme Court cases that address the relativity of law.

REFERENCES

Abbott, J. H. (1981). *In the belly of the beast: Letters from prison*. New York, NY: Random House.

Alexander, K. (1997). Zero for conduct: After bearing the child of a 13-year-old student, a sixth-grade teacher may be heading for prison. *People Weekly, 48* EC:A19823594.

Andrews, D. A., Zinger, I., Hoge, R. D., Bonta, J., Gendreau, P., & Cullen, F. T. (1990a). Does correctional treatment work? A clinically relevant and psychologically informed meta-analysis. *Criminology, 28,* 369–404.

Andrews, D. A., Zinger, I., Hoge, R. D., Bonta, J., Gendreau, P., & Cullen, F. T. (1990b). A human science approach or more punishment and pessimism: A rejoinder to Lab and Whitehead. Criminology, *28,* 419–29

Associated Press. (1998). Teenage dad overjoyed about new daughter with ex-teacher. *Johnson City Press,* October 19.

Becker, D. & Olavarrieta, C. D. (2013). Decriminalization of abortion in Mexico City: The effects on women's reproductive rights. *American Journal of Public Health, 103,* 590–3.

Bernard, T. J. & Engel, R. S. (2001). Conceptualizing criminal justice theory. *Justice Quarterly, 18,* 1–30.

Blum, A. (1980). Medicine vs. Madison Avenue: Fighting smoke with smoke. *Journal of the American Medical Association, 243,* 739–40.

Brown, S. E. (1982). *Hidden assaults and the tobacco industry*. Paper presented at the annual meeting of The American Society of Criminology. Toronto, Canada.

Burton, V. S., Jr., Dunaway, R. G., & Kopache, R. (1993). To punish or rehabilitate? A research note assessing the purposes of state correctional departments as defined by state legal codes. *Journal of Crime and Justice, XIV,* 177–88.

CDC. (2008). Abortion surveillance–United States, 2005. *Surveillance Summaries, 57,* 1–32.

Cloud, J. (1998). A matter of hearts. *Time, 151* EC:A20534677.

Cocca, C. E. (2002a). The politics of statutory rape laws: Adoption and reinvention of morality policy in the states, 1971–99. *Polity, 35,* 51–73.

Cocca, C. E. (2002b). From "Welfare Queen" to "Exploited Teen": Welfare dependency, statutory rape, and moral panic. *NWSA Journal, 14,* 56–79.

Cullen, F. T. (2005). *The twelve people who saved rehabilitation: How the science of criminology made a difference.* The American Society of Criminology 2004 presidential address. *Criminology, 43,* 1–42.

Curra, J. (2000). *The relativity of deviance.* Thousand Oaks, CA: Sage.

Dowd, M. (2002). Driving while female. *New York Times,* November 17.

Dreyfuss, R. (1999). Big tobacco rides east. *Mother Jones Magazine,* January/February.

Drug Policy Alliance. (2002a). *Drug by drug.* http://www.lindesmith.org/drugbydrug/cocainecrack.

Drug Policy Alliance. (2002b). *Drug by drug: Overview.* http://www.lindesmith.org/drugbydrug.

Drug Policy Alliance. (2011). *Drug war by the numbers.* http://www.drugpolicy.org.

Durkheim, E. (1893/1933). *The division of labor in society.* (G. Simpson, Trans.). New York, NY: The Free Press.

Durkheim, E. (1895/1958). *The rules of sociological method.* (S.A. Soloway & J.H. Mueller, Trans.). Glencoe, IL: The Free Press.

Fleishman, J. (2006). *latimes.com/news.* Feb. 9.

Fogel, D. (1975). *We are the living proof. The justice model for corrections.* Cincinnati, OH: Anderson Publishing Co.

Fox News (2006). *Fox News broadcast.* March 22.

Fradella, H. F. & Brown, K. (2005). Withdrawal of consent post-penetration: Redefining the law of rape. *Criminal Law Bulletin, 41,* 3–23.

Frank, D. J., Hardinge, T., & Wosick-Correa, K. (2009). The global dimensions of rape-law reform: A cross-national study of policy outcomes. *American Sociological Review, 74,* 272–90.

Galliher, J. F. & Walker, A. (1977). The puzzle of the social origins of the Marihuana Tax Act of 1937. *Social Problems, 24,* 367–76.

Georgia Code Annotated (1984). *Georgia Code Annotated A416–6–2.* (1984).

Goode, E. (2001). *Deviant behavior* (6th ed.). Upper Saddle River, NJ: Prentice Hall.

Grasmick, H. G., Davenport, E., Chamelin, M. B., & Bursik, R. J. (1992). Protestant fundamentalism and the retributive doctrine of punishment. *Criminology, 30,* 21–45.

Hasday, J. E. (2000). Contest and consent: A legal history of marital rape. *California Law Review, 88,* 1373–1506.

Intl-tobacco@essential.org (2000). *Women, girls and tobacco: An appeal for global action.*

Johnson City Press. (1987). *Sodomy: Crimes against nature law pressed.* March 29.

Johnson City Press. (1993). *Judge rejects woman's pleas to free attacker.* Associated Press. November 13.

Johnson City Press. (2002a). *Lounges ad featuring king draws Thai diplomat's ire.* Associated Press. June 30.

Johnson City Press. (2002b). *Couple to be stoned to death for affair*. August 30.

Johnson City Press. (2002c). *Stoning sentences surge in Nigeria*. September 15.

Johnson City Press. (2003). *Senate OKs bill setting up state lottery*. April 24.

Kraska, P. B., Bussard, C. R., & Brent, J. J. (2010). Trafficking in bodily perfection: Examining the late-modern steroid market place. *Justice Quarterly, 27*, 159–85.

Logan, C. H. & Gaes, G. G. (1993). Meta-analysis and the rehabilitation of punishment. *Justice Quarterly, 10*, 245–63.

McLellan, A. (1991). Post-penetration rape: Increasing the penalty. *Santa Clara Law Review, 31*, 779.

Martinson, R. (1974). What works?–Questions and answers about prison reform. *The Public Interest*, (Spring), 22–54.

Morgan, J. T. (2013). *Ignorance is no defense: A teenager's guide to Georgia law*. Decatur, GA, Westchester Legal Press.

Morgan, J. T. & Parker, W. (2010) *Ignorance is no defense: A college student's guide to North Carolina Law*. Decatur, GA, Westchester Legal Press.

Morral, A. R., McCaffrey, D. F., & Paddock, S. (2002). Reassessing the marijuana gateway effect. *Addiction, 97*, 1493–1504.

People Weekly. (1998). *Family man: Teenage lover of Mary Kay Letourneau writes book about their romance*. EC:53150648.

Pollock, J. M. (2013). *Criminal Law* (10th ed.). Boston, MA: Anderson/Elsevier.

Radelet, M. L. & Akers, R. L. (1996). Deterrence and the death penalty: The views of the experts. *The Journal of Criminal Law and Criminology, 87*, 1–16.

Reinarman, C. (2000). The social construction of drug scares. In P. A. Adler, & P. Adler (Eds.), *Constructions of deviance: Social power, context and interaction*. 3rd edition (pp. 147–58). Belmont, CA: Wadsworth.

von Hirsch, A. (1976). *Doing justice*. New York, NY: Hill and Wang.

Wilson, J. Q. & Herrnstein, R. (1985). *Crime and human nature*. New York, NY: McGraw-Hill.

Wolfgang, M. E. (1958). *Patterns in criminal homicide*. Philadelphia, PA: University of Pennsylvania Press.

Zimmer, L. & Morgan, J. (1997). *Marijuana myths, marijuana facts: A review of the scientific evidence*. New York, NY: Lindesmith Center.

Production of Crime Statistics

LEARNING OBJECTIVES

After reading Chapter 3, you should be able to:

- Identify the three main sources of crime statistics in the United States.
- Discuss the strengths and weaknesses of each of the crime sources.
- Explain the difference between "macro" and "micro" level theories of crime.
- Explain what a longitudinal study is and state why such studies are important for understanding the causes of crime.
- Detail the history of the development of the UCR.
- List the eight crimes that comprise the Crime Index.
- Identify the serious crimes that are excluded from the Crime Index.
- Explain how the NIBRS differs from the UCR.
- Discuss the advantages of the NIBRS relative to the UCR.
- Provide a detailed description of the NCVS.
- Discuss the validity of self-report measures of crime.
- Explain strategies that have been developed to increase the validity of self-report measures of victimization and offending.

Crime statistics are a vital part of the study of crime. Theories of crime causation often are grounded in crime statistics, and popular and professional perceptions of the extent and distribution of crime are shaped by this information. Public response to crime and criminals is largely based upon views regarding the perceived seriousness and magnitude of the "crime problem." During the 1970s and again in the late 1980s, the United States experienced an increase in both violent and property crime. According to media reports, based on statistics released by the Federal Bureau of Investigation (FBI), crime was growing at alarming rates. Since 1991, however, the crime rate has declined steadily. Furthermore, even during the recent economic recession, the crime rate continued to fall, much to the puzzlement of criminologists. This 20-plus year decline in crime rates has resulted in historically low levels of crime, although many citizens continue to fear for their safety and are purchasing firearms to protect themselves and their homes.

While most information about crime in America is based on police data, in this chapter we examine three major sources of crime statistics:

- Uniform Crime Reports (UCR)
- National Crime Victimization Survey (NCVS)
- Self-report data (SRD)

The **Uniform Crime Reports (UCR)** consist of information collected by local police departments and forwarded to the FBI. The **National Crime Victimization Survey (NCVS)** is conducted jointly by the U.S. Census Bureau and the U.S. Department of Justice. Independent researchers carry out self-report surveys, which provide **self-report data (SRD)**. Other data are obtained from qualitative strategies that include in-depth interviews, observational studies, life histories, and case studies. These latter sources have provided criminology with classic studies of criminal lifestyles. Focusing on an individual or a small group, these qualitative case studies have been largely descriptive; providing detailed information about a wide range of criminal activities: a professional thief (Sutherland, 1937), a professional fence (Klockars, 1974; Steffensmeier, 1986), a drug-dealing community (Adler, 1992), gang members (Campbell, 1991; Decker & Van Winkle, 1996; Miller, 2001), burglars (Wright & Decker, 1994), robbers (Wright & Decker, 1997), and drug dealers (Jacobs, 1999; Jacques & Wright, 2011) among others. Although these works are rich and colorful in their descriptions of individuals, groups, or subcultures, problems of validity and reliability affect the generalizability of these accounts. Emphasis in this chapter will be upon quantitative sources of crime statistics.

REVIEW OF ELEMENTARY RESEARCH METHODOLOGY

A review of elementary research methodology might prove beneficial prior to discussing crime data sources. To facilitate the reading of this and later chapters that review empirical tests of major theoretical propositions in criminology, the following methodological concepts will be considered:

- Independent and dependent variables;
- Correlation and causality;
- Cross-sectional and longitudinal research designs;
- Micro-level and macro-level analyses;
- Sampling;

- Research designs; and
- Validity and reliability.

Generalizability, validity, and reliability are key issues involved in all the social sciences. Research designs attempt to ensure that the work is sound enough so that its findings are not limited to the specific case or cases examined. For example, if we seek to know what causes crime, we could ask people we know why they broke the law. Such an approach will provide some information about why people violate the law, but will it allow us to make generalizations? That is, will it truly explain all criminal acts? In all probability, it will not. Will asking five friends why they drink alcohol even though they are under age provide an explanation of the causes of crime? Such simplistic approaches might strike you as humorous, but many people base their understandings of crime on such unscientific "research." No wonder so much confusion exists with regard to what to do about crime in society.

How then can the issue of crime causation be studied? First, there are different **levels of explanation**. The **macro level** attempts to explain crime rates, while the **micro level** seeks to understand why individuals commit crime. Macro-level researchers, for instance, might attempt to interpret variations in homicide rates across time or societies, or differences between cities. In such work, the **dependent variable**, the thing to be explained, is homicide rates. The **independent variable**, the thing you believe explains the dependent variable, might be ethnic diversity or the percentage of the population living in poverty. Both the independent and dependent variables are measured in terms of a large social unit. The homicide rate usually refers to the number of murders per 100,000 people. Ethnic diversity would be measured in terms of the relative distribution of people identified as white, African-American, Hispanic, Asian, and other, while the percentage living in poverty would be the percentage of the population living below the poverty line of $23,850 for a family of four in 2014. Notice, these three measures do not focus on any one person. Rather, they represent group-level information that can be obtained from the U.S. Census Bureau and from law enforcement records. The macro-level approach assumes that societal factors help to explain individual behavior. This theoretical framework will be discussed in greater detail in Chapter 7.

At the micro level, the purpose of research is to explain individual behavior and often involves a social-psychological approach. Instead of trying to explain variations in the homicide rate, a micro-level design would seek to interpret variations in individual behavior. Now the dependent variable would be murder and whether an individual committed this act. Independent variables might be individual income (thus allowing classification of an individual as being poor or not poor) and the individual's race. Micro-level measures of this type are usually obtained from individuals through interviews or questionnaires.

An important issue is **generalizability**, the extent to which the research can be generalized; that is, can inferences be made beyond the immediate individual or place studied? Generalizability is achieved through sound research design and sampling procedures. Research designs can be considered blueprints that tell the researcher how to proceed, beginning with how units of analysis are to be selected for study.

Much of the early work in criminology and criminal justice relied upon **cross-sectional research designs** in which data are collected at one time point. Public opinion polls or voter preference polls are examples of surveys that interview a cross-section of people about their opinions on a specific topic.

Longitudinal research designs collect information across time. This allows for examining changes over time and also allows for establishing correct temporal ordering of variables, an important concern in testing criminological theory. Early self-report studies interviewed youths at one point in time and obtained information about their families, school performance, and their attitudes about a number of things. Simultaneously, the researchers collected information about the youngsters' involvement in criminal activity during an earlier period. The researchers then used current attitudes (independent variables) to explain past criminal activity (dependent variable). This interpretation, however, is temporally incorrect. The independent variable needs to occur prior to the dependent variable. Longitudinal research collects information at a minimum of two time periods. Independent variables are obtained in the first measurement and the dependent variable in the second.

To make inferences beyond the specific subjects, some form of *probability* sampling should be used (e.g., simple random, stratified, cluster). This means that every subject or case to which one hopes to be able to generalize has an equal probability of being selected for inclusion in the study. To be able to generalize about the difference in homicide rates between large and small cities, in the example above, the researcher would have to include small and large cities in the sample, and those cities should be drawn from a comprehensive list of all cities. This could be achieved by putting the names of all small cities (i.e., less than 250,000 population) into a hat and selecting five of them for study. Five large cities (i.e., more than 500,000 population) could be similarly selected. This represents a **stratified probability sampling** procedure in which the population is divided into appropriate categories and then sampled within these strata. In this manner, the study results can be said to be representative of all cities included in the two strata. Simply selecting two cities out of convenience would not produce generalizable data that could necessarily be considered as representative of all small cities.

If, in our macro-level study, we find that cities with wide ethnic diversity and high rates of poverty have higher crime rates, can we conclude that these two variables cause crime? We cannot. Our finding would show that these independent variables are related to, or correlated with, homicide rates. Before we can conclude that they are a cause of the differences in rates, we would have to meet two additional criteria. First, the independent variables must have been measured at a time preceding the measurement of homicide rates. For something to be a cause of something else, it has to occur prior to the thing you are trying to explain. Second, other potential causal factors need to be controlled.

HIGHLIGHT 3.1 TEMPORAL ORDERING

Let us assume that we are interested in exploring the relationship between poverty and crime. A survey has been conducted in which respondents have answered the following two questions: "Are you currently employed?" and "During the past year did you break into a building to steal something?" Based on our analysis, we find that people who are unemployed are more likely to report committing a burglary. Now that we have found a correlation between these two variables, does this mean that unemployment causes property crime? No—if anything, these data would be more supportive of the conclusion that breaking into a building to steal something causes a person to lose their job; crime causes unemployment! This cross-sectional example shows the fallacy of asking questions about current statuses and inferring a causal connection to past behavior. To partially remedy the situation, the question could have been, "Were you employed last year?"

Instead of ethnic diversity and poverty causing homicide, geographic location, unemployment, and availability of handguns might be the real explanation of different homicide rates. Without controlling for such potential variables, it is not possible to make causal inferences.

Thus, while there may be a **correlation** between two things (e.g., the more of one is associated with more of the other), **causality** entails more than just establishing a relationship. Before it can be said that poverty causes crime, for example, three criteria need to be met: (1) it must be shown that the variables are correlated, (2) temporal ordering must be established (the independent variable must precede the dependent variable), and (3) rival or other potential explanatory factors need to be controlled (see Highlight 3.1). Having reviewed these essential elements of research methodology, we turn our attention to crime statistics.

HISTORY OF OFFICIAL CRIME STATISTICS

Knowledge about the extent and distribution of crime in the United States prior to the twentieth century was based primarily upon local arrest statistics, court records, and jail and prison data. There had been no systematic attempt to estimate the extent of crime in society at large. Thorsten Sellin, an early commentator on crime figures, cautioned against the use of court and prison records. He wrote that "the value of a crime for index purposes decreases as the distance from the crime itself in terms of procedure increases" (1931:346). Given the reliance upon arrest and trial statistics, no clear picture of the amount of crime in pre-twentieth century America can be formulated.

In 1870, when Congress created the U.S. Department of Justice, it mandated that the Attorney General report crime statistics annually. This reporting, however, did not materialize. Nor did a resolution to the same effect, passed in St. Louis at the 1871 convention of the National Police Association (the forerunner of the International Association of Chiefs of Police; IACP), have success. By the 1920s, however, police professionals had become concerned about media portrayals of crime waves. This led the IACP to establish a Committee for Uniform

Crime Records to develop a procedure for collecting information about the amount of crime across the nation. The task proved particularly complicated because no two states defined all crimes in the same manner. In 1929, a final version of the data collection instrument was distributed to police departments, and a total of 400 agencies submitted their crime reports to the FBI the following January. A similar situation exists today with respect to information regarding officer-involved shootings. While it is a relatively rare event, although without accurate data, we do not know how rare or common it actually is, police use of force results in hundreds of deaths in the United States each year as well as an unknown number of nonfatal injuries. Little is known about this politically charged issue (recall the August 2014 fatal shooting of an unarmed teenager in Ferguson, MO) since neither the police nor any other agency collects systematic information about the events. In Highlight 3.2, Professor David Klinger argues for the development of a national database on officer-involved shootings.

HIGHLIGHT 3.2 OFFICER-INVOLVED SHOOTINGS

Professor David Klinger, an expert on officer-involved shootings, contributed the following argument for the creation of a national database on officer-involved shootings:

> The ultimate power of all nation-states is the power to kill its citizens. In the United States, this power is lawfully wielded at two points in the criminal justice process: At the end, after a citizen has been found guilty of a capital crime and is executed in prison, and at the beginning, when a police officer uses deadly force to seize a citizen whose behavior is deemed to present a serious threat to the safety of officers or other citizens. While research has demonstrated that police officers kill far more people in public than executioners kill convicts in prisons, we do not have any real sound sense of just how many people American police officers kill each year, because there is no sound national base that tracks this information.

As is the case with many crime- and justice-related matters, the Federal Bureau of Investigation (FBI) keeps some records about the use of deadly force by police officers. As part of their Supplementary Homicide Report (SHR) program, the FBI collects data from police agencies on what they call the "killing of a felon by a law enforcement officer in the line of duty." Unfortunately, many police agencies do not participate in the SHR program and research has demonstrated that the SHR numbers

for many of the agencies that *do report* are lower than what internal police records say are the number of people killed by these agency's officers (e.g., Sherman and Langworthy, 1979; Klinger 2012). Consequently, we know that the FBI's SHR figures undercount—by some unknown degree—the number of citizens killed by U.S. police officers each year.

Beyond the fact that the SHR does not provide an accurate picture of the number of citizens killed by the police, the FBI data contain no information whatsoever about those officer-involved shootings that do not result in the death of any citizen. Research (e.g., Fyfe, 1978; White, 2006) has repeatedly shown that most of the people struck by police bullets survive their wounds and that many of the people shot at by police officers are not hit by any of the bullets fired at them. Given that the vast majority of people shot at by police do not die, even if the SHR provided an accurate count of the number of citizens killed by the police, it would provide a misleading picture of how often police officers exercise their powers to use deadly force against citizens.

Because the paucity of data means that we have no clear idea of how often police officers shoot at citizens, many scholars (including those who sat on the National Research Council Committee to Review Police Policy and Practices; Skogan and Frydl, 2004) have called for the development of a national database to track all instances in which our nation's police officers discharge their firearms at citizens. Such a database is needed so that we can obtain a clear picture of how often U.S. police officers shoot at, wound, and kill citizens. Beyond this, a comprehensive database that tracked all shootings would provide vital information about the circumstances in which officers shoot, the backgrounds of the officers and citizens involved in such events, and other matters (e.g., the types of weapons citizens were armed with when the police shot at them) that can assist us in developing a comprehensive picture of when and how our nation's police officers exercise the ultimate power they have to take the life of citizens at the outset of the criminal justice process.

HIGHLIGHT 3.3 INTERNATIONAL CRIME DATA

Since 1970, the United Nations has collected data on crime and the operation of the criminal justice systems of member nations. The first survey results published in 1977 covered the period 1970–75 and represented data from 64 nations. The United Nations Surveys of Crime and Trends and Operations of the Criminal Justice System (UNCJS) are conducted every five years and the Fifth UN survey included reports from 103 nations. Similar to the American UCR, the UNCJS collects information on murder, rape, robbery, assault, and theft. Information on other crimes is also collected but cultural and societal variations in definitions and standards makes analysis of crimes such as bribery, fraud, and drug offenses more difficult. While some claim that there are too many inconsistencies in reporting to make this a useful source of information (Aebi, 2002), others note the value of these data. In support of this latter position, the following standards of the UNCJS are cited: it represents official data from each country; it provides standard definitions and classifications of crimes, it provides regular and ongoing reporting of UN member nations, and it contributes to development of a universal methodology for collecting international crime (Fairchild & Dammer, 2001).

Comparative criminologists, researchers interested in the study of crime in different countries, currently are confronted with problems similar to those encountered earlier in the twentieth century by American criminologists (see Highlight 3.3). Not only do crime definitions differ substantially from one nation to the next, but recording of crime data varies to an even greater degree. In spite of these problems, the field of comparative criminology is expanding as the globalization of the world continues (see, for example, Gang Feature 3.1).

With respect to the Uniform Crime Reports, police departments initially submitted crime data voluntarily; the FBI had no statutory authority to demand compliance. Currently, more than 18,000 law enforcement agencies representing about 95 percent of the nation's population report to the FBI (for an excellent overview of the historical development of the UCR, consult Barnett-Ryan, 2007). This high rate of reporting stems in part from the fact that many states now have the power to demand, with the force of state law, crime statistics from local jurisdictions (Maltz, 1977, 1999). Reporting statistics to the FBI, however, remains a voluntary practice that often has more to do with departmental prestige than it does with coercion. Within the law enforcement subculture, failure to participate in the FBI's UCR system implies that a law enforcement agency is not "professional."

GANG FEATURE 3.1   THE EUROGANG PROGRAM OF RESEARCH: A MULTI-METHOD, MULTI-SITE DESIGN FOR COMPARATIVE GANG RESEARCH

The Eurogang Program of Research: A Multi-method, Multi-site Design for Comparative Gang Research

Throughout this textbook we feature research on youth gangs to highlight relevant issues in each chapter. However, gang research suffers from shortcomings found in other research arenas, such as problems of measurement and data collection methods. Much of the former gang research has applied varying definitions of gangs, been limited to research in a single location (neighborhood or city), focused on a single gang or small group of gang members, and/or used one method (survey, observational, in-depth interviews, archival) to study gangs. Thus, when differences have been found, it is not clear whether such differences represent real differences or are the result of methodological and definitional differences. The Eurogang Program represents an international collaboration of researchers and policy makers that has attempted to introduce common standards to the study of gangs.

In 1998, the Eurogang group met for the first time to determine whether there were indeed youth gangs in Europe. After much discussion, the consensus was "yes." To facilitate gang research, members in the group worked to establish a common definition and common instruments that could be used across multiple contexts and in a variety of cultures. The first task was to agree on a definition. Since the word "gang" does not translate into all other languages with the same meaning, it became necessary to develop a consensus definition. After numerous discussions, the following definition was proposed: a gang is "any durable, street-oriented youth group whose involvement in illegal activity is part of its group identity." Once agreement had been reached on the definition, the next challenge was how to implement this definition. While a researcher can ask a survey participant "are you a member of a gang?" it is not feasible to ask "are you a member of a durable, street-oriented youth group whose involvement in illegal activity is part of its group identity?"

To capture the essence of this definition, the group developed a series of questions that could be combined to identify individuals who would be considered gang members. These questions were translated into a number of languages (e.g., Dutch, French, German, Norwegian, Russian, Spanish) and then pretested before being finalized. These questions were then incorporated into a youth survey, an expert survey (to be administered to adults knowledgeable about the youth situation, including police officers, youth workers, and teachers), as well as an outline for conducting ethnographic research. The Eurogang group recognized the shortcomings of prior research and encouraged researchers to include multiple methodologies in their research designs. Another goal of the group is to foster multi-site research that will allow for understanding similarities and differences that may be a result of contextual settings (such as neighborhood, city, or nation).

For more information on this international collaborative effort, consult Esbensen and Maxson (2012), Klein (2009), and Weerman et al. (2009), or log onto the Eurogang website: http://www.umsl.edu/~ccj/eurogang/euroganghome.htm.

Description of the UCR

The UCR consist of two components, Part I (Index) and Part II (non-Index) offenses. Part I offenses include those illegal acts considered to be particularly serious that "occur with sufficient frequency to provide an adequate basis for comparison" (U.S. Department of Justice, 1980:3). Eight crimes comprise the Part I **Index crimes**. From most to least serious (important with regard to the **Hierarchical Rule** described below), they are:

1. Criminal homicide;
2. Forcible rape;
3. Robbery;

4. Aggravated assault;
5. Burglary;
6. Larceny-theft;
7. Motor vehicle theft; and
8. Arson (added in 1979).

Absent from this list are serious crimes such as kidnapping, embezzlement, corporate fraud, and other white-collar offenses. These latter crimes, the FBI argues, occur too infrequently or do not readily come to the attention of the police, and therefore, would not provide a consistent or comparable measure across time or across jurisdictions. One might reasonably question the exclusion of white-collar crimes from the Index offenses. Recent experience suggests that these types of offenses are neither rare nor lacking in serious consequences. During the past 25 years, a number of high-profile cases (Michael Milken, Bernie Madoff's Ponzi scheme) as well as industry-wide insider trading and antitrust violations led to the near collapse of the global economy (see Chapter 12). However, focus on the eight traditional Part I offenses in media reporting diverts attention from these serious white-collar violations. As a result of the selection of acts included in the Crime Index, public perception about the nature, extent, and seriousness of illegal behavior becomes biased toward "street" crime and ignores "suite" crime.

The **crime rate** is calculated by dividing the number of crimes committed by the population in a given jurisdiction. This resultant number is then multiplied by 100,000. In this manner, the figure is standardized, enabling comparison across different localities. A city of 20,000 people with 200 crimes reported to the police, for example, has a crime rate of 1,000 (200/20,000 × 100,000). This crime rate would compare unfavorably to that of a city with 2,000,000 inhabitants and 5,000 crimes reported to the police (a crime rate of 5,000/2,000,000 × 100,000 = 250).

Each year, the FBI attempts to guarantee consistent practices across jurisdictions by distributing to each law enforcement agency a *Uniform Crime Reporting Handbook*, containing guidelines to be followed in recording crimes. Highlight 3.4 provides an example of instructions for recording robbery.

Part II offenses include most other crimes not itemized in Part I. Twenty specific crimes and a catchall "other" category are in this section, including other assaults, embezzlement, vandalism, sex offenses, drunkenness, and status offenses (i.e., juvenile acts, such as truancy, which are defined as criminal only because of the person's age). Information regarding the frequency and distribution of these crimes is rarely reported to the media by the FBI. Therefore, the public

Bernard L. Madoff, the accused mastermind of a $50 billion Ponzi scheme, leaves Federal Court in New York in January 2009.

CREDIT: AP Photo/Stuart Ramson.

HIGHLIGHT 3.4 UCR GUIDELINES FOR THE RECORDING OF ROBBERY

3. Robbery

(Crime against property, score one offense per distinct operation.)

Definition: The taking or attempting to take anything of value from the care, custody, or control of a person or persons by force or threat of force or violence and/or by putting the victim in fear.

Robbery is a vicious type of theft in that it is committed in the presence of the victim. The victim, who usually is the owner or person having custody of the property, is directly confronted by the perpetrator and is threatened with force or is put in fear that force will be used. Robbery involves a theft or larceny but is aggravated by the element of force or threat of force.

In the absence of force or threat of force, as in pocket-picking or purse-snatching, the offense must be classified as larceny rather than robbery.

However, if in a purse-snatching or other such crime, force, or threat of force is used to overcome the active resistance of the victim, the offense is to be classified as strong-arm robbery.

In analyzing robbery, the following subheadings are used:

3.a.   Firearm

3.b.   Knife or cutting instrument

3.c.   Other dangerous weapon

3.d.   Strong-arm—hands, fists, feet, etc.

Armed robbery, categories 3.a.–3.c., are incidents commonly referred to as "stickups," "hijackings," "holdups," and "heists." Robberies wherein no weapons are used may be referred to as "strong-arms" or "muggings."

In any instance of robbery, score one offense for each distinct operation including attempts. Do not count the number of victims robbed, those present at the robbery, or the number of offenders when scoring this crime.

In cases involving pretended weapons or those in which the weapon is not seen by the victim but the robber claims to have one in his possession, classify the incident as armed robbery and score it in the appropriate category. If an immediate "on view" arrest proves that there is no weapon, the offense may be classified as strong-arm robbery.

Score One Offense for Each Distinct Operation

3.a Robbery—Firearm

Count one offense for each distinct operation in which any firearm is used as a weapon or employed as a means of force to threaten the victim or put him in fear.

3.b Robbery—Knife or Cutting Instrument

Score one offense for each distinct operation in which a knife, broken bottle, razor, or other cutting instrument is employed as a weapon or as a means of force to threaten the victim or put him in fear.

3.c Robbery—Other Dangerous Weapon

3.d Robbery—Strong-Arm—Hands, Fists, Feet, etc.

In this category of robbery, enter one offense for each distinct operation in which a club, acid, explosive, brass knuckles, or other dangerous weapon is used.

This category includes muggings and similar offenses where no weapon is used, but strong-arm tactics (limited to the use of personal weapons such as hands, arms, feet, fists, teeth, etc.) are employed to deprive the victim of his property.

Source: U.S. Department of Justice (1980). Uniform Crime Reporting Handbook. Washington, DC: U.S. Department of Justice.

---

rarely learns about the extent of "nonserious" crimes such as hazing and statutory rape (sexual intercourse with a minor).

In addition to information about the number and types of crimes committed and where they occur, the FBI also provides data about characteristics and consequences of crimes, (e.g., degree of injury, monetary loss, and personal characteristics of the victim and offender). This information permits criminologists to examine relationships between variables that could help to explain the causes of crime. As might be expected, crime is not equally distributed in the population; some groups tend to commit (or, at least, get caught engaging in) more illegal acts than others. Explanations for these differentials challenge both theory builders and those seeking to control crime.

The UCR also collects data about law enforcement agencies. This allows planners to evaluate issues such as the effect of police department size on the number of arrests and convictions, the desirability of various types of shift assignments, and hiring trends in law enforcement with regard to sex, race, and educational level. The UCR thus provides a wealth of information not just about crime, but also about aspects of the criminal justice system. The data published in the quarterly and annual reports represent but a fraction of what is gathered. For those interested, UCR data are available online (http://www.fbi.gov/ucr/ucr.htm).

The police, as noted earlier, record crimes differently for Part I and Part II offenses. Part I or Index offenses consist of crimes known to the police, including both crimes the police themselves discover and crimes reported by citizens. For most offenses, especially property crimes, citizen reports are the major source of information about crime. One study found that only 1.6 percent of the robberies and 0.4 percent of household burglaries were discovered at the scene by the police (Gove et al., 1985). Thus, while UCR data are referred to as "official statistics," the data are primarily a product of police response (reactive behavior) and not of police patrol (proactive behavior).

Given their reliance upon citizen reports, the Part I statistics are the result of a three-stage process:

1. Citizens must decide whether a crime has been committed;
2. If citizens determine that a crime has been committed, they must decide whether to report the act to the police; and
3. Once the act has been reported, an officer must decide:
   (a) Whether a crime has occurred;
   (b) How to classify it; and
   (c) Whether to record it.

UCR data, therefore, are several stages removed from the actual crime. Recall Sellin's warning about the value of crime statistics decreasing as one becomes further removed from the crime itself. But remember that reported crime is more proximate to the actual offense than is arrest or conviction.

Part II crimes in UCR statistics represent only crimes that result in an arrest. This makes it difficult to compare Part II crimes with Part I offenses. Arrest statistics provide a distorted picture of "non-serious" crimes because only a fraction of crimes known to the police are cleared by an arrest. This again illustrates the importance of trying to obtain data about crime as close to the criminal act as possible.

Strengths of the UCR

Despite various shortcomings, to be discussed in the following section, the UCR are an important source of information about crime in U.S. society. The collaborative effort between the FBI and local, county, and state law enforcement agencies minimizes redundancy. Also, the data offer nation-wide crime statistics, which allow for city and regional comparisons. The comparisons are facilitated by the uniform guidelines and definitions provided by the FBI's *Uniform Crime Reporting Handbook*. Presumably, the same criminal act committed in Cullowhee, North Carolina, would be recorded in the same manner if committed in Irvine, California. It then becomes possible to compare the relative safety of these two communities as well as to evaluate the performance of the police agencies in solving and preventing crime. The FBI, however, routinely warns against making such comparisons because, despite the *Handbook* advice, law enforcement agencies sometimes employ idiosyncratic methods to record crimes for FBI purposes. In one Ohio city, "stolen" cars were not entered into official records until 24 hours after the initial report. In another Ohio city, about the same size as the first, "stolen" cars were recorded at the time they were reported missing. Not surprisingly, the second city showed a much greater rate of auto theft than the first, although the true rates actually might have been quite similar. Along these same lines, Gang Feature 3.2 highlights the importance of developing consistent criteria for identifying gang members and measuring gang-related crime.

Another advantage of the UCR is that the statistics have been collected and stored since 1930 and are updated monthly. Policy analysts and the public can therefore make annual crime rate comparisons. It also is possible to examine crime trends, be they overall crime rates or rates for specific crimes. For instance, researchers can analyze the crime of rape and compare it to the crime trend in general. In 1960, however, significant changes in recording practices were made that no longer allow direct comparisons with earlier years.

Weaknesses of the UCR

An obvious shortcoming of the UCR Crime Index is its emphasis upon conventional street crimes and its exclusion of other serious crime. As evidence of the inherent problems associated with the Crime Index, reporting of the Crime Index was suspended in 2000 until a more precise estimate of crime could be developed (Barnett-Ryan, 2007). The UCR definition of serious crime deflects attention from such illegal acts as corporate violence, political crime, and computer fraud. People may be misled into believing that they are most endangered by murderers or robbers, when in fact the personal and financial costs of corporate and political crime far exceed those of conventional street crimes (Simon & Eitzen, 1990; and Kappeler et al., 1993). In their award-winning book *Myths that Cause Crime*, Harold Pepinsky and Paul Jesilow (1984) devoted a chapter to the misconception that white-collar crime is nonviolent. Among the figures they cite are the following: each year 10,000 lives are lost due to unnecessary surgery and 20,000 persons are killed because of errors in prescribing drugs. The authors point out that numerous birth defects were caused by the premature marketing of thalidomide by

GANG FEATURE 3.2 DEFINITIONAL ISSUES: TWICE AS GREAT, OR HALF AS GREAT?

Definitional Issues: Twice as Great, or Half as Great?

What is a gang and what determines whether a crime is gang related? These are two important questions that should be addressed prior to any discussion about gangs. Yet, it is surprising the extent to which these questions are either ignored or readily dismissed. Articles, whether academic or media generated, in which gangs and gang activity are described include a diverse population, often failing to qualify the scope of the topic. Thus, depending upon an author's interest or focus, a gang may be comprised of any, or all, of the following: youthful offenders, drug dealing posses, bikers, neighborhood cliques, prisoners, or any other specifically defined group of three (and in some jurisdictions only two) or more individuals whose members engage in criminal activity. These are quite distinct groups and descriptions of one cannot be generalized to the other. In spite of the absence of a common definition of gangs, it is not uncommon to hear or read about gangs, gang members, and gang activity as if these were synonymous terms. While failure to define the groups and activities included in such discussions may result in general confusion about the nature of the problems, there are more serious ramifications from a policy perspective. With respect to gangs and the attention they have drawn in the past 20 years, it is important to be able to identify the magnitude of the problem, both in terms of gang membership and level of gang-related crime. Given the diverse definitions, such simple objectives are difficult to attain. Here we provide an example of definitional differences from law enforcement.

Los Angeles and Chicago are often identified as the two cities with the most pronounced gang presence in the United States. In an interesting project, Cheryl Maxson and Malcolm Klein (1990, 2002) compared "gang-related" homicides in these two cities. This research highlights the difficulty of comparing crime rates among different jurisdictions.

In Los Angeles, both the L.A. Police Department and Sheriff's Department rely upon a "gang member" definition to classify crimes as gang-related. That is, any crime committed by a gang member is considered to be gang related, i.e., any crime in which either the suspect or victim is on file as an active gang or associate gang member is so classified. The driving force behind this policy, then, is the identification of gang members. Both L.A. law enforcement agencies use the following criteria to identify gang members:

- An individual admits to membership in a gang.

- A reliable informant identifies an individual as a gang member.

- An informant of untested reliability identifies an individual as a gang member and it is corroborated by independent information.

- An individual resides in or frequents a particular gang's area and affects its style of dress, use of hand signs, symbols, or tattoos, and associates with known gang members.

- An individual has been arrested several times in the company of identified gang members for offenses which are consistent with usual gang activity.

Additionally, when there are strong indications that an individual has a close relationship with a gang but does not fit the above criteria, that person is then identified as a "gang associate."

In contrast to Los Angeles, the Chicago Police Department utilizes a "gang motive" definition to classify a crime as gang related. Under this definition, a crime "is considered gang-related only if it occurs in the course of an explicitly defined collective encounter between two or more gangs." Importantly, under this definition, criminal and violent activity engaged in by gang members outside of the gang context is NOT considered gang related. Clearly, such disparate standards will have substantial effects on the volume of gang-related offenses.

Maxson and Klein (1990, 2002) examined gang homicides in Chicago and Los Angeles. They found that the Los Angeles homicide rate was reduced approximately 50 percent when the more restrictive gang motive standard was used to classify homicides in that city. In an examination of the relative prevalence of these two definitional approaches, Maxson and Klein (2002) found about an equal number of jurisdictions use each standard. In spite of these different standards, they concluded: "An examination of factors associated with gang member and gang motivated homicides suggests that the qualities of these homicides do not differ dramatically and it is 'appropriate' to make cross-city comparisons about gang and nongang homicides regardless of definition used" (Maxson & Klein, 2002:182). However, with respect to the prevalence of gang homicides, Maxson and Klein urge caution when comparing homicide rates across different jurisdictions.

the Richardson-Merrell Company in the 1960s. Chapters 11 and 12 examine more closely the issues of such forms of white-collar crime. Included in debates about the Affordable Care Act (i.e., Obamacare) in 2013 was the fact that thousands of Americans die each year because of "errors" made by medical professionals.

The UCR also can be a tool for political manipulation. Police administrators sometimes rely upon these data to justify requests for additional money for personnel, equipment, and training. At other times, the Crime Index can be manipulated by a department to indicate exemplary performance (i.e., reducing crime rates or increasing clearance rates). This can be achieved by failing to record some crime reports or by negotiating with offenders to plead guilty to a number of offenses, some of which they may not have committed, in return for a reduced sentence. This most frequently occurs with property offenses, which traditionally have low clearance rates. The police can sometimes solve or "clear" as many as 200 burglaries by bargaining with one suspect. These data become an in-house self-evaluation of police performance.

Several problems also arise from recording practices. While the *Uniform Crime Reporting Handbook* specifies definitions and procedures to be followed, different departments and regions of the country may still adhere to idiosyncratic standards. While it may be accurate to state that "a rose is a rose is a rose," it is not necessarily the case that a rape is a rape is a rape. See, for example, the analysis by Duncan Chappell and his colleagues (1971) of how Boston police reports of rape differ in both vocabulary and style (and particularly in terms of the kinds of acts that are defined as rape) from the reports of Los Angeles police. Cultural standards, level of police professionalism, and staffing patterns can lead to the same behavior being recorded differently in different jurisdictions. Take the case of a 19-year-old female college student who claims that she was raped, beaten, and robbed while hitchhiking home from a fraternity party. Does the officer record this as a rape, a robbery, or an assault? The answer is; it all depends. A chauvinist officer might believe that a woman hitchhiking alone at night is "asking for it," and therefore, the officer might ignore the rape allegation. A different officer may record the event as a rape. (See Chapter 11 for more discussion of rape.) UCR instructions mandate that the crime be tabulated in the most serious category, known as the *Hierarchical Rule*. If the student was robbed and raped, the crimes would appear only as a rape (and not as a robbery), but if she were killed, the crimes would be classified as a homicide (and not as a rape).

Another problem concerns the manner in which crimes are counted. Instructions direct law enforcement agencies to tally each distinct property crime as one offense. If, for example, ten rooms in a hotel were burglarized, these offenses should be recorded as one burglary, but if ten apartments in an apartment complex were burglarized, the crimes should be recorded as ten burglaries. For personal offenses, such as robberies, the number of victims is immaterial for tabulating purposes, as is the number of offenders. If two robbers confront five patrons in a bank, only one robbery is said to have occurred. These definitional rules tend to underestimate the extent of certain offense types and clearly make direct comparison with **victimization surveys** and self-report surveys inappropriate. For instance, while the UCR procedures would classify the above bank robbery as *one offense*, victimization surveys would identify *five victims* while a self-report survey would produce *two offenders*.

Crime rates also can be misleading. Take, for instance, the city of Las Vegas, or any other resort community. These places are inundated by visitors, some of whom inevitably commit crimes. Yet, the crime rate is calculated in terms only of the number of people in the resident population, not in terms of the true total of people that might become either offenders or victims. And because rates are calculated in terms of a jurisdiction's population, serious errors in determining the number of people living in an area—not an uncommon problem—can affect the accuracy of crime rates.

A further criticism of the Crime Index is its reactive nature. Law enforcement agencies rely primarily upon the willingness of private citizens to report crime. Yet, there are numerous reasons why individuals might choose not to report known crimes to the police. One estimate is that only 35 percent of the crimes that take place annually are reported to the police (Harlow, 1986). Reasons most frequently mentioned for not reporting crime are:

- A belief that the event is not important enough to report; and
- A feeling, particularly for violent crimes, that the act is a private or personal matter.

Other reasons include:

- A belief that the police cannot or will not do anything about a report;
- A fear that an individual's own criminal behavior (as in prostitution or drug dealing) may be exposed;
- A fear that a person's or a business's reputation may be damaged by publicity resulting from reporting;
  - A fear of reprisal, as in some cases of domestic violence; and
  - A disagreement with the legal definition; or
  - A belief that the behavior is not wrong or that the criminal act was justified.

In addition to these reasons for not reporting crimes to the police, during the past few years, a number of people have failed to report crime in response to a stop-snitching movement in some communities. In Highlight 3.5, Professor Lee Slocum describes findings from her research examining youths' willingness—or reluctance—to report observed illegal activities.

HIGHLIGHT 3.5 STOP SNITCHING: WHY DON'T KIDS REPORT CRIMES TO THE POLICE?

In 2004, the issue of crime reporting captured the public's attention with the release of a video in Baltimore called *Stop F*%$ing Snitching,* which threatened violent retaliation for cooperating with the police. Although the creators of the video stated that the intent of their work was to discourage criminals from snitching on their associates in return for leniency from law enforcement and not to discourage citizens from reporting crime to the police, the stop-snitching mantra spread to the general public (Brown, 2007). Police departments and prosecutors have claimed that the resulting culture of silence has made it increasingly difficult for them to solve crimes and convict offenders (Kahn, 2007).

A study by Slocum, Taylor, Brick, and Esbensen (2010) indicates that not everyone has bought into this code of silence. Using survey data collected from a sample of middle-school youths, they found most youths are likely or are very likely to report burglary (62 percent), the attack on a stranger on the street (50 percent), and stealing from a store (45 percent). However, almost a quarter of the students abided by a code of silence and would not report these crimes.

The researchers were interested in identifying what explains these differences between youths in reporting attitudes. They hypothesized that the willingness to report crimes depends on where a youth lives, their perceptions of the community and law enforcement, and their personal experiences. In keeping with these hypotheses, they found that youths were less willing to report crimes when they live in poorer neighborhoods. Other community characteristics, such as minority/immigrant concentrations and

residential mobility were not associated with reporting intentions. The researchers found that personal characteristics of the students also were related to reporting. Specifically, delinquent youths were more reluctant to report, perhaps because they worry about drawing attention to their misbehavior. Youths were also less willing to report when they held negative views of the police. Reporting was more likely when youths were aware of services to help victims of crime and when they believe that young people can play a positive role in the community. They suggest that these factors signal to youths that the community takes crime seriously and that concrete benefits may emerge from reporting. Finally, perceived victimization risk was positively associated with willingness to report, indicating that teenagers might report because they have faith that the police and other authority figures can do something about crime. Additional analyses indicated that the reason youths living in poor neighborhoods are reluctant to report crimes is because they are more involved in delinquency and have more negative perceptions of the police than their counterparts living in more economically advantaged communities.

Slocum and colleagues conclude that the key to combatting the code of silence is to foster positive relations between youths and the police, integrate youths into the community, and establish and make youths aware of services to help victims of crime. Programs that target delinquency more generally also should have a positive impact on attitudes toward reporting crimes. These interventions may be particularly beneficial in poor communities, where the code of silence has a stronger foothold.

A NEW LOOK TO THE UCR: NATIONAL INCIDENT-BASED REPORTING SYSTEM

Given the number of criticisms of the UCR and the growing complexity and diversity of crime, the **National Incident-Based Reporting System (NIBRS)** was introduced in 1984 to meet the needs of law enforcement agencies, and incident-level data were being collected by the end of the 1980s (U.S. Department of Justice & Federal Bureau of Investigation, 2011). NIBRS was developed to address two primary goals:

- To enhance the quantity, quality, and timeliness of crime statistical data collected by the law enforcement community; and

- To improve the methodology used for compiling, analyzing, auditing, and publishing the collected crime data.

Whereas the traditional UCR system required tallying the number of occurrences of Part I offenses as well as arrest data for Part I and Part II offenses, NIBRS requires more detailed reports and allows for recording of multiple offenses, thus eliminating the Hierarchical Rule which led to recording of only the most serious offense. Agencies using NIBRS collect data regarding individual crime incidents and arrests and submit them in "reports" detailing each incident. This procedure provides much more thorough information about crimes than did the summary statistics of the traditional UCR system.

NIBRS abandoned the use of Part I and Part II offenses in favor of Group A and Group B classifications. Part I offenses focused on "street offenses" and ignored "suite offenses." Group A is considerably more inclusive of a wide array of criminal activity. Detailed information recorded for each of the 22 Group A offenses include crime circumstances, victim and offender information, arrestee data, and information about the extent of damage to both person and property.

The following offenses are included in Group A:

1. Arson
2. Assault
3. Bribery
4. Burglary
5. Counterfeiting
6. Vandalism
7. Drug Offenses
8. Embezzlement
9. Extortion
10. Fraud
11. Gambling Offenses
12. Homicide
13. Kidnapping
14. Larceny/Theft
15. Auto Theft
16. Pornography
17. Prostitution
18. Robbery
19. Sex Crimes, Force
20. Sex Offenses
21. Stolen Property
22. Weapon Violation

Offenses included in Group B consist of the following:

1. Bad Checks
2. Curfew/Vagrancy
3. Disorderly Conduct

4. DUI
5. Drunkenness
6. Family Offense
7. Liquor Violations
8. Peeping Tom
9. Runaway
10. Trespass
11. All Other

South Carolina was the first state to "pilot" this new program and by 1988, NIBRS was approved for general use (U.S. Department of Justice & Federal Bureau of Investigation, 2006). In 2012, 6,113 agencies in 36 states and representing 33.4 percent of participating agencies reported more than 5 million crime incidents (http://www.fbi.gov/news/news_blog/nibrs-crime-statistics-report-for-2012-is-sued). While the NIBRS data are not a nationally representative sample of law enforcement agencies or criminal incidents, they are one of the few multijuris-dictional data sources available for examining offenders, victims, situational characteristics, and police arrest/clearance status in crime incidents.

Strengths of NIBRS

NIBRS provides a number of improvements over existing measures such as the UCR, NCVS, and self-reports. A thorough critique by Maxfield (1999:145) sug-gests the following benefits of NIBRS over existing alternatives: (1) incident- and victim-level analysis can be disaggregated to local jurisdictions and aggregated to intermediate levels of analysis; (2) incident details supporting analysis of ancil-lary offenses (drugs, weapons) and crime situations are available; (3) separable individual, household, commercial, and business victimizations are included; (4) data on incidents targeting victims under age 12 are available; (5) a broader range of offense categories, including those affecting abstract victims, are avail-able; (6) allowance for examination of nonhousehold-based individual victims and other incidents that are difficult to measure with household-based surveys; (7) individual-level information about offenders from arrest records and victim reports are available; and, (8) information about the residual status of victims and offenders is included. These advances have a number of practical implica-tions for communities and law enforcement agencies. Faggiani and McLaugh-lin (1999), for example, demonstrate how local law enforcement agencies can engage in "tactical crime analysis" using NIBRS data by examining local crime patterns and then using this information to strategically target crimes and areas. They also have important implications for researchers who seek to better under-stand the nature and scope of criminal incidents.

Weaknesses of NIBRS

Maxfield (1999:145–46) also summarizes a number of limitations of NIBRS relative to existing sources of crime data. First, like the UCR, NIBRS data include only crimes reported to police and retained by police recordkeeping systems, thus excluding unreported and unrecorded crimes. Second, the inflexibility of the NIBRS specifications creates a considerable reporting burden on participating local agencies. This may explain why NIBRS has been adopted primarily by smaller agencies in smaller states, with the nation's largest cities and agencies lagging behind. Third, different types of agencies have different organizational incentives. The FBI and other national agencies are most interested in a national monitoring system and national-level research application, while local and state submitting agencies are more concerned with local record-keeping requirements, analysis to support local operations, and conservation of resources for data systems that have local applications. Fourth, the age and complexity of the NIBRS record structure and concomitant size of data files present unfamiliar challenges to researchers, analysts, and computer hardware and software. For example, Dunn and Zelenock's (1999) analyses of 1996 NIBRS data illustrate difficulties associated with analyzing millions of records and the need for powerful computer hardware and software to process the information. Fifth, a number of uncertainties exist concerning the error structure of incident-based measures generally and NIBRS data specifically. Other issues associated with NIBRS include Snyder's research (1999) which reported that juveniles accounted for a disproportionate amount of robbery clearances in NIBRS relative to other data sources. Addington (2004, 2006) identified limitations in the NIBRS data concerning murder incidents, particularly as they pertain to police clearance rates.

Recent Studies Using NIBRS

Despite these limitations, NIBRS provides a promising approach to the study of crime for both researchers and practitioners. Examinations by Chilton and Jarvis (1999) and Rantala and Edwards (2000) of NIBRS data relative to other sources of crime data have generally found that NIBRS presents a suitable complement to more commonly utilized sources such as the NCVS and UCR. Additionally, Akiyama and Nolan (1999) and Dunn and Zelenock (1999) present clear descriptions for users of the data and highlight the versatility of incident-based measures. This versatility is illustrated as NIBRS data have been used to examine a variety of topics ranging from descriptions of criminal incidents to characteristics of offenders as they pertain to official agency processing (e.g., Addington, 2006; Taylor et al., 2009) to tests of criminological theories. Studies have used NIBRS to examine a wide range of crimes, ranging from child abuse (Finkelhor & Ormrod, 2001) and hate crimes (Strom, 2001; Messner et al., 2004) to intimate partner violence (Thompson et al., 1999; Vasquez et al., 2005) and differences between lethal and nonlethal assaults (Chilton, 2004).

Some concern has been expressed regarding the possible effect on crime rates of this new recording system. Ramona Rantala and Thomas Edwards (2000) conducted an examination of this very issue. They compared crime rates in more than 1,000 agencies that have adopted the NIBRS system and found that while the crime rates under NIBRS were greater, the difference was relatively small. They found that on average the violent crime rate was less than 1 percent higher and the property crime rate slightly more than 2 percent higher under NIBRS guidelines compared to the traditional UCR system.

ALTERNATIVE MEASURES OF CRIME

The UCR have been the primary source of crime statistics in the United States for more than 80 years, but there has been a continuous search for alternative and better measures. Two other data sources that rely upon surveys to obtain data on criminal behavior have been developed. Self-report studies request individuals to indicate the type and amount of criminal behavior in which they have engaged. Victimization surveys ask respondents to indicate the types of crimes of which they have been victims. Advocates of these approaches claim that they provide a clearer picture of criminal activity than does the UCR. Others argue that they provide an alternative enumeration.

Self-report Studies

The history of self-reported delinquency (SRD) studies has been one of methodological improvements. Self-report studies generally have relied upon responses from juveniles and have been influential in the development of theories explaining the etiology (causes) of delinquency. The labeling perspective, for instance (see Chapter 9), was largely influenced by early self-report studies. Likewise, integrated theoretical models and developmental and life-course criminology (discussed in Chapter 10) are also tied closely to self-report studies.

Early self-report studies were conducted by Austin Porterfield (1946) and by James Wallerstein and Clement Wyle (1947). It was not until the work of Short and Nye (1957), however, that self-report measures received serious attention. A description of five major self-report studies highlights not only the methodological improvements made in this data collection technique, but the extent to which this technique has been adopted by criminological researchers, especially during the past 40 years.

Short and Nye (1957)

James F. Short Jr. and F. Ivan Nye's pioneering work revealed a totally different image of the juvenile delinquent and the extent of delinquency than official records had portrayed. Two different samples of adolescents completed questionnaires: one consisted of youth enrolled in the ninth through twelfth grades in three schools in the state of Washington, while the other was comprised of institutionalized delinquents. Responses to 23 questions inquiring about rule and law violations showed little difference between the two groups. The finding that parents' socioeconomic background and the quality of family life were not related to delinquency was of special significance. This finding contradicted a "truism" about the causes of delinquency: that it is caused by poverty and/or by broken homes.

There were several methodological problems with the Short-Nye scale. The respondents had been requested to identify all those rules and regulations that they had broken since beginning grade school. Response categories were:

1. Very often
2. Several times
3. Once or twice
4. No

Of the 23 rule violations included in the inventory, seven were selected to comprise a delinquency scale. But, the high-school-aged respondents were being asked to recall events that had occurred as long as 10 years earlier, and to indicate approximately how often they had engaged in such behavior. Furthermore, the response categories did not allow the researchers to differentiate adequately between habitual and infrequent "delinquents."

Take, for example, the item "skipped school without a legitimate excuse." In the course of 10 years, an individual may have "skipped" once a year. This is certainly more than once or twice and more than several times. Is it "very often"? It is not possible to differentiate between this respondent and the person that also has skipped school ten times, but all in the past year.

Another methodological problem raised with the Short-Nye scale is its emphasis upon what can be considered "trivial" offenses. Behaviors such as defying parental authority and skipping school can hardly be equated in terms of seriousness with **Part I crimes** such as robbery and assault. By including trivial behaviors in their delinquency scales, researchers tend to overestimate the amount of delinquency. This inclusion of what some scholars have referred to as typical adolescent behavior may have contributed to findings such as the absence of a relationship between social class and delinquency (Tittle et al., 1978).

THE NATIONAL YOUTH SURVEY

A major study utilizing self-report research methods was conducted by Delbert Elliott and his colleagues at the University of Colorado. The National Youth Survey (NYS), begun in 1977, is based on a probability sample of youth in the continental United States (Elliott et al., 1985). The initial sample consisted of 1,726 male and female adolescents. The panel (the same youths), which was originally between the ages of 11 and 17, was interviewed ten times, annually until 1981 and then again in 1984, 1987, 1990, 1993, and 2002. This last wave provides data about a national sample of young adults from 36 to 42 years of age. Then in 2003, the original respondents, their spouses or partners, their parents, and their children aged 11 and older, were all interviewed.

Unlike prior self-report studies, the NYS measurement of delinquency was geared to approximate the UCR crime categories. Consequently, 40 items were developed that measured all but one of the UCR Part I offenses (homicide) and 60 percent of Part II offenses (see Highlight 3.6).

HIGHLIGHT 3.6 SELF-REPORTED DELINQUENCY AND DRUG-USE ITEMS AS EMPLOYED IN THE NATIONAL YOUTH SURVEY

How many times in the past year have you:

1. Purposely damaged or destroyed property belonging to your parents or other family members?
2. Purposely damaged or destroyed property belonging to a school?
3. Purposely damaged or destroyed other property that did not belong to you (not counting family or school property)?
4. Stolen (or tried to steal) a motor vehicle such as a car or motorcycle?
5. Stolen (or tried to steal) something worth more than $50?
6. Knowingly bought, sold, or held stolen goods (or tried to do any of these things)?
7. Thrown objects (such as rocks, snowballs, or bottles) at cars or people?
8. Run away from home?
9. Lied about your age to gain entrance or to purchase something; for example, lying about your age to buy liquor or to get into a movie?
10. Carried a hidden weapon other than a plain pocketknife?
11. Stolen (or tried to steal) things worth $5 or less?
12. Attacked someone with the idea of seriously hurting or killing him/her?
13. Been paid for having sexual relations with someone?
14. Had sexual intercourse with a person of the opposite sex other than your wife/husband?
15. Been involved in gang fights?
16. Sold marijuana or hashish ("pot," "grass," "hash")?
17. Cheated on school tests?
18. Hitchhiked where it was illegal to do so?
19. Stolen money or other things from your parents or other members of your family?
20. Hit (or threatened to hit) a teacher or other adult at school?
21. Hit (or threatened to hit) one of your parents?
22. Hit (or threatened to hit) other students?
23. Been loud, rowdy, or unruly in a public place (disorderly conduct)?
24. Sold hard drugs, such as heroin, cocaine, and LSD?
25. Taken a vehicle for a ride (drive) without the owner's permission?
26. Bought or provided liquor for a minor?
27. Had (or tried to have) sexual relations with someone against their will?
28. Used force (strong-arm methods) to get money or things from other students?
29. Used force (strong-arm methods) to get money or things from a teacher or other adult at school?
30. Used force (strong-arm methods) to get money or things from other people (not students or teachers)?
31. Avoided paying for such things as movies, bus or subway rides, and food?
32. Been drunk in a public place?
33. Stolen (or tried to steal) things worth between $5 and $50?
34. Stolen (or tried to steal) something at school, such as someone's coat from a classroom, locker, or cafeteria, or a book from the library?
35. Broken into a building or vehicle (or tried to break in) to steal something or just to look around?
36. Begged for money or things from strangers?
37. Skipped classes without an excuse?
38. Failed to return extra change that a cashier gave you by mistake?
39. Been suspended from school?
40. Made obscene telephone calls, such as calling someone and saying dirty things?

Source: *U.S. Department of Justice, Sourcebook of Criminal Justice Statistics* (1989). Table 3.109, pp. 330–1.

The self-report instrument included two separate response sets. Respondents interviewed during January and February were instructed to indicate how many times in the past year ("from Christmas a year ago to the Christmas just past") they had committed each specified offense. If the individual indicated ten or more times, this was followed with a validity check; respondents were asked whether the behavior was done:

1. Once a month
2. Once every 2–3 weeks
3. Once a week
4. 2–3 times a week
5. Once a day
6. 2–3 times a day

Agreement between the two responses could then be checked, and when this was done, a high level of agreement was found. The advantage of instructing the youths to answer for the interval between Christmases is that Christmas usually is a salient event that permits the time period to be more clearly identified than would be true if asked about the past year.

Frequency counts allow researchers to examine repeat violators. At the low end of the frequency scale, no differences were found between subgroups (e.g., social class, age, and race). Among high-frequency offenders (those identified as engaging in patterned delinquent behavior), however, differences by race and social class were discovered: lower-class youths and African Americans appeared more frequently in the high-frequency offender group than whites and middle-class youths (Elliott & Ageton, 1980). Highlighting the importance of replication (i.e., repetition of a previous study to test the reliability of the initial findings), a subsequent analysis utilizing data from the first five years of the NYS (1977–81) found that once social class was controlled, differences by race disappeared (Huizinga & Elliott, 1987).

PROGRAM OF RESEARCH ON THE CAUSES AND CORRELATES OF DELINQUENCY

In 1986, the Office of Juvenile Justice and Delinquency Prevention (OJJDP) in the U.S. Department of Justice awarded funds to three research projects to conduct self-report studies to examine the causes and correlates of delinquency in high-risk neighborhoods. All three projects used a core of SRD items that represent a refinement of the NYS items. Two of the projects (Huizinga et al., 1991; Loeber et al., 1991) included children as young as seven in the samples. Prior self-report studies, as noted above, had focused almost exclusively on junior and senior high school youths. A **cohort study** is a form of longitudinal study using cohorts, that is, groups of people who share a common characteristic or experience within a defined period. Inclusion of the younger cohorts in this study allowed for a better determination of early life experiences associated with delinquent or problem behavior. Another methodological issue was the time interval between data collection points. Two of the studies (Loeber et al., 1991; Thornberry et al., 1991) conducted interviews every six months, while the Huizinga et al. (1991) research adhered to an annual schedule. The three projects submitted a three-volume report to OJJDP in 1994 (Huizinga et al., 1994b). The project staffs have provided contributions to the understanding of a number of topics including gang behavior (Bjerregard & Smith, 1993; Esbensen & Huizinga, 1993; Thornberry et al., 1993, 2003), gun ownership (Lizotte et al., 1994, 2000; Bjerregard & Lizotte, 1995), victimization (Esbensen & Huizinga, 1991; Esbensen et al., 1999), consequences of arrest (Huizinga & Henry, 2008), and risk factors and resiliency (Huizinga et al., 1994a; Loeber et al., 1995; Thornberry et al., 1995, 2000; Kelley et al., 1997).

THE PROJECT ON HUMAN DEVELOPMENT IN CHICAGO NEIGHBORHOODS

The National Institute of Justice and the John D. and Catherine T. MacArthur Foundation collaborated on an ambitious research endeavor (Farrington et al., 1986; Tonry et al., 1991; Earls & Reiss, 1993). Beginning in 1988, teams of researchers worked on development of a research design and data collection instrument. After six years of planning, the project implemented the research design in 1994 and began collecting data in 1995. A probability sample of 80 Chicago neighborhoods was selected for the longitudinal study. During the first wave of interviews, 6,234 children from seven cohorts (ages 0, 3, 6, 9, 12, 15, and 18 years) were surveyed. Eighty-four percent were successfully re-interviewed during the second wave of data collection in 1997–8. In addition to the longitudinal study, the Project on Human Development in Chicago Neighborhoods includes a community survey in which community residents in each of Chicago's 343 neighborhoods are interviewed. Observational studies were also conducted from 1996 through 2000. This project included many of the characteristics, research design, and measurement of the OJJDP projects. One notable addition was the inclusion of the birth cohort; pregnant women whose unborn children were monitored throughout pregnancy and after birth. Another feature of this study was the planned collection of medical data that allowed for testing the role of some physiological factors on crime causation. A number of publications have already been produced by members of the research team conducting this extensive study (e.g., Duncan & Raudenbush, 1998; Sampson & Bartusch, 1998; Raudenbush & Sampson, 1999; Sampson et al., 1999; Morenoff et al., 2001; Sampson, 2002, 2012).

THE INTERNATIONAL SELF-REPORT DELINQUENCY STUDY

While much of the self-report research has been conducted in the United States, one international effort offers a more global approach to the study of crime. The product of a NATO-sponsored workshop convened in the Netherlands in 1988 (Klein, 1989), this international project led to data collection efforts in 13 countries (Belgium, Canada, France, Germany, Greece, Italy, the Netherlands, Northern Ireland, Spain, Sweden, Switzerland, the United Kingdom, and the United States). Every effort was made to use comparable sampling techniques and to employ similar methods of questionnaire administration. As with all comparative research, problems such as language, legal statutes, and cultural variations greatly complicated the undertaking. Preliminary comparisons between the countries have shown a considerable degree of consistency with regard to the correlates of self-reported delinquency (Junger-Tas & Klein, 1994). This initial effort was subsequently labeled the International Self-Report Delinquency Study 1 (ISRD-1).

Lessons learned from ISRD-1 informed the second round of the International Self-Report Delinquency Study (known as ISRD-2) which was conducted between November 2005 and February 2007 (Enzmann et al., 2010). One of the more noticeable differences between ISRD-1 and ISRD-2 was the increase in the number of participating countries; ISRD-2 included more than 71,000 survey respondents in 31 nations. Fifteen countries represent Western Europe: Austria, Belgium, Denmark, Finland, France, Germany, Iceland, Ireland, Italy, the Netherlands, Norway, Portugal, Spain, Sweden, and Switzerland. Ten countries from Eastern Europe participated: Armenia, Bosnia-Herzegovina, Cyprus, the Czech Republic, Estonia, Hungary, Lithuania, Poland, Russia, and Slovenia. In addition, Canada and the United States represented North America, and four countries represented Central America: Aruba, the Netherlands Antilles, Suriname, and Venezuela. *Juvenile Delinquency in Europe and Beyond: Results of the Second International Self-Report Delinquency Study* by Junger-Tas and her colleagues (2010) provides a comprehensive country-specific report of findings from this multinational comparative research project.

This multinational self-report study was driven by several objectives, but of primary importance was (1) to determine if the **prevalence** of delinquent behavior was similar across national boundaries, (2) to examine if the relationship between offending and demographic variable (i.e., sex and age) held across countries, and (3) to assess whether other correlates with offending (i.e., the role of peers and family) were similar among the different nations. Considerable differences were found for overall delinquency prevalence rates with rates ranging from more than 40 percent in Ireland to only 13 percent in Venezuela. Prevalence rates for serious offending ranged from a high of 8 percent in Germany to less than 2 percent in several countries (including Portugal, the Czech Republic, Armenia, Lithuania, and Slovenia). While the prevalence rates varied, more consistency was found with respect to the correlates of delinquency. Sex and age differences in offending were less pronounced than official data would suggest. A number of theoretical constructs behaved similarly across the different national samples. For example, associating with delinquent peers was related to self-reported offending, as was unstructured socializing. This large-scale, multinational study confirms a number of findings from single-country studies but also identifies some interesting and unique differences among countries (see the volume by Junger-Tas et al. 2010).

Strengths of SRD

Self-report studies were introduced during the 1940s and 1950s to provide an alternative measure to the UCR. It was argued that a substantial **"dark figure" of crime** existed, that is, that the police were being informed about or discovering only a relatively small fraction of the crime that was occurring.

UCR data are at least one step removed from the actual crime, and therefore, are subject to bias, distortion, and reporting errors. Self-report studies go straight to the point of investigation, to the perpetrator; they do not rely upon second- or third-hand accounts. It is, therefore, possible to ascertain the amount of "secret deviance" (Becker, 1963) or the dark figure of crime (Biderman et al., 1967; Reiss, 1967).

The self-report technique, in addition, is not subject to manipulation or politicization, as are UCR data. The police cannot alter SRD to suit economic or political needs. In this regard, the SRD can become a measure of police performance and effectiveness.

Weaknesses of SRD

Since the first use of SRD, numerous methodological improvements have been made. While self-report studies have been conducted primarily with adolescent populations, this sample bias has been addressed in recent years. The self-report technique has been used in the study of adult prisoners (e.g., Petersilia et al., 1977; Greenwood & Abrahamse, 1982; Horney & Marshall, 1992; Horney et al., 1995) and this survey method has gained increasing usage with other adult samples, especially as longitudinal samples of youth have been followed into adulthood. Representative of this trend are the NYS, the OJJDP funded Causes and Correlates Program, the Dunedin (New Zealand) Study (Moffitt et al., 2001 and Silva & Stanton, 1996), and the Chicago Neighborhoods study.

Other problems, however, persist. Emphasis upon trivial offenses before the NYS research made it difficult, if not impossible, to draw any meaningful comparisons between official crime rates and self-reported crime rates.

Other criticisms of self-report measures include the time frame under consideration and the response categories provided. The time frame used in the reporting period may affect the validity of the data. It is difficult for respondents to recall accurately events that occurred 3, 5, or 10 years ago. They may forget or, if the time periods are not clearly identified, respondents may include events that occurred outside of the relevant interval. **Telescoping** refers to projecting an event outside the time period being studied. A calendar year period, as used in the NYS, better permits comparison with the annual UCR figures. The truncated responses of most self-report surveys do not allow for examination of high-frequency offenders and tend to group occasional and frequent offenders. This provided a distorted view of the offending behavior.

Methodological concerns have also been raised. These include:

- Sampling;
- Selective loss;

- Falsification, validity, and reliability;
- Interviewer measurement error; and
- Memory decay.

The majority of self-report studies have utilized limited samples of city, county, or state populations. Such samples may well provide unrepresentative information about the true nature and extent of crime.

The problem of **selective loss** or sample mortality is closely associated with the sampling issue. Whenever researchers study less than the entire population about which they desire to make inferences, the possibility of sampling error arises. Once a sampling technique and a sample have been selected, researchers must deal with the fact that some people will refuse to participate, while others will be unreachable. To what extent do these nonresponses bias the results? Initial loss rates of approximately 25 percent are common. While comparisons can be made based on certain demographic information that may be known about the nonrespondents, it is impossible to determine the full extent to which the nonrespondents may be similar to or different from survey participants.

Falsification is obviously another important matter. Is it not naive to believe that an individual will admit to a perfect stranger in an interview or on a questionnaire that the individual has engaged in criminal acts? Numerous studies have been conducted to assess the extent of falsification. John Clark and Larry Tifft (1966), using polygraphs in order to try to determine the amount of lying, found very little. Martin Gold (1966) utilized community informants to investigate over-reporting and under-reporting of illegal activity; he concluded that self-reports were valid measures. Others have studied individuals already known to have committed certain offenses or have scrutinized police records in order to verify self-report information (Hirschi, 1969; Elliott & Ageton, 1980; Hindelang et al., 1981). In their review of the literature, Robert Hardt and Sandra Peterson-Hardt (1977) concluded that the self-report method appears to provide valid and reliable measures of criminal activity.

Related to falsification is the role of the interviewer in the data collection process. An interviewer's characteristics and attitudes may affect the reporting of behaviors by respondents, which would amount to **interviewer measurement error.** Race, sex, social class, and attitudes all have been examined. This research (Schuman & Converse, 1971; Bradburn & Sudman, 1979) suggests that attempts to match respondents with interviewers who have similar demographic characteristics can reduce response error. In a study of interviewer effect upon self-reported delinquency, however, Esbensen (1983:66) concluded that "the effect of any single variable is likely to be minimal." Finally, **memory decay** refers to respondents' loss of memory over time.

Victimization Studies

The development of victimization surveys was sponsored by the President's Commission on Law Enforcement and Administration of Justice in the 1960s (Biderman et al., 1967; Ennis, 1967; Reiss, 1967). The best known of the three major early studies is that by the National Opinion Research Center (Ennis, 1967). This work used a sample of 10,000 households (33,000 individuals) in the continental United States. A household representative answered questions for all of its members, unless there had been a criminal victimization. In that case, the interviewer would question the victim about the incident. These early surveys found that victimization for Index crimes was substantially greater than the crime rate reported by the UCR. The victimization rate for rape, for example, was eight times greater than the UCR figure, while the surveys indicated about five times as many assaults.

Numerous methodological concerns were raised after the initial surveys were completed. They included:

- The time period to be used;
- The likelihood that one member of the household would know of or remember criminal victimizations of others;
- The sample size required to measure crime victimization accurately; and
- The frequency with which such a survey should be conducted.

Pre-tests conducted in 1970 and 1971 answered many of the concerns, such as whether a victim would report victimization to an unknown interviewer. James Garofalo and Michael Hindelang (1977) conducted a reverse-records check in which a total of 982 victims identified from police records in three cities (Washington, Baltimore, and San Jose) were interviewed by U.S. Census Bureau workers. More than 70 percent reported their known victimization to the interviewers. The rate of reporting specific types of crime varied considerably; 88 percent of the sample reported burglaries, but only 47 percent mentioned assaults. Person-to-person crimes, such as assault and rape, especially those committed by acquaintances, were less likely to be reported than were victimizations by strangers. This may be attributable to forgetfulness or repression, but Arnold Binder and Gilbert Geis (1983) suggest that in the case of wife-beating and rape, a woman may not want to jeopardize her relationship with a husband or boyfriend attacker and, therefore, will not report the crime to interviewers. Only 54 percent of victims raped by a person known to them reported the victimization, for example, while 84 percent of those raped by a stranger mentioned the crime to survey interviewers. A second factor found to affect responses was the time frame. In the San Jose study, 81 percent of the victimizations known to have occurred one to three months prior to the interview were reported, while only 67 percent of those that took place 10 to 12 months earlier were reported to the interviewers.

San Jose and Dayton were used to examine the possible effect of having one household member screen questions (household-respondent method), as opposed to having each household member screen questions about his or her own victimization (self-respondent method). The self-respondent method resulted in twice as many reports of robberies, 50 percent more reports of aggravated assaults, and 20 percent more reports of rape. Thus, the household-respondent method provides a substantial underestimate of criminal victimization.

THE NATIONAL CRIME VICTIMIZATION SURVEY (NCVS)

The National Crime Victimization Survey (NCVS), originally known as the National Crime Survey or the NCS, was begun in 1972 under the auspices of the Law Enforcement Assistance Administration (LEAA). It consisted of two separate components, one a sample of American cities and the other a national sample. Between July 1972 and May 1975, studies were carried out in 26 different American cities, 13 of which were surveyed twice. On the basis of a representative probability sample of housing units, approximately 10,000 households with about 22,000 eligible respondents (persons above the age of 12) were surveyed in each city. A separate sample of businesses was also contacted in each city. Anywhere from 1,000 to 5,000 businesses were included, on the basis of the city size. This study of businesses, however, was later discontinued.

For the national survey, households and businesses were chosen on the basis of a stratified multistage cluster sample, which identified a total of 72,000 households. During the first full year of data collection in 1973, interviews were completed with more than 145,000 residents, ages 12 and over residing in 65,000 households (Rennison & Rand, 2007). Residents in each of the selected households were subsequently interviewed during successive months. In this manner, the entire sample was interviewed in six months, at which point the cycle was repeated. Each household address was visited a maximum of seven times during three years before it was rotated out of the sample and replaced by a new household address. This procedure produces a panel design that allows the same households to be queried over a period of time. It also provides the opportunity to control for the problem of telescoping by comparing the most recently reported victimizations with responses from the previous interview. Budget cuts during the past several years, however, have reduced the sample size of households to slightly more than 40,000 and have increased reliance on telephone surveys to collect the data.

The NCVS, initially supervised by LEAA, is now conducted by the U.S. Census Bureau for the U.S. Bureau of Justice Statistics. In 1992, the U.S. Department of Justice introduced a redesigned NCVS (U.S. Department of Justice, 1997). New screening procedures using detailed cues to help respondents recall crime incidents resulted in considerably higher reported levels of victimization, especially for simple assaults and crimes committed by nonstrangers. Of notable interest is the change in the measurement of rape and sexual assault (Bachman & Taylor, 1994). While these types of victimizations were previously obtained through indirect questioning, the redesigned NCVS includes specific questions about these victimizations. To measure rape, the respondents are asked: Have you been forced or coerced to engage in unwanted sexual activity by (a) someone you didn't know, (b) a casual acquaintance, or (c) someone you know well? As a result of these types of changes to the survey, researchers must weigh the data collected before 1992 to study long-term trends in victimization. Figure 3.1 provides an example of the types of questions asked of respondents in the NCVS.

FIGURE 3.1

Sample questions from the National Crime Victimization Survey.

INDIVIDUAL'S PERSONAL CHARACTERISTICS

17. NAME

PGM 4

Last

First

18. Type of interview

401

1 ☐ Per. – Self-respondent
2 ☐ Tel. – Self-respondent
3 ☐ Per. – Proxy } Fill 13 on cover page
4 ☐ Tel. – Proxy
5 ☐ Noninterview — Fill 19-28 and 14 on cover page

19. Line No.

402

Line No.

20. Relationship to reference person	21. Age last birthday	22a. Marital status THIS survey period	22b. Marital status LAST survey period	23. Sex	24. Armed Forces member	25a. Education -highest grade	25b. Education -complete that year?	26. Attending college	27. Race	28. Hispanic origin
403	404	405	406	407	408	409	410	411	412	413
01 ☐ Husband		1 ☐ Married	1 ☐ Married	1 ☐ M	1 ☐ Yes		1 ☐ Yes	1 ☐ College/ University	1 ☐ White	1 ☐ Yes
02 ☐ Wife		2 ☐ Widowed	2 ☐ Widowed	2 ☐ F	2 ☐ No		2 ☐ No		2 ☐ Black	2 ☐ No
03 ☐ Son		3 ☐ Divorced	3 ☐ Divorced					2 ☐ Trade/ school	3 ☐ Amer. Indian, Aleut, Eskimo	
04 ☐ Daughter	Age	4 ☐ Separated	4 ☐ Separated			Grade		3 ☐ Voca- tional school		
05 ☐ Father		5 ☐ Never married	5 ☐ Never married						4 ☐ Asian, Pacific Islander	
06 ☐ Mother			6 ☐ Not inter- viewed last survey period					2 ☐ Not at all		
07 ☐ Brother									5 ☐ Other	
08 ☐ Sister										
09 ☐ Other relative										
10 ☐ Nonrelative										
11 ☐ Ref. person										

29. Date of interview ⟶

PGM 5

501 ☐☐ ☐☐ ☐☐
Month   Day   Year

30. Before we get to the crime questions, I'd like to ask you about some of YOUR usual activities. We have found that people with different lifestyles may be more or less likely to become victims of crime.

On average, during the last 6 months, that is, since _____, 19___, how often have YOU gone shopping? For example at drug, clothing, grocery, hardware and convenience stores. *(Read answer categories until respondent answers yes.)*

Mark (X) the first category that applies.

502
1 ☐ Almost every day (or more frequently)
2 ☐ At least once a week
3 ☐ At least once a month
4 ☐ Less often
5 ☐ Never
6 ☐ Don't know

31. On average, during the last 6 months, how often have you spent the evening out away from home for work, school or entertainment? *(Read answer categories until respondent answers yes.)*

Mark (X) the first category that applies.

503
1 ☐ Almost every evening (or more frequently)
2 ☐ At least once a week
3 ☐ At least once a month
4 ☐ Less often
5 ☐ Never
6 ☐ Don't know

32. On average, during the last 6 months, how often have you ridden public transportation? *(Read answer categories until respondent answers yes.)*

Do not include school buses.

Mark (X) the first category that applies.

504
1 ☐ Almost every day (or more frequently)
2 ☐ At least once a week
3 ☐ At least once a month
4 ☐ Less often
5 ☐ Never
6 ☐ Don't know

If unsure, ASK OR VERIFY –

33a. How long have you lived at this address?
(Enter number of months OR years.)

505 _____ Months (1-11) – **SKIP** to 33b

OR

506 _____ Years (Round to nearest whole year) – Fill Check Item A

CHECK ITEM A How many years are entered in 33a?

☐ 5 years or more – **SKIP** to 36a
☐ Less than 5 years – Ask 33b

33b. Altogether, how many times have you moved in the last 5 years, that is, since _____, 19___?

508 _____ Number of times

FIGURE 3.1
(Continued)

INDIVIDUAL'S SCREEN QUESTIONS

36a. I'm going to read some examples that will give you an idea of the kinds of crimes this study covers.

As I go through them, tell me if any of these happened to you in the last 6 months, that is since _____ ____, 19___.

Was something belonging to YOU stolen, such as –

(a) Things that you carry, like luggage, a wallet, purse, briefcase, book –

(b) Clothing, jewelry, or calculator –

(c) Bicycle or sports equipment –

(d) Things in your home – like a TV, stereo, or tools –

(e) Things from a vehicle, such as a package, groceries, camera, or cassette tapes –

OR

(f) Did anyone ATTEMPT to steal anything belonging to you?

Briefly describe incident(s)

MARK OR ASK –

36b. Did any incidents of this type happen to you?

| 532 | 1 ☐ Yes – **What happened?** *Describe above* |
| | 2 ☐ No – ***SKIP** to 40a* |

36c. How many times?

| 533 | |
| Number of times (36c) |

40a. (Other than any incidents already mentioned,) since _____ ____, 19___, were you attacked or threatened OR did you have something stolen from you –

(a) At home including the porch or yard –

(b) At or near a friend's, relative's, or neighbor's home –

(c) At work or school –

(d) In places such as a storage shed or laundry room, a shopping mall, restaurant, bank, or airport –

(e) While riding in any vehicle –

(f) On the street or in a parking lot –

(g) At such places as a party, theater, gym, picnic area, bowling lanes, or while fishing or hunting –

OR

(h) Did anyone ATTEMPT to attack or ATTEMPT to steal anything belonging to you from any of these places?

Briefly describe incident(s)

MARK OR ASK –

40b. Did any incidents of this type happen to you?

| 532 | 1 ☐ Yes – **What happened?** *Describe above* |
| | 2 ☐ No – ***SKIP** to 41a* |

40c. How many times?

| 533 | |
| Number of times (40c) |

HIGHLIGHT 3.7 FUTURE DIRECTIONS OF THE NCVS

Professor Janet Lauritsen from the University of Missouri-St. Louis has been working with the NCVS for a number of years and is assisting the Bureau of Justice Statistics in its efforts to enhance the design of the NCVS. She was asked to comment on the future directions of the NCVS. Her comments follow:

The methodological strengths and weaknesses of the NCVS recently were studied by a panel of the National Academy of Sciences' Committee on National Statistics to determine how the quality and relevance of the victimization data can be improved (Groves and Cork, 2008). The panel reported that due to a series of cost and budget restrictions, the NCVS was in danger of becoming unable to fulfill its principal purpose of providing annual estimates of the levels and changes in rates of victimization. The panel offered many recommendations to the Bureau of Justice Statistics to ensure that the data remain valuable and relevant to the nation. Some of the recommendations were technical in nature, such as increasing the sample size so that rare types of victimization could be estimated with more precision. Other recommendations

focused on improving its usefulness, such as finding ways to design the survey so that victimization rates could be estimated for states and large cities.

Based on many of the panel's suggestions, the Bureau of Justice Statistics has been conducting new research that will be used to inform a second redesign of the NCVS. These ongoing studies are exploring the strengths and weaknesses of a variety of new methods, such as how to count series or repeat victimizations, how the addition of new attitudinal questions might affect victims' reports of crime, and how to best administer the survey to ensure that survey participation rates remain high and costs remain affordable. In addition, a newly formed panel of the Committee on National Statistics is in the process of examining state-of-the-art evidence to determine what methods produce the most reliable and valid estimates of rape and sexual assault. Many other research and design projects are currently underway, and the results will be used by the Bureau of Justice Statistics to inform how victimization in the United States will be measured in the future.

In 2008, the National Research Council of the National Academies published its review for the Bureau of Justice Statistics (see also Highlight 3.7). The panel conducting the review consisted of 13 researchers and statisticians with familiarity with the NCVS and issues associated with conducting large-scale surveys intended to provide national estimates of the behavior in question. The Chair of the panel, Robert Groves, was subsequently selected by President Obama to oversee the 2010 U.S. Census. Issues examined included cost; inability to provide local or smaller geographic estimates due to sampling error associated with the "small" sample once you get down to the state and metro levels; reduction in sample size since 2005 when the sample decreased to 38,000 households instead of 45,000 as in 1996; going from six-month to annual; and, using the first wave of interviews instead of treating it as a "bounding" wave, that is, establishing a baseline for subsequent reporting of victimizations.

Other countries have also initiated victimization surveys and in 1988 an ambitious multinational crime victimization survey was launched. See Highlight 3.8 for an overview of the International Crime Victimization Survey (ICVS), which has now been conducted four times in more than 70 countries.

Strengths of Victimization Surveys

The NCVS had been heralded as the solution to the crime measurement issue, but it also proved far from a perfect enumeration of crime. Nevertheless, the

HIGHLIGHT 3.8 THE INTERNATIONAL CRIME VICTIMIZATION SURVEY

In 1988, three European criminologists, Jan van Dijk, Pat Mahew, and Martin Killias, developed the first large-scale international victimization survey. This initial effort provided the stimulus for the International Crime Victimization Survey (ICVS) which now has successfully collected data five times (1989, 1992–4, 1996–7, 2000, and 2004). To date, this household survey has been conducted one or more times in 72 different countries around the world. The ICVS is similar to the NCVS in that detailed information is collected from individuals concerning their experiences as victims of both property and violent crimes. Telephone surveys are conducted in most nations, but in some countries without widespread use of telephones, household visits are necessary. Data from the first four sweeps of the ICVS have provided some interesting insights to the amount of crime cross-nationally. Long considered an extremely crime-ridden society, the United States may not be that different from other nations. Victimization rates (per 100,000) for selected crimes and countries are reported for the 1997 ICVS data.

Country	Any Crime	Burglary	Contact Crimes
Argentina	87	28	37
Brazil	68	14	45
Canada	64	19	18
Egypt	69	22	32
England & Wales	63	23	17
China	52	9	13
Germany	62	12	18
Philippines	40	10	11
Poland	61	13	16
Russia	63	17	22
South Africa	64	23	29
Sweden	67	15	19
USA	64	23	20

national probability sample of residences allows for comparisons with the UCR data collected by the FBI, and this comparability has been one of the primary uses of the NCVS, a sort of validity check on the UCR. The NCVS, like the UCR, also can be used to study temporal variations in the crime rate that can provide a basis for assessing the impact of broader changes in law enforcement practices and other social factors.

Another major NCVS advantage is that a lot of information is collected about relatively few crimes. The UCR, on the other hand, collects a little bit of information about a lot of crimes. The NCVS approach allows appraisal of some of the financial and personal effects of victimization; for each specific criminal victimization, respondents are requested to supply estimates regarding the cost of materials stolen or destroyed. Due to the NCVS panel design (interviewing the same household over a period of three years), it is also possible to examine some of the psychosocial effects of victimization on crime

In-depth interviews can address the effects of victimization on crime victims over time.

CREDIT: ©iStockphoto. com/Jerry Koch.

victims over time. How are people affected by victimization? Why do victims choose to call the police? How often do victims use victims' services? Is there such a thing as "victim-proneness"? These are the types of questions that can be answered by in-depth interviews.

Weaknesses of Victimization Surveys

Caution must be exercised when interpreting NCVS data. Problems include those common to self-report studies (e.g., falsification, telescoping, validity, interviewer effect, and sampling). In addition, idiosyncrasies of the victimization data collection process draw criticism. The household-respondent method, for instance, may result in underreporting. There are some concerns that victims may under-report some types of victimizations if other members of the household are present during the interview. Although interviewers try to conduct the interview in private, this cannot always be assured. Other procedures may result in over-reporting; several of these are discussed below. Cost is also a major problem associated with victimization research. The current NCVS studies of 40,000 households represent a major financial outlay and are to some extent cost-prohibitive.

Several unique methodological issues have been raised concerning NCVS recording practices. Many of the victimizations reported, for example, represent trivial offenses, such as minor assaults that normally would not be considered crimes. Prior to the redesign of the NCVS in 1992, rape was measured indirectly. In the earlier surveys, the woman was not asked if she had been raped. Instead, if she answered "yes" to one of the following questions: Did anyone threaten to beat you up or threaten you in some way? or Did anyone try to attack you in some other way? then her answer was tabulated as a rape. Such methodological problems may go a long way toward explaining some of the differences in NCVS and UCR findings that are discussed in Chapter 4.

A second recording difficulty is that victimization surveys record crimes perpetrated against individuals and households, regardless of where the incident occurred. Thus, the victimization data cannot be used to provide crime estimates for any specific neighborhood, city, or state. This practice means that the victimization data cannot be compared to UCR data for specific geographical areas and that we cannot learn whether, for example, victims in one city are more likely to report crime to the police than victims in another city.

Another peculiarity of victimization recording that leads to under-reporting is the use of what are referred to as "series incidents." This offense category includes incidents such as school bullying and spouse abuse, which have no clear-cut beginning or end. In the NCVS, discrete events typically are counted. Therefore, when spouse abuse is reported, it becomes difficult for the victim to separate one incident from another and to provide a count of the number of times the incidents occurred. When a father or husband regularly mistreats his children or spouse, for example, is this a single incident or two or three or many more? In such cases, the NCVS uses a separate series incidence measurement procedure that gathers details about only the most recent incident. These series incident reports are not included in some of the victimization rates reported on official publications. Consequently, the NCVS underestimates the incidence of domestic violence and other crimes that involve a continuing relationship between offender and victim.

Problems shared by the NCVS with the self-report technique revolve around the data collection method. Reliability studies have found that individuals vary in their reporting of victimization, depending upon their educational level and the type of crime committed. "In 1976, for example, persons with college degrees recalled three times as many assaults as those with only an elementary education" (Gove et al., 1985:460). The majority of assaults reported in victimization surveys are relatively trivial, with many involving no injury. This raises the question of whether an assault or an intended assault, as defined by law, actually occurred (Gove et al., 1985).

Examinations of interviewer impact in self-report studies have indicated little or no significant effect. However, Summer Clarren and Alfred Schwartz (1976:129) concluded: "the upper bound for the number of 'crimes' that could be elicited is limited only by the persistence of the interviewer and the patience of the respondent." Interestingly, the very crimes that tend to be both overreported and underreported (rape, assault, petty theft, and series incidents) are those most affected by the ability and the patience of the interviewers.

COMPARISON OF UCR, SRD, AND NCVS DATA SOURCES

The three measures of crime just reviewed paint different pictures of the extent and distribution of crime in the United States. This highlights the importance of understanding the merits of the particular source. According to the UCR, for example, crime increased from 1960 through 1990 and has been declining since 1991, but both the NCVS and SRD suggest relative stability and even a decline since 1973 (Menard, 1987; U.S. Department of Justice & Federal Bureau of Investigation, 2011). Certainly, these contradictory conclusions about crime trends cannot both be valid! But, alas, given the different measurement (e.g., crimes included, populations covered, and recording policies), it is possible that each source is correct in its own particular way. Biderman and Lynch (1991) have provided an excellent critique of the UCR and the NCVS, concluding that once their different methodologies are considered, the findings are not as disparate as it appears. A more recent assessment of longer trends in the UCR and NCVS shows that the two estimates have become more similar over time (Lynch & Addington, 2007), perhaps because the police are recording more of the incidents that come to their attention and because victims are more likely to report violence to the police now compared to the past (Baumer & Lauritsen, 2010).

Robert O'Brien (1985), in providing what is considered by many to be the best review of the three data sources, points out that there are definitional differences between the three. For example, neither the victimization nor the self-report studies include homicide, while the NCVS excludes commercial larceny. With respect to populations covered, the UCR is said to represent 95 percent of the U.S. population, the NCVS is a national probability sample of persons over the age of 12. To date, there is no comparable self-report study of a national probability sample of adults that is conducted on an annual basis.

Both the NCVS and SRD yield information about actual behavior (i.e., victimization and offending, respectively), while the UCR is largely a reactive measure of police response to citizen complaints. Given these differences, one has to ask, "Do these sources actually measure the same phenomenon?" While no clear consensus exists in the field (e.g., O'Brien, 1985; Biderman & Lynch, 1991; Blumstein et al., 1991; Menard, 1992), let us consider the example of a convenience store robbery in which five customers are present. The UCR guidelines instruct the police to record this as one criminal event, thus reporting it as one robbery. The NCVS, however, treats the individual as the reporting unit so, if all five victims were participants in the NCVS, then five robbery victims would be tallied. This example illustrates that these two data sources may well measure different aspects of the same phenomenon. To better understand the crime problem and criminal justice response to crime, it is of utmost importance to realize the extent to which the data source shapes the picture of crime. These differences will be discussed more fully in Chapter 4.

SUMMARY

Crime statistics are essential to criminology. Knowledge of the extent and distribution of crime in society shapes both criminological theories and criminal justice policy. This chapter reviewed three major sources of crime data. Crime statistics are inherently quantitative, allowing for computation of crime rates (UCR) or prevalence rates (SRD and NCVS). These data permit researchers and policymakers to examine crime trends and to evaluate the impact of various criminal justice programs.

The UCR are the result of information supplied by local law enforcement agencies to the FBI. This measure of crime was first collected in 1930 and today represents approximately 95 percent of the nation's population. Most attention is paid to the Part I offenses (also referred to as Index crimes), which include particularly serious and relatively frequently occurring crimes (homicide, rape, robbery, aggravated assault, burglary, larceny-theft, motor vehicle theft, and arson). The FBI tabulates the information submitted by local law enforcement agencies and issues quarterly and annual reports that typically are summarized by the media. These data are largely responsible for the public's perception of the extent of crime in the United States. As with any data, the UCR have both positive and negative aspects associated with their use and interpretation.

Self-report studies, an alternative measure of crime, were introduced during the 1940s. They ask survey respondents to identify illegal or deviant acts they have committed during some specified period. Researchers have continued to improve upon the SRD method and this data source is widely used to test and develop theories of crime.

Victimization studies were introduced in the mid-1960s and provide a third source of information on crime. Similar to the SRD, victimization studies use surveys and ask people directly about crimes that have been committed against them or their households. The National Crime Survey, conducted by the U.S. Census Bureau, provides annual data on the victimization rate for the population at large, as well as for subgroups. As with the self-report method and all data collection methods, victimization studies have a number of methodological weaknesses, but they provide a valuable alternative source of information that is not available in police data and that has improved our understanding of the extent and distribution of crime.

KEY TERMS AND CONCEPTS

Causality

Cohort Study

Correlation

Crime Rate

Cross-sectional Research Designs

"Dark Figure" of Crime

Dependent Variable

Falsification

Frequency

Generalizability

Hierarchical Rule

Independent Variable

Index Crimes

Interviewer Measurement Error

Levels of Explanation

Longitudinal Research Designs

Macro Level

Micro Level

National Crime Victimization Survey (NCVS)

National Incident-Based Reporting System (NIBRS)

Part I Crimes

Part II Crimes

Prevalence

Reliability

Self-Report Data (SRD)

Stratified Probability Sampling

Selective Loss

Telescoping

Uniform Crime Reports (UCR)

Validity

Victimization Surveys

KEY CRIMINOLOGISTS

Albert D. Biderman	David Huizinga	Robert J. Sampson
Delbert S. Elliott	Josine Junger-Tas	Thorsten Sellin
James Garofalo	Rolf Loeber	James F. Short Jr.
Michael Hindelang	F. Ivan Nye	Terence P. Thornberry

DISCUSSION QUESTIONS

1. What is the "dark figure" of crime, and what measures have been developed to address this biased description of crimes in the United States?

2. Explain why some critics of the UCR data argue that the Part I/Index offenses do not accurately reflect the true amount or distribution of crime in the United States.

3. Discuss the relative strengths and weaknesses of the UCR as an indicator of crime in the United States.

4. It is silly to think that people will actually tell the truth to researchers who conduct self-report studies. Do you agree or disagree with this statement? Why or why not?

5. Comparative studies of the causes of crime can be insightful but at the same time difficult to implement. What can be learned from comparative studies, and what are some of the difficulties associated with conducting cross-national research?

6. Victimization studies provide an alternative view of crime in society. Describe the NCVS and identify the types of information this survey provides that is not available in the UCR.

REFERENCES

Addington, L. A. (2004). The effect of NIBRS reporting on item missing data in murder cases. *Homicide Studies, 8,* 193–213.

Addington, L. A. (2006). Using NIBRS murder data to evaluate clearance predictors: A research note. *Homicide Studies, 10,* 140–52.

Adler, P. A. (1992). *Wheeling and dealing: An ethnography of an upper-level drug dealing and smuggling community* (2nd ed.). New York, NY: Columbia University Press.

Aebi, M. (2002). *Counting rules as the main explanation of cross-national differences in recorded crime.* Paper presented at the Annual Meeting of the European Society of Criminology. Toledo, Spain, September.

Akiyama, Y. & Nolan, J. (1999). Methods for understanding and analyzing NIBRS data. *Journal of Quantitative Criminology, 15,* 225–38.

Bachman, R. & Taylor, B. M. (1994). The measurement of family violence and rape by the redesigned national crime victimization survey. *Justice Quarterly, 11,* 499–512.

Barnett-Ryan, C. (2007). Introduction to the uniform reporting program. In J. P. Lynch, & L. A. Addington (Eds.), *Understanding crime statistics: Revisiting the divergence of the NCVS and UCR* (pp. 55–89). New York, NY: Cambridge University Press.

Baumer, E. P. & Lauritsen, J. L. (2010). Reporting crime to the police, 1973–2005: A multivariate analysis of long-term trends in the NCS and NCVS. *Criminology, 48,* 131–85.

Becker, H. S. (1963). *Outsiders: Studies in the sociology of deviance.* New York, NY: The Free Press.

Biderman, A. D. & Lynch, J. P. (1991). *Understanding crime incidence statistics: Why the UCR diverges from the NCVS.* New York, NY: Springer-Verlag.

Biderman, A. D., Johnson, L. A., McIntyre, J., & Weir, A. (1967). *Report on a pilot study in the District of Columbia on victimization and attitudes toward law enforcement.* Washington, DC: President's Commission on Law Enforcement and Administration of Justice.

Binder, A. & Geis, G. (1983). *Methods of research in criminology and criminal justice.* New York, NY: McGraw-Hill.

Bjerregard, B. & Lizotte, A. J. (1995). Gun ownership and gang membership. *The Journal of Criminal Law and Criminology, 86,* 37–58.

Bjerregard, B. & Smith, C. (1993). Gender differences in gang participation, delinquency, and substance use. *Journal of Quantitative Criminology, 9,* 329–55.

Blumstein, A., Cohen, J., & Rosenfeld, R. (1991). Trend and deviation in crime rates: A comparison of UCR and NCVS data for burglary and robbery. *Criminology, 29,* 237–63.

Bradburn, N. M. & Sudman, S. (1979). *Improving interview method and questionnaire design.* San Francisco, CA: Jossey-Bass.

Brown, E. (2007). *Snitch: Informants, cooperators, and the corruption of justice.* New York, NY: Public Affairs.

Campbell, A. (1991). *The girls in the gang* (2nd ed.). New York, NY: Basil Blackwell.

Chappell, D., Geis, G., Schafer, S., & Siegel, L. (1971). Forcible rape: A comparative study of offenses known to the police in Boston and Los Angeles. In J. M. Henslin (Ed.), *Studies in the sociology of sex* (pp. 161–90). New York, NY: Appleton-Century-Crofts.

Chilton, R. (2004). Regional variations in lethal and non-lethal assaults. *Homicide Studies, 8,* 40–56.

Chilton, R. & Jarvis, J. (1999). Using the national incident-based reporting system (NIBRS) to test effects of arrestee and offender characteristics. *Journal of Quantitative Criminology, 15,* 207–24.

Clark, J. P. & Tifft, L. L. (1966). Polygraph and interview validation of self-reported deviant behavior. *American Sociological Review, 31,* 516–23.

Clarren, S. N. & Schwartz, A. I. (1976). Measuring a program's impact: A cautionary note. In W. Skogan (Ed.), *Sample surveys of the victims of crime* (pp. 121–34). Cambridge, MA: Ballinger.

Decker, S. H. & Van Winkle, B. (1996). *Life in the gang: Family friend, and violence.* New York, NY: Cambridge University Press.

Duncan, G. J. & Raudenbush, S. W. (1998). Assessing the effects of context in studies of child and youth development. *Educational Psychologist, 34,* 29–41.

Dunn, C. S. & Zelenock, T. J. (1999). NIBRS data available for secondary data analysis. *Journal of Quantitative Criminology, 15,* 239–48.

Earls, F. J. & Reiss, A. J., Jr. (1993). *Annual report of the program on human development and criminal behavior for the John D. & Catherine T. MacArthur Foundation.* Cambridge, MA: Harvard School of Public Health.

Elliott, D. S. & Ageton, S. S. (1980). Reconciling race and class differences in self-reported and official estimates of delinquency. *American Sociological Review, 45*, 95–110.

Elliott, D. S., Huizinga, D., & Ageton, S. S. (1985). *Explaining delinquency and drug use*. Beverly Hills, CA: Sage Publications.

Ennis, P. (1967). *Criminal victimization in the United States: A report of a national survey*. Washington, DC: President's Commission on Law Enforcement and Administration of Justice.

Enzmann, D., Marshall, I. H., Killias, M., Junger-Tas, J., Steketee, M., & Gruszcynska, B. (2010). Self-reported youth delinquency in Europe and beyond: First results from the Second International Self-Report Delinquency Study in the context of police and victimization data. *European Journal of Criminology, 7*, 159–83.

Esbensen, F.-A. (1983). Measurement error and self-reported delinquency: An examination of interviewer bias. In G. P. Waldo (Ed.), *Measurement issues in criminal justice* (p. 66). Beverly Hills, CA: Sage Publications.

Esbensen, F.-A. & Huizinga, D. (1991). Juvenile victimization and delinquency. *Youth and Society, 23*, 202–28.

Esbensen, F.-A. & Huizinga, D. (1993). Gangs, drugs, and delinquency in a survey of urban youth. *Criminology, 31*, 565–89.

Esbensen, F.-A. & Maxson, C. L. (2012). *Youth gangs in international perspective: Results from the Eurogang Program of Research*. New York, NY: Springer.

Esbensen, F.-A., Huizinga, D., & Menard, S. (1999). Family context and victimization. *Youth and Society, 31*, 168–98.

Faggiani, D. & McLaughlin, C. (1999). Using national incident-based reporting system data for strategic crime analysis. *Journal of Quantitative Criminology, 15*, 181–91.

Fairchild, E. & Dammer, H. R. (2001). *Comparative criminal justice systems* (2nd ed.). New York, NY: Wadsworth.

Farrington, D. P., Ohlin, L. E., & Wilson, J. Q. (1986). *Understanding and controlling crime: Toward a new research strategy*. New York, NY: Springer-Verlag.

Finkelhor, D. & Ormrod, R. (2001). *Child abuse reported to police. Juvenile justice bulletin (May)*. Washington, DC: U.S. Department of Justice, Office of Justice Programs, Office of Juvenile Justice & Delinquency Prevention.

Fyfe, J. J. (1978). *Shots fired: An examination of New York City Police firearms discharges*. Ann Arbor, MI: University Microfilms International.

Garofalo, J. & Hindelang, M. J. (1977). *An introduction to the national crime survey*. Washington, DC: National Criminal Justice Information and Statistics Service, Law Enforcement Assistance Administration, U.S. Department of Justice.

Geller, W. & Michael, J. S. (1992). *Deadly force: What we know: A practitioner's desk reference on police-involved shootings*. Washington, DC: Police Executive Research Forum.

Gold, M. (1966). Undetected delinquent behavior. *Journal of Research in Crime and Delinquency, 3*, 27–46.

Gove, W. R., Hughes, M., & Geerken, M. (1985). Are uniform crime reports a valid indicator of the index crimes? An affirmative answer with minor qualifications. *Criminology, 23*, 451–502.

Greenwood, P. W. & Abrahamse, A. (1982). *Selective incapacitation*. Santa Monica, CA: RAND Corporation.

Groves, R. M. & Cork, D. L. (2008). *Surveying victims: Options for conducting the National Crime Victimization Survey. National Research Council*. Washington, DC: The National Academies Press.

Hardt, R. H. & Peterson-Hardt, S. (1977). On determining the quality of the delinquency self-report method. *Journal of Research in Crime and Delinquency, 14*, 247–61.

Harlow, C. W. (1986). *Reporting crimes to the police*. Washington, DC: The Criminal Justice Archive and Information Network.

Hindelang, M. J., Hirschi, T., & Weis, J. G. (1981). *Measuring delinquency*. Beverly Hills, CA: Sage Publications.

Hirschi, T. (1969). *Causes of delinquency*. Berkeley, CA: University of California Press.

Horney, J. & Marshall, L. H. (1992). Risk perceptions among serious offenders: The role of crime and punishment. *Criminology, 30*, 575–94.

Horney, J., Osgood, D. W., & Marshall, L. H. (1995). Criminal careers in the short-term: Intra-individual variability in crime and its relation to local life circumstances. *American Sociological Review, 60*, 655–73.

Huizinga, D. & Elliott, D. S. (1987). Juvenile offenders: Prevalence, offenders, and arrest rates by race. *Crime & Delinquency, 33*, 206–23.

Huizinga, D. & Henry, K. L. (2008). The effect of arrest and justice system sanctions on subsequent behavior: Findings from longitudinal and other studies. In A.M. Liberman (Ed.), *The long view of crime: A synthesis of longitudinal research* (pp. 220–54). New York, NY: Springer.

Huizinga, D., Esbensen, F., & Weiher, A. W. (1991). Are there multiple paths to delinquency? *Journal of Criminal Law and Criminology, 82*, 83–118.

Huizinga, D., Esbensen, F., & Weiher, A. W. (1994a). Examining developmental trajectories in delinquency using accelerated longitudinal designs. In E. G. M. Weitekamp, & H. J. Kerner (Eds.), *Cross-national longitudinal research on human development and criminal behavior*. Dordrecht, The Netherlands: Kluwer.

Huizinga, D., Loeber, R., & Thornberry, T. P. (1994b). *Urban delinquency and substance abuse*. Washington, DC: U.S. Department of Justice.

Jacobs, B. A. (1999). *Dealing crack: The social world of streetcorner selling*. Boston, MA: Northeastern University Press.

Jacques, S. & Wright, R. (2011). Informal control and illicit drug trade. *Criminology, 49*, 729–65.

Junger-Tas, J. & Klein, M. (1994). *International self-report delinquency survey*. Amsterdam: Kugler Publishers.

Junger-Tas, J., Marshall, I. H., Enzmann, D., Killias, M., Stetete, M., & Gruszcynska, B. (Eds.), (2010). *Juvenile delinquency in Europe and beyond: Results of the second international self-report delinquency study*. Berlin, Germany: Springer.

Kahn, J. (2007). The story of a snitch. *The Atlantic Monthly*, April. Available online at www.theatlantic.com/doc/200704/stop-snitching.

Kappeler, V. E., Blumberg, M., & Potter, G. W. (1993). *The mythology of crime and criminal justice*. Prospect Heights, IL: Waveland Press.

Kelley, B. T., Huizinga, D., Thornberry, T. P., & Loeber, R. (1997). *Epidemiology of serious violence*. Washington, DC: U.S. Department of Justice.

Klein, M. W. (1989). *Cross-national research in self-reported crime and delinquency*. Dordrecht, Netherlands: Kluwer.

Klein, M. W. (2009). *The street gangs of Euroburg*. Bloomington, IN: IUniverse.

Klinger, D. A. (2012). On the problems and promise of research on lethal police violence: A research note. *Homicide Studies, 16*, 78–96.

Klockars, C. B. (1974). *The professional fence*. New York, NY: The Free Press.

Lizotte, A. J., Tesoriero, J. M., Thornberry, T. P., & Krohn, M. D. (1994). Patterns of adolescent firearms ownership and use. *Justice Quarterly, 11*, 51–73.

Lizotte, A. J., Krohn, M. D., Howell, J. C., Tobin, K., & Howard, G. J. (2000). Factors influencing gun carrying among young urban males over the adolescent-young adult life course. *Criminology, 38*, 811–34.

Loeber, R., Green, S. M., Keenan, K., & Lahey, B. B. (1995). Which boys will fare worse? Early predictors of the onset of conduct disorder in a six year longitudinal study. *Journal of the American Academy of Child and Adolescent Psychiatry, 34*, 499–509.

Loeber, R., Stouthamer-Loeber, M., Van Kammen, W., & Farrington, D. (1991). Initiation, escalation and desistance in juvenile offending and their correlates. *Journal of Criminal Law and Criminology, 82*, 36–82.

Lynch, J. P. & Addington, L. A. (Eds.), (2007). *Understanding crime statistics: Revisiting the divergence of the NCVS and UCR*. New York, NY: Cambridge University Press.

Maltz, M. D. (1977). Crime statistics: A historical perspective. *Crime & Delinquency, 23*, 32–40.

Maltz, M. D. (1999). *Bridging gaps in police crime data*. Washington, DC: U.S. Department of Justice.

Maxfield, M. G. (1999). The national incident-based reporting system: Research and policy implications. *Journal of Quantitative Criminology, 15*, 119–49.

Maxson, C. L. & Klein, M. W. (1990). Street gang violence: Twice as great or half as great? In C. R. Huff (Ed.), *Gangs in America* (pp. 71–100). Newbury Park, CA: Sage Publications.

Maxson, C. L. & Klein, M. W. (2002). Defining gang homicide: An updated look at the member and motive approaches. In J. Miller, C. L. Maxson, & M. W. Klein (Eds.), *The modern gang reader* (3rd ed)(p. 182). Los Angeles, CA: Roxbury Press.

Menard, S. (1987). Short-term trends in crime and delinquency: A comparison of UCR, NCS and self-report data. *Justice Quarterly, 4*, 455–74.

Menard, S. (1992). Residual gains, reliability, and the UCR-NCS relationship: A comment on Blumstein, Cohen, and Rosenfeld. *Criminology, 30*, 105–13.

Messner, S. F., McHugh, S., & Felson, R. B. (2004). Distinctive characteristics of assaults motivated by bias. *Criminology, 42*, 585–618.

Miller, J. (2001). *One of the guys: Girls, gangs, and gender*. New York, NY: Oxford University Press.

Moffitt, T. E., Caspi, A., Dickson, N., Silva, P., & Stanton, W. (2001). Males on the life-course persistence and adolescence-limited antisocial pathways: Follow-up at age 26. *Development and Psychopathology, 13*, 355–75.

Morenoff, J. D., Sampson, R. J., & Raudenbush, S. W. (2001). Neighborhood inequality, collective efficacy, and the spatial dynamics of urban violence. *Criminology, 39*, 517–59.

National Research Council (2008). *Surveying victims: Options for conducting the national crime victimization survey*. Washington, DC: The National Academies Press.

Nye, F. I. (1958). *Family relationships and delinquent behavior*. New York, NY : John Wiley and Sons.

O'Brien, R. M. (1985). *Crime and victimization data*. Beverly Hills, CA: Sage Publications.

Pepinsky, H. E. & Jesilow, P. (1984). *Myths that cause crime*. Cabin John, MD: Seven Locks Press.

Petersilia, J., Greenwood, P. W., & Lavin, M. (1977). *Criminal careers of habitual felons*. Santa Monica, CA: RAND Corporation.

Porterfield, A. L. (1946). *Youth in trouble*. Fort Worth, TX: Leo Potisham Foundation.

Rantala, R. R. & Edwards, T. J. (2000). *Effects of NIBRS on crime statistics*. Washington, DC: U.S. Department of Justice, Office of Justice Programs.

Raudenbush, S. W. & Sampson, R. J. (1999). Econometrics: Toward a science of assessing ecological settings, with application to systematic social observation of neighborhoods. *Sociological Methodology, 29*, 1–41.

Reiss, A. J., Jr. (1967). *Studies in crime and law enforcement in major metropolitan areas*. Washington, DC: President's Commission on Law Enforcement and Administration of Justice.

Rennison, C. M. & Rand, M. (2007). Introduction to the National Crime Victimization Survey. In J. P. Lynch, & L. A. Addington (Eds.), *Understanding crime statistics: Revisiting the divergence of the NCVS and UCR* (pp. 7–54). New York, NY: Cambridge University Press.

Sampson, R. J. (2002). Transcending tradition: New directions in community research, Chicago style—The American Society of Criminology 2001 Sutherland Address. *Criminology, 40*, 213–30.

Sampson, R. J. (2012). *The great American city: Chicago and the enduring neighborhood effect*. Chicago, IL: University of Chicago Press.

Sampson, R. J. & Bartusch, D. (1998). Legal cynicism and (subcultural?) Tolerance of deviance: The neighborhood context of racial differences. *Law and Society Review, 32*, 777–804.

Sampson, R. J., Morenoff, J. D., & Earls, F. J. (1999). Beyond social capital: Spatial dynamics of collective efficacy for children. *American Sociological Review, 64*, 633–60.

Schuman, H. & Converse, J. M. (1971). The effects of black and white interviewers on black responses in 1968. *Public Opinion Quarterly, 35*, 49–68.

Sellin, T. (1931). The basis of a Crime Index. *Journal of Criminal Law and Criminology, 22*, 335–56.

Sherman, L. W. &. Langworthy, R. H. (1979). Measuring homicide by police officers. *Journal of Criminal Law and Criminology, 70*, 546–60.

Short, J. F., Jr. & Nye, F. I. (1957). Reported behavior as a criterion of deviant behavior. *Social Problems, 5*, 207–13.

Silva, P. & Stanton, W. (1996). *From child to adult: The Dunedin Multidisciplinary Health and Development Study*. Auckland, NZ: Oxford University Press.

Simon, D. R. & Eitzen, D. S. (1990). *Elite deviance* (3rd ed.). Newton, MA: Allyn and Bacon.

Skogan, W. & Frydl, K. (2004). *Fairness and effectiveness in policing: The Evidence*. Washington, DC: National Academies Press.

Slocum, L. A., Taylor, T. J., Brick, B. T., & Esbensen, F.-A. (2010). Neighborhood structural characteristics, individual-level attitudes, and youths' crime reporting intentions. *Criminology, 48*, 1063–1100.

Snyder, H. N. (1999). The overrepresentation of juvenile crime proportions in robbery clearance statistics. *Journal of Quantitative Criminology, 15*, 151–61.

Steffensmeier, D. (1986). *The fence: In the shadow of two worlds*. Totowa, NJ: Rowman and Littlefield.

Strom, K. J. (2001). *Hate crimes reported in NIBRS, 1997–1999. Bureau of Justice Statistics Special Report (September)*. U.S. Department of Justice, Office of Justice Programs, Bureau of Justice Statistics.

Sutherland, E. H. (1937). *The professional thief*. Chicago, IL: University of Chicago Press.

Taylor, T. J., Holleran, D., & Topalli, V. (2009). Racial bias in case processing: Does victim race affect police clearance of violent crime incidents? *Justice Quarterly, 26*, 562–91.

Thompson, M. P., Saltzman, L. E., & Bibel, D. (1999). Applying NIBRS data to the study of intimate partner violence. *Journal of Quantitative Criminology, 15,* 163–80.

Thornberry, T. P., Huizinga, D., & Loeber, R. (1995). The prevention of serious delinquency and violence: Implications from the Program of Research on the causes and correlates of delinquency. In J. C. Howell, B. Krisberg, J. D. Hawkins, & J. J. Wilson (Eds.), *A sourcebook: Serious, violent, & chronic juvenile offenders* (pp. 213–37). Thousand Oaks, CA: Sage Publications.

Thornberry, T. P., Krohn, M. D., Lizotte, A. J., & Chard-Wierschem, D. (1993). The role of juvenile gangs in facilitating delinquent behavior. *Journal of Research in Crime and Delinquency, 30,* 55–87.

Thornberry, T. P., Wei, E. H., Stouthamer-Loeber, M., & Van Dyke, J. (2000). *Teenage fatherhood and delinquent behavior.* Washington, DC: U.S. Department of Justice.

Thornberry, T. P., Krohn, M. D., Lizotte, A. J., Smith, C. A., & Tobin, K. (2003). *Gangs and delinquency in developmental perspective.* New York, NY: Cambridge University Press.

Thornberry, T. P., Lizotte, A. J., Krohn, M. D., Farnworth, M., & Jang, S. J. (1991). Testing interactional theory: An examination of reciprocal causal relationships among family, school, and delinquency. *Journal of Criminal Law and Criminology, 82,* 3–35.

Tittle, C., Villemez, W., & Smith, D. (1978). The myth of social class and criminality: An empirical assessment of the empirical evidence. *American Sociological Review, 43,* 643–56.

Tonry, M., Ohlin, L. E., & Farrington, D. P. (1991). *Human development and criminal behavior: New ways of advancing knowledge.* New York, NY: Springer-Verlag.

U.S. Department of Justice (1980). *Uniform Crime Reporting Handbook.* Washington, DC: U.S. Department of Justice.

U.S. Department of Justice (1989). *Sourcebook of Criminal Justice Statistics – 1989.* Washington, DC: U.S. Department of Justice.

U.S. Department of Justice (1997). *Effects of the redesign on victimization estimates.* Washington, DC: U.S. Department of Justice.

U.S. Department of Justice & Federal Bureau of Investigation (2006). *National Incident-Based Reporting System (NIBRS) frequently asked questions [online].* Available at http://www.fbi.gov/ucr/faqs.htm. Retrieved May 30, 2006.

U.S. Department of Justice & Federal Bureau of Investigation (2011). *Crime in the United States, 2010.* Washington, DC: U.S. Department of Justice, Federal Bureau of Investigation.

Vasquez, S. P., Stohr, M. K., & Purkiss, M. (2005). Intimate partner violence incidence and characteristics: Idaho NIBRS 1995 to 2001 data. *Criminal Justice Policy Review, 16,* 99–114.

Wallerstein, J. S. & Wyle, C. J. (1947). Our law-abiding lawbreakers. *Probation, 25,* 107–12.

Weerman, F. M., Maxson, C. L., Esbensen, F.-A., Aldridge, J., Medina, J., & van Gemert, F. (2009). *Eurogang Program Manual: Background, development, and use of the Eurogang instruments in multi-site, multi-method comparative research.* http://www.umsl.edu/~ccj/eurogang/euroganghome.htm.

White, M. D. (2006). Hitting the target (or not): Comparing characteristics of fatal, injurious and noninjurious police shootings. *Police Quarterly, 9,* 303–30.

Wright, R. T. & Decker, S. H. (1994). *Burglars on the job: Streetlife and residential break-ins.* Boston, MA: Northeastern University Press.

Wright, R. T. & Decker, S. H. (1997). *Armed robbers in action: Stickups and street culture.* Boston, MA: Northeastern University Press.

Distribution of Crime

LEARNING OBJECTIVES

After reading Chapter 4, you should be able to:

- Describe crime trends in the United States over the past 40 years.
- Describe the geographical and temporal distribution of crime in the United States.
- Discuss differences in crime rates between the United States and other industrialized nations and identify reasons for these differences.
- Compare and contrast differences in crime trends between the UCR and NCVS.
- Discuss the different perspectives on female crime associated with the liberation and post-liberation explanations.
- Indicate why the UCR data may not be well suited to provide information on offenders and victims.
- Explain what is meant by the term "age-crime curve."
- Identify some of the problems associated with measuring social class.
- Discuss the role of race and social class in offending rates.

To explain the causes of crime, it is important to know who is committing crime, who is being victimized, and when and where crimes are being committed. This information can also be utilized by criminal justice practitioners to evaluate the effectiveness of crime-fighting techniques and to discover matters requiring greater attention. Similarly, a portrait of criminal activity conveys information about sore points in the social system, and how the system is failing to persuade people to act in legal ways. Unless you are persuaded that genes are destiny, that is, that criminal activity is predestined for some people, a logical deduction is that each society creates its own criminals.

A number of factors must be considered when discussing the distribution of crime. First, it is essential to determine how many crimes and what types of crimes are being committed; in other words, what is the volume of crime? A second issue is who is committing the offenses? What are the offenders' social characteristics, i.e., gender, age, race, ethnicity, and social class? The characteristics of victimized individuals and their relationships to offenders are also important. Are they strangers, friends, or relatives? Are they youthful or aged? Other matters of importance in the study of crime are the geographical and temporal distributions. Do crime rates, for example, vary by region of the country and by community size? And what about crime trends over time? And during what times of the year, week, and day do particular crimes most occur? These and other aspects of the distribution of crime are examined in the present chapter.

VOLUME OF CRIME: UNIFORM CRIME REPORTS

The Uniform Crime Reports (UCR) are a major source of information detailing the extent of crime in the United States (see Chapter 3). Published annually by the Federal Bureau of Investigation in the U.S. Department of Justice, these data become available in late fall for the previous year. Table 4.1 depicts, for 2012, the number of Index crimes reported to and recorded by the police, as well as a breakdown by crime type.

TABLE 4.1 Total Number of Major Crimes Reported to and Recorded by the Police, 2012		
United States Population 313,914,040		
	Number	Rate[1]
Crime Index Total	10,189,900	3,246.1
Violent crime	1,214,462	386.9
Murder	14,827	4.7
Forcible Rape	84,376	26.9
Robbery	354,520	112.9
Aggravated Assault	760,739	242.3
Property Crime	8,975,438	2,859.2
Burglary	2,103,787	670.2
Larceny-theft	6,150,598	1,959.3
Motor vehicle theft	721,053	229.7

[1]Rate per 100,000 people

Source: U.S. Department of Justice (2013). *Crime in the United States*, 1993–2012. Washington, DC: U.S. Government Printing Office.

A total of 10,189,900 Index crimes were recorded in 2012 by reporting law enforcement agencies. Of these, 88 percent were property offenses (burglary, larceny-theft, and motor vehicle theft), while 12 percent were violent offenses (murder, forcible rape, robbery, and aggravated assault). The distribution of violent and property offenses in the United States is reasonably similar to that found in other industrialized nations.

Historically, the United States has experienced violent crime rates significantly higher than other industrialized nations. The decline in violent crime during the past decade, however, has reduced the disparity between the United States and other industrialized nations. In a cross-national comparison of violent crime rates, Steven Messner and Richard Rosenfeld (2007) report that the rate of robbery is now greater in France and England and Wales than it is in the United States. The U.S. robbery rate from 2000–2 of 145.9 robberies per 100,000 residents, however, while no longer the highest, was more than 60 percent higher than the average rate (89.8) for 15 other industrialized countries. While the disparity in rates has declined, the U.S. violent crime rate remains well above the average among other industrialized nations. Messner and Rosenfeld (2007) maintain that the difference in violence between the United States and other countries is further witnessed in the greater likelihood of the use of firearms in robberies (more than ten times more likely in the United States than in England and Wales) and homicides. Since the publication of the Messner and Rosenfeld book, *Crime and the American Dream*, the American crime rate has continued to decline and in 2012, the robbery rate was 112.9 per 100,000. The American homicide rate of 4.7 homicides per 100,000, while declining, remains significantly higher than that found in other industrialized nations.

Freda Adler (1983) insists that we should study nations not obsessed with crime in order to determine what sociocultural factors tend to inhibit criminal activity. She suggested that nations with low crime rates exhibit a greater sense of community and greater congruence in norms than do societies showing high crime rates. The lesson from these diverse inquiries is that, although the distribution of violent and property crimes may be similar for industrialized nations, crime rates can vary dramatically from country to country.

The crime rate in the United States of 3,245 means that in 2012, approximately 32 Index offenses were reported for every 1,000 people living in the United States; this figure, however, may be a conservative estimate because offenses sometimes have multiple victims. To obtain a more comprehensive picture of the volume of crime, we should also look at UCR Part II offenses. Approximately 10 million arrests were made in 2012 for these crimes, which include drug violations, embezzlement, vagrancy, sexual assaults, and driving under the influence of alcohol or other drugs. Recall, only those crimes resolved by an arrest are tabulated in this category. Underestimation is especially characteristic for offenses that are private in nature and exceptionally difficult to detect, such as gambling, fraud, drug use, and sex crimes. If we assume an arrest rate of 50 percent (which is probably high given that only 12 percent of burglaries and car thefts are cleared by an arrest), this would indicate that there were more than 20 million Part II crimes committed in the United States in 2012. In addition to these Part II offenses, there were more than 10 million Index offenses reported during the 2012 calendar year; thus, there were in excess of 30 million crimes committed in the United States in 2012. Remember, this figure includes only those crimes that come to the attention of the police; millions more crimes remain undetected. It should also be noted that many of these crimes are of a nonserious nature.

Geographical Distribution

Where do these crimes occur? If you are planning to move, what is the safest place in the nation? Table 4.2 provides answers to these two questions by geographical region, although some criminologists argue that regional and idiosyncratic recording differences may well account for a substantial part of these different rates. In terms of violent crime, avoid the southern states if you want to minimize your odds of being murdered, raped, or assaulted. While these states have 37.4 percent of the population, they account for 43.6 percent of murders and 42.9 percent of assaults. On the other hand, if you want to reduce the probability that your car will be stolen, stay out of the western states. While these states account for 23.4 percent of the population, 37.0 percent of all car thefts are recorded in the west. In general, the southern and western states should be avoided if you fear crime. The percentage of crimes committed in these states notably exceeds their population percentage. Conversely, the states comprising the northeastern area of the United States are your best bet for reducing the likelihood of becoming a crime victim. While comprising 17.8 percent of the U.S. population, these states account for only 16.0 and 12.9 percent of violent and property crimes respectively.

Temporal Distribution

When do crimes occur? When are we most apt to be victimized? Is crime increasing? These are practical questions that are of concern not only to researchers and practitioners, but to all of us. UCR data suggest that while crimes are distributed fairly evenly throughout the year, fewer crimes tend to be committed during the months of January and February. Conversely, slightly more crimes are committed during the warmest summer months (July and August) and during December.

These seasonal fluctuations may be attributable to climatic conditions. People are less mobile and more apt to stay at home during cold, snowy seasons. Thus, fewer opportunities exist to commit crimes. With people remaining at home, for instance, burglars are less likely to find suitable targets. In the hot summer months, people are outdoors more and away on vacations. These factors improve the chances of interpersonal violence among strangers and increase the number of potential unoccupied "hits" for burglars.

During December, more murders, robberies, and burglaries are committed than in any other month. This phenomenon may be closely associated with the pressures and expectations surrounding the holiday season. With the emphasis upon buying gifts, the need for money is heightened. Researchers have also

TABLE 4.2 Geographic Distribution of Crime in the United States, 2012 UCR Data[1]

Region	Percent of the Population	Percent of Violent Crimes	Percent of Murder	Percent of Rapes	Percent of Robberies	Percent of Aggravated Assaults	Percent of Property Crimes	Percent of Burglaries	Percent of Larceny-thefts	Percent of Motor Vehicle Thefts
Northeast	17.8	16.0	14.2	13.0	19.1	15.0	12.9	11.2	13.9	9.7
Midwest	21.4	19.7	21.1	25.3	19.6	19.0	20.7	20.6	21.0	18.6
South	37.4	40.9	43.6	37.6	37.2	42.9	42.2	45.0	42.1	34.8
West	23.4	23.4	21.0	24.0	24.1	23.1	24.2	23.2	23.0	37.0

[1]Because of rounding, the percentages may not add to 100.0

Although arson data are included in the trend and clearance tables, sufficient data are not available to estimate totals for this offense. Therefore, no arson data are published in this table.

Source: U.S. Department of Justice (2013). *Crime in the United States, 2012.* Washington, DC: U.S. Government Printing Office.

indicated that family holidays such as Christmas lead to increased tension and interpersonal hostility, which are likely to trigger assaults and homicides. Familial and acquaintance interpersonal violence (including homicide, rape, and assault) accounts for more than 50 percent of all such offenses.

Most crimes are likely to be committed during the evening and nighttime hours and over the weekend, especially from Friday evening through Saturday night. For some crimes, such as burglaries, motor vehicle thefts, and larceny-thefts, it is difficult to determine when the crime actually occurred. If someone has been out of town for two weeks and upon returning discovers his or her house burglarized and car stolen, it usually is impossible to determine when during the two-week period the crime occurred. Generally, the crime is considered to have taken place immediately prior to being reported. Consequently, the tabulated figures may not be accurate indicators of the actual time of the offenses.

Fluctuations in crime rates over time have been closely studied. Generally, the discussion focuses on the immediate past and on the American crime scene. Messner and Rosenfeld (1994), for instance, found U.S. homicide rates in excess of 8 per 100,000 during the 1920s and 1930s. They then fell below five per 100,000 during the 1950s, only to increase to more than eight homicides per 100,000 during the 1970s and 1980s. During the last few years of the twentieth century and the first decade of the twenty-first century, the U.S. murder rate fell and, in 2012, the murder rate was below five per 100,000 inhabitants. To understand the current situation better, it is beneficial to examine historical and international crime trends. In their historical analysis, Ted Robert Gurr and associates (1977) reported finding a U-shaped curve in the rates of criminal violence, with high rates in the early 1800s that declined until the Great Depression and then rose rapidly throughout the twentieth century. More long-term analyses, however, suggest that homicides and assaults are substantially lower now than they were in thirteenth-century England, when homicide rates were 10 to 20 times greater than the current rate (Hagan, 1994). Thus, while crime and violence are widely regarded as a major social problem and one that keeps getting worse, historical data suggest that things have been bad for a long time, and may actually be getting better.

With respect to recent trends, UCR crime totals skyrocketed during the 1960s and 1970s, suggesting a serious crime wave. Figure 4.1 presents a 40-year summary of the number of crimes recorded by the police from 1973 through 2012. Crime rates peaked in 1980, declined steadily until 1984, and then increased each year through 1991. Then, in spite of dire predictions of continuing increases in crime, especially violent youth crime, the crime rate began to decline, falling by 2012 to a rate (3,245 per 100,000) well below that recorded in 1973 (4,154 per 100,000). Does this mean that the police are doing a better job of deterring crime than they did in the late 1980s and the early 1990s? Does it mean that the "get-tough" policies of the past several presidential administrations have been successful? Are such policies as determinant sentencing, "three-strikes" legislation, and mandatory arrest policies responsible for the declining crime rate?

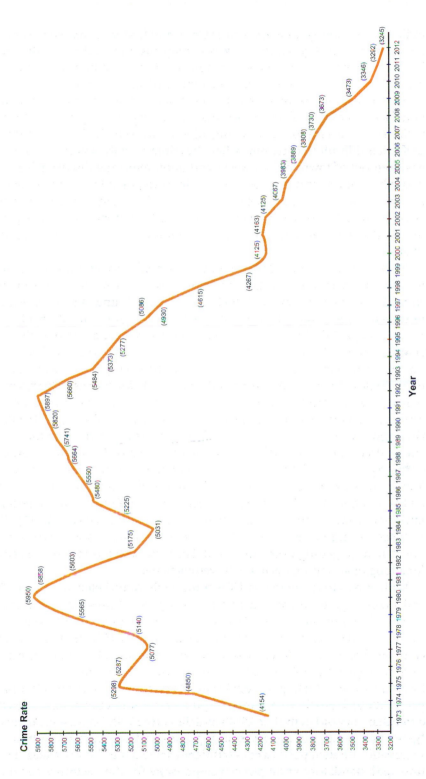

Crime Rate

Year

FIGURE 4.1

Forty-year crime trend: UCR data, 1973–2012.

Source: U.S. Department of Justice. (2013). *Crime in the United States, 2012*. Washington, DC: U.S. Government Printing Office and Table 1 (http://www.fbi.gov/about-us/cjis/ucr/crime-in-tha-u.s/2012/crime-in-the-u.s.-2012/tables/1tabledatadecoverviewpdf/table_1_crime_in_the_united_states_by_volume_and_rate_per_100000_inhabitants_1993-2012.xls).

Some persons have made such claims, although no evidence has been presented to support them. Or is the trend toward community-oriented policing having its desired effect? What about the role of noncriminal justice factors such as the "booming" economy of the 1990s, the low unemployment rate, or the aging of the American population? Al Blumstein and a number of other colleagues have addressed the declining crime rate in several publications (Blumstein & Wallman, 2000; Blumstein, 2001).

In March 1985, the California Attorney General convened a conference to discuss why the crime rate was falling. A number of noted scholars gave presentations, with each providing a favorite explanation, ranging from demographic changes to prison policies to early prevention programs. There was little consensus regarding the reasons for the four-year decline in crime rates from 1981 to 1984. One speaker (Geis, 1986:31) noted, however, that the conference should have addressed a different issue: "Why, despite its downward movement, does the crime rate in the United States remain so stunningly high in comparison to that of other advanced nations?" Given the subsequent increase in crime rates from 1984 to 1991, perhaps this was a correct perspective. This question is perhaps even more relevant today than it was in 1985, for despite a 20-year decline, the American violent crime rate and the incarceration rate remain higher than those of any other industrialized nation.

VOLUME OF CRIME: NATIONAL CRIME VICTIMIZATION SURVEY most acc.

Victimization rates reported by the National Crime Victimization Survey (NCVS; described in Chapter 3) suggest that the crime rate is considerably higher than that reported by the UCR. The NCVS estimated that more than 26 million criminal victimizations occurred in 2012 (6.8 million violent crimes and 19.8 million property crimes), excluding murder, kidnapping, commercial burglary, and robbery, as well as victimless crimes such as drug abuse, prostitution, and drunkenness. These latter crimes are excluded largely because of the cost of data collection and the difficulty of securing satisfactory information.

Violent crimes (rape, personal robbery, and assault) accounted for 25.6 percent of the NCVS victimizations (compared with 12 percent in the UCR). The remaining 74.4 percent of reported victimizations involved property crimes, with thefts from households accounting for 57.5 percent of all reported victimizations, burglaries represented another 14.2 percent, and motor vehicle thefts accounted for 2.4 percent. Table 4.3 provides a summary of the number and the rate of victimizations recorded by the NCVS.

Victimization rates are generally reported per 1,000 persons or 1,000 households. The overall victimization rate for violent crimes for people over the age of 12 in 2012 was 26.1; this figure is approximately seven times the rate reported by the UCR. The NCVS reports property crimes primarily as household victimizations, which makes comparisons between UCR and NCVS data difficult. The NCVS household crime rate of 155.8, however, was more than six times

TABLE 4.3 Victimizations by Crime Type, NCVS, 2012

	Number of victims	Rate[1]
All Crimes	26,465,570	
Violent Crime	6,842,590	26.1
Rape/sexual assault	346,830	1.3
Robbery	741,760	2.8
Assault	5,754,010	22.0
Aggravated assault	996,110	3.8
Simple assault	4,186,390	15.8
Domestic violence	1,259,390	4.8
Intimate partner violence	810,790	3.1
Stranger violence	2,710,110	10.3
Violent crime with injury	1,573,460	6.0
Property Crime	19,622,980	155.8
Burglary	3,764,540	29.9
Motor vehicle theft	633,740	5.0
Theft	15,224,700	120.9

[1] Rate per 1,000 persons aged 12 and older. Property crimes per 1,000 households.

Source: U.S Department of Justice. (2013). *Criminal Victimization in the United States, 2012.* Washington, DC: U.S. Department of Justice.

the UCR crime rate for property victimization. Overall, the NCVS victimization rates are significantly greater than those reported by the UCR.

Geographical Distribution

NCVS data about the geographic distribution of crime complement the UCR data. Table 4.4 presents information about the distribution of crime by region and community size for 2012. Rural areas, with a violent crime rate of 20.9 per 1,000 population aged 12 and over, appear to be the safest areas to live relative to sub-urban (23.8 per 1,000) and urban (32.4 per 1,000) locations. Consistent with the impression provided by the UCR data, the NCVS data indicate that the Northeast has the lowest household property crime rate, although it has a higher violent crime rate than both the South and Midwest. In marked contrast to the UCR, the South does not have the highest rate of violent crime; in fact it is only two-thirds the rate of violence reported in the West. What accounts for such disparate findings? Is it a product of the level of police professionalism in these different areas? Is it an artifact of differential reporting of crime by residents of the western states relative to those in the southern states? Which measure (the UCR or NCVS) provides the most accurate picture? Review Chapter 3 for discussion of these questions.

TABLE 4.4 Location and Type of Victimization, NCVS 2012 Data		
Location	Violent Crime[1]	Household Property Crime[2]
All	26.1	155.8
Northeast	24.7	116.9
Midwest	23.9	153.1
South	22.1	143.4
West	35.5	210.5
Urban	32.4	187.0
Suburban	23.8	138.9
Rural	20.9	142.9

[1] Rate per 100,000 population age 12 and over.

[2] Rate per 1,000 households.

Source: U.S Department of Justice. (2013). *Criminal Victimization in the United States, 2012*. Washington, DC: U.S. Department of Justice.

The NCVS also reports that most crimes of violence (robberies and assaults) occur in a public place such as on the street, in a parking garage, or in a commercial building. Rape, on the other hand, is most likely to take place in the victim's home or some other place known to the victim. Furthermore, almost 63 percent of rape victims know their assailants and are victimized in their own homes or at the home of an acquaintance. Contrary to popular perception, the NCVS data indicate that women face a greater risk of rape once they enter their homes than they do getting there. Victims raped by strangers account for one-third of victims and, unlike the acquaintance rape victims, are more likely to be victimized in a public place such as on a street, in a park or playground, or in a commercial establishment.

Temporal Distribution

Crimes of personal violence, according to NCVS figures, are slightly more likely to be committed during the daytime (53%), although 31 percent occur between 6 p.m. and midnight. Slightly more than one-half (50.5%) of all robberies involving injuries take place during this six-hour period. Household crimes are less likely to be committed at night (33%) than during the daytime (40%), but given the nature of property crime, the time of many crimes cannot be accurately determined (27%).

A different picture from the UCR data is found with respect to victimization trends during the 1970s and 1980s. While some annual fluctuations can be observed between 1973 and 1992, the overall pattern was quite stable (see Figure 4.2). In fact, the 1992 violent crime victimization rate of 3,210 is virtually the same as the rate of 3,260 recorded in 1973. With the redesign of the NCVS in

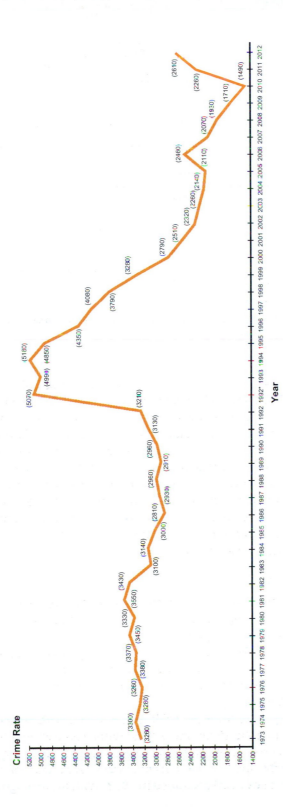

Crime Rate

Year

FIGURE 4.2

Victimization rates for violent crimes per 100,000 persons age 12 and over: 1973–2012.

Source: U.S. Department of Justice. (2013). *Crime in the United States, 2012.* Washington, DC: U.S. Government Printing Office and Bureau of Justice Statistics NCVS Victimization Analysis Tools at www.bjs.gov.

*The NCS underwent a redesign in 1992 that coincided with the renaming of the survey to the NCVS. The redesign led to higher rates of reporting of some offenses, especially rape/sexual assault. The two reports for 1992 reflect the change associated with the redesign.

1992, historical comparisons became problematic. However, since 1993, when the NCVS violent victimization rate peaked, there has been an overall decline in reported victimizations, falling to a rate of 2,610 per 100,000 in 2012. This decline in the number and rate of victimizations mirrors the decline reported in the UCR. A similar pattern is evident for property crime rates.

VOLUME OF CRIME: SELF-REPORT STUDIES

Self-report data (SRD) are not directly comparable to the UCR or NCVS for one important reason: the only national studies conducted to date have been limited to the self-reported behavior of youths and young adults. Self-report studies also employ a different procedure for reporting crime rates than UCR or NCVS. Two measures are currently in use: **prevalence rates** and **frequency rates**. Prevalence refers to the number of persons in a population that report one or more offenses of a given type within a specified period. The prevalence rate is typically expressed as a proportion of persons in the population who have reported some involvement in a particular offense or set of offenses. Frequency or **individual offending rates** (also called lambda) refer to the number of offenses that occur in a given population during a specified time interval. Individual offending rates may be expressed as an average number of offenses per person or as the number of offenses per some population base. While prevalence rates are informative, indicating the number of different persons involved in criminal acts, individual offending rates are more comparable to the UCR and NCVS data.

The best countrywide SRD are from the National Youth Survey (NYS; see Chapter 3), although these data are quite dated at this time. Prevalence rates for youths aged 15 to 21 in 1980 indicate that 65 percent reported committing at least one of the 24 offenses included in a delinquency scale. The prevalence rate for Index offenses was, however, only 12 percent. Individual offending rates for 1980 indicate that an average of 32 offenses were committed per person. The majority of the offenses, however, were status offenses or public disorder crimes. Serious offenses accounted for only 1 percent of all reported offenses in 1980. Furthermore, the individual offending rate for Index offenses was only 0.6 per person. With an adolescent population of approximately 29 million, a prevalence rate of 12 percent suggests that 3.5 million youths commit at least one Index offense per year.

Geographical Location

In terms of where crimes are committed, the situation reported in UCR and NCVS data is not found for the NYS data. Both prevalence and frequency rates reveal lower rates of delinquency for rural youths as compared to urban youths, but these differences are not statistically significant. Suburban rates tend to be more similar to the urban than the rural figures. Elliott et al. (1983:90–91) commented that:

> the difference in prevalence rates on the global delinquency scales appeared to reflect higher prevalence rates for urban and suburban

youth in relatively nonserious forms of delinquency. The only systematic differences on incidence scales also involved a relatively nonserious offense scale—minor theft. There was little evidence that urban, suburban and rural youth differ with regard to reported incidence or prevalence rates on the serious nonviolent or serious violent offense scales.

Temporal Distribution

The NYS is a longitudinal study in which the same individuals were interviewed from 1977 through 2003. While comparisons can be made over time, a major problem is that changes in the rates may reflect changes in the cohort. As they age, persons begin to engage in different types of behavior. That is, to what extent do temporal changes reflect **maturation effects**? For example, the delinquent behaviors of youths aged 11–17, as the cohort was in 1976, may be both qualitatively and quantitatively different from the behaviors of 15–21-year-olds in 1980. Given this limitation of the data, it is preferable not to make assumptions about temporal patterns.

DISTRIBUTION OF CRIME BY GENDER

A major shortcoming of criminology has been the tendency to exclude females from the field of study. Traditionally, theories of crime have been concerned primarily with the behavior of males and research has been largely limited to male samples. The exclusion of women has been due in part to the notably low rates of female involvement in crime as indicated by official arrest records; females accounted for approximately 26 percent of all arrests in 2012 (2,474,637 females were arrested compared with 6,972,023 males; see Table 4.5). Additionally, it was long assumed that females primarily engage in sexual offenses, making their behavior tangential to any serious study of criminality. As a result, the major criminological theories may suffer from a lack of generalizability to females and our understanding of **gender and crime**, or the distribution of crime by gender may be biased. Throughout this text, we will attempt to address this deficiency by calling attention to research and theoretical formulations that include females or focus on females.

Perspectives on Female Crime

Examples of early justifications for excluding females are provided prior to a summary of the gender-crime issue. William Kvaraceus commented that "[t]he majority of delinquent girls, regardless of their reason for referral [to the juvenile court] are in some degree sexually delinquent" (1945:116). Albert Cohen declared that girls were beyond the scope of his theory. He stated:

> The most conspicuous difference between male and female delinquency
> is that male delinquency . . . is versatile and female delinquency is
> relatively specialized. It consists overwhelmingly of sexual delinquency
> (1955:45).

TABLE 4.5 Sex of Offenders by Offense Type, UCR, 2012

UCR Index Offense	Males	Females
Total Arrests	6,972,023	2,474,637
	73.8%	26.2%
Murder and nonnegligent manslaughter	7,549	965
	88.7%	11.3%
Forcible rape	13,840	131
	99.1%	0.9%
Robbery	70,059	10,428
	87.0%	13.0%
Aggravated assault	232,041	69,024
	77.1%	22.9%
Burglary	184,249	36,035
	83.6%	16.4%
Larceny-theft	568,859	431,637
	56.9%	43.1%
Motor vehicle theft	43,176	10,068
	81.1%	18.9%
Arson	7,283	1,599
	82.0%	18.0%

Source: U.S. Department of Justice. (2013). *Crime in the United States*, *2012*. Washington, DC: U.S. Government Printing Office.

Richard Cloward and Lloyd Ohlin (1960) acknowledged that female gang members existed, but they concluded that they were affiliated with and subordinate to groups of male delinquents. Because the female members were not a real threat on their own, Cloward and Ohlin (1960) eliminated women from further consideration in their theoretical work. Females were also readily dismissed in Hirschi's (1969:35) *Causes of Delinquency*, in which he spelled out his version of social control theory and specifically stated: "In the [data] analysis that follows . . . the females disappear." Gang Feature 4.1 questions the assumptions that involvement in criminal activity and membership in gangs are primarily a male phenomenon.

Not all criminologists, however, ignored the criminal activity of women. In *The Criminality of Women* (1961), Otto Pollak argued that crime data underreport female crime. He cited a number of factors for this, including the petty nature of the majority of women's offenses and the likelihood that men who are victims of crimes committed by women do not report them. He also believed that male police officers often face a conflict when dealing with female offenders because

GANG FEATURE 4.1 DEMOGRAPHIC CHARACTERISTICS OF GANG MEMBERS

Demographic Characteristics of Gang Members

While the gang literature is voluminous, little consensus exists with regard to the nature of gangs, especially with regard to gender and racial composition. The common stereotype is that gangs are primarily a male phenomenon and that females serve largely in an auxiliary capacity. Likewise, media presentations portray gang membership as a minority phenomenon, with nonminority youths virtually absent. Results from relatively recent research suggest that these common assumptions may be erroneous. As discussed in Gang Feature 3.2 in Chapter 3, the extent of the gang problem is largely determined by the definition employed. The same applies to the nature and composition of gangs. Different definitions and different methodologies result in different pictures. Much of the gang research has relied on case studies in which researchers observed specific individuals and/or specific gangs identified by knowledgeable informants. These descriptive accounts provide very rich descriptions of these gangs. However, they provide only part of the overall picture. Findings from surveys of larger, more general samples of adolescents have included questions about gang involvement and gang activity. These surveys have produced a different picture than the one provided by the case studies. But, again, they provide only part of the picture. Law enforcement data are similar in nature to the information gleaned from case studies. One of the issues is the nature of the sample. In general surveys, both gang and nongang individuals are surveyed. These surveys generally are restricted to younger samples, including respondents as young as 10 years of age. Case studies are usually restricted to gangs and active members, which by default results in older samples, generally 16 and older. It should not be surprising that these different methodologies produce different estimates about the gender and racial composition of gang members.

The police data and case studies reinforce the notion that most gang members are male and from racial minorities. These estimates indicate that more than 90 percent of gang members are male and that 90 to 95 percent of the gang members are minority. Thus, the picture emerges that the gang problem is indeed one that should focus on minority males. A different picture emerges from the general surveys; one that indicates that such attention on minority males is misplaced. These general surveys have found females to account for 30 to 40 percent of active gang youths, more than twice the highest estimates given by case studies and law enforcement data. With respect to race and ethnicity, most of the surveys have been limited to "high-risk" areas and therefore largely comprised of racial and ethnic minorities. One large-scale survey of almost 6,000 eighth-grade students conducted in 11 American cities examined the racial and gender composition of delinquent youth gangs (Esbensen & Winfree, 1998). The authors found that 25 percent of the gang members were white and that 38 percent of the gang members were females. Interestingly, data from a survey of Dutch youths revealed similar results: the majority of self-identified gang members were native Dutch (i.e., not ethnic minorities as indicated by police data), and 40 percent were females (Esbensen & Weerman, 2005). In subsequent school-based surveys, Esbensen and Carson (2012) and Weerman (2012) reported findings consistent with the earlier estimate: approximately one-third of the gang members are girls and gang members tend to reflect the ethnic/racial composition of their neighborhoods. As with other general surveys, these estimates differ substantially from the "official" figures. The authors caution that different methodologies (e.g., general surveys compared with case studies), sampling frames (e.g., survey of 13- to 15-year-olds versus observation of 18- to 25-year-old biker gangs), and definitional issues (e.g., restricting gang membership to criminally involved gangs instead of all youth groups), are likely the source of these different pictures of gangs. At the same time, they also maintain that it is important to consider all of these sources when assessing the nature and extent of the gang problem and when considering community response to gangs and gang activity.

of a sense of "chivalry" and preconceived notions about women. As a result, the officers are less likely to suspect and arrest female offenders. Furthermore, data indicate that women are more likely to be acquitted than men. All told, then, the crimes of women are underreported, less likely to be detected, and even when detected, treated more leniently.

Discussing the masked criminality of the female, Pollak argued that to a large extent this has to do not only with the types of crimes committed by women (illegal abortions, thefts by prostitutes of their customers' possessions, domestic thefts), but also with the innate secrecy of women. He argued that the deceitfulness of women is not only socially induced, but also related to the female physiology. Pollak believed that women acquire the confidence to deceive men through their sexual play-acting, faked sexual response, and menstruation. With the assurance gained in their power to deceive men, women are able to commit crimes that go undetected.

Although there is no apparent support for the work of Pollak, some criminologists accepted his premises. The notion that women are able to conceal their deviance through their legitimate and traditional roles has found its way into a number of studies of female crime. At the same time, Pollak's work has been bitingly criticized by feminist criminologists who find it superficial, misogynistic, and highly overstated. In one of the more subtle critiques, Meda Chesney-Lind and Randall Sheldon (1998) label as "fascinating and contorted" his attempts to explain why "precocious biological maturity" accounts for female but not male sexual delinquency.

Explanations of Female Crime

Studies of women in general increased in the 1970s; this was true in criminology as well. For the first time, substantial numbers of female criminologists entered the field, and many of them focused on the female offender. No longer was the study of the female offender restricted to physical and psychological factors; cultural and social structural variables began to be scrutinized. Criminologists argued that when women break the law, they often do so in their role as women, that is, they go from shoppers to shoplifters and check writers to check forgers.

Dale Hoffman-Bustamonte (1973) emphasized the idea that women are socialized very differently than men. Boys, besides being allowed much greater freedom than girls while growing up, are encouraged to be more aggressive, ambitious, and outgoing. Girls are expected to be nonviolent, hence they do not possess the technical skills to commit violent acts. (Consult also the works of Boocock 1972 and Schur 1984.) An example is the reaction parents typically have to their children's participation in fights. For a son involved in a fight, the response may be, "I hope he looks worse than you." Such comments are rarely directed to daughters. Young boys may be discouraged from starting fights, but they are taught not to back down if hit by another boy.

Moreover, in our culture, boys are taught how to fight and that it is appropriate to stop when the opponent is down; this training is not given to young girls. When girls fight, they frequently bite, scratch, and pull hair. This behavior is socially defined as unseemly. Although typically they are not as strong as boys, girls can be much more vicious in fights than boys.

Available data show that when women commit violent crimes, their victims are often relatives or lovers. For homicide, the weapon most often used is a kitchen implement, usually a knife. Even when women commit violent crimes, they utilize gender-specific weapons. In her study of female robbers, Jody Miller (1998) reported that women generally targeted female victims and, when weapons were used, they were more likely to use knives. This choice of weapon is in sharp contrast to male robbers' reliance on guns to intimidate their victims.

Role theory, as it presently stands, is a starting point in the development of a feminist criminology. However, as Carol Smart (1976:69) has suggested, "The study of gender roles cannot be, and to be fair, is probably not intended to provide a complete analysis of the [crime] phenomenon." She asserted that role theory must be situated within "a theory which can account for the specifically differentiated roles as well as other features of human activity" (1976:70).

Law enforcement officers handcuff an unidentified woman. Studies of female criminality increased in the 1970s, but were rare before that time.

CREDIT: AP Photo/Stephen Monahan via the Lindsay Letter.

Liberation and Crime

At the same time the women's movement gathered momentum, the crime rate of women appeared to be increasing. As a result, criminologists began examining the link between liberation and crime. In *Sisters in Crime*, Freda Adler (1975:12–13) stated:

> Women are no longer indentured to the kitchens, baby carriages or bedrooms of America. . . . Allowed their freedom for the first time, women . . . by the tens of thousands—have chosen to desert those kitchens and plunge exuberantly into the formerly all male quarters of the working world. . . . In the same way that women are demanding equal opportunity in the fields of legitimate endeavor, a similar number of determined women are forcing their way into the world of major crimes.

Adler connected the rise in female crime with the rise in women's assertiveness brought about by the women's movement. She contended that there were now fewer restraints on women and greater pressure on them from their enhanced positions. Because of this, women were becoming susceptible to the same criminogenic forces that men faced. Therefore, it was likely that with the convergence of role expectations, female crime would begin to resemble male crime. Adler's prediction of an increase in the rate of female involvement in conventional "street crimes" has been realized in official data. Between 1973 and 2012, female arrests for Index offenses increased 114.6 percent while the male rate increased by 9.6 percent (see Table 4.6).

While Adler utilized data from case studies to support her position, Rita James Simon (1975) in *The Contemporary Woman and Crime* examined the statistical picture of female crime over a number of decades. To examine the possible

TABLE 4.6 **Sex of Persons Arrested for Index Offenses in 1973 and 2012 and Percentage Change**

	1973		2012		% Change 1973–2012	
	Males	Females	Males	Females	Males	Females
All arrests	5,502,284	997,580	6,028,378	2,140,934		
Percent	84.7%	15.3%	73.8%	26.2%	9.6%	114.6%
Index Crime total[1]	1,112,485	256,739	972,218	477,107		
Percent	81.3%	18.7%	67%	33%	−12.6%	85.8%
Violent crime	260,800	29,582	278,167	60,074		
Percent	89.8%	10.2%	80.1%	19.9%	6.6%	133.5%
Property crime[1]	851,685	227,157	694,051	417,033		
Percent	78.9%	21.1%	62.5%	37.5%	−18.5%	83.6%

[1] After 1978, arson is included as an Index and property crime.

Source: U.S. Department of Justice. (1974). *Crime in the United States, 1973*. Washington, DC: U.S. Government Printing Office; http://www.fbi.gov/about-us/cjis/ucr/crime-in-the-u.s/2012/crime-in-the-u.s.-2012/tables/33tabledatadecoverviewpdf.

effect of the women's movement on the criminality of women, Simon utilized data on the status of women in the labor force, marriage and fertility rates, income, and education, as well as crime statistics. She concluded that some types of crimes (predominantly white-collar offenses) will increase, while other types (violent crimes, in particular) will decrease. These changes, she believed, will occur because of the change in the position of women in society. Furthermore, Simon concluded that as women are accepted into various legitimate fields that have been dominated by men, the criminal justice system will come to deal with women more like men. As a result, women will no longer benefit from "chivalrous" treatment by the police and the courts.

Although the works of Adler and Simon broke new ground, their data and methods of analysis have received considerable criticism. Adler also has been taken to task for assuming that becoming criminal results from being liberated, as the majority of women involved in crime seem to have been influenced very little by the women's movement. Those most touched by the movement tend to be educated and from middle- or upper-class families, while women found in crime statistics tend to be less educated and from the lower class.

Research reported by Helen Boritch (1992) also suggests that Simon and others may have been mistaken in their assumptions that historically, women have been treated more leniently than men by the criminal justice system. Her analysis of court processing from 1871 to 1920 in Middlesex County, Ontario, revealed that women were more likely to receive prison sentences and to incur longer sentences than men.

There continues to be a lack of agreement regarding the rate of female offending and reasons associated with differences in rates of male and female offending. More recent research by Janet Lauritsen, Karen Heimer, and James Lynch (2009), however, reveals that the gender gap in offending is narrowing. Utilizing both UCR and NCVS data, they examined trends in violent offending and victimization from 1973 to 2005. In a response to a critique by Schwartz et al. (2009), Heimer and her colleagues (2009:436) concluded that:

> Males remain more violent than females. Nonlethal violent offending has been decreasing for both genders over time. However, the decreases have not been of the same magnitude across gender, and we observed that the gender gap has narrowed over time. We do not find this surprising, given the social and economic changes that have occurred in terms of gender (in)equality since the early 1970s.

They suggest that the time has come to "move beyond the debate over whether these changes in offending have occurred and focus research efforts on explaining the reasons for differential changes in female and male rates of violent offending" (Lauritsen et al., 2009:392).

Post-liberation Explanations

During the past 30 years, a number of researchers and theorists have in fact examined post-liberation explanations of female offending. John Hagan, John H. Simpson, and A. Ronald Gillis (1979, 1985, and 1987) proposed a **power-control model** of delinquency to explain why girls commit fewer delinquencies. They suggest that daughters are more closely controlled by the patriarchal family than are sons. This control is perpetuated in female peer groups where dependence, passivity, and compliance are reinforced. Furthermore, because women's access to the reward structure of the social system is markedly more restricted than males, Hagan and his associates also link the sexual stratification of crime to the sexual stratification of work.

These ideas have been refined and expanded in a series of articles in which authority in the family and youth power are examined in conjunction with the family's position in the social order. In the estimation of Hagan, Simpson, and Gillis (1985, 1987), it is the presence of power and the absence of control that creates conditions in which delinquency can occur (see also Blackwell, 2000). Given the greater control of women and their lack of power, their lower rate of offending should not come as a surprise.

Research exploring factors associated with adolescent crime, however, has failed to identify different causal or explanatory models for female and male delinquency. Maude Dornfeld and Candace Kruttschnitt studied the effects of family risk factors, such as parental divorce, maternal alcohol abuse, and harsh discipline, and concluded that "while we would not deny that there are gender-specific risk factors . . . we would deny that responses to those risk factors can be predicted solely on the basis of sex" (1992:414). Similarly, results of a multinational longitudinal analysis reported by Avshalom Caspi and his colleagues (1994) indicate that the same three personality scales were correlated with both male and female delinquency.

A growing body of research continues to identify more similarities in the causal explanations of female and male offending than differences. Giordano and Rockwell (2000), for instance, tested the efficacy of differential association theory in explaining serious offending. They found that the social learning concepts of differential association theory were equally applicable to female offenders in their study as they were to male offenders. In a similar vein, Miller (1998) found that, while the actual methods of committing robberies differed between males and females, the motivations underlying the robberies were similar. In their examination of delinquents, Liu and Kaplan (1999) not only found similar patterns of involvement in delinquency, but also identified similar mediating variables exerting the same effect on female and male offending. Esbensen and Deschenes (1998) examined the role of gender in explaining gang membership. They found some modest differences in explanatory models for males and females; the social learning models were quite similar for the boys and girls, but the social control models indicated different explanatory factors explained male and female gang affiliation. In yet another investigation into gender differences, Heimer and DeCoster (1999) explored the effects of familial controls on male and female offending. They found that "girls are less violent than boys mainly because they are influenced more strongly by bonds to family, learn fewer violent definitions, and are taught that violence is inconsistent with the meaning of being female" (1999:303).

UCR Data on Gender and Crime

Many of the reported UCR crimes are never solved, and no information about the offender becomes known. It therefore is necessary to rely upon arrest data for demographic information. This may result in a biased sample in that older, smarter, and occasional offenders probably are less likely to be arrested. Other factors such as sex, race, and social class also may affect police officers' decisions to arrest or not to arrest an individual. Caution must be used, therefore, when employing arrest data to determine the pattern of crime.

Table 4.6 shows that, of the 1,449,325 arrests for Index crimes in 2012, 33 percent were of females. This figure is slightly more than the percentage of females accounting for all arrests (26.2%), suggesting that females, when they commit crimes, are more likely to be arrested for serious crimes than are their male counterparts. In contrast to data from 1973, there appears to have been a major change in the offending levels of women. In 1973, women accounted for only 15 percent of all arrests. Does this change in the percentage of arrests accounted for by women reflect a change in female offending? While some may conclude that to be the case, another possibility, consistent with the liberation perspective described above, is that there has been a change in police response to female offenders, with officers increasingly arresting females for offenses that previously would not have resulted in arrest.

Analysis of crime trends from 1973 to 2012 by gender shows that female arrest rates increased significantly while arrest rates for males declined. Arrests of males for Index offenses were 12.6 percent lower in 2012 compared with 1973, while female arrests increased 85.8 percent. The increase in violent offending is the most pronounced with arrests of females increasing by 133.5 percent compared with a 6.6 percent increase for males. The question remains, however, does this increase in female arrests reflect an actual increase in female activity or a change in criminal justice processing? In an attempt to examine this issue, David Huizinga and Finn Esbensen (1991) compared data from the 1978 NYS with data from the 1989 Denver Youth Survey. Limiting the NYS sample to urban youths, they examined male and female delinquency rates. Contrary to UCR arrest data, they found the 1989 respondents reported slightly lower rates of offending, although the differences were not statistically significant.

NCVS Data on Gender and Crime

Information regarding the sex of property offenders is unavailable in the NCVS because these offenders are not usually seen by their victims. It is therefore only possible to compare victimization data for crimes of violence in which there is personal contact. The NCVS data reveal a greater level of female participation in violent crimes than does the UCR. The NCVS data indicate that the perceived sex of offenders in single-offender victimizations (that is, the gender of the offender as reported by the victim) is 90 percent male and 10 percent female. This distribution is fairly consistent across offense types; the only exceptions are that rapists tend to be predominately male (99%).

SRD on Gender and Crime

Although official records indicate that variations in the rates of offending for males and females are significant, self-report data provide a very different picture. In a study of 820 males and females in Oakland, California, Michael J. Hindelang (1971) found that female delinquency was not as specialized as others had claimed. He concluded (1971:533):

> The patterns of female delinquent involvement, although at a reduced frequency, parallel quite closely the pattern of male delinquency. . . . Most and least frequent activities among the males and females are nearly identical. The finding is at odds with the conception of female delinquents as engaging primarily in "sex" delinquencies.

Furthermore, from his reanalysis of ten self-report studies, Joseph Weis (1980) concluded that "sex differences are small and the percentages of both sexes involved in a wide variety of offenses are large." Other SRD indicate the same patterns. Steven Cernkovich and Peggy Giordano's (1979) analysis of a sample from a Midwestern community showed similar patterns of delinquent behavior among the sexes, as did Rachelle Canter's (1982) analysis of five panels of the NYS data. Gender differences are most pronounced for the serious and violent offense categories. For prevalence rates, the male-to-female sex ratios are approximately 3:1 for Index offenses. The ratio for frequency rates is closer to 5:1. Translated into percentages, this suggests that females commit approximately 20 percent of the serious crimes reported by persons aged 15 to 21 years. This figure is quite consistent with NCVS data but twice the rate reported by UCR arrest data. According to SRD data, female offending appears to be very similar to male criminality, except that the former occurs at a less frequent rate.

DISTRIBUTION OF CRIME BY AGE

Next to gender, age is the personal characteristic that appears to be the best predictor of involvement in criminal activity. This age-crime relationship is so prevalent that street crime is often perceived as synonymous with youth. Some social scientists have argued that much of what is called criminal or delinquent activity is no more than behavior that is a "normal" part of growing up (e.g., Jolin & Gibbons, 1987). Consistent findings across cultures confirm the **age-crime curve**; that is, crime rates follow a fairly consistent pattern across cultures, with initiation occurring in late childhood or the early teen years, escalating through the mid-teens, and then tapering off in the late teens and early twenties. The shape of this curve is remarkably similar across societies, but the age of initiation and the peak years of criminal activity vary to some degree.

Arrest data in Table 4.7 highlights the extent to which crime increases with age and then declines in the mid-to late twenties. The percent of arrests accounted for by different age groups tends to increase for both violent and property crime through the late twenties and then declines. Youths under the age of 22 account for a disproportionate amount of all arrests, including 37.6 percent of property crimes, 28.5 percent of violent crimes, and 31 percent of homicides and nonnegligent manslaughters. It is important to note that these arrest data may partially reflect differential enforcement practices or inexperience on the part of youthful offenders.

Victimization data on the perceived age of offenders in single-offender violent victimizations are consistent with the UCR data: 31 percent of such offenders were judged to be less than 21 years of age, compared to 30 percent in the UCR data. The NYS data also support the general finding that delinquent behavior increases through early adolescence, reaches a plateau through the late teen years, and then gradually declines through the twenties.

Criminal Careers Debate

During the past 25 years, criminological attention has been paid to the concepts of "criminal careers" and "career criminals." The term **criminal career** assumes that criminal activity is similar to other occupations, with a beginning, a period of activity, and an ending or **termination** of the career. **Career criminal** is a term synonymous with the more familiar concept of "habitual offender." The

TABLE 4.7 Age of Persons Arrested, UCR 2012

	Total all ages	Under 16	16–18	19–21	22–24	25–29	30–34	Over 34
All arrests	9,446,660	474,471	930,351	1,244,206	1,083,786	1,444,699	1,137,938	3,131,209
Total percent distribution[1]	100.0	5.0	9.9	13.1	11.5	15.3	12.0	45.2
Murder and non-negligent manslaughter	8,514	141	837	1,642	1,281	1,455	983	2,175
Murder and non-negligent manslaughter percent distribution[1]	100.0	1.7	9.8	19.3	15.0	17.1	11.5	25.5
Violent crime[2]	404,037	22,302	41,056	51,788	47,099	63,112	49,961	128,719
Violent crime percent distribution[1]	100.0	5.5	10.2	12.8	11.7	15.6	12.4	32
Property crime[2]	1,282,906	110,468	193,359	179,526	133,994	174,791	135,686	355,082.0
Property crime percent distribution[1]	100.0	8.5	15.1	14.0	10.4	13.6	10.6	27.8

[1] Because of rounding, the percentages may not add up to 100.0.

[2] Violent crimes are offenses of murder and nonnegligent manslaughter, forcible rape, robbery, and aggravated assault. Property crimes are offenses of burglary, larceny-theft, motor vehicle theft, and arson.

Source: U.S. Department of Justice (2013). *Crime in the United States, 2012*. Washington, DC: U.S. Government Printing Office.

criminal career literature is largely an outgrowth of prediction models and the attempt to identify the costs of crime relative to the costs of incarceration.

The notion of **selective incapacitation** as a crime-fighting tool gained popularity during the Reagan administration (1980–8). This policy advocates incarcerating career criminals and other high-rate offenders in order to reduce societal costs (e.g., economic and personal injury costs). For each high-rate offender incarcerated, the number of crimes that would have been committed if that individual were not confined can be estimated. Associated with the policy of locking people up in order to prevent future crimes is the need to be able to predict high-rate offenders and to determine the length of their careers (e.g., will it be necessary to confine these people for life or will they terminate their criminal activity at some earlier point?). This policy of incapacitation has contributed to an explosion in the number of people behind bars in the United States; so much so that some states are suffering fiscal problems associated with funding of their correctional systems. Criminologists refer to this policy as **mass incarceration**. In Highlight 4.1, Professor Michael Campbell details some of the societal problems associated with the policy of mass incarceration.

Michael Gottfredson and Travis Hirschi (1986, 1988, and 1990) have been outspoken opponents of the value of the criminal career paradigm, as well as of longitudinal research to conduct evaluative studies of criminal careers.

HIGHLIGHT 4.1 MASS INCARCERATION

Beginning in the late 1970s, states across the United States started sending more people to prison and kept them behind bars longer for many types of criminal offenses. Increases in violent crime were often cited as the justification for sending more people to prison, and over time state prison populations became overcrowded and states began building more facilities. At the same time, politicians at the state and national level increasingly focused on crime and disorder and called for harsher punishment and more aggressive policies. The heightened political focus on crime led to the passage of much stricter drug laws, harsh sentences for repeat and violent offenders, and a decline in the use of parole as a way to manage prison populations. Between 1975 and 2000, the nation's incarceration rate increased by more than 400%, and today the United States has by far the world's highest incarceration rate and imprisons people at levels four times higher than other comparable democracies.

Scholars refer to this new era of increasing imprisonment as "mass incarceration." The masses that have been most directly affected by the nation's increasing use of prisons are disproportionately poor, have low levels of educational attainment, and are people of color. By 2000, nearly one in nine African-American men were under some form of criminal justice surveillance, and prisons had replaced military service and education as key socializing institutions. The nation's "War on Drugs," which began in the early 1980s under President Ronald Reagan, greatly expanded the size and power of law enforcement across the nation. Police used aggressive tactics that primarily targeted the open drug markets of inner-city neighborhoods and arrested, charged, and convicted a dramatically larger number of drug offenders. In the late 1980s, more than half of those behind bars were serving time for drug and nonviolent crimes. Then, in 1994 President Bill Clinton signed a new criminal justice law that pumped billions of dollars into prison expansion and required states to pass laws that ensured long prison sentences.

But it was not only the scale of the use of imprisonment that changed. The consequences of a prison conviction also became more severe. Employers enforced strict limits on who qualified for jobs and often omitted people convicted of (or sometimes just charged with) crimes. The federal government refused public assistance to people convicted of drug crimes, including public housing, student loans, and welfare payments. This meant that those people from the nation's poorest communities who had been convicted of a crime were less likely to find employment or housing upon their release, and that they would likely struggle to procure basic necessities as states lowered eligibility. Recent scholarship has shown how these policies have had stark consequences for urban neighborhoods where large proportions of young men are imprisoned. Incarceration undermines the family networks that often lead to lower rates of criminal offending over time, and men who are in prison cannot provide support for their children and other family members. Mass incarceration has not stopped violence or eliminated drug markets in these communities, but it directly affects the lives and family networks of millions of the nation's poorest citizens, especially those from historically disadvantaged groups. For further discussion of the effects of mass-incarceration policies, consult Beckett and Sasson (2000), Braman (2004), Western (2006) or Campbell and Schoenfeld (2013).

They maintain that the effect of age on crime is invariant. Historical and cross-cultural research, they maintain, shows that the age-crime curve has remained relatively unchanged for 150 years. If, in fact, crime peaks at age 16 or 17 and declines steadily throughout the remainder of the life-cycle, then Gottfredson and Hirschi suggest "maturational reform" best accounts for the decline. **Desistance** in criminal activity is "change in behavior that cannot be explained and change that occurs regardless of what else happens" (Gottfredson & Hirschi, 1990:136). This is consistent with their belief that criminal behavior is a result of low self-control, which is a relatively stable propensity that varies across individuals and explains differences in rates of criminal activity. Self-control is (or is not) inculcated early in the socialization process and is largely a result of child-rearing practices. To understand the causes of criminal activity, it is necessary to examine early childhood experiences and measure individual self-control. Other factors are of secondary importance.

In contrast to Gottfredson and Hirschi (1990), Blumstein et al. (1988a, 1988b) are vocal proponents of the criminal career paradigm. They state that criminal careers can be measured in terms of the "longitudinal sequence of offenses committed by an offender who has a detectable rate of offending during some period" (Blumstein et al., 1988a:2). They invoke such terms as **initiation** or onset, continuity, duration, individual offending rates (or **lambda**), **escalation**, desistance, and termination. Longitudinal research is clearly a necessity to study criminal careers. Questions arise concerning the causes of crime, but also of interest are factors associated with increased frequency of crime commission, escalation of the seriousness of offending, and, importantly, desistance of law-violating behavior. Can escalation and termination be explained simply as results of low self-control in the case of the former and maturation in the case of termination? This surely oversimplifies. Blumstein and colleagues cite prior research to support their position that different factors explain the onset and termination of criminal activity and that age is part of this overall criminal career perspective. In Chapter 10 we examine this debate in greater detail.

DISTRIBUTION OF CRIME BY RACE

Race is a third personal characteristic considered to be highly correlated with crime rates. The common notion is that African Americans and some other minorities are overrepresented in crime statistics, and this indeed does appear to be the case when we examine UCR data. The NCVS data also show a disproportionate number of perceived offenders to be African American. Most of the self-report studies, however, (including the NYS) do not find the same magnitude of differences in crime rate by race.

Table 4.8 shows that, on the basis of arrest statistics, African Americans commit violent crimes at a rate considerably disproportionate to the size of their population. While African Americans comprise less than 15 percent of the American population, they account for 38.5 percent of arrests for violent crimes. Does this discrepancy suggest that there is discrimination within the criminal justice system? A study by Robert Sigler and Melody Horn (1986) found that when the researchers controlled for economic status, race did not appear to have an effect on the likelihood of arrest,

A protester holds a sign in Miami, Florida, in December 2014. Nationwide protests against decisions not to prosecute white police officers involved in the killing of black men highlight the sticky question of the relationship between race and crime. It is clear that disproportionate minority processing by the criminal justice system is in effect, but the question is why.

CREDIT: AP Photo/Lynne Sladky.

TABLE 4.8 Distribution of Crime by Race, UCR, 2012

	Total	White	Black	Other
Total Arrests	9,390,473	6,502,919	2,640,067	247,487
Percent[1]	100.0	69.3	28.1	2.6
Index Crime[2]	1,677,785	1,103,196	529,051	45,538
Percent[1]	100.0	65.8	31.5	2.7
Violent crime[2]	402,470	236,394	155,088	10,988
Percent[1]	100.0	58.7	38.5	2.7
Property crime[2]	1,275,315	866,802	373,963	34,550
Percent[1]	100.0	68.0	29.3	2.7

[1] Because of rounding, the percentages may not add up to 100.0.

[2] Violent crimes are offenses of murder and nonnegligent manslaughter, forcible rape, robbery, and aggravated assault. Property crimes are offenses of burglary, larceny-theft, motor vehicle theft, and arson.

Source: U.S. Department of Justice. (2013). *Crime in the United States, 2012*. Washington, DC: U.S. Government Printing Office.

although once arrested, African Americans were more likely to be incarcerated. A number of studies examining sentencing decisions have confirmed the finding that African Americans are more likely to receive prison sentences, and often harsher ones, than are whites (Chiricos & Crawford, 1995; Everett & Nienstadt, 1999; Spohn & Holleran, 2000; Steffensmeier et al., 1998). This is quite clearly seen in the disparate sentencing guidelines associated with powder cocaine and crack cocaine. However, in a study examining sentencing decisions in Pennsylvania, Darrell Steffensmeier and Stephen Demuth (2001) found that Hispanic defendants received the harshest sentences for both drug and nondrug offenses; whites received the least severe treatment, with African-American defendants in the middle.

The NYS data tend to refute the UCR data. With regard to serious and violent offenses, there did not appear to be any racial difference in the rates of crime commission by the fifth year of the study and when social class was controlled, the race relationship disappeared (Huizinga & Elliott, 1987). These findings suggest that some degree of disproportionate minority contact with and processing by the criminal justice system is in effect.

DISTRIBUTION OF CRIME BY SOCIAL CLASS

An enduring debate in criminology centers on the relationship between **social class and crime**. This apparently simple issue remains unresolved despite numerous attempts at resolution. Support can be found for both positive and negative relationships between social class and crime. Charles Tittle, Wayne Villemez, and Douglas Smith (1978), using their meta-analysis of 35 studies, concluded that the link between social class and criminality was a myth. Their article stimulated a proliferation of new research and critical reactions. John Braithwaite (1981), for example, in an ambitious secondary analysis, found that 81 percent of 224 studies reported an inverse relationship between social class and crime (i.e., the lower the social class, the more criminal activity). Introduction of the underclass concept by William Julius Wilson (1987) spawned further research into this area and the re-emergence of gangs has been linked to the development of an urban **underclass**—a portion of the population outside the mainstream of the American occupational system (e.g., Hagedorn, 1988; Vigil, 1988). Charles Tittle and Robert Meier (1990) conducted a critical review of research published during the 1980s and concluded that support of the socioeconomic status (SES)–delinquency relationship was generally weak and inconsistent.

Much of this debate has been spurred by self-report research. Empirical evidence and theoretical works prior to 1960 accepted the relationship between lower class and criminality as an a priori assumption; researchers sought to account for the higher rates of criminal conduct among the lower class. Walter Miller (1958), for example, suggested that the lower class had unique "focal concerns" that placed a cultural value on behaviors resulting in conflict with middle-class beliefs (see Chapter 8). Richard Cloward and Lloyd Ohlin (1960) proposed a set of postulates referred to as "differential opportunity theory" (see Chapter 7). Others suggested that persons in the lower class commit more criminal acts due to their "blocked" opportunities to legitimate means for achieving success. Little empirical evidence existed to dispute the researchers' assumption that the lower class was more criminal. Elijah Anderson (1994, 1999) has proposed a variant of Miller's focal concerns (see Chapter 8). He suggests that inner city, lower-class African Americans subscribe to a "code of the streets," which puts them into direct conflict with middle-class values. This street code emphasizes a reliance on the threat and use of violence to gain and maintain respect. Several studies have found that those individuals who subscribe to a code of the street have considerably higher rates of violence (Stewart & Simons, 2006, 2010; Stewart et al., 2006). Research by Terrance Taylor and his colleagues (2010) found that the street code was not limited to African-American youths but also explained higher rates of offending among Hispanic and white youths.

With the introduction of self-report techniques in the late 1950s and 1960s, new evidence was presented that coincided with the emergence of a new theoretical perspective: labeling theory (see Chapter 9). A number of these studies found no relationship between social class and self-reported juvenile crime. This conclusion supported the argument that it was not that the lower class committed more crime, but rather that this social class–criminality relationship was an artifact of discretionary practices within the criminal justice system. The police, for instance, were more likely to stop and arrest members of the lower class. Similarly, once arrested, lower-class individuals faced a greater likelihood of being convicted and sentenced to prison than did their middle-class counterparts (Evans, 1978; Aaronson et al., 1984).

Not only did these self-report findings fuel a major theoretical debate, but they also raised methodological concerns regarding the measurement of both social class and of criminal activity. Was criminal activity to be defined as the commission of illegal acts or as the official detection and labeling of such acts? Furthermore, should the scope of criminality be confined to the "street crimes" identified in the UCR Index offenses or should there be a broader conception of crime? Answers to these questions will shape, to a large extent, the results of the social class–criminality debate.

There is also the issue of discretionary (or discriminatory) practices within the criminal justice system. To what extent, the labeling theorists would ask, is it possible to discern the difference between behavior and differential response to behavior? Darrell Steffensmeier and Robert Terry (1973) conducted a study of shoplifters and found that the same behavior resulted in different outcomes depending upon the sex and apparent social class of the "criminal." Other studies have reported similar findings, leading to the view that a "Pygmalion effect" or self-fulfilling prophecy may explain the seeming relationship between social class and crime.

The latter question reflects the political nature of crime. When a criminologist or a politician defines crime, that person makes an ideological statement with a number of important implications. If, for example, we define embezzlement, tax evasion, insider trading, and Ponzi schemes as Index offenses, who will the criminals be? Obviously, these are crimes more likely to be committed by members of the middle and upper classes (e.g., Bernie Madoff) and not by the lower class (see, for example, the research reported by Willott et al., 2001). Conversely, if we define serious crime as burglary, robbery, and larceny-theft, then who will the criminals be? The definition of crime has major repercussions for our view of who the criminals are and for how we, as a society, proceed to "fight" crime.

It is no easy task to define social class. If we agree that social class is a composite measure of education, income, and occupation, how do we measure these variables? How do we measure educational attainment: number of years in school, highest grade completed, informal training, or some combination of the preceding? Depending upon the decision, the results may be quite different.

What about income? Does this refer to individual, family, or household income? The researcher also must decide whether to measure gross or net income on a monthly, annual, or possibly even on an average annual basis. A further problem is how to ask questions regarding income. Americans typically find inquiries regarding their income more personal and sensitive than those dealing with either illegal or sexual activity.

On the face of it, it seems obvious that a college dean has higher occupational prestige than a data processor at the computer center. But if you were a researcher interested in determining family social class, how would you decide the social class of a college dean whose husband was a data processor? This is but one issue involved in "operationalizing" concepts such as social class. Another concern is whether to use an individual-, family-, or neighborhood-level measurement of social status.

Given this definitional uncertainty, it is not surprising that neither the UCR nor the NCVS record data regarding the offender's social class. From where, then, does the bulk of this information come? Much of it derives from qualitative and impressionistic opinions formulated into theoretical statements that posit an inverse relationship between social class and criminal behavior. Robert Merton's (1938) pioneering publication is a classic example. On the basis, in part, of empirical observation of who was being arrested and incarcerated, Merton argued that a disjunction between socially accepted means and culturally specified goals was the cause of criminal behavior. He stated that this goals-and-means disjunction was most pronounced among the lower classes. This statement, as will be considered further in Chapter 7, was based upon the belief that all Americans aspire to the same things, but that access to successful achievement of these goals is contingent upon location in the class structure. With everyone seeking wealth, power, and prestige, the members of the lower classes experience the greatest frustration in realizing their dreams. Frustrated lower-class individuals use illegitimate avenues through which to achieve material success.

This theoretical orientation was perpetuated by Miller (1958), Cohen (1955), and Cloward and Ohlin (1960). Empirical studies were relegated the task of *post hoc* confirmation of these theorists' assumptions. Utilizing samples of prisoners, the studies generally confirmed the theoretical statements. Regardless of how the researchers operationalized social class, the findings were remarkably consistent: the lower classes were disproportionately represented among the inmate population. But, as suggested above, to what extent do these official statistics reflect differential rates of offending or discretionary practices within the criminal justice system? Self-report studies have failed to resolve this argument. While a number of researchers have suggested that the social class–crime relationship is a myth (Tittle et al., 1978; Krohn et al., 1980), others have argued that methodological weaknesses are the source of the confusion (Clelland & Carter, 1980; Elliott & Ageton, 1980; Braithwaite, 1981; Brown, 1985; Tittle & Meier, 1990). Obviously the relationship between social class and crime requires better, more extensive research. In one study, Wright and colleagues (1999:176) found that SES has both a positive and a negative effect on delinquency: "low SES promoted delinquency by increasing individuals' alienation, financial strain, and aggression and by decreasing educational and occupational aspirations, whereas high SES promoted individuals' delinquency by increasing risk taking and social power and by decreasing conventional values." This research suggests the importance of examining the mediating variables between social class and behavior.

VICTIMS OF CRIME

Criminal victimization in the United States, as measured through the earlier version of the NCVS, declined from 1981 through 1992. Under the revised format of the NCVS, victimizations peaked in 1993 at 43,547,000 and are significantly lower in 2012 with 26,465,570 victimizations reported in that year. The UCR, SRD, and, limitedly, the NCVS provide information about offenders. This information serves as the basis for not only theory development, but also criminal justice policy formation. Knowledge about crime victims is also important for understanding crime and developing measures to effectively deal with crime. Who are these victims? Who is most likely to be victimized? These are questions the NCVS is ideally suited to answer.

Much of the information collected for the NCVS is tabulated by household characteristics. The term household refers to a dwelling unit and its occupants. Household victimization is determined by the occurrence of a burglary, auto theft, or household theft, or is counted if a household member was a crime victim, no matter where the crime occurred. According to the NCVS household survey data, approximately one out of every ten (9%) American households experienced some form of property crime victimization in 2012. Table 4.9 summarizes the characteristics of households

TABLE 4.9 Rates of Property Crimes per 1,000 Households, by Race, Hispanic Origin, Income, and other Household Characteristics, 1995 and 2012		
Characteristics of Household or Head of Household	Rates of Property Crime per 1,000 Households	
	1995	2012
Race		
White	272.9	150.1
Black	322.3	174.7
Other	292.6	151.6
Hispanic Origin		
Hispanic	364.1	199.2
Non-Hispanic	272.7	149.9
Household Income		
Less than $7,500	290.7	253.5
$7,500–14,999	256.1	233.3
$15,000–24,999	286.9	192.4
$25,000–34,999	283.0	169.7
$35,000–49,999	293.6	152.8
$50,000–74,999	317.1	149.4
$75,000 or more	336.1	148.1

Source: U.S Department of Justice. (1997). *Changes in Criminal Victimization, 1994–1995.* Washington, DC: Bureau of Justice Statistics. Generated using the NCVS Victimization Analysis Tool at www.bjs.gov. November 12, 2014.

victimized in 2012. In general, households with the highest victimization rates were found in the western states, had annual household incomes of less than $15,000, the head of household was black, and were located in an urban area. These patterns of victimization have remained quite similar to those reported in 1995.

Household Income

The overall likelihood of property victimization is greatest for households with annual family incomes of less than $7,500. That is, the number of property crimes per 1,000 households decreased steadily with increased household income in 2012. For households making less than $7,500 per year, the property victimization rate was 253.5 per 1,000 households, compared to a rate of 169.7 for households with $25,000 to $34,999 and a rate of 148.1 for households earning more than $75,000 per year.

Personal victimizations provide a more consistent picture of crime victims. Those most likely to be victims of violent crimes are the poor; the rate of reported violent crime victimization for all types of personal victimizations decreased with income. As reported in Table 4.10, the rate of personal victimizations for

TABLE 4.10 Rate of Violent Victimization by Demographic Characteristic of Victims, 2012

Demographic characteristic	Violent Crime Rate[1]
Total	26.1
Sex	
Male	29.1
Female	23.3
Race/Hispanic origin	
White	25.2
Black/African American	34.2
Hispanic/Latino	24.5
American Indian/Native Alaskan	46.9
Asian/Native Hawaiian/	
Other Pacific Islanders	16.4
Two or more races	42.8
Income	
Less than $7,500	75.4
$7,500–14,999	40.6
$15,000–24,999	37.1

TABLE 4.10 *continued*

$25,000–34,999	26.7
$35,000–49,999	25.3
$50,000–74,999	22.0
$75,000 or more	21.1
Age	
12–17	48.4
18–24	41.0
25–34	34.2
35–49	29.1
50–64	15.0
65 or older	5.7
Marital status	
Never married	40.7
Married	13.5
Widowed	8.3
Divorced	37.8
Separated	83.1

[1] Rate per 1,000 persons aged 12 and older.

Source: U.S Department of Justice. (2013). *Criminal Victimization in the United States, 2012.* Washington, DC: U.S. Department of Justice.

persons in households with incomes of less than $7,500 (75.4 per 1,000 persons age 12 and over) is more than three times the rate of those people living in households with $75,000 or more (21.1).

Geographical Location

Urban households had higher property victimization rates per 1,000 households (187.0) than both suburban (138.9) and rural (142.9) households (see Table 4.4). This pattern was also found for personal victimizations, with urban areas again having the highest rates for all crime types. With respect to region of the country, the western states are definitely the ones to be avoided from a crime victimization perspective. For both household crimes and personal crimes, the West has rates significantly higher than any other region. The Northeast appears to be the safest region, consistently reporting the lowest rates of victimization.

Race and Ethnicity

With regard to **race and crime**, in 2012, Hispanic households (199.2 per 1,000 households) had substantially higher victimization rates than did

African-American (174.4) and white (150.1) households. Hispanic households had higher rates of both theft and motor vehicle theft but African-American households reported the highest rates of burglary. Personal victimizations (see Table 4.10) displayed a slightly different pattern; in 2012 Hispanics reported a lower rate (24.2 per 1,000 persons aged 12 and older) than African Americans (34.2) and similar to whites (25.2). American Indians/Native Alaskans and individuals indicating that the head of household was of two or more races had the highest personal victimization rates (46.9 and 42.8 respectively).

Gender

Males are significantly more likely to commit crime than are females. Likewise, males tend to be victimized more often than females. The difference between male and female victimization rates, however, has decreased steadily. In 1995, males (54.4 per 1,000 persons) reported almost 50 percent more personal victimizations than did females (38.5 per 1,000 persons). By 2012, the male rate was only slightly greater than the female rate of victimization (29.1 versus 23.3). Most of this difference between males and females is attributed to the higher rates of victimization for robbery and aggravated assault among males.

Age

Contrary to popular opinion, the elderly are the least likely to be victims of crime. Teenagers are the most likely to experience a personal crime. In fact, the victimization rate of 48.4 per 1,000 persons aged 16–19 is more than eight times the victimization rate (5.7) for those age 65 and older. For each specific offense type, teenagers have the highest risk of victimization. With respect to simple assaults, for example, teenagers are more than twice as likely as 35-to 49-year-olds to be victims, yet 25 times more likely to be victimized than are those persons 65 and older.

SUMMARY

We have described in this chapter the volume and distribution of crime in the United States. Not only is it of interest to criminologists to be aware of geographical, temporal, and social characteristics of crime, but it is also vital for criminal justice policymakers to be cognizant of this information. The three dominant sources of crime data, the UCR, the NCVS, and SRD, provide somewhat different pictures about the nature of crime.

The UCR portray the United States as experiencing a skyrocketing increase in crime throughout the 1960s and 1970s, peaking in 1980, and declining through 1984, before rising again from 1985 through 1991 and declining again since 1992. In contrast, the NCVS data show a relatively stable crime rate through the 1970s and 1980s. Of particular note, however, is the fact that both of these measures of crime in the United States have reported a persistent decline in crime since 1992. In fact, according to both sources, the crime rate in 2010 was at an historic low.

The UCR are limited to crimes recorded by the police, while the NCVS reflects crimes reported to interviewers. These different methodologies may account in part for some of the discrepancy in the actual number of crimes. In general, the NCVS and self-report studies list a crime rate from two to ten times that reported by the UCR. Gove et al. (1985) and others have suggested that these sources are measuring different domains of behavior and, therefore, the sources reach different results.

There is greater agreement with respect to specific characteristics of the distribution of crime and of offenders. The general picture is that crime is concentrated in urban areas, overall crime rates are highest in the West, and most crimes are committed between 6 p.m. and 6 a.m. Criminals are likely to be males under the age of 25. Additionally, African Americans, according to UCR and NCVS data, are overrepresented in the population of offenders. Self-report data, however, do not support this conception. The same is true for the offender's social class. While neither UCR nor NCVS provide information about the perpetrator's social class, the common assumption has been that members of the lower class commit a disproportionate share of all crimes. Self-report data provide contradictory evidence on this matter. Social class of offenders, thus, remains a hotly debated topic in criminology.

Data from the NCVS provide a picture of crime victims. Contrary to common stereotypes, the individuals most likely to be victimized are young African-American and Hispanic males residing in urban areas. Households with the highest probability of victimization are those with six or more occupants, with a Hispanic or African-American head of the household, in urban areas, and with low incomes (this is especially the case for victimization of a violent crime).

KEY TERMS AND CONCEPTS

Age-Crime Curve

Career Criminal

Criminal Career

Desistance

Escalation

Frequency Rates

Gender and Crime

Geographical Distribution (of Crime)

Individual Offending Rates

Initiation

Lambda

Mass Incarceration

Maturation Effects

Power-Control Model

Prevalence Rates

Race and Crime

Selective Incapacitation

Social Class and Crime

Temporal Distribution (of Crime)

Termination

Underclass

Victimization Rates

KEY CRIMINOLOGISTS

Freda Adler

Alfred Blumstein

John Braithwaite

Michael Gottfredson

John Hagan

Karen Heimer

Travis Hirschi

Janet Lauritsen

Steven Messner

Richard Rosenfeld

Rita Simon

Charles Tittle

DISCUSSION QUESTIONS

1. Discuss the merits of the following statement: female offenders have been systematically excluded from criminological research and therefore it is difficult to assess whether there has been an increase in female crime or whether the reported increase is only a reflection of the recording of behavior that was previously ignored.
2. According to both the UCR and NCVS, crime has been declining for the past 20 years. However, if one were to base their opinion on media accounts, crime is rampant and increasing. Which of these positions do you support, and why?
3. On the basis of the three data sources discussed in this chapter (UCR, NCVS, and SRD), provide a description of the personal and social characteristics that describe offenders and victims of crime.
4. Relying upon both the UCR and NCVS data, describe the trend in violent crime rates during the past 30 years in the United States.

REFERENCES

Aaronson, D. E., Dienes, C. T., & Musheno, M. C. (1984). *Public policy and police discretion: Processes of decriminalization.* New York, NY: Clark Boardman.

Adler, F. (1975). *Sisters in crime.* New York, NY: McGraw-Hill.

Adler, F. (1983). *Nations not obsessed with crime.* Littleton, CO: Fred B. Rothman.

Anderson, E. (1994). The code of the streets. *The Atlantic Monthly, 273,* 80–94.

Anderson, E. (1999). *Code of the streets: Decency, violence, and the moral life of the inner city.* New York, NY: W.W. Norton & Company.

Beckett, K. & Sasson, T. (2000). *The politics of injustice: Crime and punishment in America.* Thousand Oaks, CA: Pine Forge Press.

Blackwell, B. S. (2000). Perceived sanction threats, gender, and crime: A test and elaboration of power-control theory. *Criminology, 38,* 439–88.

Blumstein, A. (2001). Why is crime falling—Or is it? In *Perspectives on crime and justice: 2000–2001 lecture series* (pp. 1–34). Washington, DC: U.S. Department of Justice, Office of Justice Programs, National Institute of Justice.

Blumstein, A. & Wallman, J. (2000). *The crime drop in America*. New York, NY: Cambridge University Press.

Blumstein, A., Cohen, J., & Farrington, D. (1988a). Criminal career research: Its value for criminology. *Criminology*, *26*, 1–36.

Blumstein, A., Cohen, J., & Farrington, D. (1988b). Longitudinal and criminal career research: Further clarifications. *Criminology*, *26*, 57–76.

Boocock, S. S. (1972). *An introduction to the sociology of learning*. Boston, MA: Houghton-Mifflin.

Boritch, H. (1992). Gender and criminal court outcomes: An historical analysis. *Criminology*, *30*, 293–325.

Braithwaite, J. (1981). The myth of social class and criminality reconsidered. *American Sociological Review*, *46*, 36–57.

Braman, D. (2004). *Doing time on the outside: Incarceration and family life in urban America*. Ann Arbor, MI: University of Michigan Press.

Brown, S. E. (1985). The class-delinquency hypothesis and juvenile justice system bias. *Sociological Inquiry*, *55*, 212–23.

Campbell, M. C. & Schoenfeld, H. (2013). The transformation of America's penal order: A historicized political sociology of punishment. *American Journal of Sociology*, *118*, 1375–423.

Canter, R. J. (1982). Sex differences in self-report delinquency. *Criminology*, *20*, 373–93.

Caspi, A., Moffitt, T. E., Silva, P. A., Stouthamer-Loeber, M., Krueger, R. F., & Schmutte, P. (1994). Are some people crime-prone? Replications of the personality-crime relationship across countries, genders, races, and methods. *Criminology*, *32*, 163–95.

Cernkovich, S. A. & Giordano, P. C. (1979). On complicating the relationship between liberation and delinquency. *Social Problems*, *26*, 467–81.

Chesney-Lind, M. & Sheldon, R. G. (1998). *Girls: Delinquency and juvenile justice* (2nd ed.). Belmont, CA: West/Wadsworth.

Chiricos, T. G. & Crawford, C. (1995). Race and imprisonment: A contextual assessment of the evidence. In D. Hawkins (Ed.), *Ethnicity, race and crime*. Albany, NY: State University of New York Press.

Clelland, D. & Carter, T. J. (1980). The new myth of class and crime. *Criminology*, *18*, 319–36.

Cloward, R. & Ohlin, L. (1960). *Delinquency and opportunity*. New York, NY: The Free Press.

Cohen, A. K. (1955). *Delinquent boys*. New York, NY: The Free Press.

Dornfeld, M. & Kruttschnitt, C. (1992). Do the stereotypes fit? Mapping gender-specific outcomes and risk factors. *Criminology*, *30*, 397–419.

Elliott, D. S. & Ageton, S. S. (1980). Reconciling race and class differences in estimates of delinquency. *American Sociological Review*, *45*, 95–110.

Elliott, D. S., Huizinga, D. H., Knowles, B. A., & Canter, R. J. (1983). *The prevalence and incidence of delinquent behavior: 1976–1980, National Youth Survey report number 26*. Boulder, CO: Behavioral Research Institute.

Esbensen, F.-A. & Carson, D. C. (2012). Who are the gangsters? An examination of age, race/ethnicity, sex, and immigration status of self-reported gang members in a seven-city study of American youth. *Journal of Contemporary Criminal Justice*, *28*, 462–78.

Esbensen, F.-A. & Deschenes, E. P. (1998). A multisite examination of youth gang membership: Does gender matter? *Criminology*, *36*, 799–827.

Esbensen, F.-A. & Weerman, F. M. (2005). Youth gangs and troublesome youth groups in the United States and the Netherlands: A cross-national comparison. *European Journal of Criminology*, 2, 5–37.

Esbensen, F.-A. & Winfree, L. T. (1998). Race and gender differences between gang and non-gang youth: Results from a multi-site survey. *Justice Quarterly*, 15, 505–26.

Evans, M. (1978). *Discretion and control*. Beverly Hills, CA: Sage Publications.

Everett, R. S. & Nienstadt, B. C. (1999). Race, remorse and sentencing reduction: Is saying you're sorry enough? *Justice Quarterly*, 16, 99–122.

Geis, G. (1986). On the declining crime rate: An exegetic conference report. *Criminal Justice Policy Review*, 1, 16–36.

Giordano, P. C. & Rockwell, S. M. (2000). Differential association theory and female crime. In S. S. Simpson (Ed.), *Of crime & criminality* (pp. 3–24). Thousand Oaks, CA: Pine Forge Press.

Gottfredson, M. R. & Hirschi, T. (1986). The true value of lambda would appear to be zero: An essay on career criminals, criminal careers, selective incapacitation, cohort studies, and related topics. *Criminology*, 24, 213–33.

Gottfredson, M. R. & Hirschi, T. (1988). Science, public policy, and the career paradigm. *Criminology*, 26, 37–56.

Gottfredson, M. R. & Hirschi, T. (1990). *A general theory of crime*. Stanford, CA: Stanford University Press.

Gove, W. R., Hughes, M., & Geerken, M. (1985). Are uniform crime reports a valid indicator of the index crimes? An affirmative answer with minor qualifications. *Criminology*, 23, 451–502.

Gurr, T. R., Grabosky, P. N., & Hula, R. C. (1977). *The politics of crime and conflict: A comparative study of four cities*. Beverly Hills, CA: Sage Publications.

Hagan, J. (1994). *Crime and disrepute*. Thousand Oaks, CA: Pine Forge Press.

Hagan, J., Gillis, A. R., & Simpson, J. (1985). The class structure of gender and delinquency: Toward a power-control theory of common delinquent behavior. *American Journal of Sociology*, 90, 1151–78.

Hagan, J., Simpson, J. H., & Gillis, A. R. (1979). The sexual stratification of social control: A gender-based perspective on crime and delinquency. *British Journal of Sociology*, 30, 25–38.

Hagan, J., Simpson, J., & Gillis, A. R. (1987). Class in the household: A power-control theory of gender and delinquency. *American Journal of Sociology*, 92, 788–816.

Hagedorn, J. M. (1988). *People and folks: Gangs, crime and the underclass in a Rustbelt city*. Chicago, IL: Lakeview Press.

Heimer, K. & DeCoster, S. (1999). The gendering of violent delinquency. *Criminology*, 37, 277–317.

Heimer, K., Lauritsen, J. L., & Lynch, J. P. (2009). The National Crime Victimization Survey and the gender gap in offending: Redux. *Criminology*, 47, 427–38.

Hindelang, M. J. (1971). Age, sex, and the versatility of delinquent involvements. *Social Problems*, 18, 522–35.

Hirschi, T. (1969). *Causes of delinquency*. Berkeley, CA: University of California Press.

Hoffman-Bustamonte, D. (1973). The nature of female criminality. *Issues in Criminology*, 8, 117–36.

Huizinga, D. & Elliott, D. S. (1987). Juvenile offenders: Offender incidence and arrest rates by race. *Crime & Delinquency*, 33, 206–23.

Huizinga, D. & Esbensen, F. (1991). *Are there changes in female delinquency and are there changes in underlying explanatory factors?* Paper presented at the annual meeting of the American Society of Criminology.

Jolin, A. & Gibbons, D.C. (1987). Age patterns in criminal involvement. *International Journal of Offender Therapy and Comparative Criminology, 31*, 237–60.

Krohn, M.D., Akers, R.L., Radosevich, M.J., & Lanza-Kaduce, L. (1980). Social status and deviance: Class context of school, social status, and delinquent behavior. *Criminology, 18*, 303–18.

Kvaraceus, W. (1945). *Juvenile delinquency and the school*. Yonkers, NY: World Book Company.

Lauritsen, J.L., Heimer, K., & Lynch, J.P. (2009). Trends in the gender gap in violent offending: New evidence from the National Crime Victimization Survey. *Criminology, 47*, 361–400.

Liu, X. & Kaplan, H.B. (1999). Explaining the gender difference in adolescent delinquent behavior: A longitudinal test of mediating mechanisms. *Criminology, 37*, 195–215.

Merton, R.K. (1938). Social structure and anomie. *American Sociological Review, 3*, 672–82.

Messner, S. & Rosenfeld, R. (1994). *Crime and the American dream*. Belmont, CA: Wadsworth.

Messner, S. & Rosenfeld, R. (2007). *Crime and the American dream* (4th ed.). Belmont, CA: Wadsworth.

Miller, J. (1998). Up it up: Gender and the accomplishment of street robbery. *Criminology, 36*, 37–66.

Miller, W.B. (1958). Lower class culture as a generating milieu for gang delinquency. *Journal of Social Issues, 14*, 5–19.

Pollak, O. (1961). *The criminality of women*. New York, NY: Barnes.

Schur, E.M. (1984). *Labeling women deviant: Gender, stigma, and social control*. New York, NY: Random House.

Schwartz, J., Steffensmeier, D., Zhong, H., & Ackerman, J. (2009). Trends in the gender gap in violence: Reevaluating NCVS and other evidence. *Criminology, 47*, 401–26.

Sigler, R.T. & Horn, M. (1986). Race, income, and penetration of the justice system. *Criminal Justice Review, 11*, 1–7.

Simon, R. (1975). *The contemporary woman and crime*. Rockville, MD: National Institute of Mental Health.

Smart, C. (1976). *Women, crime and criminology: A feminist perspective*. London, UK: Routledge.

Spohn, C. & Holleran, D. (2000). The imprisonment penalty paid by young, unemployed, Black and Hispanic male offenders. *Criminology, 38*, 281–306.

Steffensmeier, D.J. & Demuth, S. (2001). Ethnicity and judges' sentencing decisions: Hispanic-Black-White comparisons. *Criminology, 39*, 145–78.

Steffensmeier, D.J. & Terry, R.M. (1973). Deviance and respectability: An observational study of reactions to shoplifting. *Social Forces, 51*, 417–26.

Steffensmeier, D.J., Ulmer, J., & Kramer, J. (1998). The interaction of race, gender, and age in criminal sentencing: The punishment cost of being young, black, and male. *Criminology, 36*, 763–97.

Stewart, E.A. & Simons, R.L. (2006). Structure and culture in African-American adolescent violence: A partial test of the code of the street thesis. *Justice Quarterly, 23*, 1–33.

Stewart, E. A. & Simons, R. L. (2010). Race, code of the street, and violent delinquency: A multilevel investigation of neighborhood street culture and individual norms of violence. *Criminology, 48,* 569–605.

Stewart, E. A., Schreck, C. J., & Simons, R. L. (2006). "I ain't gonna let no one disrespect me": Does the code of the street increase or decrease violent victimization among African American adolescents? *Journal of Research in Crime and Delinquency, 43,* 427–58.

Taylor, T. J., Esbensen, F.-A., Brick, B., & Freng, A. (2010). Exploring the measurement quality of and attitudinal scale of street code-related violence: Differences across groups and contexts. *Youth Violence and Juvenile Justice, 8,* 187–212.

Tittle, C. & Meier, R. F. (1990). Specifying the SES/delinquency relationship. *Criminology, 28,* 271–99.

Tittle, C., Villemez, W., & Smith, D. (1978). The myth of social class and criminality: An empirical assessment of the empirical evidence. *American Sociological Review, 43,* 643–56.

U.S. Department of Justice. (1974). *Crime in the United States, 1973.* Washington, DC: U.S. Government Printing Office.

U.S. Department of Justice. (1997). *Changes in criminal victimization, 1994–95.* Washington, DC: U.S. Department of Justice.

U.S. Department of Justice. (2010). *Criminal victimization in the United States, 2008 statistical tables.* Washington, DC: U.S. Department of Justice.

U.S. Department of Justice. (2013). *Crime in the United States, 2012.* Washington, DC: U.S. Government Printing Office.

Vigil, J. D. (1988). *Barrio gangs: Street life and identity in Southern California.* Austin, TX: University of Texas Press.

Weerman, F. M. (2012). Are the correlates and effects of gang membership sex-specific? Troublesome youth groups and delinquency among Dutch girls. In F.-A. Esbensen & C. L. Maxson (Eds.), *Youth gangs in international perspective: Tales from the Eurogang Program of Research* (pp. 271–87). New York, NY: Springer.

Weis, J. G. (1980). *Sex differences: Study data publications.* Seattle, WA: Center for Law and Justice.

Western, B. (2006). *Punishment and inequality in America.* New York, NY: Russell Sage Foundation.

Willott, S., Griffin, C., & Torrance, M. (2001). Snakes and ladders: Upper middle-class male offenders talk about economic crime. *Criminology, 39,* 441–66.

Wilson, W. J. (1987). *The truly disadvantaged: The inner city, the underclass, and public policy.* Chicago, IL: University of Chicago Press.

Wright, B. R. E., Caspi, A., Moffitt, T. E., Miech, R. A., & Silva, P. A. (1999). Reconsidering the relationship between SES and delinquency: A causation but not correlation. *Criminology, 37,* 175–94.

PART 2

Theories of Crime

The first four chapters have provided a foundation for the study of criminology. There is little professional consensus regarding the definition of criminology or the bounds of criminological inquiry, but there are certain elements that most criminologists regard as basic. Crime as it is defined in criminal codes is something with which the criminologist must be conversant. For many criminologists, explaining violations of legal codes is the *raison d'être* of criminology. Other criminologists view reactions to antisocial or deviant behaviors, whether the behaviors are officially proscribed or not, as central to the field of criminology. It should be stressed that criminology is a science, and as such it is comprised of an empirical and a theoretical component. Measuring crime and related variables, discussed in the preceding two chapters, are major concerns within the empirical domain. The following six chapters turn to the theoretical dimension.

There are basic questions that deserve attention before a review of major theories of crime. These include: "What is theory?" "Why is theory so important to the criminological enterprise?" Students and even criminal justice practitioners often lament that theory is boring and not pertinent to the "real world," that is, to practical concerns. But theory that is alien to the real world is, very simply, poor theory.

The fundamental purpose of theory is to explain things that can be observed. The scientific approach requires that theory be subjected to the test of observation. Propositions that facilitate prediction of the phenomena of interest should be derivable from theories. If a proposed explanation or theory fails the tests of observation and prediction, then it should be rejected. Criminological theories seek to arrive at explanations that account for behaviors defined as criminal. If, for example, a theory (assuredly a far-out theory) implicates blue eyes as a causal factor in embezzlement, but blue-eyed persons do not appear disproportionately in representative samples of embezzlers, the theory is discarded. New ideas for the explanation of embezzlement can then be advanced as the scientific interplay of theory and research continue.

Criminologists study crime, criminals, and societal reactions to crime and criminals, accumulating an abundance of facts in the process. These facts should be used as building blocks for theory construction because it is theory that provides meaning to what often seem to be unrelated facts. Theory incorporates propositions that relate two or more concepts in such a fashion that they then can be subjected to the tests of observation and prediction. Thus, the scientific approach is self-correcting in the sense that theories failing to explain and predict should be discarded or revised. Without formal theory development and testing, myths regarding the causes of crime are apt to flourish. This brings us to the pragmatic justification for the study of theories of crime: its implications for crime-related public policy.

First, it is important to recognize that virtually everyone holds some view about the causes of crime and, by implication, about how to prevent, control, and respond to it. College and university students, brick masons, physicians, ministers, nuns, bank presidents, and persons from every walk of life are likely to believe that they know the causes of, and consequently the cures for, criminality. Think of the occasions on which you have heard persons react to discussions of crime or delinquency by exclaiming: "It's in the genes," "They're from the wrong side of town," "They got in with the wrong crowd," or "Those kids need to have their butts kicked." Each of these reactions reflects one or more formal theories. Unfortunately, nonspecialists often adopt simplified explanations and solutions for complex problems such as crime. Such public opinion, whether informed or uninformed, can affect crime control policy, sometimes making things worse rather than improving them.

All criminal justice practitioners embrace some theoretical perspective regarding the causes of crime. These practitioners may not be fully aware that they do this, and their thinking may be ill-formed, but at least in part, their ideas likely guide their behavior. A probation officer, for instance, will be "tough" or "sympathetic" with delinquents depending on his or her beliefs regarding the roots of the misbehavior. The question is not whether criminal justice practice is in need of theory, but rather whether criminal justice policy and practice will be guided by the best possible theory or by theory that is randomly formed, nonsystematic, and unable to pass scientifically rigorous tests. The "real world" of criminal justice turns on theory, but unfortunately, it is often a very poor understanding rather than the best that criminology has to offer. Theory inevitably influences criminal justice policy. A particularly important reason for studying formal criminological theories is to enhance the prospects that sound theory will dominate criminological programs.

Criminology poses many intriguing questions. One of the most absorbing is the age-old question of "Why?" "Why do people commit crime?" "Why do others conform?" "How can we explain or understand crime and criminality?" This section of the text explores a variety of theoretical perspectives on such matters. The theoretical viewpoints are presented in a historical framework. The historical format has merit beyond its organizational value because theoretical notions spawned in a given era often reflect the social, political, and economic character and circumstances of the time. While studying society can tell us much about crime, the reverse is also true.

Deterrence and Rational Choice Theories of Crime

LEARNING OBJECTIVES

After reading Chapter 5, you should be able to:

- Describe how crime was understood and responded to in the preclassical era.
- Explain the logic and reasoning of the founders of the classical school of criminology.
- Discuss contemporary research assessing the deterrence doctrine, explaining both distinct research methodologies and findings.
- Display a proficient vocabulary of concepts incorporated in contemporary deterrence research.
- Explain routine activities theory as it applies to both victims and offenders.

One of the most widely debated premises underlying attempts to explain crime, among both criminologists and lay persons, is the role of choice. At issue is the degree to which offenders are or are not driven by rational decision making. Both **deterrence theory** and other explanations falling within the larger **rational choice** paradigm assign a greater role to rational decision making on the part of the criminal offender than do other approaches. Both are rooted in **utilitarianism**, the notion that public policy decisions should maximize pleasure, while minimizing pain among the general citizenry. The assumption of rational calculation among criminals is oftentimes viewed as being directly at odds with other theories of crime, although most contemporary criminologists envision rationality as falling more on a continuum than in a dichotomy. Moreover, the value of merging different perspectives (theoretical integration) has increased substantially in recent years.

Classical criminology provides the origin of the concept of deterrence. It represents the first effort to explain crime as a product of natural rather than supernatural forces. At its core is the belief that persons consider the prospects of punitive sanctions before making a decision to commit a crime. This line of thinking provided the rationale for development of contemporary Western criminal justice systems and served as the dominant explanation of crime from the late eighteenth to the late nineteenth century. The last one-third of the twentieth century witnessed a resurgence of the deterrence concept and it continues as a popular theory of crime today.

This chapter begins with an examination of the social context within which classical criminology emerged, a time referred to as the **preclassical** era. The unfolding of classical criminology and its impact is then detailed. The chapter then turns to an examination of the development of contemporary deterrence concepts and the move toward a broader rational choice perspective. The evolution of routine activities theory in recent decades is reviewed as a leading rational choice perspective that is distinct from deterrence.

PRECLASSICAL VIEWS OF CRIME

Criminology, historically speaking, is a very young field of study. Although norms and regulations of human behavior have always been critical matters in all societies, little intellectual energy was focused on these issues for thousands of years. It was not until the latter part of the eighteenth century that crime was explained as a natural rather than a supernatural phenomenon. Prior to that, crime was attributed to the devil, demons, witches, and various other evil spirits, which were thought to be acting through the offending party.

A major rationale for the application of punishment has been retribution or revenge. In early times, revenge often served as the sole motive for dealing with crime (Schafer, 1976). During periods in which systems of private, kinship, religious, and state-controlled revenge prevailed, little attention was focused on the causes of crime or on how responses to crime might be useful for crime control or prevention. There was nothing in the early days that approached formal systems of criminal justice. Revenge served to placate and sometimes to compensate victims of crime.

During the earliest period of private revenge, life was, as Thomas Hobbes (1651/1962:100) described it, "a war, as is of every man, against every man . . . and the life of man, solitary, poor, nasty, brutish, and short." Each individual had to provide for his or her own security and, when that security was violated, the individual had to exact whatever revenge was deemed appropriate and feasible. This state of affairs proved socially dysfunctional, in part because the distinction between victim and offender became blurred. The strength of the party desiring revenge was the only control over the severity of punishment, and the offender was likely to retaliate, thereby setting in motion a spiral of violence.

The problem was intensified when the parties in the revenge cycle were kinship groups rather than individuals. Attacks came to be interpreted as affronts to an entire family, tribe, or clan. Retaliation, in turn, was directed toward any or all members of the offender's kinship group. This widening of the revenge cycle was known as **blood feuding**. What had been a feud between two individuals in an earlier era now became a conflict between kinship groups.

Blood feuds became so disruptive that they posed a threat to the stability of the social order in the Middle Ages. Feudal lords began to capitalize on superstitions regarding the causes of crime and to support a religiously oriented approach to punishing offenders, whom the lords often declared to be possessed. This eliminated the need for private and kinship revenge. These types of revenge were supplanted by punishment in God's name, which was controlled by representatives of the church and state. Punishments were defined as appeasement, not just of the victims, but of God. Those committing crimes were regarded as evil and sinful persons.

Persecution justified by law has been traced as far back as the fourth century A.D. (Newman, 1978), but it reached a pinnacle during the period of the **Holy Inquisition**, which extended from the twelfth century through the eighteenth century. Henry Lea's (1887/1955) massive three-volume work, *A History of the Inquisition of the Middle Ages,* opens with a discussion of the crisis of authority faced by the Roman Catholic Church at the close of the twelfth century. This unsettled condition led to an alliance between church and state that provided the framework for the Inquisition. The historical significance of this age for criminological thought cannot be overstated, as "the inquisitorial process, based upon torture, had become the groundwork of all criminal procedure" (Lea, 1866/1973:86).

The Inquisition took place in most European countries throughout the Middle Ages and led to widespread imprisonment, torture, and execution, which were measures designed to extract confessions and to punish the heretical (Newman, 1978). Actually, the inquisitors and other secular authorities administered the punishments because the Church was prohibited from shedding blood. The words of a thirteenth-century inquisitor, however, reflect the movement's attachment to the Church:

> The object of the Inquisition is the destruction of heresy. Heresy cannot be destroyed unless their defenders and fautors [practitioners] are destroyed, and this is effected in two ways, viz., when they are converted to the true Catholic faith, or when, on being abandoned to the secular arm, they are corporally burned (Lea, 1887/1955, Vol. 1:535).

Secular authorities had no real choice in the matter. If they refused to carry out the inquisitorial sentence and burn the heretics, they themselves were threatened with excommunication and risked being labeled heretical. The title page of *Malleus Maleficarum,* a fifteenth-century witch hunters' manual, notes: "Not to believe in witchcraft is the greatest of heresies" (Kramer & Sprenger, 1486/1928). Most secular authorities, however, were enthusiastic about carrying out their duties "to do with them what was customary to be done with heretics"—that is, to burn them alive (Lea, 1887/1955:537–38).

The cruelty and injustice of the Inquisition represent a horrible chapter in the history of crime and punishment. The witch hunters brought the full machinery of the State to bear on their unfortunate victims. These terrible deeds offer lessons of contemporary significance (Geis & Bunn, 1981). As did witch hunters in the past, do we still have "criminal" scapegoats? Are we still sometimes misled by authorities who define crime in their own interest or out of ignorance, as authorities did in dealing with witchcraft? It was not social deviants or misfits that participated in the torture and killing of thousands of innocent persons labeled "witches." It was respectable members of society, such as the clergy, lawyers, and eminent figures, including the English physician and philosopher, Sir Thomas Browne (Geis & Bunn, 1981). This awful historical episode bears remembering when analyzing contemporary crime and punishment.

As the State assumed full responsibility for crime, brutal punishment became more common, reaching its height in the seventeenth and eighteenth centuries. Death had always been the major method of punishment in the Western world, but it was extended to all felonies in seventeenth-century England (Newman, 1978). Moreover, the death penalty was not administered quickly or humanely. Hanging could produce slow death, with the executioner tugging at the legs of the condemned to finish the job. Gruesome practices were often a part of the criminal process. Although English common law prohibited torture (Langbein, 1977; Heath, 1982), it was sometimes used in Star Chamber proceedings and in the process of *peine forte et dure*, which consisted of stretching the accused on his back and stacking iron weights on him until he died or agreed to plead to the charge. It was important to both the accused and his family that he not plead guilty, for so long as the individual died without pleading, thus remaining unconvicted, his property was passed on to his family. If he were convicted, his property could be confiscated (Maestro, 1973).

Torture in England was never as severe as that employed throughout continental Europe (Newman, 1978). In France, before the Revolution, the accused could be taken from his or her home by the *gendarmerie* (the secret police), tried without any defense, and condemned to death. Paul Lacroix (1963:416) describes the barbaric means of execution by fire used at one time in France:

> [A] stake was erected on the spot specially designed for the execution, and round it a pile was prepared, composed of alternate layers of straw and wood, and rising to about the height of a man. Care was taken to leave a free space round the stake for the victim, and also a passage by which to lead him to it. Having been stripped of his clothes, and dressed in a shirt smeared with sulphur, he had to walk to the center of the pile through a narrow opening, and was then tightly bound to the stake with ropes and chains. After this, faggots and straw were thrown into the empty space through which he had passed to the stake, until

he was entirely covered by them; the pile was then fired on all sides at once.

Burning alive was the usual punishment for heresy, but even more extraordinary tortures were reserved for perpetrators of what were considered the worst crimes, such as regicide (the killing of a king). The execution of Damiens, the mentally disturbed assassin of King Louis XIV, who was subjected to a variety of preliminary tortures before his **quartering** (described below), vividly illustrates the cruelty of those times:

> In the torture chamber Damiens' legs were placed in devices called "boots," which could be squeezed gradually by means of wedges. After the insertion of eight wedges at intervals of fifteen minutes, every insertion being accompanied by horrible screams, the doctors who had been called to be present at the operation decided that it was not possible to continue "without the danger of an accident." The victim was then taken to the place of execution, in front of the Paris City Hall. The site was filled with all the Parisian rabble, wishing to enjoy the spectacle. French and Swiss guards kept order on all the surrounding avenues. The prisoner was placed on the scaffold and tied with ropes applied to his arms and legs. First, his hand was burned in a brazier filled with flaming sulphur. He was then pinched with red-hot tongs on his arms, his thighs and his chest. On his open wounds molten lead and boiling oil were poured. This operation was repeated several times and every time the most horrible screams came from the wretched creature. After that, four big horses, whipped by four attendants, pulled the ropes rubbing against the inflamed and bleeding wounds of the patient. The pulling and shaking lasted a full hour. The arms and legs became more and more distended but remained attached to the body. The executioners then cut some of the tendons, and with some more pulling the limbs finally separated. Damiens, despite having lost two legs and one arm, was still breathing and died only when the second arm was detached from his bloody torso. Arms, legs, and body were all thrown into a fire that had been prepared near the scaffold (Maestro, 1973:14–15).

Other means of execution employed well into the eighteenth century included drowning, burying alive, beheading, stoning, and breaking on the wheel. Forms of nonlethal corporal punishment in Europe and the American colonies included the stocks, pillories, whipping,

A "rack" on exhibit. Preclassical responses to crime, deviance, or unpopularity tended to be harsh, cruel, and inhumane. One of the best known devices, the rack was first used in ancient Egypt and Babylonia and became standard equipment in every dungeon of the Roman Empire.

CREDIT: AP Photo.

mutilation, and branding. These gruesome preclassical practices served as the catalyst for a powerful reform movement in the understanding of crime and the administration of justice (Scott, 1938/1959).

THE CLASSICAL SCHOOL OF CRIMINOLOGY

The arbitrary administration of justice and the cruel punishments in medieval Europe, which continued into the eighteenth century, provided fertile ground for the emergence of the classical school of criminology. This school offered the first naturalistic explanation for crime and superseded centuries of interpreting crime as a supernatural phenomenon. The classical school was the dominant perspective for approximately one century, but then fell into disrepute, particularly among American criminologists, with the surge of positivism (described in the following chapter). Many criminologists, however, still highly regard classical thought because it represented a tremendous humanitarian reform. It also provided the fundamental rationale for most criminal codes of the Western world, and in recent years classical thought has reemerged by forming the basis of contemporary rational choice theories of crime.

The classical school of criminology must be interpreted in the context of **the Enlightenment**, for this school was a product of that larger reform movement. Rationalism, intellectualism, and humanitarianism were pitted against ideas stressing the divine rights of royalty and the clergy (Johnson, 2003). The founding classicists extended the views of the progressive thinkers of that era to the arena of criminal law and its administration. Charles Montesquieu's 1748 publication of *Espirit des lois* (*The Spirit of the Laws*) was an important prelude to the classical school. This work examined the administration of criminal law and repudiated torture and other abuses. Voltaire's campaign against these widespread injustices also predated the classical school. In 1762, Voltaire successfully lobbied for the rehabilitation (postmortem declaration of innocence) of Jean Calas, a Protestant merchant in Toulouse who had been falsely convicted of murdering his son for planning to convert to the Catholic faith. Calas's son in fact was mentally ill and had committed suicide, but Calas was painfully executed by means of the infamous wheel (Bien, 1960). In that same year, Jean-Jacques Rousseau (1762/1948) published *The Social Contract*, which, along with similar works, formed the basis of the classical school of criminology. The two foremost representatives of classical criminology are Cesare Beccaria and Jeremy Bentham.

CESARE BECCARIA—FATHER OF CLASSICAL CRIMINOLOGY

Cesare Beccaria (1738–94) was born in Milan, Italy. He was the oldest of four children in a modestly wealthy aristocratic family. His early education, which he found to be a stifling experience, was at a Jesuit school; his teachers viewed him as moody and disinterested. Mathematics was Beccaria's forte, earning him the nickname "Little Newton" among his peers. At the age of 20, he completed the Doctor of Law degree at the University of Pavia.

Beccaria experienced more than his share of hardships, beginning with his father's refusal to approve his marriage to the woman of his choice. His father placed him under house arrest for three months to dissuade him from marrying Teresa Blasco (Phillipson, 1923/1970). A father at that time had the power to enforce his will under the doctrine *of patria potestas,* a Roman rule that gave fathers virtually unchecked power over the lives of their children. The couple finally wed despite this opposition, but they were forced to live in poverty. Subsequently, however, Beccaria's relations with his family were restored, and he moved back home, where he spent the remainder of his life. Other difficult times in Beccaria's life included the death of Teresa when he was 35, the death of his younger daughter when he was 50, and a succession of suits filed against him by his relatives. Beccaria was shy and modest, so he preferred to avoid the public eye. He was also obese, as he was inordinately fond of fine food and wine.

An important formative point in Beccaria's career came when he joined with two friends, Pietro and Alessandro Verri, to form a literary club, the Academy of Fisticuffs, which met in the Verri home to discuss topics of literary and social interest. Pietro Verri suggested that Beccaria undertake a critical essay on the administration of criminal law. In nine months, Beccaria completed *Dei delitti e delle pene (On Crimes and Punishments),* which was published in 1764. Slightly more than 100 pages long, the book was written in a straightforward, readable style. Both the author and publisher initially remained anonymous because Beccaria said that he had no desire to become a martyr. These were not times conducive to marching to the beat of a different drummer; the cost of criticizing church and state could be severe.

On Crimes and Punishments sets forth the central tenets of the classical school of criminology. As the embodiment of an overdue reform movement, it proposed "practically all of the important reforms in the administration of criminal justice and in penology which have been achieved in the civilized world since 1764" (Monachesi, 1972:49). It was an immediate success, and in a short time was translated into French, English, German, Spanish, Dutch, Polish, and a few years later, into Russian, Greek, and other languages. The work was praised by the intellectuals of Beccaria's time, including Voltaire, Diderot, Rousseau, and Hume, although many chose to emphasize Beccaria's utilitarian positions to the neglect of his powerful advocacy of human rights. Traditional jurists and religious zealots defended the system of criminal law that Beccaria attacked; Beccaria became fearful when the inquisitors commissioned a critique of his book. The inquisitors proclaimed that "all sensible people have found that the author of the book *On Crimes and Punishments* is an enemy of Christianity, a wicked man and a poor philosopher" and charged Beccaria with sedition and impiety (Maestro, 1973:64). *On Crimes and Punishments* was placed on the Index of books condemned by the Catholic Church and remained on the list until the abolition of the Index in 1962. Fortunately, the provincial governor interceded on Beccaria's behalf, and the attacks on his work, as so often happens, thrust it further into the public limelight.

In his introduction to Marcello Maestro's biography of Beccaria, Norval Morris observed that the views expressed in *On Crimes and Punishments* "were set deep in established writings" (1973:ix). In particular, social contract theorists such as Hobbes, Locke, Hume, and Rousseau provided a point of departure for Beccaria, who saw punishment as an unfortunate necessity in the prevention and control of crime:

> Laws are the conditions under which independent and isolated men united to form a society. Weary of living in a continual state of war, and enjoying a liberty rendered useless by the uncertainty of preserving it, they sacrificed a part so that they might enjoy the rest of it in peace and safety. . . . Some tangible motives had to be introduced, therefore, to prevent the despotic spirit, which is in every man, from plunging the laws of society into its original chaos. These tangible motives are the punishments established against infractors of the laws (Beccaria, 1764/1963:11–12).

Despite this advocacy of punishment, however, Beccaria first and foremost was a humanitarian legal reformer. He vehemently advocated the principle *nullum crimen sine lege* ("no crime without law") and specified criteria for the enactment and administration of criminal codes. Beccaria staunchly supported the separation of powers between legislative and judicial functions in criminal law. Beccaria (1764/1963:13–14) phrased it in this manner:

> Only the laws can decree punishments for crimes; authority for this can reside only with the legislator who represents the entire society united by a social contract. . . . The sovereign, who represents the society itself, can frame only general laws binding all members, but he cannot judge whether someone has violated the social contract. . . . There must, therefore, be a third party to judge the truth of the fact. Hence the need for a magistrate whose decisions, from which there can be no appeal, should consist of mere affirmations or denials of particular facts.

Moreover, Beccaria argued that, in criminal cases, judges "cannot have the authority to interpret laws, and the reason, again, is that they are not legislators. . . . Nothing can be more dangerous than the popular axiom that it is necessary to consult the spirit of the laws" (1764/1963:14–15). Beccaria was clearly reacting against the abuses of his time, as judicial proceedings were notoriously arbitrary and inconsistent.

Another important vein of classical thought involved the nature of criminal harm. Beccaria asserted that the essence of crime was harm to society. He did not see the law as an instrument for preventing all misdeeds of humankind; he believed that this purpose would be impossible and undesirable. Instead, Beccaria stated that criminal law should be employed only to control behavior that is harmful to society and that punishment can be justified only insofar as it is proportionate to the harm done.

At the heart of classical thought is the notion that "[i]t is better to prevent crimes than to punish them" (Beccaria, 1764/1963:93). Prevention, Beccaria and other classicists argued, was to be accomplished through the mechanism of deterrence, which was founded upon certain assumptions regarding human nature. Deterrence employs threats of punishment to influence behavior. It assumes that people are *rational*, that their behavior is a product of **free will**, and that they are **hedonistic**, that is, that their goal is to increase pleasure and/ or to reduce pain. Rational beings are capable of making decisions in a logical, calculating fashion by taking cognizance of the costs and benefits of alternative courses of action. Having free will, they can act as they choose.

If specific assumptions underlying a theory of crime are faulty, the theory itself will lack validity. Are the assumptions undergirding classical deterrence theory tenable? Beccaria and his contemporaries had no doubt that they were, although they never tested their ideas empirically. There is a good deal of "common sense" evidence supporting their assumptions and the concept of deterrence. Much of our day-to-day behavior seems to parallel the model of rational, freely willed, hedonistic behavior. Take a student who arises from bed late one morning (having made an earlier decision to sleep just a bit longer), looks at her watch and, being rational, concludes that she has a choice to make. She can take time for breakfast or she can go to her criminology class. Although she might later attempt to convince her criminology instructor otherwise, after considering the consequences of alternative decisions (e.g., the pleasure of a tasty breakfast versus the pain of hunger), she is free to go to class or to breakfast. The decision seems to involve the rational exercise of free will. The process is hedonistic because it is couched in terms of seeking pleasure (good breakfast and grades) versus avoidance of pain (missing breakfast and attending a purportedly boring criminology lecture).

The deterrence doctrine and its assumptions regarding human nature permeate social relations and institutions. Parents and teachers incorporate the "carrot and the stick" principle to influence the behavior of children. Both the threat of punishment to deter undesirable behavior and the offer of rewards to elicit desired behavior assume that human beings are hedonistic actors. Adults experience the same manipulation from employers who pose threats of disciplinary action and offer promises of pay raises. These tactics can be used to support the assertion that threats of sanctions deter crime. Notice how drivers reduce their speed or come to a complete stop at a stop sign if they see a patrol car there, or consider how teenagers drinking alcohol in public attempt to camouflage their drinks when they see the police approaching. Despite such common sense validation of propositions, criminologists, as scientists, are obliged to remain skeptical of such evidence. The scientific approach requires that observations be recorded in a systematic manner to avoid the error of "selective observation" (seeing that which supports but overlooking that which contradicts a particular theoretical premise). In short, common-sense postulates supported by anecdotes often prove to be incorrect.

Beccaria enumerated three principles of punishment that became the hallmark of classical deterrence doctrine. Assuming that people are rational, hedonistic, and that they exercise free will, it followed for him that crime control is a function of the **certainty**, **severity**, and **celerity** (speed) of punishment. He believed that through proper manipulation of these factors, crime can be prevented. To neglect these principles, or as Beccaria and his contemporaries witnessed in eighteenth-century Europe, to apply them in an arbitrary and inconsistent fashion, is to encourage crime. As people fail to believe in the negative consequences of law-violating behavior, they become less likely to conform to legal mandates. Persons that covet the property of another are more apt to steal that property if the prospects of punishment seem relatively low, temporally distant, or not severe.

The first principle of deterrence maintains that, as the perceived certainty of punishment increases, the probability of norm violations declines. Conversely, as Beccaria expressed it, "undoubtedly ignorance and uncertainty of punishments add much to the eloquence of the passions" (1764/1963:17). Laws, he argued, must be very clear and must be consistently enforced.

The second principle of deterrence states that, as the punishment response becomes swifter, the probability of norm violation declines. Conversely, procrastination in regard to punishment increases the probability of norm violations. Beccaria (1764/1963:56) explained the principle in this manner:

> I have said that the promptness of punishments is more useful because when the length of time that passes between the punishment and the misdeed is less, so much the stronger and more lasting in the human mind is the association of these two ideas, crime and punishment; they then come insensibly to be considered, one as the cause, the other as the necessary inevitable effect.

The message is that both prosecution of suspects and punishment of convicted offenders should be conducted expeditiously.

The third principle of punishment in classical deterrence dogma addresses severity. The severity of punishment was accorded less importance than certainty and celerity; Beccaria felt that "the certainty of punishment, even if it be moderate, will always make a stronger impression than the fear of another which is more terrible but combined with the hope of impunity" (1764/1963:58). He maintained that the severity of punishment was justifiable and that it accomplished a desired deterrent effect, but only up to a certain point:

> For a punishment to attain its end, the evil which it inflicts has only to exceed the advantage derivable from the crime. . . . All beyond this is superfluous and for that reason tyrannical (1764/1963:43).

JEREMY BENTHAM—UTILITARIANISM AND CLASSICAL THOUGHT

Jeremy Bentham (1748–1832) expressed admiration for Beccaria's work and shared many of his views, while contributing his own ideas to the classical school. Like Beccaria, Bentham is recognized more for his contributions as a criminal law reformer than as a theoretician. As Gilbert Geis observed, "the practical results, rather than the theoretical heritage he left behind, stand as major monuments to Bentham. He was not a great philosopher, but he was a great reformer" (1972:66).

Bentham was born in London. He was extraordinarily precocious, reading Latin at four years of age and French soon after. He began the study of law at Oxford at the age of 12, but he was never pleased with his schooling. After a brief encounter with the practice of law, Bentham retreated from the profession of which he was so critical, choosing to devote his life to scholarship. He was a prolific writer, addressing a wide array of subjects.

Bentham displayed a number of eccentricities. He was withdrawn, having few close personal relationships, and he never married, although at the age of 57 he proposed to a woman of many years' acquaintance. He led a regimented life of study and writing, accented by devotion to music, gardening, and animals. His dietary habits were simple. His personality, according to Coleman Phillipson (1923/1970), was complex and comprised of "an extraordinary mixture of antithetical characteristics" (1923/1970:150) but also was child-like in many respects. One of Bentham's more remarkable actions was the incorporation of instructions in his will that his body be dissected and the skeleton displayed in a London university, where it sits today, clad as in life and crowned with a wax image of his head.

Odd personal traits aside, Bentham, like Beccaria, responded to the arbitrariness, inconsistency, and cruelty in the administration of justice in his time. He advocated that punishment should not be guided by retribution, but rather by the aim of preventing crime. In agreement with Beccaria, he defined crime as an offense detrimental to the community. At the heart of Bentham's punishment philosophy was utilitarianism, which he referred to as the "greatest happiness principle." According to this principle, actions should be judged according to whether, on balance, they contribute to the happiness and benefit of humankind. Criminal acts detract from the collective happiness and therefore should be prevented. This, Bentham reasoned, can be accomplished because people carefully weigh the costs and benefits of their actions:

> Nature has placed mankind under the governance of two sovereign masters, pain and pleasure. It is for them alone to point out what we ought to do, as well as to determine what we shall do. . . . They govern us in all we do, in all we say, in all we think (1789/1973:66).

This weighing of pleasure versus pain, which Bentham called felicity or hedonistic calculus, can allow the legal system to function as a deterrent of criminal behavior. By manipulating the pain of punishment, the pleasure stemming from criminal behavior may be outweighed.

A common feature of the classical theorists was their focus on criminal law and their neglect of criminals. This can be understood in the context of the times, as the law was administered in an arbitrary and capricious manner. With this emphasis on statutes and the administration of justice, however, the neglect of the offender detracted from criminological theorizing. The major weakness of Bentham's work was "its total failure to consider criminals as human beings, as live, complicated, variegated personalities" (Geis, 1972:53). Bentham's felicity calculus rested on a series of overly simplistic assumptions regarding human nature. Consequently, while his ideas contributed immensely to the reform of the criminal law and its administration, they fell short as an attempt to explain why criminals violate the law.

IMPACT OF CLASSICISM

The classical school represents the emergence of modern criminological thinking, usurping the earlier view that crime is a supernatural phenomenon. Yet in the years following its enunciation, significant deficiencies in this perspective became evident. The simplistic assumptions regarding the motivations of offenders, failure to scrutinize criminals as persons, and neglect of scientific evaluation of classical propositions eventually contributed to bypassing this school of thought in favor of the positivistic explanations of crime discussed in the following chapter. The impact of classicism on the practice of criminal justice, however, never faltered. Many of the operational premises of Western criminal justice systems, and especially the rights accorded the accused, can be traced to the works of Beccaria, Bentham, and other classicists. Criminal law and procedure, as well as penology and policing, were profoundly affected by this reform movement.

CRIMINAL LAW AND PROCEDURE

Because the classicists focused on the failure of the law to provide a rational framework for the control of criminal behavior, many of their most noteworthy contributions were in the reform of criminal codes and procedures. Legislators such as Sir Samuel Romilly became staunch advocates of legal reform derived from classical principles. Romilly served in the English Parliament from 1806 to 1818, introducing a large number of bills to eliminate barbaric punishments and to facilitate consistency and certainty of punishment. These reforms, however, were not easily accomplished, as witnessed by a portion of an 1813 parliamentary address by Romilly, following defeat of a bill that he had introduced in order to abolish disemboweling and quartering:

> I cannot but confess that I feel some disappointment and much mortification at the resistance to the bill now before us. I had flattered myself that at least in this one instance I should have secured your unanimous concurrence. I certainly did not foresee that in an English House of Commons in the nineteenth century, one voice would have been heard in defense of a law which requires the tearing out of the heart and bowels from the body of a human being, while he is yet alive, and burning them in his sight (Phillipson, 1923/1970:274).

Legal reforms and protections of the accused advocated by the classicists ultimately spread throughout the Western world. In America, such luminaries as John Adams, Benjamin Franklin, and Thomas Jefferson acknowledged a debt to Beccaria. Classical influence is obvious in the French Declaration of the Rights of Man, the English Reform Act of 1832, and the Constitution of the United States. Classical principles include the right of the accused to have a public trial by a jury of peers, the assistance of legal counsel, an opportunity to present evidence on his or her own behalf, and protections derived from the notion that a person is legally innocent of a crime until proven guilty beyond a reasonable doubt. Equally significant are the reductions in the repertoire of corporal punishments, abolition of torture, which became defined as cruel and unusual punishment, and diminution of capital punishment. All of these reforms were stimulated by classical thought. In short, the totality of Western criminal law, including the behaviors proscribed, procedures for prosecution, and the array of punishments for offenders, was revolutionized.

PENOLOGY

The classical epoch also infused a wide range of changes in the practice of penology. Until then, incarceration was predominately in two settings. One was the gaols (a British spelling of jail), which were used for relatively short-term detention of persons accused of crimes and awaiting trial, for the condemned awaiting execution or corporal punishment, and for debtors. Conditions in these facilities were awful; those confined were not segregated by age, sex, or reason for incarceration. The other leading mode of confinement was within convict galleys, called hulks. These were dilapidated ships plagued by unsanitary conditions and inadequate food and supplies, resulting in shocking mortality rates. Otherwise, punishment of criminals was corporal or by transportation to such sites as the American colonies and, later, Australia.

Imprisonment under relatively humane conditions, in lieu of these more brutal punishments, was one of the innovations fostered by the classical school. The penitentiary arose, and although conditions were extremely harsh by today's standards (e.g., use of solitary confinement in the Pennsylvania system and enforced silence in the congregate system in New York), they represented a vast improvement over the gaols and hulks. The latter were abolished, as was the practice of transportation, and prisoners generally came to be segregated by age and sex. Even some measure of rehabilitative effort was introduced to facilitate Bentham's "subserviency to reformation," the view that a penalty that reduces offenders' motivation to crime is superior to one that does not.

It was in the context of the move to substitute prisons for existing modes of punishment that Bentham advocated the **Panopticon**, an elaborate prison design. He spent several years and most of his assets seeking to promote this project. In the end, however, the English Parliament rejected it, although some of his ideas filtered to other countries, where they had a limited impact. The Panopticon plan consisted of a circular guard house with wings of cells protruding from it so that guards could maintain observation from that central location along all corridors. This architectural concept is evident in the short-lived Pennsylvania system of prisons. Another major feature, anticipating today's trend toward private management of correctional institutions, was the idea of contract management.

POLICING

Reform principles of the classical school of criminology extended into the realm of policing. These reforms took longer, though, because of intense political controversy. In the decade following the death by suicide of Romilly, Sir Robert Peel, serving as Home Secretary, pursued the challenging task of police reform. Modern law enforcement in England and America began with Peel's introduction of the **London Metropolitan Police Act of 1829**. The measure passed both houses of Parliament after several years of adroit political maneuvering by Peel. Widespread resistance had to be overcome because English citizens had a marked distrust of centralized government (Lyman, 1964; Critchley, 1972). Police reforms implemented in France and other continental European countries had increased the power of central government, and the fear was that police power would be similarly used in England. This profuse mistrust of police authority continued after Peel's new police, dubbed "Bobbies" and "Peelers" for their initiator, took to the streets. The public was so antagonistic that "policemen attempting to control traffic were ridden down and lashed with whips" (Critchley, 1972:54). In some instances, Bobbies were killed with impunity. After a few years, however, the new approach to policing, rooted in classical criminology, achieved popularity in London and became the model for police reform throughout England. The same model found its way to America and provided the founding philosophy for municipal policing, which began with the formation of the Boston Police Department in 1838.

Robert Peel. Modern law enforcement in England and the United States began with Peel's introduction of the London Metropolitan Police Act of 1829.

CREDIT: Wikipedia.org.

At the core of Peel's reform legislation was the goal of deterring crime. In instructions to the first two commissioners of the London Metropolitan Police, Peel stated, "It should be understood, at the outset, that the principal object to be attained is the prevention of crime. . . . The absence of crime will be considered the best proof of the complete efficiency of the police" (Lyman, 1964:133). Following classical propositions, it was believed that crime could be deterred by police patrol. If the police were randomly moving about, dressed in recognizable uniforms, the potential offender would conclude that it was unwise to commit an offense because of the increased risk of apprehension. The higher certainty of punishment would, it was believed, outweigh the benefit to be derived from the offense.

The perception of the police as a deterrent force persisted for nearly 150 years after the Peelian Reform without being seriously questioned. In America, August Vollmer's classic police administration text maintained that patrol "is society's best defense against the criminal. The mere sight of uniformed officials diligently patrolling beats is often sufficient to deter the community's weaker members from committing legal infractions" (1936:217). O.W. Wilson and R.C. McLaren, two more leading authorities on police administration, similarly advocated the deterrent effect of a police presence. They saw patrol as the "backbone" of policing and concluded that "an impression of omnipresence is created by frequent and conspicuous patrol" (1972:320). In recent decades, however, police authorities began to consider the deterrent effect of police patrol an open empirical question rather than the essence of crime prevention.

CONTEMPORARY DETERRENCE THEORY

Although criminologists largely dismissed the ideas of the classical school early in the twentieth century, neither legislators nor police administrators did. This schism of theory and practice retarded the growth of criminological wisdom. Little effort was made to blend the classical notions of deterrence with dominant sociological perspectives to see if they could explain more crime together than separately. In a further contribution to the theoretical divide, deterrence and labeling (examined in Chapter 9) predict fully opposite impacts of criminal justice sanctions. The central thesis of deterrence maintains that punishment diminishes crime, while labeling theory asserts that punishment increases crime. According to deterrence theory, a person's criminal activity will decline as a result of being caught and punished. Labeling theory suggests that the person will be driven by punishment into further crime.

As deterrence theory has advanced, criminologists have recognized that sanctions can at times deter future offending, while at other times or among different subjects, amplify misconduct. Robert Morris and Alex Piquero (2013), for example, found that arrests of chronically offending or even moderately repeating juvenile delinquents increased their offending, but not that of less serious delinquents. Similarly, Gary LaFree and his colleagues (2009) found that while both deterrent and amplification or **backlash effects** occurred in response to crackdowns on IRA terrorists in Northern Ireland, the backlash effect was the larger. This is now a broad concern within the counterterrorism community, but there is reason to believe the concept may be applicable across a broad range of offenders. In short, deterrence theory no longer presumes that punishment always yields only positive results, but that it sometimes makes matters worse. What is important is the net effect of enhancing sanctions. So long as punishment responses inhibit more crime than they cause, they may represent a valuable addition to our crime prevention arsenal.

Until recent years, however, such sophisticated and objective analyses of sanctions were not offered. To the contrary, ideological bias left issues of deterrence ignored for decades. Ideological predispositions led to empirically unfounded conclusions, some suggesting that deterrence works and some that it does not. At the turn of the twentieth century, Enrico Ferri asserted that "we have but to look about us . . . to see that the criminal code is far from being a remedy against crime, that it remedies nothing" (1901/1968:231). At mid-century, Harry Barnes and Negley Teeters, in their influential criminology text, drew the same untested conclusion, asserting that "the claim for deterrence is belied by both history and logic" (1951:338). In the late 1960s, a leading criminology text continued to offer a similar unsubstantiated assertion to the effect that deterrence "does not prevent crime in others or prevent relapse into crime" (Reckless, 1967:508).

It is clear that both theory and research on the effects of sanctions have progressed exponentially. Both exponents and opponents of deterrence theory maintain that their viewpoints are congruent with common sense. Deterrence advocates cite as proof of deterrence the marked reduction in the speed of traffic when vehicles approach a visible patrol car. Deterrence opponents, on the other hand, point to the large number of persons in prison for the second or third time as proof that deterrence does not work. However, it is not sound to infer from the decelerating vehicles that, in general, "deterrence works," and certainly, the fact that some persons repeatedly violate the law does not repudiate deterrence doctrine. Discussions of deterrence commonly rely on these unwarranted inferences, a fact well illustrated by the wry analysis of Frank Zimring and Gordon Hawkins. They refer to one of their analogies as the **tiger prevention fallacy** (Zimring & Hawkins, 1973:28):

> A man is running about the streets of mid-Manhattan, snapping his fingers and moaning loudly, when he is intercepted by a police officer. This conversation follows:

P.O.:   What are you doing?
Gtlm: Keeping tigers away.
P.O.:   Why, that's crazy. There isn't a wild tiger within five thousand miles of New York City!
Gtlm: Well then, I must have a pretty effective technique!

The issue highlighted by the tiger prevention tale, as Gibbs (1975) stressed, is that deterrence is an inherently unobservable phenomenon. We cannot see that which is prevented, yet absence of the prevented occurrence does not establish a deterrent effect. Contrary assertions, however, are common among deterrence exponents. Conclusions that low levels of deviance can be credited to threats of sanction reflect the tiger prevention fallacy. While the tiger tale is a facetious illustration, serious assertions regarding criminal justice successes are sometimes equally silly. One of the text authors often provides an illustrative example wherein his local police made a pronouncement to the news media in the early days of crack cocaine as a popular drug. They assured the media that the locality was unfazed by this new drug. When asked why, the police spokesperson said something to the effect that "these drug dealers know that we won't put up with it!" The media naively accepted this ridiculous claim, but of course crack later arrived in the small town and persisted in the drug culture for years. The problem finally declined, not because of police activity, but as a consequence of other illegal drugs displacing the crack market. So much for the "crack prevention fallacy!"

Opponents of deterrence often arrive at a similarly flawed, but reversed inferential conclusion. Zimring and Hawkins (1973) have summarized this fallacy as the **warden's survey**. In this analogy, they refer to numerous prison wardens (and others) who have concluded that deterrence does not work based upon their observations of convicted offenders. Their fallacious conclusion is derived from "experience with groups of men who have evidently not been deterred or they would not be in prison" (Zimring & Hawkins, 1973:31). Logically, if deterrence could be observed, it would be located among populations of nonoffenders. By this criterion, sanctions could only be judged to be effective deterrents if there were a complete absence of crime.

Criminologists for most of the twentieth century tried to refute the deterrence doctrine with materials that were variations of the warden's survey and with data indicating that murder rates are higher in jurisdictions using capital punishment. Criminal justice practitioners, on the other hand, typically have erred in the direction of the tiger prevention fallacy, exhibiting an unfaltering faith in deterrence theory. Charles Tittle (1980:1) summarized the situation succinctly by noting that "on one hand there was a strong but uncritical belief among the general population and criminal justice practitioners that sanctions do curtail deviance, and on the other hand there was a strong but uncritical belief among academics that they do not."

Criminologists virtually rediscovered the deterrence question about 40 years ago. Johannes Andenaes's (1952, 1966) conceptual analyses served as the harbinger of this re-examination, while the empirical endeavors of Gibbs (1968) and Tittle (1969) fueled an explosion of research activity in the 1970s. It was a unique combination of trends and circumstances that set the stage for this reconsideration of deterrence theory. First, much attention focused on empirical evidence suggesting that rehabilitation, the logical policy derivative of **positive criminology** (see Chapter 6), had not succeeded in substantially reducing recidivism. Reviews of rehabilitative programs had concluded as much in the late 1960s and early 1970s (e.g., Bailey, 1966; Wilkins, 1969; Hood, 1971; Kassebaum et al., 1971). Robert Martinson's (1974) generalization that "nothing works" in efforts to rehabilitate offenders helped open the door to deterrence research even wider. In the ensuing decades conceptualization of the concept has made enormous strides.

CONCEPTUALIZING DETERRENCE

The conceptual roots of deterrence lay in the work of Cesare Beccaria and Jeremy Bentham. The theoretical propositions of the utilitarian thinkers see crime as a negative function of the certainty, severity, and speed of punishment. In other words, as punitive responses to crime increase in these three contexts, it is expected that the frequency of crime will decline. Moreover, the concept was proposed as a general theory of crime; that is, an explanation that applies to all people and all types of crime (Exum, 2002). As far as it goes, this assertion seems plausible. The deterrence propositions of rational choice theory, however, have "come a long way" since Beccaria brought them to the forefront (Pratt, 2008: 43).

Certainty

Modern research has focused mostly on the certainty of punishment, the dimension also most emphasized by the early classicists. Quite a substantial body of evidence has emerged that higher certainties of punishment are associated with lower levels of crime. In short, there is a strong consensus that certainty of punishment is the most important of the three elements of punishment. Given that the certainty of punishment deters, however, how much certainty is required? How sure must the potential offender be that punishment will follow to be dissuaded from the prohibited behavior? Some studies of the relationship between crime clearance (arrest) and crime rates show that no deterrent effect exists until arrest probability attains some minimal level (Tittle & Rowe, 1974; Brown, 1978; Brown, 1981; Loughran et al., 2012). This threshold for the operation of deterrence is called a **tipping level** and adds another layer of complexity to the original deterrence proposition. It is one of many factors upon which modern-day criminologists understand deterrence to be contingent.

Severity

Deterrence theory also suggests that, all else being equal, crime should decrease as punishment severity increases (Andenaes, 1966; Zimring & Hawkins, 1973). Rarely, however, is all else equal. Beccaria and Bentham were cautious about declaring that deterrent effects are contingent upon the severity of punishment. Less is known about the effects of punishment severity, but among the studies completed, most have not supported the deterrence proposition and the consensus has been that the severity of punishment does not matter. A study comparing the effects of prison to probation, conducted by Cassia Spohn and David Holleran (2002), is representative. Comparing three groups of felons (drug, drug-involved, and nondrug), they found recidivism was both more frequent and occurred more quickly for all three types of offenders if they were sentenced to prison rather than probation. In other words, rather than a deterrent effect, the more severe punishment (imprisonment) had the opposite impact: a criminogenic or crime-enhancing result. The **criminogenic** effect was even more pronounced among the drug offenders. Spohn and Holleran (2002) concluded that the contemporary punitive emphasis on crime, especially drug crimes, is misguided and counterproductive, given what we are learning about the severity of punishment. Another study, however, reached contrary conclusions although it looked at only one type of crime. Greg Pogarsky (2002), in studying the drinking and driving habits of college students, found that the severity of punishment held even more deterrent effect than did the certainty, so long as only "deterrable" subjects were considered. Similarly, Silvia Mendes (2004) has argued that certainty and severity are of equal importance. This issue of who and what type of crimes might be more deterrable is an interesting topic that will be examined in much more detail later in this chapter.

Speed

If detection and punishment do follow criminal behavior, how quick must the punitive response be to have an effect? The American machinery of justice typically moves very slowly. Might this delay or cancel the effects of a punishment response that is, or is presumed to be, sufficiently certain? Some would suggest that it does, while others have contended that delays in punishment cause further suffering and trepidation, thus actually enhancing deterrent effects. To date, however, few empirical efforts have been undertaken to examine the importance of swift punishment in creating deterrence.

Contemporary Concepts

Another basic conceptual issue concerns the punishment itself. What, in fact, is punishment? Legal sanctions currently in use include fines, denial of privileges such as holding a driver's license, community supervision such as probation, confinement in jails and prisons, and capital punishment. Graeme Newman (1983) maintained that a return to corporal punishment would be a valuable addition to our repertoire of punishments. Others argue for elimination of some current punishments, most notably capital punishment. There are political and cultural limits on the use of sanctions. Although the execution of speeders and subsequent display of their heads beside the posted speed limits in early twentieth-century Peking may have had a significant deterrent impact, most of us probably would not want to resort to such extreme measures to deter speeders (Griffiths, 1970).

If punishment does deter crime, what should we see? There are distinctly different possibilities. It is theoretically possible to completely deter any given individual from any specific form of criminal conduct. If an individual entirely refrains from commission of a criminal act out of fear of legal sanctions, we have **absolute deterrence** (Gibbs, 1975; Tittle, 1980). Remember, however, the tiger prevention fallacy, reminding us that the absence of offending behavior by a particular person does not demonstrate absolute deterrence because abstention may be for a variety of reasons other than threat of sanctions. An alternative possibility is for the threat of sanctions to result in less law violation, but not complete conformity to the law. Such a reduction is referred to as **marginal or restrictive deterrence**. Reductions may be in the form of less frequent, less conspicuous, or less flagrant violations. That is, fear of sanctions may lead potential offenders to be much more cautious, while continuing some offending.

Crime Displacement

This is another conceptual possibility in the assessment of deterrent effects. **Crime displacement** refers to changing the manner of lawbreaking in the face of threats that enhance the perceived certainty or severity of punishment.

Displacement represents shifts in times, places, and forms of crime (Reppetto, 1976). Increased deterrent effects for robbery, for example, could lead to increases in other offenses. Rather than ceasing their criminal activity, robbers who conclude that risks of sanctions for robbery have become excessive may become burglars. Robbers who decide that the risks of robbery have become too great at particular hours or in particular neighborhoods may commit robberies at other times or in other places. Consequently, it is important to think in terms of net changes in crime rates that might result from modifications in sanctioning perceptions. If 20 nighttime robberies in a downtown precinct are deterred by focusing efforts on that problem, but ten more burglaries, five more daytime robberies, and five more suburban robberies occur, crime may have been displaced, but not deterred.

Finally, it is important to distinguish between **objective punishment properties** and **perceptions of punishment** certainty and severity. The effectiveness of sanctions will necessarily be mediated through perceptions of them. Robert Apel (2012) recently published a thorough review of the labyrinth of perceptual deterrence research. He points out that perceptions of sanctions among the general public are generally quite inaccurate. Subjects may over- or underestimate the objective certainty and severity of punishment. Underestimating the objective properties of punishment has been dubbed the **base rate fallacy**. The "base rate" is the expected rate of punishment certainty or severity and the fallacy is ignoring or underestimating that objective level of certainty or severity of punishment. To illustrate, one of the authors often provides the example of convicted offenders using phrases such as, "I thought I was too smart to get caught," or the offender reincarcerated for new offenses declaring, "I thought I'd learned where I messed up and wouldn't get caught again." Whether a reflection of an overly optimistic personality or poor judgment skills, such offenders exemplify the base rate fallacy. They conclude that they are exempt from the base odds of getting caught. A recent examination of this overconfidence found consistent support for high-school offenders (Loughran et al., 2013). Others may be deterred because they grossly overestimate sanctions, or perhaps because they are not experienced in the world of deviance, they naively misread the risks. Either way, personal or vicarious experiences can facilitate periodic "resetting" or "updating" of perceptions.

Figure 5.1 displays the causal deterrence linkage between objective prospects of punishment (arrests, convictions, etc.), perceptions of punishment prospects, and offending behaviors. Unfortunately, recent research has not been kind to this model. Greg Pogarsky and his colleagues (2005), for

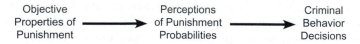

FIGURE 5.1
Objective-perceptual punishment linkage.

example, found the process of forming perceptions of punishment risks to be quite complex, noting in particular that it appears to vary across types of offending. Similarly, Kleck et al. (2005) failed to find support for any linkage between objective punishments delivered by the criminal justice system and individual perceptions of punishment. Without this linkage the logic of general deterrence is undermined.

GENERAL AND SPECIFIC DETERRENCE

Punishment has the potential to deter prohibited behaviors through two distinct processes. Most frequently, when criminologists or criminal justice practitioners speak of deterrence, they refer to general deterrent practices. **General deterrence** involves punitive sanctions (real or perceived) designed to influence the behavior of individuals other than those punished. The sanctioned offender serves as an example to *others* that might contemplate illegal behavior so that, through the rational-calculative process assumed by deterrence theory, additional law-breaking is prevented.

Publicity is an essential component of the general deterrence process, for the wider the dissemination of sanctioning information, the greater is the potential impact of that information. Publicity designed to deter unlawful behavior usually takes the shape of media campaigns or informal word-of-mouth. It may communicate accurate information regarding the sanctioning process or utilize distorted messages designed to serve as scare tactics. Further, it may focus on specific offenses (e.g., a message that drug dealers are severely penalized) or general compliance with the law (e.g., a communication that "crime does not pay").

General deterrence theory is a utilitarian scheme with crime-reducing benefits predicated on increasing public perceptions of the certainty, celerity, and/or severity of punishment. One concern is the ethical aspects of punishment. General deterrent effects, many criminologists fear, can be just as readily achieved by punishment of an innocent party that is widely believed to be guilty as by punishment of the factually guilty party. An even more likely scenario is the application of exceptionally severe punishments to offenders that, for reasons unrelated to the gravity of their crimes, have captured the public eye. In both cases, general deterrent effects might be realized, but they would be rooted in actions that are considered unjust from other than a utilitarian vantage point.

Specific deterrence (also called special, individual, and particular deterrence) seeks to discourage the *sanctioned individual* from engaging in future misconduct. Rather than being designed to affect others, it is intended to "teach a lesson" to the criminal. Like general deterrence, specific deterrence is founded on principles of hedonistic calculus (an assumption that human nature leads people to pursue pleasure and avoid pain). The focus, however, is on how punishment actually is experienced rather than publicity about the punishment of others. Apprehension and punishment may lead an offender to an upward reassessment of punishment probabilities, thereby changing his or her cost-benefit calculus and reducing the likelihood of additional crime. Surprisingly, however, a number of researchers (e.g., Pogarsky & Piquero, 2004) have found just the opposite. They suggest that this might be due to (1) a "selection" process, whereby the most committed offenders tend to be caught and (2) a "resetting" phenomenon analogous to that of the gambler believing that their bad luck will not continue. Likewise, the apprehended offender erroneously concludes that they are unlikely to again face arrest and sanction. There are several ways, drawing from other theoretical perspectives, in which efforts to achieve specific deterrence might produce results opposite of those desired. Labeling theory, for example, as previously mentioned, predicts increases in deviant behavior as a consequence of punishment. This is based on the notion that punishment stigmatizes persons, restricting their legitimate opportunities for such things as jobs, associates, and recreation (see Chapter 9). Note, however, that while labeling is essentially the opposite of specific deterrence, it is not necessarily inconsistent with general deterrence. Punishment may increase criminal behavior among those punished, while reducing offenses among the general population that learns about the punishment.

DETERRENCE AND INDIVIDUAL TRAITS

The bold assumption of the classical theorists was that *all* persons follow the same calculus in making choices to commit or not commit crimes. While it did not take long to recognize that children and the insane did not fit this thinking, it was not until the new era of deterrence was opened in the closing decades of the twentieth century that criminologists began to recognize that there are many more exceptions. Criminologists now have far more complex conceptual schemes for estimating the effectiveness of sanctions in deterring people from engaging in criminal and delinquent behavior.

Perhaps the greatest shortcoming of classical criminology was a naive and overly simplistic view of human beings. This raises the important question of whether some persons are more deterrable than are others. In recent years, criminologists have identified a host of individual characteristics that might be differentially related to deterrability. For example, persons who place a premium on delayed gratification (i.e., future-oriented) are believed to be more subject to control by sanctioning than present-oriented or impulsive individuals. The impulsive person may reflect less on the consequences of acts and therefore be less affected by them. This bears some resemblance to the concept of low self-control discussed in Chapter 8. Recent research incorporating that concept has indicated that low self-control may be characteristic of persons that are unreceptive candidates for deterrent effects (Piquero & Tibbetts, 1996; Tibbetts & Myers, 1999). These studies have suggested that those with high self-control may be deterrable, at least through informal or shaming mechanisms, while those with low self-control may not be deterrable at all. Individuals also differ in their penchant for taking risks. Those stimulated by the thrill of risk-taking should be less deterrable than those daunted by risk. Biological makeup, surveyed in Chapter 6, may also drive susceptibility to threats of sanctions. Rates of arousal of the cerebral cortex, imbalances in neurotransmitters, or brain damage resulting from environmental insults (e.g. lead poisoning in early development) all may render subjects inept in assessing risks and/or rendering rational decisions. Finally, the outlook of the personality may be associated with deterrability. Optimists may underestimate the prospects of apprehension and punishment, and consequently, may be less responsive to deterrent efforts. Pessimists, to the contrary, may overestimate the likelihood of punishment, which enhances their deterrability.

A number of demographic attributes also appear to be associated with differences in sanction effectiveness. Older persons, for example, owing to their greater stake in the established social order, and perhaps greater experience, tend to be more responsive to sanction threats than younger persons. Second, although relatively little attention has been focused upon deterrability by race, considering the weight assigned to race in other criminological contexts, it is reasonable to suspect possible differences. Both Bishop (1984) and Tittle (1980), for example, found strong empirical support for the notion that African Americans are more responsive to formal sanction threats than are whites, although it is not clear why this might be the case. One possibility is that African Americans believe that they will be dealt with more harshly if apprehended and convicted. Brenda Blackwell and her colleagues (1994) also found African Americans to hold higher perceptions of risks of legal sanctions, but lower perceptions of threats of informal sanctions. Similarly, in their examination of deterrent effects on DUI, Rodney Kingsnorth and his colleagues (1993) did find that punishments were perceived quite differently, depending upon one's location in the social stratification system. Higher class people were particularly averse to the prospects of spending time in jail. It is, of course, likely that social standing alters one's perceived utility of some types of crime.

We know that gender is the best single predictor of criminality (see Chapter 4), suggesting, to the extent that deterrence factors explain criminal involvement, that females are more responsive to threats of punishment than are males. Evidence regarding the role of gender and formal sanctioning systems, however, has been mixed. In a study of student cheating (Tittle & Rowe, 1973), females were found to be more responsive to sanction threats, and greater special deterrent effects following DUI convictions have been found for females (Kingsnorth et al., 1993). Other studies have found no difference by sex (e.g., Anderson et al., 1977; Finken et al., 1998) or greater deterrent effects for males (e.g., Silberman, 1976; Bishop, 1984; Miller & Anderson, 1986). This confusion, however, may be resolved by considering the role of informal sanctions in controlling deviance. It has been forcefully argued that women are typically controlled by informal mechanisms, while, for males, it is more often necessary to resort to formal social control (Hagan et al., 1979). Females are more responsive to shaming in patriarchal cultures because they are socialized to be more dependent on the family. "The female is thus always more socially integrated, always more susceptible to shaming by those on whom she is dependent, and never quite as free to make deviant choices as the male" (Braithwaite, 1989:92). It may be that females are far more receptive to deterrent threats than males, but that they occur within the family, prior to any need for intervention on the part of formal agents of social control. Recent studies of gender and sanctions have supported the position that females are more responsive to informal sanction threats (Grasmick et al., 1993a; Tibbetts & Herz, 1996), while tests of formal deterrent effects have still failed to show significant and consistent gender differences (Carmichael et al., 2005).

What is at stake for the individual may also be a determining factor in shaping his or her deterrability. What one has the potential to lose through the sanctioning process and what one stands to gain through rule violation may inform the decision-making process. The more one has to lose through sanctioning the more deterrable they should be, and conversely, the more one believes they could gain through deviant means the more difficult to deter they should be. An informative study of cheating among college students reviewed later in this chapter, for example, found that those with higher grades (more to lose) were more easily deterred, while those with low grades (less to lose) were less deterrable.

Table 5.1 summarizes differential deterrent effects by individual characteristics that have been postulated. A lot of research is needed to arrive at a fuller understanding of these individual differences. What should be clear, however, is that it is far more complex than just assuming all actions taken by all persons are equivalent "choices." Contemporary deterrence theorists do not accept the classical premise that all persons are alike, but rather recognize a myriad of differences that impact individual deterrability. **Bounded rationality** is a more limited understanding of "the social, physical, and situational context in which criminal decisions are made as well as the offenders' perceptions of the world around them" (Copes & Vieraitis, 2009:242). In short, the contemporary view of rational decision making as bounded incorporates diverse individual differences.

Following the logic that individuals may be more or less deterrable, Greg Pogarsky (2002) has developed a tripartite conceptual schema of deterrability (see Figure 5.2). At one end of the continuum are the **incorrigible**, those who do not hold potential to be significantly affected by threats of punishment. Sex offenders, for example, have notoriously high recidivism rates. They are widely viewed as offenders with psychological or biological disorders that undermine their ability for the rational calculus on which the deterrence doctrine is based. At the opposite polar extreme lie **acute conformists**, individuals who require no threat of punishment to compel conformity because other forces prevent them from violating the rules. Many persons, for example, are deterred by extralegal sources so that threats of legal sanctions are not needed to insure conformity. It is the middle category, which Pogarsky identifies as the *deterrable* that are relevant to formal sanction threats. Consequently, he argues that studies of formal sanction threats should limit the search for deterrent effects to this group. Findings may be skewed in research that mixes deterrable subjects with the incorrigible and acute conformists.

TABLE 5.1 Deterrent Effects by Individual Characteristics

Individual Characteristics	Deterrability
Future-oriented/delays gratification	High
Present-oriented/impulsive	Low
High self-control	High
Low self-control	Low
Low risk-taker	High
High risk-taker	Low
Authoritarian	High
Nonauthoritarian	Low
Pessimist	High
Optimist	Low
Older	High
Younger	Low
Black	High
White	Low
(Sparse research)	
Higher classes	High
Lower classes	Low
Female	High
Male	Low
Much to lose and little to gain	High
Little to lose and much to gain	Low

Incorrigible   Acute Conformist

Deterrable

FIGURE 5.2
Pogarsky's individual deterrability continuum.

Bruce Jacobs (2010), however, has proposed that the matter of deterrability may be even more complex, requiring a careful examination of *sensitivity to risk* across individuals. Jacobs reviewed a wide variety of actual crime vignettes to illustrate wide variation in levels of risk evident across crime scenarios. In short, the work of some offenders seems remarkably cautious and calculated while that of others appears foolhardy from a rational sanction-avoidance framework. Deterrability, then, is a function of both criminal commitment or motivation and **risk sensitivity**.

DETERRENCE AND TYPES OF CRIME

The classical theorists did not foresee variations in deterrability across types of crime either. The same logic that applies to individuals, however, can be used to analyze varying types of crime. This is helpful because different forms of crime attract different sorts of persons who will vary in terms of the individual characteristics discussed in the previous section. It is likely, for example, that the sex offender will possess more of the traits that render them less deterrable than would typically be the case for many other offenders.

In short, crimes may be conceptually ranked along a continuum from most to least deterrable through an exercise similar to the above examination of individual deterrability. Following classical assumptions, it has been frequently postulated that those crimes that are more rational or "normal" will be more deterrable than those that are less so. The deterrability of behaviors becomes doubtful to the degree that irrationality appears. Insider stock trading and child molesting are divergent examples on the rationality continuum. It would be presumed that the potential inside stock trader would give careful consideration to punishment prospects and, if those prospects were perceived as relatively certain and severe, the individual would opt not to commit the crime or to do so less often or less flagrantly. Conversely, potential child molesters would seem to be less capable of conforming to norms governing sexual activity with children even if they perceive the risk of punishment as very likely and severe.

William Chambliss proposed similar deterrability concepts. He defined **instrumental crime** as "instrumental to the attainment of some other goal" and **expressive crime** as one "committed because it is pleasurable in and of itself" (1967:708). The distinction is between gain and passion, with the latter being more difficult to control. The role of emotion in decision making has continued to occupy a central role among deterrence theorists. Sex crimes, for example, are typically seen as falling far on the emotional or expressive end of this continuum. To the extent that an offense is less rational, it ought to be more difficult to deter. Researchers have, in fact, found some empirical support for the notion that emotion undermines rational decision making among sexual offenders (e.g., Loewenstein et al., 1997; Bouffard, 2002). Various **visceral states** propel people to behave in particular ways, as opposed to their choosing among alternative paths. Obviously, for example, pedophiles do not so much choose to seek out children for sexual activity as they feel driven or compelled to pedophilic sexual outlets. For many pedophiles to "choose" appropriate (legal) adult sexual partners is likely as difficult as it might be for a nonpedophile to choose children as sexual partners or for heterosexuals to elect same-sex partners. The emotional constitution for these particular "choices" would be lacking. Consequently, to deter an individual from seeking sexual activity, or any other outlet that is emotionally compelling, is a challenging task to say the least.

Differential deterrent effects have often been noted by theorists regarding crimes against property as compared to those against persons. Property crimes have generally been regarded as most amenable to deterrence, largely because they seem to be more rational and instrumental.

The age-old distinction between crimes *mala prohibita* (wrong because prohibited) and *mala in se* (wrong in themselves) also has been postulated as a differentiating factor in deterrability. The rationale in suggesting that *mala prohibita* offenses are more responsive to threats of legal sanction is that conformity is fully reliant on those formal sanctions, as there are no informal sanctions (Andenaes, 1966). Parking regulations, for example, would not be observed if there were no legal sanctions, according to this argument. No other social control mechanisms would substitute. Offenses *mala in se*, to the contrary, hardly need legal sanctions to forestall widespread violations. "If the threats of legal punishment were removed, moral feelings and the fear of public judgement [*sic*] would remain as powerful crime prevention forces, at least for a limited period" (Andenaes, 1966:957). Incest, Andenaes notes, is probably not very responsive to legal control, but even in the absence of legal prohibition, few would violate this norm. Many, however, undoubtedly would park where they pleased in the absence of legal regulation.

The locale of the offense may also figure into deterrence. A crime that must be committed in a public setting is likely to be more responsive to legal threats than one that can be perpetrated in private. For example, picking flowers in a public park is probably more readily deterred than assault inside a house. Prostitution by a streetwalker is likewise probably more deterrable (or displaceable) than prostitution by a call girl.

The range and force of motivations vary immensely from one type of crime to another. Any of these differences may be related to the prospects for effective deterrence. Table 5.2 summarizes the differentiating factors that have been discussed. In the following pages, specific offenses will be used to illustrate the operating principles of deterrence.

Deterring Campus Deviance

The forms of crime and deviance that impel deterrent efforts are often weighty matters. A more zingy introduction to application of deterrence concepts can be enjoyed by examining some rather inane, albeit relatively innocuous, campus deviance before turning to the more staid topics of intimate partner violence and homicide.

Starting with professors' violations of campus parking regulations, William Chambliss (1966) took advantage of a natural experiment, a crackdown on university parking violations, to see how faculty members responded to increased sanction threats. He concluded that increased certainty and severity (bigger fines) largely deterred this form of professorial deviance. Even where it did not absolutely deter illegal parking, Chambliss found marginal deterrent effects in the form of limiting violations

TABLE 5.2 Differential Deterrent Effects by Crime	
Characteristic of Crime	Deterrability
Rational	High
Irrational	Low
Instrumental	High
Expressive	Low
Property (nonviolent)	High
Persons (violent)	Low
Mala prohibita	High
Mala in se	Low
Public	High
Private	Low

to much shorter periods of time and restricting them to locations thought be infrequently patrolled.

Moving on to more grievous (from a professorial vantage) misconduct, Charles Tittle and Allan Rowe (1973) were perhaps the first criminologists to test deterrence theory on academic cheating among college students. Through an artful, even if mischievous, experimental design they feigned student self-grading of quizzes administered at the end of prior class meetings and operationalized "cheating behavior" as the difference between professorial grading on the QT and self-assigned grades. Surprisingly (not!), there was considerable variation on this cheating index. Professors Tittle and Rowe applied various "treatments" throughout the course by making classroom announcements (moral appeals, spot-checking, snared and punished cheaters) and tracking corresponding shifts in cheating. The moral appeals did not reduce cheating, but threats of sanction did. Many investigations of deterrence and student cheating have been undertaken in the years since Tittle and Rowe's initial foray into this realm of deviance. Most have concurred that student cheating is deterrable. Daniel Nagin and Greg Pogarsky (2003) observed that their test cheaters also reported more past illegal and deviant behaviors than did noncheating students. These inquiries have also advanced many of the personal characteristics that facilitate or hinder deterrent effects. Among them has been the widespread finding that males are less responsive to sanctions than females (Gibson et al., 2008; Nagin and Pogarsky, 2003), which provides valuable clues for understanding motivations to offend.

Deterring Intimate Partner Violence

Characteristics of the far more serious crime of assaulting a spouse or partner, in contrast to the errant students and professors, suggest low deterrability. The behavior appears to be irrational, expressive, quite violent, and likely to take place in private. Moreover, such behavior historically has been culturally condoned (e.g., Walker, 1979; Brown, 1984) and arguably continues so to some degree. Given a theoretical framework generally suggesting low deterrability, the outcome of the watershed **Minneapolis Domestic Violence Experiment** (Sherman & Berk, 1984) was quite surprising.

The design of this important study provided for random assignment of three police responses to cases of misdemeanor domestic assault: (1) arrest of the offender; (2) separation of the parties; or (3) some sort of advice, including mediation. Police officers responding to domestic violence calls were instructed to intervene as dictated by the color of the form appearing on top of their report pad. Cases were then followed for six months to determine if the assaulters recidivated, as measured by additional reports to the police and periodic interviews with the victims. The lowest rate of repeat assaults (13 percent) was obtained when the offenders had been arrested, a middle level (18.2 percent) followed advice or mediation, while the highest incidence of new assaults came after separation. The researchers concluded that "swift imposition of a sanction of temporary incarceration may deter male offenders in domestic assault cases. . . . In short, criminal justice sanctions seem to matter for this offense in this setting with this group of experienced offenders" (Sherman & Berk, 1984:270). Thus, special deterrence was thought to be operating even for this theoretically unpromising type of crime.

The Minneapolis study, in combination with feminist activism and civil suits seeking equal protection of the laws for battered women, had an unprecedented impact on police policy. Arrest quickly became the policy and legal standard for misdemeanor domestic assault cases (Brown, 1990). Arrests of men who had committed misdemeanor assaults against their partners moved from a rarity in 1984 when the study was reported to the typical response well before the close of the decade and soon became commonplace. Ironically, however, the changes in law have also led to dramatic increases in arrests of women, and have created a sense of ambivalence among some feminist criminologists (Chesney-Lind, 2002).

While the impact of the Minneapolis experiment, combined with other social forces, was rapid and substantial, a series of six replication studies (Omaha, Milwaukee, Charlotte, Colorado Springs, Dade County, and Atlanta) reflected the complexity of deterrence propositions. Lively debate was stimulated because the conclusions of the evaluators of these six studies were quite divergent. While some found special deterrent effects of arrest, others did not. Still others found that arrest *increased* recidivism among marginal offenders, those who may have felt they had nothing to lose. In Milwaukee, for example, unemployed suspects were more likely to assault their partners again if arrested (Sherman et al., 1992). Similar results emerged in Omaha (Dunford, 1992) and Colorado Springs (Berk et al., 1992). A more recent study analyzing National Crime Victimization Survey (NCVS) data, however, found no evidence that offenders with less to lose would be more likely to repeat the assaults if arrested (Felson et al., 2005).

A number of criminologists have attempted to reanalyze data from this collective set of studies to determine what overall conclusions can be supported. David Sugarman and Sue Boney-McCoy (2000) undertook a meta-analysis, a complex statistical technique for assessing a group of studies, and concluded that there was a deterrent effect overall. Similarly, Christopher Maxwell and colleagues (2002) combined all individual cases (4,032) of males assaulting their partners from five of the six replicating studies. They then analyzed that larger data set, concluding that "there were consistently smaller rates of subsequent victimization and recidivism among the suspects assigned to the arrest treatment versus the nonarrest interventions" (2002:66). Regarding policy direction, they went on to state that their findings "support the continued use of arrests as a preferred law enforcement response for reducing subsequent victimization of women by their intimate partners" (2002:69). The NCVS data (Felson et al., 2005), however, contradicted the finding that arrest deters. They failed to find significant reductions in recidivism for perpetrators of domestic violence who were arrested, although they did observe that mere reporting of offenses to the police yielded some deterrent effect.

The evidence for deterring the crime of misdemeanor assaults of women in domestic settings is mixed and complex. The consensus seems to be that there is some special deterrent effect, varying by characteristics of the offender. Unfortunately, differences in deterrability by persons, even when clearly understood, complicate the task of policy development. If arrest deters some assaulters, but escalates the violence of others, police policy for responding to these crimes becomes far more difficult to formulate. Nevertheless police responses to domestic violence have been fundamentally reshaped and will not return to the era of nonarrest of perpetrators. The policy debate has shifted by and large to the prosecutorial stage.

In a further reflection of the complexity of efforts to deter intimate partner violence, questions have surfaced in recent years regarding appropriate levels of prosecutorial discretion. At issue is whether offices of prosecutors should be organized around evidence-based approaches to domestic violence cases, inferring mandatory prosecution or "no-drop" policies, or follow a victim-centered approach that allows victims considerable input in the prosecutorial decision. The debate over appropriate reactions to abusers has become so strident that Candace Kruttschnitt concluded that it "has come full circle" (2008:629). On the one hand, it is argued that prosecution deters repeat offenses (special deterrence). On the other hand, it is countered that aggressive prosecution can have the unintended consequences of injecting additional strain into the lives of victims (e.g., multiple court appearances), disempowering them (undermining future cooperation with the criminal justice system), and even increasing the risk of future assaults for some (Buzawa & Buzawa, 2008). A recent comparison revealed no difference in recidivism rates for domestic assaults in Brooklyn, which has a no-drop policy, and the Bronx, New York, where there is a victim-driven decision regarding the prosecutorial decision (Davis et al., 2008). Mixed evidence regarding deterrent effects, combined with concern about unintended consequences has led some to conclude that the victim's wishes should be followed. Jo Dixon (2008), for example, suggested that the problem of domestic violence would be better served if the courts made an effort to go beyond mere deterrent effects to address the social roots of the problem. The most recent studies have fueled the debate. Mary Finn's (2013) comparison of evidence-based and victim-centered jurisdictions in metropolitan Atlanta, Georgia led her to the conclusion that the victim-centered approach could be credited with prevention of more psychological and physical abuse. In critiquing Finn's work, however, Richard Peterson (2013) cautioned that there are far too many distinctions between the policies and practices of prosecutorial offices to effectively label them as evidence-based or victim-centered. He points out that both Atlanta jurisdictions deploy victim advocates and domestic violence investigators, suggesting that such measures as these might be more important than how prosecutorial decisions are made. He concludes (p. 479) that "all District

A lethal injection gurney used in Florida. Do executions deter crime or yield a brutalization effect? In 2006, Florida state prison workers botched a lethal injection so badly that the U.S. Supreme Court temporarily stopped executions across the country.

CREDIT: AP Photo/Fla. Dept. of Corrections, File.

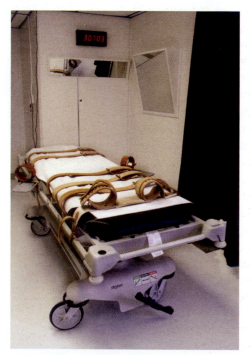

Attorneys, whether they use a victim-centered or evidence-based prosecutorial policy, should consider using a broad, victim-centered approach that empowers victims to address their needs."

Another recent direction taken in responding to domestic violence has been the sentencing of offenders to rehabilitative-oriented batterer programs. While these programs do monitor the offenders and extend accountability, the rehabilitative goal is at their core and runs counter to the notion of deterrence. However, evaluations have largely been unsupportive of their success in reducing recidivism. A recent assessment of batterer programs in the Bronx, New York, found that offenders who were required to complete the programs displayed the same rates of recidivism as those who were not assigned to them (Labriola et al., 2008). Clearly, however, the popularity of batterer rehabilitative programs in recent years reflects the shifting sands of domestic violence policy.

Deterring Homicide

Research regarding the deterrability of murder has been almost entirely limited to the capital punishment debate, neglecting the possibility that alternative sanctions could yield deterrent effects. This could be addressed by studying, for example, the potential of sentences of life-without-parole (LWOP) versus executions in deterring others from committing homicides. The U.S. Supreme court ruling in *Furman v. Georgia* (1972) led to a moratorium on executions until *Gregg v. Georgia* (1976). After the *Gregg* decision, executions increased for over three decades, but have seen modest declines in recent years because advances in DNA testing revealed that more innocent people have been put to death than was previously thought. A majority of nations no longer include the death penalty in their legal codes, and the United States is the only democratic, industrialized nation that continues capital punishment. China, Iran, and Saudi Arabia are the only countries that utilize the death penalty more than the United States (Amnesty International, 2012). The capital punishment debate is laden with matters of incapacitation, retribution, and other moral issues, but the focus here is on the question of deterrent effects.

Empirical evidence regarding the capital punishment deterrence hypothesis has been accumulating for many decades, beginning with studies by Sutherland (1925) and Sellin (1952). Most of this research has failed to find deterrent effects, with the most notable exception of the findings of economist Isaac Ehrlich (1975). (For a review of this body of research, see Bedau, 1997 and Bailey & Peterson, 1999.) Some research (e.g., see Bowers, 1988; Cochran et al., 1994; Bailey, 1998; Stack, 1998) has even unveiled evidence that executions serve to desensitize some people to the value of human life, actually leading to increases rather than declines in homicide. This finding, antithetical to a deterrent effect of capital punishment, is called the **brutalization effect**.

The new millennium has witnessed renewed debate regarding potential deterrent effects of capital punishment, though the weight of evidence continues to be stacked heavily against the proposition that executing murderers will deter others from committing murder. Because a very large portion of homicides are "crimes of passion," they do not fit well with a theory rooted in the notion of rational choices. The most recent studies suggesting a possibility of limited deterrent effects, however, seem more driven by statistical analyses than by theoretical propositions. An analysis of month-by-month executions and homicides in Texas undertaken by Kenneth Land and his co-researchers (2012) reflects much of the current debate. Their research is instructive for several reasons. First, since executions are "rare events" in most states, distributions are not stable enough across time to meet the assumptions of statistical tests, nor do they seem sufficient to coincide with the underlying logic of deterrence theory. Commenting on the Land et al. research, Fagan, Geller & Zimring (2012:587) noted that "nearly all researchers agree that if we could observe a deterrent effect, it would be in Texas." Indeed, over the course of the 14-year period (1994–2007) that Land and colleagues reviewed, some 335 persons were executed by the state of Texas; two per month on average. Second, the study found *both* a deterrent *and* a brutalization effect as well as some temporal displacement, with only a modest net deterrent effect. This is consistent with findings in other locales and time frames (e.g. Cochran and Chamlin, 2000), and is further evidence of the complexity of estimating deterrent effects. In addition, critical theoretical linkages for the Land et al. findings to support a deterrence conclusion are either missing or contradictory. Most troubling is that reductions in homicides were found for those that involved no other felonies, while those accompanied by other felonious acts showed a net brutalization effect. Reacting to this logical theoretical disconnect, Radelet (2012:576) proclaimed: "If one believes these findings, then the types of murders that result in executions (those that are especially premeditated or 'cold and calculated,' those with accompanying felonies, and those done with a motive of pecuniary gain) are not deterred, but those done in moments of passion (barroom brawls and murder during a heated domestic argument) are deterred." This finding clearly fails to line up with the premises of deterrence theory. To further exacerbate the incongruency of deterrence theory and the Land et al. research findings, not only were the hard-core offenders not deterred, but they displayed a variation of the brutalization effect. As Sonja Siennick (2012:536) commented in an editorial introduction to the Texas findings, the threat of death "actually makes hardened criminals' offenses more deadly by motivating them to eliminate witnesses." Still another chasm between deterrence theory and empirical findings is that media analyses of execution publicity, a primary vehicle for altering perceptions of the risk of execution, are minimal at best (Hjalmarsson, 2012).

Although many criminologists aspire to answering questions sufficiently to inform policy and the prescription for doing so is scientific study, death penalty research has been a manifest failure in this regard. There is widespread agreement that statistical analysis of numbers of executions and crime rates has failed to document either deterrent or brutalization effects (e.g. Charles & Durlauf, 2013; Durlauf et al., 2013; Manski & Pepper, 2013). The contrariety of studies and the empirical–theoretical dissonance belie any general conclusions. Instead, the empirical evidence regarding the death penalty deterrence–brutalization effect is more of a "muddle" (Fagan et al., 2012). Returning to the theoretical foundations of deterrence, however, suggests that appreciable deterrence effects from executions are unlikely.

EXTRALEGAL SANCTIONS: SHAME AND EMBARRASSMENT

Assessing the impact of extralegal or informal sanctions, along with those imposed by the justice system, has been considered for some time. Johannes Andenaes (1968) spoke of legal prohibitions functioning as a "moral jolt" awakening offenders or potential offenders to the realization of the extent to which society condemns a particular act. This engenders shame, guilt, or other informal socially induced controls that bring the offender back into conformity or hold the conformist in line. In this manner, criminal sanctions may serve to validate or strengthen norms. Emile Durkheim saw **normative validation** as the principal impact of punishment on crime, arguing that witnessing the official sanctioning of a norm violation reinforces a person's view of that behavior as deviant.

Several relationships between these legal and extralegal forms of sanctions are possible if, in fact, deviant behavior can be deterred. They can have deterrent effects that are independent, contingent on each other, or that interact. Consider, as an example, that Joe or Jane College was tempted to smoke marijuana for the first time, but after thinking about it, decided that it was not worth the risk. The issue is the nature of the threat that was perceived as making the behavior too hazardous. If the student was deterred by fear of arrest, fines, or a criminal record, formal sanction mechanisms were operative. If, on the other hand, the student opted not to smoke a joint out of concern that his or her parents, coach, criminology professor, or other persons perceived as disapproving would come to know about it, informal sanction threats were the deterring element. If it was reasoned that the police might detect the violation, leading to exposure of the misconduct to those significant others, this suggests that the deterrent effects of informal sanctions are contingent upon formal sanctions. Finally, the would-be deviant might have concluded that legal problems (e.g., court appearance, fines), combined with social disapproval, outweighed the satisfaction that might be derived from getting high. Thus, formal and informal mechanisms would have interacted to achieve deterrent effects.

There is considerable agreement that informal sanction threats accomplish substantial deterrent effects, perhaps exceeding formal threats. Early findings of the potency of extralegal sanctions in deterring deviance have led sociologists in particular to develop broader models of control that incorporate extralegal and particularly moral factors. Jack Gibbs (1989) has gone so far as to argue that control should serve as the central notion of sociology, so one might deduce that a sociological approach to explaining crime should be expanded to include extralegal normative violations and controls. The thin, and perhaps arbitrary, line between violation of extralegal and legal norms is quite evident in considering the full gamut of social control attributable to the informal dimension of deterrence. Only a quite small portion of norms are ever assimilated into criminal codes and subjected to legal control. Yet extralegal deterrence may play similar roles in the control of rude and obnoxious, but legal, behavior and in controlling violations of criminal codes. Thomas Scheff (1988) has noted that we rarely have to rely on formal sanctions to accomplish social control. Control is instead maintained by a subtle reward of deference extended by others, instilling the emotion of inner pride, and by the withholding of deference (punishment) that generates the emotion of shame.

Shaming has emerged as perhaps the foremost concept in criminological thinking for the informal control of crime and deviance. John Braithwaite (1989), one of the leading theorists to focus on the role of shaming in deterring crime, notes that it may consist of a wide range of social reactions to undesired behavior ranging from "a frown . . . a turning of the back, a slight shaking of the head . . . direct verbal confrontation . . . indirect confrontation by gossip . . . [or] . . . officially pronounced by a judge from the bench" (1989:57–58). Braithwaite, like many other criminologists, has concluded that the prospects of sanctions or shaming being imposed by significant others (e.g., relatives or friends) are much more effective in preventing crime than are the formal threats of the criminal justice system. Moreover, he argues, successful socialization within the family through the vehicle of shaming implants a conscience that will be on duty all of the time, in effect delivering an immediate punishment for every transgression, as opposed to the relatively remote prospects of being caught and shamed for any given violation. Shaming, in other words, builds a conscience or moral awareness which then becomes a more controlling factor than the threat of shaming per se. The key concept for crime prevention is to provide a means of reintegration of the offender into the law-abiding community. Its antithesis is stigmatization, or labeling, which is exactly what Terance Miethe and his colleagues (2000) found in their evaluation of a drug court intended to deter recidivism through shaming. Harold Grasmick and his colleagues (Grasmick & Bursik, 1990; Grasmick et al., 1993b; Grasmick & Kobayashi, 2002) have extended contemporary informal deterrence theory to draw a distinction between shame, conceptualized as internalized guilt feelings, and **embarrassment**, the loss of respect in the eyes of significant others.

Numerous researchers have found more empirical support for shame/embarrassment, informal sanctions, than for the formal threats of justice systems. For shoplifting and drunk driving, Stephen Tibbetts and Denise Herz (1996) found that perceived threats of shame were the most important factor. Similarly, both Tibbetts and Myers (1999) and the Cochran et al. (1999) studies of academic cheating among college students found shame to be the explanation most supported. In a survey of jail inmates, Alicia Sitren and Brandon Applegate (2012) found support for feeling shame, but not for formal deterrence for drunk driving, using drugs, and minor theft. Focusing on a more contextually confined form of deviance, lewd behavior at Mardi Gras, David Redmon (2002) failed to find support for deterrent effects of external sources of control in the domains of family, work, and general community. Examining workplace rule violations within a Japanese hospital, Harold Grasmick and Emiko Kobayashi (2002) found that shame (but not embarrassment) was the strongest predictor of conformity. Barak Ariel (2012), however, found that neither "moral persuasion" nor formal sanction threats enhanced tax compliance among Israeli businesses. But in yet other cultural settings, Russia and the Ukraine, Charles Tittle and his team of researchers (2011) found that both certainty and severity of social sanctions deterred both property and violent offenses, while no deterrent effects were found for formal threats of punishment. Yet they failed to replicate these findings in Greece.

Some criminologists suggest that the role of religion in social control has been underestimated or simply ignored. Recent research, however, suggests that religion may be a critical tool in implementing effective informal controls. In a recent study, for example, Andrew Spivak and his colleagues (2011) found in a sample of college students that drinking violations were more effectively deterred through the vehicles of both shame and embarrassment for those who (1) ascribed to a literal interpretation of the Bible and (2) felt that problem drinking constituted a sin. While many value debates are spurred within religious discussions, it does appear that religiosity may facilitate informal deterrence mechanisms through shame and embarrassment. Those effects may not hold up for behaviors more broadly condemned than campus drinking, however, just as the law is not necessary to deter the most abhorrent categories of crime.

A RATIONAL CHOICE PERSPECTIVE

The concept of crime deterrence emerged as the centerpiece of the classical school of criminology. Its fundamental propositions remain at the heart of the broader rational choice framework, but as the past several pages illustrate, have experienced a conceptual explosion. While anchored in the original classical deterrence concepts, the contemporary rational choice perspective is far more complex. A recent presentation of "thoughtfully reflective decision making," tested with longitudinal data and analyzed through binomial and logistic regression models, serves as an example of both the conceptual and methodological advances (Paternoster et al., 2011). Such remarkably sophisticated works addressing deterrence and rational choice could not have been envisioned just a few years ago and are beyond the imagination of the classical founders.

Rational choice expands conventional deterrence research by incorporating many more variables in the reasoning process and by considering choices, not only of potential offenders, but of victims as well. Research regarding the process of choosing crime has revealed it to be a far more complex process than was envisioned by the earlier classical deterrence theorists. Nor do the choices end with choosing or not choosing crime. The offender must decide on the type of crime (Guerette et al., 2004), where and when to commit it, elect a *modus operandi*, determine what to do afterwards, and so forth. Conceptualizing robbers as "purposeful foragers," Bernasco & Block (2009), for example, found that the presence of drug and prostitution markets attracted robbers while other community characteristics served to discourage them. Whatever the degree of rationality, choices are an ongoing process among both victims and offenders from the rational choice perspective and these choices are impacted by many different factors. The rational choice perspective has also paved the way for a number of additional practical crime prevention foci. Studies of victimization, defensible space designs, crime displacement, hot spots, and routine activities are all highly visible examples within the criminological literature that arguably fall within the rational choice framework. As with more conventional deterrence research, these topics assume that rationality underlies decisions to violate the law, but go on to include other variables. Environmental cues, for example, become important input in the offenders' larger reasoning process. The victim as well serves as a variable within the crime equation and even becomes the primary focus in many theoretical frameworks within the rational choice model. Neither rational choice, however, nor any of its specific derivatives should be considered a theory of crime in the strictest sense. Rather, they are perspectives that incorporate a choice variable within complicated crime equations.

ROUTINE ACTIVITIES: VICTIMS AND OFFENDERS

Routine activities theory (RAT), sometimes referred to as a lifestyle approach, was first introduced by Lawrence Cohen and Marcus Felson (1979) to explain escalating official crime rates during the 1970s, but has since evolved (see Felson 1994; 1998; 2002). Following the re-emergence of the rational choice perspective, RAT has garnered extensive attention. By 2004, Cohen and Felson's seminal piece had climbed to the thirteenth most cited work in the *American Sociological Review* (Jacobs, 2005), and interest in the approach has since continued to grow. As a rational choice theory, it argues that available opportunities are an important component in crime calculus. Choices in lifestyle on the part of potential victims may create or curtail crime opportunities for the motivated offender. Because of this focus on the lifestyle or routines of victims, many criminologists argue that RAT is really not a theory of crime at all, but a theory of victimization. In recent years, however, criminologists have increasingly applied the concept to offenders as well. A person's lifestyle may expose them to opportunities or experiences that increase their odds either of engaging in criminal behaviors or of being victimized.

At the heart of RAT are three premises, often referred to as the **crime triangle**. It is when these three elements are present at any point in space and time that a crime occurs. Thus the crime is seen as an "event" that requires both victim and offender roles. The lifestyle of either, or both, can help explain the occurrence or nonoccurrence of criminal events. The first component necessary for a crime is the presence of **motivated offenders**. The early de-emphasis on motivation explains why routine activities was construed as a theory of victimization rather than of offending. No attention was extended to what motivated offenders until recent years. It was assumed that there is always an ample supply and that these motivated offenders would commit crime whenever viable opportunities were encountered. Note that this assumption is in line with the reasoning of the classical school. Human nature is such (hedonistic) that people will offend whenever there is sufficient opportunity.

The presence of **suitable targets** is the second requirement of the routine activities explanation of victimization/offending. Something of value to the potential offender must be available. It could be appealing property or it could be an outlet for emotionally satisfying activity such as an expression of anger or hatred, the pursuit of excitement or fulfilling of sexual or other drives. In short, there must be something that tempts the hedonistic calculus of the would-be offender.

The crime triangle is completed by the **absence of capable guardians**. Neither persons nor other agents are present to protect the property or vulnerable persons. Capable guardians may take many different forms, depending on the context. It might mean that a person is home, a security guard is on duty, that passersby are likely, that neighbors are at home, doors are locked, cameras are installed, or dogs are present. The impact of guardians is reflected in recent research (Tillyer & Tillyer, 2014) substantiating that daytime robbery victims are less likely to be injured than nighttime victims because the robbers will expect a higher likelihood of third-party intervention from persons going about legitimate routine activities. A recent burglary pandemic in a resort community also serves as a narrative on forethought of guardianship among burglars. The community was struck with a chance storm that disrupted power. Knowing that tourists would vacate the resort homes rather than endure a night without power, the burglars took advantage of decayed guardianship (lack of human presence, deactivated camera and alarm systems) to reward themselves with flat-screen televisions (suitable targets) and other manageable goods from nearly half of the homes in the community.

Cohen and Felson (1979) contended that certain social changes had facilitated increases in suitable targets and declines in the presence of capable guardians. For example, they argued that increased levels of females in the workforce had resulted in more homes being left unoccupied (absence of capable guardians) during the day, which provided increased opportunities for burglars. Though it sounds like a dark and ironic twist of fate, recent research by Stewart J. D'Alessio and his colleagues (2012) found support for this prediction. They observed that increases in unemployment were associated with decreases in daytime residential burglaries. Just as Cohen and Felson hypothesized, it appears that more time at home, sadly as a function of unemployment, insulates the home from burglary by providing capable guardianship during the daytime hours most appealing to burglars. At the same time, Cohen and Felson maintained that technological developments resulted in more portable, but valuable, items that could be targeted by thieves in homes, automobiles, or with persons. This tendency has exploded in more recent years with the spread of items such as cellular telephones, flat-screen televisions, and laptop computers.

Routine Activities of Victims

The study of victims of crime, a subfield of criminology called **victimology**, received quite a boost in interest as a consequence of the popularity of RAT. For many years the theory focused almost exclusively on how the routines or lifestyles of persons related to their risk of becoming victims of crime. Fundamentally, the theory proposes that victimization risk is a function of how people pattern their behavior. If one stays home less often, for example, the reduction in capable guardianship of their home translates to an increased risk of crime being committed against their home property. By the same token, as one more frequently ventures away from home, the risk of victimization against their person expands due to the greater likelihood of crossing paths with a motivated offender. So as predicted by RAT, Min Xie and her colleagues (2012) found that increases in the women's participation in the labor market were associated with their more frequently being victims of violent crime perpetrated by both strangers and nonintimate acquaintances, though simultaneously associated with decreases in violent victimization by intimate acquaintances. Similarly, a well-recognized fact among criminologists (but seen in reverse by widespread lay myth) is that the elderly are far less frequently victims of crime than are the more youthful because they place themselves less at risk. They less often go out late at night, go out by themselves or go to bars. Going to bars, as an example, clearly places one at higher risk of victimization. To take the point further, as did Elizabeth Mustaine and Richard Tewksbury (1998), who people go to bars with, how long they stay, how drunk they get, and what time they leave all factor into the quality of guardianship. In interviews with 16,000 adults across the United States, Richard Felson and Keri Burchfield (2004) found that young males were especially at risk of being physically assaulted when they were out drinking. They observed heightened risks of sexual assault for both males and females.

Similarly, Bonnie Fisher and her colleagues (1998:702) found "that students who partied on campus several nights per week and were more likely to take recreational drugs were more likely to be a victim of on-campus violent crime." But far less than a "night on the town" can place one at a degree of risk. Mustaine and Tewksbury's (1998) research, for example, found that just frequently eating out, leaving home to study, and belonging to more clubs and organizations significantly increased risk of both minor (less than $50) and major (more than $50) theft victimizations. Similarly, Verna Henson and William Stone (1999) found that most crimes on a college campus were thefts resulting from dormitory rooms being left unlocked. Because victimization is a function of lifestyle, those who are victims once are more likely to be targeted by offenders again.

The most rapidly growing form of victimization in recent years has been in the virtual realm. Bradford Reyns (2013), for example, found that persons incorporating online banking and shopping, emailing/text messaging or downloading media in their routines increased their risk of identity theft by 30–50 percent for each behavioral pattern. Similarly, Billy Henson and his associates (2011) found that 42 percent of their sample of college student social network users had been victims of unwanted contact or sexual advances, harassment, or threats. While most did not reveal their physical addresses online, an array of information was made available that did place them at risk of being tracked and stalked. They found that females were victimized at nearly twice the rate of males. Risk of victimization increased along with the number of social sites used and with frequency of updating their sites. Not surprisingly, allowing strangers to visit their sites increased victimization 2.6-fold. Surprisingly, and unfortunately, victimization was not reduced by deploying the privacy features of social networks.

In a study of high school seniors and college freshmen, Catherine Marcum and her colleagues (2010) applied a routine activities framework to examine differences in victimization by sex. They drew a number of analogies to more traditional forms of victimization that have been examined through the lens of routine activities. For example, they noted that just as spending time away from home is a risk factor, "one way to leave the protection of home and become exposed to potential victimization is to go onto the Internet" (2010: 417). They found support for routine activities hypotheses in general, as well as differences across gender, just as has been the case with an array of conventional offenses. They found especially high victimization for males and females in high school and college, particularly for email, chat rooms, and instant messaging. In routine activities jargon, this was interpreted as exposure to more motivated offenders. Providing personal information online was further associated with being targeted, the virtual version of target suitability. Capable guardianship, however, was not accomplished through deploying protective software. Again, that is, using protective software failed to reduce victimization. For the high school seniors, however, having someone present in the room as they undertook online activities did significantly reduce victimization. This suggests that parents, teachers, and others can effectively contribute to capable guardianship to insulate highschoolers from online victimization.

Given that much of RAT research has focused on the role of the victim and college campuses, relevant questions you might ask yourself from this perspective would scrutinize your habits. Do you conduct yourself in such a way as to minimize risk of victimization? Or do you do things that place you at risk of victimization? Do you spend a lot of time online? Do you post revealing information or "meet" people online? If so, you are risking exposure to more motivated offenders and rendering yourself a more suitable target. Do you lock your doors when you leave home? Do you ever leave your keys in your car or car doors unlocked? Taking steps to minimize risk of your property being stolen by attending to such mechanical details is referred to as **target hardening**. This can be extended to your personal safety. Do you go out late? Do you frequent bars? Do you drink often or large amounts on some occasions? Do you know the persons with whom you socialize or do you sometimes find yourself out with people you really do not know? Tragic murders of promising young women, such as those of criminal justice student Imette St. Guillen in New York and high-school graduate Natalie Holloway, celebrating in Aruba, highlight the ideological debate about the victim role in crime. When some commentators alluded to their late-night drinking with strangers, others cried foul, saying that raising these points smacked of "blaming the victim." From a criminological routine activities perspective, while the offenders bear no less responsibility for their horrendous crimes, the victims' late night drinking without the presence of friends who might provide capable guardianship were part of the equation.

> Some scholars have avoided the study of the victim's role in violence because they anticipate an accusation that they are 'blaming the victim' (Felson & Burchfield, 2004:855).

Others tread very lightly, almost apologetically, for exploring the victim's role in the crime. In her examination of sexual assaults Sherley, for example, cautions:

> Certainly, examining the victim as an attractive target should in no way imply that victims somehow contribute to their own victimization (2005:99).

She later reiterates:

> Again, it is not being suggested that sexual assault victims in any way contribute to their own victimization (2005:104).

Yet lifestyle theories seem inevitably to lead to an ideological deadlock, at least for those who are ideologically inflexible. To gain causal insight into criminal events, informed by the role of the victim, it is essential that the analyst separate causation from blame or moral accountability. While blame and accountability must remain squarely assigned to the offender, the contribution of lifestyle theories is that victim lifestyle is part of the equation. Whether a victim's lifestyle or routines causally contribute to burglary by frequent vacationing, leaving their home vulnerable, or to crimes against the person by frequenting pubs, the legal and moral responsibility of the offender is unaltered. Yet an unavoidable Catch-22 remains. Deviant or just more active lifestyles bear more risk of victimization than do conforming or less active ones. This is why the elderly are the least victimized, and young adults the most victimized, groups in our society. Recognizing these facts regarding the distribution of victimization is not necessarily "blaming the victim," and certainly removes no responsibility (legally or morally) from the offender. At some point, however, degrees of blame or personal responsibility can be inferred by the victim's actions, triggering an ideological debate about "blaming the victim." For example, the victim's behavior may reflect gaps in judgment, low self-control, risk-taking, or other flawed characteristics. In that vein, it can be argued that young men are at high risk of physical assault when drinking because "intoxicated men are more provocative" (Felson & Burchfield, 2004:848). Or others may conclude that with the majority of prostitutes reporting physical assaults (e.g., Dalla, 2002), such work is too risky. As criminologists, however, our work "should be based on 'causal analysis' and should leave 'blame analysis' to the criminal justice system" (Felson & Burchfield, 2004:856). Likewise, while ideological weighting of victim behaviors may be inevitable, it is not an appropriate task for the criminologist in seeking to explain criminal events.

Another telling, but sensitive issue, is the widespread observation that victims, like offenders, often repeat the experience. This seems to defy the old saying, "once bitten twice shy," something that Margit Averdijk (2011) recently analyzed with longitudinal data. While it seems logical to predict that victims suffering loss or harm would take extensive steps to prevent a repeat experience, limited changes were observed in post-victimization routine activities. While violent victimizations were followed with some declines in shopping time and time away from home, less serious transgressions were not followed with much lifestyle change. This makes sense from the perspective of cost-benefit analysis. Since we take pride in our freedom and loss of freedom may be seen as of the "costs" of victimization, many victims will refuse to succumb to the experience by limiting their routines. Others may be unable to do so due to the necessity of work, travel, and other obligations. If one lives in a "risky" neighborhood, he or she may not be able to afford relocation, and so forth. In other words, there may be structural forces that undermine many crime prevention remedies consistent with routine activities theory.

Routine Activities of Offenders

Of late, criminologists have examined the routines of offenders with the idea that this may help to explain patterns of offending, just as lifestyle activities of potential victims might identify victimization risk levels. In fact, there is a strong correlation between being a victim and a perpetrator of crime. That is, deviant lifestyles are predictive of both victimization and offending. Elizabeth Mustaine and Richard Tewksbury (1999) examined their sample of college students to determine the role of lifestyle or routine activities in explaining drunk driving. Note that this shift in focus, from victim to offender, suggests skepticism regarding the first premise of routine activities theory—the assumption that there are ample motivated offenders, only needing to come in contact with a suitable target in the absence of capable guardianship. Mustaine and Tewksbury's approach suggests that motivated offenders are not just randomly distributed, but rather that they too are products of particular situations that are created by lifestyle choices and other factors influencing people's routines. Demographic characteristics account for some of the differences in patterns of drinking and driving, especially gender, with males reporting higher rates. More directly relevant to the motivation to offend, however, are lifestyle choices. Both males and females were more likely to drive drunk when they drank away from home, were more tolerant of other illegal behavior, drank more frequently, and engaged in other forms of illegal behavior.

A study of property and violent offenses by Icelandic adolescents also applied a routine activities framework, integrating it with social control and learning theories (see Chapter 8). The authors of the study, Jon Gunnar Bernburg and Thorolfur Thorlindsson (2001), urged that the motivation of offenders not be taken for granted, but that criminologists seek to determine if motivation is shaped by the social context in which the offender is located. They specifically examined factors like having delinquent friends (learning theory) and lack of attachment with authority figures such as parents and teachers (control theory) as rendering youths who encounter opportunities for delinquency more likely to be motivated to pursue them. In other words, they found that delinquency was not a result of opportunities alone. It was more a result of certain learning experiences and inadequate social bonding, combined with routine activities that present opportunities for misconduct. This suggests two important things about routine activities; first, that it may shed light on offending as well as victimization, and second, that routine activities can be enhanced by combining or integrating it with other perspectives.

A similar approach was taken by Martin Schwartz and his colleagues (2001) in analyzing Canadian data on male sexual victimization of females among college and university students. Somewhat differently, however, they construed peer attitudes not as a learning component to be combined with routine activities, but rather as an "index of motivation." In this vein, they concluded that "motivated offenders exist because they have developed certain attitudes and behaviors as a result of encouragement and support by other males" (2001:646). They also found that offenders were more likely to be heavy drinkers. Reviewing the victimization patterns among women, they found that those who drank more, used recreational drugs more frequently, and those who partook of these activities with dating partners, had increased risk of victimization. In short, males who had been encouraged by peers to victimize females (emotionally or physically), who drank more, and who drank with dating partners were more likely to be motivated offenders, and to view females who were drinking and/or consuming drugs in the course of dating as suitable targets for sexual victimization.

Hate crimes have also been analyzed from a routine activities framework. The practice of "claping" Amish minorities examined by Bryan Byers and Benjamin Crider (2002) serves as an example. Claping is a term for the perpetration of predatory crimes against the Amish by non-Amish persons, usually adolescents, rooted in anti-Amish biases. The term is the counterpart to "clape," a derogatory noun of unknown origin used in reference to Amish persons by the offenders. Typical illustrations of claping offered by Byers and Crider are "dusting," speeding past Amish buggies to irritate the occupants with a cloud of dust; "flouring," the unleashing of a bag of flour on Amish buggies while driving past; and vandalism directed at Amish property such as blowing up mailboxes and turning over outhouses.

Utilizing a methodology of interviewing offenders in a U.S. community with an appreciable Amish population, the authors argued that claping fit all three elements of routine activities theory. Motivation was particularly reflected in anti-Amish bias, a view that they were different and that their conduct was sometimes perceived by the offenders as provocative. Claping was also spontaneously motivated as an exciting activity to relieve boredom. Access to an automobile was essential, and in the context of adolescents driving around seeking fun, the pattern of offending could be interpreted as a youthful bonding experience to relieve boredom and act upon anti-Amish biases. Thus motivation appears not to be just random, but a product of other social forces.

The Amish were depicted as suitable targets because they were perceived by offenders as "easy" targets, as they would do little to protect themselves and were readily identifiable because of their distinct appearance and practices. The lack of capable guardianship was explained by the low likelihood of the Amish reporting victimization and the perceived social acceptance of claping. Because claping seemed widely viewed as mischievousness rather than crime, the expectation was that social sanctions were unlikely.

Some lifestyle choices present conceptual problems for routine activities theory. Richard Spano and his fellow researchers (2008) recently pointed this out in regard to gang membership, carrying guns, and employment. While the dominant view is that gang membership is part of a deviant identity that increases risk of victimization (and offending), some have argued that it can also provide capable guardianship. Some gang members identify a need for protection as a key motivation in electing to join. Similarly, as Spano et al. (2008) note, carrying a gun is viewed by most criminologists as part of a risky deviant lifestyle. Yet it can be construed as enhancing guardianship. Conversely, conventional wisdom long held that employment insulated youths from a variety of troubles, but recent research has belied this assumption. Regarding victimization, routines such as transportation and late hours can place one at more risk and the earnings may render them a more suitable target. Data for impoverished urban minority youths collected by Spano et al. (2008) reinforced the complex nature of how these three domains of routine activity relate to risk of victimization.

HOW RATIONAL IS CHOICE?

Economists analyze economic behavior from a rational choice perspective. They presume, whether one is buying toothpaste or a new car, that each individual will make the decision that is most favorable to them. In classical terms, the consumer will maximize utility. It is assumed that the purchase decision will be rational and very predictable. That is, two different persons will typically make the same choice. If the same brand and size of toothpaste is available at two stores, and the same car at two dealerships, the two businesses with the lowest prices will make the sales. Gary Becker (1968) was one of the first economists to apply this model to the study of crime, but he has been followed by many others. Moreover, many criminologists have accepted the economic model. But can we safely assume that potential offenders (or consumers, for that matter) are rational beings who will make like decisions? On reflection, this seems to be a rather bold assumption.

In a highly regarded book on the rational choice perspective, Kenneth Tunnell (1992) points out that cognitive psychologists have adopted a different model of human decision making. People are seen as less than fully rational. Oftentimes they do not make decisions that would appear to be in their own best interest for a variety of reasons. First, people do not always have all of the information they need to make informed decisions, and even if they do, may not have the capacity to optimally process that information. Their analytical abilities may be impaired by alcohol or other drugs, by cognitive deficiencies, or negative learning experiences. Moreover, they may assess things quite differently than some of us, given their life experiences. As Alfred Blumstein (1998:134) noted, "This problem of differential deterrability is particularly acute for crimes involving individuals who see no particular options in the legitimate economy, for whom life in the street is very risky anyway, and who have not been effectively socialized against committing crime. . . . Even though prison may not be a very attractive option, its disutility is likely to be far less than it is to middle-class populations." The personalities, experiences, and options that we all bring to bear on a given choice in life are so diverse that it is quite naive to assume that we will all assess the situation similarly and arrive at similar choices.

How much variation is there in the availability of choices or options from one person to the next? If one person has far fewer options than the next, are they making choices in the same sense? As one of the authors frequently asks of students, "how many of you chose to attend this university?" Almost all will assert that they did, but what does it say that most are from the immediate region, that most work while going to school and that many are first generation college students? When asked what opportunities to attend more prestigious schools were declined within that decision-making process, most have the same answer: none. Upon closely examining the route to the particular university it turns out that, for many, there were not a lot of decisions, but rather a path of many forces that propelled them to that particular place at that point in time. Yet that is not to say there were no choices made along the way and, in the final analysis, a decision was made to complete the admission application and to come to campus. The question here may be, can we best understand their enrollment by looking at where they are from, what kind of family influences they experienced in their formative years, and their financial standing? Or can we best explain their presence at the university in terms of those final rational decisions to complete an application and drive to the campus? Virtually every human being makes some rational choices, but the question would seem to be what is the relative weight of those choices and the many factors that shape the context of decision making?

There is a distinction between rationally choosing and just doing something. It is a distortion of the concept of choice to say that a duck chooses to go to water and swim. It may also be a stretch to explain, say, Mary Kay Letourneau's conviction for the rape of a 13-year-old boy as a rational choice, or to construe the conduct of many offenders as the outcome of thoughtful deliberation. More insight into these and many crimes can be gained by examining the forces that limit choices, render the offender less able to analyze situations than would a more conforming citizen, and why society chooses to react as it does to particular behaviors. It has been argued that the shortcoming of the rational choice perspective has been its failure to reconcile rationality with the observation that criminals often display impulsiveness, moral ambiguity, and expressive motivations to offend (de Haan & Vos, 2003). In short, much criminal behavior, while rational steps may be taken, is far more reflective of emotional drives that seem to fly in the face of what many people would consider rational and deliberate choices.

Box 5.1 summarizes media reports of what most of us might cynically dismiss as the acts of "stupid criminals." Indeed, many of these crime news

BOX 5.1 RATIONAL CRIMES OR STUPID CRIMES?

- A 24-year-old city police officer in Tennessee who was assigned to teach in the Drug Abuse Resistance Education (DARE) program pleaded guilty to contributing to the delinquency of a minor. This was based on an incident in which the car he was riding in was stopped by a state trooper at 2:30 A.M. on Main Street of a nearby small town. He was a passenger in the car with two 17-year-olds, one of whom was consuming beer that he had purchased.

- A Seattle, Washington, woman was arrested for dancing topless for two hours on top of an electrical tower along a busy commuting thoroughfare during the morning rush hour. She was drinking vodka as she danced, spitting it and lighting it on fire. It was later reported that she was formerly a male, but was undergoing sex change surgery. Indecent exposure and trespassing charges were filed.

- An Ohio man was arrested on drug trafficking charges after depositing $300,000 cash, contained in grocery bags, in a bank account, and declaring himself unemployed on routine depository papers.

- A Toronto, Canada, man, on trial for murder, elected to serve as his own attorney. He had told a prison guard, "You guys are always picking on me because I killed some white bitch."

- Murder charges were filed against an ex-policeman in Detroit in the 1999 slaying of his wife and son. In 1975 he had been found not guilty by reason of insanity in the deaths of his first wife and their two children.

- A Tennessee community college astronomy teacher was convicted of stealing an antique telescope lens from a Cincinnati observatory. He had donated it to the college where he was employed.

- One of four armed robbers was killed and six customers wounded in a foiled attempt to rob a bar filled with off-duty policemen. They were gathered to hear a performance of the "Pigs in a Blanket" band, comprised of police officers.

- A Bristol, Tennessee, man arrived an hour and a half late at his hearing on auto theft and drug charges. He was arrested because he drove to the hearing in a stolen car.

- A 32-year-old Newport, Tennessee, man was arrested on the courthouse lawn right after kissing his 17-year-old bride to seal their wedding vows. A passing deputy recognized the groom as an individual with an outstanding theft warrant. He approached the newlyweds, handcuffed the groom and escorted him in to the jail. The official conducting the wedding observed that the bride was left "standing at the altar" and was "really upset." The Circuit Judge released him on bond the following day so that the couple could go on their honeymoon.

- The Circuit Judge alluded to in the above scenario was charged a few months later with public intoxication and destruction of county property. Enraged over the County Commission's investigation of a friend's trash disposal company, the judge ransacked the office of the County Executive while he and others stood by in dismay. Police officers finally escorted the judge out the back door. Friends noted that he had been under a lot of stress, as his mother had recently died and his home had burnt. He was hospitalized for depression after the incident.

- A 36-year-old Tennessee man pleaded guilty to a charge of voluntary manslaughter. The charge arose from an incident in which he and his wife were drinking with another man and the defendant fell asleep. When he awoke and found his wife having sex with the other man, he shot him four times.

- A Florida man shot and killed his wife's lover in a Starbucks coffee shop, then fatally shot himself. His wife had been planning to leave him for the victim.

- A Tennessee sheriff was charged with burglarizing the home of, and assaulting the son of, his chief deputy. The event occurred during a night that the sheriff's niece was spending in the home of the alleged victim, who claimed that the sheriff was in uniform at the time. The 19-year-old niece's father was charged, along with the sheriff.

releases are of the caliber to earn mention in outlets such as the Charlotte-based "John-Boy and Billy" radio show's "Dumb Crook News," *The Stupid Crook Book* (Gregory, 2002), or Butler and Ray's (2000) *The World's Dumbest Criminals.* They are, however, real and in some cases very tragic. Clearly, each of these crimes were less than fully rational, or at least rewards and sanctions were weighted quite differently than they would be by more law-abiding citizens. If indeed, these are stupid crimes, can we still assume, as do deterrence and rational choice theorists, that crimes are a product of rational (or at least bounded rational) choice?

Note that several threads of commonality run through these crime scenarios. Most involved emotionally charged issues. Some involved alcohol impairment. Clearly, most of the offenders displayed a distorted focus on potential benefits of their crime (whether financial or emotional satisfaction) to the neglect of likely costs in any calculations they made. In some cases it is difficult to imagine that even minimal calculation took place. It would appear that like the duck going to water, they just did it. Would a highly (or even minimally) rational actor have made choices such as those reflected in Box 5.1? Alas, a plethora of episodes are potential material for stupid/dumb criminal shows and books. The next three chapters offer some insight regarding these rather widespread, but relatively unthinking offenders.

SUMMARY

In seeking to explain crime, one of the most debated issues is the role of choice and the issue of how rational any decision making is on the part of offenders. The concept of deterrence, with its origins in the classical school of criminology, assumed a high degree of rationality. It was intended to be a general theory of crime: that is, one that explains all types of crime and offenders. Contemporary deterrence theory and the broader rational choice framework envision choice in somewhat more relative terms, a bounded rationality, that recognizes variations in levels of choice and rationality. Criminology is a relatively new field of inquiry. Explanations of crime as a natural phenomenon began only with the classical school in the eighteenth century. Before that, crime was viewed as a supernatural occurrence. Response to it often was irrational. Church and state joined forces to produce a period of gruesome and barbaric responses to crime and deviance. Throughout Europe, people were tortured and executed for all manner of offenses, real and imagined. It was this epoch of atrocities that provided the backdrop for the beginning of criminology: a reform movement referred to as the classical school of criminology. Classical criminology emerged in the latter part of the eighteenth century as part of the Enlightenment. Led by Cesare Beccaria and Jeremy Bentham, it stressed a fair and rational response to crime, asserting that human beings could thereby be deterred from criminal behavior. Beccaria and Bentham asserted that this could be accomplished through assuring relative certainty, celerity, and severity of punishment. Most criminologists emphasize the contributions of the classical school of criminology to humanitarian reform of the administration of justice more than to theoretical ideas. The school's work led to substantial mitigation of the harshness of punishment and established most of the rights and protections of the accused now regarded as fundamental to Western justice. It also provided the theoretical premises of Western legal codes and the Peelian principles of policing that have dominated both England and America for more than 150 years. Deterrence theory was neglected in the United States in favor of sociological positivism for nearly 100 years, although it had provided the theoretical foundation for the practice of criminal justice for more than two centuries. The last one-third of the twentieth century witnessed a re-examination of the deterrence doctrine and initiation of research to test it. The long delay in subjecting the perspective to scientific scrutiny can be attributed to its ideological ingredients. The notion of deterrence pits those sympathetic to punitive responses to crime against others with a distaste for punishment. An **anti-rehabilitation movement**, that is, the decline of faith in rehabilitation that characterized the 1970s, along with a generally more conservative political climate, did however, increase receptivity to research regarding deterrence.

Deterrence doctrine identifies certainty, severity, and celerity of punishment as key elements in a rational decision-making process aimed at deciding between criminal and noncriminal paths of conduct. With renewed conceptual attention, this central thesis has been expanded to incorporate a range of further contingencies for deterrent effects. One view that has been increasingly emphasized is the importance of distinguishing perceptions from objective characteristics of punishment, with more importance attributed to the former as an element in the deterrence of crime. Another important differentiation is between general and specific deterrence, the former consisting of punishment designed to influence decisions of persons other than the punished individual, while the latter is intended to modify the behavior of that person. Third, recognition of degrees of deterrence is now deemed possible. Absolute deterrence, the complete avoidance of criminal behavior due to fear of punishment, is one extreme, while restrictive or marginal deterrence recognizes modifications of criminal conduct short of abstention. Finally, the role of informal sanctions and other extralegal variables has been given particular attention and now is being widely credited as more important to potential deterrent processes than legal factors. This contemporary perspective on deterrence is actually part of a broader rational choice framework for understanding crime. While threats of punishment sometimes deter criminal behavior, such effects can vary according to both types of crimes and persons. In fact, individual deterrability is now conceptualized as falling along a continuum. While some of us are good candidates for sanctions because we are potentially deterrable, others are incorrigible (undeterrable) while still more are acute conformists who never require threats of sanctions to ensure conformity. The more deterrable crimes probably include acts that are more rational, instrumental (designed to meet goals), nonviolent, *mala prohibita* in nature, and those that must be committed in public. Examples of previously studied potentially deterrable offenses reviewed in this chapter include professors violating parking regulations and cheating college students. Woman battering, on the other hand, has generated mixed evidence, but largely favorable toward the deterrence doctrine. Research examining the effects of capital punishment has failed to document general deterrent effects. Persons thought more deterrable include those with low commitment to crime as a way of life, amateurs, and those that see themselves as having more to lose, such as their employability. A number of personality and demographic factors also have been suggested as relevant to deterrence.

Rational choice theory includes more than just deterrence. Perspectives rooted in rational choice, however, are not theories in the conventional sense of explaining crime. Routine activities or lifestyle theory, for example, is widely viewed as an analytical framework for understanding victimization patterns. It conceptualizes victimization as the result of convergence of motivated offenders, attractive targets, and a lack of capable guardians at some point in space and time. Recent research, however, has also examined the effect of lifestyle routines in terms of prospects for offending. Whether crime is largely a product of choices and, if so, how those choices are made is a major topic of debate within criminology. Many criminal events appear not to be very rational choices at all, or at least reflect patterns of decision making quite different from those more typically seen among law-abiding citizens. Positivistic theories reviewed in the following three chapters are quite at odds with the rational choice approach.

KEY TERMS AND CONCEPTS

Absence of Capable Guardians	Free Will
Absolute Deterrence	General Deterrence
Acute Conformists	Hedonistic
Anti-Rehabilitation Movement	Holy Inquisition
Backlash Effects	Incorrigible
Base Rate Fallacy	Instrumental Crime
Blood Feuding	London Metropolitan Police Act of 1829
Bounded Rationality	Mala in Se
Brutalization Effect	Mala Prohibita
Certainty, Severity, and Celerity	Marginal (Restrictive) Deterrence
Classical Criminology	Minneapolis Domestic Violence Experiment
Crime Displacement	
Crime Triangle	Motivated Offenders
Criminogenic	Normative Validation
Deterrence Theory	Objective Punishment Properties
Embarrassment	Panopticon
The Enlightenment	Perceptions of Punishment
Expressive Crime	Positive Criminology

Preclassical Criminology

Quartering

Rational Choice

Risk Sensitivity

Routine Activities Theory (RAT)

Shaming

Specific Deterrence

Suitable Targets

Target Hardening

Tiger Prevention Fallacy

Tipping Level

Utilitarianism

Victimology

Visceral States

Warden's Survey

KEY CRIMINOLOGISTS

Cesare Beccaria

Jeremy Bentham

Lawrence Cohen

Marcus Felson

Robert Martinson

Raymond Paternoster

Sir Robert Peel

Alex Piquero

Greg Pogarsky

Sir Samuel Romilly

Charles Tittle

CASES

Furman v. Georgia, 428 U.S. 238 (1972)

Gregg v. Georgia, 428 U.S. 153 (1976)

DISCUSSION QUESTIONS

1. Explain the relevance of the Holy Inquisition to preclassical understanding of crime.

2. Describe the three principles of punishment as delineated by Cesare Beccaria.

3. How did the Peelian reform movement introduce principles of classical criminology into practice? How do these ideas continue to impact policing?

4. Distinguish general from specific deterrence, and provide examples of each.

5. What types of crime are most and least deterrable? Why?

6. What crimes have you been deterred from committing? What crimes have you not been deterred from committing?

7. Has fear of shame or embarrassment ever prevented you from misbehaving?

8. What is the crime triangle? Describe examples of each part.

9. Is it more accurate to stereotype criminal behavior as "stupid" or as "smart"? What are the implications of your answer for deterrence theory?

REFERENCES

Amnesty International. (2012). *Facts and figures on the death penalty.* http://www.amnesty.org/en/news/death-penalty-2011-alarming-levels-executions-few-countries-kill-2012–03–27.

Andenaes, J. (1952). General prevention—illusion or reality? *Journal of Criminal Law, Criminology, and Police Science, 43*, 176–98.

Andenaes, J. (1966). The general preventive effects of punishment. *University of Pennsylvania Law Review, 114*, 949–83.

Andenaes, J. (1968). Does punishment deter crime? *Criminal Law Quarterly, 11*, 76–93.

Anderson, L.S., Chiricos, T.G., & Waldo, G.P. (1977). Formal and informal sanctions: A comparison of deterrent effects. *Social Problems, 25*, 105–15.

Apel, R. (2012). Sanctions, perceptions, and crime: Implications for criminal deterrence. *Journal of Quantitative Criminology, 29*, 67–101.

Ariel, B. (2012). Deterrence and moral persuasion effect on corporate tax compliance: Findings from a randomized controlled trial. *Criminology, 50*, 27–70.

Averdijk, M. (2011). Reciprocal effects of victimization and routine activities. *Journal of Quantitative Criminology, 27*, 125–49.

Bailey, W.C. (1966). Correctional outcome: An evaluation of 100 reports. *Journal of Criminal Law, Criminology, and Police Science, 57*, 153–60.

Bailey, W.C. (1998). Deterrence, brutalization and the death penalty: Another examination of Oklahoma's return to capital punishment. *Criminology, 36*, 711–33.

Bailey, W.C. & Peterson, R.D. (1999). Capital punishment, homicide, and deterrence: An assessment of the evidence. In M.D. Smith, & M.A. Zahn (Eds.), *Studying and preventing homicide*. Thousand Oaks, CA: Sage.

Barnes, H.E. & Teeters, N.K. (1951). *New horizons in criminology* (2nd ed.). New York, NY: Prentice Hall.

Beccaria, C. (1764/1963). *On crimes and punishments.* (H. Paolucci, Trans.) Indianapolis, IN: Bobbs-Merrill.

Becker, G. (1968). Crime and punishment: An economic approach. *Journal of Political Economy, 76*, 493–517.

Bedau, H.A. (1997). *The death penalty in America: Current controversies*. New York, NY: Oxford University Press.

Bentham, J. (1789/1973). *Political thought.* New York, NY: Barnes and Noble.

Berk, R.A., Campbell, A., Klap, R., & Western, B. (1992). A Bayesian analysis of the Colorado Springs Spouse Abuse Experiment. *Journal of Criminal Law and Criminology, 83*, 170–200.

Bernasco, W. & Block, R. (2009). Where offenders choose to attack: A discrete choice model of robberies in Chicago. *Criminology, 47*, 93–130.

Bernburg, J.G. & Thorlindsson, T. (2001). Routine activities in social context: A closer look at the role of opportunity in deviant behavior. *Justice Quarterly, 18*, 543–67.

Bien, D.D. (1960). *The Calas affair.* Princeton, NJ: Princeton University Press.

Bishop, D.M. (1984). Legal and extralegal barriers to delinquency: A panel analysis. *Criminology, 22*, 403–19.

Blackwell, B.S., Grasmick, H.G., & Cochran, J.K. (1994). Racial differences in perceived sanction threat: Static and dynamic hypotheses. *Journal of Research in Crime and Delinquency, 31*, 210–24.

Blumstein, A. (1998). U.S. criminal justice conundrum: Rising prison populations and stable crime rates. *Crime & Delinquency, 44*, 127–35.

Bouffard, J. A. (2002). The influence of emotion on rational decision making in sexual aggression. *Journal of Criminal Justice, 30*, 121–34.

Bowers, W. J. (1988). The effect of executions is brutalization, not deterrence. In K. C. Haas, & J. A. Inciardi (Eds.), *Capital punishment: Legal and social science approaches.* Newbury Park, CA: Sage Publications.

Braithwaite, J. (1989). *Crime, shame and reintegration.* Cambridge, UK: Cambridge University Press.

Brown, D. W. (1978). Arrest rates and crime rates: When does a tipping effect occur? *Social Forces, 57*, 671–81.

Brown, S. E. (1981). Deterrence and the tipping effect. *Southern Journal of Criminal Justice, 6*, 7–15.

Brown, S. E. (1984). Police responses to wife beating: Neglect of a crime of violence. *Journal of Criminal Justice, 12*, 277–88.

Brown, S. E. (1990). Police responses to wife beating: Five years later. *Journal of Criminal Justice, 18*, 459–62.

Butler, D. & Ray, A. (2000). *The world's dumbest criminals.* Nashville, TN: Rutledge Hill Press.

Buzawa, E. S. & Buzawa, A. D. (2008). Courting domestic violence victims: A tale of two cities. *Criminology & Public Policy, 7*, 671–85.

Byers, B. D. & Crider, B. W. (2002). Hate crimes against the Amish: A qualitative analysis of bias motivation using routine activities theory. *Deviant Behavior, 23*, 115–48.

Carmichael, S., Langton, L., Pendell, G., Reitzel, J. D., & Piquero, A. R. (2005). Do the experiential and deterrent effect operate differently across gender? *Journal of Criminal Justice, 33*, 267–76.

Chambliss, W. J. (1966). The deterrent influence of punishment. *Crime & Delinquency, 12*, 70–75.

Chambliss, W. J. (1967). Types of deviance and the effectiveness of legal sanctions. *Wisconsin Law Review, 1967*, 703–19.

Charles, K. K. & Durlauf, S. N., (2013). Pitfalls in the use of time series methods to study deterrence and capital punishment. *Journal of Quantitative Criminology, 29*, 45–66.

Chesney-Lind, M. (2002). Criminalizing victimization: The unintended consequences of pro-arrest policies for girls and women. *Criminology & Public Policy, 1*, 81–90.

Cochran, J. K. & Chamlin, M. B. (2000). Deterrence and brutalization: The dual effects of executions. *Justice Quarterly, 17*, 685–706.

Cochran, J. K., Chamlin, M. B., & Mark, S. (1994). Deterrence or brutalization? An impact assessment of Oklahoma's return to capital punishment. *Criminology, 32*, 107–34.

Cochran, J. K., Chamlin, M. B., Wood, P. B., & Sellers, C. S. (1999). Shame, embarrassment, and formal sanction threats: Extending the deterrence/rational choice model to academic dishonesty. *Sociological Inquiry, 69*, 91–105.

Cohen, A. K. & Felson, M. (1979). Social change and crime rates: A routine activities approach. *American Sociological Review, 44*, 214–41.

Copes, H. & Vieraitis, L. M. (2009). Bounded rationality of identity thieves: Using offender-based research to inform policy. *Criminology and Public Policy, 8*, 237–62.

Critchley, T. A. (1972). *A history of police in England and Wales.* Montclair, NJ: Patterson Smith.

D'Alessio, S. J., Eitle, D., & Stolzenberg, L. (2012). Unemployment, guardianship and week-day residential burglary. *Justice Quarterly, 29*, 919–32.

Dalla, R. L. (2002). Night moves: A qualitative investigation of street-level sex work. *Psychology of Women Quarterly, 26*, 63–74.

Davis, R. C., O'Sullivan, C. S., Farole, D. J., & Rempel, M. (2008). A comparison of two prosecution policies in cases of intimate partner violence: Mandatory case filing versus following the victim's lead. *Criminology & Public Policy, 7*, 633–62.

de Haan, W. & Vos, J. (2003). A crying shame: The over-rationalized conception of man in the rational choice perspective. *Theoretical Criminology, 7*, 29–54.

Dixon, J. (2008). Mandatory domestic violence arrest and prosecution policies: Recidivism and social governance. *Criminology & Public Policy, 7*, 663–70.

Dunford, F. W. (1992). The measurement of recidivism in cases of spouse assault. *Journal of Criminal Law and Criminology, 83*, 120–36.

Durlauf, S. N., Fu, C., & Navarro, S., (2013). Capital punishment and deterrence: Understanding disparate results. *Journal of Quantitative Criminology, 29*, 103–21.

Ehrlich, I. (1975). The deterrent effect of capital punishment: A question of life and death. *American Economic Review, 65*, 397–417.

Exum, M. L. (2002). The application and robustness of the rational choice perspective in the study of intoxicated and angry intentions to aggress. *Criminology, 40*, 933–66.

Fagan, J., Geller, A., & Zimring, F. E., (2012). The Texas deterrence muddle. *Criminology and Public Policy, 11*, 579–91.

Felson, M. (1994). *Crime and everyday life: Insights and implications for society*. Thousand Oaks, CA: Pine Forge Press.

Felson, M. (1998). *Crime & everyday life* (2nd ed.). Thousand Oaks, CA: Pine Forge Press.

Felson, M. (2002). *Crime & everyday life* (3rd ed.). Thousand Oaks, CA: Sage.

Felson, R. B. & Burchfield, K. B. (2004). Alcohol and the risk of physical and sexual assault victimization. *Criminology, 42*, 837–59.

Felson, R. B., Ackerman, J. M., & Gallagher, C. A. (2005). Police intervention and the repeat of domestic assault. *Criminology, 43*, 563–84.

Ferri, E. (1901/1968). Three lectures given at the university of Naples, Italy—April 22, 23, and 24, 1901. In S. Grupp (Ed.), *The positive school of criminology*. Pittsburgh, PA: University of Pittsburgh Press.

Finken, L. L., Jacobs, J. E., & Laguna, K. D. (1998). Risky drinking and driving/riding decisions: The role of previous experience. *Journal of Youth and Adolescence, 27*, 493–512.

Finn, M., (2013). Evidence-based and victim-centered prosecutorial policies. *Criminology & Public Policy, 12*, 443–72.

Fisher, B. S., Sloan, J. J., Cullen, F. T., & Chunmeng, L. (1998). Crime in the ivory tower: The level and sources of student victimization. *Criminology, 36*, 671–710.

Geerken, M. & Gove, W. R. (1977). Deterrence, overload and incapacitation: An empirical evaluation. *Social Forces, 56*, 424–27.

Geis, G. (1972). Jeremy Bentham. In H. Mannheim (Ed.), *Pioneers in criminology*. Montclair, NJ: Patterson Smith.

Geis, G. & Bunn, I. (1981). Sir Thomas Browne and witchcraft: A cautionary tale for contemporary law and psychiatry. *International Journal of Law and Psychiatry, 4*, 1–11.

Gibbs, J. P. (1968). Crime, punishment, and deterrence. *Southwestern Social Science Quarterly*, *48*, 515–30.

Gibbs, J. P. (1975). *Crime, punishment, and deterrence*. New York, NY: Elsevier.

Gibbs, J. P. (1989). *Control: Sociology's central notion*. Champaign, IL: University of Illinois Press.

Gibson, C. L., Khey, D., & Schreck, C. J. (2008). Gender, internal controls, and academic dishonesty: Investigating mediating and differential effects. *Journal of Criminal Justice Education*, *19*, 2–18.

Grasmick, H. G., Bursik, R. J., Jr. (1990). Conscience, significant others, and rational choice: Extending the deterrence model. *Law and Society Review*, *24*, 837–61.

Grasmick, H. G. & Kobayashi, E. (2002). Workplace deviance in Japan: Applying an extended model of deterrence. *Deviant Behavior*, *23*, 21–43.

Grasmick, H. G., Blackwell, B. S., Bursik, R. J., Jr. (1993a). Changes in sex patterning of perceived threats of sanctions. *Law and Society Review*, *27*, 679–705.

Grasmick, H. G., Bursik, R. J., Jr. & Arneklev, B. J. (1993b). Reduction in drunk driving as a response to increased threats of shame, embarrassment, and legal sanctions. *Criminology*, *31*, 41–67.

Gregory, L. (2002). *The stupid crook book*. Kansas City, MS: Andrews McMeel Publishing.

Griffiths, J. (1970). The limits of criminal law scholarship. *Yale Law Journal*, *79*, 1388–1474.

Guerette, R. T., Stenius, V. M. K., & McGloin, J. M. (2004). Understanding offense specialization and versatility: A reapplication of the rational choice perspective. *Journal of Criminal Justice*, *33*, 77–87.

Hagan, J., Simpson, J. H., & Gillis, A. R. (1979). The sexual stratification of social control. *British Journal of Sociology*, *30*, 25–38.

Heath, J. (1982). *Torture and English law: An administrative history*. Westport, CT: Greenwood.

Henson, B., Reyns, B. W., & Fisher, B. (2011). Security in the 21st century: Examining the link between online social network activity, privacy, and interpersonal victimization. *Criminal Justice Review*, *36*, 253–68.

Henson, V. A. & Stone, W. E. (1999). Campus crime: A victimization study. *Journal of Criminal Justice*, *27*, 295–307.

Hjalmarsson, R., (2012). Can executions have a short-term deterrence effect on non-felony homicides? *Criminology & Public Policy*, *11*, 565–72.

Hobbes, T. (1651/1962). *Leviathan*. London, UK: Collier-MacMillan.

Hood, R. G. (1971). Research on the effectiveness of punishments and treatments. In L. Radzinowicz & M. E. Wolfgang (Eds.), *Crimes and justice* (vol.3). New York, NY: Basic Books.

Jacobs, B. A. (2010). Deterrence and deterrability. *Criminology*, *48*, 417–41.

Jacobs, J. A. (2005). ASR's greatest hits: Editor's comment. *American Sociological Review*, *70*, 1–3.

Johnson, H. A. (2003). *History of Criminal Justice*. Cincinnati, OH: Anderson.

Kassebaum, G., Ward, D. A., & Wilner, D. M. (1971). *Prison treatment and parole survival: An empirical assessment*. New York, NY: John Wiley and Sons.

Kingsnorth, R. F., Alvis, L., & Gavia, G. (1993). Specific deterrence and the DUI offender: The impact of a decade of reform. *Justice Quarterly*, *10*, 265–88.

Kleck, G., Sever, B., Li, S., & Gertz, M. (2005). The missing link in general deterrence research. *Criminology*, *43*, 623–59.

Kramer, H. & Sprenger, J. (1486/1928). *Malleus maleficarum*. London, UK: John Rodker.

Kruttschnitt, C. (2008). Editorial introduction: The effect of "no-drop" prosecution policies on perpetrators of intimate partner violence. *Criminology & Public Policy*, *7*, 629–32.

Labriola, M., Rempel, M., & Davis, R. C. (2008). Do batterer programs reduce recidivism? Results from a randomized trial in the Bronx. *Justice Quarterly*, *25*, 252–82.

Lacroix, P. (1963). *France in the Middle Ages*. New York, NY: Frederick Ungar.

LaFree, G., Dugan, L., & Korte, R. (2009). The impact of British counterterrorist strategies on political violence in Northern Ireland: Comparing deterrence and backlash models. *Criminology*, *47*, 17–46.

Land, K. C., Teske, Jr., R., & Zheng, H. (2012). The differential short-term impacts of executions on felony and non-felony homicides. *Criminology & Public Policy*, *11*, 541–64.

Langbein, J. (1977). *Torture and the law of proof*. Chicago, IL: University of Chicago Press.

Lea, H. C. (1866/1973). *Torture*. Philadelphia, PA: University of Pennsylvania Press.

Lea, H. C. (1887/1955). *A history of the inquisition of the Middle Ages*. New York, NY: Russell Sage Foundation.

Loewenstein, G., Nagin, D., & Paternoster, R. (1997). The effect of sexual arousal on expectations of sexual forcefulness. *Journal of Research in Crime and Delinquency*, *34*, 443–73.

Loughran, T. A., Paternoster, R., Piquero, A. R., & Fagan, J. (2013). A good man always knows his limitations: The role of overconfidence in criminal offending. *Journal of Research in Crime and Delinquency*, *50*, 327–58.

Loughran, T. A., Pogarsky, G, Piquero, A. R., & Paternoster, R. (2012). Re-examining the functional form of the certainty effect in deterrence theory. *Justice Quarterly*, *29*, 712–41.

Lyman, J. L. (1964). The Metropolitan Police Act of 1829. *Journal of Criminal Law, Criminology and Police Science*, *55*, 141–54.

Maestro, M. (1973). *Cesare Beccaria and the origins of penal reform*. Philadelphia, PA: Temple University Press.

Manski, C. F. & Pepper, J. V. (2013). Deterrence and the death penalty: Partial identification analysis using repeated cross sections. *Journal of Quantitative Criminology*, *29*, 123–41.

Marcum, C. D., Ricketts, M. L., & Higgins, G. E. (2010). Assessing sex experiences of online victimization: An examination of adolescent online behaviors using routine activities theory. *Criminal Justice Review*, *35*, 412–37.

Martinson, R. (1974). What works?—Questions and answers about prison reform. *Public Interest*, *35*, 22–54.

Maxwell, C. D., Garner, J. H., & Fagan, J. A. (2002). The preventive effects of arrest on intimate partner violence: Research, policy and theory. *Criminology & Public Policy*, *1*, 51–80.

Mendes, S. M. (2004). Certainty, severity, and their relative deterrent effects: Questioning the implications of the role of risk in criminal deterrence policy. *Tennessee Electronic Library*, 1–15.

Miethe, T. D., Lu, H., & Reese, E. (2000). Reintegrative shaming and recidivism risks in drug court: Explanations for some unexpected findings. *Crime & Delinquency*, *46*, 522–41.

Miller, J. L. & Anderson, A. B. (1986). Updating the deterrence doctrine. *Journal of Criminal Law and Criminology*, *77*, 418–38.

Monachesi, E. (1972). Cesare Beccaria. In H. Mannheim (Ed.), *Pioneers in criminology* (pp. 36–50). Montclair, NJ: Patterson Smith.

Montesquieu, C. L. (1748/1900). *The spirit of the laws*. New York, NY: Appleton.

Morris, N. (1973). Foreword. In M. Maestro (Ed.), *Cesare Beccaria and the origins of penal reform*. Philadelphia, PA: Temple University Press.

Morris, R. G. & Piquero, A. R. (2013). For whom do sanctions deter and label? *Justice Quarterly, 30*, 837–68.

Mustaine, E. E. & Tewksbury, R. (1998). Predicting risks of larceny theft victimization: A routine activity analysis using refined lifestyle measures. *Criminology, 36*, 829–58.

Mustaine, E. E. & Tewksbury, R. (1999). Assessing the likelihood of drunk driving: Gender, context and lifestyle. *Journal of Crime and Justice, 22*, 57–93.

Nagin, D. S. & Pogarsky, G. (2003). An experimental investigation of deterrence: Cheating, self-serving bias, and impulsivity. *Criminology, 41*, 167–94.

Newman, G. (1978). *The punishment response*. Philadelphia, PA: J.B. Lippincott.

Newman, G. (1983). *Just and painful. A case for the corporal punishment of criminals*. New York, NY: Macmillan Publishing Company.

Paternoster, R., Pogarsky, G., & Zimmerman, G. (2011). Thoughtfully reflective decision making and the accumulation of capital: Bringing choice back in. *Journal of Quantitative Criminology, 27*, 1–26.

Peterson, R. R. (2013). Victim engagement in the prosecution of domestic violence cases. *Criminology & Public Policy, 12*, 473–80.

Phillipson, C. (1923/1970). *Three criminal law reformers*. Montclair, NJ: Patterson Smith.

Piquero, A. & Tibbetts, S. G. (1996). Specifying the direct and indirect effects of low self-control and situational factors in decision-making: Toward a more complete model of rational offending. *Justice Quarterly, 13*, 481–510.

Pogarsky, G. (2002). Identifying "deterrable offenders: Implications for research on deterrence. *Justice Quarterly, 19*, 431–52.

Pogarsky, G. & Piquero, A. R. (2004). Studying the reach of deterrence: Can deterrence theory help explain police misconduct? *Journal of Criminal Justice, 32*, 371–86.

Pogarsky, G., Kim, K., & Paternoster, R. (2005). Perceptual change in the National Youth Survey: Implications for deterrence theory and offender decision-making. *Justice Quarterly, 22*, 1–29.

Pratt, T. (2008). Rational choice theory, crime control policy, and criminological relevance. *Criminology & Public Policy, 7*, 42–52.

Radelet, M. L. (2012). The death penalty in Texas. *Criminology & Public Policy, 11*, 573–78.

Reckless, W. C. (1967). *The crime problem* (4th ed.). New York, NY: Appleton-Century-Crofts.

Redmon, D. (2002). Testing informal social control theory: Examining lewd behavior during Mardi Gras. *Deviant Behavior, 23*, 363–84.

Reppetto, T. C. (1976). Crime prevention and the displacement phenomenon. *Crime & Delinquency, 22*, 166–77.

Reyns, B. W. (2013). Online routines and identity theft victimization: Further expanding routine activity theory beyond direct-contact offenses. *Journal of Research in Crime and Delinquency, 50*(2), 216–38.

Rousseau, J.-J. (1762/1948). *The social contract*. London, UK: Oxford University Press.

Schafer, S. (1976). *Introduction to criminology*. Reston, VA: Reston Publishing.

Scheff, T. J. (1988). Shame and conformity: The deference-emotion system. *American Sociological Review, 53*, 395–406.

Schwartz, M. D., DeKeseredy, W. S., Tait, D., & Alvi, S. (2001). Male peer support and a feminist routine activities theory: Understanding sexual assault on the college campus. *Justice Quarterly, 18*, 623–49.

Scott, G. R. (1938/1959). *The history of corporal punishment*. London, UK: Torchstream.

Sellin, T. (1952). Murder and the death penalty. *Annals of the American Academy of Political and Social Science, 284*, 1–166.

Sherley, A. J. (2005). Contextualizing the sexual assault event: Images from police files. *Deviant Behavior, 26*, 87–108.

Sherman, L. W. & Berk, R. A. (1984). The specific deterrent effects of arrest for domestic assault. *American Sociological Review, 49*, 261–72.

Sherman, L. W., Schmidt, J. D., Rogan, D. P., Smith, D. A., Gartin, P. R. & Cohn, E. G. (1992). The variable effects of arrest on criminal careers: The Milwaukee Domestic Violence Experiment. *Journal of Criminal Law and Criminology, 83*, 170–200.

Siennick, S. E. (2012). Deterrence and the death penalty. *Criminology & Public Policy, 11*, 535–38.

Silberman, M. (1976). Toward a theory of criminal deterrence. *American Sociological Review, 41*, 442–61.

Sitren, A. H. & Applegate, B. K. (2012). Testing deterrence theory with offenders: The empirical validity of Stafford and Warr's model. *Deviant Behavior, 33*, 492–506.

Spano, R., Freilich, J. D., & Bolland, J. (2008). Gang membership, gun carrying, and employment: applying routine activities theory to explain violent victimization among inner city, minority youth living in extreme poverty. *Justice Quarterly, 25*, 381–410.

Spivak, A. L., Fukushima, M., Kelly, M. S., & Jenson, T. S. (2011). Religiosity, delinquency, and the deterrent effects of informal sanctions. *Deviant Behavior, 32*, 677–711.

Spohn, C. & Holleran, D. (2002). The effect of imprisonment on recidivism rates of felony offenders: A focus on drug offenders. *Criminology, 40*, 329–58.

Stack, S. (1998). The effect of publicized executions on homicides in California. *Journal of Crime and Justice, 21*, 1–16.

Sugarman, D. & Boney-McCoy, S. (2000). Research synthesis in family violence: The art of reviewing the research. *Journal of Aggression, Maltreatment & Trauma, 4*, 55–82.

Sutherland, E. H. (1925). Murder and the death penalty. *Journal of Criminal Law and Criminology, 15*, 522–29.

Tibbetts, S. G. & Herz, D. C. (1996). Gender differences in factors of social control and rational choice. *Deviant Behavior, 17*, 183–208.

Tibbetts, S. G. & Myers, D. L. (1999). Low self-control, rational choice, and student test cheating. *American Journal of Criminal Justice, 23*, 179–200.

Tillyer, M. S. & Tillyer, R. (2014). Violence in context: A multilevel analysis of victim injury in robbery incidents. *Justice Quarterly, 31*, 767–91.

Tittle, C. R. (1969). Crime rates and legal sanctions. *Social Problems, 16*, 408–23.

Tittle, C. R. (1980). *Sanctions and social deviance: The question of deterrence*. New York, NY: Praeger.

Tittle, C. R. & Rowe, A. R. (1973). Moral appeal, sanction threat, and deviance: An experimental test. *Social Problems*, *20*, 488–98.

Tittle, C. R. & Rowe, A. R. (1974). Certainty of arrest and crime rates: A further test of the deterrence hypothesis. *Social Forces*, *52*, 455–62.

Tittle, C. R., Botchkovar, E. V., & Antonaccio, O. (2011). Criminal contemplation, national context, and deterrence. *Journal of Quantitative Criminology*, *27*, 225–49.

Tunnell, K. D. (1992). *Choosing crime: The criminal calculus of property offenders*. Chicago, IL: Nelson-Hall.

Vollmer, A. (1936). *The police and modern society*. College Park, MD: McGrath.

Walker, L. (1979). *The battered woman*. New York, NY: Harper and Row.

Wilkins, L. T. (1969). *Evaluation of penal measures*. New York, NY: Random House.

Wilson, O. W. & McLaren, R. C. (1972). *Police administration* (3rd ed.). New York, NY: McGraw-Hill.

Xie, M., Heimer, K., & Lauritsen, J. L. (2012). Violence against women in U.S. metropolitan areas: Changes in women's status and risk, 1980–2004. *Criminology*, *50*, 105–44.

Zimring, F. E. & Hawkins, G. J. (1973). *Deterrence: The legal threat in crime control*. Chicago, IL: University of Chicago Press.

CHAPTER 6

Individual Theories of Crime
A Biosocial Perspective

The previous chapter examined the emergence of criminology with the classical school, heavily identified with the Italian reformer, Cesare Beccaria. This school of thought emerged in the context of the Western world's revolution against the dominance of royalty and the church with burgeoning Enlightenment thought. As the first natural explanation of crime, it represented what Thomas Kuhn (1970) called a **paradigm revolution**. This is a dramatic shift in the theoretical orientation, and especially the underlying assumptions, for explaining a phenomenon. This rational choice or free will outlook dominated criminological thought for about a century before another paradigm revolution occurred. This chapter begins with a review of the social context that set the stage for a paradigm shift into **positivism**.

It was dramatic scientific developments in the late nineteenth century that provided fertile ground for the emergence of positive criminology. Charles Darwin's *On the Origin of Species* (1859/1964) and *The Descent of Man*

(1871/1964) set the intellectual tone. The Darwinian context cannot be overstated. There was optimism that science could provide the answers to many questions and solutions to diverse human problems. Darwin's works were widely read and very influential examples of this emerging scientism. Thus it is not surprising that criminologists turned to science or that the earliest positivists emulated Darwin's theories. Cesare Lombroso is typically recognized as the father of modern or positivistic criminology and one of the key ideas in his earlier works was that of **atavism**, a view of criminals as a throwback to an earlier and more primitive evolutionary stage. In seeking to explain crime in terms of biological evolution Lombroso was clearly following in the footsteps of the giant scientific figure that Darwin represented.

The shift to positivism as a new paradigm for understanding crime is of far greater importance than any specific theories within that framework. Initially, positivism embraced biological variables, attempting to explain crime in terms of biological makeup predisposing some people to commit crime. It later incorporated psychological variables, and as Chapters 7 and 8 reveal, ultimately came to be dominated by social factors for most of the twentieth century. Thus positivism takes many different forms, and oftentimes positivists with different disciplinary identities will disagree sharply over what variables might explain crime. Generally, we can divide positivist thinking into biological, psychological, and sociological camps. Recognizing that the theories falling into the positive criminological paradigm are so diverse, it is important to understand what they have in common.

The common ground of all positivistic theories can be seen more clearly by focusing on two aspects of the concept: **empiricism** and **determinism**. First, positivism presumes that knowledge can be discovered only by means of observation and experience. It insists that criminologists employ the scientific method to seek answers to their questions. Thus positivism is rooted in the collection of empirical data, thereby shifting the focus from crime to criminals. Classical criminologists, by contrast, were philosophers. They only had to engage in armchair theorizing about crime because they assumed there were no individual differences between criminals and noncriminals in need of explanation. Differences in the criminal justice system were what were thought to matter. This leads to the second element within positivism. It assumes that individual differences are rooted in factors beyond, or at least not entirely within, the control of individuals. Thus the offender's behavior is "determined" by something other than her or his free-willed choice. In other words, there are forces that shape people and their behavior. As positivism came to life in criminology, the view was that offenders were products of biological deficiencies.

Every theory offers a prescription for dealing with crime. Positivism and rational choice are characterized not only by antithetical assumptions, but also by diverse policy implications. Given the positivists' dismissal of free will, punishing criminal behavior becomes both morally objectionable and unfruitful. Positivism instead calls for the medicalization of criminality. Following this **medical model**, the causes of crime are sought, and once identified, a cure is within reach.

As with disease, it is assumed that discovery of cause is the first step toward cure. Thus, while deterrence theorists advocate the fashioning of punishments to fit the crime, positivists favor the tailoring of treatments to fit the criminal.

Positivism dominated American criminology for most of the twentieth century and provided the rationale for many policy developments. It had wide effects on the practice of penology, even leading to the adoption of the more contemporary "corrections" title that is consistent with criminological applications within the medical model framework. It gave rise to the *indeterminate* (open-ended) *sentence*, which calls for release of the offender once deemed cured or rehabilitated. *Community corrections*, including the practices of probation and parole, are also part and parcel of positivism. Prediction tables used by parole boards are an empirical tool for helping to determine when an offender is likely rehabilitated, meriting release. Moreover, the wide ranges of treatments that have been tried in correctional settings are rooted in positivistic theories of crime.

Positivism obviously can be used to justify greater intervention in the lives of offenders than is the case with rational choice theories, because the express goal of the positive doctrine is to help, not punish, the individual. This is a concern regarding contemporary positivism, given some lessons of history. It raises moral and political questions regarding the limits of intervention in the name of rehabilitation. The question is, even given the knowledge that a strategy is effective, what is morally permissible? Group counseling? Psychotherapy? Administration of drugs or hormones? Dietary controls? Monitoring of associations with other persons? Lobotomies? Sterilization? As Stanley Grupp (1968:8) noted nearly half a century ago, "the problems posed by the potential tyranny of the expert remain as ominous today as ever." Many criminologists continue to echo this caution. Table 6.1 highlights some of the differences between positivism and the classical rational choice perspective.

Reviewing the history of rational choice thinking, we saw that deterrence, the foremost theory derived from the paradigm, emerged in the late eighteenth

TABLE 6.1 Comparison of Positive and Rational Choice Paradigms

Positive	Rational Choice
Focuses on criminals	Focuses on crime
Assumes individual differences	Assumes no individual differences
Assumes deterministic forces	Assumes free will
Rooted in biology, psychology, or sociology	Rooted in philosophy, especially utilitarianism
Applicable at individual level to address differences rooted in biology, psychology, or social environment	Applicable at group level only (no individual differences)
Calls for medical model applications (treatment) to individuals	Calls for criminal justice system applications (punishment) to individuals

century. It was then largely supplanted by positivism about 100 years later, only to reemerge in the last three decades of the twentieth century, and continues to thrive today. A similar fate befell biological positivism. Biologically based criminology emerged as the foremost perspective for conceptualizing crime with Cesare Lombroso's *L'uomo delinquente* in 1876. Although this work was not translated to English (as *Criminal Man)* until 1911 (Lombroso-Ferrero, 1911/1972), and then not fully, the influence of Lombroso was quickly felt throughout the Western world, including the United States (Rafter, 1992). He ushered in positivistic thinking under the umbrella of **criminal anthropology**, which he defined as the study of the "organic and psychic constitution" of abnormal (criminal) persons (Lombroso-Ferrero, 1911/1972:5). Biological criminology began to lose ground in the eyes of U.S. criminologists, however, in the 1920s 1930s. A temporary death knell of the perspective was then rung by two factors. First, the close association of biological explanations of human behavior, including crime, with the Nazi and Fascist movements led to their being inextricably tied to racist ideology. The fact that extreme biological positivism was advocated by Hitler and Mussolini and used as the basis for genocidal policies established a political climate that rejected and remained unreceptive to biological variables and crime for decades. This is a debate that, as will be seen, persists yet today. Second, any study of the history of the discipline of criminology must acknowledge the crucial role played by Edwin Sutherland in shaping the field. He was a sociologist who sought to elevate criminology to a respectable status within that discipline and to disassociate it from biology, psychology, and other disciplines. He was very successful on both counts, steering mainstream criminology down a sociological path from the 1940s through the remainder of the twentieth century. As a result of these two factors, it has been noted that, "By mid-century, biological explanations for crime were passé, disreputable, and perhaps even taboo. They were unthinkable and even unmentionable" (Wright & Miller, 1998). Sociological variables still dominate criminology, but it has increasingly become interdisciplinary in recent years. In fact, **biosocial criminology** has emerged as a widespread specialty, marked by the emergence of texts and courses following that perspective.

THE HISTORY OF BIOLOGICAL POSITIVISM

The early history of biological positivism is reviewed before turning to contemporary biological and biosocial theories of crime. That early story begins with a more detailed look at the life and works of Cesare Lombroso, who is widely credited with founding criminological positivism.

Cesare Lombroso (1835–1909)

Cesare Lombroso was born in Verona, Italy, one of the few cities of the era that allowed a Jewish boy to attend high school. He went on to obtain a medical degree from the University of Pavia in 1858. The early part of his career was spent as an army physician, followed by work in several hospitals for the insane. From 1876 until his death he was a professor at the University of Turin. He led a peaceful life as a productive scholar, with the devoted following of two daughters (Gina and Paola), a son-in-law (William Ferrero), and many students.

It is important to reemphasize that Lombroso's development of biological positivism was, as with most theorists and theories, a logical extension of the intellectual thought of his time. Not only did he follow Darwin's model, but also built upon the earlier work of others who had addressed crime within a biological framework. Franz Joseph Gall (1758–1828), for example, preceded Lombroso in popularizing **phrenology**, which associated criminality with abnormalities in the brain that they believed could be identified externally, earning them the nickname of "skull-feelers."

Lombroso's daughter, Gina, noted after his death a turning point in his career. While performing an autopsy on a violent criminal, Lombroso observed an unusual cranial depression, similar to that found in rodents, birds, and lower types of apes. His daughter later would describe the impact of this discovery on her father:

> At the sight of the skull, says my father, I seemed to see all at once, standing out clearly illumed as in a vast plain under a flaming sky, the problems of the nature of the criminal, who reproduces in civilized times characteristics, not only of primitive savages, but of still lower types as far back as the carnivore (Lombroso-Ferrero, 1911/1972:6–7).

This discovery laid the foundation for Lombroso's subsequent theoretical work. Adopting a social Darwinian perspective, he maintained that humans demonstrate different levels of biological development. Certain characteristics, such as the cranial depression he had found, marked for Lombroso an atavistic person, that is, a person possessing qualities of more primitive ancestors. Lombroso classified such biological throwbacks as a **born criminal**, and in his earliest work, he insisted that all criminals were atavistic. By the time of his death, though, he had backed away, saying that born criminals accounted for about one-third of the law-breaking population. The other two-thirds were **criminaloids**, or minor offenders.

The following list offers a brief sample of the wide range of characteristics set forth by Lombroso to identify atavistic criminals:

- The criminal skull tends to be larger or smaller than the average skull common to the region or country from which the criminal hails;
- Prominent frontal sinuses and excessive development of the femoral muscles, a characteristic common for primates and carnivores;
- Excessively large jaws and cheekbones;
- An asymmetrical physiognomy in which eyes and ears are frequently situated at different levels, or are of unequal size;
- Shifty eyes or hard expression in eyes;

- Unusually large or small ears, or ears standing out from the face as in chimpanzees;
- A flattened nose is common among thieves while murderers showed an aquiline nose, like the beak of a bird of prey; and
- Rapists and murderers are likely to have fleshy, swollen, and protruding lips. Swindlers have thin, straight lips (Excerpted from Lombroso-Ferrero, 1911/1972:24).

In one study, Lombroso compared two groups of criminals to presumptively noncriminal Italian soldiers. He reported that only 11 percent of the soldiers had three or more of the anomalies indicative of biological inferiority, while 35 and 40 percent of the criminal groups had three or more such defects (see Figure 6.1).

Charles Thomas and John Hepburn (1983:146) argue that history has been far too generous with Lombroso, that he "had the effect of blocking our progress for more than a quarter of a century." Although sociological positivism ultimately supplanted the biological (and psychological) versions, a **Statistical School** preceded Lombroso with initiation of the scientific study of crime by nearly half a century. A.M. Guerry (1802–66), a French social statistician, was the first to analyze ecological (geographic-based) data in a search for relationships between crime and social characteristics. The best known representative of this school was Adolphe Quetelet (1796–1874), a Belgian who is revered as the "father of modern statistics." Quetelet refuted the notion of free will and sought explanations of crime, or what he called propensities for crime, through analysis of social data (Quetelet, 1833/1984). A third major figure in this largely unheralded school was Henry Mayhew (1812–87), an Englishman who took essentially a sociological approach in analyzing both official data and detailed observations. It is one of the ironies of history that individual-based positivism, led by a Lombrosian biological perspective and later psychological

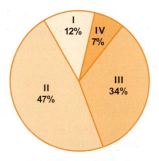

Criminals Guilty of Homicide and
Sentenced to Penal Servitude

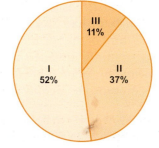

Noncriminal Italian Soldiers

FIGURE 6.1

Percentage distribution of skull anomalies found by Lombroso.

I	=	No anomalies of skull
II	=	One or two anomalies of skull
III	=	Three or more anomalies of skull
IV	=	Five or more anomalies of skull

factors, won out over the socially oriented statistical school that closely paralleled mainstream twentieth century criminology.

Lombroso and the Female Offender

Unlike the relatively rapid development in this period of theories to explain the behavior of male offenders, there were few facts and ideas about female offenders. Lombroso, however, with his son-in-law, William Ferrero, in 1895, became a pioneer in the study of crime by women when he published *The Female Offender*, employing the same analytical framework used in his earlier work.

The authors measured various body parts and noted physical irregularities in women in prison and before the courts. They associated female offending with features such as occipital irregularities, narrow foreheads, prominent cheekbones, and a "virile" form of face.

Lombroso and Ferrero reported fewer degenerative physical characteristics among female offenders than they had found among men. Prostitutes were said to have more atavistic qualities than other female offenders, because they mostly offended against what Lombroso believed to be "female decency." The "evil tendencies" of women offenders were said to be more numerous and varied than those of men (1895:151). Their "maternal instincts" and "ladylike" qualities were said to be suppressed and they were depicted as more merciless in their violent offenses than their male counterparts. Female criminals were believed by Lombroso and Ferrero to be overgrown children with no moral sense.

The study by Lombroso and Ferrero of female offenders has deservedly received harsh criticism, and both their methods and theoretical assumptions have been attacked. Among other things, they generalized from small numbers of offenders and control groups. They failed to consider more plausible explanations for the alleged findings on body build and criminal behavior. A deformed physique, for instance, can make it difficult to obtain a job and to form satisfactory personal relationships which, in turn, can encourage crime. They also confused biological and environmental factors, grouping under biology such matters as tattooing, drinking, and overeating. In addition, their assumptions regarding women had no scientific basis. That the female offender was declared to be more ruthless and merciless than the male had much more to do with the fact that she had deviated from her stereotypical sex-role identity than with her actual behavior. The observation of Paul Topinard, a French contemporary of Lombroso, that pictures of Lombroso's supposedly atavistic criminals looked much like those of his own academic friends succinctly pinpointed the inadequacy of Lombroso's work (cited in Tarde, 1912:270).

Enrico Ferri (1856–1928)

Enrico Ferri was born the son of a poor Italian shopkeeper and was a politically active member of the Socialist party for most of his life. A pivotal point in his career came when he sent Lombroso a copy of his dissertation, which critiqued the classical school and its assumption of free will. Lombroso's response,

Ferri reminisced years later, had been complimentary, but qualified; Lombroso insisted that "Ferri isn't positivist enough!" Ferri, upon being informed by a friend of this, retorted, "What! Does Lombroso suggest that I, a lawyer, should go and measure the heads of criminals in order to be positivist enough!?" (cited in Sellin, 1968:17–18). The two men soon became close colleagues, and Ferri ultimately incorporated anthropometric methods into his positive approach to criminology.

Under Ferri's influence, positivism developed into a multiple factor approach, seeking many different causes for a single criminal act, an approach that had an immense impact on American criminology (Grupp, 1968). Ferri also argued, in opposition to the classical tradition, that different punishments should be accorded criminals committing similar crimes, with the penalty to be tailored to the background and traits of the offenders as these are seen to predict future acts.

Ferri's study of crime in France and Italy showed that, with the exception of infanticide (the killing of an infant) and patricide (the murder of one's own father), crimes against the person occur with greatest frequency during the summer months. He attributed the higher summer rate chiefly to three circumstances: (1) the physiological effects of heat, which leave a large surplus of energy, (2) the better nourishment of the population in the summer, and (3) an enhanced irritability due to oppressive temperatures and humidity (Ferri, 1917). Ferri (1917:54) also joined with Lombroso and his fellow positivists in challenging the free will assumption that largely underlays the work of the classical theorists:

> How can you still believe in the existence of a free will, when modern psychology, armed with all the instruments of positive modern research denies that there is any free will and demonstrates that every act of a human being is the result of an interaction between the personality and the environment of man? . . . The positive school of criminology maintains . . . that it is not the criminal who wills: in order to be a criminal it is rather necessary that the individual should find himself permanently or transitorily in such personal, physical, and moral conditions, and live in such an environment, which become for him a chain of cause and effect, externally and internally, that disposes him toward crime.

Although Ferri succeeded in chronicling the strength of the positive approach to criminology, his career, ironically, exemplified what became the transitory downfall of biological positivism. Ferri displayed a naive faith in the promise of scientism to address crime, failing to question whether scientists and politicians might abuse such power. Ferri ended his career as a Fascist, declaring that "the Fascist government . . . has accepted and is putting into effect some of the principles and the most characteristic practical proposals of the positive school" (cited in Sellin, 1968:32). For a powerful emotional and historical sense of how Nazi and Fascist ideology corrupted scholarly inquiry, review the 2006 film, *The Good German*. The plot depicts George Clooney playing the role of a German literature professor who gradually succumbs to political pressure and abandons fundamental academic values to gain favor with the Nazi regime.

Raffaele Garofalo (1852–1924)

Raffaele Garofalo rounded out the trio of pioneering Italian criminological positivists. Garofalo rejected the legal definition of crime for a sociological approach. He thought offenders against the person lacked the natural moral sentiment of "pity," while property offenders were deficient in "probity" (honesty), a conclusion easy enough to reach after the crime has occurred, but singularly difficult to demonstrate in regard to particular individuals prior to the offense. Garofalo believed in ridding society of criminal offenders (those "inassimilable to the particular conditions of the environment") and thereby helping along the Darwinian thesis of selection of the fittest (Allen, 1960:254–76). The peril of such extreme views is reflected in the fact that Garofalo, like Ferri, became an activist in the Italian Fascist movement under Benito Mussolini. He viewed it as legitimate for the state to intervene in the natural evolutionary process, as depicted by Darwin, and to execute, imprison, or transport inferior criminally inclined persons.

Charles Goring (1870–1919)

Although it also highlighted biological determinism, Charles Goring's *The English Convict* (1913), the result of 13 years of work, undermined Lombroso's ideas about "born criminals." Goring criticized Lombroso for relying on observations rather than instruments for measurement, and he provided quotations from Lombroso's work to demonstrate its recourse to nonscientific language. One such observation was a story of a woman accused of poisoning her victims with arsenic. "The bust which we possess of this criminal," Lombroso had written, "so full of virile angularity, and above all, so deeply wrinkled, with its Satanic leer, suffices of itself to prove that the woman in question was born to do evil, and that, if one occasion to commit it had failed, she would have found others" (Goring, 1913:15). Such Lombrosian hyperbole led Goring to conclude that "as a result of this attitude of mind, of its haphazard method of investigation, of its desire to adjust fact to theory, rather than to formulate a theory by observation of fact—as a result of all this, we have . . . an organized system of self-evident confusion whose parallel is only to be found in the astrology, alchemy, and other credulities of the Middle Ages" (Goring, 1913:15).

For his part, Goring, a medical officer in the English prisons, collaborated with the famous statistician Karl Pearson to

Biological determinism is plagued by a history of despicable inhumanity. Here German Chancellor Adolf Hitler gestures during a speech in May 1937. As one of the most notorious tyrants in world history, Hitler launched the holocaust as a "final solution" to what he called the "Jewish problem."

CREDIT:
AP Photo.

study 3,000 recidivist convicts and a large number of noncriminals. Goring summarized his work in the following terms:

> The preliminary conclusion reached by our inquiry is that [the] anthropological monster has no existence in fact. The physical and mental constitution of both criminal and law-abiding persons, of the same age, stature, class, and intelligence, are identical. There is no such thing as an anthropological criminal type (Goring, 1913:370).

Nonetheless, Goring found support for the position that persons of different constitutional types were likely to commit certain kinds of crimes (Beirne, 1993). Goring claimed, for instance, that offenders convicted of crimes of violence were characterized by strength and "constitutional soundness" considerably above the average of that of other criminals, and that burglars, thieves, and arsonists "as well as being inferior in stature and weight, are also relative to other criminals and the population at large, puny in their general bodily habit" (Goring, 1913:200). Goring also found that convicts were one to two inches shorter than noncriminals and weighed three to seven pounds less. He thought these results were a general indication of hereditary inferiority. Contemporary criminologists would ask whether the relative shortness and lesser weights were the result of poor nutrition, itself associated with class position, and insist on inclusion of social class measures as control variables.

Earnest A. Hooton (1887–1954)

The next major entrant into the debate regarding physiological causation in crime was Earnest A. Hooton, a Rhodes Scholar and Harvard University physical anthropologist, who published *The American Criminal: An Anthropological Study* (1939a) and *Crime and the Man* (1939b). Hooton was a renowned, but very controversial figure, even in his own time. He was convinced that crime could only be understood through biology and therefore was adamantly opposed to social and cultural anthropology and to the emergence of sociology as the leading criminological framework. He summarized his view of the criminal offender in the following way:

> Criminals are organically inferior. Crime is the resultant of the impact of environment upon low grade human organisms. It follows that the elimination of crime can be effected only by the extirpation of the physically, mentally, and morally unfit, or by their complete segregation in a socially aseptic environment (Hooton, 1939a/1969:309).

Such words, suggesting the killing off of those alleged to be unfit on the highly arguable ground that they would inevitably commit criminal acts, would echo ominously when soon afterwards a similar reasoning provided the rationale for the genocidal tactics of the Nazi regime in Germany (Kuhl, 1994). (If you watch *The Good German*, keep in mind the expositions of Professor Hooton.)

Hooton arrived at his conclusions from a massive study of more than 17,000 persons, including 14,000 prisoners. He offered innumerable distinctions between those caught for committing crime and his control group, a listing quite reminiscent of Lombroso's atavists. There were, however, very serious methodological flaws in Hooton's work. As did Lombroso, he confused inherited traits with conditions that are the result of environmental influences, such as tattooing. Indeed, what would Hooton make of the contemporary prevalence of tattoos among university students and professors? Besides, the group which he compared the prisoners to was a haphazard collection of firefighters, sunbathers, and hospital outpatients. In addition, it is illogical to maintain that because certain traits are observed in a studied population these traits are the cause of their behavior.

Nicole Rafter's review of Hooton's career depicts him as "an offbeat eugenicist." While eugenics was at the heart of his view, leading him to favor birth control, sterilization, and even euthanasia, he distanced himself from racism, taking the position that crime was committed by "morons and other degenerates who could be found in every race" (Rafter, 2004:757). It was striking that, although a staunch eugenicist, he not only decried Nazis as "vicious subhumans," but served on the editorial board of the National Association for the Advancement of Colored People. Perhaps Hooton's most lasting contribution was to keep the pulse of biological criminology beating, however slightly, through the middle portion of the last century. This was accomplished primarily through his influence on other criminologists, particularly Sheldon and Eleanor Glueck and William Sheldon, all on the Harvard faculty as well.

William Sheldon (1898–1977)

Constitutional Psychology was the name attached to the biological approach developed by William Sheldon in *Varieties of Delinquent Youth* (1949), a study of 200 young men referred to a Boston rehabilitation facility. Sheldon (1949:5) argued that the body is really "an objectification, a tangible record, of the most long-standing and most deeply established habits that have been laid down during a long succession of generations."

Sheldon built upon the work of Ernst Kretschmer (1925), who believed that there were three distinctive bodily forms—**somatotypes**—and that persons with particular types were likely to behave in particular ways. The types were labeled **endomorph** (soft and round), **mesomorph** (muscular), and **ectomorph** (lean) (see Figure 6.2). Specific temperaments were said to be associated with each body type: endomorphy, for instance, "is manifested by relaxation, conviviality, and gluttony for food, for company and for affection and social support" (Sheldon, 1949:25). See Highlight 6.1 for an interesting note on Sheldon's data collection methods.

Sheldon found delinquents to be decidedly high in mesomorphy and low in ectomorphy. His sample was too small to be used to relate body types to specific offenses, but Sheldon argued in colorful language that he had substantiated

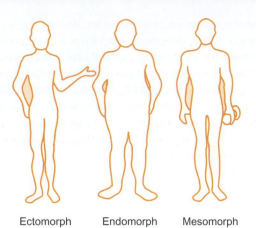

FIGURE 6.2
Somatotypes.

Ectomorph   Endomorph   Mesomorph

HIGHLIGHT 6.1 NUDE POSTURE STUDIES OF STUDENTS CREATE STIR

All college freshmen from several Ivy League and other prestigious schools were required to pose nude for photos, from the 1940s through the 1960s. They were taken by William H. Sheldon, who believed there was a relationship between body shape and intelligence and other traits. Sheldon's work has since been dismissed by most scientists as quackery.

Much of Sheldon's work has been destroyed by participating schools, but it was discovered that the Smithsonian Institution retains a collection of nude photos, including pictures of Hillary Rodham Clinton, George H.W. Bush, and Diane Sawyer. A spokesperson for the

Smithsonian indicated that they are now sealed, but previously were made available to students and researchers. At issue is whether they should be destroyed or retained for their historical value. The stir was created when alumni of schools such as Yale and Mount Holyoke read a report in the *New York Times Magazine* about the collection. They then began calling their alma maters, some distraught and others mildly amused, to find out what would become of the photos.

Source: Adapted from AP report by B. Greenberg in the *Johnson City Press*, January 21, 1995.

Hooton and further demonstrated the significance of criminal anthropology for understanding law-breaking:

> Hooton is one of a small group of contemporaries who have resolutely persisted in the retention of common sense in the formula for academic science. He considers it a datum of common sense that there are structurally superior and inferior organisms, and that a relationship must exist between structural and behavioral inferiority (Sheldon, 1949:752).

Sheldon's results were supported in a 1950 study by Sheldon Glueck and Eleanor Glueck, a research team based at the Harvard Law School, who matched 500 delinquents and nondelinquents. Delinquents were found to be considerably more mesomorphic than nondelinquents and their ranks contained a much lower proportion of ectomorphs (Glueck & Glueck, 1950).

Scathing critiques from within the mainstream criminological community of scholars met the work of William Sheldon and the Gluecks. Edwin

Sutherland, for instance, preeminent in the field at the time, faulted Sheldon on nine major points. His criticisms ranged from Sheldon's sloppy definition of delinquency to his statistical techniques. Orthodox criminological thought continues to give Sheldon's work low marks. Robert Sampson and John Laub (1990), however, have raised a revisionist voice, insisting that there was more to these early efforts than that for which they have been given credit. Sampson and Laub insist that Sutherland and the sociologists were intent on turning the study of crime into an exclusively sociological enterprise, and that they overreacted to the efforts of potential intruders to capture some of what they regarded as their intellectual turf.

CRIMINAL HEREDITY: THE BAD SEED THEORY

Efforts have been made to link genetic traits to criminal behavior by studying families in which criminal activity was widespread through generations, an approach called **eugenics** in its early days of popularity. In the closing decades of the nineteenth century and opening decades of the last century, there was a strong premise that nature played a stronger role than did nurture. Thus observation of widespread deviant behavior within a family was viewed as explicable by genetics, with little thought given to environmental influences or the need to control for other factors that might cause both deviance and particular biological characteristics. No one stopped to think, for example, that both stunted growth and deviance could be products of social disadvantage. It was concluded by many biological theorists that differences in the physiques of offenders must be the cause of observed patterns of deviance.

One of the early classics in the study of "degenerate" families is Henry Goddard's *The Kallikak Family* (1912/1955). Goddard traced two lineages of Martin Kallikak (a fictitious name), a member of an upstanding family: the **Kallikak family**. While a militiaman during the American Revolution, Kallikak met a **feebleminded** (then the label for a person functioning below the normal intellectual range, but above the level designated "idiot") girl by whom he became the father of a feebleminded son. This child was given the name of the father in full, and "thus has been handed down to posterity the father's name and the mother's mental capacity" (Goddard, 1912/1955:18). Of the 480 descendants that Goddard could trace from the union, 36 were illegitimate, 33 prostitutes, 24 alcoholics, three epileptics, 82 died in infancy, three were criminals, and eight kept houses of prostitution. The 496 descendants from Martin's marriage to a "respectable" woman of "good family" all were described as "normal" except for two alcoholics and one person said to be sexually promiscuous.

The difficulty with this study, of course, is that it proclaims the significance of heredity as the cause of the problems, but is quite unable to separate nature from nurture. Goddard attended to this problem but never appreciated how his words undercut his own argument. He observed that the feebleminded offspring "married into families, generally of about the same type" while "all of the legitimate children of Martin, Sr., married into the best families in their state, the descendants of colonial governments, signers of the Declaration of Independence, soldiers, and even founders of a great university" (Goddard, 1912/1955:19–30). Goddard had clearly demonstrated intergenerational continuity of behavior but utterly failed to separate genetic and environmental influences.

Another widely cited early study of family history is Richard Dugdale's *The Jukes: A Study in Crime, Pauperism, Disease and Heredity* (1877). Dugdale began his work with Ada Jukes (fictitious name) and located more than 1,000 of her descendants, including 140 criminals, 280 paupers, 40 persons with venereal disease, and assorted other deviants. In short, the Jukes name, like the Kallikak's, has lived in infamy for generations. In 1911 Dugdale's research was revised and expanded by a eugenicist, Arthur H. Estabrook (1916), whose work was published in *The Jukes in 1915*. Highlight 6.2 points to the ideological bias that played a part in driving the family studies approach and the inhumane policies for which they ultimately provided support.

Family pedigree studies such as those of the Jukeses and the Kallikaks fueled the eugenics movement that blossomed in the late nineteenth and early twentieth centuries. These ideas informed government policy for contending with crime, mental health, and other social ills. The U.S. Supreme Court case of *Buck v. Bell, Superintendent* (1927) exemplifies the impact of the eugenics movement on law. In an opinion delivered by the renowned and otherwise largely progressive Justice Oliver Wendell Holmes Jr., the court ruled that the State of Virginia had the authority to administer involuntary surgical sterilization on "feebleminded" and other "unfit" persons if the superintendent of a state institution deemed it in the best interest of society. The subject of the appeal before

---

HIGHLIGHT 6.2 BAD SEED OR BAD SCIENCE: REFLECTING ON THE JUKES FAMILY AS VICTIMS OF IDEOLOGICAL BIAS

The **Jukes family** has stood in social science history for more than one century as the epitome of a genetically flawed family, teeming with crime, mental illness, poverty, and a host of other social defects. They were used to provide the academic evidence of the power of genetics in transmitting such defective character, leading eugenicists' calls for sterilization, lobotomies, isolation, and even extermination.

The recent finding of archives from the original studies of the fictitiously named Jukes, undertaken first by Richard Dugdale and updated by Arthur Estabrook, cast a dark cloud over the Jukes research. The work appears to have been ideologically driven to bolster the views of the eugenics movement that was a craze in the early 1900s.

Dugdale's work was often misrepresented as purely supporting a biological explanation of the Jukes' deviance, while Estabrook has been accused of knowingly misrepresenting the data. He did not, for example, point out that some of the lineage became lawyers, real estate brokers, and fulfilled other respectable roles. He also withheld the information that Ada Jukes' husband was a descendant of a governor. Estabrook did reveal that the Jukeses were not comprised of a single family, but rather were a composite of several families, including such surnames as Miller, Bank, and Bush.

Source: Adapted from Christianson, S. (2003). *The New York Times*, February 8.

the court was Carrie Buck, a young woman who was the offspring of a feeble-minded woman and who had already given birth to a feebleminded illegitimate child. In Justice Holmes's words, "It is better for all the world, if instead of waiting to execute degenerate offspring for crime, or to let them starve for their imbecility, society can prevent those who are manifestly unfit from continuing their kind . . . Three generations of imbeciles are enough" (*Buck v. Bell*, 1927). The law permitting involuntary sterilization of humans continued in Virginia until 1974. Highlight 6.3 describes how individuals who were sterilized by the North Carolina Eugenics Board are seeking compensation for their injuries.

As the twentieth century unfolded, criminologists became increasingly uncomfortable with biological explanations of crime. By mid-century, biological accounts were in disrepute and a sociological approach came into dominance. The rejection of genetics and other biological factors in explaining crime was more a reflection of ideology than science. The abuse of human rights, supported on the grounds of eugenic interpretations of social problems, reached a dreadful height with the rise of the Nazi and Fascist parties in Europe and eruption of World War II. Because biological theorizing was used as an intellectual justification for denying human rights and seeking extermination of peoples, the perspective was spurned by most in the criminological community. The overwhelming rejection of a biological criminological perspective was not the result of cumulative scientific research, but primarily an ideological response to horrific abuses of

HIGHLIGHT 6.3 NORTH CAROLINA VICTIMS OF FORCED STERILIZATION PROJECT SEEK COMPENSATION

From 1929 until 1974, the state of North Carolina sterilized more than 7,000 individuals. Approximately 85 percent of the sterilized victims were females, and 64 percent of victims after 1950 were nonwhite females. Individuals were often referred to the Eugenics Board for sterilization because they were labeled "feebleminded," promiscuous, mentally unstable, or an unruly or disorderly delinquent. North Carolina had one of the most versatile sterilization referral policies. Other states that had sterilization policies at that time required that victims be institutionalized or jailed, while North Carolina allowed social workers, educators, and doctors to refer noninstitutionalized victims. In 1974, a federal lawsuit was filed by the American Civil Liberties Union against the North Carolina Eugenics Board on behalf of a number of sterilization victims. In the end, the jury found that the state of North Carolina did not violate victims' rights to procreation, and the case was denied to be heard by United States Supreme Court.

Delores Elaine Riddick was sterilized after she had been raped by an older neighborhood acquaintance while walking home from a party. From a troubled background, Delores' estranged father reportedly signed the sterilization order, even though it was reported that he was illiterate and he did not have custody of Delores at that time. "They cut me open like I was a hog," she stated. In 2009 Governor Beverly Perdue provided funding for the Justice for Sterilization Victims Foundation. The commission ultimately recommended compensation in the amount of $50,000 per victim of the sterilization project. North Carolina became the first state to compensate victims of eugenics when Governor Pat McCrory signed the bill in 2013.

Adapted from: http://abcnews.go.com/US/wireStory?id=14306999&singlePage=true.

http://rt.com/usa/north-carolina-eugenics-program-932/

science. An unfortunate consequence was the stymieing of progress in objective understanding of the role that biological factors play in the generation of crime and deviance.

Contemporary Biological Perspectives

Criminology, many believe, is once again in the midst of a dramatic shift insofar as the role it extends to biology in understanding crime. As Nicole Rafter (2004:736) concluded, "today biological explanations are again gaining credibility and are joining forces with sociological explanations in ways that may soon make them equal partners." A recent review of "the genetic turn in sociology," published in the widely circulated *Chronicle of Higher Education* (Shea, 2009), painted a similar picture of a growing acceptance of biological factors in the well-established "parent" discipline. The *Chronicle* article noted that leading sociology journals have begun publishing papers that focus on the role of biology in understanding human behavior and that even a subfield of gene–environment interactions is emerging in the sociology departments of some universities. Some, however, are less optimistic about the progress that has been made toward including modern biological insights within criminological circles. John Wright and his colleagues (2008a) reviewed the prevalence of biological focus among the faculty and dissertations of doctoral programs in criminology and criminal justice, finding little scholarly focus in the area. Similarly, they lamented, only 4 percent of the articles published in four premier criminology journals over the preceding dozen years were biologically informed. Similarly, too, a national survey regarding public perceptions of the role of biology in crime causation found low levels of support among lay persons (Gajos et al., 2014). Given the revolutionary advances across numerous realms of biological research, their findings seem rather remarkable, but are quite clear. While they did find that 60 percent of those interviewed agreed that neurological problems could lead to criminal behavior, nearly two-thirds felt that genetic factors did not play a role. Moreover, 93 percent viewed environmental variables as playing a larger role than genetics in crime causation. Thus, the level of acceptance and impact of the growing *biosocial criminology* movement is a debatable question in the eyes of some.

Delightfully, Richard Wright and Mitchell Miller (1998:14) identified an earlier edition of this text as meriting "praise for unusually good coverage of biocriminology," a tradition that has been continued in conjunction with the revitalization of this perspective. They only faulted the presentation for its mention of association of the perspective with racism. Similarly, Wright et al. (2008a) object that, "To this day, introductory criminology textbooks link biological theorizing with the repulsive practices that accompanied Hitler and Mussolini . . ." These abuses are part of history, forewarning criminologists to remain on guard to prevent new ethical misuses of science. Yet at the same time, as reviewed below, striking advances in knowledge about biology and human behavior have been discovered in recent years. The science of criminology is obligated to incorporate these emerging findings in the quest to explain crime and deviance.

Although many of the same debates persist, and others have emerged, the differences have narrowed substantially. Perhaps the most important change is that few theorists now propose to explain crime and deviance solely through biological variables. Those who incorporate biological variables are unlikely to consider themselves biocriminologists, eugenicists, or criminal anthropologists. The more common identities are as biosocial, biopsychological, sociobiological, or psychobiological criminologists, or as interdisciplinary criminologists. This reflects a growing tendency to incorporate or "integrate" (see Chapter 10) variables within theories that are derived from a much wider range of "parent disciplines," including biology.

Along with becoming far more multidisciplinary, biologically inclusive criminology has moved in a less deterministic direction. The debate is framed not so much in a **nature vs. nurture** format, but rather in a nature *and* nurture perspective. Well-known biosocial criminologist John Wright noted in a Visiting Scholar lecture delivered at Western Carolina University that there is "no single gene for crime," but rather "that for the vast majority of people, it is always a combination of their genetic architecture, their experiences, and what they have been socialized to do" (Wright, 2009). Biological theories no longer see crime as biological destiny, but as outcomes that are the sum of biological **risk factors**, combined with a wide range of environmental influences. These risk factors impact the statistical probability of criminal behavior, while recognizing a complex path between biology and crime. Clearly, not all persons who suffer from bouts of depression, have high testosterone levels, or who are genetically programmed to be aggressive will become involved in crime. The more risk factors present, however, the greater the odds of criminal behavior. The environment, in turn, can either further enhance risk of criminality or may serve to insulate the biologically at-risk person from a criminal path.

Although criminology has been decidedly moving in a multidisciplinary direction, some resistance in mainstream criminology (the more sociologically oriented) to theories of criminal behavior that rely upon physiological variables continues. This is partly based on ethical concerns, a fear that identification of biological deficiencies may be more likely to lead to unacceptable interventions in the lives of subjects than if they displayed only social risk factors. Although some researchers focusing on physiological factors have emphasized that we can identify those at risk and devise policies to do "good" things for them (e.g., develop programs for prenatal care, provide opportunities that will help insulate genetic "time bombs," etc.), concern remains that biology tends to hold more implications for doing "bad" things to people. This is where the historical abuses of eugenicists and racists haunt criminological research. It is difficult to discount a history that includes sterilization, lobotomies, institutionalization of persons classified as "feebleminded," and political agendas to annihilate races of people politically designated as inferior. Even Paul Billings, himself a clinical geneticist at Stanford University, echoes such concerns: "It's not the genes that cause violence in our society. It's our social

---

HIGHLIGHT 6.4 GENETIC CONTROVERSY REIGNS

How controversial are genetics in explaining human behavior? Nikolas Rose (2000), an expert on biology and crime, has pointed out that we exist in a "biologized culture"— one that increasingly turns to genetics to explain human diversity in all dimensions. From athletic performance to intellectual capacity to artistic talent, human performances are increasingly linked to genetics, raising concerns about genetic alterations being employed to produce the ideal offspring. But of concern to criminologists is the other end of the continuum, the role of genetics in producing "problem" behaviors. Thus geneticists have claimed genetic links to schizophrenia, bipolar disorder (manic depression), alcoholism, aggression, and various forms of crime.

Does the focus on genetic predisposition alarm you? It does alarm some people. In 1992 a conference titled Genetic Factors in Crime: Findings, Uses, and Implications was funded by the National Institutes of Health (NIH). It was to bring together researchers from many disciplines on the campus of the University of Maryland to share their research findings on genetics and crime. But it did not take place as scheduled. In the face of accusations by some leaders of African-American groups that this could facilitate racism, NIH suspended funding. The conference finally went forward, still under protest, in 1995.

---

system" (Stolberg, 1993: A18). Highlight 6.4 examines the controversy that continues over the role of biology in explaining problem behavior, including crime.

The difficulty is that persons displaying traits (social, psychological, or biological) placing them at risk for delinquent and criminal behavior can always be discriminated against, potentially even before displaying the "problem" behavior. The search for a biological precursor of criminal activity is fueled by a desire to locate characteristics that will effectively identify the potential lawbreaker. If low intelligence or high testosterone levels are likely to lead to illegal behavior, it might make sense to locate people with such traits and seek to remedy them or to isolate or more carefully monitor those who have them. Unfortunately, ideology bears heavily on the identification of risk factors. When the risk factors are located in genetics, suspicions, some of them also rooted in ideology, come to the forefront.

Biosocial criminology argues that criminal behavior results from the combination of biological, psychological, and sociological risk factors. Biological risk factors include variables such as genetics, brain structure and functioning, neurotransmitters, and other physiological characteristics. Psychological risk factors refer to cognitive processes and attitudes that place one at risk for antisocial behavior. Such psychological risks may include neuropsychological factors (e.g., low self-control, poor decision-making skills), antisocial attitudes, and mental disorders (e.g., depression, bipolar disorder, schizophrenia). In other words, the approach is quite interdisciplinary, although a number of biosocial models may not explicitly include psychological variables. This is due in part to researchers' uncertainty on whether psychological factors originate from biological or sociological forces. Nonetheless, some biosocial models do explicitly include psychological variables. Finally, sociological risk factors refer to environmental and social causes of offending, such as delinquent peer association, poor parental supervision, and stressful life circumstances.

According to biosocial criminology, there are at least four ways in which biological, psychological, and sociological risk factors come together to produce antisocial behavior: (1) an additive biosocial model, (2) a correlated biosocial model, (3) a sequential biosocial model, and (4) a multiplicative biosocial model (Raine et al., 1997; Rutter et al., 2006). First, biological and sociological risk factors may additively combine to influence antisocial behavior (see Figure 6.3).

This model, referred to as the **additive biosocial model**, argues that individuals will be most likely to engage in antisocial behavior when they have *both* biological *and* sociological risk factors; thus, a biological risk factor (or sociological risk factor) alone will not result in maladaptive behavior. Instead, it is the independent effects of nature *and* nurture that cause behavior. The model is referred to as the additive biosocial model because the risk associated with the biological and sociological factors adds up in a linear, cumulative fashion. An example of the additive biosocial model is presented in Figure 6.4.

It illustrates that individuals who only have a biological risk factor commit, on average, two crimes per year. Similarly, individuals who only have a sociological risk factor (but who do not have a biological risk factor) commit two crimes per year. Individuals who have both a biological and a sociological risk factor, however, commit approximately four crimes per year. This example shows that the risk associated with the biological factor (i.e., two crimes) additively combines with the risk from the sociological factor (i.e., two crimes) to influence the number of crimes committed (two + two = four crimes in total).

The second type of biosocial effect is referred to as the **correlated biosocial model**, also referred to as a **gene–environment correlation**. This model states

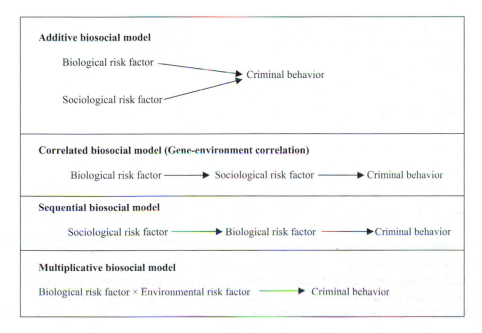

FIGURE 6.3
Illustrations of biosocial theoretical models.

FIGURE 6.4
Example of an additive
biosocial model.

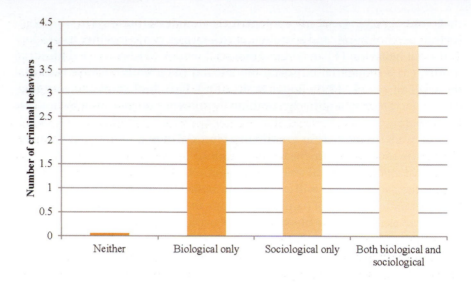

FIGURE 6.4
Example of an additive biosocial model.

that biological risk factors may be indirectly related to individuals' criminal behavior via their interactions with the social environment. That is, biological factors may increase the likelihood that individuals will be exposed to a particular environment and that they will evoke certain responses from others. Individuals' interactions with the environment, in turn, increase their chances of engaging in crime. For example, individuals who have a genetic proclivity for risky or antisocial behavior are likely to select themselves into environments that allow this behavior to be expressed. They may "hang out" in bars or nightclubs that tolerate and provide opportunities for antisocial behavior (e.g., dark, little to no security, no rules), rather than well-lit establishments that have ample security and that do not tolerate criminal behavior. Once they enter into the criminogenic bar or nightclub, they are then free to engage in antisocial behavior. Applied to the biosocial model, this example may be written as:

Individual likes antisocial behavior → Selects a bar that permits antisocial behavior → Individual engages in antisocial behavior.

Arousal theory appears to readily blend with the notion that individuals with low arousal of the cerebral cortex will require a lot of stimulation to achieve a feeling of emotional and physical balance. More technically, arousal involves a series of complex interactions between the anatomical nervous system (controlling bodily functions such as resting heart rate), the neuroendocrine system (regulating vital hormones such as testosterone) and the cerebral cortex (driving rational decision making). Thus persons with a low state of arousal will actively seek out stimulation through exciting and risky activities. While this need can be satisfied through involvement in conventional and legal hobbies, sports, and occupational endeavors, it can also be met through delinquent and criminal activities. Thus arousal theory predicts that conforming individuals with low rates of arousal will pursue hobbies such as motorcycling, parachuting, rock climbing, martial arts, and such. Similarly, they will be attracted to work in fields such as tree trimming, mining, agriculture, or law enforcement. Conversely, those with high arousal, the superoptimally stimulated, will prefer hobbies such as stamp collecting, chess or photography and occupations that will limit them to indoor work and minimum conflict. Where this perspective intersects with environmental variables is a matter of the availability of needed stimulating experiences. Those with low arousal (a biological force) and foreclosed opportunities (an environmental factor) will respond to the availability of illegal stimuli. Finding youths with low resting heart rates to be disproportionately motivated for both violent and nonviolent delinquency, Jill Portnoy and colleagues (2014) noted that the policy implication is to create stimulating prosocial activities for youths with low states of arousal.

An interesting application of arousal theory by Lee Ellis (1996) sheds new light on the consistent finding that religiosity is negatively associated with criminal behavior. He argued that those with low arousal of the cerebral cortex are less likely to be involved in religious ceremonies because these tend to be more serene than stimulating. At the same time, provocative deviant activities would provide needed "thrills". The superoptimally aroused, on the other hand, would tend to find tranquil religious services quite satisfying while being repelled by the risks of deviance.

A third type of biosocial model, called the **sequential biosocial model**, argues that individuals' environments may influence their biological functioning (environment → biological functioning). For instance, hundreds of studies have reported that early childhood abuse and neglect influence functioning of the hypothalamic-pituitary-adrenal axis, the dopamine system, the serotonin system, and brain regions that are responsible for negative emotions and self-regulation (Andersen & Teicher, 2009). Studies have also found that environments can influence the expression of our genes. This phenomenon, referred to as an **epigenetic effect**, occurs when exposure to certain environments causes genes to "shut off" (i.e., slow down or stop protein production) or "turn on" (i.e., begin or increase protein production).

Some of the classic epigenetic studies were conducted by Weaver and his colleagues (2004, 2007). The researchers found that a specific gene (glucocorticoid receptor gene) was "shut off" (i.e., methylated) among young rats who had neglectful mothers (i.e., low intimate contact), but the gene was functioning normally among young rats who did not have neglectful mothers. This particular gene is important because it is part of a system that is responsible for our anxiety, fear, and sensitivity to stress; thus, if it is shut off, individuals and animals are more anxious, more fearful, easily frustrated, and have trouble recovering from a stressful event. What was particularly interesting about this study was that it also found that the effects of neglect could be reversed. That is, young rats from neglectful mothers who were "adopted out" to loving caring mothers had their glucocorticoid gene turned back on; their gene started functioning the same as those in pups from loving mothers. Subsequent studies have found that the environment can influence the expression of more than 900 genes (Weaver et al., 2006). Applied to traditional sociological criminology, these findings suggest that strains (see Chapter 7) and weakened social bonds (see Chapter 8) may have biological consequences (in addition to sociological and psychological consequences), and these consequences may help to explain behavior.

Finally, the last type of biosocial effect discussed here is the multiplicative biosocial model. The **multiplicative biosocial model** states that individuals who have both a biological and a sociological risk factor engage in an exponentially higher level of criminal behavior than individuals who have only a biological or only a sociological risk factor. This model is different than the additive biosocial model because it argues that synergy between biological and sociological risk factors increases criminal behavior above and beyond the additive effects of biology and environment. For instance, let us return to our previous example where individuals who only have a biological risk factor commit two crimes per year, and individuals who only have a sociological risk factor (i.e., poverty) commit two crimes per year. Under the additive model, it was expected that individuals who had both the biological and environmental risk factor would commit four crimes, on average, per year (see Figure 6.5). Contrary to the additive model, the multiplicative biosocial model would predict that individuals who have both biological and sociological risk factors would commit five or more crimes per year (or any number of crimes larger than four, the combination of the independent effects). While the difference between the additive and multiplicative model seems very mathematical in nature, it also has important conceptual implications. The additive model states that the addition or

FIGURE 6.5
Example of a multiplicative biosocial model.

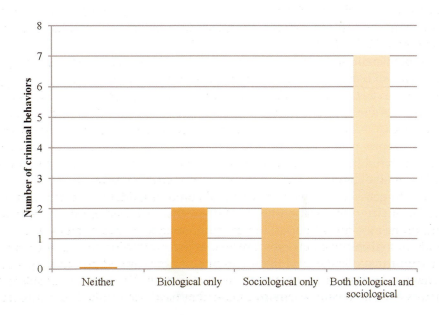

combination of a biological and sociological risk factor can moderately increase the risk of criminality by summing across all risk factors. The multiplicative model, however, states that the synergy between the biological and sociological risk factors can have severe or disastrous effects. It is analogous to chemical interactions whereby a given chemical or drug has little or no physiological impact unless ingested in combination with other substances, but in combination can be substantial or even lethal. Similarly, biological and sociological risk factors may work together to enhance the negative (or positive) effects of each other.

One form of the multiplicative biosocial model is the **gene × environment interaction**. The gene × environment interaction occurs when the effect of the environment on behavior varies by one's genetic composition. For instance, a negative social environment may have a strong effect on criminal behavior for those who are genetically predisposed toward antisocial behavior, while the same negative environment may have little to no effect on criminal behavior for those who are not genetically prone to maladaptive behavior. The landmark gene × environment interaction study for criminal behavior was conducted by Caspi and colleagues (2002). Their research group found that a variant of the monoamine oxidase A (MAOA) gene interacted with childhood maltreatment to influence delinquent and criminal behavior. More specifically, the authors found that maltreated children who had the low activity allele (i.e., the "genetic risk" factor) had significantly higher levels of conduct disorder, convictions for violent crimes, self-reported disposition toward violence, and antisocial personality disorder, compared to maltreated youths who did not have the genetic risk (i.e., environmental risk only), and compared to nonmaltreated youths who did have the low activity allele (i.e., biological risk only). Since the publication of Caspi et al. (2002), scores of other studies have found that genetic variants related to the neurotransmitter and hormone systems interact with various environments to influence criminal behavior and substance use (Boisvert & Vaske, 2011).

Another example of the multiplicative biosocial model is when two biological factors interact to influence behavior. That is, maladaptive behavior may occur when genes interact with other genes, or when genes interact with other biological functions (e.g., hormones, neuropeptides). A gene X gene interaction is referred to as **epistasis**. Epistasis occurs when one genetic variant enhances (or mutes) the effect of another genetic variant on a phenotype (any measurable traits such as criminal behavior); thus, gene A may have a strong or weak effect on behavior Y, depending upon the person's score on gene B.

The four models above provide the theoretical guidelines to conducting biosocial criminological research. The models, however, are quite general and do not specify which biological components are most relevant to the study of maladaptive behavior. Further, many criminologists are not familiar with the particular biological components that are related to antisocial behavior. In light of these issues, the next section discusses the biological factors and the biosocial environments that have been linked to antisocial behavior. The biological factors include genetics, brain structure and function, neurotransmitters, and hormones. The criminogenic biosocial environments that may influence antisocial behavior include obstetric factors, exposure to toxins, and very early stressful life events. While other environments may increase the risk of antisocial behavior, these environmental factors have known biological consequences that are relevant to the study of criminal behavior. It is likely that future research will expand upon this list and elucidate the neurobiological consequences of other environments (e.g., delinquent peer association).

Genetics

The study of genetics and behavior is broken down into two subcategories: behavioral genetics and molecular genetics. Behavioral genetics attempts to answer the question: "How important are genetics and environments to the study of antisocial behavior?" Behavioral genetic models can tell us what percentage of variation in a behavior is attributable to genes or the environment. **Molecular genetics**, on the other hand, addresses the question: "Which specific genetic variants are important to the study of antisocial behavior?" Thus, behavioral genetics is much more general in nature, while molecular genetics is more specific in that it tries to pinpoint particular genetic variants that are important to cognition and behavior.

Behavioral Genetics

The broad research question for **behavioral genetics** is the relative contribution of genetics and environment to any given phenotype. A *phenotype* is any observable human trait, from hair color and height to musical talent and athleticism. The criminological focus in behavioral genetics is on behavioral phenotypes such as aggression, violence, and criminality. Under the behavioral genetics model, researchers can estimate how much variance in antisocial behavior is attributable to genetics and environment. Researchers estimate how much variation in behavior is due to genetics through a **heritability coefficient** (h^2). The heritability coefficient ranges from 0 to 1, with a score of 0 indicating that genetics does not explain any individual differences in antisocial behavior and a score of 1 indicating that 100 percent of the variance in antisocial behavior is explained by genetics. To illustrate variability in heritability coefficients, it would be 0 for explaining the language that people speak because linguistic abilities are not inherited at all, but rather are acquired through learning from one's environment. Near the other end of the heritability continuum, height yields a coefficient of approximately 0.90, reflecting the fact that it is about 90 percent determined by our genetic structure (Rowe, 2002).

In behavioral genetics, the potential environmental influences are subdivided into shared and nonshared categories. **Shared environmental influences** are the common social experiences within a family that make siblings similar. Examples of shared environmental influences may include their standard of living and neighborhood experiences. Each member of the family also experiences environmental interactions specific to them, referred to as **nonshared environmental influences**. Examples are accidental injuries sustained during delivery or after birth, influences from different peers, or unique treatments within the family and so forth. Nonshared environmental influences are unique to each child and therefore promote differences between siblings. One recent study, for example, found that identical twins whose mothers were disengaged from one of the pair were more likely to have self-control problems and to become involved in delinquency (Beaver, 2008).

Researchers have used two different behavioral genetic methodologies to investigate the contributions of genetics and environment to antisocial behavior: adoption studies and twin studies. Adoption studies begin by tracking the development of youths who are adopted soon after birth and who are adopted by nonfamily members. These studies assess the contributions of genetics and environmental factors to a phenotype by examining whether adopted children resemble their biological parents in terms of antisocial behavior more than their adoptive parents. The key concept in adoption and twin studies is **concordance**, which refers to the portion of cases wherein both family members display the same behavioral outcome. If adopted children resemble their biological parents more so than their adoptive parents (i.e., greater concordance with biological parents than adoptive), this suggests that genetic factors are important to explaining their behavior. For instance, researchers would state that criminality was genetically transmitted if an adoptee engaged in criminal behavior and a biological parent has a history of criminal behavior, but the adoptive parents did not engage in criminal behavior. On the other hand, if the adoptee resembled his or her adoptive parents more than their biological parents (i.e., greater concordance with adoptive parents than biological), this would make a case for the relevance of environmental factors in antisocial behavior. This is the most classic type of design used in adoption studies, but it is important to note that there are other designs that can be used with adoptees (Plomin, 1990).

Early adoption studies examined concordance rates between adoptees and their parents (biological and adoptive) to examine the role of genetics in behavior. An early study by R.R. Crowe (1972) determined that adopted children whose biological mothers had criminal records displayed higher levels of criminal involvement than those whose biological mothers had no such records. In a larger study of adopted persons, Barry Hutchings

Dr. Nancy Segal, center, co-director of the University of Minnesota project Twins Reared Apart, poses with twins who were separated at birth. The study explores the relative importance of heredity and environment by investigating what similarities are shared by separated twins.

CREDIT: AP Photo.

FIGURE 6.6
Distribution of adopted Danish males aged 30–44 years by criminal record of their adoptive and biological fathers.

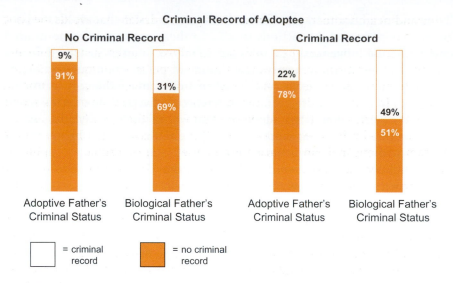

Criminal Record of Adoptee

No Criminal Record

9%
91%
Adoptive Father's Criminal Status

31%
69%
Biological Father's Criminal Status

Criminal Record

22%
78%
Adoptive Father's Criminal Status

49%
51%
Biological Father's Criminal Status

☐ = criminal record   ▇ = no criminal record

Source: Adapted from B. Hutchings & S.A. Mednick (1977). "Criminality in Adoptees and Their Adoptive and Biological Parents: A Pilot Study." In S.A. Mednick & K.O. Christiansen (Eds.) *Biosocial Bases of Criminal Behavior*, pp. 127-141. New York, NY: Gardner Press.

and Sarnoff Mednick (1977), using Danish data, found an increasing tendency for males to have criminal records if their fathers (adoptive or biological) had criminal records, with the tendency more pronounced if the biological father was the offender. Figure 6.6 displays a portion of their findings. Hutchings and Mednick (1977) suggest that poor heredity may make people more vulnerable to endangering social circumstances because they suffer from a genetic disadvantage that places them in a position in society in which they are more likely to succumb to crime.

More recently, adoption studies have used sophisticated statistical techniques to estimate the contributions of genetics, shared environments, and nonshared environments to antisocial behavior. Overall, these studies suggest that the heritability of antisocial and criminal behavior is approximately 0.30 to 0.40 (Boisvert, 2009; Moffitt, 2005). Shared environments explain little to no variation in antisocial behavior, and nonshared environments explain the remaining 60–70 percent. It is important to note that the estimate of nonshared environments also includes estimates of measurement error (inherent in studying human behavior), and thus it is difficult to assess the contributions of nonshared environments accurately. While this estimate suggests that genetic factors are important to the explanation of antisocial behavior, adoption studies, like all studies, have their limitations. One limitation to adoption studies is that adoption agencies tend to place children in stable family homes. This limitation is referred to as **selective placement bias**. Selective placement bias can lead to a lack of variation in the adoptive family environment, and ultimately lead researchers to underestimate the importance of the environment.

Twin studies are another type of behavioral genetic design that avoids the issue of selective placement bias.

Twin studies have become a mainstay in efforts to assess genetic influence among biological relatives. We know that, on average, siblings share 50 percent of their genes, 25 percent in the case of half-siblings. The same is true for dizygotic (DZ) or "nonidentical" twins, as they are the product of two separate eggs being fertilized and developing simultaneously. Biologically, they are siblings sharing a birthdate. Monozygotic (MZ) or "identical" twins, however, have the same genetic makeup because they are the result of a single egg splitting, being fertilized, and developing at the same time. Since identical twins share 100 percent of their genes, theoretically they should be exactly the same once nonshared environmental influences are controlled.

Johannes Lange's *Crime as Destiny* (1930) pioneered the exploration of criminal concordance. He found much more concordance for MZ than for DZ twin brothers, consistent with genetic explanations of criminality. Probably the most cited twin study is Karl O. Christiansen's (1977) work undertaken in Denmark. He examined records for a large cohort and found the following rates of criminal concordance: 35 percent for MZ males; 13 percent for DZ male twins; 21 percent for MZ females; and 8 percent for DZ female twins.

The cumulative results of behavioral genetics research, overall, suggest that genetics explains approximately 50 percent of the variation in delinquent and criminal behavior, with nonshared environments explaining approximately 40 percent. Shared environments tend to explain only a trivial amount of variation in delinquent and criminal behavior (Moffitt, 2005). For instance, a recent meta-analysis of 38 twin and adoption studies revealed that genetic factors explain 56 percent, nonshared environment explains 31 percent, and shared environment explains 11 percent of the variation in antisocial personality and behavior (Ferguson, 2010). Other meta-analyses also show that approximately 40 percent of the variation in a variety of behaviors (i.e., intelligence, perceptual-motor skills, language, mental disorders, substance use) is explained by genetics; thus suggesting that genetics may underpin a wide range of behaviors (Malouff et al., 2008).

The advances of the biosocial perspective in recent years may seem straightforward and unarguably scientific. Accordingly, one might presume that the earlier ideological and paradigmatic clashes over the role of biological variables in explaining crime and deviance would be a historical footnote. Yet just as the ninth edition of *Criminology: Explaining Crime and Its Context* was being readied for press, a virtual firestorm of disagreement emerged in *Criminology*, the top journal of the American Society of Criminology. On the one hand, it is abundantly clear that the biosocial perspective has become deeply intertwined with mainstream theorizing and research within the discipline. On the other hand, this combative exchange suggests that considerable suspicion and intolerance remains and may stymie continued movement toward a more inclusive criminology. Others might read the debate as a matter of criminologists within this subfield as talking "past" and not to one another. In any event, a review of that vigorous debate will render an appreciation for the depth of the rancor, as well as the points of disagreement, that continues to encroach on biological discussions. Students with particular interest in the area are encouraged to pursue the original sources for more technical depth and to trace any further evolution of these topics.

The debate was launched with the publication of an article by Callie Burt and Ronald Simons (2014). Offering caveats that they were not motivated to press the field toward extreme social determinism and that criminologists can only ignore biological variables "at our own peril" (p. 251), they go on to present a contentious critique of the full gamut of heritability studies. The bulk of their discussion focuses on twin and adoption studies, offering several rationales for discounting their findings. They contend that adoption studies overestimate heritability and underestimate environmental influences because of shortcomings: cases of late separation of offspring from their biological parents coupled with the cogency of early bonding, selective placement, and prenatal (e.g. lead, nicotine, alcohol) influences.

Burt and Simons's review of twin studies focuses on their implicit assumption that MZ and DZ twins experience "equal" shared environmental influence, an **equal environment assumption (EEA)**. They identify a variety of factors that suggest this assumption is untenable and, importantly, assert that they substantially inflate h^2, the heritability coefficient, rendering the twin study design "patently invalid" (p. 233), "preposterous" (p. 236), and built upon a broader logic plagued by "fatal flaws" (p. 223). Beyond specific methodological concerns, Burt and Simons (2014) offer a broader conceptual critique and some sweeping conclusions. They assert that because genes and the environment operate through a complex interactive process, "it is biologically nonsensical to attempt to partition genetic from environmental influences" (p. 225). This leads them to "call for an end to heritability studies in criminology" (p. 225) and to profess that for criminologists to engage in such studies "does a disservice to both scientific and public knowledge" (p. 246).

To no great surprise, a group of criminologists heavily invested in behavioral genetics, including heritability studies (Barnes et al., 2014), were quick to respond vigorously. Substantively, they elected to focus on the EEA of twin studies, predicated on their reading of Burt and Simons that (a) this was the thrust of their presentation and that (b) other behavioral genetics research designs yield much the same results. At the same time, some of their more acrimonious retorts challenged the scholarly virtues of the Burt and Simons paper. J. C. Barnes and his colleagues (2014) objected that "Burt and Simons called for a *de facto* form of censorship" (p. 589). They insisted that the critique of heritability studies was "seductive, especially for the uninformed about behavioral genetics and for those ideologically opposed to biology" (p. 590), but that "they misquoted scholars," "misrepresented study findings," and "labeled political ideologues as 'experts' in behavioral genetics" (p. 591).

Returning to the Barnes et al. (2014) response to the contention that the EEA is so extensively violated in twin studies as to constitute a "fatal flaw," they presented an exhaustive review of 61 previous assessment works. Their conclusion from this body of literature was that the bulk of them, particularly those that empirically assessed EEA, indicated that any violations of the assumption have not led to significantly biased (inflated) estimates of h^2. They go on to delineate another assumption, **random mating**, that also underlies twin study designs. In short, the supposition is that partners selected for reproductive purposes are not predisposed to carry any particular phenotypes in their genetic makeup. For example, it would assume that any given individual is not more or less likely to mate with another person that is tall or short, dark or fair-skinned, nondrinker or heavy drinker, drug-free or drug-addicted, and so forth. As with the EEA, it is clear that there will be degrees of departure from the ideal premise of the statistical model. The difference is that violations of this assumption will have the effect of attenuating h^2 and, conversely, inflating the shared environment correlation. This is so because the statistical model sets the odds of DZ twin offspring (as with singular) being like a parent at .5. All else being equal (i.e. random mate selection), there is a 50 percent chance that the child of a tall mother will be genetically programmed to grow tall. To the extent that tall women elect to mate with tall men, the .5 assumption underestimates the genetic contribution to height if DZ and MZ twins are compared. Likewise, and directly relevant, the offspring of both parents at risk for substance abuse will have greater genetic influence toward such risk than will one born to parents, only one of whom is so at risk. Thus the contention of Barnes and colleagues (2014) is that an h^2–inflating EEA violation, to the extent that it has such an effect, is more than offset by violation of the random mating assumption that deflates h^2 and inflates environmental correlations. Their conclusion is that the claim that violating the EEA inflates h^2 "is unequivocally incorrect" (p. 610), leaving the larger image portrayed by Burt and Simons a "social construction of reality" (p. 611).

Following convention for academic exchanges in scholarly journals, the editor of *Criminology* commissioned an additional pair of exchanges between the groups (Burt & Simons, 2015; Wright et al., 2015). Those rejoinders, predictably, failed to unveil much common ground between the camps. Burt and Simons (2015) reiterated that their intent was to "*reinvigorate biological research in criminology by pointing it away from a misguided gene-centric model.*" They draw on a recent book by Aaron Panofsky (2014) attributing a "hitting them over the head style" among behavioral geneticists, entailing the depiction of critics "as mortal enemies and attacking them in spectacular, polemical fashion". "The task was not to seek synthesis, integration, or sober rational persuasion but to engage in polemical scientific attack, declaring themselves as crusaders who would rout the antigenetics heresy gripping behavioral science" (Panofsky, 2014:142, as cited in Burt & Simons, 2015). Burt and Simons argued that their work had been oversimplified as a methodological statistical critique of heritability studies when "*the crux of our argument against heritability studies is conceptual.*" In this vein, they reasserted their position that the relative contribution of genes and environment cannot be assessed because there is "a much more complicated, interactive reality."

For their part, John Wright and the other members of the behavioral genetics responding team (2015) objected that Burt and Simons had shifted from a 20-page methodological/statistical and two-page conceptual critique in their original paper to a position that the core of their argument was conceptual. To the substance of the conceptual argument, Wright et al. (2015) concede that genes and environment are connected in complex ways, but insist that heritability studies are valid and can separate genetic from environmental forces. They remain concerned that the call to ban heritability studies was methodologically unfounded, but, of more concern, runs "contrary to the canons of science."

This fiery debate highlights two issues in the continuing nature and nurture discussion. First, it demonstrates that strong substantive disagreements (conceptual, theoretical, methodological, statistical) persist. Second, it is evident by the tone of the exchange that biosocial criminology has some way to go to fully shed its emotional and ideological backdrop. Despite the strident antagonism and intellectual clash evident in this exchange, it is clear that biological variables now have a firm foothold in criminological inquiry. It will be exciting to see how both the evidence and ideological dispositions unfold in years to come. Indeed, the spiritedness and rapid evolution of this shift to accommodate biological variables, beyond shining a broader lens on our understanding of crime and deviance, lends an invigorating jolt to the criminological enterprise. Despite the tenor of the debate just reviewed, it seems that the antagonists agree that biology will bolster our understanding of crime and deviance and that molecular genetics holds promise in that regard. That is an encouraging sign.

Molecular Genetics

Criminologists may use molecular genetic methods to identify the specific genetic variants that are associated with higher levels of antisocial and criminal behavior. Social scientists tend to focus on genetic variants that are related to neurotransmitter and steroid hormone systems (e.g., estrogen, glucocorticoids, androgens), since these systems are tightly linked to individuals' psychology and decision making. Thus, it is believed that the causal chain linking genes to behavior may look like:

genetic polymorphism → change in neuropsychology → change in behavior.

Scientists emphasize that there is not a "crime gene." Instead, they recognize that criminal behaviors are complex and that hundreds or thousands of genetic variants may underlie them. That is, researchers believe that criminal behavior is a **polygenic disorder**, or that multiple genes work together to produce a phenotype. For instance, Comings and colleagues (2000) conducted a study of adolescents and found that ten genetic variants were related to conduct disorder, seven variants were related to oppositional defiant disorder, and ten genetic variants were related to attention deficit disorder. Their study was one of the first attempts to examine the polygenic nature of antisocial behavior. However, their investigation was limited to only 42 genetic variants, and it is likely that hundreds of variants contribute to antisocial behavior.

What are these genetic variants? In short, a genetic variant (or difference in DNA) is referred to as a *polymorphism* in the molecular genetics literature. DNA consists of genetic letters (A, C, T, G) that are strung together and provide instructions for the production of certain amino acids. A change in the genetic letters or nitrogen bases signifies a difference in the amino acid produced. More specifically, a change in the genetic letters (i.e., an extra letter, a letter deleted, or a different letter substituted) may represent a specific amino acid being produced less, or a different amino acid being produced all together. For instance, a switch in the sequence from CCA to CAA means that the amino acid glutamine (CAA) will be produced instead of proline (CCA). This is important because changes in amino acids may lead to changes in proteins, and changes in proteins lead to changes in chemicals and structures within our brain and body. Thus, a change in the foundation—DNA—can have ramifications throughout the body, and it may influence how we perceive and interact with the world.

Researchers have found that genetic variations, called **polymorphisms**, related to the serotonin, dopamine, and enzymatic systems (i.e., monoamine oxidase or MAO) are associated with antisocial and criminal behavior (Boisvert & Vaske, 2011). For instance, studies have shown that individuals who carry the short allele of the serotonin transporter polymorphism (5-HTTLPR) have a higher risk of attention deficit hyperactivity disorder (ADHD), oppositional defiant disorder (ODD), aggressive behavior, violent offending, chronic offending, alcohol abuse, and other drug abuse problems than individuals who carry the long allele. The 5-HTTLPR polymorphism occurs because 44 genetic letters (or base pairs) are deleted from a region in the serotonin transporter gene. This deletion results in less protein for serotonin transporters, and fewer transporters may ultimately lead to less serotonin activity overall (Vaske, 2011). It is widely documented that low serotonin activity is associated with impulsive and aggressive behaviors.

Other studies have found that dopaminergic polymorphisms (in the dopamine transporter gene) and enzymatic polymorphisms (in the MAOA gene) are related to antisocial behavior. While studies have linked genetic polymorphisms to antisocial behavior, it should be noted that the effect of individual genetic polymorphisms on antisocial behavior is relatively small. Individual genetic polymorphisms rarely explain more than 2 percent of the variation in an antisocial behavior. However, researchers believe that these individual polymorphisms combine with other polymorphisms and environments to produce behavior; thus, studying the effects of individual genes may underestimate the effects of genetics on behavior. At this point in the science, researchers are just now beginning to develop methods (called quantitative trait locus analysis) that combine the effects of multiple genetic polymorphisms and then examine their combined effect on behavior. It will be interesting to see how such methods will shape our understanding of genetics and behavior in the coming years.

Genetic variants often are linked to behavior because these variants influence the structure and functioning of the brain, neurotransmitters, and hormones. This is an area of growing research within the biosocial perspective. The following sections will briefly review the specific brain regions, neurotransmitters, and hormones that may be associated with antisocial behavior.

Brain Structure and Function

Brain structure refers to the volume or density of gray and white matter in the brain, while brain functioning refers to the amount of blood flow and glucose metabolism within the brain. Healthy brains require the structure or machinery of the brain to be intact, as well as a normal rate of blood flow and energy consumption. A deficit in one's brain structure means that a certain region of the brain is small or missing altogether. A deficit in one's brain functioning, on the other hand, suggests that a brain region may not be receiving enough oxygen or glucose (i.e., energy) to function. Thus, individuals need their brain structure and functioning to be intact, in order for "normal" behavior to emerge.

In the early 1990s, researchers began using magnetic resonance imaging technologies to examine whether structural and functional deficits were related to antisocial behavior. They found that a number of regions in the prefrontal cortex, temporal cortex, and limbic system were particularly relevant to the explanation of antisocial behavior. The prefrontal cortex is considered the most evolved region of the brain, and it is responsible for higher order cognitive processes, such as problem solving, decision making, self-regulation, and meta-cognition. Raine and colleagues (2000) found that the volume of gray matter in the prefrontal cortex was 11 percent smaller among individuals who were diagnosed with antisocial personality disorder, compared to healthy controls and psychiatric controls.

A myriad of studies in recent years have found deficiencies in the frontal lobe in particular, but also the temporal lobe, limbic system, and paralimbic system of the brain, to be associated with both cognitive problems and deviant behavior. Structures and functional abnormalities in the brain may lead directly to aberrant behavior, for example, by undermining control of emotions. But these brain deficiencies may also result in cognitive disabilities that, in turn, may be linked to behavioral problems. A learning disorder could lead to problems with school adjustment or peer relationships that, in turn, lead to misconduct. Note that these brain deficiencies could be either inherited or the result of injuries to the brain from inadequate prenatal care, injuries, substance abuse, or toxic environments.

While structural and functional abnormalities are important for behavior, they are only one part of the picture. The brain also has a number of neurotransmitters, enzymes, and hormones that influence cognition and behavior.

Neurotransmitters and Enzymes

Neurotransmitters are considered the brain's chemical messengers. They take information from one neuron to the next neuron, where the message is then processed. As shown in Figure 6.7, there is a small gap that separates one

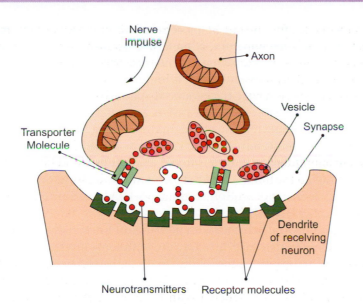

Nerve
Impulse

Axon

Vesicle

Synapse

Transporter
Molecule

Dendrite
of receiving
neuron

Neurotransmitters   Receptor molecules

FIGURE 6.7
Neurotransmission.

neuron from the next. This gap is referred to as the synaptic cleft. Electrical energy cannot travel across the synaptic cleft, and so brain cells communicate to each other through chemical messages. To communicate, presynaptic neurons release chemical messages or neurotransmitters into the synaptic cleft. The neurotransmitters travel across the synaptic cleft, and then attach to a protein structure on the postsynaptic neuron called a receptor. Once the receptor "catches" the neurotransmitter, the chemical message triggers an electrical response in the postsynaptic neuron and the electrical message is sent to the neuron's cell body where it is processed. After the neurotransmitter has transmitted its message, it is released from the receptor and it floats back into the synaptic cleft. The neurotransmitter is then removed from the synaptic cleft by being returned to the presynaptic neuron or it is degraded by an enzyme, such as MAOA or COMT.

While there are currently more than 100 identified neurotransmitters, criminal behavior is most often linked to monoamine neurotransmitters, such as dopamine, serotonin, and monoamine oxidase. **Dopamine** is relevant to a wide range of behaviors and skills, as it plays a role in movement, learning, concentration, and any pleasurable or rewarding experiences. Studies have shown that low levels of dopamine are related to an inability to concentrate and higher levels of depression, while higher levels of dopamine have been linked to aggression, paranoia, negative emotionality, and hyperactivity. Dopamine is also a key component to addictive behaviors, such as substance abuse. For instance, Buckholtz and colleagues (2010) recently found that individuals with higher scores on an impulsive psychopathy trait scale had a greater release of dopamine in response to a dopamine stimulant (amphetamine), compared to individuals with lower scores on the impulsive psychopathy scale. These findings suggest that impulsive individuals may be more sensitive to the rewarding effects of amphetamine and other dopamine stimulants (e.g., cocaine, alcohol), and they may be more likely to develop drug dependency problems.

Serotonin is a neurotransmitter that is important for the regulation of emotions, cognition, and behavior. It is produced in both the central nervous system (CNS) and in the intestines, but researchers are not sure whether intestinally produced serotonin can cross the blood–brain barrier and influence cognition. Low levels of CNS serotonin have been linked to higher levels of impulsivity, sensation seeking, aggression, oppositional defiant disorder, and depression. A meta-analysis of 20 studies revealed that there was a moderate negative association between a measure of serotonin activity (5-HIAA) and antisocial behavior (Moore et al., 2002). Other studies have examined the association between serotonin and antisocial behavior with measures of intestinally produced serotonin. These studies often have mixed results, with some investigations showing higher levels of serotonin corresponding with antisocial behavior, and other studies finding that low levels of serotonin place one at risk for maladaptive behavior. Researchers tend to focus on the association between CNS serotonin and antisocial behavior, given that serotonin is synthesized in the brain and can directly influence brain functioning.

Monoamine oxidase (MAO), unlike dopamine and serotonin, is an enzyme that is responsible for degrading excess monoamine neurotransmitters (serotonin, norepinephrine, and dopamine), after neurotransmission is complete. Research has shown that high levels and low levels of MAO may lead to maladaptive behavior, and so MAO must be in a moderate range for optimal functioning. Ellis (1991) reviewed the research on MAO and antisocial behavior, and found that low MAO levels were associated with defiance of punishment, impulsivity, childhood hyperactivity, sensation seeking, poor academic performance, extraversion, and recreational drug use. Further, a case study of a Dutch criminal family revealed that the antisocial males had low levels of MAOA (one version of MAO), and that their MAOA deficiencies were the result of a genetic polymorphism in the MAOA gene (Brunner et al., 1993). These findings indicate that low MAO activity may place one at risk for antisocial behavior.

While current research focuses on the roles of dopamine, serotonin, and MAO in offending, there are a host of other neurotransmitters that may be relevant to the etiology of antisocial behavior. These include amino acid neurotransmitters such as gamma aminobutyric acid (GABA) and glutamate, and the biogenic amine neurotransmitter noradrenaline. GABA and glutamate have been linked to substance use issues, and noradrenaline has been associated with sensation seeking. Neuropeptide neurotransmitters, such as vasopressin and corticotropin releasing hormone (CRH), may also be important for antisocial behavior. CRH is important for regulating one's response to stressors, and thus individuals with hyperactive CRH systems may be overly sensitive to stress or strain. As described in Robert Agnew's General Strain Theory (see Chapter 8), strain or stressful life events may lead to higher levels of antisocial behavior and substance use.

Hormones

Research has found that sex hormones and stress hormones are related to anti-social behavior. One of the most widely studied sex hormones in criminological research is **testosterone**. Numerous studies have reported that testosterone is positively correlated with violent offending, sex offending, drug offending, antisocial behavior, alcoholism, physical aggression, sensation seeking, and callousness (Ellis et al., 2009). The positive correlation between testosterone and antisocial behavior has been found across studies that vary in age of respondents (children vs. adults), country in which the study was conducted (Europe vs. United States), and measures of antisocial or aggressive behavior (official report, self-report, experimental tasks). While studies have reported an association between testosterone and antisocial behavior, researchers are unsure *why* testosterone is linked to antisocial behavior. Perhaps testosterone has a direct effect on brain functioning, or perhaps it indirectly influences behavior by altering gene expression. In addition, it is important to recognize that environmental factors, such as winning a competition or a fight, can cause testosterone levels to briefly rise; thus, associations between testosterone and antisocial behavior may actually reflect the effects of environmental factors more so than testosterone.

The most widely publicized source of excessive testosterone is the use of anabolic steroids by competitive athletes seeking every edge to enhance their strength and endurance. There is a convincing body of scientific evidence that these steroids, a synthetic derivative of testosterone, have a host of deleterious side effects. Most relevant to criminology are the mood swings and aggressiveness that are manifested in what is popularly termed "steroid rage." An array of anecdotal cases suggest that anabolic steroids are associated with violent behavior.

Imbalance in female hormones is similarly suspect in the eyes of some. Premenstrual syndrome (PMS) suffered by some women has been hypothesized to be associated with psychological as well as physical changes. In fact, PMS is a recognized excuse from criminal culpability in France and has been introduced in American and English courts with varying degrees of success. Yet some respond that PMS is more an ideological construct than a biological force.

Stress hormones, such as cortisol, have also been linked to antisocial behavior. Cortisol is responsible for helping people "calm down" or recover after a stressful event. Researchers have hypothesized that deficits in cortisol should be related to higher levels of antisocial behavior. Indeed, a number of studies have found that cortisol levels are much lower among antisocial populations compared with nonoffender populations (Ellis et al., 2009).

Environments that Impact Biology

When criminologists study the effects of environment on crime, they typically focus on the adolescent years. This constrains their view to environments such as delinquent peers, poor parental supervision, and strained teacher–youth relationships. Developmental psychologists, however, tend to emphasize the effects of prenatal and perinatal environments on biological functioning and behavior. During pregnancy and infancy the brain undergoes rapid periods of development during the first 33 months of life (9 months gestation, first 24 months of life). This is often referred to as a **critical period** in development. For instance, the number of synapses (or connections between brain cells) in the prefrontal cortex peaks around 12 months of age, and then steadily declines over time (Huttenlocher, 1994). By age 2, the brain has reached 80 percent of its adult weight (Kretschmann et al., 1986).

Since the brain is undergoing many developmental changes in the first 33 months of life, it may be more sensitive to insults and toxins during this time period. Indeed, research has shown that injury or exposure to toxins during the first 33 months often leads to deficits in brain structure/function and cognition, but that the same environmental insults may not lead to cognitive impairments if the negative environment is experienced after the "critical period" (Riva & Cazzaniga, 1986). Researchers have a special term that they use to describe the effects of an environment on brain structure and functioning: **brain plasticity**. Brain plasticity acknowledges that the environment, especially very early environments, can shape brain development.

In light of the evidence on critical periods and brain plasticity, researchers have focused on prenatal and very early childhood environments that may place one at risk for antisocial behavior. These environments include (but are not limited to) obstetric factors (e.g., pregnancy complications, prenatal substance use, low birth weight or early term birth), exposure to toxins (e.g., lead), and early childhood stress (e.g., neglect and abuse). Prenatal and very early environments may increase one's risk of antisocial behavior because these environments lead to changes in individuals' biological, psychological, and sociological systems. For instance, early childhood neglect and abuse may lead to (1) biological changes such as high levels of dopamine, lowered serotonin levels and deficits in the prefrontal cortex, (Andersen & Teicher, 2009); (2) psychological changes such as impulsivity, anger, depressive thoughts, irritability or frustration, and anxiety; and (3) sociological changes such as attention seeking behavior, changes in peer groups, or weakening of attachments with family, teachers, or other social support/control systems (Lansford et al., 2002).

One widespread environmental neurotoxin is lead. The neurological effects are so thoroughly documented that federal legislation required its removal from gasoline, paint, and other products many years ago, but it persists in old paint and other features of impoverished environments. The **Cincinnati Lead Study (CLS)** has followed a cohort of persons born in such neighborhoods, characterized by extremely high levels of environmental lead concentrations, resulting in extraordinarily high rates of lead poisoning. (Dietrich et al., 2001; Wright et al., 2008b, 2009). The researchers measured blood lead levels at the prenatal stage, at age 6, and an average level across childhood to age 6. The findings of the CLS are quite sobering. From among 248 subjects followed, 800 arrests were generated and nearly two-thirds had at least one arrest with a mean of 5.2 each. Lead poisoning undermines brain development by stifling synapse formation. This reduces the travel of neurotransmitters, and correspondingly, lowers arousal of the cerebral cortex. This results in an array of cognitive deficiencies and lower intelligence scores (Needleman & Gatsonis, 1990). The end result is disproportionate contact with the criminal justice system.

BIOLOGY, MENTAL DISORDERS, AND CRIME

Some forms of mental illnesses are now well understood to be products of biological forces such as ones that have been discussed in this chapter. Two particularly widespread diseases that are risk factors for crime and deviance are **bipolar disorder** and **schizophrenia**.

Bipolar disorder or manic depression is one such form of mental illness. It is estimated that about one percent of the general population has bipolar disorder (Barondes, 1997; Papolos & Papolos, 1999). The consensus is that the condition is caused by deficiencies in the autonomic nervous system's ability to regulate emotion. There are thought to be inappropriate levels of or an imbalance between neurotransmitters such as serotonin, norepinephrine, and dopamine, causing emotions to alternate from one extreme to another. In effect, the bipolar individual can fluctuate from having a very low to a very high arousal threshold. Bipolar disorder is a heritable trait, with at least the potential for its development being genetically transmitted. Studies have identified polymorphisms that place persons at risk for bipolar and other mood disorders by disrupting neurotransmission (Leon et al., 2005). Durand and Barlow (2000), for example, found a concordance rate of 80 percent for identical twins, compared with 16 percent for fraternal twins. Recent studies have found flawed genes that are risk factors for bipolar disorder (Zhou et al., 2009). Like other biological predictors of criminality, bipolar disorder is a "time bomb" that may be detonated by stressful life events. Once triggered, the disorder becomes a cyclical process, with wide variation in the timing of relatively normal, manic, and depressive stages.

While most agree that great strides have been made in controlling the disorder with drugs, recurring patterns of deviance are quite common among bipolar persons. Unfortunately, medications have side effects and very frequently the individual will discontinue their use, while hiding the change from others. Much of the deviant behavior thought to result from bipolar disorder is not designated criminal at any given time or place, but nevertheless, is very disruptive of relationships. The disorder, for example, is associated with poor judgment, deceit, and manipulations of others. Sexual deviance and financial irresponsibility are common domains of misconduct, with infidelity or excessive spending causing the collapse of many personal relationships. Bipolar individuals typically follow a line of rational argumentation to support even the most bizarre patterns of behavior and often lead secretive lives. Consequently, patterns of deviance are frequently successfully hidden, even from close family members, for extended periods of time. Moreover, deviant episodes are separated by periods of normal behavior and exceptional levels of creativity or other forms of productivity are widespread among bipolar individuals. Many gifted artists, actors, and intellectuals, for example, have been afflicted with the illness. But, left untreated, and particularly in combination with other characteristics predictive of criminal behavior, bipolar disorder is associated with even the most serious forms of crime.

Schizophrenia also affects about one percent of the population (Lachenmeyer, 2000), but is much more disruptive to the person's life-course and more associated with crime. The illness usually begins early in life and is characterized by dramatic misperceptions of the world and inappropriate emotions. It is not a well-understood disease, but the consensus is that it is also rooted in neurobiology. Zacarias Moussaoui, the bumbling al-Qaeda operative convicted in conjunction with the infamous 9/11/01 attacks, is one of the most well-known criminals diagnosed as schizophrenic.

SUMMARY

This chapter tells the story of a second major paradigm shift in the history of criminology. It began in an era of scientific revolution, with Charles Darwin at the forefront. This led to adoption of the positive paradigm, marked by its adherence to the scientific method and presumption of determinism. Positive criminology first took the biological route, but this waned by the mid-twentieth century, displaced by a sociological approach. Over the last couple of decades, however, a biosocial perspective has re-emerged and garnered an appreciable following in criminological circles.

Biological explanations of the causes of criminal behavior got off to a poor start because of the crude methods of measurement, their ethnocentric biases, and primitive theoretical thinking. In the closing years of the twentieth century, however, changes in the criminological landscape began to provide much more room for biosocial variables. They became much less deterministic, far more interdisciplinary, and had availability of dramatically better measurement instruments. While some heated debated continues, as reviewed in this chapter, it is evident that biosocial criminology is becoming a quite viable subfield and increasingly informing the general body of criminological knowledge.

In the biosocial arena, behavioral genetic and molecular genetic studies have revealed that genetics may be related to antisocial behavior. It is important to remember, however, that the path between genetics and offending is most likely not direct. Instead, it is more likely the case that genetics influence one's cognitive skills, personality, and a host of risk factors, including serious mental illnesses, that place individuals at higher risk for crime and deviance. In addition, genetics and other biological risk factors may, in some cases, lead to antisocial behavior only when they are paired with a criminogenic environment. Both nature *and* nurture, many criminologists now agree, must be taken into account in explanations of antisocial behavior.

HIGHLIGHT 6.5 THE DEBATE OVER POLICY IMPLICATIONS OF BIOSOCIAL CRIMINOLOGICAL RESEARCH

In 2009, an Italian inmate had his prison sentence reduced by one year because a number of biological tests revealed that he had structural abnormalities in his brain and that he carried the "risk" allele (or variant) of five genes linked to antisocial behavior. One of the genetic variants was the low activity allele of the (MAOA) gene. This case, along with others, has caused lawmakers and researchers to question the role of biosocial research in how the justice system responds to criminal behavior. Should biological risk factors be considered mitigating factors, like mental disorders? Should defendants with biological risk factors receive shorter sentences? If individuals and offenders do have biological deficits, how should the justice system treat those deficits? Incarceration? Sterilization? One suggestion has been to provide enrichment programs for those who are identified as having biological risk factors. If antisocial behavior is a product of environment and biology, then enrichment programs that improve environmental conditions may mask or "offset" any of the negative effects of the biological risk factor.

Source: Adapted from Feresin, E. (2009). *Nature News*. October 30.

The long hesitance of criminologists to consider biosocial explanations of criminal behavior, given a historical review, is quite understandable. Early biological theories stigmatized groups of individuals in society and provided a foundation for atrocious public policies, such as sterilization and eugenics. However, evidence is mounting that behavior is partially a function of biology. If we choose to ignore an aspect of our humanity and development because of the possibility of extremist public policies, we will essentially be paralyzed, because every theory has the possibility of creating dangerous policies when taken to the extreme. See Highlight 6.5 in regards to policy concerns. Instead of solely focusing on the potential harms of biosocial criminology, individuals should expand their discussion to include what the biosocial perspectives can add to our understanding of behavior and interventions.

Despite questions regarding the policy implications of biosocial criminology, it is clear that at least the immediate direction for criminology will include the integration of more variables from a wider range of categories, including the biological realm. The coming years almost surely will see more attempts to develop general theories of crime that will incorporate a range of biological variables and combine them with environmental influences.

KEY TERMS AND CONCEPTS

Additive Biosocial Model

Arousal Theory

Atavism

Behavioral Genetics

Biosocial Criminology

Bipolar Disorder

Born Criminal

Brain Plasticity

Cincinnati Lead Study (CLS)

Concordance

Correlated Biosocial Model

Criminal Anthropology

Criminaloids

Critical Period

Determinism

Dopamine

Ectomorph

Empiricism

Endomorph

Epigenetic Effect

Epistasis

Equal Environment Assumption (EEA)

Eugenics

Feebleminded

Gene–Environment Correlation

Gene × Environment Interaction

Heritability Coefficient

Jukes Family

Kallikak Family

Medical Model

Mesomorph

Molecular Genetics

Monoamine Oxidase (MAO)

Multiplicative Biosocial Model

Nature vs. Nurture

Neurotransmitters

Nonshared Environmental Influences

Paradigm Revolution

Phrenology

Polygenic disorder

Polymorphisms

Positivism

Random Mating

Risk Factors

Schizophrenia

Serotonin

Selective Placement Bias

Sequential Biosocial Model

Shared Environmental Influences

Somatotypes

Statistical School

Testosterone

KEY CRIMINOLOGISTS

J. C. Barnes

Callie Burt

Karl O. Christiansen

Charles Darwin

Richard Dugdale

Lee Ellis

Arthur H. Estabrook

William Ferrero

Enrico Ferri

Raffaele Garofalo

Eleanor Glueck

Sheldon Glueck

Henry Goddard

Charles Goring

A. M Guery

Earnest Hooton

Cesare Lombroso

Terrie Moffitt

Adolphe Quetelet

William Sheldon

Edwin Sutherland

John Wright

CASE

Buck v. Bell, Superintendent, 274 U.S. 200 (1927)

DISCUSSION QUESTIONS

1. Describe the impact of Charles Darwin on criminological thought.

2. How can it be said that Cesare Lombroso advanced the field of criminology?

3. How do the core concepts and assumptions of positivism differ from the classical or rational choice school of thought?

4. In what ways has biological criminology threatened humanity? Could it do so again? Why or why not?

5. What kinds of biological risk factors did early biological theories focus on? On what types of biological and biosocial risk factors do contemporary biosocial theories focus?

6. What were two factors that led to the rejection of early biological theories?

7. How do the four contemporary biosocial models explain antisocial behavior?

8. What are the major points of contention regarding the value of heritability studies to understanding crime?

9. How is mental illness related to genetics? To crime? What forms of mental illness are both widespread and risk factors for antisocial behavior?

REFERENCES

Allen, F.A. (1960). Raffaele Garofalo. In H. Mannheim (Ed.), *Pioneers in criminology* (pp. 254–76). London, UK: Stevens.

Andersen, S.L. & Teicher, M.H. (2009). Desperately driven and no brakes: Developmental stress exposure and subsequent risk for substance abuse. *Neuroscience and Biobehavioral Reviews, 33,* 516–24.

Barnes, J.C., Wright, J.P., Boutwell, B.B., Schwarts, J.A., Connally, E.J. Nedelec, J.L. & Beaver, K.M. (2014). Demonstrating the validity of twin research in criminology. *Criminology, 52,* 588–626.

Barondes, S.H. (1997). *Mood genes: Hunting for origins of mania and depression.* New York, NY: W.H. Freeman.

Beaver, K.M. (2008). Nonshared environmental influences on adolescent delinquent involvement and adult criminal behavior. *Criminology, 46,* 341–70.

Beirne, P. (1993). *Inventing criminology: Essays on the rise of "homo criminals".* Albany, NY: State University of New York Press.

Boisvert, D. (2009). *Rethinking Gottfredson and Hirschi's general theory of crime: A behavioral genetic approach.* Unpublished thesis. Cincinnati, OH: University of Cincinnati.

Boisvert, D. & Vaske, J. (2011). Genes, twin studies, and antisocial behavior. In A. Somnit & S.A. Peterson (Eds.), *Biology and politics: The cutting edge* (pp. 159–83). Bingley, UK: Emerald Group Publishing Limited.

Brunner, H.G., Nelen, M., Breakefield, X.O., Ropers, H.H., & van Oost, B.A. (1993). Abnormal behavior associated with a point mutation in the structural gene for monoamine oxidase A. *Science, 262,* 578–80.

Buckholtz, J.W., Treadway, M.T., Cowan, R.L., Woodward, N.D., Benning, S.D., Li, R. (2010). Mesolimbic dopamine reward system hypersensitivity in individuals with psychopathic traits. *Nature Neuroscience, 13,* 419–21.

Burt, C.H. & Simons, R.L. (2014). Pulling back the curtain on heritability studies: Biosocial criminology in the postgenomic era. *Criminology, 52,* 223–62.

Burt, C.H. & Simons, R.L. (2015). Heritability studies in the postgenomic era: The fatal flaw is conceptual. *Criminology, 53,* 103–12.

Caspi, A., McClay, M., Moffitt, T.E., Mill, J., Martin, J., Craig, I.W. (2002). Role of genotype in the cycle of violence in maltreated children. *Science, 297,* 851–54.

Christiansen, K.O. (1977). A preliminary study of criminality among twins. In S.A. Mednick & K.O. Christiansen (Eds.), *Biosocial bases of criminal behavior* (pp. 89–108). New York, NY: Gardner.

Christianson, S. (2003). Bad seed or bad science: The story of the notorious Jukes family. *The New York Times,* February 8.

Comings, D.E., Gade-Andavolu, R., Gonzalez, N., Wu, S., Muhleman, D., Blake, H. (2000). Multivariate analysis of associations of 42 genes in ADHD, ODD and conduct disorder. *Clinical Genetics, 58,* 31–40.

Crowe, R.R. (1972). The adopted offspring of women criminal offenders: A study of their arrest records. *Archives of General Psychiatry, 27,* 600–603.

Darwin, C. (1859/1964). *On the origin of the species.* Cambridge, MA: Harvard University Press.

Darwin, C. (1871/1964). *The descent of man.* New York, NY: D. Appleton.

Dietrich, K.N., Ris, M.D., Succop, P.A., Berger, O.G., & Bornschein, R.L. (2001). Early exposure to lead and juvenile delinquency. *Neurotoxicology and Teratology, 23,* 511.

Dugdale, R.L. (1877/1910). *The Jukes: A study in crime, pauperism, disease, and heredity.* New York, NY: G.T. Putnam's Sons.

Durand, V.M. & Barlow, D.H. (2000). *Abnormal psychology: An introduction.* Scarborough, Ontario: Wadsworth.

Ellis, L. (1991). Monoamine oxidase and criminality: Identifying an apparent biological marker for antisocial behavior. *Journal of Research in Crime & Delinquency, 28,* 227–51.

Ellis, L. (1996). Arousal theory and the religiosity-criminality relationship. In P. Cordell & L. Siegel (Eds.), *Readings in Contemporary Criminological Theory* (pp. 65–83). Boston, MA: Northeastern University Press.

Ellis, L., Beaver, K.M., & Wright, J.P. (2009). *Handbook of crime correlates.* London, UK: Academic.

Estabrook, A.H. (1916). *The Jukes in 1915.* Washington DC: The Carnegie Institute of Washington.

Feresin, E. (2009). Lighter sentence for murderer with "bad genes": Italian court reduces jail term after tests identify genes linked to violent behaviour. *Nature News, October, 30,* 2009.

Ferguson, C.J. (2010). Genetic contributions to antisocial personality and behavior: A meta-analytic review from an evolutionary perspective. *The Journal of Social Psychology, 150,* 160–80.

Ferri, E. (1917). *Criminal sociology* (J.I. Kelly & J. Little, Trans.). Boston, MA: Little, Brown.

Gajos. J.M., Beaver, K.M., Gertz, M. & Bratton, J. (2014). Public opinion of genetic and neuropsychological contributors to criminal involvement. *Journal of Criminal Justice Education, 25*(3), 368–85.

Glueck, S. & Glueck, E. (1950). *Unraveling juvenile delinquency*. Cambridge, MA: Harvard University Press.

Goddard, H.H. (1912/1955). *The Kallikak family*. New York, NY: Macmillan Publishing Company.

Goring, C.B. (1913). *The English convict: A statistical study*. London, UK: His Majesty's Stationery Office.

Greenberg, B. (1995). *Ivy League Photos locked up/subjects could include Bush, Hillary Clinton*. Associated Press, January 21.

Grupp, S. (1968). *The positive school of criminology: Three lectures by Enrico Ferri*. Pittsburgh, PA: University of Pittsburgh Press.

Hooton, E.A. (1939a/1969). *The American criminal: An anthropological study*. Westport, CT: Greenwood.

Hooton, E.A. (1939b). *Crime and the man*. Cambridge, MA: Harvard University Press.

Hutchings, B. & Mednick, S.A. (1977). Criminality in adoptees and their adoptive and biological parents: A pilot study. In S.A. Mednick, & K.O. Christiansen (Eds.), *Biosocial bases of criminal behavior* (pp. 127–41). New York, NY: Gardner.

Huttenlocher, P.R. (1994). Synaptogenesis, synapse elimination, and neural plasticity in human cerebral cortex. In C.A. Nelson (Ed.), *Threats to optimal development* (Vol. 27, pp. 35–54). Hillsdale, NJ: Lawrence Erlbaum Associates.

Kretschmann, H.J., Kammradt, G., Krauthausen, I., Sauer, B., & Wingert, F. (1986). Brain growth in man. *Bibliotheca Anatomica, 28*, 1–26.

Kretschmer, E. (1925). *Physique and character: an investigation of the nature of constitution and of the theory of temperament*. London: Trubner & Co., Ltd.

Kuhl, S. (1994). *The Nazi connection: Eugenics, American racism, and German national socialism*. New York, NY: Oxford University Press.

Kuhn, T.S. (1970). *The structure of scientific revolution* (2nd ed.). Chicago, IL: University of Chicago Press.

Lachenmeyer, N. (2000). *The outsider*. New York, NY: Broadway.

Lange, J. (1930). *Crime as destiny* (C. Haldane, Trans.). New York, NY: Boni.

Lansford, J.E., Dodge, K.A., Pettit, G.S., Bates, J.E., Crozier, J., & Kaplow, J. (2002). A 12-year prospective study of the long-term effects of early child physical maltreatment on psychological, behavioral, and academic problems in adolescence. *Archives of Pediatrics & Adolescent Medicine, 156*, 824–30.

Leon, S.L., Croes, E.A., Sayed-Tabatabaei, F.A., Claes, S., Broeckhoven, C.V., & van Dujin, C.M. (2005). The Dopamine D4 Receptor Gene 48-Base-Pair_repeat Polymorphism and Mood Disorders: A Meta-Analysis. *Biological Psychiatry, 57*, 999–1003.

Lombroso, C. (1876). *L'uomo delinquente: studiato in rapporto alla antropologia, alla medicina legale, ed alle discipline carcerarie*. Milan, Italy: Hoepli.

Lombroso, C. & Ferrero, W. (1895). *The female offender*. London, UK: Unwin Fisher.

Lombroso-Ferrero, G. (1911/1972). *Criminal man*. Montclair, NJ: Patterson Smith.

Malouff, J. M., Rooke, S. E., & Schutte, N. S. (2008). The heritability of human behavior: Results of aggregating meta-analyses. *Current Psychology, 27*, 153–61.

Moffitt, T. (2005). Genetic and environmental influences on antisocial behaviors: Evidence from behavioural-genetic research. *Advances in Genetics, 55*, 41–104.

Moore, T. M., Scarpa, A., & Raine, A. (2002). A meta-analysis of serotonin metabolite 5-HIAA and antisocial behavior. *Aggressive Behavior, 28*, 299–316.

Needleman, H. L. & Gatsonis, C. A. (1990). Low-level lead exposure and the IQ of children. *The Journal of the American Medical Association, 263*, 673–78.

Novak, M. A. & Harlow, H. F. (1975). Social recovery of monkeys isolated for the first year of life: Rehabilitation and therapy. *Developmental Psychology, 11*, 453–65.

Panofsky, A. (2014). *Misbehaving in science: controversy and the development of behavior genetics.* Chicago, IL: University of Chicago Press.

Papolos, D. F. & Papolos, J. (1999). *The bipolar child.* New York, NY: Broadway Books.

Plomin, R. (1990). *Nature and nurture: An introduction to human behavioral genetics.* Pacific Grove, CA: Brooks/Cole Publishing Company.

Portnoy, J., Raine, A., Chen, F. R., Pardini, D., Loeber, R., & Jennings, J. R. (2014). Heart Rate and antisocial behavior: The mediating role of impulsive sensation seeking. *Criminology, 52*(2), 292–311.

Quetelet, A. (1833/1984). *Research on the propensity for crime at different ages* (S. F. Sawyer, Trans.) Cincinnati, OH: Anderson Publishing Co.

Rafter, N. H. (1992). Criminal anthropology in the United States. *Criminology, 30*, 525–45.

Rafter, N. H. (2004). Earnest A. Hooton and the biological tradition in American criminology. *Criminology, 42*, 735–71.

Raine, A. & Yang, Y. (2006). Neural foundations to moral reasoning and antisocial behavior. *Scan, 1*, 203–13.

Raine, A., Brennan, P. A., & Farrington, D. A. (1997). Biosocial basis of violence: Conceptual and theoretical issues. In A. Raine, P. A. Brennan, D. P. Farrington, & S. A. Mednick's (Eds.), *Biosocial bases of violence* (pp. 1–20). New York, NY: Plenum Press.

Raine, A., Lencz, T., Bihrle, S., LaCasse, L., & Colletti, P. (2000). Reduced prefrontal gray matter volume and reduced autonomic activity in antisocial personality disorder. *Archives of General Psychiatry, 57*, 119–27.

Riva, D. & Cazzaniga, L. (1986). Late effects of unilateral brain lesions sustained before and after age one. *Neuropsychologia, 24*, 423–28.

Rose, N. (2000). The biology of culpability: Pathological identities in a biological culture. *Theoretical Criminology 4*, 5–34.

Rowe, D. C. (2002). *Biology and crime.* Los Angeles, CA: Roxbury.

Rutter, M., Moffitt, T. E., & Caspi, A. (2006). Gene-environment interplay and psychopathology: Multiple varieties but real effects. *Journal of Child Psychology and Psychiatry, 47*, 226–61.

Sampson, R. J. & Laub, J. H. (1990). Crime and deviance over the life course: The salience of adult social bonds. *American Sociological Review, 55*, 609–27.

Sellin, T. (1968). Enrico Ferri: Pioneer in criminology. In S. Grupp (Ed.), *The positivist school of criminology: Three lectures by Enrico Ferri* (pp. 361–83). Pittsburgh, PA: University of Pittsburgh Press.

Shea, C. (2009). The nature-nurture debate, redux. *The Chronicle of Higher Education*, B6–B9.

Sheldon, W. (1949). *Varieties of delinquent youth.* New York, NY: Harper and Row.

Stolberg, S. (1993). Fear clouds search for genetic roots of violence. *Los Angeles Times (Orange Cty. ed.)*, Dec. 30, Al, A18.

Tarde, G. (1912). *Penal philosophy* (R. Howell, Trans.). Boston, MA: Little, Brown.

Thomas, C.W., & Hepburn, J.R. (1983). *Crime, criminal law, and criminology*. Dubuque, IA: William C. Brown.

Vaske, J. (2011). *Genes and abuse as causes of offending*. El Paso, TX: LFB Scholarly.

Weaver, I.C.G., Meaney, M.J., & Szyf, M. (2006). Maternal care effects on the hippocampal transcriptome and anxiety-mediated behaviors in the offspring that are reversible in adulthood. *Proceedings of the National Academy of Sciences of the United States of America*, *103*, 3480–85.

Weaver, I.C.G., Cervoni, N., Champagne, F.A., D'Alessio, A.C., Sharma, S., Seckl, J.R. (2004). Epigenetic programming by maternal behavior. *Nature Neuroscience*, *7*, 847–54.

Weaver, I.C.G., D'Alessio, A.C., Brown, S.E., Hellstrom, I.C., Dymov, S., Sharma, S. (2007). The transcription factor nerve growth factor-inducible protein A mediates epigenetic programming: Altering epigenetic marks by immediate-early genes. *The Journal of Neuroscience*, *27*, 1756–68.

Wright, J.P. (2009). *Visiting scholar lecture at Western Carolina University: Who is winning the nature/nurture war? Insights from the study of violence*. http://fpame-diaserver.wcu.edu/~static/johnwright.mov. Summarized in *The Carolina Criminologist*, 1,2:1–3, 10–11.

Wright, R.A., & Miller, J.M. (1998). Taboo until today? The coverage of biological arguments in criminology textbooks, 1961 to 1970 and 1987 to 1996. *Journal of Criminal Justice*, *26*, 1–19.

Wright, J.P., Boisvert, D., & Vaske, J. (2009). Blood lead levels in early childhood predict adulthood psychopathy. *Youth Violence and Juvenile Justice*, *7*, 208–22.

Wright, J.P., Beaver, K.M., DeLisi, M., Vaughn, M.G., Boisvert, D., & Vaske, J. (2008a). Lombroso's legacy: The miseducation of criminologists. *Journal of Criminal Justice Education*, *19*, 325–38.

Wright, J.P., Dietrich, K.N., Ris, M.D., Wessel, S.D., Lanphear, B.P., & Hornung, R.W. (2008b). Association of prenatal and childhood lead concentrations with criminal arrests in early adulthood. *PLOS Medicine*, *5*, PMCID:PMC2674320.

Wright, J.P., Barnes, J.C., Boutwell, B.B., Schwartz, J.A., Connally, E.J., Nedelec, J.L. & Beaver, K.M. (2015). Mathematical proof is not minutiae and irreducible complexity is not a theory: a final response to Burt and Simons and a call to criminologists. *Criminology*, *53*, 113–20.

Zhou, X., Tang W., Greenwood T.A., Guo, S., He, L., Geyer, M.A., & Kelsoe, J.R. (2009). Transcription factor SP4 is a susceptibility gene for bipolar disorder. *PLOS ONE* 4:e5196

Social Structure Theories of Crime

LEARNING OBJECTIVES

After reading Chapter 7, you should be able to:

- Discuss the historical development of strain theory in American criminology.
- Identify Durkheim's five modes of adaptation to structural stress.
- Discuss the differences in Durkheim's and Merton's assumptions about the sources of stress in society.
- Explain how Cloward and Ohlin expanded Merton's theory of anomie by integrating the influence of both legitimate and illegitimate opportunity structures.
- Identify policies for reducing crime that are based on Cloward and Ohlin's opportunity theory.
- Elaborate on Messner and Rosenfeld's Institutional Anomie Theory, and explain how these criminologists attribute crime to the "American dream."
- Identify at least three main criticisms of social strain theory.
- Explain how General Strain Theory addresses some of the major criticisms of social strain theory.
- Identify at least three policies or programs that, from the perspective of a strain theorist, would reduce crime.
- Identify how social disorganization theory explains crime rates.
- Describe the Chicago Area Project, including its underlying theoretical justification.
- Discuss the role of immigration on crime rates.

The preceding chapter reviewed biological perspectives that locate the cause of crime in individual human differences. This chapter and the two that follow present the sociological orientation that has dominated American criminology since the 1920s.

Sociologists envision crime, delinquency, and deviant behavior as the product of social forces rather than of individual differences. Most sociological theories fit the positivist mode in that they contend that these social forces push or influence people to commit crime. Even at this broad level of categorization, however, the perspectives are not pure. **Sociobiology**, for instance, combines social and biological variables to explain crime. Many sociologists incorporate psychological factors in their theories, and both economists and sociologists are currently pursuing classical explanations of crime. So despite the general dominance of sociology in criminological theory construction, all manner of cross-disciplinary perspectives and hybrid theories can be found. A major trend is toward integration of various theoretical perspectives, a matter considered in Chapter 10.

Classification of theories within the sociological perspective is a knotty task. We have elected to use the term "social structure" to characterize the theories reviewed in this chapter, "social process" for those in Chapter 8, and "social reaction" in reference to the theories considered in Chapter 9. We do not contend that this organization scheme is necessarily the correct one, only that it provides a useful framework for contrasting sociological explanations of crime and their underlying assumptions.

The social structure genre provides the purest sociological explanation of crime and delinquency. It links the key troubles of individuals to the social structural origins of these difficulties (Mills, 1956). Theories that are most appropriately characterized as social structural depict crime as a product of characteristics of society. Structural features that contribute to poverty, unemployment, poor education, and racism are viewed as indirect or root causes of high crime rates among members of socially deprived groups. Theories of this variety, however, are not intended to imply that only poor people commit crimes, nor do they mean that people located in the lower levels of the social structure have no choices or are devoid of responsibility for misconduct. These theories do, however, assume that crime is primarily a lower-class problem and point to flaws within the social structure that increase the odds of a person within that social stratum resorting to illegal behavior. Social structure theorists draw attention to the primarily lower-class status of the clientele of our criminal justice system. This perspective also is frequently used to explain the disproportionate involvement of minorities in crime and delinquency (e.g., Peterson et al., 2000; Messner et al., 2001; Martinez, 2003) and the effect of unemployment and other economic hardships on crime rates (e.g., Hill & Crawford, 1990; Britt, 1997; Messner & Rosenfeld, 2007). Many criminologists, however, reject the assumption that crime is primarily a lower-class phenomenon, attributing the disproportionate lower-class representation in the criminal justice system to discrimination.

Social structure theories tend to be macro-theories. They are designed specifically to account for the higher rates of crime that the perspective assumes to characterize the lower echelon of the American class structure. Consequently, some criminologists maintain that social structure theories may be properly tested only with data collected at the group level (e.g., Bernard, 1987; Messner & Rosenfeld 2007), while others (e.g., Agnew, 1987, 1999; Menard, 1995) counter that individual-level data satisfactorily mirror the group problems that social structure theories portray.

Social structure theories provided the dominant explanation of crime in the 1950s and 1960s, but they were largely supplanted in the 1970s with the rise of control (see Chapter 8) and deterrence (see Chapter 5) theories. The focus on underlying structural defects was consistent with the reformist ideal of the era. Social structure theories reflect a fundamental faith in the social system, but they seek to identify structural flaws that contribute to the genesis of crime. Social structure theorists typically fit the traditional liberal image; they tend to be persons looking for means of reform without radically altering the basic social structure. They assume consensus regarding the legitimacy of laws and seek only adjustments to assure fairness. Charles Thomas and John Hepburn (1983) illustrate this orientation by comparing social structure theorists and automobile mechanics. The mechanics strive to restore the automobile to a level of efficiency defined in terms of its original design. This is attempted by cleaning, adjusting, tuning, and replacing parts of the engine. The mechanic does not critique the basic premise of an internal combustion engine, but rather accepts it as the optimal powerhouse for the vehicle. Likewise, social structure theorists do not question the foundation of our social structure, but they suggest how the social structure can be optimized by identifying and correcting deficiencies. Other explanations of crime, however, adopt a conflict perspective and offer fundamental critiques of our social system (for examples, see Chapter 9).

There are two major variations of social structure theories. Strain theories most frequently reflect the notion that crime is an outgrowth of weaknesses in the social structure. The social ecology tradition, though it does not fit quite so neatly, is incorporated in the present chapter because its analyses of the social and economic conditions of neighborhoods contributed to the foundation of the social structure tradition.

STRAIN THEORIES

Strain theories are at the heart of the sociological bid to account for crime. The thrust of this theoretical agenda is that stress, frustration, or strain (hence the name), generally a product of failed aspirations, increase the prospects for norm violation. These theories maintain that norms are violated to alleviate the strain that accompanies failure. Blockage of legitimate goal attainment is said to encourage deviant solutions. Key objectives of strain theories, therefore, are the specification of sources of strain and of deviant adaptations. Most strain theorists reason that the structure of American society creates the greatest pressure within the lower social echelons, and consequently, these theorists focus on explaining lower-class crime. Strain also tends to be associated with distorted aspirations, unrealistic desires for attainment, and crass materialism. This goal distortion sets the stage for individual failure and the search for deviant solutions.

Emile Durkheim, an early French sociologist, stimulated the strain tradition for explaining crime and other deviant behavior. Robert Merton's revision of Durkheim's theory, thereafter, provided the foundation for contemporary understanding of this perspective in the context of American culture. Theorists such as Richard Cloward, Lloyd Ohlin, Robert Agnew, Steven Messner, and Richard Rosenfeld further extended the concept. The collective works of these scholars delineate the central tenets of strain theory.

Emile Durkheim—Origins of Social Structure Theory

Born in 1858 in France, Emile Durkheim was exposed to the confusion and turmoil of a nation adjusting to a new social order. The French Revolution of 1789 had supplanted a repressive monarchy with a representative-based republic. Following closely upon this political upheaval were the social and economic transformations brought about by the industrial revolution. Nineteenth-century France was a country in transition. The classical notion of free will was being challenged and Cesare Lombroso (see Chapter 6) had introduced his biological determinism in the middle of the nineteenth century. Toward the end of the century, Durkheim brought focus upon how the organization of society can propel people toward violating norms. In other words, Durkheim, as a sociologist, saw behavior as socially rather than individually determined.

In 1892, Durkheim received the first doctoral degree in sociology awarded by the University of Paris. His most important contribution to criminology lies in his reviving the concept of anomie, delineated most clearly in his book *Suicide: A Study in Sociology* (1897/1951). Although the term can be traced to ancient Greeks, among whom it meant "lawlessness," for Durkheim anomie represented a state of "normlessness." Because it is norms, or socially expected behavior, that control how people act, their breakdown represents a threat to social control. Durkheim hypothesized that anomie contributes to suicide. Many contemporary theorists speculate that it also is a vital factor in many types of crime.

Because sociology was a new discipline, Durkheim felt it necessary to demonstrate the utility of this perspective so that it could gain credibility. What, critics asked, could be gained by examining social institutions and group behavior that could not be understood through the analysis of individuals? To test his belief that individual behavior was shaped by larger social phenomena, Durkheim examined the most individual of all forms of deviance: the taking of one's own life. His proposition was that the basic determinants of suicide are social variables such as religion, marital status, and economic conditions. He approached the explanation of deviance on a group (or macro) level (attempting to account for rates of suicide), but the fact that his brother had taken his own life suggests that Durkheim was interested in interpreting behavior at the individual (or micro) level as well. Occasionally, he drew analogies in his book *Suicide* that reflected his concern with bridging a macro-theory with micro-level explanations.

To test his proposition, Durkheim examined suicide data from nineteenth-century Europe and descriptive data about preliterate societies. Among his findings were:

- The rate of suicide is much lower in purely Catholic countries
- Jews showed lower suicide rates than both Catholics and Protestants
- Single persons (including those divorced and separated) are more likely to commit suicide than are married persons
- Suicide rates increase steadily with age
- Suicides are more numerous during periods of economic crisis than during periods of stability
- Periods of crisis such as war and revolution are associated with higher than normal suicide rates
- The number of suicides in the military is greater than among civilians
- Suicide is found in some preliterate societies where norms stipulate that wives take their own lives when their husbands die and that servants kill themselves when their masters die

Durkheim divided these findings into four categories of suicide related to the social configuration of society: egoistic, altruistic, fatalistic, and anomic. These categories are on a macro-theoretical level because Durkheim explained deviance in terms of the organization of society and social institutions. His conclusions were supported by data showing higher rates of suicide in geographical areas reflecting the social configurations specified by the theory.

It was Durkheim's research on suicide that laid the foundation for anomie or strain theory. Anomic suicide, he postulated, occurs when rapid or extreme social change or crisis threatens group norms. People become uncertain of the appropriateness of their behavior. This results in a state of confusion or "normlessness." Durkheim's examples referred to the higher suicide rates during wars and revolutions as well as during periods of economic recession, depression, or advancement. Durkheim considered fatalistic and anomic suicide as opposites, that is, the former reflecting overcontrol while the latter represents a lack of normative control. Criminologists have extended the idea of anomie or strain to account for the genesis of crime.

Durkheim's four types of suicide are:

- **Egoistic suicide**—suicide resulting from a weakening of commitment to group values and goals, especially when the individual has come to rely primarily upon his or her own resources
- **Altruistic suicide**—suicide precipitated by an overcommitment to group values and norms
- **Fatalistic suicide**—suicide derived from excessive regulation (e.g., slavery or imprisonment)
- **Anomic suicide**—suicide that occurs when rapid or extreme social change or crisis threaten group norms

Anomie

Anomie refers to a state or a condition in society in which the norms are no longer effective in regulating behavior. How is it that norms are disrupted or the willingness to conform to norms is attenuated? In addition to crises, such as wars, Durkheim indicated that anomie also is the result of a disjunction between people's aspirations and their ability to achieve these goals. This may be brought about by rapid social change such as drastic economic growth. In nineteenth-century French society, Durkheim speculated that such economic expansion would be more likely to affect the upper and middle classes, whose expectations and aspirations expand to an insatiable level. As Durkheim (1897/1951:253) wrote:

> With increased prosperity, desires increase. . . . Overweening ambition always exceeds the results obtained, great as they may be, since there is no warning to pause here . . . since this race for an unattainable goal can give no other pleasure but that of the race itself . . . once it is interrupted the participants are left empty-handed. . . . How could the desire to live not be weakened under such conditions?

Durkheim noted a lower suicide rate among the lower classes and suggested that poverty insulated the poor from experiencing anomie and, thus, suicide. Aspirations, Durkheim felt, are class related, with the upper classes having higher goals than those below them. While stating that aspirations varied, Durkheim believed that the French Revolution had created an egalitarian society in which all members had a similar opportunity to succeed or fail. Thus, what later strain theorists referred to as the opportunity structure was considered to be a constant. Figure 7.1 illustrates Durkheim's presentation of the relationship between social class and anomie.

Durkheim maintained that a successful social structure defines reasonable limits for desires, but when social organization falters, insatiable desires are unleashed. Unlimited aspirations create pressure for deviant solutions. Recent instances of "creative accounting" practices that led to criminal charges (e.g., Enron, WorldCom, and Madoff) serve as examples of the effect of such unlimited aspirations.

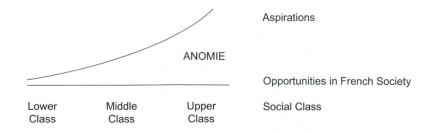

FIGURE 7.1
Durkheim's presentation of the relationship between social class and anomie.

Robert K. Merton—Social Structure and Anomie

Robert K. Merton's 1938 version of anomie theory has been acclaimed as one of the most influential developments in the study of crime and deviance. At a time when crime seemed rampant in American society, Merton presented an explanation that seemed enlightening: social conditions place pressures on people differentially throughout the class structure, and people react individually to these conditions. While Durkheim assumed that humans are naturally inclined to have unlimited desires that must be socially controlled, Merton felt that such desires are socially generated.

Merton postulated that all societies have a cultural system that (1) denotes socially approved values and goals and (2) details acceptable norms or institutionalized means for achieving these goals. Not only do these prescribed **goals and means** enable people to pursue success in appropriate ways, but at times they also exert pressure on some segments of the society to engage in nonconforming behavior in an effort to achieve success. This happens when the goals of success are emphasized more than acceptable ways of seeking that success.

American society, according to Merton, espouses one overriding goal: the acquisition of wealth. The "almighty dollar" is something for which most Americans are taught to strive. While there are culturally approved means for obtaining wealth, they are given less emphasis, and of course, not everyone succeeds through legitimate endeavors. This may result in shortcuts or in nonconforming behavior to obtain money.

The institutionalized means for pursuing wealth and status are clearly set forth in American society, but these means are not feasible for many of those at the bottom of the social structure. The "Protestant work ethic" espouses traditional middle-class values that have been popularized by American folklore. Ben Franklin's maxims, passed on from generation to generation, highlight the means to success (e.g., a penny saved is a penny earned, a stitch in time saves nine, honesty is the best policy, don't put off until tomorrow what you can do today). The means include frugality, diligence, deferred gratification, hard work, honesty, and success through self-improvement (i.e., education). Although access to the opportunity structure is not uniformly available to all, it is expected that with hard work, anyone in America can be successful. It is not uncommon for grade-school students to be told that if they work hard, they have the potential to become president. Success stories of the "self-made man" are put forth as examples of the validity of the claim that perseverance will be rewarded. The problem, however, is that many people try to achieve success but fail. Little emphasis is placed on the intrinsic rewards of adhering to the socially approved means whether or not these produce success. The attainment of wealth, Merton argued, has become such an overriding concern that little satisfaction is derived from merely playing the game honestly. Winning is what it's all about. Vince Lombardi, a revered Green Bay Packer football coach, declared, "Winning isn't everything; it's the only thing." A business writer (Tauby, 1991:59) illustrates how this theory might explain marked increases in crimes such as embezzlement by women. White-collar crimes, she wrote, "are sometimes a by-product of the American dream gone haywire, a warped form of ambition."

The legitimate means for obtaining wealth are differentially available throughout the class structure. Members of the upper class have greater access to education, important interpersonal contacts that will enhance their opportunities, and socialization that prepares them for competition in the struggle to achieve wealth and status (Mills, 1956; Domhoff, 1967; Dye, 1976). Members of the lower class experience greater stress or strain in their attempts to make money legitimately. That is also why, Merton argued, they are found in disproportionate numbers among the criminal population, the mentally disturbed, and other deviant groups. This conflict between the institutionalized means and the culturally specified goals is what causes anomie (see Figure 7.2). It is an inequitable social structure, evaluating success similarly at all social levels, that produces lower class strain and that ultimately leads to crime and delinquency. Merton (1938:680) summarized his argument in this manner:

> It is only when a system of cultural values extols, virtually above all else, certain common symbols of success for the population at large while its social structure rigorously restricts or completely eliminates access to approved modes of acquiring these symbols for a considerable part of the same population, that antisocial behavior ensues on a considerable scale.

How accurate is Merton's depiction of American society? Do you think we measure the success of ourselves and others primarily in materialistic terms? Do we value ends above means? If other concerns rival or exceed the value placed on monetary success, the notion of strain or pressure toward deviant routes to success is called into question. Similarly, if American culture emphasizes the value of following the rules as much as or more than attaining success, the theory will not hold up. To speculate on our cultural values, consider questions such as the following: Is more emphasis placed on the status and income of occupations or on whether the occupations themselves are intrinsically satisfying? Do sports revolve more around fair play or winning? Does our educational system place a higher premium on grades and diplomas or on hard work and perseverance? Does the business community more keenly

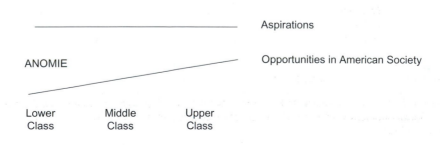

FIGURE 7.2
Merton's conception of the relationship between social class and anomie.

prize profits or integrity in business practices? Answers to such questions help to evaluate Merton's premise that goals and means are poorly integrated in our society.

To assess the applicability of Merton's version of anomie to American society, we must consider at least one other empirical issue. Are the means made available to the lower class inadequate for the goals to which society leads the lower class to aspire? Are some persons so severely handicapped by being reared in poverty, slums, and other disadvantaged environments that they do not have, or do not perceive themselves as having, reasonable opportunities to become well educated, to develop talents, and to acquire rewarding jobs? Can cultural background block people from effectively competing for the common symbols of success of which Merton wrote? If both of these conditions (overemphasis on monetary success and denial of opportunities) are met, the stage is set for strain in the lives of those located in lower strata of the social structure.

There are different ways in which people respond to this structural stress, not all of them deviant. Merton identified five individual modes of adaptation: conformity, innovation, ritualism, retreatism, and rebellion. They are depicted in Figure 7.3.

From the standpoint of criminal behavior, **conformists** are of little concern. They accept the culturally specified goals and adhere to the institutional means in their attempts to succeed, and they will continue to do so regardless of their success or failure. These are the people who hold a society together; society must be largely constituted of conformists in order to continue functioning.

Innovation is probably the most common form of adaptation to structural stress induced by the inability to legitimately achieve cultural goals. It is primarily innovators who become the focus of criminologists. Innovators aspire to attain conventional goals but use illegal means to succeed because they do not perceive themselves as having legitimate opportunities. The Wall Street broker who engages in insider trading, the individual who burglarizes homes, the person who sells his or her body, and the student who cheats on a test are examples of people who use illegitimate means to obtain desired ends. As a social structure theory, this explanation of crime points disproportionately

Modes of Adaptation		Culture Goals	Institutionalized Means
I	Conformity	+	+
II	Innovation	+	–
III	Ritualism	–	+
IV	Retreatism	–	–
V	Rebellion	±	±

FIGURE 7.3
Merton's individual modes of adaptation.

Source: Reprinted with permission of The Free Press, a Division of Simon & Schuster, Inc., from *Social Theory and Social Structure*, Revised and Enlarged Edition by Robert K. Merton. Copyright © 1968, 1967 by Robert K. Merton.

to the lower class, for which legitimate opportunities for success are less available.

Ritualists can be thought of as the opposite of innovators; they abide by the rules but have abandoned pursuit of the goals. Ritualists go through the motions but lack commitment to the attainment of wealth or status. In the authors' years of teaching, students have been encountered who could be classified as ritualists. They attend classes, read assignments, and play the role of student, with the exception that they seem oblivious regarding grades and graduation. Whether they get an "A" or a "D" on a test makes no difference. The professor who routinely comes to class, but makes few demands on students to excel, demonstrates no up-to-date knowledge of subject matter, no new approaches to teaching, and lacks enthusiasm also exemplifies the ritualist. Outside of academe, the bureaucratic worker who always follows rules to the letter but seems to have forgotten the goals of the work group demonstrates ritualism. This adaptation reduces the probability of failure. It is a "safe" approach to life.

A fourth mode of adaptation is that of the **retreatists** or societal dropouts. These people neither aspire to cultural goals nor abide by the institutionalized means. Their dropout status is characterized by transiency, drug addiction, and homelessness. While this mode of adaptation is viewed as deviant and some of the behaviors have been criminalized (e.g., vagrancy and public drunkenness), retreatists for the most part engage in crimes that have no victims except, of course, themselves. Retreatists represent the antithesis of the Protestant work ethic and middle-class values.

Rebellion is the final mode of adaptation identified by Merton. This occurs when a person rejects the goals and the means of society. Unlike the retreatist, however, the rebel substitutes a new set of values and norms for the discarded ones. Examples include the street-gang member who seeks a "rep" instead of money and uses violence and intimidation instead of hard work and honesty to achieve the goal, and the political revolutionary who employs subversive and violent acts rather than participating in the existing political system. While Merton refers to rebellion as an individual mode of adaptation, rebels are essentially societal dropouts who form a subculture with its own values and norms.

These five modes of adaptation, Merton suggested, are ways in which people respond to anomic conditions. From a criminal justice perspective, conformists and ritualists do not pose a problem. It is the innovators, retreatists, and rebels who get into trouble with law enforcement agents.

Whereas Durkheim maintained that it was the insatiable aspirations of people that led to social strain, Merton believed that it was the differential access to the means necessary for attaining success that caused stress. This focus on the opportunity structure of society shifted attention to the lower classes and to instrumental crimes such as burglary, robbery, larceny, and other crimes that would produce an economic gain. Subsequent criminologists extended this perspective, most notably, to explanations of juvenile delinquency and gang activity.

Richard A. Cloward and Lloyd E. Ohlin—Opportunity Theory

Approximately 20 years after the publication of Merton's classic work on ano-mie, Richard Cloward and Lloyd Ohlin (1960) proposed a model explaining gang delinquency that expanded upon Merton. Their extension of anomie is called **opportunity theory**. Cloward and Ohlin agreed with Merton in large mea-sure, but they believed that he had failed to acknowledge the role of illegitimate opportunity structures in the development of deviant adaptations to anomic conditions. They suggested that, just as the availability of legitimate means varies across social groups, so too does access to illegitimate opportunity structures. They argued that the delinquent activities in which one becomes immersed are a function of the delinquent opportunities that are available to that person.

Illegitimate opportunity structures, like legitimate ones, presuppose social organization or integration in order to offer illegal opportunities. "Just as the unintegrated slum cannot mobilize legitimate resources for the young, neither can it provide them with access to stable criminal careers, for illegitimate learn-ing and opportunity structures do not develop" (Cloward & Ohlin, 1960:173). According to Cloward and Ohlin, a community is considered well organized against crime if, for example, it has an active parent–teacher association, a high level of citizen involvement in local politics, a community-watch program, and groups such as the Elks Club and Daughters of the American Revolution. Con-versely, the words of "Stanley," a delinquent youth who traced his career for Clifford Shaw in *The Jack-Roller: A Delinquent Boy's Own Story* (1930/1966:54), illustrate a community well organized for aberrant behavior:

> Stealing in the neighborhood was a common practice among the children and approved by the parents. Whenever the boys got together they talked about robbing and made more plans for stealing. I hardly knew any boys who did not go robbing. The little fellows went in for petty stealing, breaking into freight cars, and stealing junk. The older guys did big jobs like stick-up, burglary, and stealing autos. The little fellows admired the "big shots" and longed for the day when they could get into the big racket.

Cloward and Ohlin maintained that persons seeking innovative solutions to their strained circumstances must learn the necessary values and skills to take advantage of the opportunity structure within their community. Traits that pro-duce success or failure in capitalizing on legitimate opportunity structures also apply to illegitimate opportunity structures. The process by which one is rejected from illegitimate endeavors is no more fair or forgiving than are the avenues through which legitimate success is sought. Those lacking the proper skills and potential will confront failure in their efforts to become, say, drug dealers.

To illustrate opportunity structures, imagine concluding that you are doomed to failure no matter how diligently you work; therefore, you seek an illegal route to success. What criminal solution would you select? A common response by college students is that they would "sell drugs." This answer reflects the oppor-tunity rationale of Cloward and Ohlin. Selling illicit drugs is one of the more salient illegal opportunities available to college students. There are two reasons for this fact. First, the college community is an organized and well-integrated environment that provides an opportunity for a profitable illicit drug venture. Second, as a college student you already have or presume that you can readily accumulate the necessary knowledge, skills, and interpersonal contacts essential to conducting such an enterprise on a college campus.

Frustrated college students, on the other hand, would be unlikely candidates for running a loan-shark operation in an urban setting or managing a "chop shop" (recycling stolen cars) in a rural community. Although these are profitable activities in a community organized for criminal activity, most college students lack the requisite skills and personality attributes to take advantage of these illegal opportunities.

Adaptation to anomie, Cloward and Ohlin argued, is associated with the environment in which an individual lives. If there are no pawn shops, fences, or willing buyers of stolen goods, then it is much less attractive to a burglar to continue to steal. There are only so many iPads and smart phones that one person can use. If the ecological area lacks an illegitimate opportunity structure, persons may turn to petty and unprofitable forms of crime or simply drop out of mainstream society. The ecological studies of Clifford Shaw and Henry McKay and other scholars in the Chicago School (discussed later in this chapter) laid the groundwork for an analysis of community organization and disorganization as elements of opportunity structures. Edwin Sutherland (1937:211) likewise anticipated the concept of differential opportunity, noting that "selection and tutelage are the two necessary elements" in becoming a professional thief. That is, success within a particular criminal subculture requires access to learning structures to allow demonstration of aptitude and acquisition of the pertinent skills. Cloward and Ohlin (1960:151) explicitly acknowledged their debt to Shaw and McKay and to Sutherland, noting that their version of strain theory contains elements of both the structure (strain) and process (learning) traditions:

> The concept of differential opportunity structures permits us to unite the theory of anomie, which recognizes the concept of differentials in access to legitimate means, and the "Chicago tradition," in which the concept of differentials in access to illegitimate means is implicit. We can now look at the individual, not simply in relation to one or the other system of means, but in relation to both legitimate and illegitimate systems.

Concerned with explaining gang delinquency, Cloward and Ohlin identified three different types of gangs: criminal, conflict, and retreatist (see Figure 7.4). Each gang type represents a specific mode of adaptation to perceived anomie. The **criminal gang**, similar to Merton's innovator, aspires to the conventional goals of society. Its access to the legitimate means for achieving success are blocked, but there is an illegitimate opportunity structure, in the form of community organization for crime, that permits the gang to achieve money and status through illegal or nonconventional means. An example would be the inner-city youth exposed to older gang members who are operating a theft

Types of Adaptation	Conventional Goals	Legitimate Means	Illegitimate Means
Criminal	+	−	+
Retreatist	−	−	−
Conflict	±	±	±

FIGURE 7.4

Cloward and Ohlin: Group adaptations to anomie.

Source: Adapted from R.A. Cloward and L.E. Ohlin (1960). *Delinquency and Opportunity.* New York: The Free Press.

ring. The youth learns the appropriate behavior and justifications from these older youths and sees them achieve success through their illegal operations. As a consequence, the youth joins the gang and ultimately moves up through its ranks. Gang Feature 7.1 highlights the importance attributed to the availability of legitimate opportunities.

Cloward and Ohlin (1960:171) described the neighborhood providing illegitimate opportunity structures in this way:

> [T]he criminal subculture is likely to arise in a neighborhood milieu characterized by close bonds between different age-levels of offenders, and between criminal and conventional elements. As a consequence of these integrative relationships, a new opportunity structure emerges which provides alternative avenues to success-goals. Hence the pressures generated by restrictions on legitimate access to success-goals are drained off. Social controls over the conduct of the young are effectively exercised, limiting expressive behavior and constraining the discontented to adopt instrumental, if criminalistic, styles of life.

When an illegitimate opportunity structure exists, Cloward and Ohlin postulated that individuals confronted with blocked legitimate opportunity structures will gravitate toward the illegitimate means and engage in behavior that will result in the attainment of conventional goals. In the event that an illegitimate opportunity structure does not exist, as when a community is disorganized, a **conflict gang** will develop (see Figure 7.5). Conflict subcultures are characterized by destructive and violent behavior. The conventional goals are abandoned and supplanted by alternative values usually emphasizing physical prowess and cunning. Conflict gangs often have been sensationalized by the media, as in movies such as *West Side Story*, *Colors*, and *Boyz in the Hood*. Cloward and Ohlin (1960:172) wrote the following about conflict gangs:

> First, an unorganized community cannot provide access to legitimate channels to success goals. . . . Secondly, access to stable criminal opportunity systems is also restricted. . . . Finally, social controls are weak in such communities. These conditions, we believe, lead to the emergence of conflict subcultures.

GANG FEATURE 7.1 GANGS AND SOCIAL STRUCTURE IN INTERNATIONAL PERSPECTIVE

During the 1990s, it became increasingly evident that the youth gang problem experienced by the United States was also occurring in Europe. Not only were gangs emerging in rural and small-town America, they were emerging in previously gang-free cities of Europe. While some of these gangs were influenced by the media (van Gemert, 2001), others developed in response to perceived structural problems associated with a lack of access to legitimate opportunities.

Three studies conducted by anthropologists and criminologists employing qualitative methodologies have documented the presence of youth gangs in the Netherlands, Norway, and Great Britain. Results from these three projects are summarized here. For a broader discussion of the emergence of gangs throughout Europe, consult the publications associated with the Eurogang Program of Research (e.g., Klein et al., 2001; Decker & Weerman, 2005; van Gemert et al., 2008; Esbensen & Maxson, 2012).

Frank van Gemert, a Dutch anthropologist, studied violent youth groups in The Hague and Rotterdam and, while he acknowledged the role of structural and cultural factors, his research led him to emphasize the impact of a juvenile lifestyle that is transmitted largely through the media. The groups he studied were involved in violent offenses but oftentimes avoided violence through the art of intimidation. Members of these groups, the Eight Tray Crips and the Eastside Crips in The Hague and the Southside First Tray Crips in Rotterdam, had not only adopted the names of a well-known American gang, they had adopted their symbols (i.e., bandanas, clothing, and hand signs). The cultural diffusion of youth culture through the media is captured in the following quote from van Gemert's work (2001:145):

> Over the past few years, Dutch youths have been attracted to video clips and compact discs with gangsta rap, in which the scene is set by young African Americans with big cars and fat gold chains, and in the company of sensual ladies. The language of these youths is characterized by hyperbole and contains many references to competition and violence. The fact that famous rappers like Tupac Shakur, Notorious B.I.G., and Stretch not only talked about the hard life of the 'hoods, but actually were killed as gangsters

in drive-by shootings, takes nothing away from their intentions.

A group of researchers (Judith Aldridge, Juanjo Medina-Ariz, and Rob Ralphs, 2012) located at the University of Manchester in the United Kingdom have been studying gangs and gang-involved youths in "Research City." Given issues of confidentiality, the researchers do not want to disclose the actual identity of their study location. From 2005 through 2008, they conducted direct observation, informal conversations, and 130 formal interviews in two broad areas of Research City. One area, Inner West, was ethnically diverse, but the gang members tended to be predominantly black Caribbean/African/Asian/mixed-race. The second area, Far West, was a housing estate on the outskirts of town, with most gang members being white. One of the interesting findings from this research project is the contrast in police identification of gang members in these two areas. While the white gang members in Far West "hung out" in public places and were viewed by residents as problematic (i.e., intimidating and harassing residents), the police did not recognize, at least officially, this area as having a gang problem. Conversely, the researchers never observed the gang members of Inner City congregating in public places or in large groups, yet the police identified this area as possessing a gang problem. Historically, however, Inner City had been home to open-market drug dealing by gang members in the 1980s and 1990s. In response to these drug markets, the police had initiated an aggressive police presence in these communities, to the point that many young people viewed the "stop and search" police policy as one of harassment. Aldridge and her colleagues suggest that this aggressive policing, in conjunction with a number of drive-by shootings, contributed to a change in gang member behavior; that is, reducing their time spent in public places. The question remains, however, why were the gang youths in Far West not recognized by the police as a gang problem worthy of the same response as the gang youths in Inner City?

In her study of gangs in Oslo, Norway, Inger-Lise Lien (2001:169) provides evidence of the cultural diffusion of youth culture described by van Gemert. The gang youths "watch American gangster movies and give themselves gangster names like Cash Money Brothers, Black Mafia

GANG FEATURE 7.1 (CONTINUED)

Society, Mafia Sisters." Lien suggests that it is the desire to obtain material goods without the legitimate means to attain them that has led to the formation of the Oslo gangs. Interviews with gang members painted a picture of pessimism about the future and concern about not finding jobs through legal channels. Additionally, many of the gang-involved youths were immigrants who felt limited in their ability to succeed in the Norwegian economy. One member of the Young Guns, for example, stated: "We were poor, and we were newcomers to Norway. . . . The boys in the Killers were second-generation immigrants. They drove around in BMWs and Mercedes. They thought they were better than us [sic], but we wanted to show them who we were, and put them in their place. This is how all this gang business started. We taught them how to respect us, and when they saw us they would tremble. We were happy."

Level of Community Organization	Availability of Illegitimate Means	
	Yes	No
Organized	Criminal	Retreatist
Disorganized	Criminal	Conflict

FIGURE 7.5
Level of community organization, availability of illegitimate means, and type of delinquent gangs.

The last of the delinquent subcultures identified by Cloward and Ohlin is the retreatist, which is composed of social dropouts (e.g., drunkards, drug addicts). While this form of behavior may be seen as individualistic, Cloward and Ohlin argue that drug users, for example, must establish contacts with others if for no other reason than to obtain drugs. Thus, retreatism is seen as a group adaptation to the blocked opportunity structure. As with the conflict subculture, retreatists experience the double frustration of having access to neither legitimate or illegitimate means. They are double losers. They may be found in unorganized communities, but are more likely to exist in organized communities. This is because (1) without illegitimate means, a criminal subculture cannot persist, and (2) in an organized community, the destructive and malicious behaviors associated with conflict gangs will not be tolerated. Thus, Cloward and Ohlin argued, youths in such a situation will resort to withdrawal and drug or alcohol use.

RECENT DEVELOPMENTS IN STRAIN THEORY

Robert Agnew—General Strain Theory

Although social strain was a dominant American sociological theory of crime during the twentieth century, it came under increasing attack during the 1970s (e.g., Hirschi, 1969; Kornhauser, 1978; Bernard, 1984). According to Robert Agnew (1992), the decline in the popularity of social strain theory can be attributed to four major criticisms:

- The focus on lower-class delinquency;
- The neglect of goals other than middle-class status and financial gain;
- The failure to consider barriers to achievement other than social class; and
- The inability to account for why only some people who experience strain turn to criminal activity.

Agnew proposes a general strain theory (GST) that addresses these criticisms.

Strain theory has historically been class-bound; that is, lower-class crime is explained as a result of blocked opportunities. In his GST, Agnew broadens the perceived sources of strain by identifying three types of strain-inducing stimuli: (1) the failure to achieve one's goals, (2) the removal of positively valued stimuli, and (3) the presence of negatively valued stimuli. Virtually everyone experiences one or more of these types of strains, but it is the individual's interpretation of the source of the strain that is the determining factor of whether illegal activity will occur. It is when these strains are seen as unjust, too great, or uncontrollable that criminal behavior is more likely to result. Agnew suggests that strain produces anger, frustration, and/ or depression and that these negative emotions are the source of illegal responses to strain.

In response to empirical tests of GST and in attempts to refine the perspective, Agnew (2001; 2004; 2006) provided expanded discussions of the role of various types of strain that contribute to criminal behavior. First, he distinguished between *objective* strains, "events or conditions that are disliked by most members of a given group" (Agnew, 2001:320), and *subjective* strains, "events or conditions that are disliked by the people who are experiencing (or have experienced) them" (Agnew, 2001:321). Acknowledging that not all people respond to the same condition in the same manner, Agnew emphasizes the need to account for the individual's subjective assessment of strain in order to understand its role in offending. A second component of Agnew's elaboration of GST consists of delineating four characteristics of strain related to crime: (1) when strain is seen as unjust, it is more likely to cause anger; (2) when strain is high in magnitude or severity, it is more likely to result in a criminal response (i.e., "it is more difficult to legally cope with a large rather than small financial problem" (Agnew, 2001:332); (3) strains associated with low social control (unemployment and homelessness) are more likely to lead to crime; and (4) strain is associated with a criminal outcome when criminal activity is seen as a means to reduce strain (i.e., the bullied child sees bullying others as a way to cope with the strain).

A third point in Agnew's (2001) elaboration of GST is the specification that while some strain will result in criminal activity, not all strain is expected to produce a criminal response. For instance, he indicates that the following types of strains should increase the likelihood of criminal activity: parental rejection; child abuse; homelessness; criminal victimization; child abuse or neglect; abusive peer relations: and the failure to achieve core goals that are not the result of conventional socialization and that are easily achieved through crime (e.g., thrill, excitement, money). On the other hand, the following types of strain should NOT increase the likelihood of crime: unpopularity or isolation from peers; excessive demands of conventional jobs that are well rewarded (long hours associated with many professional jobs); failure to achieve goals that result from conventional socialization and that are difficult to achieve through illegitimate channels (e.g., educational or occupational success); burdens associated with the care of conventional others to whom one is strongly attached, like children and sick/disabled spouses.

The failure to achieve goals includes blocked opportunity due to a person's location in the class structure, but it also can involve the failure to realize desired goals due to individual weakness or inadequacies. The fact that a 4-foot-6-inch lower-class youth is unable to make the high-school basketball team may have more to do with her height and/or ball-handling ability than with her social class standing. Agnew also suggests that strain may occur when an individual perceives the reward to be inadequate relative to the effort, especially when compared with others. Criminology professors often hear students complain, "But, I studied 10 hours for this exam. Why didn't I get an A?" Does this question indicate strain? Not in the traditional sense, but under Agnew's general strain theory we can now appreciate why this same student was caught cheating on the next exam. Agnew also postulates that criminal behavior can result from experiencing stressful life events—both the removal of positively valued stimuli and the exposure to negative stimuli. While psychologists have studied the effects of life events such as divorce, moving, changing schools, switching jobs, and death of a family member, criminologists generally have failed to consider the impact of such events on behavior. Agnew argues that such life events can contribute to social strain. Victimization, for instance, is one negative stimulus that has been linked to offending. Child abuse or wife battering also may cause stress that the individual will ultimately seek to relieve through criminal activities.

Deviance is but one possible consequence of strain. Agnew identifies a number of cognitive, emotional, and behavioral adaptations that will minimize negative outcomes and thus reduce the probability of criminal behavior resulting from strain. For instance, people can invoke one of three cognitive coping strategies: minimizing the importance of goals (i.e., it's not that important), minimizing negative outcomes (i.e., it really isn't all that bad), or accepting responsibility (i.e., it's my fault). Persons who learn to reduce the relevance of strain will be less likely to resort to antisocial behavior.

Steven Messner and Richard Rosenfeld—Crime and the American Dream

In a different vein from Agnew et al., Messner and Rosenfeld (1994; 2007; 2013) propose an explanation of social strain theory that rekindles the macro-level perspective offered by Robert Merton more than 75 years ago.

America, as we pointed out in Chapter 4, has a violent crime rate higher than most other nations. Messner and Rosenfeld (2007) maintain that the "American Dream" is the root cause of this high volume of crime. The American Dream consists of a broad cultural ethos that entails a commitment—in fact, an overcommitment—to material success through individual competition. In one of his later works, Robert Merton (1968) indicated that the American Dream is a double-edged sword—the very elements that contribute to America's success at the same time foster that "cardinal American vice, deviant behavior" (1968:200).

An emphasis on individual success tends to undermine the collective sense of community and the glorification of monetary success tends to limit aspirations to economic success. "Tasks that are primarily noneconomic in nature tend to receive meager cultural support, and the skillful performance of these tasks elicit little public recognition" (Messner & Rosenfeld, 1994:8). As an example, Messner and Rosenfeld cite education, which is largely viewed as a means to achieve economic or occupational success as an end in itself. How many students reading this text, for example, are attending college for the sole or primary purpose of learning and "expanding their horizons?" And how many are in college to obtain credentials necessary for a prestigious, high-salaried job?

Messner and Rosenfeld suggest that the American Dream has created an anomic society, one in which the attainment of goals has superseded the need to conform to legitimate means. They summarize their view in the following manner:

> Our basic thesis is that the American Dream itself exerts pressures toward crime by encouraging an anomic cultural environment, an environment in which people are encouraged to adopt an "anything goes" mentality in the pursuit of personal goals (2001:61).

This cultural environment is dominated by the economy and its interconnection with other social institutions. Messner and Rosenfeld maintain that four cultural values underscore the American Dream: achievement, individualism, universalism, and materialism.

- Achievement is considered the "defining feature of American culture." The emphasis is not on good sportsmanship, fair play, and effort; it is on winning.
- Individualism identifies the American focus on the rights of the individual to think and do as he or she sees fit. Infringement on these rights, as detailed in the Bill of Rights, would be seen as un-American.
- Universalism connotes the American ethos and the culturally shared values described by Merton in his anomie theory. Americans are encouraged to aspire to success, generally measured in terms of economic success. The pursuit of upward mobility and the evaluation of success or failure produces considerable stress throughout the society.

- Materialism, or the fetishism of money, is a distinctive American phenomenon. Money, especially the accumulation of large amounts, has become a measure of success in American society. Messner and Rosenfeld explain that "monetary success is inherently open-ended. It is always possible to have more money. Hence, the American Dream offers 'no final stopping point.' It requires 'never-ending achievement'" (2001:63–64).

This cultural emphasis on achievement, individualism, universalism, and materialism interacts with social institutions of family, education, and the polity. The pre-eminent role of economic considerations in the pursuit of success unduly affects American society in three interrelated ways:

- Devaluation of noneconomic institutional functions and roles;
- Accommodation to economic requirements by other institutions; and
- Penetration of economic norms into other institutional domains (Messner & Rosenfeld, 2001:70).

Devaluation of noneconomic goals is notably present in the educational arena. Education is seen by most as a means to an end—job acquisition or job promotion. Rarely is education seen as an end in itself. Students are encouraged to study to get good grades, not to learn for the sake of learning. Accommodation to economic requirements is evident within the family. Rarely must a parent find time for work; the trick is finding time for one's family. For instance, rather than supporting a pro-family policy that encourages and promotes parental involvement with their children, the United States, unlike most other industrialized nations, has no mandatory paid maternity or parental leave law. In fact, parents generally must take unpaid leave upon the birth of a child and are then criticized for their inappropriate priorities, placing family before work. The influence of the economy has also penetrated other aspects of American life. Business leaders have become frequent participants in the pursuit of electoral office, usually with no prior political background or experience. The assumption is that government would be better run like a business. A similar trend is also occurring in higher education where university governing bodies increasingly are turning to corporate America for recruitment of chancellors and university presidents. The glorification of the business model ignores the unique roles of government and education and succumbs to the cultural value of defining achievement through monetary success. Read an interview with Richard Rosenfeld in Highlight 7.1.

Anomic societies tend to have relatively weak and/or ineffective social control as a result of the emphasis on ends rather than means. At a local high school track meet, one of the authors observed a T-shirt with an inscription characteristic of the winning at all cost mentality—"Second place is the first loser." With this emphasis, it becomes increasingly difficult for social institutions such as the family and education to exert counterbalancing effects. "Innovation" or the use of illegitimate or illegal means (e.g., use of performance enhancing drugs among athletes) has become common throughout society.

HIGHLIGHT 7.1 INSTITUTIONAL ANOMIE THEORY AND THE CURRENT CRIME DECLINE

Interview with Professor Richard Rosenfeld, Curator's Professor of Criminology and Criminal Justice, University of Missouri-St. Louis.

Q: Institutional Anomie Theory (IAT) really focuses on explaining crime in the American context. Given this emphasis, how does your theory explain the rising crime rates in other countries? And how do you account for the fact that there has been a convergence of sorts in the crime rates of America and Western Europe?

A: When originally developed in the early 1990s, *Crime and the American Dream* focused on the special case of the high crime rates in American society compared with other developed nations. IAT emerged later as an explanation of crime that can be applied to any nation characterized by marked imbalance of its major social institutions. The theory predicts, for example, that societies in which the free-market economy dominates other institutions will exhibit comparatively high rates of serious violent and property crime. During the 1990s and into the current century, crime rates have fallen in both the United States and Europe. The theory attributes the crime drop to the economic expansion in Western nations during that period (Rosenfeld & Messner, 2009).

Homicide rates in the United States remain far higher than those in other developed societies, but over the past few decades Canada, Australia, and many European countries have surpassed the United States in levels of property crime. That is due in part to the dramatic growth in U.S. imprisonment rates. On any given day, a much larger fraction of the U.S. criminal population is behind bars than is the case elsewhere and therefore is unable to commit crimes against the general public. When the informal social controls of noneconomic institutions are weakened, only the expansion of formal social control through the police, courts, jails, and prisons can reduce crime. In its original formulation, IAT did not devote sufficient attention to the growth of mass incarceration in the United States. Although it has begun to do so recently (Rosenfeld & Messner, 2010), the theory remains a work in progress.

Q: Research suggests that opportunities for upward mobility, a core belief in IAT, have declined in American society, yet the crime rate continues to fall when IAT would have predicted an increase. How do you account for this?

A: No theory has satisfactorily explained falling crime rates in the midst of economic crisis and diminished mobility opportunities. Two such periods in American history are the Great Depression of the 1930s and the 'Great Recession' of 2008–9. One possible explanation involves the extension of social welfare protections, including the Roosevelt Administration's work and income-maintenance programs during the 1930s (Johnson et al., 2007) and the record expansion of the Food Stamp program and extension of unemployment insurance benefits during the current period. This explanation is consistent with IAT's emphasis on the role of government in curbing the periodic crises of the free-market economy. But the Great Depression and the current crisis share something else in common: record low rates of inflation. When prices rise slowly or fall, consumers feel less pressure to "trade down" to markets offering cheap goods, including the underground market for stolen goods. Property crime rates should fall as a result, and declining rates of property crime should push down violent crime rates as well (Rosenfeld, 2009). IAT looks first at changes in the economy and government's role in protecting individuals and families from the full brunt of market forces when explaining cyclical changes in crime rates.

ASSESSING STRAIN THEORIES

At the heart of the strain paradigm is the assumption that crime, delinquency, and other forms of deviance are essentially problems located in the lower strata of our social structure. The advent of self-report measures, however, brought this axiom into question. On the basis of self-report data, criminologists increasingly have attacked strain theory, suggesting that it is founded upon a "myth of social class and criminality" (Tittle et al., 1978). This myth, it is argued, is a product of inherent biases in official statistics. The justice system creates a lower-class crime problem through a class-biased enforcement response. Others contend that such criticisms represent an inaccurate **myth of classlessness** (Braithwaite, 1981).

The relationship between class and crime is critical to strain theory, and is indeed a complex issue. As we discussed in Chapter 4 of this text, the relationship between class and crime is largely shaped by how one defines and measures the two concepts. If crime is defined as street crime, as is the case with UCR Index offenses, then offenders are disproportionately from the lower class, regardless of how class is defined. If, however, one relies on self-report data, the relationship between class and crime is not so clear. While some definitions of social class are restricted to "a two-class model comprised of the really lower-class and of everyone else" (Brown 1985:213), other definitions include much finer gradations. How social class is measured has implications for the outcome of tests of strain theory.

In an interesting study of 200 "homeless" men in Edmonton, Alberta, Stephen Baron and Timothy Hartnagel combined in-person interviews with observational data to examine the relationship between homelessness and crime. They sought to determine how these homeless men accounted for their failure. From a strain theory perspective, the attribution of failure should be placed on the social structure rather than on oneself. In support of this perspective, Baron and Hartnagel (1997:425) report that "long-term unemployment and sparse employment histories tend to undermine perceptions of equal opportunity and lead the youths to blame the government, private industry, and the economy for their condition." Hoffman and Ireland (2004) undertook a study to assess the ability of Cloward and Ohlin's opportunity theory to explain differences in rates of delinquency. Utilizing data from the National Education Longitudinal Study they were able to measure both school- and individual-level measures for a sample of more than 12,000 students enrolled in 883 schools across the United States. Their findings are supportive of the role of anomie in explaining differences in delinquency; that is, they found that the disjunction between economic aspirations and educational expectations was associated with increased levels of delinquent involvement. However, contrary to the theoretical premise of opportunity theory that illicit opportunity structures help to account for variations in illegal activity, Hoffman and Ireland found no support for school-level effects on delinquency.

A more fundamental question, however, is whether strain theory must focus exclusively on the lower class. Scott Menard contends that while strain may be felt more strongly among the lower class, this does not mean that anomie "varies within the social structure. Instead, it means that the effects of anomie may be felt differently by individuals with different positions in the social structure" (Menard, 1995:137). In his investigation of Merton's anomie theory, Menard (1995) found that an individual's mode of adaptation, combined with a measure of social class, was better able to explain variations in some types of offending. Agnew's GST serves as an example of a theoretical attempt to explain the presence of criminal activity within all social class levels. The question, however, still remains: Do members of the lower class necessarily experience greater strain? Perhaps lower-class persons are not motivated by materialistic aims or middle-class success standards and, consequently, do not undergo strain. Or even if they do, might not persons of other classes experience strain as a product of other social structural features?

In their 2005 publication, Travis Pratt and Francis Cullen report on findings from a meta-analysis of 214 articles published between 1960 and 1999. They examined the extent to which empirical assessments of macro-level theories supported the underlying assumptions of those theories. Included in their macro-level assessment were the following seven perspectives: social disorganization, resource/economic deprivation, anomie/strain, social support/altruism, routine activity, rational choice/deterrence, and subcultural. Of relevance for the material discussed in this chapter, Pratt and Cullen concluded that the overall support for social disorganization theory was "fairly strong" while "anomie/ strain theory has not been adequately tested to confirm its empirical status" (Pratt & Cullen, 2005:410).

The keystone foundation of contemporary strain theory, Mertonian anomie, is often criticized for limiting its focus to property crimes. To the extent that Merton's position is read in this manner, the extension of the strain paradigm by Cloward and Ohlin has alleviated the problem, as noted by Francis Cullen (1988:233):

> [B]ecause scholars have shown that any given strain state (e.g., frustrated aspirations) can lead to a range of responses, the relationship between strain and any one form of deviance or crime is indeterminate, not etiologically specific or determinate; hence the need for a theory of intervening variables—opportunity theory—that explains why people pursue one wayward path and not another.

To a considerable extent, Messner and Rosenfeld's **Institutional Anomie Theory (IAT)** addresses both the debate about the location of strain in the class structure and the concentration on property crime. Their theoretical formulation refocuses attention to macro-level conditions and societal effects on violent offending. Mitch Chamlin and John Cochran (1995) used data from all 50 states to examine the extent to which institutional anomie theory could explain and predict rates of instrumental crime. Their findings were consistent with Messner and Rosenfeld's model, reporting that "it is the interplay between economic and other social institutions that determines the level of anomie within a collectivity and, in turn, the level of crime" (Chamlin & Cochran, 1995:423). In a subsequent assessment of the underlying assumptions of IAT, Chamlin and Cochran (2007) suggest that this theory is best suited for explaining crime in advanced western nations.

Other tests of IAT are generally supportive of the perspective. Michael Maume and Matthew Lee (2003:1168) found that IAT explained variations in homicide rates "across macrosocial units within the United States." To what extent, however, do these findings hold across nations? Remember, Messner and Rosenfeld contend that adherence to the American Dream is the source of America's high violent crime rate relative to those found in other countries. Two studies comparing homicide rates cross-culturally also report findings consistent with institutional anomie theory. Jukka Savolainen (2000) and Steven Messner and Richard Rosenfeld (1997) found that nations with higher levels of social welfare support systems had lower homicide rates. In further efforts to assess the robustness of institutional anomie theory, William Pridemore (2002) examined the effects of structural factors on homicides in transitional Russia. His findings of a strong correlation between negative socioeconomic change and homicide were consistent with Messner and Rosenfeld's predictions. However, in a subsequent examination of the relationship between socioeconomic change and serious property crime in transitional Russia, Kim and Pridemore (2004) failed to find a relationship.

The past two decades have witnessed a number of empirical tests of GST, beginning with one conducted by Robert Agnew and Helene White (1992). They found that measures of GST did a moderately good job of explaining delinquency and drug use. Measures of family, school, and neighborhood strain were significant predictors of delinquency, while the traditional measures of failure to achieve valued goals were not. They also found that these strain variables had different effects. Adolescents with delinquent friends, for example, were more susceptible to the negative effects of strain than were adolescents with pro-social peers. Paternoster and Mazerolle (1994) also found strain was associated with higher rates of delinquency when they controlled for the effect of social control and differential association variables.

Subsequent researchers have tested different aspects of GST. Mazerolle and Piquero (1998), for example, found that, in a sample of college students, some types of strain were related to feelings of anger, and that anger was predictive of violent behavior but not of other offenses (see also Mazerolle et al., 2003). Similarly, utilizing a sample of offenders, Piquero and Sealock (2000) found that of the coping strategies identified in GST, anger was predictive of interpersonal violence. Depression, on the other hand, was not predictive of offending. Brezina (1996), utilizing both cross-sectional and longitudinal data, found that strain produced negative feelings of anger and resentment that were related to increased rates of delinquent involvement. Broidy (2001), on the other hand, reported mixed support for GST. Consistent with GST, she found that strain is related to anger and other negative emotions, but that the results varied by the type of strain experienced by the individual. In an investigation of gender differences, Mazerolle (1998) did not find differential effects of the GST variables for males and females. He did, however, report slight gender differences for violent offenses. In a subsequent test of the extent to which GST accounts for both male and female offending, Piquero and Sealock (2004:146) found that the "underlying theoretical process articulated in GST may be the same and apply equally well across gender." In their examination of gender differences, however, Broidy and Agnew (1997) stated that anger, on the part of males, was more likely to result in violent offending.

Agnew's (2001; 2004) extension of his GST articulates the importance of controlling for the type of strain: some forms of strain are likely to lead to crime while others are not. In a study of street youths in Vancouver, Canada, Stephen Baron examined the effect of specific types of strain on offending and drug use. He conducted interviews with more than 400 youths between the ages of 15 and 24 and found that various aspects of GST explained violent crime, property crime, and total crime. However, "the strains Agnew outlined were not successful in predicting drug use" (Baron, 2004:474). Much of the literature assessing GST has focused on between-individual comparisons. In two recent articles, Lee Ann Slocum (2010a, 2010b) suggests that it is also important to examine within-individual patterns of offending; that is, to assess the extent to which variations in strain over time affects individuals' offending patterns. Her examination of drug use found some support that general strain is associated with continued drug use. Slocum emphasizes the importance of viewing stress as part of a dynamic process rather than as a constant force, thereby highlighting that stress is not an individual trait but rather a socially created construct. Earlier tests of the intra-individual variation in stress among incarcerated women also maintained the importance of viewing strain as a dynamic process (Slocum et al., 2005). To summarize this growing body of research dedicated to assessing the efficacy of GST in explaining diverse forms of offending, while some mixed results have emerged, there is growing support for the ability of general strain theory to account for variations in some types of criminal offending (e.g., Mazerolle & Maahs, 2000; Mazerolle et al., 2000, 2003; Agnew et al., 2002; Baron, 2004, 2007).

Policy Implications

Strain theories have straightforward implications for combatting crime. Reductions in structurally induced strain, the perspective implies, will be accompanied by declining rates of crime. A variety of approaches may serve to curtail strain, but the traditional interpretation fuses with liberal ideology. The administrations of both John F. Kennedy and Lyndon B. Johnson in the 1960s incorporated a social activism perspective that included a delinquency prevention component (Binder & Polan, 1991). Attorney General Robert Kennedy was strongly influenced by *Delinquency and Opportunity*, written by Cloward and Ohlin; Kennedy adopted it as the blueprint for the federal response to crime during his brother's presidential administration and Ohlin was appointed as a special assistant to Kennedy's President's Commission on Juvenile Delinquency and Youth Crime. After all, "Ohlin's opportunity theory was a natural for the biases of the Kennedys (particularly Robert) because it connected delinquency to problems stemming from race and poverty" (Binder & Polan, 1991:249). Upon assuming the presidency, Lyndon Johnson continued this tradition, declaring a "war on poverty" in 1964. Johnson's Great Society vision was translated into specific programs, such as Project Headstart, VISTA, Job Corps, and Upward Bound, which were designed to enhance the opportunity for poor youths to succeed in school. Similarly, the Mobilization for Youth project in the lower east side of New York City provided educational and job opportunities for deprived youths.

It is widely conceded that the programs of the 1960s designed to alleviate poverty and enhance opportunities failed. The only parties said to profit from many of these programs were "poverty pimps," that is, persons who derived a living from operating the bureaucratic structure that was ostensibly designed to fight poverty. Stephen Rose (1972) has argued that the failure of the programs was in part due to misdirecting the effort from restructuring society to attempting to change the poor. The program-

Senator Robert F. Kennedy toured the Mississippi Delta in 1967 on an anti-poverty investigation. As Attorney General, Kennedy was strongly influenced by Cloward and Ohlin's *Delinquency and Opportunity*.

CREDIT:
AP Photo/stf.

matic shortcomings of strain-derived policies may have been more a failure of implementation than theory. Others, however, contend that the programs had positive effects on participants (see, e.g., Schweinhart, 1987; Reynolds et al., 2001).

The goals–means disjuncture delineated by Merton and adopted by other strain theorists can also be translated into policy by seeking to implement changes that lower aspirations (Kornhauser, 1978). Recall that Merton asserted that it is the disproportionate American emphasis on success, coupled with restricted opportunity that generates deviance. It follows that a society de-emphasizing upward social mobility would generate less strain. This type of society, of course, is not desirable to the majority because it defies the American ideology that anyone's child can grow up to be president, or at least to be rich, if only he or she strives hard enough.

Unlike other social strain theorists, Messner and Rosenfeld call for a more drastic social policy change than that described above. Because criminal activity is a product of the anomic cultural conditions brought about by the dominance of the economy and the pursuit of monetary success, crime reduction policies need to concentrate on the underlying cultural and structural causes. That is, crime reduction policies should seek to "vitalize families, schools, and the political system." This includes such policies as the provision of family leave, job sharing for mothers and fathers, flexible work schedules, affordable child care, de-emphasis on economic role of education, enhanced use of intermediate sanctions in the criminal justice system, and implementation of social policies that "ensure that material well being is not strictly tied to economic functions and to guarantee that noneconomic roles receive meaningful financial support from collective resources" (Messner & Rosenfeld, 2001:106). More modest policy suggestions might include greater efforts at modifying teacher training to inculcate tolerance of a wider range of class-based youth characteristics. Academic and extracurricular activities could likewise be altered to enhance the odds for successful competition by lower-class youths. In short, any measures aimed at attenuation of strain induced by the social structure are policy relevant to the strain perspective.

SOCIAL ECOLOGY

Ecology is defined as "the study of the relation of the organism to its environment" (Voss & Petersen, 1971: viii). **Social ecology** focuses on the person's relation to the social environment. For criminology, this entails study of the spatial distribution of crime and delinquency.

The social ecology approach to the study of crime grew out of research conducted by members of the Department of Sociology at the University of Chicago during the first half of the twentieth century. The **Chicago School**, as it became known, emphasized the interrelationship between research and policy, which in many instances involved getting out of university offices and into the field. The idea, derived from plant ecology, was that people must be studied in their natural habitat. Robert Park, an early Chicago sociologist whose work had an impact upon criminological research and theory, viewed the city as a social organism that contains "natural areas," that is, areas characterized by ethnic groupings, homogeneous income levels, and by certain kinds of commerce or industry. Natural areas include such well-known communities as San Francisco's Chinatown, Boston's North End, and New York's Harlem. Park claimed that symbiotic relationships exist among the inhabitants of such areas and between the areas (e.g., the commercial areas depend on the residential areas for business and the residents rely on the merchants to provide food and other amenities).

Park teamed with his colleague Ernest Burgess to describe the growth of American cities. They claimed that cities expand radially from a central business area. This **concentric zone model** of city growth is depicted in Figure 7.6. Five zones, each growing gradually and invading the adjacent zone, are identified.

FIGURE 7.6
Concentric zone model.

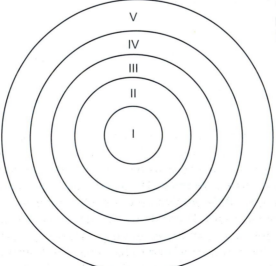

V   Commuter Zone
IV Residential Zone
III Working Class Zone
II Transitional Zone
I   Central Business District

The only limits to the concentric zones are boundaries such as lakes, rivers, highways, and railroad tracks. Zone I is the central business district, characterized by few residents and dominated by commercial establishments. Zone II is the transitional zone characterized by deteriorated housing, factories, and abandoned buildings. Generally, the poorest people in the city live in zones of transition, including the most recent immigrant groups. Zone III is the working-class area, where people escaping from the transitional zone settle. Typically, this zone has single-family tenements lining the streets. Zone IV lies in the outskirts of the city, where single-family homes with yards and garages abound. Beyond this is the commuter zone, i.e., the suburbs. Park and Burgess claimed that all cities expand and grow in this manner. As one zone becomes too confining, it encroaches upon the next zone until the original inhabitants move to the next zone. The closer they are to the central business district, the lower the quality and rental price of housing. Residents seek to migrate to outer zones as their economic positions improve. This migration pattern was adopted from the biological branch of ecology, which identified patterns of invasion, dominance, and succession.

Clifford Shaw and Henry McKay—Social Disorganization and Cultural Transmission

Clifford Shaw and Henry McKay built upon the work of Park and Burgess to study delinquency in Chicago. Using three different types of maps, Shaw and McKay (1942) plotted rates of male delinquency in Chicago between 1900 and 1933. "Spot" maps pinpointed the residences of all juveniles arrested, "rate" maps reported the percentage of juveniles with arrest records in each of 431 census tracts, and "zone" maps provided delinquency rates for each of the five zones in the concentric zone model.

Shaw and McKay examined the relationships between a number of community variables and delinquency. They found that areas with high delinquency rates were characterized by

- A decreasing population;
- A high percentage of "foreign-born" and "Negro" heads of families;
- A high percentage of families on relief;
- A low rate of home ownership; and
- Low median rental values.

Additionally, the authors located other behaviors and social phenomena common to the high-delinquency areas. Among these were high rates of truancy, infant mortality, tuberculosis, mental disorders, and adult criminality. Shaw and McKay also examined trends over time. Despite changes in the ethnic nature of the groups inhabiting the different areas, the rates of delinquency and other social problems remained relatively constant. This demonstrated that the high delinquency rates could not be attributed to the groups occupying the inner zones, but rather that the rates were related to the ecological features of those zones. For every year, the zone map of social maladies showed an inverse relationship with distance from the city center. In other words, rates were highest in the central business district and transitional zone, lowest in the commuter and residential zones, and in between in the working-class zone.

Shaw and McKay concluded that delinquency is associated with the physical structure and social organization of the city. They claimed that differential value systems existed in different communities. They wrote (1942:170–2):

> In the areas of high economic status where the rates of delinquency are low there is, in general, a similarity in the attitudes of the residents with reference to conventional values. . . . In contrast, the areas of low economic status where the rates of delinquency are high, are characterized by wide diversity in norms and standards of behavior. . . . Children living in such communities are exposed to a variety of contradictory standards and forms of behavior rather than to a relatively consistent and conventional pattern.

Shaw and McKay argued that this exposure to a multitude of different values meant that boys in these areas would come into contact with individuals involved in criminal or deviant activities.

In addition to the differential association within high-delinquency neighborhoods, Shaw and McKay described the areas as being socially disorganized, which is a concept that Cloward and Ohlin later incorporated into opportunity theory and one that has received greater attention from criminologists than have other aspects of the social ecology school. **Social disorganization** centered around three variables: poverty, residential mobility, and racial heterogeneity. These factors, depicted in Figure 7.7, are conceptualized as independent variables that generate social disorganization, which in turn contributes to crime and delinquency. The idea is that poor communities foster social disorganization because they lack the resources to address their problems. Funds are unavailable for developing viable recreation areas, for example. High levels of residential mobility contribute to anonymity. Social control declines because people do not know who belongs and who does not, inhibiting development of a sense of community. This is further exacerbated in heterogeneous communities where, because people do not come to know one another, common values fail to emerge. This absence of community values allows a tradition of delinquent behavior to develop that is handed down from one generation to the next through a process called **cultural transmission**. The breakdowns in community social control have been viewed as "a group-level analog of control theory" (Bursik, 1988:521), a perspective discussed in the following chapter.

Another characteristic of the high-delinquency areas is the presence of numerous service agencies funded and staffed by groups external to the community.

FIGURE 7.7
Causal framework of social disorganization.

Poverty
Residential Mobility ⟶ Social ⟶ Crime
Racial Heterogeneity   Disorganization   and
                                                        Delinquency

To Shaw and McKay, this situation reflected a lack of community organization and led them to launch their **Chicago Area Project (CAP)**, a delinquency prevention program. Shaw was an activist who felt an obligation to integrate research and practice. The CAP was based upon results of the ecological research as well as the biographical studies conducted by Shaw (1930/1966).

> CAP was conducted from 1932 to 1957 in three high-delinquency areas. A field worker from Shaw and McKay's Institute for Juvenile Research organized local residents to improve the community. Originally privately funded, CAP ultimately was taken over by the state of Illinois as part of its delinquency prevention program.
>
> The CAP stressed the importance of maintaining the autonomy of the community. An effort was made to avoid the imposition of Anglo-Saxon, middle-class standards on residents. The aim was to "stimulate" community organization without engineering and controlling it and to "spark" the latent potential for community control (Snodgrass, 1976:12).

Snodgrass describes Shaw's conception of "community" as that of a "folk-idealist waging an imaginary war with urban-industrial reality" (1976:13). Shaw based his model on his own experience growing up in a rural Indiana town. He believed that crime was bred in the slums of the city and that a development of community would lead to a reduction in delinquency.

While the purpose of the CAP was loosely articulated, Shaw felt that the program would be successful if it did nothing more than unite residents and reinstate the bonds of social control. In his summary of the CAP, Solomon Kobrin (1959:22), who had worked with Shaw and McKay at the Institute for Juvenile Research, wrote:

> The theory on which the Area Project program is based is that, taken in its most general aspect, delinquency as a problem in the modern metropolis is principally a product of the breakdown of the machinery of spontaneous social control. . . . [D]elinquency was seen as adaptive behavior on the part of male children of rural migrants acting as members of adolescent peer groups in their efforts to find their way to meaningful and respected adult roles essentially unaided by the older generation and under the influence of criminal models for whom the inner city areas furnish a haven.

CAP was a precursor to community prevention programs implemented during the 1960s. Snodgrass (1976) has summarized the CAP as designed to inculcate American middle-class values into slum residents in the belief that this would reduce the problems found disproportionately in these inner-city areas.

Contemporary Social Ecology

Following empirical tests of social disorganization theory in the 1950s and 1960s, there was a relative decline in theoretical and methodological interest in the social disorganization perspective. Criminologists turned largely to the labeling and conflict theories (see Chapter 9) and to social psychological perspectives such as Hirschi's social control theory, Akers' social learning theory (both discussed in Chapter 8), and increasingly to integrated theoretical models (see Chapter 10). A testament to the durability of the social disorganization perspective, however, is provided in the following conversation reported by Bursik and Grasmick: "During an annual meeting of the American Society of Criminology during the mid-1980s, we were informed that social disorganization was the 'herpes of criminology . . . once you think it is gone for good, the symptoms flare up again" (1993:30). As this quote suggests, criminologists have continued to promote the importance of community-level factors in the etiology of crime. Robert J. Bursik Jr., who received his Ph.D. from the Department of Sociology at the University of Chicago, has been one of the stronger proponents of this perspective. In 1993, he and his colleague, Harold G. Grasmick, published their widely acclaimed book, *Neighborhoods and Crime*, detailing their systemic theory of crime. In that work, they emphasize the role of social control in regulating criminal activity within the neighborhood. As the following discussion of "contemporary" social disorganization theory reflects, the work of Shaw and McKay was instrumental in stimulating a rich tradition of macro-level research examining the community context of crime.

A number of sociologists replicated the Shaw and McKay Chicago study (Lander, 1954; Bordua, 1958–9; Chilton, 1964; Quinney, 1964). These studies generally focused on variables available from the U.S. Census Bureau's decennial surveys. Representative of factors believed to be indicative of social disorganization were low median monthly rental rates, low percentage of owner-occupied homes, high percentage of nonwhites, high percentage of overcrowded homes, and high percentage of foreign-born individuals. Despite some discrepancies among the studies, the general conclusion was that social disorganization was associated with rates of officially recorded crime and delinquency. Current political debate surrounds the role of immigration on crime rates. While the influx of immigrants serves as an indicator of social disorganization, consensus is lacking on the extent to which immigration impacts crime. Highlight 7.2 provides a brief overview of this debate.

A major criticism of the work of Shaw and McKay and the four cited replications has been their dependence upon police or court records to measure delinquency. Would those same results hold for self-report data? Studies utilizing the self-report method reported contradictory conclusions. Robert Kaspis (1978) found that delinquency was higher in communities with high migration rates, but he did not find higher delinquency rates in neighborhoods where there was a higher probability of contact with adult criminals and delinquent friends, or where there was greater exposure to norms supportive of illegal behavior. Thus, Kaspis discovered only partial support for the social disorganization model.

A Liberian community in Philadelphia numbers about 15,000 in a city of 1.5 million. Although a common public perception is that immigration is linked to more crime, some contemporary research finds the opposite.

CREDIT:
AP Photo/Joseph Kaczmarek.

HIGHLIGHT 7.2 SOCIAL DISORGANIZATION THEORY AND IMMIGRATION: SOME UNEXPECTED FINDINGS

This highlight features insights from Professor Stephanie DiPietro, a criminologist who specializes in the effect of immigration on crime. When asked to comment on this relationship, she provided the following response.

The relationship between immigration and crime has been the subject of ongoing debate for more than 100 years, since the first major wave of immigrants arrived in the United States from Europe at the turn of the century. Although a common public perception is that immigration is linked to more crime, most contemporary research finds the opposite (Lee & Martinez, 2009). That is, despite popular stereotypes about immigrants being a "dangerous class," research finds nearly consistently that immigrants are less crime prone than native born Americans and that "cities of concentrated immigration are some of the safest places around" (Sampson, 2008:30). In fact, one prominent immigration scholar argued recently that the flood of immigrants to U.S. cities in the past few decades may have played a key role in the crime drop observed in the early 1990s (Sampson, 2006).

The finding that immigration is either unrelated or more often *negatively* related to crime is surprising given that some of the most well-known theoretical perspectives predict an opposite pattern. Social disorganization theory, for example, proposes that communities that are poor and have a high level of population turnover and numerous different cultures will have higher crime rates because residents in these neighborhoods are unable to work together to address commonly experienced problems such as crime (Bursik, 1988). Given that today's immigrant population, which is of predominantly Latin American, Afro-Caribbean, and Asian descent, tends to live in these types of neighborhoods, one would expect them to be disproportionately involved in crime. Rather, scholars have found substantial evidence for what has been called the "immigrant revitalization thesis," or the argument that a high concentration of immigrants in disadvantaged inner-city neighborhoods may actually improve levels of social organization by stimulating local economies, generating new opportunities for social networking, and changing the family structure in these communities (Lee & Martinez, 2002). Although future research is needed to better understand the relationship between immigration and crime at the community level, the existing research casts some doubt on the usefulness of classic theoretical perspectives such as social disorganization theory to explain this relationship. (For additional information on the immigration-crime relationship, consult DiPietro and Bursik, 2012 and DiPietro and McGloin, 2012.)

In a study of Chicago youths, John Johnstone (1978) reported that community-level characteristics proved to be the least useful in explaining delinquency rates and that there was no evidence to suggest that crime was higher for groups in economically depressed areas. A subsequent study by Johnstone (1983) examined gang behavior. In this study, he did find community poverty to be highly correlated with gang recruitment. Youth gangs were found primarily in communities characterized by social and economic deterioration. Johnstone noted that "the opportunity to gang is established by the external social environment, but the decision to do so is governed by social and institutional attachments and by definitions of self" (1983:296). In a similar vein, Anne Cattarello (2000) found that individuals who lived in socially disorganized neighborhoods were more likely to associate with delinquent peers than were youth who lived in organized communities. Furthermore, relying upon longitudinal data collected as part of an evaluation of the DARE program in Lexington, Kentucky, she concluded that all of the neighborhood variation in delinquency was mediated by the peer variables. That is, neighborhood characteristics explained variations in association with delinquent peers, which in turn accounted for differential involvement in criminal activity.

A comprehensive study of violent offenders in four cities (New York, Chicago, Miami, and Dallas) reported results similar to those of Johnstone. Jeffrey Fagan, Elizabeth Piper, and Melinda Moore (1986) interviewed violent (according to police and court records) offenders as well as comparison groups of high school students and dropouts. Analysis of both neighborhood and individual-level data led Fagan and his colleagues (1986:462) to conclude:

> Despite the disproportionate concentration of violent and serious juvenile delinquency in inner-city neighborhoods, most adolescents living in conditions of relative deprivation avoid the predictable consequences of peer, family, and social influences with respect to criminality. . . . Apparently, social and economic conditions in inner cities amplify the social processes which contribute to delinquency.

In 1989, Robert Sampson and Byron Groves published what has become a widely cited test of social disorganization theory. This classic work relied upon data from the 1982 British Crime Survey (BCS) and tested the efficacy of social disorganization theory to explain both self-reported offending and victimization. They found that "communities characterized by sparse friendship networks, unsupervised teenage peer groups, and low organizational participation had disproportionately high rates of crime and delinquency" (Sampson & Groves 1989:799). Importantly for subsequent development of this theoretical framework, Sampson and Groves noted that the levels of community organization mediated the effects of community structural characteristics. A subsequent replication of Sampson and Groves' work, utilizing data from the 1994 BCS, concluded that the earlier findings were robust and supported the social disorganization perspective (Lowenkamp et al., 2003).

Other studies utilizing self-reports have found community-level effects on rates of offending. Without exception, however, these studies find that individual-level factors have a larger effect on self-reported crime and drug use than do macro-level (i.e., measures of social disorganization) factors (e.g., Esbensen & Huizinga, 1990; Elliott et al., 1995; Oberwittler, 2004).

Another trend in recent ecological studies has been toward the inclusion of extra-community dynamics in the study of delinquency. Janet Heitgard and Robert Bursik (1987) examined the effects of neighborhood racial change and other indicators of social disorganization upon delinquency rates in adjoining areas. Their analysis showed that delinquency rates increased as a consequence of rapid compositional changes in adjoining neighborhoods. Read Robert Bursik's view of the future of social disorganization theory in Highlight 7.3.

Interesting empirical questions are still being explored by researchers utilizing the social ecology/social disorganization framework. Criminologists have incorporated new techniques (e.g., self-report and victimization data) and new approaches (e.g., examination of extra-community dynamics and a combination of individual- and community-level data). Other developments include

HIGHLIGHT 7.3 THE FUTURE OF SOCIAL DISORGANIZATION THEORY

Interview with Bob Bursik Jr., Curator's Professor of Criminology and Criminal Justice at the University of Missouri-St. Louis. Professor Bursik was asked to comment on the future of social disorganization. His response is summarized below.

After a long period during which the traditional social disorganization theory of Clifford Shaw and Henry McKay was seriously out of favor with most criminologists, the perspective was significantly revitalized during the mid to late 1980s. The hallmark of this rejuvenation was the reformulation of the key concept of disorganization in terms of the ability of relational networks to exercise processes of informal social control that would decrease the likelihood of problematic behaviors within a residential neighborhood, most notably crime. Given its grounding in the systemic theory of urban structure, this came to be known as the systemic social disorganization perspective.

Over the next decade, this perspective eventually evolved into the "collective efficacy" model of Robert Sampson and his associates, which emphasized the degree to which community residents believed that they could count on their fellow neighbors to help mutually solve problems that may arise; an excellent review of these developments can be found in Kubrin and Weitzer (2003). During the course of that evolution, a growing body of evidence suggested that the relational ties emphasized by the systemic model were neither necessary nor sufficient for the control of crime, and that their relevance primarily was in the degree to which they heightened that sense of efficacy.

I believe that such conclusions are premature for two reasons. First, a small but important series of studies (especially those employing ethnographic research strategies) consistently has documented the relevance of certain network characteristics with distinctly systemic implications, such as reciprocated exchanges and negotiated coexistence. Second, these aspects of relational networks are nearly impossible to capture with the traditional quantitative data collection methodologies that have been used to date. As a result, I think that some of the most important systemic predictions about the structural aspects of relational networks and the informal control of crime have yet to be statistically tested.

Similar measurement limitations also plagued the study of peer group processes and delinquency until the Add Health project introduced a unique "saturation sampling frame" into its study design, which meant that for a small subset of the schools in which it collected data, *everyone* was interviewed, thereby facilitating a very nuanced examination of the structures of these groups. I think that the use of a similar strategy, in which all residents of a small subset of face blocks embedded within larger communities are interviewed, is the future of large-scale, quantitative neighborhood studies. Unless that, or some similarly network-based data collection approach, is adopted, only ethnographic studies restricted to one or (at best) a handful of neighborhoods will be able to generate insights into the full role that relational networks play in the control of crime and delinquency.

Note: The Add Health study (The National Longitudinal Study of Adolescent Health) is a longitudinal study of a nationally representative sample of adolescents in grades 7–12 in the United States during the 1994–5 school year. For more information, consult the Add Health Web site: http://www.cpc.unc.edu/projects/addhealth.

the expanded use advanced statistical tools and software (e.g., factor analysis, hierarchical and multi-level modeling) that allow inclusion of a large number of community variables (see, for example, Scheuerman & Kobrin, 1986; Simcha-Fagan & Schwartz, 1986) as well as examination of trends over time (e.g., Bursik, 1986). The social disorganization hypothesis requires longitudinal data because it predicts that community changes will be followed by shifts in rates of crime and delinquency. In one study examining a decade of changes in two Baltimore neighborhoods, for example, Ralph Taylor and Jeanette Covington (1988) found that increased social disorganization was followed by increases in violent crime.

The popularity of social ecology declined concomitantly with increases in the popularity of strain and, particularly, of control and deterrence theory. Much of the initial decline of criminological focus on the ecological perspective can be attributed to W.S. Robinson's (1950) clarification of a significant inferential error that often plagued ecological studies. Robinson aptly pointed out that ecological (group-level) correlations cannot substitute for individual-level correlations. Because, for example, the economic resources of communities are associated with rates of crime in those communities does not necessarily mean that the same statistical relationship holds on an individual level. This problem, termed the **ecological fallacy**, may have unduly discouraged criminologists from analyzing ecological data because of their abiding interest in explaining and predicting criminality on an individual level (Bursik, 1988). During the past 25 years, however, the potential for integrating macro-level with micro-level theories has been given more attention (e.g., Hagan, 1989; Short, 1989). The social ecology framework is experiencing a significant resurgence in efforts to understand the causes of crime and delinquency (Wikstrom & Loeber, 2000; Sampson 2002; Sampson et al., 2002; Kubrin & Stewart, 2006; Steenbeek & Hipp, 2011).

SUMMARY

This chapter has examined social structure theories. The theories subsumed under this category have three common characteristics. They portray crime as a product of deficiencies in the social structure, such as poverty and the lack of educational opportunity. Another feature is their focus on the lower-class milieu as the source of crime. Because they view crime as a lower-class problem, social structure theorists focus on lower-class segments of society in seeking to explain crime. Some criminologists, however, have applied strain theories to white-collar offenses and others to explain increases in crimes by women. Third, this is a macro-theory tradition. Social structure theories are designed to account for variations in rates of crime among groups, not to explain individual-level criminality.

Strain theory is one of the purest sociological approaches to understanding crime. It is rooted in Emile Durkheim's concept of anomie, or normlessness, but was given its contemporary usage by Robert Merton. Strain or frustration is considered a product of failure that is likely to be disproportionately experienced within the lower class because of structural limitations on opportunities. This failure may elicit innovative or deviant responses to meet culturally emphasized success goals, primarily the goals of material acquisition and higher status. Richard Cloward and Lloyd Ohlin extended the concept with their opportunity theory, pointing out that resorting to illegitimate means to success is not always a readily available option. Instead, they argued, illegitimate opportunity structures are governed by factors such as social organization in a manner similar to legitimate opportunities.

Strain theories were popular in the 1960s and provided the basis for a number of social programs. The success of policies derived from the strain tradition, however, has been marginal at best. In addition, the assumption that crime is a lower-class problem has sparked a major debate within criminological circles. Questions have also been raised regarding the picture of delinquency as portrayed by each of the major strain theories. Criminologists such as Robert Agnew with his GST and Steven Messner and Richard Rosenfeld in *Crime and the American Dream*, however, have re-energized the strain tradition. It appears that this theoretical perspective will continue to contribute to the evolution of our understanding of crime for some time.

The social ecology school laid much of the framework for strain theories, but also contributed to the formulation of theories that can be classified primarily as social process perspectives. Social ecology is patterned after the study of plants and their environment, applying the principles from that field to the study of humans and their social environment. The concept of social disorganization is one of the primary contributions of this perspective and has implications for both the social structure and the cultural deviance theories. Socially disorganized communities lack stability and the necessary resources to formulate or accomplish collective goals, which leads to higher rates of crime.

KEY TERMS AND CONCEPTS

Altruistic Suicide

Anomie

Chicago Area Project (CAP)

Chicago School

Concentric Zone Model

Conflict Gang

Conformists

Criminal Gang

Cultural Transmission

Ecological Fallacy

Goals and Means

Innovation

Institutional Anomie Theory (IAT)

Myth of Classlessness

Opportunity Theory

Rebellion

Retreatists

Ritualists

Social Disorganization

Social Ecology

Social Structure Theories

Sociobiology

Strain Theories

KEY CRIMINOLOGISTS

Robert Agnew

Robert J. Bursik Jr.

Richard Cloward

Emile Durkheim

Charis Kubrin

Henry McKay

Robert Merton

Steven Messner

Lloyd Ohlin   Clifford Shaw

Richard Rosenfeld   Lee Ann Slocum

Robert J. Sampson   Edwin Sutherland

DISCUSSION QUESTIONS

1. Explain how self-report studies brought into question one of the underlying assumptions of strain theory.

2. Contrast Durkheim's and Merton's versions of strain in society. Make sure to discuss the role each theorist attributed to aspirations/goals and opportunities/means for success in society.

3. Cloward and Ohlin proposed their opportunity theory of strain theory in 1960. Discuss how this theoretical perspective proved especially relevant for social policy development during the 1960s.

4. "Second place is the first loser." Explain how this statement captures the essence of Messner and Rosenfeld's Institutional Anomie Theory.

5. What is the theoretical framework for the widely cited Chicago Area Project (CAP)? Describe the CAP and then explain the theoretical rationale underlying the program.

REFERENCES

Agnew, R. (1987). On "testing structural strain theories." *Journal of Research in Crime and Delinquency, 24,* 281–86.

Agnew, R. (1992). Foundation for a general strain theory of crime and delinquency. *Criminology, 30,* 47–87.

Agnew, R. (1999). A general strain theory of community differences in crime rates. *Journal of Research in Crime and Delinquency, 36,* 123–55.

Agnew, R. (2001). Building on the foundation of general strain theory: Specifying the types of strain most likely to lead to crime and delinquency. *Journal of Research in Crime and Delinquency, 38,* 319–61.

Agnew, R. (2004). A general strain theory approach to violence. In M. A. Zahn, H. H. Brownstein, & S. L. Jackson (Eds.), *Violence: From theory to research* (pp. 37–50). Cincinnati, OH: LexisNexis/Anderson Publishing.

Agnew, R. (2006). *Pressured into crime: An overview of general strain theory.* Los Angeles, CA: Roxbury Publishing Company.

Agnew, R. & White, H. R. (1992). An empirical test of general strain theory. *Criminology, 30,* 475–99.

Agnew, R., Brezina, T., Wright, J. P., & Cullen, F. T. (2002). Strain, personality traits, and delinquency: Extending general strain theory. *Criminology, 40,* 43–71.

Aldridge, J., Medina-Ariz, J., & Ralphs, R. (2012). Counting gangs: Conceptual and validity problems with the Eurogang definition. In F.-A. Esbensen, & C. L. Maxson (Eds.), *Youth gangs in international perspective: Tales from the Eurogang program of research* (pp. 35–51). New York, NY: Springer.

Baron, S.W. (2004). General strain, street youth and crime: A test of Agnew's revised theory. *Criminology, 42,* 457–83.

Baron, S.W. (2007). Street youth, gender, and financial strain and crime: Exploring Broidy and Agnew's extension of general strain theory. *Deviant Behavior, 28,* 273–302.

Baron, S.W. & Hartnagel, T.P. (1997). Attributions, affect, and crime: Street youths' reactions to unemployment. *Criminology, 35,* 409–34.

Bernard, T.J. (1984). Control criticisms of strain theories: An assessment of theoretical and empirical adequacy. *Journal of Research in Crime and Delinquency, 21,* 353–72.

Bernard, T.J. (1987). Testing structural strain theories. *Journal of Research in Crime and Delinquency, 24,* 262–80.

Binder, A. & Polan, S.L. (1991). The Kennedy-Johnson years, social theory, and federal policy in the control of juvenile delinquency. *Crime & Delinquency, 37,* 242–61.

Bordua, D.J. (1958-9). Juvenile delinquency and anomie. *Social Problems, 6,* 230–38.

Braithwaite, J. (1981). The myth of social class and criminality reconsidered. *American Sociological Review, 46,* 36–37.

Brezina, T. (1996). Adapting to strain: An examination of delinquent coping responses. *Criminology, 34,* 39–60.

Britt, C.L. (1997). Reconsidering the unemployment and crime relationship: Variations by age group and historical period. *Journal of Quantitative Criminology, 13,* 405–28.

Broidy, L.M. (2001). A test of general strain theory. *Criminology, 39,* 9–35.

Broidy, L.M. & Agnew, R. (1997). Gender and crime: A general strain theory perspective. *Journal of Research in Crime and Delinquency, 34,* 275–306.

Brown, S.E. (1985). The class-delinquency hypothesis and juvenile justice system bias. *Sociological Inquiry, 55,* 213–23.

Bursik, R.J., Jr. (1986). Ecological stability and the dynamics of delinquency. In A.J. Reiss, & M.H. Tonry (Eds.), *Crime and community* (pp. 35–66). Chicago, IL: University of Chicago Press.

Bursik, R.J., Jr. (1988). Social disorganization and theories of crime and delinquency: Problems and prospects. *Criminology, 26,* 519–51.

Bursik, R.J., Jr. & Grasmick, H.G. (1993). *Neighborhoods and crime.* New York, NY: Lexington Books.

Cattarello, A.M. (2000). Community-level influences on individuals' social bonds, peer associations, and delinquency: A multilevel analysis. *Justice Quarterly, 17,* 33–60.

Chamlin, M.B. & Cochran, J.K. (1995). Assessing Messner and Rosenfeld's institutional anomie theory: A partial test. *Criminology, 33,* 411–29.

Chamlin, M.B. & Cochran, J.K. (2007). An evaluation of the assumptions that underlie institutional anomie theory. *Theoretical Criminology, 11,* 39–61.

Chilton, R.J. (1964). Continuity in delinquency area research: A comparison of studies for Baltimore, Detroit, and Indianapolis. *American Sociological Review, 29,* 74–83.

Cloward, R.A. & Ohlin, L.E. (1960). *Delinquency and opportunity: A theory of delinquent gangs.* New York, NY: The Free Press.

Cullen, F.T. (1988). Were Cloward and Ohlin strain theorists? Delinquency and opportunity revisited. *Journal of Research in Crime and Delinquency, 25,* 214–41.

Decker, S. H. & Weerman, F. M. (2005). *European street gangs and troublesome youth groups.* Lanham, MD: AltaMira Press.

DiPietro, S. & Bursik, R. J. , Jr. (2012). Studies of the new immigration: The dangers of pan-ethnic classifications. *The Annals of the American Academy of Political and Social Science, 641,* 247–67.

DiPietro, S. & McGloin, J. M. (2012). Differential susceptibility? Immigrant youth and peer influence. *Criminology, 50,* 711–42.

Domhoff, G. W. (1967). *Who rules America?* Englewood Cliffs, NJ: Prentice Hall.

Durkheim, E. (1897/1951). *Suicide: A study in sociology* (J. A. Spaulding & G. Simpson, Trans.) New York, NY: The Free Press.

Dye, T. R. (1976). *Who's running America? Institutional leadership in the United States.* Englewood Cliffs, NJ: Prentice Hall.

Elliott, D. S., Wilson, W. J., Huizinga, D., Sampson, R. J., Elliott, A., & Rankin, B. (1995). The effects of neighborhood disadvantage on adolescent development. *Journal of Research on Crime and Delinquency, 33,* 389–426.

Esbensen, F.-A. & Huizinga, D. (1990). Community structure and drug use: From a social disorganization perspective. *Justice Quarterly, 7,* 691–709.

Esbensen, F.-A. & Maxson, C. L. (2012). *Youth gangs in international perspective: Results from the Eurogang Program of Research.* New York, NY: Springer.

Fagan, J., Piper, E., & Moore, M. (1986). Violent delinquents and urban youth. *Criminology, 24,* 439–71.

Hagan, J. (1989). Micro and macro-structures of delinquency causation and a power-control theory of gender and delinquency. In S. E. Messner, M. D. Krohn, & A. E. Liska (Eds.), *Theoretical integration in the study of deviance and crime* (pp. 213–27). Albany, NY: State University of New York Press.

Heitgard, J. L. & Bursik, R. J., Jr. (1987). Extracommunity dynamics and the ecology of delinquency. *American Journal of Sociology, 92,* 775–87.

Hill, G. D. & Crawford, E. M. (1990). Women, race, and crime. *Criminology, 28,* 601–26.

Hirschi, T. (1969). *Causes of delinquency.* Berkeley, CA: University of California Press.

Hoffman, J. P. & Ireland, T. O. (2004). Strain and opportunity structures. *Journal of Quantitative Criminology, 20,* 263–92.

Johnson, R. S., Kantor, S., & Fishback, P. V. (2007). *Striking at the roots of crime: The impact of social welfare spending on crime during the Great Depression.* National Bureau of Economic Research working paper no. 12825 (January).

Johnstone, J. W. C. (1978). Social class, social areas, and delinquency. *Sociology and Social Research, 63,* 49–72.

Johnstone, J. W. C. (1983). Recruitment to a youth gang. *Youth and Society, 14,* 281–300.

Kaspis, R. E. (1978). Residential succession and delinquency. *Criminology, 15,* 459–86.

Kim, S. W. & Pridemore, W. (2004). Social change, institutional anomie and serious property crime in transitional Russia. *The British Journal of Criminology, 4,* 81–97.

Klein, M. W., Kerner, H. J., Maxson, C. L., & Weitekamp, E. G. M. (2001). *The Eurogang paradox: Street gangs and youth groups in the U.S. and Europe.* Dordrecht, Netherlands: Kluwer Academic Publishers.

Kobrin, S. (1959). The Chicago area project: A 25-year assessment. *Annals of the American Academy of Political and Social Science, 322,* 19–29.

Kornhauser, R. R. (1978). *Social sources of delinquency*. Chicago, IL: University of Chicago Press.

Kubrin, C. E. & Stewart, E. A. (2006). Predicting who reoffends: The neglected role of neighborhood context in recidivism studies. *Criminology, 44*, 165–97.

Kubrin, C. E. & Weitzer, R. (2003). New directions in social disorganization theory. *Journal of Research in Crime and Delinquency, 40*, 374–402.

Lander, B. (1954). *Towards an understanding of juvenile delinquency*. New York, NY: Columbia University Press.

Lee, M. T. & Martinez, R., Jr. (2002). Social disorganization revisited: Mapping the recent immigration and black homicide relationship in Northern Miami. *Sociological Focus, 35*, 365–82.

Lee, M. T. & Martinez, R., Jr. (2009). Immigration reduces crime. An emerging scholarly consensus. In W. McDonald (Ed.), *Immigration, crime and justice* (pp. 3–16). Bingley, UK: Emerald Group Publishing Ltd.

Lien, I.-L. (2001). The concept of honor, conflict and violent behavior among youths in Oslo. In M. W. Klein, H.-J. Kerner, C. L. Maxson, & E. G. M. Weitekamp (Eds.), *The Eurogang paradox: Street gangs and youth groups in the U.S. and Europe* (pp. 165–74). Dordrecht, Netherlands: Kluwer Academic Publishers.

Lowenkamp, C. T., Cullen, F. T., & Pratt, T. C. (2003). Replicating Sampson and Grove's test of social disorganization theory: Revisiting a criminological classic. *Journal of Research in Crime and Delinquency, 40*, 351–73.

Martinez, R., Jr. (2003). Moving beyond black and white violence: African American, Haitian, and Latino homicides in Miami. In D. F. Hawkins (Ed.), *Violent crime: Assessing race & ethnic differences* (pp. 22–43). New York, NY: Cambridge University Press.

Maume, M. O. & Lee, M. R. (2003). Social institutions and violence: A sub-national test of institutional anomie theory. *Criminology, 41*, 1137–72.

Mazerolle, P. (1998). Gender, general strain, and delinquency: An examination. *Justice Quarterly, 15*, 65–91.

Mazerolle, P. & Maahs, J. (2000). General strain and delinquency: An alternative investigation of deviant adaptations. *Justice Quarterly, 17*, 73–78.

Mazerolle, P. & Piquero, A. (1998). Linking exposure to strain with anger: An investigation of deviant adaptations. *Journal of Criminal Justice, 26*, 195–211.

Mazerolle, P., Piquero, A., & Capowich, G. E. (2003). Examining the links between strain, situational and dispositional anger, and crime: Further specifying and testing general strain theory. *Youth & Society, 35*, 131–57.

Mazerolle, P., Burton, V. S., Jr., Cullen, F. T., Evans, T. D., & Payne, G. L. (2000). Strain, anger, and delinquency adaptations: Specifying general strain theory. *Journal of Criminal Justice, 28*, 89–101.

Menard, S. (1995). A developmental test of Mertonian theory. *Journal of Research in Crime and Delinquency, 32*, 136–74.

Merton, R. K. (1938). Social structure and anomie. *American Sociological Review, 3*, 672–82.

Merton, R. K. (1968). *Social theory and social structure*. New York, NY: The Free Press.

Messner, S. F. & Rosenfeld, R. (1994). *Crime and the American dream*. Belmont, CA: Wadsworth.

Messner, S. F. & Rosenfeld, R. (1997). Political restraint of the market and levels of criminal homicide: A cross-national application of institutional anomie theory. *Social Forces, 75*, 1393–1416.

Messner, S. F. & Rosenfeld, R. (2001). *Crime and the American Dream* (3rd ed.). Belmont, CA: Wadsworth.

Messner, S. F. & Rosenfeld, R. (2007). *Crime and the American Dream* (4th ed.). Belmont, CA: Wadsworth.

Messner, S. F., & Rosenfeld, R. (2013). *Crime and the American Dream* (5th ed.). Belmont, CA: Wadsworth.

Mills, C. W. (1956). *The power elite*. New York, NY: Oxford University Press.

Oberwittler, D. (2004). A multilevel analysis of neighbourhood contextual effects on serious juvenile offending: The role of subcultural values and social disorganization. *European Journal of Criminology, 1*, 201–35.

Park, R. E., Burgess, E. W., & MacKenzie, R. D. (1928). *The City*. Chicago, IL: University of Chicago Press.

Paternoster, R. & Mazerolle, P. (1994). General strain theory and delinquency: A replication and extension. *Journal of Research in Crime and Delinquency, 31*, 235–63.

Peterson, R. D., Krivo, L. J., & Harris, M. A. (2000). Disadvantage and neighborhood violent crime: Do local institutions matter? *Journal of Research in Crime and Delinquency, 37*, 31–63.

Piquero, N. L. & Sealock, M. D. (2000). Generalizing general strain theory: An examination of an offending population. *Justice Quarterly, 17*, 449–84.

Piquero, N. L. & Sealock, M. D. (2004). Gender and general strain theory: A preliminary test of Broidy and Agnew's gender/GST hypotheses. *Justice Quarterly, 21*, 125–58.

Pratt, T. C. & Cullen, F. T. (2005). Assessing macro-level predictors and theories of crime: A meta-analysis. In M. Tonry (Ed.), *Crime and Justice: A Review of Research* (Vol. 32, pp. 373–450). Chicago, IL: University of Chicago Press.

Pridemore, W. A. (2002). Vodka and violence: Alcohol consumption and homicide rates in Russia. *American Journal of Public Health, 92*, 1921–30.

Quinney, R. (1964). Crime, delinquency, and social areas. *Journal of Research in Crime and Delinquency, 1*, 149–54.

Reynolds, A. J., Temple, J. A., Robertson, D. L., & Mann, E. A. (2001). Long-term effects of an early childhood intervention on educational achievement and juvenile arrest: A 15-year follow-up of low-income children in public schools. *Journal of the American Medical Association, 285*, 2339–78.

Robinson, W. S. (1950). Ecological correlations and the behavior of individuals. *American Sociological Review, 15*, 351–57.

Rose, S. M. (1972). *The betrayal of the poor: The transformation of community action*. Cambridge, MA: Schenkmann.

Rosenfeld, R. (2009). Crime is the problem: Homicide, acquisitive crime, and economic conditions. *Journal of Quantitative Criminology, 25*, 287–306.

Rosenfeld, R. & Messner, S. F. (2009). The crime drop in comparative perspective: The impact of the economy and imprisonment on American and European burglary rates. *British Journal of Sociology, 60*, 445–71.

Rosenfeld, R. & Messner, S. F. (2010). The normal crime rate, the economy, and mass incarceration: An institutional-anomie perspective on crime-control policy. In S. H. Decker, & H. Barlow (Eds.), *Criminology and public policy: Putting theory to work* (pp. 45–65). Philadelphia, PA: Temple University Press.

Sampson, R. J. (2002). Transcending tradition: New directions in community research, Chicago Style—The American Society of Criminology 2001 Sutherland Address. *Criminology, 40*, 213–30.

Sampson, R. J. (2006). Open doors don't invite criminals: Is increased immigration behind the drop in crime? *New York Times*, Op-Ed, March 11.

Sampson, R. J. (2008). Rethinking crime and immigration. *Contexts, 7*, 28–33.

Sampson, R. J. & Groves, W. B. (1989). Community structure and crime: Testing social-disorganization theory. *American Journal of Sociology, 94*, 774–802.

Sampson, R. J., Morenoff, J. D., & Gannon-Rowley, T. (2002). Assessing "neighborhood effects": Social processes and new directions in research. *Annual Review of Sociology, 28*, 443–78.

Savolainen, J. (2000). Inequality, welfare state, and homicide: Further support for the institutional anomie theory. *Criminology, 38*, 1021–42.

Scheuerman, L. A. & Kobrin, S. (1986). Community careers in crime. In A. J. Reiss, & M. H. Tonry (Eds.), *Crime and Community* (pp. 67–100). Chicago, IL: University of Chicago Press.

Schweinhart, L. J. (1987). Can preschool programs help prevent delinquency? In J. Q. Wilson, & G. C. Loury (Eds.), *From children to citizens* Vol. 3. (pp. 135–53). New York, NY: Springer-Verlag.

Shaw, C. R. (1930/1966). *The Jack-Roller: A delinquent boy's own story*. Chicago, IL: University of Chicago Press.

Shaw, C. R. & McKay, H. D. (1942). *Juvenile delinquency in urban areas*. Chicago, IL: University of Chicago Press.

Short, J. F., Jr. (1989). Exploring integration of theoretical levels of explanation: Notes on juvenile delinquency. In S. E. Messner, M. D. Krohn, & A. E. Liska (Eds.), *Theoretical integration in the study of deviance and crime* (pp. 243–59). Albany, NY: State University of New York Press.

Simcha-Fagan, O. & Schwartz, J. E. (1986). Neighborhood and delinquency: An assessment of contextual effects. *Criminology, 24*, 667–99.

Slocum, L. A. (2010a). General strain theory and continuity in offending over time: Assessing and extending GST explanations of persistence. *Journal of Contemporary Criminal Justice, 26*, 204–23.

Slocum, L. A. (2010b). General strain theory and the development of stressors and substance use over time: An empirical assessment. *Journal of Criminal Justice, 38*, 1100–112.

Slocum, L. A., Simpson, S., & Smith, D. A. (2005). Strained lives and crime; Examining individual variation in strain and offending in a sample of incarcerated women. *Criminology, 43*, 1067–1110.

Snodgrass, J. (1976). Clifford R. Shaw & Henry D. McKay: Chicago criminologists. *British Journal of Criminology, 16*, 1–19.

Steenbeek, W. & Hipp, J. R. (2011). A longitudinal test of social disorganization theory: Feedback effects among cohesion, social control and disorder. *Criminology, 49*, 833–71.

Sutherland, E. H. (1937). *The professional thief*. Chicago, IL: University of Chicago Press.

Tauby, L. A. (1991). Other women's money. *Working Women*, December, 56–59.

Taylor, R. & Covington, J. (1988). Neighborhood changes in ecology and violence. *Criminology, 26*, 553–89.

Thomas, C. W. & Hepburn, J. R. (1983). *Crime, criminal law and criminology*. Dubuque, IA: William C. Brown.

Tittle, C., Villemez, W., & Smith, D. (1978). The myth of social class and criminality: An empirical assessment of the empirical evidence. *American Sociological Review, 43*, 643–56.

van Gemert, F. (2001). Crips in orange: Gangs and groups in the Netherlands. In M. W. Klein, H.-J. Kerner, C. L. Maxson, & E. G. M. Weitekamp (Eds.), *The Eurogang paradox: Street gangs and youth groups in the U.S. and Europe* (pp. 145–52). Dordrecht, Netherlands: Kluwer Academic Publishers.

van Gemert, F., Peterson, D., & Lien, I.-L. (2008). *Street gangs, migration and ethnicity*. Cullompton, Devon, UK: Willan Publishing.

Voss, H. L. & Petersen, D. M. (Eds.), (1971). *Ecology, crime and delinquency*. New York, NY: Appleton-Century-Crofts.

Wikstrom, P. O. & Loeber, R. (2000). Do disadvantaged neighborhoods cause well-adjusted children to become adolescent delinquents? *Criminology, 38*, 1109–42.

Wilson, W. J. (1987). *The truly disadvantaged: The inner city, the underclass, and public policy*. Chicago, IL: University of Chicago Press.

Social Process Theories of Crime

While social structure theories address variations in rates of crime across structural conditions, **social process theories** most commonly attempt to explain how individuals become law violators. This focus on social interactions or processes experienced by individuals, as opposed to structural matters, represents a shift from macro theory to micro theory. Social process theories redress errors that arise when social structure theories are applied at the individual level. Traditional strain theories, for instance, are rooted in the premise that the social structure generates disproportionate pressure upon members of the lower class to violate norms. The implication is that individuals subjected to economic disadvantage will resort to criminal or delinquent solutions, while the well-to-do, because of the absence of structurally induced strain, will not. This clearly can be misleading, because most people subjected to the stress of poverty do not become criminals, while some people who do not experience poverty become offenders.

Unlike most social structure theories, social process theories typically do not approach crime and delinquency as primarily a lower-class problem; one of their strengths is that their explanatory power cuts across social classes and economic strata. The social process perspective is bolstered by self-report findings, reviewed in Chapter 4, which suggest that both delinquency and crime are more equally distributed across social classes than official data indicate.

At the same time, social process theories are consistent with a pattern of crime and delinquency weighted toward members of the lower class. Features of the social structure may unevenly expose members of the lower class to adverse social processes, which in turn could translate to higher rates of deviance. It is the interactions of individuals with more immediate groups, such as family and peers, however, that may push those individuals toward or pull them away from lawbreaking. In the social process framework, these are the key to explaining behavior. Each individual will learn values of either conformity or deviance through these social processes. Some theories within this tradition assert that the social processes one experiences may provide, or fail to provide, restraints against norm violations. The emphasis is on the interactions experienced within groups significant to the individual.

Three forms of social process theories are discussed in this chapter: *social learning, culture conflict*, and *social control.* These approaches share the premise that groups influence the individual. They are often termed **social psychological theories** (as an alternative to the social process label) because they incorporate both group (social) and individual (psychological) variables. This perspective, then, seeks to integrate macro-level and micro-level explanations of crime, and social and psychological explanations, and also to account for crime across all social classes.

Attempts to categorize theories, however, are rarely endorsed with unanimity. A debate between Barbara Costello (1997, 1998) and Ross Matsueda (1997) illustrates the problem. Following the lead of Ruth Kornhauser (1978), Costello (1997:405) asserted that "differential association theory is the best known variation of the cultural deviance perspective." In response, Matsueda (1997:447) asserted that Kornhauser, and thus Costello, "faltered seriously when she reduced differential association theory to the ridiculous assumptions of 'cultural deviance theory'." The issue is embedded in how Edwin Sutherland's theory of differential association is read. His work is outlined in the following section.

LEARNING CRIMINAL BEHAVIOR

The first group of social process theories is rooted in the notion that criminal behavior is learned in a social context. The learning perspective assumes that law-breaking values, norms, and motives are acquired through interaction with others. The requisite skills and techniques are likewise learned, although their content varies widely with the complexity of the crime. Because these theories envision criminal behavior as a product of the same learning processes as non-criminal behavior, crime is construed as "normal" rather than "pathological." The task of **learning theories** is to detail the process through which criminal patterns are cultivated. In the 2005 presidential address to the American Society of Criminology, Julie Horney (2006) proposed that a broad version of Skinnerian rooted learning theory holds potential to organize much of our knowledge about criminal behavior.

Edwin H. Sutherland—Differential Association

Edwin Hardin Sutherland (1883–1950) was born in Nebraska and, after earning a Ph.D. in sociology at the University of Chicago, held professorial appointments at William Jewell College (Liberty, Missouri), the University of Illinois, the University of Minnesota, the University of Chicago, and served as department head at Indiana University (Odum, 1951). Sutherland is probably the most widely known criminologist, and **differential association** is the most prominent theory of criminal behavior. Sutherland's theory can be considered the first truly sociological effort to explain crime. His intent was to displace the biological and psychological explanations that were dominant early in the twentieth century. Independent of the merit of differential association as an explanation for crime, its role in bringing the field of criminology under the sociological umbrella is of immense importance.

Differential association was influenced by several intellectual traditions. First, the theory was an extension of the French criminologist Gabriel Tarde's (1843–1904) "laws of imitation," a social explanation of the origins of crime formulated late in the nineteenth century in response to the Lombrosian accounts (Vine, 1972).

Three other lines of thought had substantial influence on Sutherland's development of differential association: symbolic interactionism, cultural transmission, and culture conflict. Studying under George Herbert Mead (1863–1931) at the University of Chicago sensitized Sutherland to the **symbolic interaction** premise that people conduct themselves according to the meaning that things have for them. Consequently, Sutherland thought in terms of the meanings that individuals assign criminal conduct or, in other words, of the emergence of value systems. Symbolic interactionism led him to consider how values favorable or unfavorable to criminal behavior are learned and interpreted in interaction with others.

The tradition of ecological research at Chicago contributed to the conceptualization of differential association by suggesting that the community environment plays a key role in crime and delinquency. The findings of Shaw and McKay (see Chapter 7) that crime and delinquency tend to appear in neighborhoods with particular physical and social features, and that criminal values are transmitted just as are language and other cultural traits (i.e., **cultural transmission**), set the stage for explaining law-violating conduct as a product of learning. Their idea of social disorganization as the failure of a community

What is being learned? A group of children of Ku Klux Klan members play at a rally.

CREDIT:
AP Photo/Pat Sullivan.

to support crime-inhibiting conditions also was consistent with a learning explanation of criminal misconduct. Sutherland shifted the focus from the community (macro) to an individual (micro) level by addressing in differential association the process through which a person learns the criminal behavior patterns found in the community.

Culture conflict theorists such as Thorsten Sellin (1938) added to the Chicago ecological data an interpretation that subcultures such as those in the impoverished and socially disorganized neighborhoods studied by Shaw and McKay are characterized by their own conduct norms. These norms are contrary to those of the larger culture and become a source of conflict because behavior that is normal in the context of some subcultures constitutes crime in the eyes of the larger society. Sutherland drew upon this idea, along with those of cultural transmission and social disorganization, to develop differential association as an explanation for crime. Extending Figure 7.7, Figure 8.1 summarizes the framework underlying differential association. It depicts factors such as poverty, residential mobility, and racial heterogeneity as contributing to social disorganization, which in turn, engenders culture conflict. Values and behavioral patterns culturally transmitted in socially disorganized neighborhoods produce culture conflict.

Differential association suggests that persons socialized in disorganized neighborhoods are likely to have associations that will encourage criminal adaptations. In contrast, individuals from socially organized neighborhoods are more likely to experience noncriminal associations. In later versions of differential association, Sutherland substituted differential social organization for social disorganization, noting that community organization represents a continuum rather than a dichotomy. What he drew from his close association with the Chicago School was an awareness that crime is socially distributed and a belief that it is learned behavior. The need was to understand that learning process.

FIGURE 8.1
Ecological heritage of differential association.

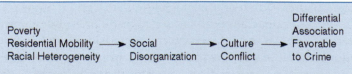

| Poverty Residential Mobility Racial Heterogeneity | → | Social Disorganization | → | Culture Conflict | → | Differential Association Favorable to Crime |

Finally, Sutherland's own research endeavors contributed to differential association. In *The Professional Thief* (1937), he identified the careful tutelage necessary for both admittance to and practice of the trade. Best known of Sutherland's works is *White Collar Crime* (1949), which demanded that crime be defined to include offenses of persons in the upper socioeconomic class. He pointed out that the crime picture was skewed by the neglect of such offenses in the justice process and in official crime statistics. He observed, "This bias is quite as certain as it would be if the scholars selected only red-haired criminals for study and reached the conclusion that redness of hair was the cause of crime" (1949:9). This concern goes to the heart of differential association because the theory is intended to account for all crime, including both the white-collar and street varieties. This was made explicit in the characterization of the goal of the theory as the development of a set of scientific "interrelated general propositions, to which no exceptions can be found" (Sutherland & Cressey, 1974:72). Differential association seeks to explain factors associated with crime (e.g., age, race, gender, socioeconomic status) but not causally related to it. Sutherland sought to identify processes common to offenders who are old and young, African-American and white, male and female.

Differential association was expounded primarily in Sutherland's classic textbook, which extended through 11 editions during a period of nearly 70 years. The first edition was published in 1924 as *Criminology*. Differential association first appeared in a crude form in the second (1934) edition, entitled *Principles of Criminology*. The theory was made explicit in the form of seven principles in the third (1939) edition. The final version of the theory, consisting of nine principles, was presented in the fourth (1947) edition. Following Sutherland's death, his student, Donald R. Cressey (1919–87), revised the next six editions (1955–78), but never modified Sutherland's last statement of differential association. Cressey felt that the theory should be tested extensively prior to subjecting it to modification. The final edition was published in 1992 with a revision by David Luckenbill.

Principles of Differential Association

The nine principles of differential association theory are presented in Box 8.1. These propositions specify "the process by which a particular person comes to engage in criminal behavior" (Sutherland & Cressey, 1974:75).

The principle that criminal behavior is learned provides the foundation for differential association. This expressly rules out heredity, human nature, and innovation as causes of aberrant behavior. Persons are not, as George Thorogood sings, "born to be bad," nor do they invent deviant behavior. They are taught how to behave, or misbehave, in a social context. This provides a sharp contrast with some other theories. Classical criminology and its deterrence propositions assume that human nature motivates the offender and focuses on how that proclivity might be curtailed. Likewise, **control theory**, which we shall turn to later in this chapter, rests on the premise that people will engage in crime or delinquency if not controlled. Which do you regard as the most plausible starting point for explaining

BOX 8.1 PRINCIPLES OF DIFFERENTIAL ASSOCIATION

1. Criminal behavior is learned.

2. Criminal behavior is learned in interaction with other persons in a process of communication.

3. The principal part of the learning of criminal behavior occurs within intimate personal groups.

4. When criminal behavior is learned, the learning includes:

   a. techniques of committing the crime, which are sometimes very complicated, sometimes very simple;

   b. the specific direction of motives, drives, rationalization, and attitudes.

5. specific direction of motives and drives is learned from definitions of the legal codes as favorable or unfavorable.

6. A person becomes delinquent because of an excess of definitions favorable to violation of law over definitions unfavorable to violation of law.

7. Differential associations may vary in frequency, duration, priority, and intensity.

8. The process of learning criminal behavior by association with criminal and anticriminal patterns involves all of the mechanisms that are involved in any other learning.

9. While criminal behavior is an expression of general needs and values, it is not explained by those general needs and values, since noncriminal behavior is an expression of the same needs and values.

Source: Adapted from Sutherland, E.H., & Cressey, D.R. (1974). *Criminology* (9th ed., pp. 75–76). Philadelphia, PA: J.B. Lippincott.

crime? Are we destined to offend if not discouraged by external forces or are we disinclined to commit criminal acts until we are taught to do so? Each theory of crime rests on certain assumptions that may not be scientifically resolvable.

The second and third principles of differential association specify that criminal behavior is learned primarily in interaction with significant others such as family and friends. The emphasis placed on parental influence in childrearing illustrates widespread endorsement of these points. It is taken for granted that children will learn language, eating habits, personal hygiene, and a host of other behaviors from their parents. Differential association extends this learning process to the realm of crime. As the associations of youths (i.e., their circle of significant others) expand, it is expected that conduct initially shaped by parents will increasingly come under the influence of peers, often arousing concern of the parents about the company kept by their offspring.

Media influence upon learning is minimized in Sutherland's theory. Contemporary thought questions this, but the nature of media has changed dramatically since the formulation of differential association. Television, for example, was not introduced until after the birth of the theory. Virtual interaction and learning are phenomena that Sutherland could not have remotely foreseen, but a recent study of digital pirating supports the conclusion that both criminal motivations and techniques are learned online (Holt & Copes, 2010). Given this contextual shift, it may not be inconsistent to incorporate media influences into the third principle. Highlight 8.1 reviews a media issue that received a lot of attention.

In the fourth principle, learning techniques of committing crime is said to be much less important than learning the mindset (motives, drives, rationalizations, attitudes) conducive to criminal behavior. So learning the values or

HIGHLIGHT 8.1 MASS MEDIA AND VIOLENCE

Do rock and rap lyrics cause violent behavior? In 1993 the rap song, "Cop Killer," by Ice-T was banned in a number of jurisdictions. Did this song promote and cause kids to kill cops, as its critics proclaimed? According to Dennis R. Martin, President of the National Association of Chiefs of Police, 144 U.S. police officers were killed in the line of duty during 1992. Did "Cop Killer" contribute to any of these deaths? Martin seems to think so and bases his opinion on a brief review of a case involving the wounding of two police officers by four juveniles in Las Vegas. Given that at least 1.5 million persons had listened to the original cut prior to its banning, Mark Hamm and Jeff Ferrell point out the absurdity of establishing a cause and effect relationship between the song and police deaths. They comment that

this argument "intentionally engineers self-serving moral panic around rap music, and obstructs solutions to the sorts of problems which rap portrays."

They point out that Ice-T is not the first artist to include a "cop killer" theme in music. Eric Clapton's recording of "I Shot the Sheriff" had far greater sales and never suffered any sort of moral or political condemnation. A number of other songs have been equally graphic of violence toward police without public censure.

Source: Hamm, M.S., & Ferrell, J. (1994). Rap, cops, and crime: Clarifying the "Cop Killer" controversy. *ACJS Today*, Vol. 13, No. 1 (May/June).

---

attitudes, often referred to as **attitude transference** in contemporary criminological literature (Kobayashi et al., 2011), to facilitate deviant behavior is the bedrock of differential association theory. While a particular mindset is essential, familiarity with technique relates to the type of crime perpetrated and to success in completing it without detection. Some crimes entail learning complex techniques. Studies of white-collar criminals (Sutherland, 1949), confidence men (Maurer, 1974), and professional thieves (Sutherland, 1937) illustrate the considerable skills that must be mastered to pursue these criminal paths. Many offenses, however, require little or no skill. Learning the motives and drives, which results in "a relatively constant desire or persistent urge to do illegal things" (Tittle et al., 1986:414) is, on the other hand, a requisite of criminal behavior. Similarly, criminal behavior is supported by learning rationalizations and attitudes that define it as acceptable. Persons may, for example, steal or rape because they have been taught specific attitudes and rationalizations, but the skills necessary for such crimes usually are minimal.

Definitions favorable and unfavorable to violations of the law, identified in the fifth statement, provide the key to differential association because they determine the values or mindset of the individual. We all are exposed to some mixture of definitions regardless of with whom we associate. Definitions favorable to violation of the law may be learned from law-abiding persons and, conversely, values supportive of legal codes may be acquired from even hardcore criminals. All of us as children received from our parents or parental figures some definitions favorable to law violation. Examples include observing parents ignoring speed limits, discussing ways to cheat on income tax returns, bringing materials home from the workplace and failing to return excessive change dispensed by cashiers. Accompanying these offenses are attitudes and rationalizations: "The traffic is light and the posted speed limit is too low"; "Taxes are too high"; "Nobody at work was going to use these materials"; "They shortchanged me plenty of times."

A definition unfavorable to legal codes does not require that a violation occur. Conveyance of values, even some that are intended to be positive, may be sufficient to constitute such a definition. The law-abiding parent who maintains that stealing to feed one's children is acceptable is providing a definition favorable to law violation, even though the intent is probably to bolster a sense of commitment to family. A parent confined to a penitentiary, on the other hand, may impress upon his or her visiting offspring that stealing is always wrong. In both circumstances, the young person would receive a mix of definitions. The same is true with peers. Consistent with Sutherland's crime proposition number five, Daniel Ragan (2014) found that adolescent alcohol consumption was influenced not just by alcohol use by peers, but by their attitudes toward it.

The sixth statement of differential association specifies that an excess of definitions favorable to violation of law over definitions unfavorable embodies "the principle of differential association" (Sutherland & Cressey, 1974:75). It is the weight of definitions favorable to law violation, which may be construed as a ratio, that determines learning of criminal patterns:

$$\frac{\text{definitions favorable to violation of law}}{\text{definitions unfavorable to violation of law}}$$

These definitions are virtually illimitable and occur throughout life, with a person becoming delinquent (criminal) when the ratio exceeds unity.

It is not clear whether Sutherland meant to provide a single ratio incorporating all definitions favorable and unfavorable to crime or specific ratios for each type of crime (Tittle et al., 1986). Both the general and specific interpretations have been adopted to test the theory. While the general interpretation seems to be more widely entertained, it is evident that one may also learn only specific types of crime. A college student, for example, may be exposed to an excess of definitions favorable to smoking marijuana, but may have little association with definitions favorable to robbery.

All associations do not carry equal weight. The theory projects variation in terms of frequency, duration, priority, and intensity. Frequency refers to how often exposure to definitions occurs, and duration refers to the length of each exposure. Priority specifies the time that particular associations are initiated. Definitions absorbed in early childhood are said to have greater impact than those in later life. Intensity reflects the degree of identification with particular associations. The more a child identifies with a person, the more weight will be attributed to the definitions provided by that person. To bring the ratio specified by statement six into accord with proposition seven, it would be necessary to weight the formula by these factors; this task is one that admittedly "would be extremely difficult" (Sutherland & Cressey, 1974:76).

The final two statements of differential association provide further linkage to general learning principles. They emphasize that criminal behavior is learned in the same manner as other behavior, and that both types of behavior are products of similar needs and values. Of course, criminologists usually focus on the

HIGHLIGHT 8.2 CAN SUBCULTURES BE "KYND?"

This section of your textbook reviews several major theoretical perspectives on subcultural explanations of crime. That focus is not surprising, as this is a criminology text that summarizes both competing and complementary approaches to explaining crime and delinquency. Yet, as Sutherland noted, learning is a normal process, and we can learn good as well as bad values and behaviors. Moreover, as has been emphasized, "good" and "bad" attitudes and behavior are relative, often in the eye of the beholder. It follows that subcultures, and the values they impart, are not inherently "bad." To maintain otherwise would condemn all minority groups to a deviant status.

A recent application of differential association theory to learning within a subcultural setting serves as an interesting illustration. Pamela Hunt (2010) examined the learning of norms within jamband subcultures and found some support for Sutherland's learning principles. She delineated the values at the core of "Deadhead" and similar "jamband subcultures" as: "kindness, generosity, tolerance, and acceptance" (p. 522), values collectively denoted within the subculture as "kynd." Ironically, the group's overconformity to such positive values may be regarded as deviant, an interesting extension of our discussion of relativity into the realm of "positive" deviance. As differential association predicts, Hunt found that absorption of these "kynd" values varied along with the frequency, intensity, and priority (although not for duration) of associations with the subculture. Thus, as Sutherland predicted, "kynd" behaviors, as well as violent, cruel, or selfish ones are subject to a learning process and this, in part, may be a function of subcultural affiliations.

Source: Hunt, P.M. (2010). Are you kynd? Conformity and deviance within the jamband subculture. *Deviant Behavior*, *31*, 521–51.

process of learning "bad" behaviors, but in an interesting twist Pamela Hunt (2010) examined the subcultural learning of "kindness" among "Deadheads" and "jambands," as described in Highlight 8.2.

Criticisms of Differential Association

The major criticisms of differential association have focused on the theory's testability, causal framework, and breadth. Perhaps the most serious criticism is that the theory is not verifiable through empirical testing. Concepts incorporated in the theory (e.g., definitions, association, excess) were vaguely and imprecisely explained, leaving researchers to generate their own operational definitions (Tittle et al., 1986). There have been notable disparities both in operational definitions of the theory's concepts and in the research findings seeking to test the theory. Similarly, as noted above, measuring the ratio of definitions favorable to violation of the law to those unfavorable is impracticable (Tittle et al., 1986; Matsueda, 1988).

Charles Tittle and his colleagues (1986) focused on deficiencies in the causal framework set out by Sutherland. Differential association presumes, for example, that definitions acquired in association with others lead to behavioral patterns. In other words, some associations were thought to cause criminal behavior and others to cause noncriminal behavior. The reverse, however, is also plausible. Persons may engage in criminal conduct, for whatever reasons, and then seek out particular associations to match their criminal values and activities; this is a "birds of a feather" interpretation. Another possibility is that the relationship between associations and behavior may be reciprocal, that is, both may influence one another simultaneously. The causal nexus is also complicated by the possibility of intervening variables. Tittle et al. (1986) found, for example, that excess associations with criminal definitions led to criminal behavior only through intermediary factors such as criminal motivations.

Differential association is widely criticized as being so broad that, in attempting to explain all criminal behavior, the theory succeeds in explaining none. Ironically, other critics have faulted the theory for not attempting to answer enough questions. Specifically, some criminologists object that differential association fails to account for why people form the associations that they do. This criticism, however, overlooks the evolution of differential association, which shows that while it was formulated to account for individual criminal behavior, it was closely wed to macro-level explanations of crime. Sutherland learned from his professors at Chicago that features of the social structure generate normative conflict and that this determines a person's associations. Differential association theory examines the impact of those associations. Craig Reinarman and Jeffrey Fagan summarized Sutherland's view by noting "that while crime is caused by differential association with others from whom one learns an excess of definitions favorable to law violation, the probability of such differential association is a function of differential social organization" (1988:311).

Testing Differential Association

Despite the difficulties, many criminologists have attempted to test differential association and continue to do so many decades after its introduction. It is widely observed that there is a strong correlation between parental criminal behavior and that of the parents' offspring, consistent with learning theory. Sutherland certainly highlighted the role of parents in providing definitions favorable/unfavorable to aberrant behavior. In a recent study of nearly 7,000 Dutch people, the relationship between offenses of fathers and their children was traced, revealing a dynamic process wherein the father's convictions increase the likelihood of offspring convictions (Van de Rakt et al., 2010). This elevated risk of criminal conviction persists for some years, albeit with a gradual decay that is further slowed by additional convictions. They found these learning effects to be stronger in the adolescent years and reduced if the parents were divorced. All in all, the study found significant and appreciable criminal learning effects from fathers to children as predicted by Sutherland's differential association and other learning theories.

Deviance of one's friends is among the strongest and most consistent predictors of delinquent and criminal behavior identified to date, "with near 'law-like' regularity" (Young et al., 2013). This finding has held up fairly consistently across a number of offense categories, age, gender, and a range of cultural settings. Misconduct has also been observed, whether the "friend" variable was measured as total number of deviant friends, their proportion, or the total number of offenses reported by friends. The key concept proposed by Sutherland and echoed by many other learning theorists is one of *balance*. That is, as the level of exposure to deviant influences increases, risk of learning or absorbing the values underlying those behaviors increases. Analysis of two of the largest American data sets on delinquency (The National Longitudinal Study of Adolescent Health or "Add Heath" and The Gang Resistance Education and Training or "G.R.E.A.T" evaluation) suggests that levels of impulsivity or self-control help to stipulate the relationship between friends and delinquency (Thomas & McGloin, 2013). Deviant friendship networks were found to be associated with higher levels of delinquency for youths low on impulsivity (high self-control), while those high on impulsivity (low self-control) were most likely to have more delinquent involvement if they reported more time "hanging out" with peers. The theoretical reasoning for these observations was that a slower historical adoption of friends' deviant values unfolds for youths with higher self-control in contrast to a rapid response of the more impulsive juvenile to situational contingencies that arise in the course of unstructured and unsupervised time with peers.

The influence of "best" friends has also been examined in a couple of studies, both looking at adolescents in grades 7 through 12. Jean Marie McGloin (2009) looked at the **deviance gap** between a subject and whom they identified as their best friend. That is, the difference in the level of deviance between the two was the focus of inquiry. It was hypothesized that it is the span of that gap, or relative deviance imbalance between the two, that exerts a delinquency influence. In short, and consistent with Sutherland's original ideas, the expectation was that individuals will seek to balance their levels of deviant activities with those of their best friend. Indeed they found that each party in a friendship dyad tended to gravitate toward the behavioral pattern of their counterpart across time. The influence of "best" friend relative to other friends was examined in a different way by Carter Rees and Greg Pogarsky (2011), and they found that the collective impact of other friends was as great as that of the best friend, consistent with delinquent behavior tending to be a group phenomenon rather than something that occurs in just pairs. The principle they drew from their findings was that "one bad apple may not spoil the whole bunch" (p. 217).

How many youths hear from a parent the sarcastic old cliché, "If your friends jumped off a bridge, would you do it too?" Holly Miller (2010) drew on this witticism in titling her paper reporting testing of the dynamics of the process whereby youths learn from their friends. From administering questionnaires to Mexican-American adolescents enrolled in grades 9 through 12 in South Texas, she found some to be more susceptible to peer influence than others. Moreover, she observed that more delinquent behavior, especially serious offending, was reported by those scoring higher on measures of susceptibility to peer influence. This was found for both males and females and applied to susceptibility to influence for both delinquent and nondelinquent activities. In short, some adolescents more readily succumb to peer pressure than do others, and this plays a role in causing delinquency. As Miller (2010) noted, this finding can have important policy implications. As all attentive parents fear, exposure to delinquent peers may enhance risk of involvement in delinquency. The susceptibility finding, however, suggests the possibility of insulating adolescents from delinquent influences by lowering susceptibility as well as by avoiding associations.

Applications of Differential Association

Returning to academic cheating provides a familiar and less somber paragon of differential association in action than some examples to follow. John Stogner and his colleagues (2013) collected survey data from undergraduate college students, finding that nearly 40 percent reported engaging in some form of "e-cheating" (electronic cheating). Of three theoretical frameworks tested for explaining this unscrupulous behavior, the most support was found for social learning theory. Included among the strongest variables to explain both "e-cheating" and forms not reliant upon technological aids were associations with best friends, longest friends, those seen most often, and those with whom the most time was spent. This suggests that efforts might be undertaken on campuses to strengthen the moral climate in relation to academic honesty and perhaps to determine whether students might cheat because they have an exaggerated view of how common it is among their friends.

One form of violence that fits differential association and other versions of learning theory is the widely observed intergenerational transmission of intimate partner violence often referred to as a **cycle of violence**. What we know is that there is a strong likelihood for both patterns of offending and victimization to be passed from one generation to the next, and learning theories provide the best framework for explaining this fact. Victims of partner violence, "like their abusers, tend disproportionately to come from families of origin in which violence and aggression were directly and/or vicariously experienced." The relationship between victim and offender appears even stronger. The "bi-directionality or 'mutual combatancy' prevalent in many intimate partner relationships suggests that both parties . . . may also co-share the roles of victim and offender . . ." (Cochran et al., 2011:792). The application of learning theories to both offenders and victims of partner violence is explained by Cochran and his colleagues (2011: 794) like this:

> Witnesses of family violence, experiencing it, seeing it modelled, reinforced, and justified, can become so inured to it that they can become readied and accustomed targets suitable for their own victimization, especially repetitive victimization. Such witnesses internalize family norms which may serve to neutralize the stigma of intimate partner violence, to accept it as normal, and perhaps even to approve of it under certain circumstances.

An important scientific goal is to generate theories of crime and deviance that can be generalized cross-culturally. Sutherland was especially motivated to develop a general theory of crime. Differential association, and Ronald Akers's expansion to social learning theory discussed in the next section, are among the repertoire of theoretical frameworks to have fared well in that regard. In testing attitude transference from parents and peers among college students in the United States and Japan, Emiko Kobayashi and colleagues (2011) found strong support. At the same time, however, they observed an interesting distinction. They found not only that parental, relative to peer, influence declined among Japanese students, but that it became negative as peer attitudes were controlled. That is, Japanese college students were more likely to report both deviant attitudes and behavior if their parents disapproved than if they approved. Kobayashi and colleagues speculated that the less individualistic culture and more lax child discipline could account for the lesser parental influence. A similar finding with high school students in Korea (Hwang & Akers, 2006) bolsters suspicion that Eastern/Western cultural distinctions could lead to different patterns in learning influences among significant others.

Learning theories, and especially differential association, were found in a meta-analysis of 133 studies published between 1974 and 2003 to fare very well (Pratt et al., 2010). Associations and definitions favorable to crime were found to impact behavior at levels similar to self-control variables (discussed later in this chapter) and greater than rational choice/deterrence (Chapter 5). This led the analysts to conclude "that it deserves its status as one of the core perspectives in criminology" (Pratt et al., 2010: 790). Yet recent criticisms have emerged to suggest that these persistent correlations may be artifacts of flawed measurement (Young et al., 2013).

Misperceptions of peer deviance are of concern, particularly the projection of one's own deviance to others. These methodological critiques led the research team of Young et al. (2013:78) to conclude that their results "At a minimum . . . suggest that learning theorists might have overstated the strength of the relationship between perceived peer deviance and personal behavior. . . ." Their findings resonate with the broader pattern of criminologists continually contriving a more tangled causal understanding of crime and deviance.

Social learning theorists have expanded and modified differential association to incorporate the principle of B.F. Skinner's operant conditioning (e.g., Glaser, 1956; Jeffery, 1965; Adams, 1973; Akers, 1973). Daniel Glaser's (1956) **differential identification** is a variation of learning theory that specifies the degree of identity with a person, real or imaginary, as the key to adoption of values predisposing a person to criminal or law-abiding behavior. This modification allows a learning role for the media. A public figure such as an athlete, according to differential identification, might have more influence on a person than individuals with whom the person interacts directly. A film character, "Rambo," for instance, may be the source of greater value inculcation than real persons with whom the individual has face-to-face interaction.

Ronald Akers—Social Learning Theory

Ronald Akers (1985) expanded Sutherland's differential association theory by adding components of operant (voluntary response) and respondent (involuntary response) conditioning. While implied in Sutherland's sixth proposition,

Akers formalized the extent to which learning is the result of exposure to both conforming and criminal behavior and definitions. Akers assumes that criminal behavior does not differ as behavior from normative conduct and both forms of behavior can be explained by his **social learning theory**. Accordingly, Akers identifies four key elements that help to shape behavior:

- Differential associations;
- Definitions;
- Differential reinforcement; and
- Imitation.

Differential associations refer to the process detailed by Sutherland, including the learning of definitions favorable or unfavorable to the law through a process of social interaction. Definitions apply to one's own attitudes; including orientations, rationalizations, definitions of the situation, and other evaluative aspects of right and wrong. These definitions include both general (i.e., religious and other moral values and norms that are unfavorable to nonconforming behavior) and specific beliefs (i.e., definitions that direct the person to commit particular acts). For example, a person may believe in the general validity of the legal order while at the same time disagree with rules regulating "victimless" crimes. This person can rationalize that while it may be illegal to smoke marijuana, it is a matter of individual choice with no victim and, therefore, it is acceptable.

Differential reinforcement consists of the actual or anticipated consequences of engaging in specific behavior. Rewards or other positive consequences will reinforce the desirability of the behavior whereas punishments will serve as a deterrent. In addition to direct rewards, Akers includes "the whole range of actual and anticipated, tangible and intangible rewards. . . . Social rewards can be highly symbolic . . . fulfilling ideological, religious, political, or other goals" (Akers, 1994:99).

Imitative behavior may also occur independent of the learning process. In some situations, observation of behavior committed by a revered role model (and observed consequences of the behavior) may result in imitative behavior. This possibility, however, is more pronounced for first-time or exploratory behavior than it is for explaining continued behavioral patterns.

Akers suggests that these components are part of a complex learning process and that criminal behavior can be expected when it has been differentially reinforced and defined as desirable. This social learning process is summarized as:

> one in which the balance of learned definitions, imitation of criminal or deviant models, and the anticipated balance of reinforcement produces the initial delinquent or deviant act. The facilitative effects of these variables continue in the repetition of acts, although initiation becomes less important than it was in the first commission of the act. After initiation, the actual social and nonsocial reinforcers and punishers affect whether or not that act will be repeated and at what level

of frequency. Not only the behavior itself, but also the definitions are affected by the consequences of the initial act. Whether a deviant act will be committed in a situation that presents the opportunity depends on the learning history of the individual and the set of reinforcement contingencies in that situation (Akers, 1994:99).

One can see that Akers's version of social learning theory includes aspects of Sutherland's differential association as well as a number of characteristics of rational choice theory (see Chapter 5). In fact, Akers has made the argument that rational choice theory is no more than a variant of social learning theory and that it has nothing new to offer (Akers, 1990). Empirical tests of Akers's advancement of differential association have been quite supportive, including cross-cultural (e.g. Tittle et al., 2012) applications.

CULTURE CONFLICT AND CRIME

Culture conflict theory is closely allied with versions of learning theory. The focus is on the normative content of cultures and how members of groups are recipients of attitudes and values transmitted through a learning process. Norms are seen as being passed down in the same manner as other cultural traits. When behaviors rooted in the values of one subculture conflict with those of society at large, problems arise. This conflict of values and their associated behaviors can cause criminal or delinquent behavior; this effect represents a perspective on the origins of crime called **culture conflict** or **cultural deviance**.

Because the basic framework of culture conflict is anchored in the learning process, it is included in this chapter. Culture conflict, however, is one of the most difficult perspectives to categorize. Contrary to the larger social process tradition, culture conflict largely depicts crime as a lower-class problem by focusing on what is learned in subcultural settings. Three variations of culture conflict are discussed in the following sections (Wolfgang and Ferracuti's "subculture of violence," Anderson's "code of the street," and Miller's "focal concerns") and describe law violation exclusively as a lower-class phenomenon, while Sellin's "culture conflict" theory more broadly implicates social class as a major source of culture conflict and crime. In addition, the perspective readily lends itself to macro-theoretical conceptualization and analysis, although social process theories typically focus on the micro level. Competing explanations for a "Southern culture of violence" draw on social class and broader social traits. Like differential association, the origins of culture conflict theory are linked to the ecological findings of the Chicago School. The discovery of Shaw and McKay that crime and delinquency persisted in impoverished and socially disorganized neighborhoods, despite the different ethnic backgrounds of new waves of inhabitants, suggested subcultures as a source of law-violating behavior. Both the ecological and culture conflict perspectives display features that cross the social structure and process boundaries, and for that reason, these perspectives might best be conceptualized as bridging theories (Williams & McShane, 1998).

Like strain theories described in the previous chapter, culture conflict theories locate the cause of crime and delinquency in subcultural features. The causal schemes delineated, however, are quite distinct. While traditional strain theorists see deviance as a product of frustration experienced by lower-class persons upon failure to reach goals derived from the dominant middle-class culture, the culture conflict perspective views deviance as conformity to norms of a subculture that run counter to those of the dominant group. Because law-breaking behavior is learned as part of the content of a subcultural code, it is construed as normal rather than pathological.

The popularity of culture conflict theories has declined in recent years. While there are a number of reasons for this decline, J. Mitchell Miller and his colleagues (1997) identify ideology as the primary factor. The first blow to their position came from the rise of conflict-based theories in the 1970s (see Chapter 9). This perspective located the crime problem with the state and the elite who dominate it, a position quite contrary to identifying subcultures as being at the root of the problem. More recently, calls for "political correctness" have implied that attributing crime to subcultural differences is labeling the subcultures as inferior, drawing focus away from social conditions, and perhaps reflecting racism.

Thorsten Sellin—Conflict of Conduct Norms

Thorsten Sellin (1897–1994) first stressed culture conflict as an explanation of crime and delinquency, drawing liberally from ideas of the Chicago School and those of Sutherland. Sellin (1938:62) noted that Shaw's ecological studies identified neighborhood characteristics that "give rise to social attitudes which conflict with the norms of the law." He also credited Sutherland's concept of differential association with providing the sociological framework for culture conflict theory. Sutherland had served on the delinquency subcommittee of the Social Science Research Council. Under the auspices of the council, Sellin's major statement on culture conflict was issued in his 1938 monograph, *Culture Conflict and Crime.*

Sellin was born in Sweden but immigrated to North America with his family at the age of 17. He earned a Ph.D. in sociology at the University of Pennsylvania and taught there from 1921 to 1968 (Laub, 1983). He served as mentor to a number of accomplished criminologists, most notably Marvin Wolfgang, with whom Sellin collaborated on several research projects. Aside from his seminal work on culture conflict, Sellin has made major contributions in a wide range of areas, including crime statistics and capital punishment.

In a 1979 interview, Sellin said that he had not offered culture conflict as a theory to explain crime, but rather as "an attempt to give a new slant, a new inspiration . . . to the field" (Laub, 1983:174). It was Sellin's concern with the development of the scientific stature of criminology that led him in this direction. His work succeeded in moving criminology away from a legalistic and toward a normative definition of crime (see Chapter 1). Noting that the legal definition of crime was inadequate to develop laws of human behavior, as social science requires, Sellin argued that the task of criminology is to explain violation of conduct norms. The Catch-22 is that conformity to the norms of many subcultures may contradict norms of the dominant culture, placing members of those subcultures in the position of violating the norms of some social group no matter how they conduct themselves. Sellin's concept of culture conflict sensitized criminology to the relativity of conduct norms and, therefore, of crime. Crime, then, may be explained in terms of conduct norms learned in a subculture that does not shape legal codes.

Given the context of the times, Sellin often focused on the immigration of persons to America. He cited, for example, a case in which a "Sicilian father in New Jersey killed the 16-year-old seducer of his daughter, expressing surprise at his arrest since he had merely defended his family honor in a traditional way" (1938:68). This illustrates **primary culture conflict**, the collision of norms from distinct cultural systems. Being reared and acculturated in one country obviously presents degrees of challenge to normative adaptation in the new country. Sellin's work also delineated **secondary culture conflict**, which occurs with the evolution of subcultures in a heterogeneous society. This type of conflict of conduct norms is characteristic of contemporary America, exemplified by the law violations of groups such as juvenile gangs in urban ghettos, drug-oriented subcultures, outlaw motorcycle gangs (see Quinn & Koch, 2003), and racist cliques (see Pridemore & Freilich, 2006).

Marvin Wolfgang and Franco Ferracuti— Subculture of Violence

Sellin's protégé, Marvin Wolfgang (1925–98), teamed with the Italian criminologist Franco Ferracuti to extend the concept of culture conflict in their **subculture of violence** theory (Wolfgang & Ferracuti, 1967). The theory is not intended to explain all violent behavior, but only assaults and homicides that occur spontaneously or in what is popularly termed the heat of passion. Most violence is of this variety rather than of a premeditated nature or of psychotic origin. Spontaneous violence is particularly prevalent among late adolescent to middle-age males in lower-class settings.

Wolfgang and Ferracuti's efforts represent an early attempt to integrate theoretical explanations for crime into a single framework. Wolfgang contributed the sociological perspective characteristic of North American criminology, drawing heavily from culture conflict, ecological studies, and a variety of learning theories. Ferracuti, on the other hand, brought to their collaborative effort the medical and biological paradigms that have dominated European criminology. Their theory also draws freely on psychological variables, combining them with social factors, as is characteristic of social process theories.

The theory contends that the subculture of violence "is only partly different from the parent culture. . . . It cannot be *totally* different from the culture of which it is a part" (Wolfgang & Ferracuti, 1967:100). A subculture need not display violence as "the predominant mode of expression," but a "potent theme of violence" differentiates the subculture from the larger culture. A subculture of violence exists when, in some social situations, "a violent and physically aggressive response is either expected or required" (1967:159). Members of the subculture are obliged to resort to violence to defend their "honor." An attack on one's manliness, that is, on a man's physical prowess or sexuality, for example, demands violent retaliation. A formative influence on the subculture of violence theory can be seen in Wolfgang's earlier homicide research, as reflected in the concluding chapter of *Patterns in Criminal Homicide* (1958/1975:329):

> Our analysis implies that there may be a subculture of violence which does not define personal assaults as wrong or antisocial; in which quick resort to physical aggression is a socially approved and expected concomitant of certain stimuli. . . . A conflict or inconsistency of social norms is most apparent, and the value-system of the reference group with which the individual differentially associates and identifies, determines whether assaultive behavior is necessary, expected, or desirable in specific social situations. When an insult or argument is defined as trivial and petty by the prevailing culture norms, but as signals for physical attack by a subcultural tradition, culture conflict exists.

Wolfgang and Ferracuti conceded that social structure or other factors may be responsible for the emergence of the subculture, but they explained the continuity of the subculture through a learning process. Learning is facilitated by positive reinforcement of violent behavior and, conversely, imposition of negative sanctions upon failure to respond violently to the appropriate stimuli. Lower-class males who inhabit the locale of a subculture of violence and who are not hesitant to respond to perceived insults with skillfully deployed violence are accorded prestige, while those males who use nonviolent means of conflict resolution are scorned and ostracized. Because members of the subculture learn violence as a normal way to manage interpersonal conflict, guilt is obviated. Social control strategies of the dominant culture, therefore, are circumvented by the learned values and norms of the subcultures. This suggests that the spontaneous violent behavior generated by subcultural values might best (or only) be contained by decomposing the subculture. Urban renewal efforts to disperse low-income housing over wider areas are designed, in part, for this purpose.

Sandra J. Ball-Rokeach (1973) undertook one of the first empirical tests of the subculture of violence thesis. She found little relationship between stances on "machismo" values delineated by Wolfgang and Ferracuti and self-reported participation in interpersonal violence, leading to the conclusion "that values play little or no role as determinants of interpersonal violence" (1973:742–43). Noting the lack of empirical support for any of the subcultural theories of violence, Thomas Bernard (1990) tested a variation not rooted in violence. He drew on prior research suggesting that "angry aggression" develops among the "truly disadvantaged" as a consequence of racial discrimination and low social position in the urban environment. The violent subcultural setting described by Wolfgang and Ferracuti, in other words, might be attributable to the social structure rather than value systems unique to that environment.

Elijah Anderson—Code of the Street

A more recent approach to explaining the disproportionate violence among young African-American males living in impoverished areas has been proposed by Elijah Anderson (1999). The **code of the street** that he details sounds very similar to the "honor" that Wolfgang and Ferracuti described. Studying underclass African-American youths in Philadelphia, he contrasted families reflecting the "street code" with "decent" families subscribing to mainstream cultural values, finding that street socialization was associated with violence. Affiliation with a family subscribing to a decent value system, Anderson argued, provides some insulation from violent delinquent involvement. As Anderson explains, the individual committed to the street code feels compelled to risk their life in violent confrontations if "dissed" (disrespected). The code, like the subculture of violence, requires the resident to project toughness, engage in violent posturing, and to be willing to resort to violence. Abiding by this code provides the otherwise unsuccessful young man with a sense of self-worth. The attitudes and posturing, in turn, feed a cycle of violence. Young men who are "strapped" (carrying firearms) or conceal "blades" (knives) are primed for violence, as are those they encounter.

Where Anderson's code of the street differs from the subculture of violence and other culture conflict theories that preceded it is in identifying the origins of the cultural content. Anderson offers a connection to social structure theories, reasoning that the street code develops in response to poverty, discrimination, family disruption, and other structural problems. That is, social structural deficiencies lead to adoption of the street code as an alternative set of values, while they, in turn, lead to increased levels of violence. In other words, this theory operates on two levels: the neighborhood structural and individual levels. Recent research (Stewart & Simons, 2010) provides evidence of the link between the two. In poor and disrupted neighborhoods, youths adopt "street" values. Even "decent" kids fear they must reflect an image of living up to the code of the street to acquire status and relative safety. Research findings addressing Anderson's assertion of the protective power of decent parenting in underclass neighborhoods has been mixed.

While subcultural theories as a group have generated less interest in recent years, tests and applications of Anderson's "code of the street" have garnered a fair amount of attention. One recent study (Mears et al., 2013) used it as the theoretical groundwork to test the prison importation model, the contention that prison environments exhibit uncommon cultural belief systems because inmates import, or bring them with them, from subcultural settings outside of the prison. They found that inmates with greater affirmation of the principles of the code later admitted to more violent behavior within prison than those who did not believe in it. Similarly, in assessing the role of gang affiliation with adherence to the street code, Matsuda et al. (2013) found "overwhelming" support for the conclusion that gang joiners are more code-driven than nonjoiners. Studies such as these suggest that the code of the street, as delineated by Anderson, permeate offender subcultures.

The street code appears to reach well beyond discrete offender subcultures, however. In a study of homeless youths in Toronto, Canada, Stephen Baron's (2013) research design suggested that those who adopt the code may become less responsive to threats of legal sanctions, which indicates an important linkage of the street code with deterrence theory. Jeffrey Nowacki's (2012) examination of the role of gender, a variable largely dismissed by Anderson, found that some girls had adopted the code. Although the proportion was less than among males, this finding also points to broader potential application of the theory. An even more expansive deployment of street code theory led to observations of a sexually deviant cybercommunity (Roberts & Hunt, 2012), identifying parallels between the cultural norms of that setting and those enumerated in Anderson's theory.

Holli Drummond and her colleagues (2011) tested the theory with a sample of African-American youths in Mobile, Alabama. They found four forms of violence predicted by embracement of the code and that the code's acceptance was strongly related to a sense of "hopelessness." Moreover, they found that lack of parental monitoring and poor sense of community were keys to the emergence of feelings of hopelessness. This process is depicted in Figure 8.2. Drummond et al. (2011: 214) concluded, "The complexity of this mediational model is perhaps the most important contribution of our study."

Like many other contemporary perspectives, a particular strength of the street code is its connection or integration of different theoretical perspectives, the social structure and culture conflict traditions in this case. Note that the values incorporated in the cultural component of the street code hold a strong resemblance to those identified in Walter Miller's earlier culture conflict theory.

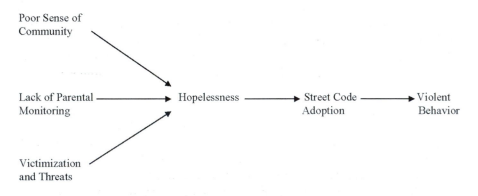

FIGURE 8.2
Mediational model of street code and violence.

Source: Adapted from Drummond, H., Bolland, J.M., & Harris, W.A. (2011). Becoming violent: Evaluating the mediating effect of hopelessness on the code of the street thesis. *Deviant Behavior, 32*, 191–223.

Walter Miller—Lower-class Focal Concerns

Walter Miller (1920–2004) is best known for his theoretical contribution to understanding gang delinquency as laid out in a journal article published in 1958. This work focused on features of lower-class culture, attributing delinquency to a distinct normative structure that conflicts with norms of the dominant culture. As with other theories falling within the culture conflict tradition, Miller's theory is grounded in learning theory and ecological data. To the extent that the norms learned in lower-class settings depart from those of the dominant middle-class culture, the stage is set for culture conflict.

While Miller's (1958) classic article provides important theoretical insight, it is especially noteworthy that it was the product of a then unique and expansive gang delinquency project that is receiving renewed attention. His book manuscript (about 900 pages) detailing this work, *City Gangs*, was not published until 2011, after Scott Decker, a criminology professor at Arizona State University, acquired Professor Miller's archives. Miller was trained as a cultural anthropologist, leading him to employ an ethnographic (descriptive) research strategy in directing outreach workers interacting with members of seven gangs under the rubric of the Boston Special Youth Program over a three-year period (1954–7) in Roxbury, Massachusetts, just outside of Boston. From 204 gang members (154 male and 50 female), they generated no less than 20,000 field contact records, each containing an array of data. As Decker points out in his Foreword to *City Gangs*, Miller's project was "the first federally funded gang outreach program in the United States" (Miller, 2011: 12) and was far ahead of its time in many respects. His efforts predated many methodological and theoretical directions of contemporary criminology. Miller and his team were paying attention to female delinquents, life-course issues, and family ties decades before these became popular concerns among gang researchers.

To return to Miller's theoretical contributions, field observations led him to conclude that lower-class persons display a set of **focal concerns** that distinguish them from the mainstream of American society. While similar to values, these focal concerns have the scientific advantage of being directly observable in the behavior of subjects and, at least arguably, of being more descriptively neutral. The six focal concerns identified by Miller are summarized in Table 8.1.

Trouble

Miller concluded that members of the lower class are preoccupied with the prospect of their activities leading to **trouble**, which results in unwanted interference from representatives of the dominant culture. This concern with "getting into trouble" does not reflect identification with the norms of middle-class culture, but rather trepidation about the potential complications for life that deviation from such norms brings. Truancy, for example, may lead to threatening inquiry from school officials or human service professionals. Cohabitation, if discovered by social workers, may lead to the withholding of welfare benefits. At the heart of trouble, however, is the potential for arrests, fines,

TABLE 8.1 Walter Miller's Lower-Class Focal Concerns

Dimension	Definition
Trouble	Interference from official social control agents of the dominant culture
Toughness	Distorted image of masculinity
Smartness	Skill and ability to dominate verbal exchanges pertinent to the lower-class environment
Excitement	Relieving the monotonous routine of lower-class existence through emotion-arousing entertainment that often violates norms of the dominant culture
Fate	Belief in little control over the forces shaping one's life
Autonomy	Ambivalence regarding freedom from external control reflected in overt resentment of control, but covert pursuit of control

Source: Adapted from Miller, W.B. (1958). Lower-class culture as a generating milieu of gang delinquency. *Journal of Social Issues*, *14*(3), 5–19.

court appearances, jail sentences, and similar inconveniences generated in response to drinking sprees, fights, or other illegal behavior. The behavior may conform to subcultural expectations, but trouble represents its undesirable consequences. A lower-class male recurrently involved in law-violating behavior may be revered as a "good old boy" or a "stand-up guy," but at the same time decried as "always in trouble." Individuals have to decide whether to conduct themselves as the subcultural standards encourage or to avoid trouble. Miller noted that potential for trouble serves as a negative criterion for mate selection in the lower class, in contrast to the potential for success and achievement that are accorded priority in the middle class. Trouble, then, is met with ambivalence in lower-class culture.

Toughness

The **toughness** dimension of lower-class focal concerns, Miller suggested, may be a reaction to the female-dominated households that are prominent in the lower-class environment. Lacking male role models, lower-class boys develop patterns of behavior that distort masculinity. Strength, physical skills and prowess, and bravery in the face of threats are emphasized, while intellectual and cultural foci of the upper classes are actively disdained. Boys who are upwardly mobile, scholastically successful, or who develop artistic talents are labeled "queer," "sissy," or "pansy," while tattoos are considered masculine. Take note that tattoo artistry has been culturally redefined in recent years, having previously been restricted to a few specific and mostly deviant subcultures. Homophobia (irrational fear of, aversion to, or discrimination against homosexuality or homosexuals) is rampant among lower-class males; characteristics of males that depart from a narrow perception of masculinity are labeled pejoratively. Overt expression of affection among males is taboo; bantering and roughhousing are encouraged.

Trouble may be a sequel to preoccupation with toughness. Determination to demonstrate one's masculinity through physical combat typically generates behavior defined by legal codes as disruptive, disorderly, or assaultive. This and other dimensions of lower-class focal concerns can be seen as inherently contradictory to the codified norms of the middle class.

Smartness

While intellectual accomplishment, as reflected by formal education or command of traditional and organized bodies of knowledge, is met with contempt in the lower class, being streetwise is highly valued. The lower-class male is provided an opportunity to learn particular skills or to foster **smartness** in the lower-class milieu and is judged by his success in cultivating those "smarts." Smartness is the ability to manipulate and outwit others through skillful deployment of verbal and psychological skills. The lower-class male, for example, takes pride in outmaneuvering the police and other representatives of the dominant culture in verbal exchanges, making their antagonists appear naive and foolish. There is a continuous flow of aggressive repartee in the ribbing, kidding, and teasing that transpires. These exchanges often consist "of increasingly inflammatory insults, with incestuous and perverted sexual relations with the mother a dominant theme" (Miller, 1958:10). Mastery of these skills can place an individual even higher in social rank than the "tough guy." The "smart guy" is also admired as one who reaps benefits from others with a minimum of physical effort. Con men, card sharks, and persons in similar roles fit this perception of success or "having it made."

Excitement

While the daily routine of lower-class existence can be exceedingly boring, the humdrum of "hanging out" or monotonous jobs are interspersed by a periodic "night on the town," particularly on weekends. Thrill or **excitement** is actively sought on these occasions. Toughness and smartness are acted out and the tediousness of daily routine is replaced with use of alcohol and drugs, gambling, music, and sexual quests. An evening filling the expectation of excitement typically consists, although not in any predetermined order, of getting high, becoming boisterous, having sexual encounters, and demonstrating toughness through verbal exchanges or fighting. Fixation on excitement permeates lower-class culture and generates ambivalence because of its potential for trouble.

Fate

Lower-class culture depicts the future as a matter of **fate** rather than a product of education, hard work, saving, and other paths subsumed under the middle-class focus on deferred gratification. One is "lucky" or "unlucky" and, although luck is seen as prone to shift, the future is not seen as subject to control. Belief in fate complements smartness; both, for example, support gambling while denigrating the value of work. Preoccupation with fate is reflected in the prominence of gambling in lower-class settings (e.g., playing pool, rolling dice, booking bets) and in the content of many body tattoos (e.g., "lucky," "born to lose"). Fate also interfaces with the other focal concerns of the lower class; gambling and tattooing, for example, may also exemplify toughness and excitement, while raising prospects of trouble.

Autonomy

The final dimension of Miller's lower-class focal concerns is reflected in "a strong and frequently expressed resentment of the idea of external controls, restrictions on behavior, and unjust or coercive authority" (Miller, 1958:12). This control theme runs rampant through country music, exemplified in songs such as Johnny Paycheck's "Take This Job and Shove It" and a plethora of prison songs, including Johnny Cash's "Folsom Prison Blues" and "Doin' My Time." Ironically, **autonomy** or freedom from external intervention and control is precluded by enactment of the other focal concerns. A lifestyle revolving around the lower-class focal concerns almost inevitably leads to trouble and the intervention of social control agents representing the dominant culture. Autonomy, in other words, reflects the resentment of the lower class toward culture conflict.

Analysis of Focal Concerns

Do you see evidence of these focal concerns in lower-class environments? Are they different from the values or concerns of the middle class? If so, does preoccupation with these concerns frequently lead to conflict with the law? These are some of the empirical questions that must be addressed before accepting or rejecting Miller's theory. Miller's perspective offers a sharp contrast with the strain tradition's premise that lower-class and middle-class persons subscribe to essentially the same values, but that lower-class persons resort to crime and delinquency out of frustration resulting from failure to live up to those expectations.

Both perspectives also have important philosophical implications. Strain theory's presumption that middle-class values must logically be coveted by the lower class might be considered presumptuous and chauvinistic. Conversely, Miller's lower-class focal concerns resemble stereotyping and bigotry. Miller's proposition is also a radical notion rooted in conflict rather than consensus theory. The fundamental idea is that different social classes subscribe to contradictory norms and that the more powerful classes impose their moral views on the less powerful through legal channels.

A number of criticisms have been leveled at Miller's theory. Some have noted that it is difficult for middle-class persons to observe lower-class settings without injecting class bias. Second, this theory, like any others, only addresses male delinquency. Others have concluded that the theory is tautological. Miller observed the behavior of persons in a lower-class milieu to identify their focal concerns and then used those focal concerns to account for their behavior. Little research has been undertaken to test the theory and, given the difficulty of observing and interpreting focal concerns or other value-related phenomena, it will be difficult to do so. Nevertheless, the unique assumptions of the theory have ensured its prominent place in discussions of the causes of crime and delinquency.

Southern Culture of Violence

The Southern region of the United States has a long history of violence, especially high homicide rates. Criminologists have long struggled to explain this **Southern culture of violence**, drawing on two primary perspectives. One group has focused on structural disadvantages such as poverty, lower educational attainment, a history of slavery, racism, and lasting effects of the Civil War and Reconstruction Era. Others have taken a cultural approach, contending that the South has a distinct cultural composition that is more hospitable to violence as a means of resolving disputes. The latter approach holds much in common with Sellin's culture conflict perspective, Wolfgang and Ferracuti's subculture of violence thesis, Miller's focal concerns, and other culture conflict approaches. The Southern culture of violence theme has been proffered for decades, but was revitalized with the publication of Richard Nisbett and Dov Cohen's *Culture of Honor* in 1996. They pegged a "code of honor" as a key element of southern culture that equips males to quickly retaliate in the face of insults as a matter of pride or manliness. At the heart of their reasoning lies immigration patterns whereby the South was predominantly settled by Scotch-Irish Celtics who brought a unique cultural heritage that was permeated with justifications for violence. For details, see Grady McWhiney's (1988) *Cracker Culture: Celtic Ways in the Old South*. Among the most salient cultural features are emphases on resorting to violence in confronting insults (with offense easily taken), conservative Old Testament religious views, and resentment of authority. Nisbett and Cohen traced early patterns of Celtic settlement and contended that their culture persisted because they tended to move into sparsely populated highland areas and continue the tradition of a herding lifestyle. The argument is that protecting the herd requires self-sufficiency and the lack of justice authorities (who were ill-respected anyway) required quick meting out of social control to both thieves and the disrespectful. The Nisbett and Cohen treatment has spawned a number of re-examinations of (sub)cultural explanations of the historically high rates of violence and homicide in the South.

Viviana Andreescu and her co-researchers (2011) undertook a test of subcultural propositions across 406 Appalachian counties. Consistent with Nisbett and Cohen, they found that the highest rates of argument-related homicides occurred in the Southern Appalachian counties and that the rate was higher in those counties dominated by conservative protestant religions. Mathew Lee and associates (2009) extended the thesis to account for high rates of homicide among southern blacks as well as whites, a southern violence pairing he referred to as the **cracker culture/black redneck thesis**. Following Nisbett and Cohen's work, they contended that the Celtics (who gained the derogatory "cracker" stereotype inferring the groups' propensity to make quips or wisecracks imbued with exaggeration and bragging) laid the cultural framework of the South. That culture was so widely dispersed that over the course of 200 years portions of it were absorbed by southern blacks as well. Thus, rural southern blacks have displayed high rates of violence and carried the cultural ethos for violence into both southern and northern cities. The notion of honor described by Nisbett and Cohen (1996) and by Lee et al. (2009) that underlies violence is remarkably similar to the code of the street described by Anderson (1999). Empirical support was found for both the cracker and black redneck propositions in their examination of 1,068 counties. Specifically, an impressive 39.5 percent increase in white homicides was observed per standard deviation increase in responses to their southern culture index and a lesser, but still significant, 12 percent increase for blacks. In sum, the study provides support for the Southern culture of violence explanation for homicides and other violence and uniquely extends this argument to black homicide rates. Still, the authors caution that "cultural explanations may exist alongside and even complement structural explanations" (Lee et al., 2009: 87). Consistent with a broad direction in criminological theorizing, they are giving credence to the growing trend to integrate theoretical ideas.

While they were not purported as an explicit application of the Southern culture of violence, Heath Copes and fellow criminologists (2013) collected ethnographic accounts of barroom fighting among working-class, adult, Southern white males. The accounts offered by their subjects revealed several themes quite contrary to those of codes propounded to account for violence among the urban minority youths that informed Wolfgang and Ferracuti's subculture of violence and Anderson's code of the street. Although these bar fighters similarly exalted "manhood," "honor," and "protection," the code they espoused also included several distinct and limiting features:

- Avoiding violence absent appreciable insult or other provocation or in situations that seemed unfair
- Strong themes of moral justification
- Avoiding disabling injuries and use of weapons
- Allowing opponents to retreat, ceasing combat when signaled by dominance, and accepting the fight as bringing closure to the matter

Perhaps the most significant difference between the Southern bar-fighting code and the established subcultural violence codes is that the former, while motivating some violence, serves to reduce the severity and continuity of it within that cultural setting. Copes and his colleagues suggest that this functionality allows for persistence of such a code in an environment where the actors, working-class men, have social investments at risk. They also noted that these men took steps to "excuse" their behavior when it went beyond the bounds of their accepted code of behavior, verbal expressions evocative of neutralizing normative standards.

SOCIAL CONTROL AND CRIME

Social control, like learning and culture conflict theories, revolves around the process of socializing people. For these theories, propensity for crime or delinquency is a function of social processes. The common ground, however, ends here. Control theories represent a sharp contrast with other theoretical approaches, even those similarly classified as social process explanations.

Each variation of the control perspective rests on the premise that, if left alone, people will pursue self-interests rather than those of society. Only by intervening and nurturing persons into a controlled social existence can they be fashioned into conformity. Other social process theories, including learning and culture conflict explanations, however, take the opposing view: that human nature is good and deviance only emerges as a product of negative environmental experience. Control theory, however, views crime as predictable behavior that society has failed to bridle. Learning theories and the related culture conflict perspective depict crime as a product of criminogenic forces, while the control approach sees crime as a consequence of the failure of social constraints.

A notion of free will is relied upon to accommodate the shift in focus from criminogenic forces to social controls. As in the classical accounts of criminal behavior, control theory depicts choice as relevant to behavior. This perspective, along with the classical views reviewed in Chapter 5, departs from positivist criminology. Because it assigns choice and responsibility to the offender, the control approach is often considered a conservative account of crime and deviance.

Value consensus also lies at the basis of control theory. It is assumed that most people believe essentially in a common set of values, even if they violate them. Obtaining social conformity is a matter of applying measures to prevent people from violating the norms to which they initially are committed. Each variation of control theory depicts the controls necessary for conformity or explains how those controls are circumvented. Three major contributions to the broad social control perspective are examined in the remainder of the chapter: neutralization, social bond, and self-control.

Gresham M. Sykes and David Matza—Techniques of Neutralization

Neutralization theory made its debut with publication of an article titled "Techniques of Neutralization: A Theory of Delinquency" authored by Sykes and Matza and appearing in the *American Sociological Review* in 1957. When assessed in 2005, it ranked as the ninth most frequently cited paper published in the *American Sociological Review* with 709 cites, though testing of it has been relatively limited (Jacobs, 2005). Perhaps one of the most interesting aspects of this theory is the wide range of nonconforming behavior to which it has been applied, which suggests potential for broad generalizability. Certainly, the perspective has generated a range of provocative applications, though not the range of interest spawned by self-control theory, which we will turn to soon.

The original point of departure for **techniques of neutralization** as a theory of delinquency was Sutherland's assertion that learning criminal or delinquent behavior includes values and rationalizations as well as techniques of committing offenses. Gresham Sykes and David Matza (1957) contended that learning excuses that may be situationally invoked allows boys to engage in behavior that violates the value system to which they basically subscribe. To support this assertion, Sykes and Matza cited anecdotal evidence that offenders typically experienced feelings of guilt and shame. In addition, they observed that offenders display some selectivity in their choice of victims, tending to avoid those who more closely reflect mainstream values of society and seeking out disvalued targets. Priests and nuns, for example, enjoy relative immunity from victimization, while robbery victims are actively sought among homosexuals ("queer baiting") or alcoholics ("rolling drunks"). The point is buttressed by comments made to one of the authors by a prison inmate in regard to child molesters. The inmate noted that while we, on the outside of prisons, saw them as the "scum of society," molesters within the prison were viewed by other inmates as the "scum of the scum" and were often assaulted, robbed, and otherwise abused. Despite these qualitative observations cited in support of the assumption that offenders accept social norms and must excuse themselves from them, Tony Christensen (2010) points out that the assumption has been subjected to little empirical scrutiny.

Note that it can be acceptable to violate norms while still holding to their validity if such norms are seen as conditional. Although one is expected, for example, to be on time for social engagements and is committed to that behavioral norm, some circumstances may excuse tardiness. Norms that are codified in criminal codes, in contrast, are quite explicit in identifying excuses and mitigating circumstances. "The criminal law, more so than any comparable system of norms, acknowledges and states the principled grounds under which an actor may claim exemption. The law contains the seeds of its own neutralization" (Matza, 1964:61). These seeds lie in concepts such as intent, self-defense, insanity, and accident. The tremendous controversy over the "stand your ground" provision fueled by George Zimmerman's shooting of Trayvon Martin serves as an extraordinary example of a law possibly planting seeds for the neutralization of assaults and homicides. According to the theory of neutralization, such judicial precepts are extended well beyond their legal bounds to serve as mechanisms to relieve guilt, thus freeing a person to violate norms. Table 8.2 lists the five techniques of neutralization originally set forth by Sykes and Matza.

To allow violation of laws in which one essentially believes, while preserving self-image, neutralization must *precede* the offense. Rationalizations are excuses that *follow* norm violation and therefore do not account for the offense. This distinction raises an important methodological issue, as it disvalues the testimony of offenders following their violations as causally related to their lawbreaking. Many law violators want to excuse themselves from responsibility and will offer rationalizations to do so, but coming before the offense, neutralizations can be a causal factor.

TABLE 8.2 Gresham Sykes and David Matza's Techniques of Neutralization	
Technique	**Definition**
Denial of responsibility	Disclaiming personal accountability for law violation
Denial of injury	Claiming that the prohibited behavior is absent the element of harm
Denial of the victim	Transforming the victim of illegal behavior into a justifiable target
Condemnation of the condemners	Denouncing the persons who allege law violation
Appeal to higher loyalties	Justifying law violation by conforming to the moral demands of another group affiliation

Source: Adapted from Sykes, G.M., & Matza, D. (1957). Techniques of neutralization: A theory of delinquency. *American Sociological Review*, *22*, 664–70.

Denial of Responsibility

The **denial of responsibility** extends the legal concept of intent to dismiss responsibility for deviant actions. The strategy is echoed in assertions that the outcome was "an accident," was "not my fault," or that "I couldn't help it." Other variables allegedly beyond the offender's control are interjected to deny or mitigate responsibility for the conduct. The strategy extends beyond circumstances immediately surrounding a particular incident, enveloping factors in the social environment "such as unloving parents, bad companions, or a slum neighborhood. In effect, the delinquent approaches a 'billiard ball' conception of himself in which he sees himself as helplessly propelled into new situations. . . . By learning to view himself as more acted upon than acting, the delinquent prepares the way for deviance from the dominant normative system without the necessity of a frontal assault on the norms themselves" (Sykes & Matza, 1957:667). The inequities of our social structure can be incorporated into a mentality that is then available to neutralize norm violation by claiming a lack of personal responsibility.

Denial of Injury

A claim that no real harm was done reflects the denial of injury. This is shown in assertions such as: "They could afford it;" "I was just borrowing it;" and "They've got insurance." **Denial of injury** can be thought of as an extension of the legal category of offenses *mala prohibita*; that is, the neutralizer claims that the offense was merely a technical violation, not a moral wrong. The delinquent is only exaggerating, not departing from, the larger society's exceptions for "kid's stuff," "a little hell-raising," or "sowing wild oats."

Denial of the Victim

By denying existence of a victim, the offender dismisses the wrongfulness of the illegal conduct under the particular circumstances of its occurrence. *Denial of the victim* actually has two meanings, with distinctive implications (Minor, 1981). First, the existence of a victim is denied by the assertion that the targets of the offense are blameworthy. The victims "got what they deserved" and thus are not appropriately regarded as victims. Con men, for example, often assert that "you can't take an honest man;" he must have "larceny in his veins" (Maurer, 1974:101). Stealing from allegedly crooked merchants, defending turf from rival gangs, or assaulting homosexuals all exemplify the blameworthy victim as an excuse for transgression. Groups as notoriously deviant as the Hell's Angels stand ready to excuse law violation by assertions such as: "If any girl claims she was raped by the Angels, it was most likely because she came up and asked for it" (Thompson, 1966:246).

The second form of denial of the victim is much less extreme. "Insofar as the victim is physically absent, unknown, or a vague abstraction (as is often the case in delinquent acts committed against property), the awareness of the victim's experience is weakened . . . and it is possible that a diminished awareness of the victim plays an important part in determining whether or not this process is set in motion" (Sykes & Matza, 1957:668). The victim in this instance is not actively reputed, but does not emerge as a factor to be contended with explicitly.

Condemnation of the Condemners

By repudiating the motives and behaviors of their accusers, law violators are asserting that their own misconduct, by comparison, is less blameworthy. They shift focus from actions contemplated or undertaken to those of the group responding to the deviance, particularly agents of social control. Offenders often deride police, judges, and prosecutors as "corrupt" or "getting away with worse." To the extent that he or she is successful in changing the subject to the actions of accusers, the criminal has successfully neutralized the norms that would control his or her behavior. Sykes and Matza term this process the **condemnation of the condemners.**

Appeal to Higher Loyalties

A dilemma is encountered when a person seeks to abide by the norms of the larger society but those norms are in conflict with the behavioral demands of a smaller, but more intimate, group with which the person is affiliated. Violation of the rules of society may be neutralized by claiming loyalty to the more pressing demands of the immediate group, an **appeal to higher loyalties.** Thus, the offender may claim that the offense was necessary "to help a friend" or "for my family." This dilemma of dual loyalties, like the other techniques of neutralization, has its seeds in culturally condoned excuses. Few would blame a father who stole a drug he could not afford or otherwise acquire in order to treat his very sick infant.

Whither Now, Neutralization?

Returning to the Sutherlandian roots of neutralization, it is a fundamentally sociological perspective because neutralization strategies reflect the cultural setting in which they emerge. The situational exigencies that facilitate them are absorbed from the social environment. In Sutherland's terms, they are learned through social interaction. The evolution of neutralization theory seemingly has acquired an appreciation of this notion.

Although attention in the criminological literature has been rather sparse and sporadic since W. William Minor (1980; 1981) ushered neutralization theory into an era of careful empirical scrutiny, interest has been reinvigorated of late. Robert Agnew (1994), for example, undertook a longitudinal examination of a large sample from the National Youth Survey. His analysis revealed that violence (fighting with peers) had a "moderately large" effect on violence for those who had a lot of delinquent peers and for those who were generally quite opposed to violence. A study relying on qualitative interview data undertaken by Dean Dabney (1995) concluded that theft of drugs and supplies by hospital nurses is widespread and well accounted for by the social learning of techniques of neutralization within the workplace. Such works set the stage for reconceptualizing neutralization as varying across types of persons and their social experiences. That, in turn, led to finding much more support for neutralization, especially in the area of white-collar crime. As Paul Klenowski and his colleagues (2011: 49) recently noted, "some have claimed that neutralization theory has found its most receptive audience in studies of organizational and white-collar crime."

Interviewing imprisoned white-collar offenders, Klenowski et al. (2011) examined gender differentials in neutralizations. As expected, there were both commonalities and differences among white-collar offenders across gender. Both "appeal to higher loyalties" and "denial of responsibility" were evident among both males and females, but important nuances in invoking these rationalizations were noted. Men, for example, often couched their denial of responsibility in terms of psychological illnesses. Klenowski and his colleagues suggest that hegemonic masculinity in America requires that men be in control of themselves and their environment, thus necessitating invocation of the medical model to deviate from a normative expectation for the male role. Women, on the other hand, were free to assert more conventional versions of denial of responsibility (it's not my fault) because doing so did not threaten their ascribed gender role.

Men far more often displayed denial of injury, claim of normality (supplementing Sykes and Matza's forms), and condemnation of condemner. Women were more likely to draw upon defense of necessity (another supplementation). In sum, support was found for neutralization for white-collar offenders but with considerable variation by gender. Another examination of gender and neutralization concluded that "boys and girls are offered different techniques of neutralization by their parents and schools for physically violent behavior, which track boys toward and girls away from physical violence" (Esala, 2013:112). This finding harks back to the connection of neutralization to learning theory, suggesting that mainstream culture contributes to male youth violence, and female victimization, through transference of neutralizing strategies.

Clear expressions of neutralization have also been found in the growing problem of digital pirating (Holt & Copes, 2010). Through face-to-face interviews and virtual interaction with 34 active pirates illegally downloading movies, music, television shows, and software in five countries, pervasive examples of neutralization were evident. Denial of injury was most common with offenders, often claiming that their online thefts were a prelude to later purchases or that it was good publicity for the artist's work. Examples of condemnation of the condemners were assertions that costs were excessive and/or quality low. Online deviance has rocketed into the forefront, misbehaviors that perhaps neutralization theory can shed light on. To add to the intrigue, numerous applications of neutralization theory have been to deviant behaviors that are widely deemed bizarre, disgusting, or perverted. Interviews of inmates with histories of masturbating in front of female correctional staff (Worley & Worley, 2013) fit this category. Interesting, albeit sometimes repulsive, offender storylines consistent with all five original techniques of neutralization are quoted. In the vein of testing neutralization through application to odious, yet nonviolent offenses, online discussions of zoophilia (sexual desire and abnormal attachment to animals) among a sample drawn from discussion boards populated by over half a million users were content-analyzed (Maratea, 2011). Two of the original neutralization techniques were identified, but five additional ones delineated and illustrated.

Another potentially disquieting example assessed the behavior of mothers in subjecting daughters to child beauty pageant careers (Heltsley & Calhoun, 2003). The study followed several months of highly negative press coverage of child beauty pageants in the aftermath of the 1996 murder of young beauty queen JonBenet Ramsey. They suggested that the mothers were depicted as deviant for subjecting daughters to the regimen of beauty pageant competition. Comments solicited from the mothers reflected considerable resort to neutralization. The most frequently deployed was condemnation of the condemners. This neutralization often followed a theme that those suggesting that the children were being sexualized by the activities, thereby placing them at risk of sexual victimization, must themselves be perverts to think such a thing. A distant second most frequently used neutralization was denial of injury, the argument being along lines that the activities were far from harmful to the young girls, but, in fact, very positive experiences.

A behavior even more vehemently seen as abusive, degrading, and humiliating to women is "**hogging**," the practice of targeting overweight women for sexual exploitation. Jeannine Gailey and Ariane Prohaska (2006) examined the trend of such behavior among young men and the propensity to neutralize it. They observed that the activity unfolds in a group context when large amounts of time are spent in bars. It incorporates humor, betting, and sexual conquest, all revolving around efforts expended toward "picking up" overweight and unattractive women. Most of the "hoggers" (the deviant males) interviewed in this study thought their behavior was "normal and funny." They all offered comments that could be construed as expressions of one or more of Sykes and Matza's (1957) neutralizations. All five techniques were exemplified, with denial of victim (e.g., "she was desperate") most commonly followed by denial of responsibility ("I was drunk" or "I was really horny").

Travis Hirschi—Social Bond Theory

A leading social control explanation of crime has been Travis Hirschi's control, or **social bond theory**. Like the work of Matza, Hirschi's work rests upon the assumption that "a person is free to commit delinquent acts because his ties to the conventional order have somehow been broken" (1969:3). Rather than pointing at offenders and asking "why do they do it?" (as do strain and culture conflict theories), Hirschi inquires why the conformist does *not* violate the law. His answer is that people do not break laws to the extent that they have internalized law-abiding norms or developed social bonds. Hirschi believes that it is not necessary to identify motivations to deviance, although he acknowledges that certain forces or pressures hold the potential to be integrated with a control perspective. Humans, like other animals, will violate rules if those rules have not been socially indoctrinated as part of a moral code:

> [W]e are all animals, and thus all naturally capable of committing criminal acts. . . . The chicken stealing corn from his neighbor knows nothing of the moral law; he does not want to violate rules; he wants merely to eat corn. . . . No motivation to deviance is required to explain his acts. So, too, no special motivation to crime within the human animal . . . [is] required to explain his criminal acts (Hirschi, 1969:31).

Assuming normative consensus, weakened or broken social bonds reduce a person's "stakes in conformity." With deficient ties to the social order, deviant impulses people naturally have are likely to be acted upon. The weaker the ties, the more likely deviance is to transpire. Social bonds do not reduce motivations to offend; they only reduce the chance that a person will succumb to those motivations. Hirschi (1969:27) identified four interrelated elements of the social bond, concluding that "the more closely a person is tied to conventional society in any of these ways, the more closely he is likely to be tied in other ways."

Attachment

Sensitivity to the opinions of others is at the heart of the **attachment** element of bond theory. "The essence of internalization of norms, conscience, or superego thus lies in the attachment of the individual to others" (Hirschi, 1969:18). To the extent that an individual cares about the opinions of conventional others, she or he is controlled. A potent test of conformity of youths is their response to the query: "Do you care what your parents think?" If the answer is "no," and it is really meant, the person is relatively free to deviate from the laws of society. Attachment to parents is particularly important.

In a recent analysis of 383 youths aged 12–16, George Higgins and his colleagues (2010) found that both maternal and paternal attachment was associated with delinquent involvement. Moreover, they found this to be a dynamic process. That is, if attachment to the mother or father declined, delinquency increased, and conversely, if those attachments strengthened, this was followed by declines in adolescent misbehavior.

Originally, Hirschi (1969) asserted that this can insulate the individual from delinquency regardless of relative parental conformity. Empirical findings, however, have established that only attachment to conventional parents will insulate one from delinquency. Karen Knight and Tony Tripodi (1996), for example, found a positive relationship between attachment to family and delinquency for a sample in which more than 70 percent of the subjects had other family members who had been incarcerated. For them, family attachment was associated with more delinquency, the opposite of what control theory predicts for attachment.

A fear that the parent will learn of a violation is not essential to control behavior. It is necessary only that the person considers what the parent(s) would think of deviant actions. Only a psychological presence, in other words, is required. This trial question, do you care what your parents (would) think, can be extended to include other relatives, teachers, coaches, peers, and neighbors.

If attachment to one parent reduces the likelihood of delinquency, will attachment to two parents be better yet? Hirschi's (1969) findings and reasoning suggested not. Consequently, most research has not examined the role of one versus two parents in the attachment bond. The research of Joseph Rankin and Roger Kern (1994) raises interesting questions in this regard. First, they found "that strong attachment to both parents . . . has a greater preventive effect on delinquency than strong attachment to either one or no parent" (1994:507). This has clear implications for the quality of family relationships. Second, they found that if there is a strong attachment to only one parent, it does not matter whether it is to the father or mother. This contradicts the "tender years" legal presumption of some states that assumes children's ties to mothers are more important than those to fathers. Third, their examination of broken homes revealed findings at odds with Hirschi's argument. While Hirschi asserted that attachment to one parent in a single-parent home provides the full benefit of attachment, Rankin and Kern found less delinquency in intact homes where the youth was strongly attached to both parents.

Attachment has been accorded the most attention of Hirschi's four elements. Although the bulk of tests have examined juvenile attachments to parents and schools, others are of potential importance. Spousal attachments, for example, have been scrutinized. Michael Maume and his colleagues (2005) found that marital attachment was associated with cessation of marijuana use. John Hepburn and Marie

How important is attachment to one's parents?

CREDIT: ©iStockphoto.com/Jo Unruh.

Griffin (2004) even found that attachments were associated with reduced likelihood of recidivism among child molesters on probation. Another recent study (Thaxton & Agnew, 2004) found that attachments are nonlinear. They discovered that attachments were not only weak, but negative, for highly delinquent youths. Consequently, the effects of attachment may have been underestimated by much prior research because a linear relationship between attachment and delinquency was assumed.

Commitment

Given the assumption that people are rational, they will contemplate the consequences of actions before acting. Hirschi considered such calculations to be a **commitment** to the conventional order. Conformity is encouraged by fear of losing what you have or expect to acquire. Prospects for employment and educational opportunities, reputation, and other valued conditions will discourage delinquent behavior. The more ambitious a person is, therefore, the less likely he or she is to commit criminal offenses. The high school athlete may follow all of the coach's rules to avoid risk of suspension from competition. The college student aspiring to a career in law or criminal justice may avoid experimenting with drugs out of fear of imperiling career prospects. Even nonconventional commitments may encourage conventional conformity, as when youths who aspire to organized crime affiliation avoid forms of criminal behavior deemed inappropriate by those whose judgment is important to them. Hirschi characterized commitment as "common sense" because abiding by social rules helps to maintain and advance one's status in society.

Involvement

The notion that remaining busy in conventional activities insulates persons from unconventional behavior is commonplace. The platitude that "idle hands are the devil's workshop" echoes the idea of **involvement**. Discussing the impact of involvement, Hirschi (1969:22) noted, "To the extent that he is engrossed in conventional activities, he cannot even think about deviant acts, let alone act out his inclinations." Despite the widespread common sense assumption that involvement in legitimate activities will reduce delinquency, little empirical support has been found. The findings with sports involvement have been mixed at best and the effects of youth employment have been found to be associated with *more* delinquency rather than less, particularly as the number of work hours increase (Wright & Cullen, 2000). Not surprisingly, there has been ideological resistance to this finding. When John Wright was presenting to the American Society of Criminology early evidence of the positive relationship between youth employment and delinquency, contrary to control theory predictions, his research was greeted with a firestorm of objections that this could not be so. While the reasons appear to be quite complex (e.g., disposable income that can be used for alcohol or drugs, mixtures of different age groups, lack of supervision after work), the finding has now been replicated several times.

Belief

Hirschi's control theory postulates that, although people have been socialized into a common set of beliefs, there nevertheless is variation in the strength of their beliefs. The stronger that peoples' **belief** in the conventional order is, the less likely they are to offend. For persons with weaker belief in the law, Hirschi contends that neutralization is not essential.

Analysis of Social Bond

Hirschi is one of the few theorists to have proposed a theory of crime or delinquency that was subjected to substantial empirical testing during its developmental stages. In *Causes of Delinquency* (1969), he presented the results of self-report, police, and school data for 3,605 boys involved in the Richmond (California) Youth Project. The data supported his new version of control theory. The theory has since been buttressed by empirical testing undertaken by many criminologists (e.g., Hindelang, 1973; Conger, 1976; Hepburn, 1977; Cernkovich, 1978; Krohn & Massey, 1980; Wiatrowski et al., 1981; Lasley, 1988). While the basic framework of the theory has been challenged by only a few criminologists, it has frequently been noted that its explanatory power is weak and that it has been applied mostly to minor offenders (e.g., Cretacci, 2003).

Hirschi's (1969) original test of social bond theory excluded females, but he noted that additional studies should examine gender. A number of criminologists have since tested control theory among females and found it to have strong explanatory power. One study (Li & MacKenzie, 2003), however, found differential effects of social bonds across gender for adult subjects. The theory has also been tested across various age groups, revealing varying fits (LaGrange & White, 1985). In short, social control or bond theory has fared reasonably well in empirical tests, but appears to need elaboration and more careful specification.

A major deficiency of social control or bond theory is its failure to come to grips with causal order. It proposes that social bonds relate to delinquency; weak attachments are presumed to lead to delinquency and correlations between bonds and delinquency are so interpreted. It is just as plausible, however, that delinquent behavior causes deterioration of social bonds. Virtually all tests of control theory have relied upon cross-sectional data, thus failing to address causal order; Robert Agnew (1985; 1991), however, has examined two sets of longitudinal data for juveniles and found only very weak support. Agnew (1991:150) concluded that these data "raise further doubt about the importance attributed to Hirschi's theory."

A second damaging criticism of control theory is its neglect of the origin of social bonds and their varying strength. Control theories assert that deviant behavior is a consequence of weak bonds with the conventional order. This places a scholar attempting to explain crime or conformity in a quandary. To attribute behavior, either deviance or conformity, to the strength of social bonds is only a partial answer. If social bonds are responsible for the behavior, the obvious concern is to understand those social bonds. If, as Hirschi claims, there is variation in the strength of bonds, it becomes essential to account for such differences. One study of illicit drug use among young adults failed to find bonding differences between offenders and nonoffenders (Kandel & Davies, 1991). If anything, the drug users displayed more attachments to friends than did nonusers. This led the researchers to conclude that a cultural deviance rather than a control perspective best explained drug use.

Hirschi's version of control theory has also been criticized on theoretical grounds. Willem Schinkel (2002:140–1), in arguing that the theory is tautological, concluded that "the idea that the criminal has a weakened bond to society tells us nothing new, since the criminal is part of the nonconventional, rather than the conventional, and a criminal, someone who commits nonconventional acts, is thus by definition someone who commits less conventional acts (since these constitute the 'bond' to conventional society)."

The assumptions underlying social bond theory are also open to question. Hirschi's portrayal of the morality of "man," for example, seems to be that humans are naturally immoral. In Hirschi's view, humans will do whatever benefits them unless they are controlled by social bonds. Schinkel (2002:126) summarizes the commitment bond as "the idea that rules are obeyed out of fear for the consequences of not doing so," then asking, "Is the only thing that prevents Travis Hirschi from shooting Gilbert Geis in the head the fact that Hirschi is afraid he will spend the rest of his life in jail?" To the contrary, Schinkel argues, morality is more than a purely oppressive force. Following Kant, he argues that morality is inherent in human nature rather than absent, as Hirschi contends, with choices at the center of human existence. Thus persons are not constrained by morality, as Hirschi argues, but potentially freed by moral choices. Yet those choices cannot be as arbitrarily classified as in social bond theory. The conventional and nonconventional are not so discrete. Persons can be strongly bonded to conventional society, yet engage in nonconventional activities. This would be quite evident, for example, among crooked politicians, white-collar criminals, or abusive clergy.

The policy impact of control theory is less direct than for strain theories. It is often construed as a "common sense" perspective. Control theory is at the core of what many people attempt to do in rearing their children. As Lamar Empey (1982:268) noted, "[W]hen most people concentrate on their own children, rather than children in general, they sound like control theorists." Attachment calls for strengthening the family, schools, and other primary institutions. Most parents strive to foster the attachment of their children to conventional persons and institutions. Similarly, involvement calls for the development of playgrounds and other recreational opportunities. Among individual families this translates to encouraging children to participate in athletics, hobbies, and various extracurricular activities. Parents also press their offspring to commit to educational, professional, and other social goals, and they attempt to foster a belief in the social order so that the children will develop a stake in conformity.

Michael Gottfredson and Travis Hirschi—Self-Control

Without doubt, the notion of **low self-control** embedded in Michael Gottfredson and Travis Hirschi's (1990) "**General Theory of Crime**" has likely been the recipient of more attention in recent years than any other single theory of crime. According to this theory, crime is the result of individuals with low self-control encountering situations or opportunities in which crime will produce immediate gratification with relatively low levels of risk. They view crime as so simple, however, that opportunities are abundant, propelling anyone with low self-control into a crime-saturated abyss. Self-control is said to be taught in early childhood, implying that parental discipline and management are the only factors in explaining delinquent and adult criminal offending. Parents can instill self-control in their children by monitoring the child's behavior and recognizing and punishing misbehavior when it occurs. Failure to do this will result in low self-control. It follows that those with low self-control will have children following in their footsteps (the apple not falling far from the tree, as is popularly said), not as a result of heredity or directly learning bad behavior, but as a consequence of being reared in a manner not conducive to developing self-control.

Gottfredson and Hirschi argue that the cause of *all* crime is low self-control (thus called a *general theory*) and that this characteristic is stable across the life course and set by age eight. In other words, the individual who is prone to act out in elementary school is also likely to be involved in adolescent delinquency, adult crime, and even deviant behavior in their elder years. Low self-control, they argue, is associated not only with crime and delinquency, but also with what they call **analogous acts** or noncriminal behavior also resulting from low self-control. Examples of such imprudent behaviors are excessive drinking, smoking, illicit sex, and even accidents. That is, individuals with low self-control will consistently engage in behavior that causes problems for themselves and others. They will be inclined to pursue short-term pleasures at the expense of long-term goals. Health may be jeopardized by smoking and drinking; accidents may result from high-risk behaviors while under the influence of drugs or alcohol; criminal charges may follow violent responses to insults, and so on. As widely expressed by staff in institutional corrections environments, many offenders just do not make good choices. The reason for these poor decisions, from the Gottfredson/Hirschi perspective, is low self-control rooted in poor childhood-rearing experiences.

Low self-control is a construct that is comprised of several characteristic features. It has most been typically operationalized through the Grasmick et al. (1993) 24-item scale, consisting of six elements. Persons with low self-control are envisioned as displaying these traits:

1. Impulsiveness. The person with low self-control will have an inability to delay gratification, preferring quick pleasures and rewards.
2. Simple tasks. Activities that do not require planning or intellectual investment will be preferred over those that do.

3. Risk seeking. The excitement of risky behavior will be rewarding, while safe and careful activities will bring boredom.
4. Physicality. Physical endeavors will be preferred over intellectual activities.
5. Self-centeredness. Low self-control will be characterized by insensitivity to the needs and interests of others and excessive focus on desires for the self.
6. Temper. The person with low self-control will easily lose their temper.

Gottfredson and Hirschi rule out "positivistic" sources of low self-control such as learning or cultural transmission. Who, they ask, would intentionally pass on to their offspring the trait of low self-control, given that it is a dysfunctional trait? Analogous to Hirschi's earlier social bonding theory, it is argued that self-control is more or less low in the beginning. In the absence of effective child-drearing, low self-control will persist. If children's behavior is not monitored and deviance sanctioned over the first eight years of life, self-control will be set (or remain) at a low level. This will then persist throughout the individual's life.

Gottfredson and Hirschi see themselves as developing a theory that fills the gap between classical or deterrence ideas and positivism. While the theory is rooted in the classical hedonistic view of human nature, not all persons are equally deterrable due to variations in levels of self-control. Thus, as with a positivistic perspective, the motivation to crime (self-control) varies, but no particular motivation per se is needed, only low self-control coupled with opportunity. This, however, does not compel the person to deviance (as positivists typically assert about their independent variables). It is only a trait or personality factor that shapes choices. Gottfredson and Hirschi depict all crime as exciting, requiring little skill or planning, and providing little long-term gain.

Analysis of Low Self-control

Low self-control has consistently been found to be a strong predictor of crime and delinquency. It has generally fared well with recent cross-cultural tests, with similar results between whites and African Americans (Vazsonyi & Crosswhite, 2004), and Russian (Tittle & Botchkovar, 2005; Antonaccio & Tittle, 2008) and Swiss samples (Vazsonyi & Klanjšek, 2008), and has generally held for females, although not as strongly, as with males. Support for the strength of the self-control variable has been found for a variety of forms of serious crime, including violent offenses (Piquero et al., 2005), courtship violence (Sellers, 1999), computer crimes (Higgins et al., 2008), and fraud (Holtfreter et al., 2010).

The relationship between low self-control and a wide range of analogous or imprudent behaviors has consistently been observed as well. Low self-control has been found to be related to analogous behaviors such as academic dishonesty (Cochran et al., 1998; Meldrum & Del Rio, 2013), binge drinking (Gibson et al., 2004), and adolescent sexual behavior (Hope & Chapple, 2005). This represents an important aspect of Gottfredson and Hirschi's "general" theory, because it is intended to explain *all* aberrant behavior. This trend was continued with Michael Reisig and Travis Pratt's (2011) study of deviant social behaviors among a sample of 500 undergraduate college students. They found that those with lower self-control were more likely to admit to public flatulence (farting), use of obscene language in public places, and drunk dialing (late night phone calls while intoxicated).

Many other forms of deviance have been identified as significantly related to low self-control as well, but with the researchers finding other variables equally or more strongly related (e.g., Gibbs & Giever, 1995; Evans et al., 1997; Wright et al., 1999; Wright & Cullen, 2000; Gibson & Wright, 2001). An overall assessment of the empirical support for the theory was undertaken by Travis Pratt and Frank Cullen (2000). They also concluded that while there is widespread support for the predictive power of low self-control, other factors, particularly social learning variables, play a role as well.

Competition between self-control and learning explanations of crime and deviance have been particularly keen. There is little question that deviants of all sorts emanate from families with deviant histories and, likewise, that people bear close resemblance to their friends. Deviance of friends is a very strong predictor of deviance. The question is whether the family patterns are best explained by learning processes in deviant family environments or whether such families fail to nurture self-control mechanisms, placing offspring at risk of misbehavior due to low self-control. Among deviant friendships, the competing notions are (1) that friends are critical to learning norms and values versus (2) a mere "birds of a feather flock together" pattern, whereby those with low self-control either seek out like company (selective mixing) or whose out-of-control life styles throw them in together. Looking at 63,000 youths across the United States, Jacob Young (2011) found little support for the friendships being driven by levels of self-control, instead finding that the greater influences are age, gender, and socioeconomic status. This is more consistent with the learning account for the similarities of behavior among friends.

To return to the example of family violence discussed in the context of differential association theory, another well-known pattern of criminal behavior is that those who are exposed to family violence as children are at high risk for perpetrating family violence and/or being victims of family violence as adults. Again, self-control serves as a rival hypothesis in accounting for this pattern. Bryan Payne and his colleagues (2011) recently undertook a test of this account. To the extent that domestic violence by parents is a proxy for "bad parenting," Payne et al. (2011) reasoned that this could retard development of self-control, with subsequent low self-control accounting for adult domestic violence. They collected telephone interview data from 375 southeast Virginia residents to scrutinize that linkage. Like other researchers, they found that exposure to family violence in childhood was associated with adult partner violence and that low self-control was associated with adult partner violence. However, they did not find that exposure to violence among parents in childhood impacted levels of self-control. While they noted that there are various possible reasons for this, their research failed to support self-control over the learning account of partner family violence.

Research undertaken by Constance Chapple (2005) further supported the value of combining low self-control with variables drawn from social learning and other theoretical frameworks. She found that the presence of low self-control tends to lead to peer rejection, consistent with Gottfredson & Hirschi's contention that low self-control undermines many personal relationships, and to association with deviant peers. Both of these problems, in turn, further contribute to delinquency. Elizabeth Cauffman and her colleagues (2005) also found that while low self-control was a predictor of delinquency, so was heart rate (a biological variable) and spatial span (a neuropsychological measure) after statistically controlling for the effects of low self-control. In fact, numerous studies have found evidence that low self-control, along with ADHD and other similar constructs, is a heritable trait (Boisvert et al., 2013), while Scott Desmond and his co-researchers (2013) have found self-control to be related to religiosity. Similarly, Brianna Remster (2014) found that depression contributes to low self-control. In short, a lot of research is indicating that low self-control is produced by a variety of factors beyond poor parenting of young children. So while there is broad agreement that self-control is an important factor in crime causation, there is a lot of disagreement with Gottfredson and Hirschi's claim that it is solely the product of poor childrearing practices.

Policy implications for Gottfredson and Hirschi's theory are rather straightforward. Since the theory presumes that self-control is set early in life, it portends value in programs designed to enhance self-control among young children, especially among males and in environments plagued by poor parenting skills. A meta-analytic review of 34 studies evaluating efforts to enhance childhood self-control suggests considerable success in both improving levels of self-control and reducing delinquency (Piquero et al., 2010).

Despite the widespread attention and considerable empirical support for the role of self-control, Gottfredson and Hirschi's theory has been subjected to a variety of criticisms (see, for example, Akers, 1994; Tittle, 1995; Geis, 2000; DeLisi et al., 2003). Concerns with the theory can be conceptualized as falling into empirical and theoretical categories. The empirical issues regard how research has been conducted and its failure to find evidence supportive of the full range of claims made by Hirschi and Gottfredson. The theoretical criticisms focus on the logic of the theory.

One of the empirical matters of greatest concern is how self-control has been operationalized. The Grasmick et al. (1993) scale has been most widely used and debate has centered on whether the concept of self-control is unidimensional or best conceived as a combination of multiple factors (see Piquero et al., 2000; DeLisi et al., 2003). Some researchers maintain that self-control is a unitary concept (e.g., Nagin & Paternoster, 1994; Polakowski, 1994; Piquero & Tibbetts, 1996;), while others have concluded that the different predictive abilities of the subscales (e.g., impulsivity) indicate that it should not be considered unidimensional (Arneklev et al., 1993; Wood et al., 1993; DeLisi et al., 2003;). Injecting some further confusion, Hirschi (2004) proposed a new conceptualization of self-control that is quite similar to his original idea of social bonding.

He also added an honor-based component, tapping feelings about whether others might know and what they would think about misconduct. While this new rendition of self-control has been only scantily tested, preliminary results suggest it may yield an improved measure (Brown and Jennings, 2014).

There are also important empirical assertions in Gottfredson and Hirschi's theory that are debated. Perhaps foremost among these is depicting self-control as being set by age eight and then remaining fixed throughout one's life. Many criminologists have challenged this assertion on the basis of both logic and empirical findings. Among recent examples is the work of Callie Burt and colleagues (2014). They followed a sample of African-American youths from age 10 to 25, far beyond the years that Gottfredson and Hirschi claim to fully shape self-control. They found continual evolution of self-control for some of their subjects across this time frame and, harking back to the biological theories of Chapter 6, asserted that "adolescence is a period of dramatic biological, behavioral and social changes that . . . include substantial restructuring of the cortical regions and connections undergirding impulsivity and sensation seeking" (pp. 474–5). They close their research article proclaiming that self-control theory (SCT) "has gotten some things wrong. One of these is the stability of self-control. Evidence clearly contradicts the SCT proposition that those who were not fortunate enough to be effectively parented and, therefore, failed to develop self-control are doomed to a life of myopic decisions and negative consequences thereof" (p. 479). They concede that while self-control features a degree of stability, there is also considerable change over time, far beyond the years discounted by Gottfredson and Hirschi.

Another interesting application of the theory relates it to victimization. This nicely blends victimization studies (see Routine Activities Theory in Chapter 5), which find a great deal of crossover between victims and offenders, with efforts of self-control theory to explain offending. The idea is that repeat victimization becomes another negative life outcome of low self-control, along with delinquency, crime, and analogous behaviors (Turanovic & Pratt, 2014). It unfolds this way because low self-control is thought to prevent victims from making the necessary changes in their risky lifestyles to forestall continued victimization. Travis Pratt and colleagues undertook a meta-analysis of 66 published studies, finding that self-control was consistently associated with victimization, though not as strongly as with offending. These findings are consistent with Gottfredson and Hirschi's claim that persons with low self-control will encounter an array of problems, including unemployment, few long-term relationships, criminal activity, and accidents. These tests indicate that risk of victimization is another lifetime risk that can be added to the plight of persons with low self-control.

Theoretical concerns lie more at the heart of critiques of the general theory. One of the most widespread criticisms of the theory is that it is tautological, meaning that the logical path followed is a circular one. The issue is that self-control and the propensity toward criminal behavior/analogous acts are not independently defined, but rather, are one and the same. That is, low self-control is defined in terms of persons committing deviant acts, while the theory maintains that low self-control is the cause of deviance. Thus the hypothesis seems to be that low self-control causes low self-control. Some researchers, in fact, have used deviant behaviors as the proxy for low self-control, finding that they are predictive of other deviant behaviors (e.g., Evans et al., 1997; LaGrange & Silverman, 1999; Wright et al., 1999; Redmon, 2003). Stelios Stylianou (2002:536), however, asserts that "one cannot use crime and analogous behavior as measures of low self-control. Correlations among different criminal and analogous acts are evidence of versatility, not of causation." Such correlations can also be readily interpreted as support for learning theories rather than self-control. "A correlation between a variety of deviant behaviors could simply mean that certain social contexts are associated with learning the attitudes and techniques required for a variety of deviant behaviors" (Stylianou, 2002).

Another concern has been Gottfredson and Hirschi's relative neglect of the opportunity variable. The opportunities for crime that one encounters may be more important than his or her self-control. In the absence of opportunity, low self-control may not be very predictive of crime or analogous behaviors. Carter Hay and Walter Forrest (2008) argue that this oversimplification attenuates the explanatory power of the theory. Adding a routine activities component, they found that both unsupervised peer associations and the amount of time spent with peers independently contributed and amplified the effects of low self-control on a variety of delinquent behaviors. Others have found support for an additive effect; individuals with low self-control and with greater opportunity for engaging in criminal activity report higher levels of offending (Grasmick et al., 1993; Piquero & Tibbetts, 1996; Cochran et al., 1998; Sellers, 1999).

Other theories that have claimed to explain all crime and delinquency (e.g., classical deterrence, differential association) have encountered the criticism that they better fit some forms of behavior than others. Gottfredson and Hirschi's theory encounters this problem as well. While research has found low self-control predictive of a variety of criminal behaviors, questions remain regarding the viability of the theory for explaining all crime, especially the white-collar variety (Reed & Yeager, 1996). A conspicuous question is how a white-collar offender could exercise the requisite high self-control for occupational success, yet be propelled into offending by low self-control. Consistent with the skepticism, Andrea Schoepfer and colleagues (2014) found that low self-control explained some conventional crimes examined (e.g., shoplifting), but not the white-collar offense of illegally shredding documents for one's company. To return to the logic of the theory, Gottfredson and Hirschi maintain that all crime is spontaneous rather than planned, requires little skill, and is not very profitable. These assumptions seem to largely defy criminological understanding of white-collar, organized, and perhaps other forms of crime. It is quite plausible that low self-control could turn out to be an important concept in the understanding of some, but not all, forms of crime as the theory asserts. That is, evidence may be marshaled to support low self-control, while not supporting the general application of the theory.

SUMMARY

This chapter has examined social process theories. Those theories reviewed in this grouping analyze the social processes or interactions associated with crime. Social process theories tend to have a micro-theoretical focus; that is, they look at how individuals become law violators. A social psychological label is often ascribed to the theories because they combine sociological and psychological variables. Unlike social structure theories, most social process perspectives do not limit focus to any segment of the class structure. Three groups of theories have been subsumed under the social process category in this chapter: social learning, culture conflict, and social control.

Edwin H. Sutherland, author of the theory of differential association, is generally viewed as the prime mover of learning theory. In its final form, differential association was comprised of nine principles. The key one asserted that persons become criminal offenders through an excess of definitions favorable to violation of the law. This theory is of particular importance because it helped bring the sociological perspective to a dominant position in criminological studies in the United States. Ronald Akers's social learning theory broadened this perspective through incorporation of additional learning principles.

Culture conflict or cultural deviance theory is derived from learning theory. Its basic idea is that crime and delinquency are learned as normal behavior in a subcultural setting. Thorsten Sellin took the lead in this theoretical tradition, while Marvin Wolfgang and Franco Ferracuti followed with their "subculture of violence" theory. Walter Miller focused on the lower class, and postulated distinct focal concerns that predispose persons in that class to violate legal codes. Elijah Anderson's code of the street is the most recent well known theory following this tradition. Much criminological discussion has focused upon high rates of violence and homicide that have long characterized the Southern United States.

Control theories, as do learning and cultural deviance theories, view crime as a reflection of failure of social constraints rather than as a product of criminogenic forces. The theories are rooted in both value consensus and free will assumptions. At the heart of Gresham Sykes and David Matza's neutralization version of control theory is the idea that because people fundamentally believe in the law, they must generate a rationale to excuse law violation prior to violating. Travis Hirschi's social control or bond theory proposed four elements of a bond to society that serve to control people. He maintained that the weaker the social bonds, the less the individual is constrained by the law.

Michael Gottfredson and Travis Hirschi's low self-control is currently the most widely discussed of all theories of crime. They see self-control at the heart of not only crime and delinquency, but also analogous behaviors. It is contended that self-control is fixed by the age of eight. While the theory has been tested considerably and support has been rather consistent, it has also been vigorously criticized on theoretical grounds. The emerging consensus appears to be that while self-control is an important explanatory variable in crime and deviance, it probably emanates from more sources than early childhood-rearing experiences and unfolds over a considerably longer period of time.

KEY TERMS AND CONCEPTS

Analogous Acts

Appeal to Higher Loyalties

Attachment

Attitude Transference

Autonomy

Belief

Code of the Street

Commitment

Condemnation of the Condemners

Control Theory

Cracker Culture/Black Redneck Thesis

Cultural Deviance

Cultural Transmission

Culture Conflict

Cycle of Violence

Denial of Injury

Denial of Responsibility

Denial of Victim

Deviance Gap

Differential Association

Differential Identification

E-Cheating

Excitement

Fate

Focal Concerns

General Theory of Crime

Hogging

Involvement

Learning Theories

Low Self-Control

Primary Culture Conflict

Secondary Culture Conflict

Smartness

Social Bond Theory

Social Control Theories

Social Learning Theory

Social Process Theories

Social Psychological Theories

Southern Culture of Violence

Subculture of Violence

Symbolic Interaction

Techniques of Neutralization

Toughness

Trouble

KEY CRIMINOLOGISTS

Ronald Akers

Elijah Anderson

Donald R. Cressey

Franco Ferracuti

Michael Gottfredson

Travis Hirschi

David Matza

Walter Miller

Thorsten Sellin

Edwin H. Sutherland

Gresham Sykes

Gabriel Tarde

Charles Tittle

Marvin Wolfgang

DISCUSSION QUESTIONS

1. Describe Edwin Sutherland's contributions to the field of criminology.

2. How do people learn "bad" behavior? Can it be learned from movies, music, or video games?

3. What is the relationship between learning and culture conflict theories?

4. Distinguish between primary and secondary culture conflict.

5. Differentiate neutralization from rationalization. Discuss examples of crime and deviance that criminologists have attempted to explain through neutralization.

6. Define "analogous behaviors." How are they central to Gottfredson and Hirschi's general theory of crime?

7. Discuss criticisms that have been leveled at Gottfredson and Hirschi's general theory of crime.

REFERENCES

Adams, L. R. (1973). Differential association and learning principles revisited. *Social Problems, 20*, 458–70.

Agnew, R. (1985). Social control theory and delinquency: A longitudinal test. *Criminology, 23*, 47–61.

Agnew, R. (1991). A longitudinal test of social control theory and delinquency. *Journal of Research in Crime and Delinquency, 28*, 126–56.

Agnew, R. (1994). The techniques of neutralization and violence. *Criminology, 32*, 555–80.

Akers, R. L. (1973). *Deviant behavior: A social learning approach*. Belmont, CA: Wadsworth.

Akers, R. L. (1985). *Deviant behavior: A social learning approach* (3rd ed.). New York, NY: Wadsworth.

Akers, R. L. (1990). Rational choice, deterrence, and social learning theory: The path not taken. *Journal of Criminal Law and Criminology, 81*, 653–76.

Akers, R. L. (1994). *Criminological theories: Introduction and evaluation*. Los Angeles, CA: Roxbury.

Anderson, E. (1999). *Code of the street: Decency, violence, and the moral life of the inner city*. New York, NY: W.W. Norton.

Andreescu, V., Shutt, J. E., & Vito, G. (2011). The culture of the South: Culture of honor, social disorganization, and murder in Appalachia. *Criminal Justice Review, 36*, 76–103.

Antonaccio, O., & Tittle, C. R. (2008). Morality, self-control, and crime. *Criminology, 46*, 479–510.

Arneklev, B. J., Grasmick, H. G., Tittle, C. R., & Bursik, R. J. (1993). Low self-control and imprudent behavior. *Journal of Quantitative Criminology, 9*, 225–47.

Ball-Rokeach, S. J. (1973). Values and violence: A test of the subculture of violence thesis. *American Sociological Review, 38*, 736–49.

Baron, S. W. (2013). When formal sanctions encourage violent offending: How violent peers and violent codes undermine deterrence. *Justice Quarterly, 30*, 926–65.

Bernard, T. J. (1990). Angry aggression among the "truly disadvantaged." *Criminology, 28*, 73–96.

Boisvert, D., Wright, J.P., Knopik, V., & Vaske, J. (2013). A twin study of sex differences in self-control. *Justice Quarterly, 30,* 529–59.

Brauer, J.R., Tittle, C.R., Antonaccio, O., & Islam, M.Z. (2012). Childhood experiences and self-control. *Deviant Behavior, 33,* 375–92.

Brown, W. & Jennings, W.G. (2014). A replication and an honor-based extension of Hirschi's reconceptualization of self-control theory and crime and analogous behaviors. *Deviant Behavior, 35,* 297–310.

Burt, C.H., Sweeten, G., & Simons, R.L. (2014). Self-control through emerging adulthood: instability, multidimensionality, and criminological significance. *Criminology, 52,* 450–87.

Cauffman, E., Steinberg, S., & Piquero, A.R. (2005). Psychological, neuropsychological and physiological correlates of serious antisocial behavior in adolescence: The role of self-control. *Criminology, 43,* 133–76.

Cernkovich, S.A. (1978). *The American occupational structure.* New York, NY: John Wiley and Sons.

Chapple, C.L. (2005). Self-control, peer relations, and delinquency. *Justice Quarterly, 22,* 89–106.

Christensen, T. (2010). Presumed guilty: Constructing deviance and deviants through techniques of neutralization. *Deviant Behavior, 31,* 552–77.

Cochran, J.K., Sellers, C.S., Wiesbrock, V., & Palacios, W.R. (2011). Repetitive intimate partner victimization: An exploratory application of social learning theory. *Deviant Behavior, 32,* 790–817.

Cochran, J.K., Wood, P.B., Sellers, C.S., Wilkerson, W., & Chamlin, M.B. (1998). Academic dishonesty and low self-control: An empirical test of a general theory of crime. *Deviant Behavior, 19,* 227–55.

Conger, R.D. (1976). Social control and social learning models of delinquent behavior. *Criminology, 14,* 17–39.

Copes, H., Hochstetler, A., & Forsyth, C.J. (2013). Peaceful warriors: Codes for violence among adult male bar fighters. *Criminology, 51,* 761–94.

Costello, B. (1997). On the logical adequacy of cultural deviance theories. *Theoretical Criminology, 1,* 403–28.

Costello, B. (1998). The remarkable persistence of a flawed theory: A rejoinder to Matsueda. *Theoretical Criminology, 2,* 85–92.

Cretacci, M. (2003). Religion and social control: An application of a modified social bond on violence. *Criminal Justice Behavior, 28,* 254–77.

Crosswhite, J.M. & Kerpelman, J.L. (2012). Parenting and children's self-control: Concurrent and longitudinal relations. *Deviant Behavior, 33,* 715–37.

Dabney, D. (1995). Neutralization and deviance in the workplace: Theft of supplies and medicines by hospital nurses. *Deviant Behavior, 16,* 313–31.

DeLisi, M., Hochstetler, A., & Murphy, D.S. (2003). Self-control behind bars: A validation study of the Grasmick et al. scale. *Justice Quarterly, 20,* 241–63.

Desmond, S.A., Ulmer, J.T., & Badef, C.D. (2013). Religion, self control, and substance use. *Deviant Behavior, 34,* 384–406.

Drummond, H., Boland, J.M., & Harris, W.A. (2011). Becoming violent: Evaluating the mediating effect of hopelessness on the code of the street thesis. *Deviant Behavior, 32,* 191–223.

Empey, L. T. (1982). *American delinquency: Its meaning and construction*. Homewood, IL: Dorsey Press.

Esala, J. J. (2013). Communities of denial: The co-construction of gendered adolescent violence. *Deviant Behavior, 34*, 97–114.

Evans, D. T., Cullen, F. T., Burton, V. S., Jr., Dunaway, R. G., & Benson, M. L. (1997). The social consequences of self-control: Testing the general theory of crime. *Criminology, 35*, 475–95.

Fox, K. A., Grover, A. R., & Kaukinen, C. (2009). The effects of low self-control and childhood maltreatment on stalking victimization among men and women. *American Journal of Criminal Justice, 34*, 181–97.

Gailey, J. A. & Prohaska, A. (2006). "Knocking off a fat girl": An exploration of hogging, male sexuality, and neutralizations. *Deviant Behavior, 27*, 31–49.

Geis, G. (2000). On the absence of self-control as the basis for a general theory of crime. *Theoretical Criminology, 4*, 35–53.

Gibbs, J. J. & Giever, D. (1995). Self-control and its manifestations among university students: An empirical test of Gottfredson and Hirschi's general theory. *Justice Quarterly, 12*, 231–55.

Gibson, C. & Wright, J. P. (2001). Low self-control and co worker delinquency: A research note. *Journal of Criminal Justice, 29*, 483–92.

Gibson, C., Schreck, C. J., & Miller, J. M. (2004). Binge drinking and negative alcohol-related behaviors: A test of self-control theory. *Journal of Criminal Justice, 32*, 411–20.

Glaser, D. (1956). Criminality theories and behavioral images. *American Journal of Sociology, 61*, 433–44.

Gottfredson, M. & Hirschi, T. (1990). *A general theory of crime*. Stanford, CA: Stanford University Press.

Grasmick, H. G., Tittle, C. R., Bursik, R. J., Jr., & Arneklev, B. J. (1993). Testing the core empirical implications of Gottfredson and Hirschi's general theory of crime. *Journal of Research in Crime and Delinquency, 30*, 5–29.

Hamm, M. S. & Ferrell, J. (1994). Rap, cops, and crime: Clarifying the "Cop Killer" controversy. *ACJS Today, 13* (May/June).

Hay, C. & Forrest, W. (2008). Self-control theory and the concept of opportunity: The case for a more systematic union. *Criminology, 46*, 1039–72.

Heltsley, M. & Calhoun, T. C. (2003). The good mother: Neutralization techniques used by pageant mothers. *Deviant Behavior, 24*, 81–100.

Hepburn, J. R. (1977). Testing alternative models of delinquency causation. *Journal of Criminal Law and Criminology, 67*, 450–60.

Hepburn, J. R. & Griffin, M. L. (2004). The effect of social bonds on successful adjustment to probation: An event history analysis. *Criminal Justice Review, 29*, 46–75.

Higgins, G. E., Jennings, W. G., & Mahoney, M. (2010). Developmental trajectories of maternal and paternal attachment and delinquency in adolescence. *Deviant Behavior, 31*, 655–77.

Higgins, G. E., Wolfe, S., & Marcum, C. (2008). Digital piracy: An examination of three measurements of self-control. *Deviant Behavior, 29*, 440–60.

Hindelang, M. J. (1973). Causes of delinquency: A partial replication and extension. *Social Problems, 20*, 471–87.

Hirschi, T. (1969). *Causes of delinquency*. Berkeley, CA: University of California Press.

Hirschi, T. (2004). Self-control and crime. In R.F. Baumeister & K.D. Vohs (Eds.), *Handbook of self-regulation: Research, theory, and applications* (pp. 537–52). New York, NY: Guilford Press.

Holt, T.J. & Copes, H. (2010). Transferring subcultural knowledge online: Practices and beliefs of persistent digital pirates. *Deviant Behavior, 31*, 625–54.

Holtfreter, K., Reisig, M.D., Piquero, N.L., & Piquero, A.R. (2010). Low self-control and fraud: Offending, victimization, and their overlap. *Criminal Justice & Behavior, 37*, 188–203.

Hope, T.L. & Chapple, C.L. (2005). Maternal characteristics, parenting, and adolescent sexual behavior: The role of self-control. *Deviant Behavior, 26*, 25–45.

Horney, J. (2006). An alternative psychology of criminal behavior. *Criminology, 44*, 1–16.

Hunt, P.M. (2010). Are you kynd? Conformity and deviance within the jamband subculture. *Deviant Behavior, 31*, 521–51.

Hwang, S. & Akers, R.L. (2006). Parental and peer influences on adolescent drug use in Korea. *Asian Journal of Criminology, 1*, 59–69.

Jacobs, J.A. (2005). ASR's greatest hits: Editor's comment. *American Sociological Review, 70*, 1–3.

Jeffery, C.R. (1965). Criminal behavior and learning theory. *Journal of Criminal Law, Criminology and Police Science, 54*, 294–300.

Kandel, D. & Davies, M. (1991). Friendship networks, intimacy, and illicit drug use in young adulthood: A comparison of two competing theories. *Criminology, 29*, 441–69.

Klenowski, P.M., Copes, H., & Mullins, C.W. (2011). Gender, identity, and accounts: How white collar offenders do gender when making sense of their crimes. *Justice Quarterly, 28*, 46–69.

Knight, K.W. & Tripodi, T. (1996). Societal bonding and delinquency: An empirical test of Hirschi's theory of control. *Journal of Offender Rehabilitation, 23*, 117–29.

Kobayashi, E., Akers, R.L., & Sharp, S.F. (2011). Attitude transference and deviant behavior: A comparative study in Japan and the United States. *Deviant Behavior, 32*, 405–40.

Kornhauser, R.R. (1978). *Social sources of delinquency: An appraisal of analytic methods.* Chicago, IL: University of Chicago Press.

Krohn, M.D. & Massey, J.L. (1980). Social control and delinquent behavior: An examination of the elements of the social bond. *Sociological Quarterly, 21*, 529–44.

LaGrange, R.L. & White, H.R. (1985). Age differences in delinquency: A test of theory. *Criminology, 23*, 19–45.

LaGrange, T.C. & Silverman, R.A. (1999). Low self-control and opportunity: Testing the general theory of crime as an explanation for gender differences in delinquency. *Criminology, 37*, 41–72.

Lasley, J.R. (1988). Toward a control theory of white-collar offending. *Journal of Quantitative Criminology, 4*, 347–62.

Laub, J.H. (1983). *Criminology in the making.* Boston, MA: Northeastern University Press.

Lee, M.R., Thomas, S.A., & Ousey, G.C. (2009). Southern culture and homicide: Examining the cracker culture/black rednecks thesis. *Deviant Behavior, 31*, 60–96.

Li, S.D. & MacKenzie, D.L. (2003). The gendered effects of adult social bonds on the criminal activities of probationers. *Criminal Justice Review, 28*, 278–98.

McGloin, J.M. (2009). Delinquency balance: Revisiting peer influence. *Criminology, 47*, 439–78.

McWhiney, G. (1988). *Cracker culture: Celtic ways in the Old South.* Tuscaloosa, AL: University of Alabama Press.

Maratea, R. J. (2011). Screwing the pooch: Legitimizing accounts in a zoophilia on-line community. *Deviant Behavior, 32*, 918–43.

Matsuda, K., Melde, C., Taylor, J., Freng, A., & Esbensen, F.-A. (2013). Gang membership and adherence to the "code of the street." *Justice Quarterly, 30*, 440–68.

Matsueda, R. L. (1988). The current state of differential association theory. *Crime & Delinquency, 34*, 277–306.

Matsueda, R. L. (1997). "Cultural deviance theory": The remarkable persistence of a flawed term. *Theoretical Criminology, 1*, 429–52.

Matza, D. (1964). *Delinquency and drift*. New York, NY: John Wiley and Sons.

Maume, M. O., Ousey, G. C., & Beaver, K. (2005). Cutting the grass: A reexamination of the link between marital attachment, delinquent peers and desistance from marijuana use. *Journal of Quantitative Criminology, 21*, 27–53.

Maurer, D. W. (1974). *The American confidence man*. Springfield, IL: Charles C. Thomas.

Mears, D. P., Stewart, E. A., Siennick, S. E., & Simons, R. A. (2013). The code of the street and inmate violence: Investigating the salience of imported belief systems. *Criminology, 51*, 695–728.

Meldrum, R. C. & Del Rio, J. E. (2013). Making research methods concepts relevant for students: An illustrative study on low self-control, class attendance, and student performance. *Journal of Criminal Justice Education, 24*, 494–516.

Miller, H. V. (2010). If your friends jumped off a bridge, would you do it too? Delinquent peers and susceptibility to peer influence. *Justice Quarterly, 27*, 473–91.

Miller, J. M., Cohen, A. K., & Bryant, K. M. (1997). On the demise and morrow of subculture theories of crime and delinquency. *Journal of Crime and Justice, 20*, 167–78.

Miller, W. B. (1958). Lower-class culture as a generating milieu of gang delinquency. *Journal of Social Issues, 14*, 5–19.

Miller, W. B. (2011). *City gangs*. With Foreword by S. H. Decker. Arizona State University: http://gangresearch.asu.edu/waltermillerlibrary/walter-b.-miller-book/city-gangs-book/view.

Minor, W. W. (1980). The neutralization of criminal offense. *Criminology, 18*, 103–20.

Minor, W. W. (1981). Techniques of neutralization: A reconceptualization and empirical examination. *Journal of Research in Crime and Delinquency, 18*, 295–318.

Na, C. & Paternoster, R. (2012). Can self-control change substantially over time? Rethinking the relationship between self- and social control. *Criminology, 50*, 427–62.

Nagin, D. S. & Paternoster, R. (1994). Personal capital and social control: The deterrence implications of a theory of individual differences in criminal offending. *Criminology, 32*, 581–606.

Nisbett, R. E. & Cohen, D. (1996). *Culture of honor*. Boulder, CO: Westview Press.

Nowacki, J. S. (2012). Sugar, spice and street codes: The influence of gender and family attachment on street code adoption. *Deviant Behavior, 33*, 831–44.

Odum, H. W. (1951). Edwin H. Sutherland—1883–1950. *Social Forces, 29*, 348–49.

Payne, B. K., Triplett, R. A., & Higgins, G. E. (2011). The relationship between self-control, witnessing domestic violence, and subsequent violence. *Deviant Behavior, 32*, 769–89.

Piquero, A. R. & Tibbetts, S. (1996). Specifying the direct and indirect effects of low self-control and situational factors in offenders' decision making: Toward a more complete model of rational offending. *Justice Quarterly, 13*, 481–510.

Piquero, A. R., Jennings, W. G. & Farrington, D. P. (2010). On the malleability of self-control: Theoretical and policy implications regarding a general theory of crime. *Justice Quarterly, 27,* 801–34.

Piquero, A. R., MacIntosh, R., & Hickman, M. (2000). Does self-control affect survey response? Applying exploratory, confirmatory, and item response theory analysis to Grasmick et al.'s self-control scale. *Criminology, 38,* 897–930.

Piquero, A. R., MacDonald, J., Dobrin, A., Daigle, L. E., & Cullen, F. T. (2005). Self-control, violent offending, and homicide victimization: Assessing the general theory of crime. *Journal of Quantitative Criminology, 21,* 55–71.

Polakowski, M. (1994). Linking self- and social control with deviance: Illuminating the structure underlying a general theory of crime and its relations to deviant activity. *Journal of Quantitative Criminology, 10,* 41–78.

Pratt, T. C. & Cullen, F. T. (2000). The empirical status of Gottfredson and Hirschi's general theory of crime: A meta-analysis. *Criminology, 38,* 931–64.

Pratt, T. C., Turanovic, J. J., Fox, K. A., & Wright, K. A. (2014). Self-control and victimization: A meta-analysis. *Criminology, 52,* 87–116.

Pratt, T. C., Cullen, F. T., Sellers, L., Winfree, T., Madensen, T. D., Daigle, L. E., Fearn, N. E., & Gau, J. M. (2010). The empirical status of social learning theory: A meta-analysis. *Justice Quarterly, 27,* 765–802.

Pridemore, W. A. & Freilich, J. D. (2006). A test of recent subcultural explanations of white violence in the United States. *Journal of Criminal Justice, 34,* 1–16.

Quinn, J. & Koch, S. (2003). The nature of criminality within one-percent motorcycle clubs. *Deviant Behavior, 24,* 281–305.

Ragan, D. T. (2014). Revisiting "what they think": Adolescent drinking and the importance of peer beliefs. *Criminology, 52,* 488–513.

Rankin, J. H. & Kern, R. (1994). Parental attachments and delinquency. *Criminology, 32,* 495–515.

Redmon, D. (2003). Examining low self-control theory at Mardi Gras: Critiquing the general theory of crime within the framework of normative deviance. *Deviant Behavior, 24,* 373–92.

Reed, G. E. & Yeager, P. C. (1996). Organizational offending and neoclassical criminology: Challenging the reach of a general theory of crime. *Criminology, 34,* 357–82.

Rees, C. & Pogarsky, G. (2011). One bad apple may not spoil the whole bunch: Best friends and adolescent delinquency. *Journal of Quantitative Criminology, 27,* 197–223.

Reinarman, C. & Fagan, J. (1988). Social organization and differential association: A research note from a longitudinal study of violent juvenile offenders. *Crime & Delinquency, 34,* 307–27.

Reisig, M. D. & Pratt, T. C. (2011). Low self-control and imprudent behavior revisited. *Deviant Behavior, 32,* 589–625.

Remster, B. (2014). Self-control and the depression-delinquency link. *Deviant Behavior, 35,* 66–84.

Roberts, J. A. & Hunt, S. A. (2012). Social control in a sexually deviant cybercommunity: A capper's code of conduct. *Deviant Behavior, 33,* 757–73.

Schinkel, W. (2002). The modernist myth in criminology. *Theoretical Criminology, 6,* 123–44.

Schoepfer, A., Piquero, N. L., & Langton, L. (2014). Low self-control versus the desire-for-control: An empirical test of white-collar crime and conventional crime. *Deviant Behavior, 35*, 197–214.

Sellers, C. S. (1999). Self-control and intimate violence: An examination of the scope and specification of the general theory of crime. *Criminology, 37*, 375–404.

Sellin, T. (1938). *Culture conflict and crime*. New York, NY: Social Science Research Council.

Shigihara, A. M. (2013). It's only stealing a little a lot: Techniques of neutralization for theft among restaurant workers. *Deviant Behavior, 34*, 494–512.

Stewart, E. A. & Simons, R. L. (2010). Race, code of the street, and violent delinquency: A multi-variate investigation of neighborhood street culture and individual norms of violence. *Criminology, 48*, 569–603.

Stewart, E. A., Elifson, K. W., & Sterk, C. E. (2004). Integrating the general theory of crime into an explanation of violent victimization among female offenders. *Justice Quarterly, 21*, 159–81.

Stogner, J., Miller, B. M., & Marcum, C. D. (2013). Learning to e-cheat: A criminological test of internet facilitated academic cheating. *Journal of Criminal Justice Education, 24*, 175–99.

Stylianou, S. (2002). The relationship between elements and manifestations of low self-control in a general theory of crime: Two comments and a test. *Deviant Behavior, 23*, 531–57.

Sutherland, E. H. (1937). *The professional thief*. Chicago, IL: University of Chicago Press.

Sutherland, E. H. (1949). *White collar crime*. New York, NY: Dryden.

Sutherland, E. H. & Cressey, D. R. (1974). *Criminology* (9th ed.). Philadelphia, PA: J.B. Lippincott.

Sutherland, E. H., Cressey, D. R., and Luckenbill, D. F. (1992). *Principles of criminology* (11th ed.). Lanham, MD: General Hall.

Sykes, G. M. & Matza, D. (1957). Techniques of neutralization: A theory of delinquency. *American Sociological Review, 22*, 664–70.

Thaxton, S. & Agnew, R. (2004). The nonlinear effects of parental and teacher attachment on delinquency: Disentangling strain from social control explanations. *Justice Quarterly, 21*, 763–91.

Thomas, K. J. & McGloin, J. M. (2013). A dual-systems approach for understanding differential susceptibility to processes of peer influence. *Criminology, 51*, 435–74.

Thompson, H. (1966). *Hell's Angels*. New York, NY: Ballantine.

Tittle, C. R. (1995). *Control balance: Toward a general theory of deviance*. Boulder, CO: Westview Press.

Tittle, C. R. & Botchkovar, E. V. (2005). Self-control, criminal motivation and deterrence: An investigation using Russian respondents. *Criminology, 43*, 307–52.

Tittle, C. R., Antonaccio, O., & Botchkovar, E. (2012). Social learning, reinforcement and crime: Evidence from three European cities. *Social Forces, 90*, 863–90.

Tittle, C. R., Burke, M. J., & Jackson, E. F. (1986). Modeling Sutherland's theory of differential association: Toward an empirical clarification. *Social Forces, 65*, 405–32.

Turanovic, J. J. & Pratt, T. C. (2014). "Can't stop, won't stop": Self-control, risky lifestyles, and repeat victimization. *Journal of Quantitative Criminology, 30*, 29–56.

Van de Rakt, M., Ruiter, S., De Graaf, N. D., & Nieuwbeerta, P. (2010). When does the apple fall far from the tree? Static versus dynamic theories in predicting intergenerational transmission of convictions. *Journal of Quantitative Criminology, 26*, 371–89.

Vazsonyi, A. T. & Crosswhite, J. M. (2004). A test of Gottfredson and Hirschi's general theory of crime in African-American adolescents. *Journal of Research in Crime and Delinquency*, *41*, 407–32.

Vazsonyi, A. T. & Klanjšek, R. (2008). A test of self-control theory across different socioeconomic strata. *Justice Quarterly*, *25*, 101–31.

Vine, M. S. W. (1972). Gabriel Tarde (1843–1904). In H. Mannheim (Ed.), *Pioneers in criminology* (pp. 3–11). Montclair, NJ: Patterson Smith.

Wiatrowski, M. D., Griswold, D. B., & Roberts, M. K. (1981). Social control theory and delinquency. *American Sociological Review*, *46*, 525–41.

Williams, F. P., III & McShane, M. D. (1998). *Criminology theory: Selected classic readings* (2nd ed.). Cincinnati, OH: Anderson Publishing Co.

Wolfgang, M. E. (1958/1975). *Patterns in criminal homicide*. Montclair, NJ: Patterson Smith.

Wolfgang, M. E. & Ferracuti, F. (1967). *The subculture of violence*. London, UK: Social Science Paperbacks.

Wood, P. B., Pfefferbaum, B., & Arneklev, B. J. (1993). Risk-taking and self-control: Social psychological correlates of delinquency. *Journal of Crime & Justice*, *16*, 111–30.

Worley, R. M. & Worley, V. B. (2013). Inmate public autoerotism uncovered: Exploring the dynamics of masturbatory behavior within correctional facilities. *Deviant Behavior*, *34*, 11–24.

Wright, B. R. E., Caspi, A., Moffit, T. E., & Silva, P. A. (1999). Low self-control, social bonds, and crime: Social causation, social selection, or both? *Criminology*, *37*, 479–514.

Wright, J. P. & Cullen, F. T. (2000). Juvenile involvement in occupational delinquency. *Criminology*, *38*, 863–96.

Young, J. T. N. (2011). How do they "end up together"? A social network analysis of self-control, homophily, and adolescent relationships. *Journal of Quantitative Criminology*, *27*, 251–73.

Young, J. T. N., Rebellon, C. J., Barnes, J. C., & Weerman, F. M. (2013). Unpacking the black box of peer similarity in deviance: Understanding the mechanism linking personal behavior, peer behavior and perceptions. *Criminology*, *52*, 60–86.

Social Reaction Theories of Crime

LEARNING OBJECTIVES

After reading Chapter 9, you should be able to:

- Explain how the introduction of self-report studies influenced the growth of the labeling perspective.

- Identify the social contexts that contributed to the emergence of the conflict perspective during the 1960s and 1970s.

- Describe the process associated with primary and secondary deviation.

- Provide examples of what is meant by the term "retrospective interpretation."

- Explain the meaning of the term "dramatization of evil."

- Identify Becker's four types of deviants and their relevance for criminological theories.

- Contrast the opposing assumptions and policy recommendations of labeling and deterrence theories with respect to the consequences of formally processing suspected offenders.

- Identify the historical roots of critical criminology.

- Identify the six propositions contained in Quinney's social reality of crime perspective.

- List at least five of the recommendations for confronting crime proposed by Elliott Currie.

- Identify the five social factors that Austin Turk maintained were essential elements in the criminalization process.

Chapters 5 through 8 have examined explanations of crime in terms of the offending individual. Rational choice theorists, for example, employ the concept of free will, and argue that people are rational beings who decide whether or not to violate the law. Biogenic theorists assume that genetic or other differences place some people at high risk of law violation. Social structure and process theorists view the individual as acting within the specific contexts of his or her environment. Depending upon the nature of these contexts, persons are thought to have varying probabilities of becoming involved in criminal activity.

Contrary to these emphases, social reaction theorists focus upon social and institutional responses to the individual. These theorists are not as interested in the initial delinquency or crime as they are in the way in which the act is responded to by social control agents. Social reaction approaches view the individual as a largely passive being who is forced into the role of a criminal by societal definitions or by the reactions of others. As John Curra (2000:viii) asserts at the outset of *The Relativity of Deviance*, "deviance cannot be understood apart from its social context." The social context of crime is indeed important, serving as one of the themes of this book.

Following the introduction and proliferation of self-report methods of studying crime and delinquency, the **labeling perspective** grew both in appeal and acceptance as an explanation of crime and deviance. Labeling theorists maintain that official reactions to law violations label people as criminals and ensnare them in this deviant identity. These theorists further contend that it is not the behavior alone that affects official response, but that the physical characteristics and demeanor of the individual also play major roles in fashioning the response. An interesting study, for instance, conducted by Darrell Steffensmeier and Robert Terry (1973), found that people were much more willing to attribute illegal intentions to individuals fitting a common stereotype. The researchers had four students (two males and two females) pretend to shoplift in a department store (with the manager's knowledge and approval), and recorded witnesses' reactions to the observed behavior. A student of each sex dressed the part of a "preppy," and the other pair dressed in "hippie" fashion (during the 1960s and 1970s, hippies were portrayed as unkempt youths who used illegal drugs and, in general, were nonconformists). As you might guess, people were more likely to report the "shoplifting" of the male hippie than that of any of the others. In decreasing likelihood of being reported were the acts of the female hippie, male preppy, and finally, the female preppy. When questioned, witnesses expressed their willingness to overlook the behavior of the preppy-looking shoplifters because it was inconsistent with the witnesses' pre-established ideas, but they expected no better from "hippies." They also believed that males were more likely to deviate and therefore were more willing to attribute the shoplifting behavior to the male than the female in each pair.

The labeling perspective was widely endorsed by scholars during the 1960s and 1970s. Since then, attempts have been made to evaluate the labeling approach and to better specify its theoretical parameters (e.g., Gove, 1980; Dotter & Roebuck, 1988; Matsueda, 1992; Paternoster & Iovanni, 1989; Huizinga & Henry, 2008). By the end of the 1980s, the early promises of the labeling perspective had been battered by research results, and the theory subsequently lost much of its theoretical glitter (Wellford, 1987). Regardless, sufficient evidence continues to suggest that criminal justice intervention and processing might, in many instances, contribute to an increase in offending rather than serve as a deterrent to future law-breaking. In fact, a recent resurgence in the popularity of labeling theory indicates that many criminologists believe the theory is a viable explanation for deviance amplification, which is discussed later in this chapter. This more recent research draws from elaborations of labeling theory that emphasize the various mechanisms through which official labels lead to increased levels of deviance (e.g., Link, 1982; Matsueda, 1992; Sampson & Laub, 1997). What has come to be known as **critical criminology** also experienced a surge in popularity among American criminologists beginning in the early 1960s, then grew rapidly in the 1970s. As Ray Michalowski (1996) suggests, critical criminology is best viewed as an intellectual movement. The latter part of this chapter briefly reviews the development of critical criminology. This perspective has had substantial impact on criminological thought, even though its fundamental premises may not be widely accepted in totality. Critical criminology is now widely recognized as a competing perspective from which crime may be analyzed and has its own division within the American Society of Criminology. As will be seen, critical criminology has evolved into a very broad perspective encompassing a variety of theories.

As with each theoretical perspective, it is important to recognize the context within which it grew. The social climate in the United States in the 1960s and 1970s was dramatically shaped by the civil rights movement, the Vietnam War, the riots in Watts, Newark, and Detroit, the protests at the 1968 Democratic National Convention in Chicago, the assassinations of President John Kennedy, civil rights leader Martin Luther King Jr., and presidential candidate Robert Kennedy, and the corruption of the Nixon administration culminating with the Watergate scandal. The political and social turmoil of the times created a pervasive mistrust of government and other social institutions. It was a time of wide-scale questioning of authority.

Discriminatory practices against racial minorities and women by the criminal justice system, the educational system, and the business sector were also brought to light. Given this climate, and the active role many educators and students played in the civil rights and antiwar movements, it is not surprising that social scientists began to focus on the role played by political, economic, and other social institutions in shaping societal definitions of legal and illegal behaviors. While the U.S. Department of Justice was investing billions of dollars in law enforcement and corrections, criminologists such as William Chambliss, Austin Turk, and Richard Quinney were insisting that those in power manipulated the law for their own interests. Others, including non-conflict theorists, were documenting the deleterious societal effects of white-collar and corporate crime. The first decade of the twenty-first century bore witness to the disastrous effects of Wall Street greed, often reflected in illegal activities such as insider trading and Ponzi schemes. Perhaps it is time to direct more attention to crime in the suites rather than concentrate on crime in the streets.

LABELING THEORY

Labeling and social conflict theories provide a critical perspective for the examination of major assumptions in criminology. Labeling theory has its foundation in the works of George Herbert Mead and Charles Horton Cooley. These early twentieth-century sociologists are associated with the theoretical framework known as symbolic interaction, a perspective emphasizing individual levels of behavior, as opposed to the group-level emphasis of the social structure theorists. Cooley is best known for his development of the "looking-glass self" concept. He argued that our understanding of ourselves is primarily a reflection of our perception of how others react to us; that is, we see ourselves through others. George Herbert Mead elaborated upon this concept by focusing attention on the interaction between an emerging self and the perceptions of others' reactions to that self. According to Mead (1934), this dynamic interplay between the individual and others leads to the development of a self-concept that affects subsequent behavior.

Labeling theory is built upon this foundation. Its proponents argue that the individual is a constantly changing being who responds to others' reactions. A formal response by the criminal justice system, labeling theorists contend, forces the individual to re-assess his or her personal identity. Additionally, others who become aware of the apprehension and official response re-evaluate their opinions about the individual. This process of reassessment is the basis of the labeling perspective. Note that this is precisely the opposite of deterrence theory. Deterrence proposes to reduce future criminal or delinquent behavior through application of punitive responses, while those same punishments will cause more aberrant behavior according to labeling theory.

Consider the example of Lisa, a recent high-school graduate who plans to enroll at the state university in the fall. A week after graduation, Lisa attends a party at which cocaine and marijuana are available. She tries both drugs for the first time, and a friend gives her a small vial of cocaine for later use. On her way home, Lisa encounters a police sobriety checkpoint. While she is getting her driver's license out of her purse, the vial of cocaine accidentally falls into Lisa's lap. She is arrested on suspicion of possession of a controlled substance. After being formally processed, Lisa receives a six-month probation sentence on the condition that she enrolls in a drug treatment clinic. In the eyes of the law, she is now a convicted criminal. The personal and social ramifications of the labeling process are far greater, however, than the mere acquisition of the label "criminal." Lisa's parents, friends, neighbors, and high school teachers now see her in a different light. No longer is Lisa perceived as the intelligent, motivated young woman they had known; now she is suspect, and is viewed as a potentially bad influence on "decent" kids. Lisa's self-image also may undergo a transformation. She perceives others as avoiding her, or talking behind her back; she begins to view herself as an outsider and moves toward the acceptance of those going to the drug clinic as her true friends. The labeling process is complete: the formal label has been applied, significant others have reacted to the official label, and Lisa has accepted the label and adjusted her self-concept and peer affiliations.

While this hypothetical case may be extreme, it highlights major issues identified by labeling theorists. First, of primary importance to labeling theorists is what transpires after an act, not what caused or precipitated the act. Second, deviance is a property conferred upon an act; it is not something inherent in the act (Erikson, 1962). That is, Lisa's experimentation with cocaine and possession of the vial was not deviant until it was officially tagged as such by the arresting officer and others. Third, the labeling of an individual is a process of symbolic interaction between the "deviant" and significant others. Edwin Lemert (1951) referred to this as *secondary deviance*. Fourth, the labeling process is affected by who does the labeling and by how the labeled person reacts to the label. Fifth, the act of labeling may lead to **retrospective interpretation** of the individual's prior behavior. For example, the fact that Lisa colored her hair orange two weeks before her arrest will now be seen as "another" indication that she is indeed a drug abuser; before the new hair color had been regarded as a "phase." Sixth, a deviant label such as that of "criminal" or "drug abuser" becomes a pivotal status that overrides other personal attributes. In our example, Lisa is now defined as a drug abuser first and foremost, and this label affects how others will respond to her. Consequently, the probability of further criminal behavior (secondary deviance) is enhanced. A deterrence theorist, on the other hand, would predict less likelihood of future misconduct by Lisa as she should have learned the consequences. Highlight 9.1 provides an extreme example of the powerful effect of informal labeling by peers.

HIGHLIGHT 9.1   IS A LOSER'S LABEL WORTH KILLING OVER?

Some have concluded that in the minds of Eric Harris and Dylan Klebold, it *was*. The two boys stormed Columbine High School in Colorado, killing 13 before taking their own lives. The most common account given for this horrendous action is that they were outcasts. Their targeting of specific individuals who were popular and affiliated with mainstream groups lends credence to this interpretation.

In the aftermath of the tragedy, many high school students around the country were pledging efforts to not taunt, bully, or mock others (Miller, 1999). There has been a lot of agreement that labeling may trigger horrendous behavior on the part of those labeled as misfits, losers, and weirdos. Such tragedies may lead to reassessment of labeling in this context.

Frank Tannenbaum—Dramatization of Evil

While the 1960s and 1970s saw a proliferation of books and articles advocating the labeling perspective (e.g., Kitsuse, 1962; Becker, 1963; Goffman, 1963; Lofland, 1969; and Schur, 1973), its origins can be found in Frank Tannenbaum's 1938 publication, *Crime and the Community*. Tannenbaum sought to expand the ability of existing theories to explain criminal behavior by focusing on what transpired after an individual had been caught and identified as having violated a law. Tannenbaum termed this process of social reaction to illegal behavior the **dramatization of evil**. He contended that criminals are not inherently different from the rest of the population, but that specific acts in a person's overall repertoire of behaviors are singled out and brought to public attention. The following excerpt highlights how a person who commits a single deviant act is transformed:

> There is a gradual shift from the definition of the specific act as evil to a definition of the individual as evil, so that all his acts come to be looked upon with suspicion. . . . From the community's point of view, the individual who used to do bad and mischievous things has now become a bad and unredeemable human being. From the individual's point of view, there has taken place a similar change. . . . The young delinquent becomes bad because he is not believed if he is good (Tannenbaum, 1938:17–18).

Dramatization of evil is related to **legal relativism**, another concept introduced by Tannenbaum. Acts, he insisted, are neither inherently good nor evil; there are varying degrees of good and evil, and the social audience influences the label placed upon specific behavior. The same behavior engaged in by individuals of different social status or in varying settings may be responded to quite differently. Being drunk at a fraternity party, for example, is not treated in the same manner as drunken behavior during a final exam. What is appropriate or at least tolerable behavior in one situation may be frowned upon in another.

Edwin M. Lemert—Primary and Secondary Deviation

The next major contribution to the labeling perspective was made by Edwin Lemert in his 1951 publication, *Social Pathology*. Lemert is known particularly for distinguishing between primary and secondary deviation. **Primary deviation** refers to occasional or situational behavior that may be excused or rationalized by the actor and/or the social audience. Driving 45 miles per hour in a 30 miles-per-hour zone, for example, can be rationalized by statements such as: "Everybody else is going that fast." Being drunk in public and making obscene comments is excused when the audience is told that the group is returning from a "bachelor's party." However, when such behaviors become a regular and prominent part of the actor's identity, the situation is no longer primary deviation.

Lemert wrote that "when a person begins to employ his deviant behavior or a role based upon it as a means of defense, attack, or adjustment to the overt and covert problems created by the consequent societal reaction to him, his deviation is secondary" (1951:76). **Secondary deviation** is the result of a dynamic interaction between the individual's deviation and the societal response to the deviation. Lemert described this process in the following manner (1951:77):

The sequence of interaction leading to secondary deviation is roughly as follows:

1. Primary deviation;
2. Social penalties;
3. Further primary deviation;
4. Stronger penalties and rejection;
5. Further deviation, perhaps with hostilities and resentment beginning to focus upon those doing the penalizing;
6. Crisis reached in the tolerance quotient, expressed in formal action by the community stigmatizing of the deviant;
7. Strengthening of the deviant conduct as a reaction to the stigmatizing and penalties;
8. Ultimate acceptance of deviant social status and efforts at adjustment on the basis of the associated role.

Once the process of secondary deviation results in the labeling of an individual, it becomes extremely difficult for the person to escape classification as a deviant. Lemert maintained that official reactions such as arrests, court hearings, and investigations by public welfare agencies usually exacerbate the situation and often cause dramatic redefinitions of the self. Thus, the process of formally responding to a criminal or deviant act, Lemert would argue, is likely to cause further criminal activity.

Howard S. Becker—Secret Deviants and the Falsely Accused

Howard S. Becker was one of the more prominent proponents of labeling theory to emerge during the 1960s. His now classic work, *Outsiders: Studies in the Sociology of Deviance*, first published in 1963, delineated several key elements of labeling theory as it is known today. Among these is his assertion that deviants and criminals are themselves not a homogeneous group. Aside from the fact that someone who commits a burglary may be very different from a rapist, some individuals are labeled deviant even though they have never committed a deviant or criminal act. Still others commit law violations but are never apprehended or even detected. By grouping the vast assortment of criminals together and by including what Becker called the *"falsely accused,"* we wind up with quite a heterogeneous collection of people. Along these lines, Becker wrote (1963:9):

[S]ocial groups create deviance by making the rules whose infraction constitutes deviance, and by applying those rules to particular people and labeling them as outsiders. From this point of view, deviance is not a quality of the act the person commits but rather a consequence of the application by others of rules and sanctions to an "offender." The deviant is one to whom that label has successfully been applied; deviant behavior is behavior that people so label.

TABLE 9.1 Adaptation of Becker's Typology of Deviant Behavior

	Conforming Behavior	Norm-violating Behavior
Perceived as deviant	Falsely accused	Pure deviant
Not perceived as deviant	Conformist	Secret deviant

To amplify this belief that criminal and deviant behavior are social artifacts, Becker presented a typology depicting four different types of deviants and nondeviants. Table 9.1 presents these types. The **conformist** and the **pure deviant** are both accurately perceived by society in terms of their actual behaviors. The other two types, however, are often misjudged. The **falsely accused** have been identified as deviants or criminals, perhaps due to their sex, age, race, social status, peer group affiliation, or physical appearance. While these incorrectly placed labels may be more frequently found in nonlegal settings, studies also have documented the existence of falsely accused individuals serving long prison sentences, many on death row (Bedau & Radelet, 1987; Huff, 2002). As of November 2014, the Innocence Project, a public policy organization dedicated to exonerating wrongfully convicted individuals, reports that 321 cases have been exonerated through DNA testing (www.innocenceproject.org/, accessed November 4, 2014).

Secret deviants are able to avoid detection or witnesses may fail to impose a criminal or deviant label on the actions. According to what we know from self-report studies, *secret deviants* comprise a large group; many criminal violations are never brought to the attention of the police.

These four criminal types can cause analytical problems for criminologists. The falsely accused individual, for instance, may appear in official records as a criminal and criminologists may attempt to explain the causes of this person's criminality in the same manner as they do that of the pure deviant. Labeling theorists would contend that it is appropriate to examine the effects of the label once it has been placed, irrespective of its accuracy. This, in part, can be attributed to the conceptualization of deviance as a **master status**. Borrowing from an article by Everett C. Hughes, Becker suggested that a deviant or criminal label becomes a master status with a number of assumed auxiliary statuses. A doctor, for example, is generally assumed to be male, white, upper-middle class, and Protestant or Jewish. In the same vein, a criminal is assumed to be an undesirable person who has no respect for the law and is

Michael Hanline leaves the Ventura County Jail on November 24, 2014. The 69-year-old man spent 36 years incarcerated for a murder prosecutors now say he did not commit.

CREDIT:
AP Photo/*The Ventura County Star*, Anthony Plascencia.

likely to commit any number of offenses in order to obtain what he (being male is an auxiliary status of criminals) wants.

Another concept introduced by Becker is that of **moral entrepreneurs**, that is, individuals who either serve as rule creators or rule enforcers. Becker identified the prototype of these rule creators as a moral crusader, a person who "feels that nothing can be right in the world until rules are made to correct it" (Becker, 1963:148). Prohibitionists in their campaign against alcoholic beverages are good examples of moral entrepreneurs who wanted to impose their standards upon others. While they sometimes are viewed as busybodies, many moral crusaders are motivated by a humanitarian drive. They believe that their moral values are superior to those of others and that adoption of their positions will produce a better or more decent life for all.

We must ask, as do labeling theorists: Who creates rules and who is regulated by those rules? Becker maintained that moral entrepreneurs tend to be members of the upper classes who typically want to help those beneath them to achieve a better status. That those beneath them do not always like the means proposed for their salvation is another matter. Moral entrepreneurs seek to regulate morals—be they within the realm of alcohol, drugs, sexual activity, human reproduction (e.g., abortion), child-rearing practices, or work habits. As is central to the social reaction perspective, it is not the objective behavior of "deviants" that varies and requires explanation. It is the relative success of moral entrepreneurs in controlling deviance through redefining it to coincide with their moral perspective. One successful strategy for redefining or creating deviance is to cultivate a "moral panic"—a public perception of behaviors or groups of persons that greatly exaggerate their potential for harm to the larger society. Such a response to contemporary gangs serves as an example of moral panic as described in Gang Feature 9.1.

Edwin M. Schur—Radical Nonintervention

A controversial book by Edwin Schur epitomized the labeling perspective's position regarding the effect of processing juveniles through the justice system. Published in 1973, *Radical Nonintervention: Rethinking the Delinquency Problem* argued that nothing should be done with or to children who violate the law. The **radical nonintervention** argument proposed that most adolescent rule-breaking is petty in nature and that punishment is unnecessary. Society should take a more tolerant stance and allow adolescents to experiment with a wide array of behavioral alternatives. To do otherwise, Schur maintained, serves only to label and to isolate youths from legitimate roles.

Schur agreed with Becker that the label "delinquent" is a master status and difficult to overcome. Furthermore, due in part to the alleged discriminatory practices of the justice system, Schur contended that lower-class, African-American males are more likely to be officially labeled than are other youths. This occurs in part because of the lack of power among juveniles in general and lower-class, African-American males in particular. These individuals are, for instance, unable to pay for legal counsel or to argue effectively with the police not to press charges.

GANG FEATURE 9.1 MORAL PANIC!

In their article, "Moral Panic and the Response to Gangs in California," Jackson and Rudman examined California's response to the growing youth gang problem of the 1980s. As discussed in earlier chapters, the primary response to gangs has been suppression. Jackson and Rudman attempt to account for this public policy response based on a belief in the deterrability of these behavioral patterns.

Gangs and their members garnered the attention and interest of the media during the mid-1980s. "Gangsta rap" and "wannabe" became part of the common vernacular as MTV and VH1 exposed the world to the gang lifestyle. Gangs such as the Crips, Bloods, Vice Lords, and Gangster Disciples were featured in the evening news and in the local papers. Hollywood also joined this media frenzy, producing feature-length movies depicting the gang lifestyle, usually with an emphasis on the violence and drug dealing aspects that would appeal to movie-goers. Local, state, and federal government agencies responded to this publicity. A number of initiatives in law enforcement and in research endeavors were promoted in response to this gang phenomenon.

The popular image of gangs presented by the mass media and furthered by law enforcement was that of juveniles possessing a cache of high-power weapons and engaging in a lucrative drug trade. "These gangs were characterized either as instrumental groups or vaguely defined youth street gangs whose overriding purpose was to make large amounts of money through the distribution and sale of crack and other drugs" (Jackson & Rudman, 1993:258). The general public was left with the belief that vast profits and luxurious lifestyles were common to these "gang bangers" and that because of the money available, gang members were drawn primarily from poor and minority youths with limited legitimate employment opportunities.

Jackson and Rudman provided the following examples of how media coverage spread this image of gang members:

- With the added pressure being put on gangs dealing drugs in the Los Angeles area, we're going to see a further increase in their dealing drugs in Sacramento (Sacramento Mayor's Task Force Final Report on Drug Abuse, 1988).

- Entire Sacramento neighborhoods are now at risk of becoming the Northern California rendition of south-central L.A. because of the rock cocaine plague and the gangs that brought it here. Residents of some areas . . . contend with almost daily drive-by shootings, brawls, fights, and vandalism, not to mention the devastation wrought by those hooked on rock; prostitution, child abandonment and abuse, theft and drug-induced insanity (Sacramento Bee, 1988).

As a result also in part of deaths of innocent bystanders (frequently killed in gang "drive-bys"), the public willingly and eagerly believed reports about "the intimidation of potential witnesses to gang-related activities, reports of increasing gang violence in schools, gang graffiti, drug-related commitments to local facilities, and drug-related arrests" (Jackson & Rudman, 1993:259). This perception was associated with a concern that gangs would continue to increase in size and power unless additional resources were provided to law enforcement. There appeared to be a belief that gangs were more heavily armed than the police, and that the only way to respond to the gang problem was to increase the budgets and staff of the police.

Jackson and Rudman examined California's legislative response to gangs, concluding that the "evidence to date suggests that the nature of the reaction to the 'gang problem' in California is similar to other instances of what has been referred to as 'moral panics.' Where a perceived threat of an individual or group greatly surpasses their actual threat the setting is ripe for the characterization of it as a 'moral panic'" (Jackson & Rudman, 1993:271).

Schur also discussed the concept of retrospective interpretation, which was introduced by John Kitsuse (1962), another early advocate of the labeling perspective. Retrospective interpretation refers to the process by which people re-interpret an individual's past behavior in light of new information concerning that individual. Schur and others have argued that a delinquent label serves as a prompt for others to re-evaluate things that a child has said or done in the past and then redefine these matters so they are made consistent with the new information (e.g., the new hair color of our hypothetical Lisa is reinterpreted in light of her arrest for possession of a controlled substance).

OVERVIEW OF LABELING PERSPECTIVE

Drawing on the seminal works previously reviewed, we can summarize the labeling perspective. Because it incorporates such a wide range of thought, many view it as a general perspective for understanding crime and delinquency rather than as a concise theory. It is also seen by many to be more applicable to juveniles than to adults based upon the assumption that youths are, for better or worse, more malleable than are adults. In other words, just as it is often argued that a youth may be more amenable to rehabilitative intervention than an adult, the labeling perspective holds that interventions also have more potential for backfiring and creating a delinquent self-image among them. However, given the imperfection of the criminal justice system (many adult offenders fail to be detected and/or prosecuted while other innocent individuals are falsely convicted), the labeling perspective may nonetheless still be applicable to the processing of adults in the system.

The labeling process is a circular one as depicted in Figure 9.1. First, as efforts of moral entrepreneurs are successful in redefining more conduct as criminal or delinquent, the deviance net is broadened. Successful criminalization of more behaviors will expand the ranks of offenders. More behaviors will be

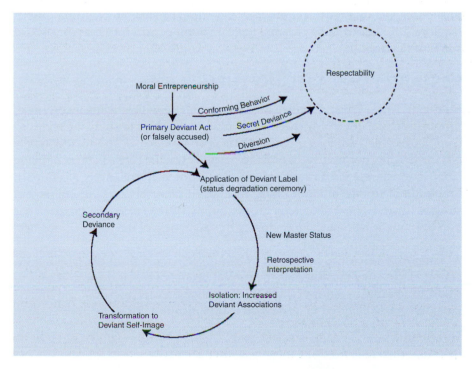

FIGURE 9.1
The labeling/deviance spiral.

construed as primary deviance and will lead to initiation of the labeling process. The process will be applied to others who are falsely accused. Otherwise, those who are conformists and secret deviants will retain respectability, while diversion programs are intended to preserve respectability for identified deviants. Those to whom the label is otherwise successfully applied become deviants as a result of status degradation ceremonies. The juvenile who is adjudicated at the conclusion of a hearing, for example, assumes the new master status of "juvenile delinquent." As a consequence of the successful labeling, the deviant is isolated from "respectable" influences and resorts to increased associations with similarly situated persons. This contributes to transformation of the person's self-image to a deviant one, setting the stage for secondary deviance. From this point, a spiral away from respectability and moving more deeply into deviance continues.

Once again, it may be helpful to frame the labeling hypothesis in terms of personal experiences and observations. Have you ever engaged in any behaviors that, if detected, could have labeled you a delinquent? Did any of your friends do so? Self-report data suggest that we would have difficulty finding anyone who did not! Perhaps you committed a few delinquent acts, got caught, were punished, and were better off for it. If not caught and adjudicated as a delinquent, maybe it would have been best if you had been. That is, punishment might keep people out of future trouble by teaching them a lesson (i.e., specific deterrence). On the other hand, it might be that being caught and officially labeled would have made you or your friend more, rather than less, likely to commit additional delinquent acts. Labeling theory maintains that kids will misbehave, but that most will outgrow it without official intervention; official labeling, it is argued, may propel a typical young person into that downward spiral of deviance.

RESEARCH ON LABELING THEORY

Charles R. Tittle (1980) identified two basic problems with labeling theory. First, propositions are not clearly specified to allow researchers to study the relationship between key variables. Second, there is an absence of data to adequately test the labeling perspective. In order to properly test the consequences of being labeled, longitudinal data are necessary and, prior to the relatively recent past, longitudinal studies in criminology have been relatively rare. Several recent studies, however, have addressed the second of Tittle's criticisms. Progress has also been made with regard to reducing the vagueness of the propositions necessary to test labeling theory.

Tittle noted that two propositions can be generated from the labeling literature. First, labeling, especially by formal agents of social control, is said to result in negative reactions by others once they become aware of the official label, a process referred to as **deviance amplification**. This response is often associated with the "attribution of bad character and stereotypical behavioral expectations" (Tittle, 1980:247). Second, labeling theorists posit that official processing is more heavily influenced by personal and social characteristics than by actual norm violations.

With respect to the first hypothesis, an early study by Richard Schwartz and Jerome Skolnick (1962) highlighted the effect of official criminal justice processing on future job employment. Four folders were prepared describing a single, 32-year-old male with a history of short-term jobs as kitchen helper, maintenance worker, and handyman. The only difference in the four folders was the applicant's reported record of criminal court involvement. Folder 1 indicated that the applicant had been convicted and sentenced for assault. Folder 2 stated that he had been tried and acquitted, while folder 3 included a letter from a judge certifying the applicant had been found not guilty. The fourth folder made no mention of a criminal record.

Twenty-five copies of each folder were sent to a sample of 100 prospective employers in a resort area. Results tended to confirm the labeling perspective. Nine positive responses were received from the folders indicating no criminal justice system involvement. This compared to lower responses for the folders with letters (six), with acquittal (three), and with a conviction (one). Schwartz and Skolnick (1962:135) commented upon this result in the following manner:

> From a theoretical point of view, the finding leads toward the conclusion that conviction constitutes a powerful form of "status degradation," which continues to operate after the time when, according to the generalized theory of justice underlying punishment in our society, the individual's "debt" has been paid. A record of conviction produces a durable if not permanent loss of status.

With the introduction of sex offender registries across the United States, one can witness the immense consequences of such a conviction. In spite of having paid their debt to society by completing their prison sentences, this master status continues to degrade their status in society (see Highlight 9.2).

In an interesting application of the labeling perspective Shadd Maruna and his colleagues (2004) turned their attention to desistance from crime, focusing less on the reactions of others than on the self-identity of the offender. While prior work has tended to examine the effects of labeling on subsequent life chances, these authors were interested in the process of desistance from crime and the establishment of an offender's credentials, or self-image, as a reformed person. One interesting outcome of their interviews with counselors and clients at a treatment facility in upstate New York was that "like social scientists, neither the clients nor counselors we interviewed had an agreed upon standard for determining whether a person has 'rehabilitated' or 'reformed'" (Maruna et al., 2004:276). In explaining the process of desistance, the researchers borrowed from Lemert's notion of primary and secondary deviation and introduced the concepts of *primary desistance*

HIGHLIGHT 9.2 IS A "SEX OFFENDER" LABEL WORTH DYING FOR?

Thomas Varnum, a convicted sex offender in Maine, concluded in 1997 that it was worth dying for a "sex offender" label. He had served three and a half years in prison for befriending a nine-year-old boy and having sex with him repeatedly over a six-month period. Paroled for a year and a half, he was employed in construction and working as a mechanic on weekends. His landlord did not know of his conviction, but said he was a good tenant. While the new Megan's Law, a version of which had passed in Maine and some 40 other states, could not be applied to him retroactively, the sheriff's department found a way. Based on an old law that allowed the release of information about convictions, deputies circulated flyers about Varnum on the road where he lived. They included his mug shot, address, and notice that he was convicted of gross sexual assault. Following neighbors' calls, Varnum's landlord asked that he move. The next evening he used a shotgun to blow the top of his head off.[1]

Another convicted sex offender, Nate Sims, chose to pack his bags and run . . . again. Sims had been convicted of the rape and sodomy of a woman and served a 20-year prison term. Upon returning to his hometown of Danville, Kentucky, he found his picture and the "sex offender" label in the newspaper. This cost him the job he had just obtained and he was arrested for violating parole by living in his car rather than his registered address. But his luck briefly changed when a local born-again Christian family offered him a bedroom in their affluent home. The couple asked, "What would Jesus do?" But their neighbors asked how they could do that and deluged them with flyers, anonymous letters, phone calls, and visits to their business. When camera crews arrived, Nate packed his bags and left his new home and another new job. These results of aggressive labeling strategies raise many questions. What are the moral rights of persons concerned with protection of their families from "risky" residents? What are the rights of "sex offenders" to re-establish their lives—to work and live somewhere?

[1]Adapted from Schwartz, J., (1998). *Johnson City Press*, 3–22–98; Breed, A.G. (1999). *Johnson City Press*, 9–2–99.

In Vermont, an online sex offender registry provides the public with a photograph of each offender, plus name, aliases, and other information.

CREDIT: AP Photo/Toby Talbot.

and *secondary desistance* to distinguish the temporary desistance all offenders experience from the "changed person" identity that only a subset experience. They suggest that desistance from crime consists of a process of negotiation that ultimately can produce a change in self-identity. This process of desistance is similar to the labeling process—only in reverse. For desistance to occur, they suggest that a "delabeling process" and "decertification" stage are important.

In an early adoption of longitudinal data to examine the labeling perspective, Suzanne Ageton and Delbert Elliott used a six-year longitudinal study of 2,617 California youths answer two questions: "Does legal processing create and/or promote an increased orientation toward delinquency?" and "What effect, if any, do other environmental and behavioral factors such as peer group affiliations and self-reported delinquent behavior play in this process?" (Ageton & Elliott, 1974:89). Their analyses showed that legal processing "creates and/or heightens an orientation toward delinquency." Furthermore, the authors also found that Anglos and males were more negatively affected by police contact than were Mexican Americans, African Americans, and females.

A more recent study of 2,614 American youths by Stephanie Wiley and Finn Esbensen (2013) confirms that official labels are associated with changes in orientations toward delinquency, as well as involvement in delinquent behavior. The researchers used a relatively new statistical technique to match three groups of individuals: (1) those who did not report official contact with the police, (2) a group that had been stopped and questioned by the police, and (3) a third group that had been arrested. Using propensity score matching, the researchers were able to match individuals on the basis of 17 covariates (e.g., demographic, attitudinal, and behavioral measures) at Time 1. This matching procedure produced three groups that were similar in all regards with the exception of their involvement with law enforcement. The researchers relied upon police contact at Time 2 and then subsequent attitudes and behavior at Time 3 to examine the effect of the police contact. By controlling for preexisting differences and by controlling for the temporal ordering of variables, the researchers were able to assess the unique effect of arrest (and being stopped) on attitudes and behavior. As labeling theorists hypothesized, the authors found that those youths who had been arrested had significantly more negative attitudes and higher rates of delinquency than those youths who had experienced no police contact. Specifically, compared with those youths with no police contact, the arrested youths were more delinquent, were more committed to deviant peers, and held more delinquent attitudes. Importantly, even those youths who reported being stopped and questioned by the police held more negative attitudes and reported higher levels of delinquency than did those youths with no contact.

Another study that used propensity score matching to examine the effects of arrest on later behavior found similar support for labeling theory. Liberman, Kirk, and Kim (2014) analyzed the relationship between arrest and later delinquency among a sample of 1,249 youths from a sample of Chicago neighborhoods. Their findings indicated that youths who were arrested committed a greater variety of offenses later on and were also more likely to commit violent offenses. In addition to increased delinquent behavior, the authors also found that arrested youths were much more likely to experience "secondary sanctioning" in the form of rearrest. Together, the results from these more recent studies provide support for the labeling perspective with contemporary datasets and more rigorous analytic methods.

Ruth Triplett (1993) also examined informal reactions in considering factors that contribute to parents labeling their children delinquent. Triplett agreed that informal responses may be more salient than formal responses because of the importance the labeled actor assigns the labeler. Being viewed as delinquent by a parent may be far more traumatic than being so labeled by an official of the juvenile justice system. Examining data from a national sample of 1,324 youths, Triplett found the parental labeling to be a function of the youths' grades, delinquent friendships, relationships with parents, parental beliefs, and race as well as their delinquent activities. These findings suggest that whether parents identify their offspring as delinquents depends more on how they fit the stereotype than on the child's actual behavior. Labeling theory asserts, however, that such labeling or stereotyping may cause further delinquent behavior.

In another study, Eric Stewart and his colleagues (2002) relied on in-depth interviews with rural Iowa families to test the extent to which delinquent behavior and subsequent arrest affected family relationships (specifically parenting practices). Importantly, the longitudinal data allowed these authors to examine the subsequent effect of parenting practices on delinquency. They concluded: "As expected, greater involvement in delinquency and poorer parenting behaviors at time 1 increased the probability of legal sanctions. Legal sanctions, in turn, predicted further increases in delinquency and decreases in parenting quality one year later at time 3" (Stewart et al., 2002:52).

Along the same lines as Stewart's research, Jon Gunnar Bernburg and his colleagues (Bernburg & Krohn 2003; Bernburg et al., 2006) analyzed data from the Rochester Youth Development Study. In their first article, Bernburg and Krohn (2003) found that arrest and juvenile justice intervention in early adolescence was negatively related to the likelihood of high school graduation, which in turn affected employment which was linked to adult crime. In addition to this mediating effect of juvenile justice intervention on high school graduation and employment, they also found the intervention to have a direct effect on adult crime. In their subsequent research, Bernburg and colleagues (2006) explored the extent to which arrest affected peer group affiliation. As Becker (1963) had hypothesized early in the history of the labeling perspective, they found that police arrest appears to influence social networks; arrested youths increased association with delinquent peers following an arrest. This change in social networks, in turn, led to an increase in subsequent offending. Other recent appraisals of labeling theory have also found support for the negative effects of both formal (Hagan & Palloni, 1990; Huizinga et al., 2003; Sweeten, 2006; Chiricos et al., 2007; Wiley & Esbensen, 2013; Wiley, Slocum, & Esbensen, 2013; Lopes et al., 2012; Kirk & Sampson, 2013; Liberman et al., 2014;) and informal labeling (Matsueda, 1992; Heimer & Matsueda, 1994; Triplett & Jarjoura, 1994). In a systematic review of longitudinal research assessing the effects of arrest on subsequent behavior, Huizinga and Henry (2008) report that the majority (17 studies) of these studies found an increase or no change in delinquency following an arrest. Only two studies reported a decrease in subsequent offending. (See Highlight 9.3 for recent research assessing the amplification of deviance hypothesis.)

Contrary to the preceding studies supportive of labeling theory, several investigations have failed to substantiate the labeling hypotheses. In an early study, Jack Foster, Simon Dinitz, and Walter Reckless (1972) learned from their study of 196 boys that only a few indicated that their public image had suffered as a consequence of their contact with authorities. For the most part, the boys did not feel that their interpersonal relationships were negatively affected, although some believed that their prospective employment might be harmed due to having a police record. In an investigation into the effect of formal processing on self-attitudes, Gary Jensen (1972) discovered a difference by race; African-American adolescents who have contact with the police are less likely to think of themselves as delinquents than are white adolescents. Jensen also reported that, in general, delinquents have lower self-evaluations than do nondelinquents.

HIGHLIGHT 9.3 LABELING THEORY—RECENT RESEARCH FINDINGS

Calls for increased attention to the multiple pathways through which official labels lead to later delinquency (e.g., Bernburg, 2009; Huizinga & Henry, 2008; Paternoster & Iovanni, 1989) have prompted researchers to use extensive longitudinal datasets to examine the labeling process in greater detail. In one such study, researchers (Wiley, Slocum, and Esbensen, 2013) used multiple analytic techniques to examine the effects of police contact (i.e., being stopped and questioned or arrested) on later delinquency. The authors relied on data from a longitudinal sample of 2,127 students enrolled in public schools in seven cities across the United States, using both propensity score matching and path analysis, to examine the effects of police contact on delinquency through three primary pathways: deviant identity and attitudes, social exclusion and attenuated prosocial bonds, and involvement

with delinquent groups. The authors found that both being stopped and questioned and arrested were linked to higher levels of delinquency, in part, through each of these mechanisms. Specifically, they found that poor grades, deviant attitudes, and delinquent peers partially explained increases in delinquency among youth who were stopped or arrested. Wiley and colleagues (2013) reported that these findings are consistent with the labeling perspective, but also noted that a large direct effect of contact on delinquency is not explained by the labeling pathways included in their study. That is, independent of the effects through deviant identity and attitudes, social exclusion and attenuated prosocial bonds, and involvement with delinquent groups, being stopped was associated with a 19 percent increase in delinquency, while being arrested was linked to a 54 percent increase in delinquency.

The study by Steffensmeier and Terry (1973) detailed at the outset of this chapter provides firm support for the effect of personal characteristics on the decision to prosecute. In a more carefully controlled study, Lawrence Cohen and Rodney Stark (1974) examined 371 shoplifting cases at a large metropolitan department store and the manager's decision whether to prosecute. Contrary to what would be predicted by labeling theorists, personal characteristics such as age, race, and sex were found to be unrelated to the decision. One variable that did help to explain the decision to prosecute was the value of the stolen merchandise. The authors concluded that deviance, at least in this setting, was not "in the eyes of the beholder."

POLICY RELEVANCE OF LABELING THEORY

Stemming in large measure from the labeling theory literature, changes in the rehabilitation model of the 1960s were evident by the mid-1970s. In particular, diversion programs aimed at preventing offenders from penetrating the formal process of the criminal justice system sprang up around the country.

While most of these programs targeted juvenile populations, the same rationale applies to adult groups. In addition to the labeling argument, the United States began experiencing drastic overcrowding in its juvenile and adult correctional facilities during the 1970s. Diversion programs were thus advocated on two fronts: avoidance of negative labeling associated with formal processing and cost savings from reducing the prison population. See Highlight 9.4 for an interesting cross-national examination of the effect of arrest on subsequent offending.

Debate soon arose about the value of diversion as a means of avoiding formal processing. A number of studies concluded that diversion resulted in

HIGHLIGHT 9.4 THE EFFECTS OF ARREST ON SUBSEQUENT BEHAVIOR: A CROSS-NATIONAL COMPARISON

The justice system in Bremen is quite lenient in its treatment of 14- to 17-year-olds in that more than 90 percent of cases referred to the prosecutor are dismissed or diverted. In the Denver study, arrest is a relatively common phenomenon with 73 percent of the males and 43 percent of the females having been arrested by age 18. The arrest figures for Bremen were 34 percent and 9 percent, respectively, for males and females. Confinement is rare in Bremen in contrast to Denver where 10–20 percent of cases result in confinement. Despite quite different justice philosophies, the prevalence of delinquency in the two cities is remarkably similar (between 62 and 69 percent of juveniles are involved in delinquent activity during the adolescent years). David Huizinga and his colleagues (2003) state; "given the substantial difference in orientation of the two systems, it is surprising that there is not a greater difference in offending."

Huizinga and colleagues were interested in the extent to which these different justice system orientations affected adolescent offending. Four different analysis strategies

(cross-tabulations, multinomial regression, event history models, and a precision control group matching analysis) produced the same results. "In all the analyses, there was very little effect of arrest on subsequent delinquent behavior. When there was an effect, arrest resulted either in maintaining the previous level of delinquency (persistence) or increasing subsequent delinquent behavior. There was essentially no indication at the individual level at either site that arrest resulted in a decrease in delinquent behavior" (2003:3).

The fact that very similar findings regarding the effect of arrest on subsequent offending were obtained in two sites with such different justice systems, one characterized as lenient and the other as punitive, suggests that the findings are quite robust. Arrest does not produce the deterrent effect that proponents of specific deterrence would predict. The authors of the study call for "greater concern about and discussion of the current U.S. orientation toward increased criminalization of behaviors and increased severity of sanctions" (Huizinga et al., 2003:5).

net-widening of the social control process (e.g., Klein et al., 1976; Dunford, 1977; Blomberg, 1980). Edwin Lemert, for example, wrote: "What began as an effort to reduce discretion in juvenile justice became a warrant to increase discretion and external control where none existed before" (1981:45). And, in a summary of studies examining the net-widening issue, James Austin and Barry Krisberg (1981:170) concluded that "diversion programs have been transformed into a means for extending the net, making it stronger, and creating new nets."

This net-widening phenomenon refers to what diversion critics see as a bastardization of the intent of the diversion programs. Instead of placing offenders who previously would have been incarcerated into diversion programs, officials put into the programs offenders who previously would have been released or would have been placed on probation, thus widening the net of official processing. Timothy Bynum and Jack Greene, for example, found that "[w]ith a 32 percent decrease in the use of consent and dismissal decisions, it is evident that a number of youths whose cases would have formerly been dismissed or handled in a consent fashion were now receiving diversion" (1984:141). Not all evaluations, however, support this conclusion. In his analysis of the flow of youths through three metropolitan juvenile justice systems, Finn Esbensen (1984:126) found that "[t]wo metropolitan diversion programs that apparently were implemented in good faith and not subverted by opponents succeeded in reducing the number of youths penetrating and being maintained in the criminal justice system."

Another criticism of diversion programs attacks the premise that negative labeling will be avoided if an individual is placed in a community treatment facility. Malcolm Klein and his colleagues (1976:110) claimed that diversion "is equally or even more encapsulating" than justice system penetration. The debate about the effect of diversion and what role it should play continues, although somewhat abated.

The late 1990s witnessed policy directions diametrically opposed to the premises of labeling theory, generally in the form of substantial increases in the harshness of responses to juvenile misconduct. In the United States, for example, legislation facilitated the transfer of juveniles to the criminal court at younger ages, for less serious offenses, and with less extensive records of delinquency. Harsher legislation was introduced in Britain as well. In his participant observation study of the juvenile justice process in a British town, Ruggiero (1997:344) concluded that the wave of more punitive juvenile delinquency legislation had the effect of generating a "climate of increased intolerance against young offenders." This more punitive legislation, in turn, served "as a catalyst for measures which were even tougher than those it established" (1997:351). That is, the "get tough on kids" message sent by the new laws led teachers, social workers, and juvenile justice personnel to resort more frequently to official sanctions to control youths. Similarly, "zero tolerance" policies in American schools spawned cases of suspensions for use of over-the-counter medications for common ailments such as menstrual cramps and headaches. One honor student was suspended for carrying a spreading knife in her lunch pail, and on several occasions, young elementary school boys were sanctioned for arguably innocuous kisses or pats that were construed as sexual harassment. In short, the trend leans toward official labeling of a broad array of youthful behaviors as delinquent. Recent years, however, have seen a reassessment of these zero-tolerance statutes and a call for a more balanced approach to school disciplinary procedures (e.g., American Psychological Association Zero Tolerance Task Force, 2008).

Aggressive policing strategies, such as stop and frisk practices, result in a disproportionate number of youths and minorities being searched and questioned by police officers in public spaces (see, for example, Jones-Brown et al., 2010; Fratello et al., 2013). As mentioned previously, research by Wiley and Esbensen (2013) indicates that simply being stopped and questioned by the police is associated with attitudes supportive of delinquency, as well as increased delinquent behavior (see also, Wiley et al., 2013). Moreover, individuals who have been publicly stopped and searched report decreased cooperation with and trust in the police, as well as embarrassment and damage to individual self-concepts (Open Society Foundation, 2013).

ROOTS OF CRITICAL CRIMINOLOGY

The theories presented in the preceding chapters are representative of a broad conceptual orientation referred to as the **consensus view** (see Chapter 1). This approach to interpreting society and social reality rests on the assumption that "a consensus of values among its members" exists and that "the state is organized to protect the general public interest" (Vold et al., 1998:235). In the event of conflict among persons or groups, the state is seen as serving as a mediator to bring about a resolution that best suits the interests of society at large.

The **conflict perspective** posits that society is composed of groups that have opposing values and interests and that the state represents the values and interests of the groups with the most power. Among the earliest systematic treatments of conflict were those by Karl Marx in the latter half of the nineteenth century. One of the applications to crime that set the stage for emergence of radical criminology in the 1960s and 1970s was George Vold's publication of *Theoretical Criminology* in 1958. These two important works are reviewed below.

Karl Marx—Conflict Theory

Much of contemporary conflict theory can be traced back to the writings of the German economist and social philosopher Karl Marx. While Marx and his colleague, Friedrich Engels, had little to say regarding crime per se, their theoretical statements about capitalist society and the history of human civilization laid the foundations for subsequent development of conflict theories in criminology.

Marx believed that the dominant feature of all societies was the mode of production, that is, the way in which people develop and produce material goods. He argued that the economic base of society shaped all social arrangements: "The mode of production of material life determines the general character of the social, political, and spiritual processes of life. It is not the consciousness of men that determines their being but, on the contrary, their social being determines their consciousness" (Marx, 1964:51). This emphasis upon the economic arena led Marx to focus much of his attention on the relationship between the producers (i.e., workers) and those who owned the means of production. Under capitalism, Marx maintained, the bourgeoisie is the dominant class that owns the means of production and the proletariat are forced to work for (or in Marxian terms, sell their labor to) the bourgeoisie. This division of labor has led to the alienation of workers.

Alienation of the proletariat from the products of their labor is indicative of an unequal distribution of property and power in society. This unequal access to property and power lays the foundation for an inevitable class conflict that Marx believed to prevail throughout all of social history. In every society, according to Marx, there exist two opposing groups: one wishing to preserve the status quo and the other attempting to modify existing relationships. This theory of social organization has provided the foundation for the conflict school of criminology in that "contemporary Marxists wish to explore ways in which law, as a form of social control, has been used to contain class struggle and maintain class divisions at different times in different societies" (Lynch & Groves, 1986:7).

Michael Lynch and Byron Groves elaborated further upon the role of contemporary Marxist criminologists:

They also seek to uncover ways in which historically generated systems of social inequality contribute to the production of specific forms of crime. In other words, Marxists attempt to make sense of crime and criminal justice by examining each in its specific social and historical context. For example, there is no reason to assume that a Roman or feudal social and economic system would produce the same types of crime as we find in our society. . . . Significant societal changes such as urbanization, industrialization, bureaucratization, and the social and technological changes that accompany them, have spawned a whole range of new behaviors (including criminal behaviors such as auto theft, computer crime, and skyjacking) and new forms of law and social control (1986:7).

The relationship between the elite and the state are viewed in two alternative ways by contemporary Marxist criminologists. **Instrumental Marxism** sees the state and criminal law as intricately linked to the bourgeoisie. That is, the economic elite use the power of the state as an instrument for the maintenance of their own power. Police, courts, and prisons serve the interests of the elite by controlling those who pose threats to the status quo. Others view this version of Marxism as naive and conspiratorial. They point out that the state, including the criminal justice system, sometimes takes actions that arguably violate the interests of the power elite. **Structural Marxism** sees the state as semi-autonomous from the power elite. While the state typically supports the power elite, thereby protecting the capitalist system, it does not always do so. In fact, occasional support of the proletariat builds credibility for the state, thus strengthening it in the long run.

Group Conflict Perspective

George Vold—Group Conflict Theory

George Vold introduced his formulation of **group conflict theory** in 1958. Vold's conceptualization is rooted in the tradition of social interaction and collective behavior theories. He viewed humans as group oriented and society as a collection of groups, each with its own interests. These groups form because members have common interests and needs that can best be met through collective action. Students in a class who feel that they have been mistreated by their instructor, for example, would be more likely to obtain redress if they banded together than if they worked individually. Their group grievances probably would carry more weight with the instructor, department head, or dean than would individual complaints.

Vold maintained that groups come into conflict with one another as the interests and purposes they serve begin to overlap and encroach. When this occurs, each group tends to defend itself. To carry the above-mentioned example further, let us assume that a professor has neither distributed a syllabus nor described the grading system to the class. After the second exam, a number of students are told that they are failing the course. Students who received scores in the 70s on the first test and in the 50s on the second test are shocked and assume an error was made. The instructor then informs them that any score of less than 60 is treated as a zero. Thus a "76" and a "0" equals a 38 average, which translates into a letter grade of F. This grading policy offends these students and they band together to preserve their "rights." Note that it was not until the power of the instructor to determine the grading system conflicted with the interests of the students who failed was there a need for the students to "defend" themselves. Vold stated that "conflict between groups tends to develop and intensify the loyalty of the group members to their respective groups" (Vold, 1958:206).

Another element of Vold's group conflict theory pertains to the distribution of power. Who, for example, enacts laws and who enforces them? Vold claimed that "those who produce legislative majorities have control over the police power and dominate the policies that decide who is likely to be involved in violation of the law" (Vold, 1958:209). Former President Reagan was able to shape the U.S. Supreme Court in his conservative image. The liberal Warren Court was largely comprised of appointees from the Kennedy and Johnson administrations. During the Rehnquist Court, we witnessed decisions that overturned or modified those made by the Warren Court. Such changes in laws alter our definitions of crime and criminals. Doctors, for instance, who perform abortions, as well as women who get abortions, possibly would be perceived and treated as criminals if the U.S. Supreme Court were to overturn the *Roe v. Wade* (1973) decision. It is unlikely, however, that the current Roberts Court will produce decisions that overturn such long-standing policies. The current court reflects a judicial balance indicative of the fact that the judges were appointed by Presidents Reagan, Clinton, Bush, and Obama.

An interesting aspect of Vold's theory is that he viewed crime and delinquency as minority group behavior. This represents an extension of his belief that human behavior is dominated by group behavior characterized by conflict. Vold wrote (1958:211): "The juvenile gang is nearly always a 'minority group,' out of sympathy with and in more or less direct opposition to the rules and regulations of the dominant majority; that is, the established world of adult values and power." Youth gangs are in large part a result of intergenerational conflict, which adults are destined to win, given their control of the legal apparatus.

Vold cautioned that, while his theory pertained to crime in general, it was most appropriate for explaining four kinds of crime:

- Crimes arising from political protest;
- Crimes resulting from labor disputes;
- Crimes arising from disputes between and within competing unions; and
- Crimes arising from racial and ethnic clashes.

While these four crime types fit quite neatly into Vold's general theoretical framework, the more individual-based crimes, such as rape, embezzlement, robbery, and fraud do not mesh as well. The growth of "**radical criminology**" in the 1970s as a phase in the critical perspective, however, fleshed out the notion of power much more clearly.

The Radical Era—1960s and 1970s

Austin Turk—Crime and the Legal Order

Turk proposed a conflict analysis of crime that closely resembles the labeling perspective. In his 1969 publication, *Criminality and Legal Order*, he wrote that "[n]othing and no one is intrinsically criminal; criminality is a definition applied by individuals with the power to do so, according to illegal and extra-legal, as well as legal criteria" (Turk, 1969:10). He maintained that the label or status of criminal is conferred upon individuals in subordinate or powerless positions in society. Conflict between groups seeking to gain or maintain control over one another characterizes society. Turk noted that "one is led to investigate the tendency of laws to penalize persons whose behavior is more characteristic of the less powerful than of the more powerful and the extent to which some persons and groups can and do use legal processes and agencies to maintain and enhance their power position vis-à-vis other persons and groups" (Turk, 1969:18).

For Turk, it is important not only to examine the behavior of the police and other enforcers, but also to scrutinize the actions of the person being apprehended. Turk wrote that "people, both eventual authorities and eventual subjects, learn and continually re-learn to interact with one another as, respectively, occupants of superior and inferior statuses and performers of dominating and submitting roles" (1969:41–2). Lawbreaking occurs when there is a failure in the system, that is, when subjects feel able to test the strength of the ability of the authority figure to control their behavior.

Criminalization, the process of being labeled criminal, requires more than law-breaking behavior. It results from the interaction between the enforcers and the alleged violators. This interaction is shaped by five social factors:

- The congruence of cultural and social norms;
- The level of organization of the subjects;
- The degree of sophistication in the interpretation of behaviors;
- The power differential between enforcers and violators; and
- The realism of moves during the conflict.

While the congruence of norms is the key variable, the other factors interact to affect the probability of conflict and of criminalization. By definition, most authority figures are part of an organized system, so it is with the violators that variation occurs. "An individual who has group support for his behavior is going to be more stubborn in the face of efforts to make him change than is someone who has only himself as an ally" (Turk, 1969:58). Thus, conflict is more likely to occur when the offender is part of an organized group.

The degree of sophistication refers to the basis or rationale used to justify behavior. Authorities generally rely upon legal norms to interpret a situation. Subjects, on the other hand, may rely upon nonlegal interpretations of behavior. They are more likely to make use of abstract justifications such as "justice" or, in the case of unsophisticated offenders, to resort to rationalizations. Conflict, Turk argued, is more likely to occur when subjects are less sophisticated. Delinquent gangs are usually organized unsophisticates, which may account for their high rate of conflict with authorities.

The fourth factor affecting the probability of criminalization is the power differential between the enforcers and violators. While enforcers generally have greater power than violators, this is not always the case: witness, for example, the ability of certain white-collar offenders and politically connected individuals to beat the criminal justice system. Turk proposed that, in general, "the greater the power difference in favor of norm enforcers over resisters, the greater the probability of criminalization" (1969:70).

The remaining moderating factor affecting criminalization is the realism of moves made by enforcers and subjects during a conflict. This refers to the appropriateness or suitability of the behavior of individuals during their interaction. A key here is the extent to which each party engages in what may be called unrealistic moves. Resisters, for example, engage in unrealistic moves when they increase the visibility or offensiveness of the behavior that initiated conflict with authorities. A marijuana user, for example, is more likely to be detected and to bring about conflict if the marijuana smoking is flagrant. The pot smoker who smokes at home and uses a breath mint prior to going out in public is engaging in realistic behavior. On the other hand, the individual who rolls a joint at the mall and goes window shopping while smoking it is engaging in what Turk would call unrealistic moves. In this latter scenario, the open disregard for current laws regulating marijuana use in most American jurisdictions make it difficult for a law enforcement official to disregard the behavior. Authorities also can be accused of making unrealistic moves if they deviate from normal legal procedures (e.g., use of excessive force during arrest).

On the basis of these dichotomies, Turk suggested that it is possible to predict the relative probability of criminalization. He claimed that the highest probability exists when:

- Both enforcers and resisters have a high congruence between cultural and social norms,
- Both groups engage in unrealistic moves, and
- The power difference clearly favors the enforcers.

Richard Quinney—The Social Reality of Crime

Richard Quinney (1970) proposed a slightly different explanation of crime and criminal behavior. Borrowing from Vold's earlier statements as well as from social interaction and learning theories, Quinney developed six propositions and associated axioms that outline his *social reality of crime* theory. These six propositions, as noted by Quinney (1970:15–23), are:

Proposition 1	(Definition of Crime): Crime is a definition of human conduct that is created by authorized agents in a politically organized society.
Proposition 2	(Formulation of Criminal Definitions): Criminal definitions describe behaviors that conflict with the interests of the segments of society that have the power to shape political policy.
Proposition 3	(Application of Criminal Definitions): Criminal definitions are applied by the segments of society that have the power to shape the enforcement and administration of criminal law.
Proposition 4	(Development of Behavior Patterns in Relation to Criminal Definitions): Behavior patterns are structured in segmentally organized society in relation to criminal definitions, and within this context persons engage in actions that have relative probabilities of being defined as criminal.
Proposition 5	(Construction of Criminal Conceptions): Conceptions of crime are constructed and diffused in the segments of society by various means of communication.
Proposition 6	(The Social Reality of Crime): The social reality of crime is constructed by the formulation and application of criminal definitions, the development of behavior patterns related to criminal definitions, and the construction of criminal conceptions.

Quinney, like the labeling theorists, views crime as the product of social definition. An important aspect of proposition 1, however, is that the definition of crime is imposed by authority figures in society. Quinney asserted that crime is a function of a stratified social system in which the actions of one group are judged and categorized by the dominant group (see Highlight 9.5 for an example).

Propositions 2 and 3 are similar to Vold's group conflict theory. Their emphasis is upon the political power that is necessary to establish definitions of criminal behavior as well as to label individuals as criminals. Throughout

---

HIGHLIGHT 9.5 AN EXAMPLE OF THE CREATION OF A SOCIAL PROBLEM

An interesting example of additional pressures on today's adolescents is the phenomenon of teenage sex. Today we are bombarded with mass media messages about teenage pregnancy and teenage motherhood and all of the associated social problems. Why does society suddenly have this new social problem? If we go back 150 years in history, were teenagers not engaging in sexual activity? Were teenage females not getting pregnant? It may be that society has not experienced change in adolescent behavior but that the social context has changed. In the early 1800s, many women were married and having babies by age 16. Since these babies were born within the confines of marriage, there was no problem. Today, however, while adolescents are entering puberty at younger and younger ages and are being exposed to increasingly explicit sexual stimulation by the larger culture, they are being told to wait until marriage before engaging in sexual activity. The mean ages at first marriage for American women and men, meanwhile, have increased steadily to the current 23 and 25 years, respectively. Due, then, to social structural changes in the marital, labor, and education arenas, contemporary adolescents are expected to refrain from engaging in behavior that their great-grandparents practiced at the same age.

American history, for example, alcohol has been, with but few exceptions, a socially accepted drug. Even in contemporary society, where drug abuse and associated problems continue to be identified as major social problems and politicians campaign on "get tough on drugs" platforms, alcohol is still seen as an appropriate, and even a glamorous, drug. After newscasters discredit the use of steroids by athletes and the consumption of cocaine by entertainers, the newscast is interrupted by advertisements promoting the use of alcohol. How is it that a drug that is responsible for far more deaths and health-related problems than all of the illegal "street drugs" combined can continue to be legal and socially approved? The first three propositions of Quinney's theory provide a possible explanation.

Proposition 4 is derived from social learning theory, more specifically from Sutherland's differential association theory. It is from an individual's interaction with others that definitions of behavior, as well as behavioral patterns, are developed. And, depending upon one's location in the class structure, there is a differential probability that the behaviors in which a person engages will be defined as criminal. An excellent example of this can be found in William Chambliss's (1973) article, "The Saints and the Roughnecks." Chambliss compared the illegal and delinquent behavior of two groups of high school boys, one made up of middle-class student leaders and the other of lower-class boys. While the latter had a reputation for being involved in delinquent activity, it was the "saints" who engaged in greater amounts and more serious illegal behavior.

Quinney's final two propositions summarize his theory of the social reality of crime. Behavior is criminalized through the exercise of power and the use of the media to foster support for the definitions of crime set forth by the powerful sector of society. Returning to our alcohol example, as long as alcohol producers and politicians can use their power to promote the glamorous and social aspects of alcohol, little will be done to outlaw this drug. True, some groups, such as Mothers Against Drunk Driving, have been able to increase awareness concerning drunk driving, but studies continue to show that not only alcohol consumption but binge drinking remain at disturbingly high levels among high school and college students. With respect to defining behavior as criminal, we can be certain that when politicians talk about law and order and getting tough on crooks, they are referring to crimes of the street, not "crimes in the suites."

William Chambliss and Robert Seidman—Law, Order, and Power

William Chambliss and Robert Seidman presented a Marxian analysis of the American justice system in their 1971 publication *Law, Order, and Power*. They examined subsystems involved in the creation and enforcement of the law (i.e., the legislature, courts, and the police), concluding that "the legal order . . . is in fact a self-serving system to maintain power and privilege" (1971:4).

The popular view of the organization of society, they argued, inhibits the majority from reaching this same conclusion. They summarized this popular view in the following manner (Chambliss & Seidman, 1971:502):

- The law represents the values of society;
- If it does not represent the values of everyone, then it at least expresses the best common denominator of the society and operates through a value-neutral governmental structure, which is ultimately controlled by the choice of the people; and
- In the long run the law serves the best interests of the society.

This myth of how the law operates, the authors claimed, is easily discredited when one examines how it works on a day-to-day basis.

Chambliss and Seidman traced the law in action by examining the legislative processes leading to rule creation. They wrote:

> [E]very detailed study of the emergence of legal norms has consistently shown the immense importance of interest-group activity, not "the public interest," as the critical variable in determining the content of legislation. To hold to the notion of natural laws emerging from the needs of society requires that we accept the highly questionable assumption that somehow interest groups operate in the best interests of society. It may be true that "what's good for General Motors is good for society," if all the members of society benefit from the triumph of special interests. Rarely does this happen. Laws inevitably improve things for some people and make things worse for others (1971:73).

In addition to the legislature, appellate courts are a primary source of rule-making. Decisions written by appellate judges serve as precedents for future court cases. Are these cases decided by neutral judges in the best interests of society? Chambliss and Seidman claimed that they are not. Judges bring to their role as decision makers their own biases and values. They undergo a socialization process that advocates the value consensus orientation. Furthermore, judges are selectively recruited from the upper echelons of American society. Chambliss and Seidman concluded that appellate judges "are necessarily biased in favor of ensuring that courts are more available to the wealthy than to the poor, and tend to produce solutions in the interests of the wealthy" (1971:113).

With respect to the role of law enforcement, Chambliss and Seidman emphasized the bureaucratic nature of the police and their connection to the political structure. The authors summarized the process of law enforcement in complex societies with the following six propositions (1971:269):

- The agencies of law enforcement are bureaucratic organizations.
- An organization and its members tend to substitute for the official goals and norms of the organization ongoing policies and activities which will maximize rewards and minimize the strains on the organization.
- This goal substitution is made possible by:
  - the absence of motivation on the part of the role-occupants to resist pressures towards goal-substitution;

- the pervasiveness of discretionary choice permitted by the substantive criminal law, and the norms defining the roles of the members of the enforcement agencies; and
- the absence of effective sanctions for the norms defining the roles in those agencies.

- Law enforcement agencies depend on political organizations for resource allocation.
- It will maximize and minimize strains for the organization to process those who are politically weak and powerless, and to refrain from processing those who are politically powerful.
- Therefore it may be expected that the law enforcement agencies will process a disproportionately high number of the politically weak and powerless, while ignoring the violations of those with power.

In summary, Chambliss and Seidman conducted an analysis of the law in action. They claimed that the law does not represent the "public interest"; rather, it represents the interests of those in power. Chambliss's (1964) analysis of the emergence of vagrancy laws is a classic illustration of this.

Contemporary Critical Thought

While all critical criminology is based on a conflict premise, it has become considerably more diverse over the past two decades, incorporating "a growing multiplicity of critical theoretical approaches" (Michalowski, 1996:13). All of these approaches explain crime as a function of the distribution of power and they are "all 'radical' in the sense that they are associated with political agendas that involve deep and fundamental social change" (Vold et al., 1998). Three important contemporary critical streams of thought are *left realism*, *feminism*, and *postmodernism*.

Left Realism

With **left realism**, radical criminologists have highlighted the crimes committed by the powerful and the effect of these "suite crimes" (i.e., white-collar offenses such as insider trading, embezzlement, and abuse of power) on the poor and working class. One problem with this perspective, however, is the lack of attention paid to "street crimes" (e.g., crimes included in the UCR Index classification). Left realists have criticized the earlier radical perspective by emphasizing the violent and costly aspects associated with conventional intra-class and intra-race crime. They maintain that while crimes of the powerful have a deleterious effect on society, so too do street crimes.

Radical criminologists historically have glamorized traditional street offenders either as modern-day Robin Hoods or as leaders of the proletarian revolution. Left realists view this romanticization as naïve and unrealistic. They claim that "street crime is 'real,' and not a moral panic created by elite opinion makers such as the media" (Schwartz & DeKeseredy, 1991:51). As such, crime control policies need to address not only the crimes of the wealthy but also the crimes committed by the poor against the poor.

The left realist movement has been most successful in establishing itself in Britain (see, for example Young, 1988). Walter DeKeseredy and Martin Schwartz (1991) suggest that left realism has failed to develop as thoroughly in the United States because of (1) the marginalization of socialists and socialist thought in America and (2) the failure to establish a dominant center of radical criminological theory at American universities.

According to two leaders of British left realism, John Lea and Jock Young (1984), the perspective is based on the following four premises:

- Street crime is a serious problem for the working class;
- Working-class crime is primarily perpetrated against other members of the working class;
- It is relative poverty, not absolute poverty, that breeds discontent and this discontent without a political solution creates crime; and
- Crime can be reduced through implementation of practical, socialist policies.

These assumptions identify poor and working-class people as those most likely to be victimized not only by the policies of the rich and powerful, but also by their similarly situated neighbors. Crime control policies, therefore, need to address both social inequality and individual depravity. Left realists have proposed a number of alternatives to conservative crime control policies. In order to reduce the further marginalization of prisoners, they recommend greater use of community service programs, victim restitution, community placements, and an overall reduction in the reliance on prison. Left realists acknowledge the importance of policing society and deterring prospective offenders, but they call for stricter civil and democratic control of the police. In addition to these specific crime control policies, Raymond Michalowski (1983) suggests that economic policies that shift the burden of the welfare state from consumers to producers would further reduce conventional crime. Among the recommended strategies are: tax surcharges on industries trying to close plants or reduce a community's work force, laws mandating the retraining of workers displaced by new technologies, and a minimum wage that is 50 percent above the poverty level.

Feminism

Feminist criminologists highlight the fact that the social world is fundamentally gendered; that is, men and women encounter different life experiences that are a product of cultural, historical, and societal processes interwoven with race and class inequalities. Feminist criminologists maintain that it is important for criminologists "to situate the study of crime and justice in the recognition that gender is an organizing principle of institutions, including criminal justice policies and practices" (Miller 2003:4).

Critical forms of **feminism** have assumed three major variations. **Radical feminism** identifies a patriarchal social order in which men dominate women as the fundamental issue. This power imbalance is the product of sexist patterns of socialization that instill a belief in male superiority. Both males and females come to accept differential gender roles that place men in positions of relative power. The solution, following this perspective, would be to alter those socialization patterns in order to equalize power among genders.

Marxist feminism sees women as dominated by men as a result of the disproportionate location of economic power among the men. As with pure Marxism, it is ownership of the means of production that underlies an imbalance of power. This serves the interest of the dominant male elite because it subjugates females to roles of sexual and domestic service. Following this perspective, the solution would be in the form of a broad redistribution of wealth that would include women as well as male proletariat.

Socialist feminism sees capitalism as inevitably flawed, producing a range of oppression, including that experienced by women. Biology also has played a role, however, in the sense that the reproductive function placed most of the burden of childbearing and rearing on women. This contributed to the formation of male dominance, and capitalism has perpetuated it. Thus, the solution is both wealth redistribution and freeing women from their disproportionate burden of childrearing responsibilities.

Postmodernism

While the paradigm shift to classicism led to a call for rationalism, and the later emergence of positivism brought science into the equation, **postmodernism** rejects the notion that rationalism and science merit a superior position in explaining the way things are. "Modern" thinking saw science as the method that holds the potential to understanding. Postmodernists believe that it is time to move on to a new way of understanding. The argument is that "truth" is not purely objective. There are many equally valid ways to pursue truth, the scientific method being only one. In fact, the scientific approach is viewed as troubling because scientists generally view themselves as "experts," thereby creating a "privileged" knowledge (Einstadter & Henry, 1995). Knowledge, from a postmodernist perspective, is viewed in egalitarian terms. Equal consideration is extended to anyone's understanding of the world. Over the past decade, this perspective has begun to appear in criminology.

The source of inequitable distribution of power is identified as language. Those who control language control the "truth." By illustration, the legalese that serves as the only acceptable language in legal proceedings does not objectively present the full truth (Milovanovic, 1994). One hires an attorney to use the necessary language to win. The defendant in a criminal case cannot simply tell his or her version of the truth. Instead, the defendant relies on a lawyer to present his or her case in legalese, which may tell a very different story. To sift through these different stories or versions of the truth, postmodernism employs a method referred to as discourse analysis. This process calls for looking not only at what is said, but how and why.

The story told by any actor is heavily influenced by particular social institutions that must be included in analysis of their story. The "truth" about educational issues, for example, as espoused by your criminology professor, will be heavily influenced by the existing institution of higher education. Your professor most likely would insist that you complete a course in criminological theory (so here you are) and probably one in statistics. She or he would probably hold to the view that these are necessary learning experiences to enable you to really understand crime. This would not be surprising, as it is the mainstream perspective within the academic discipline of criminology. The postmodernist, however, would believe that your nonexpert views are just as valid, although you might see that the "truth" about crime could only be grasped by living in a neighborhood like yours, and courses in criminology and statistics would add nothing. Applied to criminological issues, the "truth" as seen by a police officer, for example, would be largely shaped by the contemporary police institution and might be quite different from "truth" in the eyes of a citizen viewing the same scenario. Thus police may not see a particular incident as brutality, even though it is seen as such by many citizens.

Central to postmodernism is the concept of **deconstructionism**. Since conventional wisdom is primarily a product of modern rational ways of generating knowledge, primarily the scientific method, the validity of that knowledge is rejected. Thus the task comes to be deconstructing or tearing down existing bodies of knowledge. Because postmodernism calls for deconstruction of knowledge rather than creation of knowledge it is criticized as nihilistic. As Werner Einstadter and Stuart Henry (1995:280) ask, "If truth is not possible, how can we decide anything?"

RESEARCH ON CONFLICT THEORY

A number of studies have assessed the utility of the conflict perspective. These investigations generally take one of two approaches:

- Case studies testing the hypothesis that laws are formulated in the interests of those in power; and
- Empirical works examining the extent to which individuals are subject to differential processing by the criminal justice system based upon their race or socioeconomic status (SES).

With respect to the former approach, Frank Williams concluded in his review of the literature that "findings would appear to support the conflict notion that many laws are, in fact, formulated to benefit power groups" (1980:215). This conclusion is supported by the following studies of:

- Vagrancy laws (Chambliss, 1964);
- The enactment of the Marijuana Tax Act (Becker, 1963);
- The development of laws regulating theft (Hall, 1952); and
- The Prohibition movement (Sinclair, 1964).

The evidence regarding differential processing is not as supportive of the conflict perspective as it is for the development of laws. Studies have examined differential processing by race and SES for both juveniles and adults at various levels of the justice system. In an analysis of juvenile court records in a southeastern city, Timothy Carter and Donald Clelland (1979) distinguished between two types of offenses to see if the disposition received varied by the nature of the misconduct. They found greater discrimination in court dispositions for moral as opposed to traditional offenses. Moral offenses are status offenses such as incorrigibility, truancy, and runaway, as well as victimless offenses such as drug and alcohol use and sexual activity. These moral offenses, they maintained, challenge the existing social system and consequently receive harsher treatment than traditional offenses.

Robert Sampson and John Laub (1993) investigated the judicial processing of 580,000 juvenile cases in 21 states. They found that for personal, property, and drug offenses, underclass African-American males had higher rates of out-of-home placements than did white males. This pattern of juvenile justice response, they believe, is "consistent with the idea that underclass African-American males are viewed as a threatening group to middle-class populations, and thus will be subjected to increased formal social control by the juvenile justice system" (Sampson & Laub, 1993:306).

Studies of adult treatment reveal the inconsistencies encountered when testing conflict theories. In their study of police use of deadly force, David Jacobs and David Britt (1979) found that states with the greatest economic disparities experienced the largest number of police killings, while the percentage of African Americans in each state had no relationship to police killings. Similarly, Alan Lizotte (1978) found in his study of court processing in Chicago that both African-American and white laborers received longer prison terms than did white-collar workers. This finding held even when he controlled for such variables as number of prior arrests, seriousness of the case, and strength of the evidence. Contrary to Lizotte, Theodore Chiricos and Gordon Waldo (1975) reported that SES was unrelated to sentence severity in their study of more than 10,000 inmates in three southern states.

Frank Williams' review of the literature on the relationship between race and/or SES and justice system processing showed that while some of this research did support the conflict perspective, the vast majority—more than 80 percent—did not (Williams, 1980). William Wilbanks (1987) examined the literature dealing with race and the criminal justice system. Although he conceded that there may be some discrimination on the part of individuals working in the system, Wilbanks concluded that "there is insufficient evidence to support the charge that the system is racist today" (Wilbanks, 1987:8).

Cassia Spohn provides evidence to refute Wilbanks's assertion and suggests that researchers "who simply test for the direct effect of defendant race may incorrectly conclude that race does not affect sentence severity" (1994:265). Her evaluation of sentencing decisions involving a sample of all felony cases in Detroit during 1976 through 1978 found that the relationship between race and sentencing requires examination of a number of variables. Of particular importance were the observed interactions among offender race, victim race, relationship between offender and victim, and the type of crime that combined to produce different sentencing outcomes. Representative of the complexity of these interactive effects are the following specific results:

- Blacks who murder white strangers or acquaintances receive longer sentences than other defendants;
- Blacks who sexually assault white strangers, white acquaintances, or black strangers are sentenced to longer sentences than others; and
- Offenders who victimized strangers, regardless of their race or the race of their victims, were sentenced to prison at the same rate; among nonstrangers, the incarceration rate was significantly higher for black-on-white crimes than for intra-race crimes (Spohn, 1994:264).

So where does all this leave the conflict perspective? There exist some compelling arguments as well as data supportive of the hypothesis that laws are made to benefit the rich. Contradictory findings, however, underlie the question of differential treatment of the powerless within the justice system. Recent research, though, suggests that part of the inconsistency in findings may be attributable to overly simplified tests of the effect of race or class and that possible interaction effects with other key variables must be scrutinized.

POLICY RELEVANCE OF CONFLICT THEORY

To date, conflict theory per se has had little impact on the criminal justice system. Despite this, there are clear policies that can be derived from this perspective, not all of which are clearly linked with popular notions of crime fighting. Conflict theorists might maintain that President Obama's best crime-fighting proposal is the Affordable Care Act. Elliott Currie's (1985, 1989) policy recommendations reveal the emphasis of the conflict perspective on "fighting crime" through changes in social institutions other than alteration in the criminal justice system.

In his 1989 article, Currie provided 12 recommendations for confronting crime in the twenty-first century. Of these, only two emphasize justice system policies. The remaining recommendations deal with the larger socio-political environment. Citing the failure of the conservative neoclassical approach that dominated the criminal justice system during the 1970s and 1980s, the author suggested that American criminology is experiencing an "etiological crisis." A new way of thinking about crime is necessary.

Currie cited an increasing abundance of research to substantiate his recommendations. He referred to his position as a "social environmental" or "human-ecological" perspective, which is one that involves policy interventions on the individual and family level as well as on the larger social context. Currie's recommendations (1989:11–21) are:

- Expand high-quality, intensive early education along the model of Head Start;
- Expand health and mental health services for high-risk children and youths and for their parents, including high-quality prenatal and postnatal care;

- Establish a greater commitment to family support programs, especially real rather than rhetorical support for comprehensive programs against child abuse and domestic violence;
- Insist that prison time be used more constructively so that offenders leave a little smarter, a little healthier, and a little more sober;
- Establish a commitment to accessible, nonpunitive drug abuse treatment for those who need it;
- Move toward reducing inequality and social impoverishment by, among other things, increasing the minimum wage, which fell 30 percent in real terms during the 1980s, and raise women's earnings closer to those of men;
- Move toward an active labor market policy aimed at upgrading the work available to disadvantaged Americans;
- Develop a genuinely supportive national family policy that would include, for example, paid leave at the birth of a child;
- Assume greater responsibility for the economic and social stability of local communities;
- Provide a more careful research plan to examine what works for individuals at risk;
- Learn more about how to create comprehensive, preventive strategies for "high-risk" communities; and
- Attempt to understand more about why some societies have low or relatively low crime rates, while others, including our own, suffer such pervasive violence.

While not all conflict criminologists would agree with Currie's agenda, most would applaud his attempt to identify short-term as well as long-term recommendations for confronting crime in American society. His emphasis upon the causes as opposed to the consequences of behavior is not as "radical" as it was 25 years ago. From the conflict perspective, it is clear that there is more to fighting crime than merely fighting criminals.

SUMMARY

In this chapter we have examined two broad theoretical perspectives that differ from theories discussed in Chapters 5 through 8. The labeling approach focuses attention on the societal reaction to behavior and is concerned with understanding the consequences of this social response. In a similar fashion, conflict theory is interested in understanding how the social and criminal justice systems respond differentially to persons suspected of violating the law. Additionally, conflict theorists question the legitimacy of the existing social structure, maintaining that the laws and the enforcement procedures are structured to benefit the rich and punish the poor.

The labeling perspective grew in popularity through the 1960s and 1970s but lost much of its appeal as research findings failed to substantiate its claims.

Self-report studies did indicate that most people commit at least minor offenses, but subsequent evaluations did not yield substantial evidence that differential social response was responsible for the disparate rates of prosecution and incarceration. More recent work that has examined the specific mechanisms in the labeling process has provided renewed interest in and support for labeling theory, and researchers have begun to examine both the short- and long-term effects of justice system contact.

The conflict perspective has experienced a resurgence in support since the 1960s. Many attribute its renewed popularity to the social turmoil of the 1960s and 1970s. The "new criminology," as the conflict theorists have labeled their work (Taylor et al., 1973), actually consists of diverse and relatively distinct theoretical strains. All are based on the conflict perspective rooted in the works of Karl Marx and are founded on the general notion that society is comprised of groups in conflict. George Vold's development of group conflict theory preceded the 1960s resurgence of conflict criminology.

Conflict theory provided the foundation for a much broader critical criminology, beginning with the radical era of the 1960s and 1970s. Works of such theorists as Quinney, Turk, and Chambliss represent this exciting period. In the past decade, critical thought has become more diverse. Left realism, several feminist lines of thought, and postmodernism are all vibrant segments of contemporary criminological thought.

Both the broad conflict/critical and labeling perspectives discussed in this chapter have necessitated that criminologists question some of the underlying assumptions of traditional theories. As a result, criminology texts, journal articles, and papers presented at the annual meetings of the American Society of Criminology and the Academy of Criminal Justice Sciences today reflect a more critical analysis of crime and societal and criminal justice response.

KEY TERMS AND CONCEPTS

Conflict Perspective	Instrumental Marxism
Conformist	Labeling Perspective
Consensus View	Left Realism
Criminalization	Legal Relativism
Critical Criminology	Marxist Feminism
Deconstructionism	Master Status
Deviance Amplification	Moral Entrepreneurs
Dramatization of Evil	Net-Widening
Falsely Accused	Postmodernism
Feminism	Primary Deviation
Group Conflict Theory	Pure Deviant

Radical Criminology

Radical Feminism

Radical Nonintervention

Retrospective Interpretation

Secondary Deviation

Secret Deviants

Socialist Feminism

Structural Marxism

KEY CRIMINOLOGISTS

Howard S. Becker

Jon Gunnar Bernburg

William Chambliss

Edwin Lemert

Karl Marx

Richard Quinney

Edwin M. Schur

Frank Tannenbaum

Charles R. Tittle

Austin Turk

George Vold

Stephanie A. Wiley

CASE

Roe v. Wade, 410 U.S. 113 (1973)

DISCUSSION QUESTIONS

1. Some labeling theorists would argue that the best response to increased criminal activity is no response; that is, to not respond to the violation in any formal manner. Explain the rationale underlying this position.

2. Labeling theorists argue that punishment associated with a criminal act is but one aspect of the formal criminal justice processing. In addition to formal sanctions, labeling theorists suggest that other consequences of the processing have potentially greater consequences for the labeled offender. Identify what these consequences might be and discuss the research that has examined these issues.

3. Zero-tolerance laws are not supported by the tenets of the labeling perspective. What arguments would labeling theorists use to discourage the use of such laws?

4. Elliott Currie identified 12 recommendations for confronting crime. What is the rationale for the fact that only two of these recommendations dealt with justice system policies?

5. Describe the group conflict perspective proposed by George Vold.

6. "Stop and Frisk" policies unduly target young minority males and contribute to the criminalization of these young men. Do you agree or disagree with this statement?

REFERENCES

Ageton, S.S. & Elliott, D.S. (1974). The effects of legal processing on delinquent orientations. *Social Problems, 22,* 87–100.

American Psychological Association Zero Tolerance Task Force (2008). Are zero tolerance policies effective in schools? *American Psychologist, 63,* 852–62.

Austin, J. & Krisberg, B. (1981). Wider, stronger, and different nets: The dialectics of criminal justice reform. *Journal of Research in Crime and Delinquency, 18,* 165–96.

Becker, H.S. (1963). *Outsiders: Studies in the sociology of deviance.* New York, NY: The Free Press.

Bedau, H.A. & Radelet, M.L. (1987). Miscarriages of justice in potentially capital cases. *Stanford Law Review, 40,* 21–179.

Bernburg, J.G. (2009). Labeling theory. In M.D. Krohn, A.J. Lizotte, & G. Penly Hall (Eds.), *Handbook on Crime and Deviance* (pp. 187–207). New York, NY: Springer.

Bernburg, J.G. & Krohn, M.D. (2003). Labeling, life chances, and adult crime: The direct and indirect effects of official intervention in adolescence on crime in early adulthood. *Criminology, 41,* 1287–1318.

Bernburg, J.G., Krohn, M.D., & Rivera, C.J. (2006). Official labeling, criminal embeddedness, and subsequent delinquency. *Journal of Research in Crime and Delinquency, 43,* 67–88.

Blomberg, T.G. (1980). Widening the net: An anomaly in the evaluation of diversion programs. In M.W. Klein, & K.S. Teilman (Eds.), *Handbook of criminal justice evaluation* (pp. 572–92). Beverly Hills, CA: Sage.

Bynum, T.S. & Greene, J.R. (1984). How wide the net? Probing the boundaries of the juvenile court. In S.H. Decker (Ed.), *Juvenile justice policy: Analyzing trends and outcomes* (pp. 129–43). Beverly Hills, CA: Sage.

Carter, T. & Clelland, D. (1979). A Neo-Marxian critique, formulation and test of juvenile dispositions as a function of social class. *Social Problems, 27,* 96–108.

Chambliss, W.J. (1964). A sociological analysis of the law of vagrancy. *Social Problems, 12,* 67–77.

Chambliss, W.J. (1973). The saints and the roughnecks. *Society, 11,* 24–31.

Chambliss, W.J. & Seidman, R.B. (1971). *Law, order, and power.* Reading, MA: Addison Wesley.

Chiricos, T.G. & Waldo, G. (1975). Socioeconomic status and criminal sentencing: An empirical assessment of a conflict proposition. *American Sociological Review, 40,* 753–72.

Chiricos, T.G., Barrick, K., Bales, W., & Bontrager, S. (2007). The labeling of convicted felons and its consequences for recidivism. *Criminology, 45,* 547–81.

Cohen, L.E. & Stark, R. (1974). Discriminatory labeling and the five-finger discount: An empirical analysis of differential shoplifting dispositions. *Journal of Research in Crime and Delinquency, 11,* 25–39.

Curra, J. (2000). *The relativity of deviance.* Thousand Oaks, CA: Sage.

Currie, E. (1985). *Confronting crime: An American challenge.* New York, NY: Pantheon Books.

Currie, E. (1989). Confronting crime: Looking toward the twenty-first century. *Justice Quarterly, 6,* 5–25.

DeKeseredy, W. & Schwartz, M. (1991). British and U.S. left realism: A critical comparison. *International Journal of Offender Therapy and Comparative Criminology, 35,* 248–62.

Dotter, D. L. & Roebuck, J. B. (1988). The labeling approach re-examined: Interactionism and the components of deviance. *Deviant Behavior*, *9*, 19–32.

Dunford, F. W. (1977). Police diversion: An illusion. *Criminology*, *15*, 335–52.

Einstadter, W. & Henry, S. (1995). *Criminological theory: An analysis of its underlying assumptions*. Fort Worth, TX: Harcourt Brace.

Erikson, K. T. (1962). Notes on the sociology of deviance. *Social Problems*, *9*, 307–14.

Esbensen, F.-A. (1984). Net-widening? Yes and no: Diversion impact assessed through a systems processing rates analysis. In S. H. Decker (Ed.), *Juvenile justice policy: Analyzing trends and outcomes* (pp. 115–28). Beverly Hills, CA: Sage.

Foster, J. D., Dinitz, S., & Reckless, W. C. (1972). Perceptions of stigma following public intervention for delinquent behavior. *Social Problems*, *20*, 202–9.

Fratello, J., Rengifo, A. F., Trone, J., & Velazquez, B. (2013). *Coming of age with stop and frisk: Experiences, perceptions, and public safety implications*. New York, NY: Vera Institute of Justice.

Goffman, E. (1963). *Stigma*. Englewood-Cliffs, NJ: Prentice Hall.

Gove, W. R. (1980). *The labelling of deviance*. Beverly Hills, CA: Sage.

Hagan, J. & Palloni, A. (1990). The social reproduction of a criminal class in working-class London, circa 1959–80. *American Journal of Sociology*, *96*, 265–300.

Hall, J. (1952). *Theft, law and society*. Indianapolis, IN: Bobbs-Merrill.

Heimer, K. & Matsueda, R. L., (1994). Role-taking, role commitment, and delinquency: A theory of differential social control. *American Sociological Review*, *59*, 365–90.

Huff, C. R. (2002). Wrongful conviction and public policy: The American Society of Criminology 2001 presidential address. *Criminology*, *40*, 1–18.

Huizinga, D. & Henry, K. L. (2008). The effect of arrest and justice system sanctions on subsequent behavior: Findings from longitudinal and other studies. In A.M. Liberman (Ed.), *The long view of crime: A synthesis of longitudinal research* (pp. 220–54). New York, NY: Springer.

Huizinga, D., Schumann, K., Ehret, B., & Elliott, A. (2003). *The effect of juvenile justice system processing on subsequent delinquent and criminal behavior: A cross-national study*. Paper presented at the Annual Meeting of the Western Society of Criminology Vancouver, British Columbia, February.

Jackson, P. & Rudman, C. (1993). Moral panic and the response to gangs in California. In S. Cummings, & D. J. Monte (Eds.), *The origins and impact of contemporary youth gangs in the United States* (pp. 257–75). Albany, NY: State University of New York Press.

Jacobs, D. & Britt, D. (1979). Inequality and police use of deadly force: An empirical assessment of a conflict perspective. *Social Problems*, *26*, 403–12.

Jensen, G. F. (1972). Parents, peers, and delinquent action: A test of the differential association perspective. *American Journal of Sociology*, *78*, 562–75.

Jones-Brown, D., Gill, J., & Trone, J. (2010). *Stop, question, and frisk policing practices in New York City: A primer*. New York, NY: City University of New York, John Jay College of Criminal Justice.

Kirk, D. S. & Sampson, R. J. (2013). Juvenile arrest and collateral educational damage in the transition to adulthood. *Sociology of Education*, *86*, 36–62.

Kitsuse, J. I. (1962). Societal reaction to deviant behavior: Problem of theory and method. *Social Problems*, *9*, 247–56.

Klein, M. W., Teilman, K. S., Styles, J. A., Lincoln, S. B., & Labin-Rosensweig, S. (1976). The explosion of police diversion programs. In M. W. Klein (Ed.), *The juvenile justice system* (pp. 101–20). Beverly Hills, CA: Sage.

Lea, J. & Young, J. (1984). *What is to be done about law and order?* Harmondsworth, UK: Penguin.

Lemert, E. M. (1951). *Social pathology*. New York, NY: McGraw-Hill.

Lemert, E. M. (1981). Diversion in juvenile justice: What hath been wrought. *Journal of Research in Crime and Delinquency, 18*, 35–46.

Liberman, A. M., Kirk, D. S., & Kim, K. (2014). Labeling effects of first juvenile arrests: Secondary deviance and secondary sanctioning. *Criminology 52*, 345–70.

Link, B. G. (1982). Mental patient status, work, and income: An examination of the effects of a psychiatric label. *American Sociological Review, 47*, 202–15.

Lizotte, A. (1978). Extra-legal factors in Chicago's criminal courts: Test of the conflict model of criminal justice. *Social Problems, 25*, 564–80.

Lofland, J. (1969). *Deviance and identity*. Englewood Cliffs, NJ: Prentice-Hall.

Lopes, G., Krohn, M. D., Lizotte, A. J., Schmidt, N. M., Vásquez, B. E., & Bernburg, J. G. (2012). Labeling and cumulative disadvantage: The impact of formal police intervention on life chances and crime during emerging adulthood. *Crime and Delinquency, 58*, 456–88.

Lynch, M. J. & Groves, W. B. (1986). *A primer in radical criminology*. Albany, NY: Harrow and Heston.

Maruna, S., Lebel, T. P., Mitchell, N., & Naples, M. (2004). Pygmalion in the reintegration process: Desistance from crime through the looking glass. *Psychology, Crime, and Law, 10*, 271–82.

Marx, K. (1964). *Selected writings and social philosophies*. London, UK: McGraw-Hill.

Matsueda, R. L. (1992). Reflected appraisals, parental labeling, and delinquency: Specifying a symbolic interactionist theory. *American Journal of Sociology, 97*, 1577–1611.

Mead, G. H. (1934). *Mind, self, and society*. Chicago, IL: University of Chicago Press.

Michalowski, R. (1983). Crime control in the 1980s: A progressive agenda. *Crime and Social Justice, 19*, 13–23.

Michalowski, R. (1996). Critical criminology and the critique of domination: The story of an intellectual movement. *Critical Criminology, 7*, 9–16.

Miller, J. (2003). Gender, crime, and (in)justice: Introduction to the special issue. *Journal of Contemporary Ethnography, 32*, 3–8.

Miller, K. (1999). Students make pledge not to taunt outcasts. Associated Press release. *Johnson City Press*, 5–30.

Milovanovic, D. (1994). *A primer in the sociology of law*. Albany, NY: Harrow and Heston.

Open Society Foundation. (2013). *How many times have you been stopped by the police?* Video retrieved from www.opensocietyfoundations.org/voices/viewed-suspicion-twenty-years-after-stephen-lawrence.

Paternoster, R. & Iovanni, L. (1989). The labeling perspective and delinquency: An elaboration of the theory and an assessment of the evidence. *Justice Quarterly 6*, 360–94.

Quinney, R. (1970). *The social reality of crime*. Boston, MA: Little, Brown.

Ruggiero, V. (1997). Punishing children: The manufacture of criminal careers in Hellion Town. *Theoretical Criminology, 1*, 341–61.

Sampson, R. J. & Laub, J. H. (1993). Structural variations in juvenile court processing: Inequality, the underclass, and social control. *Law and Society Review, 27*, 285–311.

Sampson, R. J. & Laub, J. H. (1997). A life-course theory of cumulative disadvantage and the stability of delinquency. In T. P. Thornberry (Ed.), *Developmental Theories of Crime and Delinquency* (pp. 131–66). New Brunswick, NJ: Transaction Publishers.

Schur, E. M. (1973). *Radical nonintervention: Rethinking the delinquency problem*. Englewood Cliffs, NJ: Prentice Hall.

Schwartz, M. D. & DeKeseredy, W. S. (1991). Left realist criminology: Strengths, weaknesses, and the feminist critique. *Crime, Law and Social Change, 15*, 51–72.

Schwartz, R. D. & Skolnick, J. H. (1962). Two studies of legal stigma. *Social Problems, 10*, 133–42.

Sinclair, A. (1964). *Era of excess: A social history of the prohibition movement*. New York, NY: Harper and Row.

Spohn, C. (1994). Crime and social control of blacks: The effect of offender/victim race on sentences for violent felonies. In G. Bridges, & M. Myers (Eds.), *Inequality, crime, and social control* (pp. 249–68). Boulder, CO: Westview Press.

Steffensmeier, D. J. & Terry, R. M. (1973). Deviance and respectability: An observational study of reactions to shoplifting. *Social Forces, 51*, 417–26.

Stewart, E. A., Simons, R. L., Conger, R. D., & Scaramella, L. V. (2002). Beyond the interactional relationship between delinquency and parenting practices: The contribution of legal sanctions. *Journal of Research in Crime and Delinquency, 39*, 36–59.

Sweeten, G. (2006). Who will graduate? Disruption of high school education by arrest and court conviction. *Justice Quarterly, 23*, 547–81.

Tannenbaum, F. (1938). *Crime and the community*. Boston, MA: Ginn.

Taylor, I., Walton, P., & Young, J. (1973). *The new criminology: For a social theory of deviance*. New York, NY: Harper and Row.

Tittle, C. R. (1980). Labelling and crime: An empirical evaluation. In W. R. Gove (Ed.), *The labelling of deviance: Evaluating a perspective* (pp. 241–63). Beverly Hills, CA: Sage Publications.

Triplett, R. A. (1993). The conflict perspective, symbolic interactionism, and the status characteristics hypothesis. *Justice Quarterly, 10*, 541–56.

Triplett, R. A. & Jarjoura, G. R. (1994). Theoretical and empirical specification of a model of informal labeling. *Journal of Quantitative Criminology, 10*, 241–76.

Turk, A. (1969). *Criminality and legal order*. Chicago, IL: Rand McNally.

Vold, G. B. (1958). *Theoretical criminology*. New York, NY: Oxford University Press.

Vold, G. B., Bernard, T., & Snipes, J. (1998). *Theoretical criminology* (4th ed.). New York, NY: Oxford University Press.

Wellford, C. F. (1987). Delinquency prevention and labeling. In J. Q. Wilson, & G. C. Loury (Eds.), *From children to citizens, Volume III: Families, schools, and delinquency prevention* (pp. 257–67). New York, NY: Springer-Verlag.

Wilbanks, W. (1987). *The myth of a racist criminal justice system*. Monterey, CA: Brooks-Cole.

Wiley, S. A. & Esbensen, F.-A. (2013). The effect of police contact: Does official intervention result in deviance amplification? *Crime and Delinquency*. Published online ahead of print: doi:10.1177/0011128713492496.

Wiley, S. A., Slocum, L. A., & Esbensen, F.-A. (2013). The unintended consequences of being stopped or arrested: An exploration of the labeling mechanisms through which police contact leads to subsequent delinquency. *Criminology, 51*, 927–66.

Williams, F. P., III (1980). Conflict theory and differential processing: An analysis of the research literature. In J. Inciardi (Ed.), *Radical criminology: The coming crisis* (pp. 213–32). Beverly Hills, CA: Sage Publications.

Young, J. (1988). Radical criminology in Britain: The emergence of a competing paradigm. *British Journal of Criminology, 28*, 159–83.

CHAPTER 10

New Directions

Integration and a Life-Course Perspective

The preceding five chapters discussed theoretical paradigms that have an established history in criminological theory. In this chapter, we review several approaches to the understanding of crime that are currently eliciting considerable attention in the criminological journals. During the past 30 years, integrated theoretical models, criminal careers research, and developmental criminology have emerged as new perspectives.

Three major factors are associated with the development of these theoretical orientations. First, there has been a growing acceptance among criminologists of the limitation of existing theories. Rather than viewing the theories as competing explanations of behavior, the movement has been toward considering them as complementary. There may not be a single cause of crime; in fact, there may be multiple paths (e.g., Elliott et al., 1985; Huizinga et al., 1991; Simons et al., 1994) or different trajectories for different types of people (Moffitt, 1994; Nagin et al., 1995). Theoretical integration combines elements of the traditional perspectives to provide a more comprehensive understanding of criminal behavior.

A second development has been closely associated with the incapacitation model and the "get tough" on crime orientation associated with it. Research findings have consistently pinpointed a violent and criminally active group of offenders that account for more than one-half of all street crimes. The criminal career approach has sought to identify these high-rate offenders and to isolate factors associated with their high rates of offending. Specific guidelines for incapacitating these offenders for longer periods of time (often for life) than other offenders have been proposed in numerous jurisdictions as a way to reduce the crime rate. For example, **three-strikes legislation** (providing more punitive sentences for felons upon their third conviction) was introduced at the federal and state levels. While some legal challenges to these punitive laws have been made, the U.S. Supreme Court, in two separate decisions handed down in March 2003, upheld the constitutionality of the California legislation. A number of scholars, however, have highlighted the deleterious effects of this policy of mass incarceration (e.g., Campbell & Schoenfeld, 2013). In 2012, Californians voted to reform the original three-strikes law (Proposition 36) after recognizing its financial burden and disproportionate effects on minority and mentally ill residents (Stanford Law School Three Strikes Project and NAACP Legal Defense and Education Fund, 2013). The revision excluded nonserious, nonviolent offenses from the list of crimes eligible for life sentences under the three-strikes law and allowed prisoners who had been sentenced to life for nonviolent crimes to petition for reduced sentences.

A third factor can be seen as a combination of the two preceding approaches, resulting in the formation of developmental or life-course criminology (Loeber & LeBlanc, 1990). During the past 25 years, developmental criminology has experienced substantial growth and holds considerable promise for theoretical development (e.g., Hawkins & Weis, 1985; Sampson & Laub, 1993, 2005; Moffitt, 1994; Paternoster & Brame, 1997; Bartusch et al., 1997; Benson, 2002; Farrington, 2002; Simons et al., 2002; Thornberry et al., 2003; Laub, 2006; Melde & Esbensen, 2011, 2014).

Dale Gaines, right, poses with his sister after his March 2013 release from the Sonoma County Main Adult Detention Facility in Santa Rosa, California. Under three-strikes legislation, Gaines, a twice-convicted burglar, was destined to spend the rest of his life in prison after he tried to sell computer equipment taken in a burglary. The passage of Proposition 36 mandated the early release of thousands of lifers like Gaines.

CREDIT:
AP Photo/Jessica Spencer.

INTEGRATED THEORETICAL MODELS

The integrated approach to theory construction combines existing theories in order to explain the causes of crime better. The theories discussed in earlier chapters have not accounted for much of the variation in crime rates among subgroups of the population. Social structural theories, for example, help to explain the disproportionate representation of minorities and members of the lower classes in official measures of crime and delinquency, but they fail to explain adequately why middle- and upper-class people break the law. Travis Hirschi's social control theory attempts to account for individual variations in criminal activity, but it does not explain why members of certain groups have fewer "bonds" to conventional society. While the conflict perspective claims that the laws are enacted by the rich and powerful to their benefit, there is no consistent evidence to suggest that these statutes cause people to violate the law or that different standards are applied when processing rich or poor offenders through the justice system. Such shortcomings set the stage for new theoretical directions.

The writings of Clifford Shaw and Henry McKay (1942) represent an early attempt at integrating social disorganization and social learning theories. For Shaw and McKay, the organization and physical structure of the community was of major importance in terms of affecting behavior and interaction patterns. It was the diversity of values and behaviors in communities, however, that was instrumental in exposing youths to deviant alternatives. (See Chapter 7 to review Shaw and McKay's work.)

Richard Cloward and Lloyd Ohlin's (1960) theory of differential opportunity combines traditional strain theory with social learning theory. Societal goals can be attained through the use of legitimate or illegitimate means, depending, in part, on a person's access to different opportunity structures. A criminal subculture, for example, will develop when legitimate opportunities for success are blocked or unavailable and illegitimate means are available. This is a classic statement of strain theory: a person deviates because of some external stress. Cloward and Ohlin (see Chapter 7) built upon this strain perspective; they wrote that delinquency is group behavior requiring social support and confirmation. This social learning component maintains that behavior, as well as definitions and rationalizations for the behavior, are learned in interaction with similarly situated individuals.

The foundation for integrating different theoretical orientations thus has a history dating back to the 1940s. It was not until the 1970s, however, that the movement toward the integration of competing theoretical models was referred to in such terms and began to command interest from criminological theorists. Not all theorists, however, were receptive to this trend; some argue that the theories are incompatible because of their contradictory assumptions about the causes of behavior.

Can Theories Be Combined?

At the root of the debate about the appropriateness and utility of the integrated approach lies the issue of whether the assumptions of strain, control, and learning theories are incompatible. In her widely acclaimed book, Ruth Kornhauser (1978:23–5) provided a classification and description of the underlying assumptions of these three major theoretical models. She suggested that social structural theories assume that a general consensus exists with regard to basic values expressed in the criminal law. Violation of the law is not the result of an innate desire or tendency, but is caused by frustration brought about by barriers blocking the attainment of social goals. The source of crime, therefore, is to be found in the organization of society and in the distribution of access to legitimate means for attaining socially approved and desired objectives. Remember, for instance, the theory of anomie put forth by Robert Merton (reviewed in Chapter 7). The disjunction between cultural values and societal norms placed individuals in a state of anomie or normlessness. People responded differently to this structural stress and became conformists, innovators, ritualists, retreatists, or rebels. It is the structure of society, not a specific character trait that places the individual in the position to deviate.

In direct contrast to this assumption of the social structuralist, Kornhauser contended that social control theorists assume that humans are inherently hedonistic, self-serving creatures who will "rape, pillage, and plunder" to their hearts' content unless otherwise restrained. She maintained that these control theorists assume that all segments of the population experience the same amount of strain, in that our desires can be met only by foregoing the gratification of certain other desires. Thus, to get an "A" on your criminology exam, you will need to forgo the pleasure of attending the big social event of the semester. It is your "stake" or belief in conformity that will dictate whether you study or party. Likewise, control theorists argue, it is through the development of this stake in conformity that involvement in criminal behavior is mediated (Hirschi, 1969). This, Kornhauser wrote, is especially the case with criminal activity because illegal means are usually a faster way to satisfy our desires than the legal approach of the normative structure.

These two major theoretical orientations are diametrically opposed to one another in terms of their assumptions about the motivating factors or causes of criminal behavior. Social learning theory presents a third approach. It postulates that deviance or offending behavior is always normative, at least within some subcultural group. Stealing cars may be against the law in society at large, but within a juvenile gang studied by one of the text authors, stealing a car each week was required to maintain one's status in the group. Social learning theorists make no assumptions about the innate qualities of humans; instead, they maintain that a person is born with a "clean slate" and learns to conform to or deviate from the larger societal norms. The cause of delinquency is found in the conflicting subcultures that inevitably result in some individuals being socialized into subcultural values that conflict with what has been defined as legal by society at large. (Table 10.1 provides a summary of the underlying assumptions of these three perspectives.)

TABLE 10.1 Major Theoretical Models and Assumptions

	Strain Theory	Control Theory	Learning Theory
Assumption:	Humans are innately good.	Humans are innately evil, hedonistic.	Humans are neither good nor evil.
Cause of crime:	Frustration brought about by structural malfunction.	Unfulfilled wants fulfilled through illegal avenues due to a lack of "controls" or "bonds" to society.	Socialization into a subculture in which violation of the legal code is normative.
Question posed:	Why do people deviate from the norms?	Why do people conform to the norms?	How are norms learned?

Some theorists argue that it is impossible to combine or integrate these theories into one theoretical model. Travis Hirschi (1979:34), for example, maintained that "separate is better" and wrote that "the assumptions of strain, control, and differential association theories are fundamentally incompatible." Delbert Elliott, on the other hand, represents the integrationists in claiming that "there is nothing inherent in the form or approach to integration that precludes the reconciliation of different assumptions" (1985:132). This debate surrounds the integration perspective.

Approaches to Integration

Most early attempts to integrate theories sought to explain individual levels of behavior through a combination of social psychological theories (Conger, 1976; Cernkovich, 1978; Aultman & Wellford, 1979; Elliott et al., 1979; Johnson, 1979; Segrave & Hasted, 1983; Thornberry, 1987; Winfree et al., 1996). These models were mostly tested with self-report measures of delinquency.

The most common attempts at integration involved social control and social learning theories. Less common has been the integration of social control and strain theories, and even less common have been attempts to integrate all three of the major perspectives. Still other attempts at integration have included the labeling approach, social disorganization, conflict, and deterrence theories. The most common approach is the **end-to-end model**, which combines the theories in a sequential model so that one theoretical perspective is temporally more proximate to the actual behavior than are the other perspectives in the model (Hirschi, 1979). This approach suggests that one of the theories better explains early or prior causes of delinquency, while another is more proximate to actual precipitating factors in criminal activity (see Figure 10.1).

FIGURE 10.1
Example of an end-to-end model.

Let us look at an example of this approach. Assume that a friend of yours, Al, has just been arrested for armed robbery. You want to understand why he would do such a thing, so you go to your criminology professor to discuss it with her. Your professor asks you a lot of questions about Al, and you wind up presenting the following information.

Ever since you have known Al, he has had a bad home life and preferred hanging out with friends to being at his own home. It seemed as if his parents did not want to have anything to do with him. His parents were relatively poor and did not buy Al many presents. In school, Al did all right for a while but by sixth grade he started getting in trouble with teachers for not doing his homework. You seem to remember him ditching school beginning about then. By the time you both were in high school, you had grown apart; Al started smoking and drinking. He occasionally got in trouble at school and got suspended at least once a semester for his antics. His grades were just barely above passing, he did not study, and he did not seem to understand the need to get good grades. The kids that Al hung around with were much like him. After school and on weekends, Al and his friends would hang out and party. You had heard that they occasionally would steal things from cars and sell them to buy beer and weed. Since graduation from high school you had seen Al on occasion, and it seemed that he was still doing the same things he had done in high school.

Your professor now asks you to think about the theories that you have studied this semester. Control theory focuses on the extent to which an individual is attached to conventional adults and involved in conventional activities. We see that Al was not emotionally attached to his parents. Thus, control theorists would say that Al had a low stake in conformity. Furthermore, it appears that Al was not much involved in school. Control theorists would conclude that these facts were what caused Al to commit armed robbery.

Alternatively, strain theorists would concentrate on the fact that Al grew up in poverty and did not have many material goods as a potential source of his law-violating behavior. This situation was further aggravated by his inability to perform well in school, leading to more strain in his young life. His response to this strain was, in Merton's terminology, to become an "innovator." Learning theorists, on the other hand would emphasize the importance of Al's peer group. As his peer group changed, there was now mutual support among this group for smoking, drinking, and skipping school.

Proponents of an integrated approach would seize upon the diversity of possible explanations to account for Al's ultimate arrest. For instance, the initial weak bonds were further weakened by Al's school failure; his school failure either lowered his aspirations or he accepted the fact that he would not be able to attain the goals he had as a young child; and when Al started hanging out with a bad crowd, he found reinforcement for his own behavior. While any one of these explanations can be invoked to account for Al's criminal activity, the integration of multiple theoretical perspectives can be seen as a way of enhancing our overall understanding of criminal behavior.

Objectives of Integration

Why has criminological theory development increasingly turned to integration in recent decades? One reason is the increasingly sophisticated statistical methods available to criminologists. Early theories were usually limited to the examination of relationships between two variables; the connection, for example, between social class and crime. On occasion, a third or controlling variable would be introduced to see if there were different patterns of association. The question might be: what is the relationship between social class and crime when researchers control for race? In other words, is there a difference in crime rates for middle-class whites and lower-class whites? This level of statistical sophistication did not permit criminologists to talk about causes of crime, only correlates. When testing theories, often with the objective of suggesting policies, it is vital that the causes or precursors of the particular behavior be identified.

While it is not essential for you, at this stage, to understand fully the following discussion of statistics, a general overview will help you to appreciate the integrated models approach. The introduction of multiple regression analysis and path analysis in the social sciences provided criminologists with the statistical tools to begin to address causality. Three conditions generally must be met before it can be said that "X" causes "Y":

- The two variables must be correlated;
- X must precede Y temporally; and
- Alternative hypotheses must be eliminated.

Diagrams of causal relationships generally use the following format:

$$X \longrightarrow Y$$

The independent variable, the one hypothesized to be the cause of some phenomenon, is represented by "X" and appears to the left of the schematic representation. The dependent variable, the thing affected by the independent variable, is represented by "Y" and is to the right of "X."

A simple explanation of crime might be that social class position is a cause of criminal behavior. This would be depicted in the following manner:

$$\text{Social Class} \xrightarrow{\quad(-)\quad} \text{Criminal Behavior}$$
$$(X) \qquad\qquad\qquad (Y)$$

This example reflects the strain theory hypothesis that there is an inverse or negative relationship between social class and criminal behavior, that is, that persons in the lower class will have higher rates of criminal behavior.

The introduction of a third variable, one representing social learning theory, produces an example of an integrated model:

$$\text{Social Class} \xrightarrow{(-)} \text{Criminal Association} \xrightarrow{(+)} \text{Criminal Behavior}$$
$$(X1) \qquad\qquad (X2) \qquad\qquad (Y)$$

The integration of strain and social learning specifies the following two hypotheses:

- A negative relationship between social class and the number of friends involved in criminal activities; and
- A positive relationship between criminal associates and involvement in criminal behavior.

Remember the example of Al. He was from a relatively poor or lower-class home, he associated with a "bad crowd," and he wound up committing an armed robbery.

Models such as the one just presented can be tested empirically using multiple regression analysis. This method allows the researcher to determine the amount of variation in the dependent variable that is explained by the independent variables in the model. In a self-report survey of college students, for example, a criminologist would ask questions about:

- The student's social class background;
- The number of the student's friends that engage in criminal behavior; and
- The number of crimes that the student has committed during some time period.

Highlight 10.1 provides a sample of questions that might be used in such a survey. These questions would be asked of a sample of students. The researcher could conduct a multiple regression analysis on the data and present information regarding the strength of relationships between each variable and the extent to which all of the independent variables helped to explain criminal behavior.

HIGHLIGHT 10.1 SAMPLE QUESTIONS FOR A SURVEY TO TEST AN INTEGRATED MODEL

1. Which of the following best describes your social class?

    a) Lower class
    b) Working class
    c) Lower-middle class
    d) Middle class
    e) Upper-middle class
    f) Upper class

2. How many of your friends have done something that could have gotten them in trouble with the law during the past year?

    a) None of them
    b) A few of them

    c) Most of them
    d) All of them

3. How many times during the past year have you done each of the following things?

    a) Stolen something worth more than $5
    b) Hit someone with the idea of seriously hurting them
    c) Used a credit card without the owner's permission
    d) Used illegal drugs

Criminologists often use this statistical procedure to test the utility of their theoretical models. The explained variance of the various theories ranges from 15 percent (Cernkovich, 1978) to 52 percent (Elliott et al., 1985). The relative strengths of the theoretical models in explaining criminal behavior and of variables representing specific theoretical perspectives are influenced, in part, by the particular combinations of theories.

Social strain theory, for example, has little if any power in explaining individual differences in rates of criminal offending when combined with social learning or labeling predictors (Elliott & Voss, 1974; Aultman & Wellford, 1979; Simons et al., 1980). Compared with when each perspective is tested separately, the total explained variance of the models is increased when perspectives are combined.

In addition to the increased power of new statistical procedures, another reason for the surge of interest in the integrated approach is the inadequacy of each of the dominant perspectives to account adequately for the variation in crime rates. During the 1970s, criminology was dominated by a struggle to prove that one theory was better or more powerful than another. Elliott (1985:126) commented on this debate:

> Researchers came to recognize that these crucial tests rarely provided evidence that justified a conclusion that one hypothesis was correct and the other incorrect. At best these tests provided evidence that one hypothesis was more plausible or more powerful than the other. . . . The observation that both hypotheses might be correct and might account for independent portions of the variance in crime was typically overlooked by researchers focusing upon crucial tests, because the objective was to prove one theory right and the other wrong.

The integration approach abandons this competition between theories in favor of seeking more complete understanding of the processes leading to criminal behavior. An example of an integrated model is described in the following sections.

An Early Integrated Theoretical Model

An early example of the **integrated model approach** is the work of Delbert Elliott, Suzanne Ageton, and Rachelle Canter, which incorporates aspects of strain, social learning, and social control perspectives into a single explanatory paradigm. Their model "avoids the class bias inherent in traditional perspectives and takes into account multiple causal paths to sustained patterns of delinquent behavior" (1979:3).

As proponents of the self-report method of measuring delinquent and criminal behavior, Elliott and colleagues believe that it is not only possible, but preferable, to be able to identify individuals that are involved in habitual criminal activity. Early self-report studies found that almost all people surveyed had violated the law and that there were no race and social class differences in rates of offending. With improvements in self-report techniques, more recent studies have been able to identify serious or career offenders (e.g., Elliott et al., 1985; Farrington, 1987; Horney & Marshall, 1991; Howell 2003; Thornberry et al., 2003; Loeber et al., 2005). Refinements in self-report measures have also resulted in the identification of race and class differences once researchers controlled for both the frequency and seriousness of reported offenses (Huizinga & Elliott, 1987). Members of the lower class and racial minorities tend to report greater levels of involvement in delinquent activities. Elliott and his colleagues maintain that it is important to focus on **patterned delinquent activity** when discussing the causes and correlates of delinquency. While most people are law violators, only a minority is heavily involved in criminal activity; that minority accounts for the majority of all crime. Their model, therefore, seeks to explain patterned delinquent behavior.

The Elliott et al. (1985) theoretical model is an example of the end-to-end approach. First, the authors identify early socialization experiences as resulting in strong or weak bonds. The ideas and terminology of this stage of the integrated model are borrowed directly from Travis Hirschi's social control theory. During childhood, children develop varying levels of attachment to parents, teachers, and other conventional adults. Levels and strengths of attachments are related to the child's involvement in and commitment to conventional activities such as school, church, community athletics, and service or hobby clubs. This early socialization process determines, to a large degree, the extent to which the child will be integrated into society or, in the terminology of social control theorists, have a stake in conformity.

Second, Elliott and his colleagues argue that these early socialization outcomes are tested in late childhood and adolescence, as the child is exposed to a greater array of social institutions and experiences. During this stage, youths experience success or failure in conventional contexts such as school, clubs, work, and athletics that subsequently strengthen or attenuate the early bonds. The peer group begins to play an increasingly more important role in the life of the child. The types of peer groups to which the child is exposed serve to weaken or reinforce the early bonds as well as other social experiences. Exposure to conventional peer groups promotes conventional behaviors that lessen the probability of involvement in patterned delinquent behavior. Conversely, exposure to delinquent peer groups reinforces negative social experiences and results in a higher probability of involvement in delinquent behavior patterns. These last two stages of the model reflect the strain and learning perspectives.

An important element of the model is the notion that there are multiple paths leading to delinquent or nondelinquent behavior (Elliott et al., 1985, 1989; Huizinga et al., 1991; Moffitt, 1993; Simons et al., 1994, 2002; Thornberry et al., 2003). For example, a child who starts out with weak bonds may experience success in conventional social contexts and be exposed to conventional peers and subsequently not engage in delinquent activities. Conversely, a child who develops strong attachments to conventional society in the home may experience failure in school and other social contexts and interact with delinquent peers. Such a path would lead to a high probability of involvement

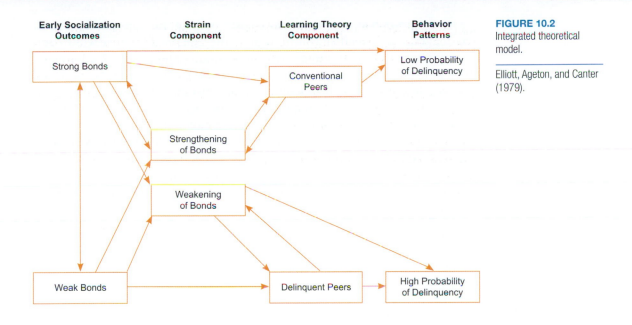

Early Socialization Outcomes	Strain Component	Learning Theory Component	Behavior Patterns

FIGURE 10.2
Integrated theoretical model.

Elliott, Ageton, and Canter (1979).

in patterned delinquent activity. Figure 10.2 summarizes this model and the multiple paths leading to delinquency.

Tests of Integrated Models

Researchers have compared the relative explanatory power of competing theories and then combined them into an integrated theoretical framework. In most instances, this has resulted in an increase in the explained variance. Another objective has been to determine if certain models are better predictors than others of specific types of behaviors. Integrated models, for example, have been used to explain general delinquency, assaultive behavior, property offenses, female delinquency, and various types of drug use. Findings reveal that the ability of a given model to explain behavior varies with the type of behavior in question.

One of the most frequent combinations of theories involves social control and social learning perspectives. Rand Conger (1976) found social control variables to be important but learning theory variables to be better predictors of delinquent behavior. He concluded that social control theory is incomplete, not incorrect. "By combining the notion that individuals are 'bonded' to others with certain principles of social learning theory, the groundwork for a stronger theory is developed. Essentially, the social learning model clarified how attachments will influence deviant behavior by including to whom one is attached in the analysis" (Conger, 1976:37).

Other studies have found similar results; each of the theoretical perspectives makes an independent contribution to the explained variance while combining them increases the total explained variance (Linden, 1978; Johnson, 1979; Johnstone, 1983; and Thornberry et al., 1991). One study of delinquency, however, found that when differential association theory is properly operationalized (i.e., the theoretical concepts are properly specified through questionnaire items), it accounts for more than one-half of the variation in reported delinquency and mediates the effects of the social control variables (Matsueda, 1982). In a test of interactional theory (an integration of social control and learning theories in which the authors stipulate that there are "feedback" loops between variables), Thornberry and colleagues reiterate the need to understand how both perspectives promote criminal behavior. They write:

> Theoretically, the long-standing debate between differential association or learning theory on the one hand and social control on the other may have unnecessarily occupied the time of theoretical criminology. The issue should not be posed as a question of whether association with delinquent peers causes delinquency, or whether adolescents, once having committed delinquent behavior, seek out and associate with others who engage in similar behaviors. . . . The present results suggest the need to specify how the reciprocal relationship between these variables develops as adolescents proceed from the initiation of delinquency to its maintenance and eventual cessation (Thornberry et al. 1994:75).

Criminologists also have tested models combining social strain and social control theories. These models generally account for less of the variation in delinquency or crime rates than do the social learning/social control approaches (Cernkovich, 1978; Segrave & Hasted, 1983). Still other theorists have integrated three or more of the dominant theoretical perspectives. While findings from these studies vary slightly, the general results consistently support the enhanced explanatory power of these integrated models (Simons et al., 1980; Winfree et al., 1981; Elliott et al., 1985, 1989).

Policy Relevance of Integrated Models

Policy recommendations are implicit in these integrated theoretical models. The integrated model proposed by Elliott and colleagues, for example, emphasizes the role of early parenting in developing the child's social bond to society. A number of researchers have evaluated proposals and programs for improving the ability of parents and parents-to-be to be effective (Loeber & Dishion, 1983; Farrington, 1987; Greenwood, 1987; Hawkins et al., 1987; Larzelere & Patterson, 1990; McCord, 1991). These ideas generally involve either the instruction of high-school students in effective parenting or the provision of training for parents of children already enrolled in school. David Hawkins and his colleagues at the University of Washington are involved in a longitudinal study evaluating a program that seeks to teach parents how better to discipline, monitor, and in general socialize their children. Other efforts to improve the child's early social bond include preschool programs such as Head Start. A longitudinal study of the Perry Pre-school Program, an experimental program to assess both short- and long-term effects of preschool participation, found that program participants not only had fewer school-related problems than the control group, but also had lower levels of involvement in delinquent and criminal behavior (Schweinhart, 1987). Integration theorists who support elements of social control theory would advocate these preventive measures.

For individuals already in the criminal justice system, rehabilitation programs incorporating efforts to strengthen the offender's attachment to society are recommended. This would include educational and vocational training as well as counseling for drug dependency and other problems. Other policy recommendations depend upon the specific model.

THE CRIMINAL CAREER DEBATE

A relatively heated controversy in criminology concerns whether criminals comprise a distinctive group within the general population. Proponents of the **criminal career** concept (Blumstein et al., 1988a, 1988b; Barnett et al., 1992) maintain that individuals can be dichotomized into active offenders and non-offenders. Critics (Gottfredson & Hirschi, 1990; Rowe et al., 1990) suggest that this is an artificial and erroneous distinction. They posit that humans possess different levels of "crime proneness" or varying propensities for crime. While this may appear to be an academic debate about the nature of crime, it has major policy ramifications. The "three-strikes" statutes enacted during the 1990s underscore its importance.

Public opinion polls continually reveal that crime is one of the major concerns reported by Americans. Media reports of random violence, gang disputes, and drug abuse appear daily and apparently contribute to the general perception that crime in America is out of control. As discussed in Chapter 4, however, while the crime rate increased from 1972 to 1991, crime has actually declined each year since 1992. Given the public concern with crime and the fear of victimization, a common political theme has been to "get tough on crime" and concern with crime-prone individuals (or career criminals) supports this approach. If it is correct that individuals can be categorized as active offenders or nonoffenders, then the argument can be made that crime rates will decrease if we identify the active offenders and imprison them. During the 1980s, we witnessed the introduction of habitual offender laws also based on the premise that life sentences for repeat offenders would protect society and reduce crime. Given the prominence of such policies in the current era, it is important that we examine their theoretical and empirical underpinnings.

The criminal career paradigm dates back to the pioneering work of Eleanor Glueck and Sheldon Glueck during the 1930s and 1940s. In their widely cited study of 500 delinquent boys and a matched sample of 500 nondelinquents, Glueck and Glueck found that the delinquent boys continued their illegal activity into adulthood. Investigation of official records and interviews with the study participants when they were 31 years old found that 62 (14 percent) of the 442 nondelinquents located had adult convictions. Of the 438 delinquents located, 354 (81 percent) had been arrested as adults. Glueck and Glueck found the following characteristics to be more descriptive of the delinquent than nondelinquent sample:

> . . . they are less adequate than the non-delinquents in capacity to operate on a fairly efficient level and have less emotional stability. . . they are more dynamic and energetic, much more aggressive, adventurous, and positively suggestible, as well as stubborn. . . more inclined to impulsive and non-reflective expression of their energy-drives. . . . Such temperamental equipment is in itself highly suggestive of the causes for their greater inclination to ignore or readily break through the bonds of restriction imposed by custom or law (Glueck & Glueck, 1950:251–2).

This early career research was largely ignored by American criminologists, in part because of the emphasis on nonsociological explanatory factors. However, Glueck and Glueck's research has been resurrected in recent years.

Research conducted by Marvin Wolfgang and his colleagues (1972) at the University of Pennsylvania also provided early fuel for the criminal career debate. Their study of a cohort of males born in Philadelphia in 1945 found that 6 percent of the 9,945 boys accounted for more than 50 percent of the officially recorded delinquent acts. More importantly, this same 6 percent accounted for 63 percent of all Index offenses. With all the caveats about relying upon official arrest data aside, the policy relevance of this finding is clear: identify and isolate this criminal 6 percent and reduce crime. For instance, several studies report that youth gang members account for approximately 75 percent of all violent offenses (Huizinga, 1997; Howell, 2003; Thornberry et al., 2003).

The criminal career research, according to Daniel Nagin and Kenneth Land (1993), was fueled by the work of two engineers concerned about the high levels of crime in New York City. They applied their mathematical training to model the effect of incapacitating offenders for varying lengths of time. In their analyses they considered both the onset and termination of criminal activity, clearly implying that criminals are distinguishable from noncriminals.

As the most vocal proponents of the career paradigm, Alfred Blumstein and his colleagues have argued that there may well be different explanatory models for the initiation, maintenance, and termination of criminal activity. Research examining criminal behavior (Blumstein & Graddy, 1982) and drug use (Esbensen & Elliott, 1994) has indeed found different explanatory factors associated with initiation and termination of the respective activities.

Widespread agreement exists regarding the sequence of illegal activity from adolescence to adulthood, and there is virtually no disagreement about the positive relationship between past and future criminal behavior. The controversy revolves around whether various types of criminals exist who have different crime histories. Michael Gottfredson and Travis Hirschi argue that crime is the product of a single underlying construct—a criminal propensity—identified as low self-control (1988, 1990). Consequently, for them, it is nonsensical to discuss criminal careers and different paths to crime. On the other hand, Arnold Barnett and his associates contend that criminal career research allows for

> the separate examination of (1) participation in offending (the distinction between those who engage in crime and those who do not); (2) characterization of the continuing criminal career, represented by the individual frequency of offending; and (3) termination of offending. Our approach allows for the possibility that different factors could influence these different facets of a criminal career, whereas the single-factor approach presumes that all aspects of a criminal career are influenced by the same factors in the same way (1992:133).

Given these diametrically opposing viewpoints, it should come as no surprise that this has been at times a heated dispute. While agreeing to comment on the two positions, Kenneth Land (1992:149) wrote that it "would be somewhat like trying to referee a fight between King Kong and Godzilla—with a substantial likelihood of being crushed in the middle, regardless of what I say." A different approach to the criminal career debate has been proposed by David Rowe, Wayne Osgood, and Alan Nicewander. They propose that an unobservable yet relatively stable set of factors accounts for an individual's "crime proneness." This **latent trait approach** assumes that there is some trait associated with the individual that determines the likelihood that the person will engage in crime. Their position:

> . . . largely falls on the side of the current debate that is articulated by Hirschi and Gottfredson. Nevertheless, we do not join Hirschi and Gottfredson in the wholesale rejection of the criminal career approach. Instead, we see merit in studying the distribution of criminal acts over individuals' lives, and we believe that a latent trait approach provides the most appropriate basis for such research (Rowe et al. 1990:238).

According to Blumstein and his colleagues, "the concept of criminal career refers to the longitudinal sequence of offenses committed by an offender who has a detectable rate of offending during some period" (1988a:2). It could be said that a one-time experimenter in crime has a criminal career spanning that one instance. Generally, however, a more restrictive interpretation is accepted. A criminal career consists of a beginning (referred to as **initiation**), a period of offending (**duration**) at some measurable level (**frequency**, or **lambda**), and a period of inactivity (variably referred to as **discontinuity** or **termination**). The term criminal career signifies the sequence of offending during some time period, not an assumption that an individual earns a livelihood through criminal activity. Blumstein and colleagues (1988b) also suggest that the criminal career paradigm does not imply that there is any special progression of behaviors or any specialization of behaviors, as Gottfredson and Hirschi (1988) have attributed to the criminal career position. In an issue of the Crime and Justice series published by the University of Chicago Press, Alex Piquero, David Farrington, and Al Blumstein (2003) provided a comprehensive review of the state of criminal career theory and research at the turn of the century. Gang Feature 10.1 reports on findings from the longitudinal studies conducted in Denver and Rochester, examining the degree to which gang membership fits into the criminal career debate.

A number of commentators have confused the criminal career research with that regarding **career criminals** (or habitual offenders). The latter would be supportive of an incapacitative model while the former would only limitedly support incapacitation. Criminal careers have a beginning and some period of active offending but, importantly, they also have periods of low offending or nonoffending. The career criminal conception assumes that the criminal

---

GANG FEATURE 10.1 ONCE IN A GANG, YOU'RE IN FOR LIFE

The title of this Gang Feature is a statement commonly heard when listening to gang members on talk shows or in interviews with the media. The gang is a lifelong commitment. To what extent is this an accurate picture? Not very, if the research literature is any indication. Several observational and qualitative studies (e.g., the research with New York City gang girls conducted by Anne Campbell and the qualitative interviews with St. Louis gang members reported by Scott Decker and Barrik Van Winkle) include discussions about members leaving the gang, but surprisingly little attention has been given to this aspect of gang life. Most attention has been to the recruitment process and the activities of the gang. Leaving the gang, as with desistance of criminal activity in the criminal career debate, deserves greater attention.

Longitudinal surveys, such as the Denver Youth Survey and the Rochester Youth Development Survey, have allowed researchers to examine the "career" of gang members. These surveys interviewed the same youths over a period of time and were able to document gang membership across time. Somewhat surprising was the finding that most gang members claim membership for one year or less. Gang membership turns out to be a fluid phenomenon, not all that dissimilar from other adolescent peer group associations.

In the Denver Youth Survey, Esbensen and Huizinga (1993) examined the relationship between gang membership and involvement in serious delinquent offending. As part of this analysis, they identified the years of actual gang membership. Of the 90 gang members in their study, only 18 of them reported being in the gang for two or more consecutive years, and only eight of these youths were in the gang for three or more years. Another 12 were members for two nonconsecutive years. In other words, 60 of the 90 gang members reported being in the gang during only one year of the four-year study.

With respect to serious delinquency, Esbensen and Huizinga report that gang membership is associated with higher rates of offending. Interestingly, the increase in offending begins in years prior to joining, but increases drastically during the year of membership. They report that gang members are more likely to commit serious crimes and, importantly, to commit them more frequently. In other publications, Thornberry et al. (1991) have reported similar results from the Rochester study, and Hill and colleagues have replicated these findings with a sample of Seattle youths (Hill, Lui & Hawkins, 2001).

activity is relatively constant. The criminal career perspective does not support the three-strikes notion as life events such as marriage, divorce, parenthood, employment, unemployment, and military service have significant impacts on patterns of offending (Horney et al., 1995). Thus, it is possible that incarceration of a three-time offender may *not* have any significant effect on the crime rate.

Policy Relevance of the Criminal Career Paradigm

The criminal career paradigm suggests that a policy of selective incapacitation will affect the crime rate. The objective is to identify career offenders, incarcerate them during their periods of high offending, and thus reduce crime. In response to this, Gottfredson and Hirschi write, "the common expectation that short-term changes in the probabilities of punishment (such as arrest) or in the severity of punishment (such as length of sentence) will have a significant effect on the likelihood of criminal activity misconstrues the nature of self-control" (1990:255–6).

In the current atmosphere of "get tough" on crime, the criminal career paradigm has attracted considerable attention. The call for more prisons, longer sentences, mandatory minimum sentences, and habitual offender laws (also referred to as "three strikes") rests largely on the belief that criminal activity can be reduced through incapacitation of offenders, especially high-rate offenders. If judges can correctly identify those individuals variably referred to as habitual offenders and career criminals, then some identifiable number of crimes can be prevented. The issue then becomes one of cost (of building and incarcerating offenders) weighed against the benefits (of crimes and social damage prevented).

The objectives of criminal career research are threefold: (1) to accurately identify the high-rate offender; (2) to identify factors associated with onset, maintenance, and termination; and (3) to determine the average number of offenses committed by each offender during some period of time. To date, the last objective has received the most attention from criminologists involved in the criminal career debate.

In 1982, Peter Greenwood co-authored the RAND Report, a survey of prisoners in three states. Greenwood determined that the average number of offenses committed by these inmates per year, while varying considerably, could be estimated at much more than 100. Thus, for every offender imprisoned, more than 100 crimes would be prevented. In a subsequent publication, Edwin Zedlewski (1987) estimated that 187 felonies are committed each year by the typical "career criminal." Other researchers have determined the offending rate to be considerably less than either of these estimates. Alfred Blumstein and Jacqueline Cohen (1979) suggest that the number of felonies committed by adult offenders is approximately ten per year. In their investigation of Nebraska prisoners, Julie Horney and Ineke Marshall (1991) found that the estimates provided by Zedlewski overestimated lambda (the frequency of offending) by 72 percent. The Horney and Marshall data rely upon an elaborate month-by-month interview schedule that allowed for finer measurement than the earlier surveys that produced higher estimates. A subsequent examination of offending differences between imprisoned and free offenders is provided by José Canela-Cacho and his colleagues, Alfred Blumstein and Jacqueline Cohen (1997). They report substantial differences between these two groups of offenders, with the incarcerated offenders committing from 10 to 50 times as many offenses a year as the free offenders. While this may seem to be a purely academic question, serious policy implications are associated with the size of lambda. Using Zedlewski's estimate, for example, led to the conclusion that spending $25 million to build more prisons to incarcerate more prisoners for longer periods of time would produce a social saving of $430 million in terms of crimes prevented. If, however, the estimates provided by Canela-Cacho and his colleagues and those reported by Horney and Marshall are correct, then the benefits of the incapacitation model reported by Zedlewski are considerably overstated.

Among criminologists, little disagreement exists regarding the futility and inappropriateness of the "three-strikes" policy. This cannot be attributed to a liberal "soft on crime" orientation but rather to empirical research. Despite the overwhelming criminological opposition, politicians and many in the general public support the three strikes approach. Why are the supposed experts being ignored? Is the politician's support based merely on re-election concerns? Why is the public so intent to put its fellow citizens away for life? These are important and interesting questions.

DEVELOPMENTAL AND LIFE-COURSE CRIMINOLOGY

The criminal career paradigm and integrated theoretical models provide a foundation for the discussion of developmental and life-course criminological theories, a perspective that has won wide acclaim in criminological circles in recent years. Developmental and life-course theories focus on the development of antisocial behavior across the life course and the various factors that promote stability and change in behavior. Similar to the criminal career paradigm, a segment of developmental and **life-course criminology (LCC)** is devoted to studying and describing the characteristics of antisocial behavior, such as the onset, escalation, variety, and desistance of such behaviors. The development of antisocial behavior may be captured by the idea of a trajectory. A **trajectory** is defined as a set of developmental sequences that describe the unfolding of a behavior over time. For instance, Loeber and colleagues (1993) described the developmental sequences that make up the trajectories for disruptive, aggressive, and covert behaviors. Their model described the initiation, progression, and specialization of disruptive, aggressive, and covert behaviors from childhood into adulthood.

A second component of developmental and life-course criminology is the study of **risk factors** that are related to the onset, escalation, generalization/

variety, and desistance of antisocial behavior. Similar to integrated criminological theories, developmental and life-course theories recognize that the causes of antisocial and criminal behavior may vary across the life course. For instance, as Elliott and colleagues' (1979) integrated model proposed, attachments to parents may be relevant to the development of antisocial behavior in childhood, while delinquent peer influences may be more important to adolescent antisocial behavior. Other criminologists have argued that antisocial behavior may be related to the same type of risk factor over time, but that the expression of that risk factor may change over time. Sampson and Laub's (1993) age-graded informal social control theory, for example, argues that weak social bonds may be related to antisocial behavior in both childhood and early adulthood, but that parental social bonds are relevant to childhood antisocial behavior while bonds to spouses and employment are more relevant in adulthood. These approaches emphasize that there may be variation in the risk factors for antisocial behavior both between domains of risk factors (i.e., different risk factors from qualitatively different domains) and within domains of risk factors (i.e., different risk factors from the same domain). This difference, while seemingly minor, enriches how we think about the risk factors for antisocial behavior, and it helps categorize the risk factors within an integrated framework. An example of this linkage of risk factors to theoretical perspectives can be found in the integrated model proposed by Esbensen and his colleagues (2010).

Developmental and life-course criminologists also recognize that risk factors develop along their own trajectories. That is, risk factors can also be described in terms of their onset, escalation, variety, and desistance. Researchers have recently begun investigating how the trajectories of risk factors parallel or overlap the trajectories of antisocial behavior. For instance, Stoolmiller's (1994) analysis of 206 boys from the Oregon Youth Study revealed that: (1) boys experienced significant increases in antisocial behavior, increases in delinquent peer association, and decreases in parental supervision from Grades 4–8; and (2) increases in delinquent peer association and increases in poor parental supervision were related to increases in antisocial behavior among boys from Grades 4–8 (see Figure 10.3). Stoolmiller also found that there was a lack of absolute and relative stability in antisocial behavior, delinquent peer association, and parental supervision from childhood into adolescence. This study was one of the first investigations to find that within- and between-individual changes in antisocial behavior were a function of within- and between-individual changes in peer association and parental supervision.

In line with Cullen's recommendations, a new division within the American Society of Criminology, The Division of Developmental and Life-course Criminology, was created in 2012. The division aims to advance the study of developmental criminology and criminal careers, as well as encourage discussions regarding developmental and life-course research and interactions among academics, practitioners, and policymakers.

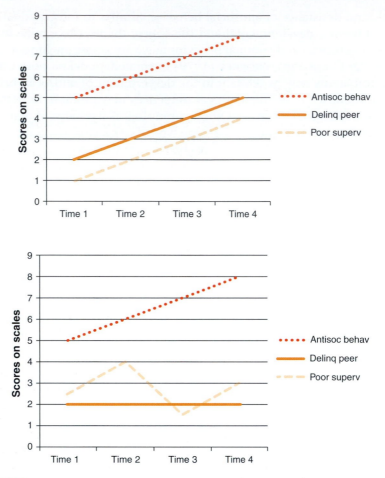

FIGURE 10.3
How changes in risk factors affect changes in antisocial behavior. One could plot the average levels of a risk factor over time and see if it parallels the average levels of antisocial behavior over time. (Top): This illustrates if the risk factor has the same trajectory as antisocial behavior. (Bottom): This illustrates if the risk factor has a different trajectory than antisocial behavior.

Study of Antisocial Behavior

Unlike traditional criminological theories that zeroed in on adolescence as the key time for delinquent behavior, developmental criminology recognizes that antisocial behavior often emerges very early in life (often as early as age 2), and that behavior continues to develop and take shape across the life course. Tremblay and colleagues (2004), for instance, observed individual differences in physically aggressive behavior (i.e., kicks, hits, bites, fights, bullies) as early as 17 months of age. Their analysis of 504 children revealed that approximately 28 percent of youths did not engage in any physical aggression, 58 percent engaged in a moderate amount of physical aggression, and 14 percent engaged in very

---

HIGHLIGHT 10.2 NEW DIRECTIONS FOR CRIMINOLOGY

Life-course and developmental criminology is quickly becoming an accepted paradigm in criminology. Two pieces of evidence to support this conclusion are the life-course symposium held at the University of Albany in April 2005 and Francis T. Cullen's 2010 Sutherland Address at the Annual Meeting of the American Society of Criminology. First, the University of Albany symposium was one of the first gatherings where criminologists collectively came together to discuss their current work in life-course/developmental criminological research, as well as the theoretical and empirical implications of the life-course paradigm. It featured presentations by Robert Sampson and John Laub (2005), Daniel Nagin and Richard Tremblay (2005), and Terence Thornberry (2005). In his concluding remarks to the symposium, Al Blumstein (2005) highlighted the value of longitudinal research designs that allow for within-individual examination of the developmental trajectories of criminal careers. Importantly, he points out that the various stages of the criminal career, such as onset of crime, have different antecedents depending upon when in the life cycle they occur. In his remarks he also emphasized the importance of collaboration: "One would hope that these important streams of research would join up in some ways so that the results would be stronger than that resulting from each of the authors alone" (Blumstein, 2005:253).

Francis T. Cullen's Sutherland Award address also highlighted the growing relevance of developmental and life-course criminology in the discipline. In his address, the sociologically-trained criminologist notes that the discipline has been devoted to **adolescence-limited criminology (ALC)** since the 1960s. ALC is a paradigm in criminology that focuses exclusively on sociological causes of crime (and patronizes individual causes of crime), it predominantly investigates the causes of adolescent delinquency, and it clutches onto deductive research while ignoring and devaluing the importance of inductive research (Cullen, 2011). When referencing ALC, he states that "although producing enormous good, (it) is now bankrupt, even if we do not realize it" (p. 289). Cullen discusses the origins of this ALC, and puts forth recommendations on where the field should move in the twenty-first century. In his "Eight Steps to Building a New Criminology," Cullen states that "LCC (life-course criminology) should replace ALC (adolescence-limited criminology) as the organizing framework for the study of crime causation," and that "nearly all serious researchers already recognize that LCC is criminology" (p. 310). He argues that one of the first steps to moving fully to a life-course criminology is by understanding how each of the traditional criminological theories (i.e., strain, differential association) are age-graded, similar to how Sampson and Laub presented an age-graded theory of informal social control. In particular, he calls on researchers to develop the area of child criminology, since many of the antecedents to life-course–persistent offending occur during infancy and childhood. Other recommendations include developing a deeper understanding of criminal decision making and understanding "individuals as they are placed into, choose, negotiate, and are constrained by different social domains" (p. 312).

---

high levels of aggression from 17 months of age until 42 months of age. Other studies have also found that a small percentage of youths exhibit high levels of antisocial and aggressive behavior very early in life, and that approximately 40 percent of the youths who exhibit severe behavioral problems early in life continue to engage in antisocial behavior at high rates in adolescence and adulthood (Robins, 1966; Mitchell & Rosa, 1981; Loeber, 1982; Patterson, 1982; Huesmann et al., 1984). These findings suggest that antisocial behavior may emerge early in development, and that these behavioral problems may persist into adolescence and adulthood.

An important concept that is used to describe the development of antisocial behavior is that of stability. **Stability** is described as the consistency of behavior over time. Researchers have identified two forms of stability: absolute stability and relative stability. **Absolute stability** refers to consistency in the average level of a trait or behavior for an individual over time. Absolute stability is used to

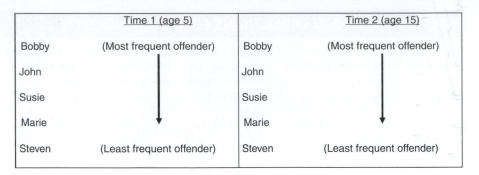

FIGURE 10.4
Relative stability in criminal offending. As illustrated, the rank ordering of the respondents does not change from Time 1 to Time 2. The lack of change in rank ordering suggests that there is perfect relative stability in criminal offending.

describe the stability of behavior *within* individuals. For example, one would say that there is absolute stability in an individual's behavior if a person committed an average of five crimes last year and he or she committed an average of five crimes during the current year; the average level for that individual did not change and it was consistent from one year to the next. **Relative stability** describes the stability of behavior *between* individuals. Relative stability is defined as consistency in the rankings of individuals on an observable characteristic over time. For example, researchers could have a list of five individuals that they rank ordered on some characteristic, such as frequency of criminal offending. Perfect relative stability would be present if the ordering of those individuals remained the same over time (see Figure 10.4), while a lack of relative stability would be present if the rank orderings of the individuals changed over time (e.g., if Marie was the most frequent offender at Time 2, while Bobby was the least frequent offender at Time 2).

Two processes that may produce stability in behavior are those of *cumulative continuity* and *interactional continuity*. **Cumulative continuity** states that antisocial behavior produces negative consequences (i.e., peer rejection, poor academic achievement, severing of parent-child bonds), and in turn these negative consequences promote the stability of antisocial behavior. Thus, cumulative continuity can be summarized as: early antisocial behavior → negative consequences → later antisocial behavior. Sampson and Laub (1993) posit that antisocial behavior leads to a "knifing off" of prosocial bonds and opportunities, and the knifing off of prosocial bonds in turn leads to the exacerbation of antisocial behavior. An example of cumulative continuity may be that individuals who are released from correctional facilities have a difficult time finding employment and stable housing once released from the institution and this lack of employment and housing causes them to return to a life of crime.

The second continuity process relevant to life-course criminology is interactional continuity. **Interactional continuity** states that: (1) individuals' traits cause them to interact in a certain way within their environment, (2) individuals tend to create the same social situations over and over again, and (3) the stability in their social interactions creates stability in individuals' behavior. That is, individuals proactively select themselves into certain environments, consistently react to environments in a certain manner, or evoke certain reactions from their environment, and these interactions promote consistency in how one behaves. For instance, individuals who are abrasive and difficult to be around tend to (1) select themselves into peer groups with other abrasive individuals (because that feels natural and people will not confront their behavior because they are all behaving that way), (2) misinterpret social cues and react to others in an abrasive way, and (3) evoke negative reactions from others (i.e., confrontation, rejection, or isolation) because of their own awkward or caustic behavior. All of these social processes cause individuals to continue in their maladaptive behavior.

Cumulative continuity and interactional continuity are two potential processes that may promote stability in antisocial behavior, but criminologists have put forth two larger perspectives to organize the processes underlying the stability of behavior. These two perspectives are the *state dependence* perspective and the *population heterogeneity* perspective. The **state dependence** position argues that early antisocial behavior indirectly increases the probability of later antisocial behavior via cumulative continuity and interactional continuity processes. That is, antisocial behavior may knife off one from prosocial opportunities and facilitate criminogenic social interactions with others. In turn, reduced prosocial opportunities and negative social interactions promote the continuation of antisocial behavior. The **population heterogeneity** approach, however, contends that early antisocial behavior is related to later criminal behavior because of some underlying propensity for antisocial behavior. For instance, Gottfredson and Hirschi's (1990) *A General Theory of Crime* proposes that individuals with low self-control will engage in antisocial behavior across the life course because they have low self-control across the life course; thus, the trait of low self-control (not sociological consequences) causes antisocial behavior in childhood, adolescence, and adulthood. These two perspectives offer competing hypotheses about the stability of antisocial behavior, with one emphasizing the role of social institutions and opportunities in creating stability (state dependence) and one emphasizing the role of personality traits or propensities (population heterogeneity) in the consistency of behavior.

The concepts of stability, state dependence, and population heterogeneity speak to the unfolding of behavior over time and how psychological or social factors can promote consistency in antisocial behavior. It is important to recognize, however, that psychological and sociological events can act as **turning points** in one's trajectory of antisocial behavior. A turning point is any significant event that increases or decreases the frequency, variety, and/or severity of antisocial behavior. For instance, Sampson and Laub's (1993) age-graded theory of informal social control argues that social transitions like getting married, going into the military, or securing a great job may cause individuals to desist or change their offending patterns.

The study of antisocial and criminal behavior is only one facet of life-course criminology. Another area is identifying the risk and protective factors that explain the stability and desistance of antisocial behavior. The next section briefly describes this aspect.

Causes of Antisocial Behavior Across the Life Course

Life-course criminology posits that the causes of antisocial behavior are multifaceted and that they may change in either type or expression across the life course. More specifically, life-course criminology argues that antisocial behavior results from the intersection of genetic/biological, psychological, sociological, and situational risk factors. Thus, unlike traditional criminological theories that focus predominantly on either genetic/biological, psychological, sociological, or situational risk factors, life-course criminology holds that all domains of risk factors are potentially important to our understanding of criminal behavior.

Life-course criminologists also assert that the risk factors for antisocial behavior may vary or differ across the life course. For instance, Lipsey and Derzon (1998) found that the strongest predictors of adolescent and adult violent behavior were different at ages 6–11 and ages 12–14. Their meta-analysis revealed that the strongest predictors of later violence were general offending and substance use at ages 6–11, but that the strongest predictors of violence were weakened social bonds to prosocial individuals and associations with deviant peers at ages 12–14. Thus, behavioral risk factors at ages 6–11 were relevant to the explanation of violent behavior in adolescence and early adulthood, while interpersonal relationships at ages 12–14 explained later violent behavior. These findings (and others) suggest that a risk factor may be relevant to antisocial behavior only at certain points in the life course.

Other theorists have argued that the same risk factor may be important to understanding antisocial behavior at two different points in the life course, but that the expression of that risk factor may change over time. Sampson and Laub (1993), for example, asserted that weakened social bonds are important to explaining antisocial behavior at all points during the life course, but that different types of social bonds may be more or less relevant to behavior at certain stages. That is, poor attachments to parents may be relevant to explaining antisocial behavior during childhood, while weakened attachments to one's spouse or workplace are more important to explaining antisocial behavior in adulthood.

One additional point that should be made is that the risk factors that promote antisocial and criminal behavior may or may not be the same factors that promote desistance from antisocial behavior. For instance, Sampson and Laub (1993) argued that weakened social bonds lead to the development of antisocial behavior among young males, and that males who strengthened their bonds in adulthood (either through marriage or work) desisted from criminal activity. Other researchers, however, have argued that the causes of crime may be quite different from the causes of desistance. Baskin and Sommers' (1998) ethnography of 170 women in New York found that women often cited a need for excitement and attachment to delinquent peers as reasons for their initial involvement in robbery but then cited financial reasons for their continued involvement in robbery. Desistance, however, was precipitated by negative social and personal experiences (i.e., illness, jail) and by changes in their self-identity. Thus, risk-seeking behavior and delinquent peers were relevant to the onset of robbery, economic or financial reasons promoted the continuity of robbery, and deterrence-based processes and a cognitive transformation were relevant to the desistance process. These results show that the predictors of the onset, stability, and desistance of antisocial behavior may be quite different.

Two specific theories that are representative of the life-course paradigm will be reviewed in the following sections: (1) Terrie Moffitt's (1993) typology of offenders and (2) Sampson and Laub's (1993) age-graded theory of informal social control.

Moffitt's Typology: Adolescence-limited vs. Life-course–persistent

Moffitt, a psychologist by training, observed that a small group of youths (5–10 percent) engage in antisocial behavior across the life course, while a large majority of youths engage in antisocial behavior only during adolescence. To describe these two groups, she created a typology of offenders, with one group described as life-course–persistent offenders and the other group referred to as adolescence-limited offenders. **Life-course–persistent offenders** typically exhibit antisocial behavior very early in life (age 3), and continue to offend late into adulthood. Their antisocial behavior is pervasive, stretching across multiple settings and engaging in various forms of antisocial behavior across the life course. **Adolescence-limited offenders** tend to begin offending during adolescence (ages 11–15), and typically desist from antisocial behavior early in their twenties. These adolescence-limited offenders resemble the life-course–persistent offenders in terms of antisocial behavior in adolescence but not in childhood or adulthood.

These two groups not only differed in their offending patterns—one concentrated in adolescence and the other with antisocial behavior diffused across settings and across developmental stages—but the groups also differed in the risk factors that drove their antisocial behavior. According to Moffitt (1993), life-course–persistent offending results from the intersection of biologically based neuropsychological problems and negative social environments. That is, youths who have neuropsychological problems (i.e., cognitive delays, poor motor skills, deficits in verbal skills and executive functioning) are at a disadvantage when learning new skills and learning to navigate their social world, but this disadvantage is exacerbated when youths are born into an unstable, chaotic, harsh, or neglectful environment. Moffitt argues that it is the interaction between biologically based neuropsychological problems/atypical neural development and criminogenic environments (biology and environment) that promotes the development of an antisocial personality and the emergence of antisocial behavior. Thus, life-course–persistent offending is most likely to occur when youths have both biological and environmental risk factors.

Biological and environmental risk factors explain the onset of offending, but the processes of interactional continuity and cumulative continuity account for the stability of antisocial behavior of life-course–persistent offenders. More specifically, youths are at risk for continuing their antisocial behavior at multiple life stages because (1) their parents may intentionally or unintentionally create a home environment that allows antisocial behavior to flourish; (2) youths may routinely misinterpret social cues and inappropriately react to social situations, which may lead to violence directly or indirectly via weakened social bonds; (3) youths may evoke negative reactions from their parents, teachers, and prosocial peers because of their bad behavior or inappropriate reactions; and (4) youths may select themselves into peer groups and settings that facilitate their antisocial behavior. Youths may also exhibit stability in their antisocial behavior because their behavior creates a series of negative consequences that may entrench them into a life of antisocial behavior. For instance, youths who engage in antisocial behavior may be rejected by prosocial peers, they may lack access and attractiveness to prosocial partners, and they may be denied positive opportunities for advancement. All of these consequences may increase the likelihood that life-course–persistent youths will continue to offend.

While the origins of life-course–persistent offending lie in biological processes and criminogenic environments, Moffitt asserted that adolescence-limited offending is a function of the developmental stage and social interactions. During adolescence, youths are caught in the *maturity gap*, or a gap between their physiological age and their social age. Adolescents are physically ready to procreate, to work, and to engage in other various "adult-like" behaviors. Society, however, does not allow adolescents to engage in a range of "adult-like" behaviors, such as going to bars or dictating how one spends his or her time. This maturity gap creates a sense of frustration and a need to assert one's independence. In an effort to appear more adult-like and to assert one's independence, youths may begin engaging in antisocial behavior—smoking, drinking, experimenting with drugs, having casual sex, and minor theft.

Typical adolescents, however, are not very skilled at engaging in even relatively minor forms of delinquency, and thus they need access to more highly skilled antisocial youths (such as life-course–persistent youths) to engage in delinquency effectively. Adolescence-limited offenders may associate with life-course–persistent peers, and they may begin to mimic their delinquent behaviors. By mimicking the behavior of life-course–persistent offenders, adolescence-limited offenders appear more "adult-like," which makes them feel good (i.e., proud) and reinforces their desire to participate in antisocial behaviors. Thus, the maturity gap creates the motivation for engaging in delinquent behavior, while social mimicry provides the instruction and reinforcement for engaging in antisocial behavior.

Moffitt asserts that most adolescence-limited offenders should desist from antisocial and criminal behavior once they begin to transition into adulthood. As youths mature, they gain access to "adult-like" opportunities, and so the internal motivation for engaging in antisocial behavior may dissipate. In addition, antisocial behavior is generally not viewed as socially acceptable as youths move into early adulthood, and so the social environment may provide less reinforcement and more punishment for antisocial behavior. As a result, most adolescence-limited offenders will reduce their offending patterns once they reach adulthood. Some adolescence-limited offenders, however, will continue to offend if they are caught in any "snares" (e.g., lack of a high school diploma, incarceration, drug addiction), which may prevent them from obtaining legitimate opportunities in adulthood.

In sum, Moffitt argued that there are two groups of offenders who typically differ in their patterns of antisocial behavior in childhood and adulthood, and who have different causal explanations for their behavior. The typology also presumed that adolescence-limited offenders' antisocial trajectories are marked by desistance as youths moved into adulthood, while life-course–persistent offenders' trajectories are marked by stability and a lack of desistance. This lack of desistance among the life-course–persistent offenders has been heavily debated by criminologists, with some criminologists arguing that all offenders begin to desist over time as a result of aging or changes in social circumstances. For instance, Sampson and Laub's (1993) age-graded theory of informal social control asserts that even life-course–persistent offenders desist from antisocial and criminal behavior as they mature and acquire social attachments to prosocial individuals; thus, all offenders have the ability to undergo drastic changes in behavior.

Sampson and Laub—Age-graded Theory of Informal Social Control

Robert Sampson and John Laub (1990; 1993; 2003; 2005; see also Laub & Sampson, 1993; 2003) have formulated a developmental model of criminal behavior based upon their re-analysis of Glueck and Glueck's (1950) *Unraveling Juvenile Delinquency* data. Their analysis of 500 delinquent boys and 500 non-delinquent boys in Boston suggested that weakened social bonds may explain the onset, stability, and desistance of antisocial behavior across the life course. Sampson and Laub argued that poor attachments to one's parents, teachers, neighborhood, and prosocial peers may place one at risk for experimenting with antisocial and criminal behavior. Antisocial behavior, however, may have a host of negative consequences (e.g., criminal justice sanctions, rejection, stigmatization) that increase the risk that individuals will continue to offend. More specifically, the authors argued that antisocial behavior may strain relationships to conventional others and conventional institutions, and these severed proso-cial relationships may cause youths to deepen their involvement in antisocial and criminal activities. The argument that early antisocial behavior leads to later antisocial behavior via weakened social bonds is consistent with the cumulative continuity hypothesis.

Sampson and Laub also asserted that social bonds may promote desistance from antisocial and criminal behavior. Quality social bonds, such as a strong marriage to a prosocial spouse or a well-paying job, may provide some level of social control over an individual's behavior and these relationships may prevent one from continuing a life of crime. When social bonds provide the individual with social capital—instrumental or affective resources—then the probability of subsequent offending will be reduced. That is, a person may not engage in criminal or antisocial behavior because they do not want to risk disappointing others or risk losing that relationship. Sampson and Laub's (1993) qualitative interviews with offenders show that social systems of recip-rocal investment, especially in marriages and families, often cause offenders to choose legitimate activities over illegitimate activities. Their subsequent work (Laub & Sampson, 2003) highlighted the importance of social bonds in the desistance process, as well as the roles of structured routine activities (i.e., involvement) and human agency (or the intentional choices and actions to avoid crime) in desistance.

One aspect of Sampson and Laub's theory that has typically received less attention is their hypothesis that structural factors may indirectly influence delinquency and criminal behavior via weakened social bonds (see Figure 10.5). Paralleling the social disorganization and collective efficacy literature, Sampson and Laub argued that structural factors (poverty, family

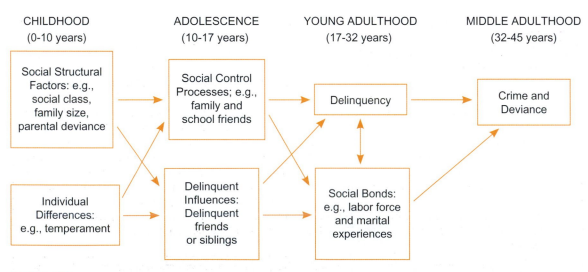

FIGURE 10.5
Sampson and Laub's developmental model.

disruption, residential mobility) may lead to higher levels of antisocial behavior because such structural factors break down individuals' ability to connect with others and to establish meaningful relationships. Without these quality relationships to informally control individuals' behavior, people are "free" to engage in antisocial behavior. More recently, researchers have attempted to explain how the breakdown of structural factors and social bonds are associated with offending by focusing specifically on how traditional markers of adulthood, such as marriage and employment, shape the life course (Blokland & Nieuwbeerta, 2005; Massoglia & Uggen, 2010; Bersani & Doherty, 2013).

See Highlight 10.3 on the Stockholm Award conferred upon Sampson and Laub for outstanding research in criminology.

Policy Implications of Developmental/Life-Course Criminology

Developmental criminology produces a multitude of recommendations for policymakers. The theoretical and empirical works suggest that interventions can occur at a number of points in the life course. In their test of the Seattle Social Development Model, for example, Huang and associates (2001:100) make five recommendations. First, intervening at only one point in the model

Could marriage be a turning point? Sampson and Laub's 1993 age-graded theory of informal social control argues that social transitions like getting married may cause individuals to desist or change their offending patterns.

CREDIT: ©iStockphoto.com/Tom England.

HIGHLIGHT 10.3 PRESTIGIOUS STOCKHOLM PRIZE AWARDED TO JOHN LAUB AND ROBERT SAMPSON

Two renowned American criminologists were awarded the Stockholm award for outstanding research in criminology in June 2011. Known especially for their contributions to the life-course perspective in criminology, they continued the longitudinal study of 500 delinquent youths implemented by Sheldon Glueck and Eleanor Glueck in the 1930s. The results have been the longest longitudinal tracing of offenders in criminology, delineated in two well-known books: *Crime in the Making: Pathways and Turning Points Through Life* (Sampson & Laub, 1993) and *Shared Beginnings, Divergent Lives: Delinquent Boys to Age 70* (Laub & Sampson, 2003).

The two primary themes of the 2011 Stockholm Criminology Symposium were Desisting from Crime: It's Never Too Late! and Contemporary Criminology. The world acclaim of Sampson and Laub's life-course work is a firm testament to the rise of the perspective in criminology. Frank Cullen's (2011) assertion that the perspective actually warrants status as a primary criminological paradigm appears to have been endorsed by the jurors for the Stockholm Prize in Criminology. While some may debate the point, without question theoretical integration is now mainstream and life-course or developmental criminology has been built on the premise of the essentiality of integration. No criminologist can ignore the evidence that has rapidly accumulated within this tradition.

Adapted from National Institute of Justice http://www.nij.gov/about/director/stockholm-prize.htm

may be a "weak" strategy. Second, the finding that there are multiple pathways to offending suggests that multiple intervention strategies may be required. Third, interventions should not only target "risk" factors, but also address "protective" factors (that is, factors that are associated with a lower prevalence of problem behavior). Fourth, research has consistently found that prior behavior influences current and future behavior. This highlights the need for early prevention and intervention strategies to reduce adult offending. Fifth, the role of the peer group is vital. Research has documented the effect of delinquent peer groups on individual behavior. Thus, disrupting these antisocial groups early in life or teaching resistance skills to negate these influences should be encouraged.

SUMMARY

Integrated theoretical models have proliferated since the 1970s and provided the groundwork for the popular contemporary life-course or developmental perspective. Several factors undergirded the emergence of integration. First, the refinement of self-report methods of data collection enabled researchers to obtain data directly from law violators. This allowed for examination of direct links between personal characteristics and behavior. Second, the increased sophistication of statistical methods has permitted researchers to look simultaneously at the effect of a number of variables upon behavior. As a result, researchers have been able to examine not only the correlates but also the causes of behavior. Third, the results of evaluations of individual theoretical perspectives failed to show high levels of explanatory power. By combining theories, criminologists have achieved a higher level of understanding of the paths or processes that produce criminal behavior.

The criminal career debate has been fueled by concern with high crime rates. Incapacitation and selective incapacitation provide quick-fix solutions to a complicated question. Unfortunately, these quick-fix solutions have failed to produce a reduction in crime. The criminal career research has identified a violent and/or highly criminal group of five to six percent of offenders who are responsible for a disproportionate amount of crime. It has not produced any prediction instrument to identify these individuals, although research suggests the importance of social events on the rate of offending among these individuals (e.g., Horney et al., 1995).

Developmental and life-course criminology have emerged as major criminological perspectives and hold considerable promise. This branch of research transcends the traditional static examination of adolescence and young adulthood and focuses on life-course trajectories. It allows for closer examination of the interplay between childhood experiences and adult behavior. A number of longitudinal panel studies have provided the type of data necessary to test developmental models.

KEY TERMS AND CONCEPTS

Absolute Stability

Adolescence-Limited Criminology (ALC)

Adolescence-Limited Offenders

Career Criminals

Criminal Career

Cumulative Continuity

Discontinuity

Duration

End-to-End Model

Frequency

Initiation

Integrated Model Approach

Interactional Continuity

Lambda

Latent Trait Approach

Life-Course Criminology

Life-Course-Persistent Offenders

Patterned Delinquent Activity

Population Heterogeneity

Relative Stability

Risk Factors

Stability

State Dependence

Termination

Three-Strikes Legislation

Trajectory

Turning Points

KEY CRIMINOLOGISTS

Alfred Blumstein

Jacqueline Cohen

Delbert Elliott

David Farrington

Michael Gottfredson

Travis Hirschi

Julie Horney

David Huizinga

Ruth Kornhauser

Marvin Krohn

John Laub

Rolf Loeber

Ross Matsueda

Terrie Moffitt

Daniel Nagin

Lee Robins

Robert Sampson

Terence Thornberry

Richard Tremblay

DISCUSSION QUESTIONS

1. Identify key assumptions underlying strain, control, and learning theories.

2. List and describe the three factors necessary for establishing causality.

3. What are the benefits of policies that are based upon the criminal career paradigm? What are some barriers to effectively implementing policies that are based upon the criminal career paradigm?

4. How does the population heterogeneity perspective explain stability in behavior? How does the state dependence perspective explain stability in antisocial behavior?

5. Moffitt and Sampson and Laub's theories are similar in many ways, but differ in other important ways. According to Moffitt and Sampson and Laub, what would be the origins of life-course offending? According to both theories, what process(es) would promote stability in antisocial behavior? According to both theories, is it likely that life-course–persistent offenders will desist from crime? What factors drive desistance in both theories?

6. How does Sampson and Laub's theory fit within the state dependence perspective? How does Moffitt's theory apply to the population heterogeneity perspective? How does Moffitt's theory apply to the state dependence perspective?

7. Following the life-course and developmental perspective, when might antisocial behavior emerge?

8. Identify key turning points discovered by developmental criminologists.

REFERENCES

Aultman, M. G. & Wellford, C. F. (1979). Towards an integrated model of delinquency causation: An empirical analysis. *Sociology and Social Research, 63,* 316–27.

Barnett, A., Blumstein, A., Cohen, J., & Farrington, D. P. (1992). Not all criminal career models are equally valid. *Criminology, 30,* 133–40.

Bartusch, D. J., Lynam, D. R., Moffitt, T. E., & Silva, P. A. (1997). Is age important? Testing a general versus a developmental theory of antisocial behavior. *Criminology, 35,* 13–48.

Baskin, D. R. & Sommers, I. B. (1998). *Casualties of community disorder: Women's careers in violent crime.* Oxford, UK: Westview Press.

Benson, M. L. (2002). *Crime and the life course.* Los Angeles, CA: Roxbury Publishing Company.

Bersani, B. E. & Doherty, E. E. (2013). When the ties that bind unwind: Examining the enduring and situational processes of change behind the marriage effect. *Criminology, 51,* 399–433.

Blokland, A. A. J. & Nieuwbeerta, P. (2005). The effects of life circumstances on longitudinal trajectories of offending. *Criminology, 43,* 1203–2140.

Blumstein, A. (2005). An overview of the symposium and some next steps. *The Annals of the American Academy of Political and Social Science, 602,* 242–58.

Blumstein, A. & Cohen, J. (1979). Estimation of individual crime rates from arrest records. *Journal of Criminal Law and Criminology, 70,* 561–85.

Blumstein, A., & Graddy, E. (1982). Prevalence and recidivism in index offenses: A feedback model. *Law and Society Review, 16,* 265–90.

Blumstein, A., Cohen, J., & Farrington, D. (1988a). Criminal career research: Its value for criminology. *Criminology, 26,* 1–35.

Blumstein, A., Cohen, J., & Farrington, D. (1988b). Longitudinal and criminal career research: Further clarifications. *Criminology, 26,* 57–74.

Campbell, M. C. & Schoenfeld, H. (2013). The transformation of America's penal order: A historicized political sociology of punishment. *American Journal of Sociology, 118,* 1375–1423.

Canela-Cacho, J. A., Blumstein, A., & Cohen, J. (1997). Relationship between the offending frequency of imprisoned and free offenders. *Criminology, 35,* 133–71.

Cernkovich, S. A. (1978). Evaluating two models of delinquency causation: Structural theory and control theory. *Criminology, 16,* 335–52.

Cloward, R. A. & Ohlin, L. E. (1960). *Delinquency and opportunity.* New York, NY: The Free Press.

Conger, R. D. (1976). Social control and social learning models of delinquent behavior. *Criminology, 14,* 17–40.

Cullen, F. T. (2011). Beyond adolescence-limited criminology: Choosing our future—The American Society of Criminology 2010 Sutherland address. *Criminology, 49,* 287–330.

Currie, E. (1989). Confronting crime: Looking toward the twenty-first century. *Justice Quarterly, 6,* 5–25.

Elliott, D. S. (1985). The assumption that theories can be combined with increased explanatory power: Theoretical integrations. In R. F. Meier (Ed.), *Theoretical methods in criminology* (pp. 123–50). Beverly Hills, CA: Sage.

Elliott, D. S. & Voss, H. L. (1974). *Delinquency and dropout.* Lexington, MA: D. C. Heath and Company.

Elliott, D. S., Ageton, S. S., & Canter, R. J. (1979). An integrated theoretical perspective on delinquent behavior. *Journal of Research in Crime and Delinquency, 16,* 3–27.

Elliott, D. S., Huizinga, D., & Ageton, S. S. (1985). *Explaining delinquency and drug use.* Beverly Hills, CA: Sage.

Elliott, D. S., Huizinga, D., & Menard, S. (1989). *Multiple problem youth: Delinquency, substance use, and mental health problems.* New York, NY: Springer-Verlag.

Elliott, D. S., Huizinga, D., & Morse, B. J. (1986). Self-report violent offending: A descriptive analysis of juvenile violent offenders and their offending careers. *Journal of Interpersonal Violence, 1,* 472–514..

Esbensen, F-A. & Elliott, D. S. (1994). Continuity and discontinuity in illicit drug use: Patterns and antecedents. *Journal of Drug Issues, 24,* 75–97.

Esbensen, F.-A & Huizinga, D. (1993). Gangs, drugs, and delinquency in a survey of urban youth. *Criminology, 31,* 565–89.

Esbensen, F.-A., Peterson, D., Taylor, T. J., & Freng, A. (2010). *Youth violence: Sex and race differences in offending, victimization, and gang membership.* Philadelphia, PA: Temple University Press.

Farrington, D. P. (1987). Early precursors of frequent offending. In J. Q. Wilson, & G. C. Loury (Eds.), *From children to citizens Volume III: Families, school, and delinquency prevention* (pp. 27–50). New York, NY: Springer-Verlag.

Farrington, D. P. (2002). *Developmental and life-course criminology: Key theoretical and empirical issues. The Sutherland award address.* Annual Meeting of the American Society of Criminology, Chicago, IL. November.

Glueck, S. & Glueck, E. (1950). *Unraveling juvenile delinquency.* Cambridge, MA: Harvard University Press.

Gottfredson, M. & Hirschi, T. (1988). Science, public policy, and the career paradigm. *Criminology*, *26*, 37–55.

Gottfredson, M. & Hirschi, T. (1990). *A general theory of crime*. Stanford, CA: Stanford University Press.

Greenwood, P. W. (1987). Care and discipline: Their contribution to delinquency and regulation by the juvenile court. In F. X. Hartman (ed.) *From children and citizens Volume II: The role of the juvenile court* (pp. 80–106). New York, NY: Springer-Verlag.

Greenwood, P. W., & Abrahamse, A. (1982). *Selective incapacitation*. Santa Monica, CA: RAND Corporation.

Hawkins, J. D. & Weis, J. G. (1985). The social development model: An integrated approach to delinquency prevention. *Journal of Primary Prevention*, *6*, 73–97.

Hawkins, J. D., Catalano, R. F., Jones, G., & Fine, D. (1987). Delinquency prevention through parent training: Results and issues from work in progress. In J. Q. Wilson & G. C. Loury (eds.) *From children to citizens Volume III: Families, school, and delinquency prevention* (pp. 186–204). New York, NY: Springer-Verlag.

Hill, K. J., Lui, C., & Hawkins, D. (2001). *Early precursors of gang membership: A study of Seattle youth*. Rockville, MD: Office of Juvenile Justice and Delinquency Prevention, United States.

Hirschi, T. (1969). *Causes of delinquency*. Berkeley, CA: University of California Press.

Hirschi, T. (1979). Separate and unequal is better. *Journal of Research in Crime and Delinquency*, *16*, 34–38.

Horney, J. & Marshall, I. H. (1991). Measuring lambda through self-reports. *Criminology*, *29*, 471–95.

Horney, J., Osgood, D. W., & Marshall, I. H. (1995). Criminal careers in the short-term: Intra-individual variability in crime and its relation to local life circumstances. *American Sociological Review*, *60*, 655–73.

Howell, J. C. (2003). *Preventing and reducing juvenile delinquency: A comprehensive framework*. Thousand Oaks, CA: Sage.

Huang, B., Kosterman, R., Catalano, R. F., Hawkins, J. D., & Abbott, R. D. (2001). Modeling mediation in the etiology of violent behavior in adolescence: A test of the social development model. *Criminology*, *39*, 75–107.

Huesmann, L. R., Eron, L. D., & Lefkowitz, M. M. (1984). Stability of aggression over time and generations. *Developmental Psychology*, *20*, 1120–34.

Huizinga, D. (1997). *Gangs and the volume of crime*. Paper presented at the Annual Meeting of the Western Society of Criminology, Honolulu, February.

Huizinga, D. & Elliott, D. S. (1987). Juvenile offenders: Prevalence, offenders, and arrest rates by race. *Crime & Delinquency*, *33*, 206–23.

Huizinga, D., Esbensen, F., & Weiher, A. W. (1991). Are there multiple paths to delinquency? *Journal of Criminal Law and Criminology*, *82*, 83–118.

Johnson, R. E. (1979). *Juvenile delinquency and its origins: An integrated theoretical approach*. New York, NY: Cambridge University Press.

Johnstone, J. W. C. (1983). Recruiting to a youth gang. *Youth and Society*, *14*, 281–300.

Kornhauser, R. R. (1978). *Social sources of delinquency*. Chicago, IL: University of Chicago Press.

Land, K. C. (1992). Models of criminal careers: Some suggestions for moving beyond the current debate. *Criminology*, *30*, 149–55.

Larzelere, R.E. & Patterson, G.R. (1990). Parental management: Mediator of the effect of socioeconomic status on early delinquency. *Criminology, 28*, 301–24.

Laub, J.H. (2006). Edwin H. Sutherland and the Michael-Adler report: Searching for the soul of criminology 70 years later. *Criminology, 44*, 235–57.

Laub, J.H. & Sampson, R.J. (1993). Turning points in the life course: Why change matters to the study of crime. *Criminology, 31*, 301–26.

Laub, J.H. & Sampson, R.J. (2003). *Shared beginnings, divergent lives: Delinquent boys to age 70.* Cambridge, MA: Harvard University Press.

Linden, R. (1978). Myths of middle-class delinquency: A test of the generalizability of social control theory. *Youth and Society, 9*, 407–32.

Lipsey, M.W. & Derzon, J.H. (1998). Predictors of violent or serious delinquency in adolescence and early adulthood. In R. Loeber, & D.P. Farrington (Eds.), *Serious and violent juvenile offenders: Risk factors and successful interventions* (pp. 86–105). Thousand Oaks, CA: Sage.

Loeber, R. (1982). The stability of antisocial and delinquent behavior: A review. *Child Development, 53*, 1431–46.

Loeber, R. & Dishion, T.J. (1983). Early predictors of male delinquency: A review. *Psychological Bulletin, 94*, 68–99.

Loeber, R. & LeBlanc, M. (1990). Toward a developmental criminology. In M. Tonry, & N. Morris (Eds.), *Crime and justice* (Vol. 12) (pp. 375–473). Chicago, IL: University of Chicago Press.

Loeber, R., Homish, L., Wei, E.H., Pardini, D., Crawford, A.M., & Farrington, D.P. (2005). The prediction of violence and homicide in young males. *Journal of Consulting and Clinical Psychology, 73*, 1074–88.

Loeber, R., Wung, P., Keenan, K., Giroux, B., Stouthamer-Loeber, M. & van Kammen, W.B. (1993). Developmental pathways in disruptive child behavior. *Development and Psychopathology, 5*, 101–33.

McCord, J. (1991). Family relationships, juvenile delinquency, and adult criminality. *Criminology, 29*, 397–417.

Massoglia, M. & Uggen, C. (2010). Settling down and aging out: Toward an interactionist theory of desistance and the transition to adulthood. *American Journal of Sociology, 116*, 543–82.

Matsueda, R.L. (1982). Control theory and differential association: A causal modeling approach. *American Sociological Review, 47*, 489–504

Melde, C. & Esbensen, F.-A. (2011). Gang membership as a turning point in the life course. *Criminology, 49*, 513–52.

Melde, C. & Esbensen, F.-A. (2014). The relative impact of gang status transitions: Identifying the mechanisms of change in delinquency. *Journal of Research in Crime and Delinquency, 51*, 349–76.

Mitchell, S. & Rosa, P. (1981). Boyhood behavior problems as precursors of criminality: A fifteen-year follow-up study. *Journal of Child Psychology and Psychiatry, 22*, 19–33.

Moffitt, T. (1993). Adolescent-limited and life-course persistent antisocial behavior: A developmental taxonomy. *Psychological Review, 100*, 674–701.

Moffitt, T. (1994). Natural histories of delinquency. In E.G.M. Weitekamp, & H. Kerner (Eds.), *Cross-national longitudinal research on human development and criminal behavior* (pp. 3–61). Boston, MA: Kluwer Academic Publishers.

Nagin, D. S. & Land, K. C. (1993). Age, criminal careers, and population heterogeneity: Specification and estimation of a nonparametric, mixed poisson model. *Criminology, 31,* 327–62.

Nagin, D. S. & Tremblay, R. E. (2005). What has been learned from group-based trajectory modeling? Examples from physical aggression and other problem behavior. *The Annals of the American Academy of Political and Social Science, 602,* 82–117.

Nagin, D. S., Farrington, D. P., & Moffitt, T. E. (1995). Life-course trajectories of different types of offenders. *Criminology, 33,* 1111–39.

Paternoster, R. & Brame, R. (1997). Multiple paths to delinquency: A test of developmental and general theories of crime. *Criminology, 35,* 49–84.

Patterson, G. R. (1982). *Coercive family process.* Eugene, OR: Castalia.

Piquero, A., Farrington, D. P., & Blumstein, A. (2003). The criminal career paradigm. In M. Tonry (Ed.), *Crime and justice: Review of research* (pp. 359–506). Chicago, IL: University of Chicago Press.

Robins, L. (1966). *Deviant children grown up.* Baltimore, MD: Williams and Wilkins.

Rowe, D. C., Osgood, D. W., & Nicewander, W. A. (1990). A latent trait approach to unifying criminal careers. *Criminology, 28,* 237–70.

Sampson, R. J. & Laub, J. H. (1990). Crime and deviance over the life course: The salience of adult social bonds. *American Sociological Review, 55,* 609–27.

Sampson, R. J. & Laub, J. H. (1993). *Crime in the making: Pathways and turning points through life.* Cambridge, MA: Harvard University Press.

Sampson, R. J. & Laub, J. H. (2003). Life-course desisters? Trajectories of crime among delinquent boys followed to age 79. *Criminology, 41,* 301–39.

Sampson, R. J. & Laub, J. H. (2005). A life-course view of the development of crime. *The Annals of the American Academy of Political and Social Science, 602,* 12–45.

Schweinhart, L. J. (1987). Can Preschool Programs Help Prevent Delinquency? In J. Q. Wilson & G. C. Loury (Eds.) *From Children to Citizens Volume III: Families, School, and Delinquency Prevention* (pp. 135–53). New York, NY: Springer-Verlag.

Segrave, J. O. & Hasted, D. N. (1983). Evaluating structural and control models of delinquency causation: A replication and extension. *Youth and Society, 14,* 437–56.

Shaw, C. R. & McKay, H. D. (1942). *Juvenile delinquency in urban areas.* Chicago, IL: University of Chicago Press.

Simons, R. L., Miller, M. G., & Aigner, S. M. (1980). Contemporary theories of deviance and female delinquency: An empirical test. *Journal of Research in Crime and Delinquency, 17,* 42–53.

Simons, R. L., Wu, C., Conger, R. D., & Lorenz, F. O. (1994). Two routes to delinquency: Differences between early and late starters in the impact of parenting and deviant peers. *Criminology, 32,* 247–75.

Simons, R. L., Stewart, E., Gordon, L. S., Conger, R. D., Elder, G. H., Jr. (2002). A test of life-course explanations for stability and change in antisocial behavior from adolescence to young adulthood. *Criminology, 40,* 401–34.

Stanford Law School Three Strikes Project and NAACP Legal Defense and Education Fund. (2013). *Progress Report: Three Strikes Reform (Proposition 36); 1,000 Prisoners Released.*

Stoolmiller, M. (1994). Antisocial behavior, delinquent peer association, and unsupervised wandering for boys: Growth and change from childhood to early adolescence. *Multivariate Behavioral Research, 29,* 263–88.

Thornberry, T. P. (1987). Toward an interactional theory of delinquency. *Criminology, 25,* 863–91.

Thornberry, T. P. (2005). Explaining multiple patterns of offending across the life course and generations. *The Annals of the American Academy of Political and Social Science, 602,* 156–95.

Thornberry, T. P., Krohn, M. D., Lizotte, A. J., Smith, C. A., & Tobin, K. (2003). *Gang and delinquency in developmental perspective.* New York, NY: Cambridge University Press.

Thornberry, T. P., Lizotte, A. J., Krohn, M. D., Farnworth, M., & Jang, S. J. (1991). Testing interactional theory: An examination of reciprocal causal relationships among family, school, and delinquency. *Journal of Criminal Law and Criminology, 82,* 3–35.

Thornberry, T. P., Lizotte, A. J., Krohn, M. D., Farnworth, M., & Sung Joon, J. (1994). Delinquent peers, beliefs, and delinquent behavior: A longitudinal test of interactional theory. (Cover story). Criminology, *32,* 47–83.

Tremblay, R. E., Nagin, D. S., Séguin, J. R., Zoccolillo, M., Zelazo, P. D., & Boivin, M. (2004). Physical aggression during early childhood: Trajectories and predictors. *Pediatrics, 114,* e43–e50.

Winfree, L. T., Esbensen, F. A., & Osgood, D. W. (1996). Evaluating a school-based gang prevention program: A theoretical perspective. *Evaluation Review, 20,* 181–203.

Winfree, L. T., Theis, H. E., & Griffiths, C. T. (1981). Drug use in rural America: A cross-cultural examination of complementary social deviance theories. *Youth and Society, 12,* 465–89.

Wolfgang, M. E., Figlio, R., & Sellin, T. (1972). *Delinquency in a birth cohort.* Chicago, IL: University of Chicago Press.

Zedlewski, E. F. (1987). *Research in brief: Making confinement decisions.* Washington, DC: National Institute of Justice.

PART 3
Types of Crime

Having examined theoretical explanations of crime, we now are ready to discuss different forms of criminal activity. The chapters in this section consider four major categories of crime and victimization: violent, economic, victimless, and youthful offending. The aim of these chapters is to offer students a taste of the kinds of events that criminologists study and to present more crime specific details. It would take several volumes much longer than this text to present a comprehensive survey of violations of criminal law. In these chapters we seek to note some highlights, to provide examples of the best research insights into the dynamics of important crimes, and to tie this material to the theories discussed in earlier chapters.

Violent and economic crimes, discussed in Chapters 11 and 12, include offenses that the average citizen most often envisions when thinking of the crime problem: murder, robbery, burglary, rape, and the so forth. Today, terrorism has joined these behaviors as a threat to peaceful existence. These crimes are important because they incite fear among the populace. Many offenses of lesser public concern, however, are more costly and harmful. Human and financial losses attributable to violent crimes pale in comparison to those caused by "white-collar crimes." The plea bargain of financier Bernard Madoff in 2009, for instance, indicated that he had bilked investors out of $65 billion (Henriques, 2011; Sander, 2009), The emotional and financial costs of unemployment and home foreclosures caused by reckless Wall Street firms' tactics during the economic meltdown that began in 2008 in the United States are incalculable.

An important issue for criminology is how wide the net of criminal law should be cast. "Crimes without victims" are said by some to be the result of an overextension of the criminal law, although others argue that criminalization of behaviors within this category such as drug use and prostitution protects the larger society from moral disintegration. As the relativity of crime instructs, "victims without crime" are the other side of the victim/offender coin. Consistent with the interactionist paradigm, the content of this chapter is deeply imbedded in and exemplifies that relativity.

A new chapter in this edition closes the book with a special focus on youth crime issues of school violence, bullying, and gangs. These are areas of much public concern and policy debate that merit special treatment. All of the types of crime and delinquency examined in these final four chapters should be viewed through the lens of the criminological foundation provided in the first unit of the book and the wide range of theories presented in the second unit of study.

Violent Crime

Violent crimes generally top the list of concerns with deviance and social control in every society. Yet as we have stressed in this text, violent crime, as with all offending, is a relative phenomenon. Violence, deployment of strong physical force, can unfold in myriad forms (e.g. martial arts, boxing, football, hunting, military training and operation, self-defense, police use of force, etc.). The varieties selected for criminalization vary across time and space and are driven by ideology. Most will agree that not all violence is bad, such as that which put down the Nazi scourge in World War II, forestalling even greater human suffering. Likewise, most Americans and many around the world felt relief, not remorse, when Osama bin Laden was shot to death amidst clandestine Special Operations activity. Depending on ideological premise, however, various violent acts come to be more broadly reacted to as unacceptable. Should waterboarding of suspected terrorists be allowed? How much physical force to discipline a child, if any, should be tolerated? Is any violence within families (e.g. pushing, slapping, restraining) ever acceptable? How about violence in sports? Recent successful lawsuits against the National Football League (NFL) for lasting effects of severe brain injuries resulting from concussions suggests reconceptualization of this popular form of acceptable violence is afoot.

Violence has long been part of our literary tradition. The classic stories of childhood are often grim and gory. Captain Hook waves a spiked arm at Peter Pan. Hansel and Gretel are about to be placed in the witch's oven. It has been argued, however, that fairy tales teach children not to imitate violence, but to overcome it (Shattuck, 1996). Murder also occurs early in the Bible when Cain slays his brother (Barmash, 2005), and theater-goers need only count the corpses in Shakespeare's *Hamlet* to appreciate the dramatic potentialities of violence (Foakes, 2003).

Of more concern are current presentations of violence on television, in motion pictures, and in video games. Events that are reasonably true to life suddenly erupt into fight sequences defying credence, with individuals seemingly inflicting punishment on each other that no human being could survive for more than a few minutes. In rapid sequence, chairs bashed over heads will be ignored and ferocious punches to the jaw will be absorbed by the hero with only a grunt. The mayhem will proceed until at last the villain succumbs.

Debate regarding acceptable cultural violence notwithstanding, many forms will be deemed unallowable at any given time and place. Violent acts prohibited by law tend to be recognized as particularly serious offenses, which leaves criminologists to address the question of why violent crimes occur. Many of the general criminological facts and perspectives reviewed in Parts 1 and 2 apply to understanding violent crime, but violence also embodies some unique parameters.

Within the general crime picture it is the case that perpetrators of violence are also disproportionately victims of crime, including violence. Moreover, these actors are not evenly distributed across gender, social class, race, age, and other demographics. Looking at serious, violent, and chronic (SVC) delinquents in Florida, Michael Baglivio and colleagues (2014) found twice as many males in the group, a figure far lower than what most research reveals. They found black youths in the SVC category twice as often as Hispanics and 2.5 times more than whites. In a manner reminiscent of Terrie Moffat's life-course persistent offenders, they found SVC offenders almost three times more likely to have had their first contact with the juvenile justice system before the age of 12. Early onset of offending tends to characterize the violent offender.

Among more notable trademarks of violent criminal events is that relational distances between victims and offenders are often closer. Much violence occurs between intimate partners, estranged partners, family members, and friends. Not only is violence more frequent among intimates, but the pattern of injuries is distinct from attacks on nonintimates (Apel et al., 2013). Heavy alcohol use is also more characteristic of violent interactions (White et al., 2012). Gang affiliation is another strong predictor of violent offending and victimization (Papachristos et al., 2013).

As with crime in general, there is no singular explanation for violent crime or for any specific form of it. It is far better to think in terms of typologies or "varieties of violent behavior" (Widom, 2014:315). Each form of violence, such as homicide or rape, can be envisioned as a pie chart with each piece of the pie representing a particular type or category of that offense with relatively distinct underlying causes. Some pieces of the pie will be very large to represent more common offender types, while others may be mere slivers to signify rare strains of crime/criminals.

Any of the theories of crime presented in Part 2 of this book may be applicable to at least some ilk of violent behavior. To recapitulate, consider some of the following as potentially promising theories to explain violent behavior. Subculture of violence theories such as those posed by Marvin Wolfgang and Franco Ferracuti or Elijah Anderson's code of the street were specifically advanced to account for violence in poverty-stricken urban minority settings. Learning theories such as Edwin Sutherland's differential association describe a process for the assimilation of violent repertoires. Robert Agnew's general strain theory facilitates understanding violence outside of subcultural settings. Similarly, the concept of low self-control holds potential for broader application. Biological and environmental variables are useful for examining violence on the individual level. In the 2013 Sutherland Address to The American Society of Criminology, Cathy Spatz Widom (2014) drew careful attention to the impact of child abuse and neglect and of post-traumatic stress disorder (PTSD) to propensity for violence. In sum, violent behavior is a complex problem to which a bevy of theoretical frameworks can be judiciously applied.

MORE RECOGNIZED FORMS OF VIOLENCE

Behaviors discussed in this section generally are viewed as serious violent crimes in America. But again what is labeled "violent crime," as we noted in earlier chapters, varies by ideology, time, locale, and observer. Assault is considered a violent crime, while failure to provide medical treatment to a pregnant woman who does not have health insurance is defined as an acceptable consequence of a market economy. The assault may involve nothing more than a pushing bout between adolescents, while the failure to provide the medical care may result in what could have been an avoidable death of the woman or of the fetus that she was carrying.

Many forms of interpersonal violence receive little attention. Violence that takes place within families and among acquaintances often does not become known to the criminal justice system. The Bureau of Labor Statistics, in its preliminary 2013 report, counted 4,405 work-related deaths for the year. The largest number of fatalities involved transportation, including highway accidents, and 9 percent were homicides that occurred in the workplace. Ninety-three percent of the victims of workplace accidents were men, and many of the deaths were the result of illegal working conditions or other violations of the criminal law (U.S. Department of Labor, 2014).

Homicide

The unlawful killing of one human being by another constitutes **homicide**. The killing must have occurred after, not before or during the birth of the victim, although groups that oppose abortion are with some success achieving the enactment of amendments to criminal laws that define an assault that kills a fetus as homicide. To be a homicide a criminal act need not be the sole cause of death, but only a recognizable causal factor. The legal definition of homicide also requires that the death occur within a year and a day from the time the injury was inflicted. In the United States there is no statute of limitations for homicide; that is, no matter how much time has elapsed since the killing, a suspected offender still can be prosecuted.

Homicide traditionally is broken down into four categories: murder, manslaughter, excusable homicide, and justifiable homicide. First-degree murder includes the attributes of premeditation and malice aforethought, the intent to kill. **Premeditation** refers to the prior formation of that intent; even a moment of such intent antecedent to the act fulfills the requirement. **Malice aforethought** is the manifestation of a deliberate intention to take the life of a fellow creature. In New York, after the 9/11 attack the legislature added "killing in the furtherance of an act of terrorism" to embrace the requirements of first-degree murder.

Second-degree murder includes malice aforethought but not premeditation. An excusable homicide is a death that occurs as a consequence of an accident perpetrated by a person performing a lawful act with ordinary caution. A boxer whose punch kills his opponent has committed an excusable homicide, as has a driver who operates his vehicle safely but runs over a child who recklessly dashed out in front of the car. Justifiable homicide involves a legal act, such as the infliction of the death penalty on a convicted felon or a killing in self-defense. In recent years, many states have abandoned the requirement that a threatened person retreat if possible and have enacted "stand your ground" self-defense statutes which legalize killing a person who is seen as endangering you. Opponents label these "Shoot First Laws" (Fontaine, 2010).

There also is a **felony-murder** doctrine, which holds that if a death occurs during the commission of a felony (say, for instance, a burglary), the perpetrator of the felony is chargeable with first-degree murder. A person setting fire to a barn might unintentionally burn to death a vagrant sleeping inside. If so, the arsonist can be charged with murder although the criminal act lacked both homicidal premeditation and malice aforethought. The felony-murder doctrine has been said to be the "most persistently and widely criticized feature of American law" (Binder, 2004:84) Guyora Binder believes that the felony-murder rule should be invoked only in cases in which the perpetrator caused death in committing a felony that inherently involved (1) violence and destruction and (2) an additional malignant purpose independent of injury to the victim. Fitting his criteria would be a case in which a rapist chokes a distraught child and unintentionally causes her death or one in which a robber holds up a motel clerk and his finger "accidentally" slips and pulls his gun trigger and kills the clerk (Binder, 2008:966–67). In 2005, the Colorado Supreme Court remanded the case of Lisl Auman, who had been imprisoned for eight years on a felony-murder charge. Auman and two male companions burglarized the house of her ex-boyfriend, retrieving some of her belongings as well as taking other things. After a wild chase, she was arrested and handcuffed in the back seat of a patrol car. Five minutes later, one of the men who had been with her shot a policeman and then killed himself. Auman was convicted of first-degree murder and sentenced to life in prison without the possibility of parole. The appellate court had no quarrel with the felony-murder element in her case, but found that the jury should have been instructed to determine whether she knowingly had entered the dwelling intending to steal or only to retrieve her own possessions (*Auman v. People*, 2005). Rather than holding a new trial, the authorities entered a bargain with Auman that led to her parole.

Manslaughter lacks the requirement of malice aforethought. In first-degree manslaughter, often called voluntary manslaughter, death results from conditions under which a fatality might reasonably have been anticipated, as in a knife fight. Illustrating first-degree manslaughter was the sentencing of two 20-year-old men and a 21-year-old woman in Florida to 15-year prison terms for having removed stop signs from a road intersection as a prank. Soon afterward, three teenagers entering the intersection drove into the path of an eight-ton truck and were killed.

Second-degree, or involuntary manslaughter, involves circumstances less closely related to the lethal outcome, as when a person dies from injuries sustained in a fall during a fist fight. A recent four-year sentence for involuntary manslaughter involved a woman and her husband whose dog broke its leash and mauled to death a resident of their apartment building (*People v. Noel*, 2005). Negligent manslaughter is used in some jurisdictions to prosecute driving fatalities.

Homicide Correlates

In the United States, the South shows the highest rate of murder, a matter that has led commentators to tag the region as marked by a **subculture of violence** (see Chapter 8). Others insist that poverty and lower educational attainment, not regional culture, are the major contributors to the higher level of violence in the South (Huff-Corzine, Corzine, & Moore, 1991).

Lifetime murder risk probabilities are based on the likelihood that a person born in a particular year will become a murder victim over the course of that person's life span, assuming that the murder rate remains stable. It is sobering to realize that the danger for an African-American urban male, a member of the highest risk group, is one chance in 24 of being murdered.

Native-American males are also at a high lifetime risk (one chance in 57) as are African-American females (one chance in 98). In comparative terms, the lifetime risk of murder for all Americans is one in 210; for motor accidents, the figure is one in 83; for airplane accidents, one in 5,000, and for crossing a road, one in 1,100. The lifetime death risk for falling is about the same as that for murder.

Trends in Homicide

Homicide, especially murder, is regarded as the most reliably measured crime because almost all the offenses become known to the police. This is not to say that every murder is discovered. Some killings may go into the record books as suicides or accidents. A husband or a wife may "accidentally on purpose" back out of the garage and run over an out-of-favor spouse. Another difficulty with homicide rates lies in the failure to discriminate among the kinds of events. There are infanticides, organized crime slayings, and lethal juvenile gang drive-by shootings, among many other forms. And there are definitional issues. Should the more than 3,000 persons killed by terrorists in the 9/11 World Trade Center disaster be counted as murder victims?

The record shows no consistent pattern for homicide in the United States. The peak homicide rate (10.2 per 100,000 population) appeared in 1980. It had fallen to 7.9 per 100,000 by 1985. It then climbed 24 percent to 9.8 in 1991 but dropped markedly in later years, and in 2013 it achieved a new low of 4.7, the lowest rate in almost half a century.

The best guess regarding the reasons for the decline was that the market for crack cocaine, which produced numerous killings, had fallen off and dealers had become more secretive and less combative (Jacobs, 2000). As Alfred Blumstein and Richard Rosenfeld (1999:1211–12) put the matter: "Whatever the drawbacks of flipping hamburgers or bagging groceries, kids are far less likely to kill or be killed working in a fast food restaurant than in selling crack on the street corner outside." Cynics note wryly that when homicide rates go down, politicians and law enforcement agencies point to their programs as responsible for the good news. But when the rates go up, the same sources maintain that conditions beyond their control, such as the age structure of the population and the disintegration of traditional family life, caused the increase.

Changes in domestic living arrangements also have contributed to the downturn in the homicide rate. There has been a sustained drop in killings during the past two decades that involve spouses, ex-spouses, and domestic partners. This decrease has been especially pronounced among African Americans and appears to be related to a corresponding drop in "domesticity," that is, declining marriage rates, increasing age at marriage, and high divorce rates (Dugan et al., 1999). Finally, higher rates of incarceration likely have played a role in lowering homicide rates by removing from street life some persons who were more likely than most others to kill.

Patterns in Criminal Homicide

The latest statistical reports on homicide indicate that some 14,827 persons were its victims in 2012. One of the classic studies of murder was undertaken by Marvin Wolfgang (1958), who analyzed Philadelphia homicides for 1948–52. Dated as the study is, most of the observed homicidal patterns continue to be seen today. Men were likely to be homicide victims on the street, while women usually were killed at home, most often in the bedroom. Men most frequently were victims of fatal domestic attacks in the kitchen, and most often were killed with a kitchen knife. Alcohol was present in nearly two-thirds of all homicide cases, and in nearly half of these cases there was alcohol consumption by both the victim and the offender. Murders were most frequent on Saturdays, and more than half of all offenses occurred between 8 p.m. and 2 a.m.

Of the offenders, more than half had a previous arrest and two-thirds of those arrests were for violent offenses. More surprisingly, 47 percent of victims, had an arrest record, over half for violent offenses. Most of the assailants were friends, relatives, or acquaintances, especially for female victims and most were intraracial crimes. Marvin Wolfgang (1958:245) introduced the important concept of **victim precipitation** to suggest that "the victim may be a major precipitating cause of his own demise." The victim-precipitated cases were those in which the victim was the first to show and use a deadly weapon or to strike the first blow in an altercation. Wolfgang found that about one-quarter of the homicides that he studied were victim-precipitated.

Mark Berg and his colleagues (2012) have more recently delved into urban subcultures of violence and how they generate both violent aggression and victimization of the same aggressors. Following the lead of Wolfgang's classic Philadelphia study and Elijah Anderson's (1999) more recent observation of the city's violent subcultures, they concluded that the "**street code**" underlies much violence.

The code defines violence as an acceptable tool for resolving conflict, places a high value on maintaining respect and a reputation for commanding it, along with little tolerance for insult. Berg's research team found that locales dominated by this street code, but not those more independent of it, displayed the offender-victim overlap that signifies victim precipitation (i.e., what behaviors, if any, on the part of victims contribute to their own victimization). In other words, both violent offending and victimization of the aggressors are products of the street code.

A plethora of other recent studies has added evidence that the honor or street code permeates inner-city settings that are economically deprived and disproportionately populated by African Americans. Analyzing patterns of homicide in Newark, New Jersey, over a 28-year period, April Zeoli and her colleagues (2014) found many spatial homicide hot spots fitting this description. Examining how group processes fueled gang shootings in Boston and Chicago, Andrew Papachristos and others (2013) discovered that adjacent turf and prior conflicts were strong predictors of fatal and nonfatal events. More than half of the homicides in both cities were gang-related, and 95 percent of the Chicago murders perpetrated with a firearm. Turf control and ongoing conflict are intimately related to street values such as respect. Examining city-level data, Kyle Burgason and his fellow researchers (2014:543) found that youthful offenders committing robberies or assaults in "those cities in which the street culture mentality is likely most entrenched, are significantly more likely to use a firearm." Doing so obviously enhances their ability to control the situation, bolstering their "rep" or "juice." The evidence is clear that a substantial portion of homicide can be attributed to urban street codes as a component of subcultures of violence.

Serial Killings and Mass Murders

Serial killings and mass murders get far more attention than their frequency merits because they are so shocking. **Serial killers** commit repeat murders over a period of time. The FBI defines the serial killer as one who kills three or more persons at different times, separated by a "cooling-off" period characterized by some conforming routines such as work or family activities. They account for only four-tenths of 1 percent of the annual homicide rate (Schlesinger, 2001) and they generally murder their victims within an hour after they abduct them (Godwin & Rosen, 2005). A subgroup of serial killers, but falling outside of the FBI definition, are "spree killers," persons who kill three or more victims at different locations within a period of hours or a few days (Hickey, 2009). Serial killers tend to be highly mobile. Their murders usually lack a personal motive because there generally has been no prior association between the victims and the offender. They frequently will prey upon drifters, teenage runaways, and others whose disappearance is less likely to provoke investigation (see Highlight 11.1 for a serial killing report from Colombia). These characteristics render the killer difficult to apprehend so that they often accrue large numbers of victims over multiple years. Some, such as London's "Jack the Ripper" and California's "Zodiac Killer," were never identified, although

HIGHLIGHT 11.1 COLOMBIAN SERIAL KILLER MURDERS 140 PEOPLE

A 42-year-old Colombian man, Luis Alfredo Garavito, confessed to having killed 140 children, usually between the ages of 8 and 16. Garavito had posed as a beggar, a cripple, and a monk at various times to gain the confidence of his victims. Their bodies later were discovered with their throats slit and showing signs of beatings and mutilation. Twenty-five skeletons of youngsters he had killed were dug up in the city of Pereira, where a mural carved into the side of an overlooking hillside now commemorates the victims.

The children were mostly from poor families and worked as street vendors. They were allowed by their parents to roam freely, often with instructions that they beg money from tourists (adapted from Newton, 2006).

recent DNA testing of the shawl of one of Jack the Ripper's victims, 126 years after her murder, has led some to conclude that it was Aaron Kosminski, a Polish-born hairdresser who spent his final years in an asylum (Edwards, 2014).

Virginia Beard and a team of researchers (2014) have analyzed 1,697 serial killers from the early 1800s through 2012, summarizing patterns of behavior. They revealed, to considerable surprise, that just over one-third had some profit motivation, even though they had removed contract killers and repeated retail robbery homicides from the database. An example they shared was Dorothea Pueue, who collected social security checks for boarders whom she had killed. Beard et al. noted that the profit motivation was particularly widespread among female serial killers, although they are quite uncommon among the group. Mutilation of corpses (16.3 percent) and desecration of bodies (9.3 percent) were the next most common features of the episodes. Collecting trophies, ranging from driver's licenses to body parts (desecration of bodies) were reported as relatively common characteristics of this type of murder. A lot of attention is accorded the most gruesome behaviors. Necrophilia (sexual acts with a corpse) was noted for 4.3 percent of offenders, including the notoriously infamous Ted Bundy and Gary Leon Ridgway, "The Green River Killer." Another 3 percent engaged in cannibalism, most notably by Jeffrey Dahmer, who was killed in prison. Body posing (3.1 percent) was represented by Albert De Salvo, aka "The Boston Strangler," tying bows under the chins of victims with the strangulating stocking. Smaller numbers of offenders used information about additional victims or locations of remains to facilitate plea bargaining or delay executions (1.8 percent) and even fewer (0.6 percent, but notably "Jack the Ripper," "The Zodiac Killer," and "The BTK Killer") taunted the police, media, or families of victims.

Karen Quinet's study found a dramatic increase in the number of prostitutes killed in serial murders during the first decade of the present century compared to the time period 1979 to 2000 (Quinet, 2011). Ridgway, named the "Green River Killer" for the site in the state of Washington where he dumped the bodies of many of his victims, may have killed 71 persons. On being sentenced to life imprisonment he told the court why he victimized prostitutes:

> I picked prostitutes as my victims because I hated most prostitutes and did not want to pay them for sex. I also picked prostitutes as victims because they were easy to pick up without being noticed. I knew they would not be reported as missing. I picked on prostitutes because I thought I could kill as many of them as I wanted without being caught (Quinet, 2011:81; see also Reichert, 2004).

Sheriff Dave Reichert, left, and "Green River Killer" Gary Leon Ridgway, right, in a video taken of a 2003 interrogation of Ridgway near Seattle. Ridgway pleaded guilty to 48 counts of aggravated first-degree murder in killings from 1982 to 1991.

CREDIT: AP Photo/ Courtesy King Co. Prosecutor's Office.

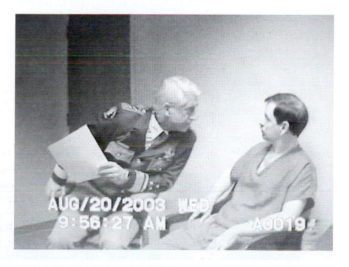

This fits a 2 percent category of serial killers identified by Beard et al. (2014) who sought out specific types of people toward whom they felt hatred. Drawing on routine activities theory, researchers found three predictive items that relate to whether a state will have a higher-than-average serial killing rate. These were (1) a larger percentage of the population living in urban areas, (2) a high divorce rate, and (3) a larger number of single-person households (DeFronzo et al., 2007).

Mass murderers are those who kill multiple victims in a single episode; they claim even fewer victims than serial murderers (Duwe, 2007). Mass murders, unlike serial killings, usually are readily resolved because the offense typically is perpetrated in an open setting and ends with the offender committing suicide or being shot or captured by the police. The mass killer may have been propelled into the murderous foray by a stressful event, such as being fired from a job; thus general strain theory offers explanation. The killers are likely to have military backgrounds, to kill strangers, to be white (by a large margin), and to be older than the average murderer (Fessenden, 2000). Table 11.1 summarizes recent (2010–13) mass shootings in the United States.

The deadliest episode of mass murder in the United States took place on the campus of Virginia Tech University in Blacksburg, Virginia, on April 16, 2007, when Seung-Hui Cho slaughtered 32 persons and wounded 23 others before killing himself. Cho had a history of mental problems (Roy, 2009). The campus killings led to attempts to pass legislation permitting students to carry weapons into classrooms so that they can allegedly protect themselves against killers. The laws are unlikely to change much except that they might make professors more careful about whom they offend and to whom they assign failing grades.

The Virginia Tech slaughter was followed on November 5, 2009, by the killing of 12 persons and the injuring of 31 others, mostly soldiers stationed at Fort Hood in Texas. The killer was a medical doctor, Major Nidal Malik Hassan, a Muslim who was hostile to the American wars in the Mideast against people of his faith. On January 8, 2011, there was another mass murder that drew headlines, when 22-year-old Jared L. Loughner killed six people, including a nine-year-old girl and a federal district judge, and severely wounded Congresswoman Gabrielle Giffords at an outdoor political rally in Tucson, Arizona.

Many wondered how the authorities had missed what in retrospect seemed obvious signs

SWAT team members head to Norris Hall, the site of a shooting on the campus of Virginia Tech in Blacksburg, Virginia, on April 16, 2007. A gunman opened fire in a dorm and then, two hours later, in a classroom across campus, killing at least 30 people in the deadliest shooting rampage in U.S. history.

CREDIT: AP Photo/Steve Helber.

HIGHLIGHT 11.2 MASS SHOOTINGS IN SCHOOLS SINCE SANDY HOOK

On December 14, 2012, 20-year-old Adam Lanza shot his mother to death, proceeding to Sandy Hook Elementary School in Newtown, Connecticut, where he killed 20 children and six adults with an assault rifle and a Glock pistol. It was second in mass shooting death tolls in American schools, following the 2007 killings at Virginia Tech University. While the tragedy led to widespread discussion about firearms regulations and monitoring of persons displaying mental health problems that could portend violence, virtually no reform transpired in the following two years. *Mother Jones*, on the second anniversary of the shooting,

identified 21 separate fatal school shooting sprees, an average of one every five weeks, since then. These events totaled 37 deaths in 16 states and 11 nonfatal wounds. Some of the cases were associated with mental health problems while others involved gang violence and domestic disputes. Weapons borne by the perpetrators included shotguns, handguns, and assault-style rifles.

Source: http://www.n-touchnews.com/news-feeds/mother-jones/4185-there-has-been-a-fatal-school-shooting-every-5-weeks-since-sandy-hook

of disturbance in the personalities of the killers. At Fort Hood, Major Hassan had accumulated poor performance ratings; Jared Loughner had been tossed out of Pima Community College because he was behaving irrationally; and Seung-Hui Cho had been described by neighbors as a man who was sullen and brooding. But it remains a considerable jump from erratic behavior to an actual act of mass murder, and it is virtually impossible to predict which of innumerable distraught behavioral symptoms will lead to violence (see, generally, Skeem & Monahan, 2011). See Highlight 11.2.

Explaining Homicide

The newcomer to criminology sometimes proclaims that those who kill must be "sick"; murderers must be driven by irrational forces. While fitting the statistically rare serial, and perhaps mass, killers, this description is not an accurate characterization of the run-of-the-mill killer. As alien as murder may seem to most of us, it preponderantly is a product of circumstances that generally make sense to the perpetrator. Donald Black (1993) insists that murder typically is a form of "self-help," the method a person who feels beleaguered uses to resolve the situation. Jack Katz (1988) interprets murder as an act of "righteous slaughter," done because the perpetrator believes that the killing is essential to achieve or to maintain a certain position, such as one of self-respect. The killer typically believes that the victim deserves his or her fate. "If we stick to the details of the events," Katz (1988:12) writes, "we can see offenders defending the good, even in what initially appears to be crazy circumstances." But Kenneth Polk notes that, while there is an element of truth in Katz's point, it falls short of explaining most homicides. What Katz did, Polk (1993:194) maintains, was to "first theorize about the nature of homicide, then [he] selectively sought out illustrations of his point to 'verify' his idealized conception of how the act proceeds."

Five postulates are said by sociologist Leonard Beeghley to offer the best theoretical construct for interpreting murder. He maintains that the high rate of homicide in the United States reflects the impact of (1) greater availability of

TABLE 11.1 Recent U.S. Mass Killings

Case	Location	Date	Year	Summary	Fatalities	Injured	Total victims	Prior signs of possible mental illness	Mental Health
Washington Navy Yard shooting	Washington, D.C.	9/16/2013	2013	Aaron Alexis, 34, opened fire in the Navy installation. The incident left 12 people dead and eight wounded. Alexis was shot dead by police.	13	8	21	Yes	Alexis had reportedly "heard voices" and had been undergoing mental health treatment in August 2013.
Hialeah apartment shooting	Hialeah, Florida	7/26/2013	2013	Pedro Vargas, 42. After setting his apartment complex on fire, Vargas killed six people in the complex, and held another two hostages at gunpoint before being killed by a SWAT team.	7	0	7	Unclear	His mother expressed concerns about her son needing a psychiatric evaluation.
Pinewood Village apartment shooting	Federal Way, Washington	4/21/2013	2013	Dennis Clark III, 27. After shooting and killing his girlfriend, Clark shot two witnesses in his aparment's parking lot and a third victim in a different apartment. Clark was killed by the police.	5	0	5	No	Unknown
Newtown school shooting	Newtown, Connecticut	12/14/2012	2012	Adam Lanza, 20. After killing his mother, Lanza drove to Sandy Hook Elementary school. There Lanza killed 20 children and six adults before committing suicide.	28	2	30	Unclear	It was reported that Lanza had a history of mental problems

Weapons obtained legally	Where obtained	Type of weapons	Weapon details	Race	Gender	Sources
Yes	Sharpshooters Small Arms Range	Sawed-off shotgun, two boxes of shells; also a .45-caliber handgun taken from a security guard he shot at the scene	Remington 870 Express 12-gauge shotgun; Beretta handgun	African-American	Male	Schmidt, M. S. (2013, September 17). State law prevented sale of assault rifle to suspect last week, officials say. *The New York Times*. Available online at www.motherjones.com/politics/2012/12/mass-shootings-mother-jones-full-data Tapper, J., Bohn, K., Borger, G., Todd, B., Levs, J. (2013, September 18). Vetting military contractors: How did navy yard gunman get in? *CNN*. Available online at www.motherjones.com/politics/2012/12/mass-shootings-mother-jones-full-data The FBI Washington Field Office. (2013, September 25). Law enforcement shares findings of the investigation into the Washington Navy Yard shootings [Press Release]. Available online at www.motherjones.com/politics/2012/12/mass-shootings-mother-jones-full-data
Yes	Florida Gun Center	9mm semiautomatic handgun	Glock 17	Latino	Male	Mazzei, P. (2013, July 31). Hialeah shooting victims' families grapple with senseless loss. *The Miami Herald*. Available online at www.motherjones.com/politics/2012/12/mass-shootings-mother-jones-full-data Pedro Vargas ID'd as gunman behind deadly rampage in Hialeah, Florida. (2013, July 27). *CBSNEWS*. Available online at www.motherjones.com/politics/2012/12/mass-shootings-mother-jones-full-data Flechas, J., & Sanchez, M. (2013, July 31). Little about Pedro Vargas' life sheds light on motive for Hialeah massacre. *Miami Herald*. Available onlline at www.motherjones.com/politics/2012/12/mass-shootings-mother-jones-full-data
Yes	Unknown	Semiautomatic handgun, shotgun	.40 caliber semiautomatic handgun, pistol grip shotgun	African-American	Male	Broom, J., & Clarridge, C. (2013, April 22) Witnesses among five dead in Federal Way. *The New York Times*. Available online at www.motherjones.com/politics/2012/12/mass-shootings-mother-jones-full-data
No	Stolen from mother	Two semiautomatic handguns, one rifle (assault), one shotgun (assault)	10mm Glock, 9mm SIG Sauer P226 semiautomatic handguns; .223 Bushmaster XM15-E2S semiautomatic rifle; Izhmash Saiga-12 12-gauge semiautomatic shotgun	white	Male	Llanos, M. (2012, December 15). Authorities ID gunman who killed 27 in elementary school massacre. *NBC NEWS*. Available online at www.motherjones.com/politics/2012/12/mass-shootings-mother-jones-full-data Jaffe, G., Duggan, P., & Lynch, C. (2012, December 14). Suspect Adam Lanza was obscure in life, now is infamous in death. *The Washington Post*. Available online at www.motherjones.com/politics/2012/12/mass-shootings-mother-jones-full-data

(Continued)

TABLE 11.1 (Continued)

Case	Location	Date	Year	Summary	Fatalities	Injured	Total victims	Prior signs of possible mental illness	Mental Health
Accent Signage Systems shooting	Minneapolis, Minnesota	9/27/2012	2012	Andrew Engeldinger, 36, went on a shooting rampage after being fired. Engeldinger killed the business owner, three fellow employees, and a UPS driver before taking his own life.	7	1	8	Yes	Reports of "paranoia and delusions."
Sikh temple shooting	Oak Creek, Wisconsin	8/5/2012	2012	Wade Michael Page, 40, opened fire in a Sikh gurdwara. Page died from a self-inflicted gunshot during a shootout with police.	7	3	10	Yes	Friends feared he was a high suicide risk. Page's nurse stated that it was obvious that he had mental health problems.
Aurora theater shooting	Aurora, Colorado	7/20/2012	2012	James Holmes, 24, opened fire in a movie theater during the opening night of "The Dark Night Rises".	12	58	70	Yes	Holmes had seen at least three mental health professionals.

Weapons obtained legally	Where obtained	Type of weapons	Weapon details	Race	Gender	Sources
Yes	Unknown	One semiautomatic handgun	9mm Glock semiautomatic handgun	white	Male	Simons, A., Furst, R., Mckinney, M., & Walsh, Paul. (2012, September 29). Gunman lost his job, then opened fire, killing five. *StarTribune*. Available online at www.motherjones.com/politics/2012/12/mass-shootings-mother-jones-full-data
Yes	Unknown	One semiautomatic handgun	9mm Springfield Armory XDM semiautomatic handgun	white	Male	Kissinger, M. (2012, August 9). Friend of Sikh temple shooter feared what he might do. *Journal Sentinel*. Available online at www.motherjones.com/politics/2012/12/mass-shootings-mother-jones-full-data
						Huus, K. (2012, September 10). Officer arriving at Sikh temple shooting: 'Time to use deadly force'. *NBC News*. Available online at www.motherjones.com/politics/2012/12/mass-shootings-mother-jones-full-data
						Murphy, K., & Hennessy, M. (2012, August 8). Sikh temple shooting: Gun shop owner says Wade Page seemed normal. *Los Angeles Times*. Available online at www.motherjones.com/politics/2012/12/mass-shootings-mother-jones-full-data
						Wisconsin temple gunman Wade Page 'shot himself in head'. (2012, August 8). *British Broadcasting Corporation*. Available online at www.motherjones.com/politics/2012/12/mass-shootings-mother-jones-full-data
Yes	Gander Mountain Stores in Thornton and Aurora, Colorado.; Bass Pro Shop in Denver, Colorado.; BulkAmmo.com	Two semiautomatic handguns, one rifle (assault), one shotgun	Two .40-caliber Glock semiautomatic handguns; .223-caliber Smith & Wesson M&P15 semiautomatic rifle; 12-gauge Remington 870 pump-action shotgun	white	Male	James holmes saw three mental health professionals before shooting. (2012, September 19). *CBS News.com*. Available online at www.motherjones.com/politics/2012/12/mass-shootings-mother-jones-full-data
						Aurora shooting prompts gun bills in big states. (2012, August 16) *Colorado 9 news.com*. Available online at www.motherjones.com/politics/2012/12/mass-shootings-mother-jones-full-data
						Frosch, D., & Johnson, K. (2012, July 20). Gunman kills 12 in Colorado, reviving gun debate. *The New York Times*. Available online at www.motherjones.com/politics/2012/12/mass-shootings-mother-jones-full-data
						Serwer, A., Suebsaeng, A., & Kroll, A. (2012, July 20) What you need to know about the Batman theater shooting. *Mother Jones.com*. Available online at www.motherjones.com/politics/2012/12/mass-shootings-mother-jones-full-data

(Continued)

TABLE 11.1 (Continued)

Case	Location	Date	Year	Summary	Fatalities	Injured	Total victims	Prior signs of possible mental illness	Mental Health
Oikos University killings	Oakland, California.	4/2/2012	2012	L. Goh, 43, a former student, opened fire in a nursing classroom. Goh was later arrested.	7	3	10	Yes	Was described as "mentally unstable" and "paranoid."
Su Jung Health Sauna shooting	Norcross, Georgia	2/22/2012	2012	Jeong Soo Paek, 59, had been kicked out after a spat. He later returned and gunned down two of his sisters and their husbands, and then committed suicide.	5	0	5	Yes	His sister worried about his homicidal tendencies.
Seal Beach shooting	Seal Beach, California	10/14/2011	2011	Scott Evans Dekraai, 42, opened fire inside a hair salon and was later arrested.	8	1	9	Yes	Evans reported suffered from bipolar disorder, mood swings, and PTSD.

Weapons obtained legally	Where obtained	Type of weapons	Weapon details	Race	Gender	Sources
Yes	Bullseye in Castro Valley, California	One semiautomatic handgun	.45-caliber semiautomatic handgun	Asian	Male	Harris, H., Richman, J., Bender, K. J., Woodall, A. & Artz, M. (2012, April 2). Former student opens fire at Oakland University, killing seven. *San Jose Mercury News.com*. Available online at www.motherjones.com/politics/2012/12/mass-shootings-mother-jones-full-data
						Crimesider staff. (2012, April 3). Gun used in Oikos University shooting rampage was bought legally, police say. *CBS News.com*. Available online at www.motherjones.com/politics/2012/12/mass-shootings-mother-jones-full-data
						Miller, T. J. (2012, April 4). One L. Goh showed violent tendencies before the Oikos University shooting. *Berkeley Patch.com*. Available online at www.motherjones.com/politics/2012/12/mass-shootings-mother-jones-full-data
Yes	Unknown	One semiautomatic handgun	.45-caliber semiautomatic handgun	Asian	Male	Green, J. (2012, February 14). Spa victim foreshadowed violence in '06 restraining order. *Gwinnettdailypost.com*. Available online at www.motherjones.com/politics/2012/12/mass-shootings-mother-jones-full-data
						Dahl, J. (2012, August 24). Shooting sprees in 2012: Crimesider reports on some of the country's worst public shootings this year. *Cbsnews.com*. Available online at www.motherjones.com/politics/2012/12/mass-shootings-mother-jones-full-data
						Bluestein, G. (2012, February 22). Victims in Korean spa shooting near Atlanta were two married couples; gunman was brother. *Chronic.augusta.com*. Available online at www.motherjones.com/politics/2012/12/mass-shootings-mother-jones-full-data
						Bluestein, G., & Martin, J. (2012, February 23). Mass shooting at spa shocks Ga. Korean community. *Onlineathens.com*. Available online at www.motherjones.com/politics/2012/12/mass-shootings-mother-jones-full-data
Yes	Unknown	Two semiautomatic handguns, one revolver	.45-caliber Heckler & Koch, 9mm Springfield semiautomatic handguns; .44 Magnum Smith & Wesson revolver	white	Male	Lloyd, L. (2011, October 13). Seal Beach shooter suffers from PTSD, names of seven dead victims released. *Laist.com*. Available online at www.motherjones.com/politics/2012/12/mass-shootings-mother-jones-full-data
						Coker, M. (2011, October 24). Six women and two men, OC homicides nos. 45-52: Massacred at beauty salon. *Blogs.ocweekly.com*. Available online at www.motherjones.com/politics/2012/12/mass-shootings-mother-jones-full-data
						Seal Beach shooting: Suspect had been ordered not to carry guns. (2011, October 13). *Latimesblogs.latimes.com*. Available online at www.motherjones.com/politics/2012/12/mass-shootings-mother-jones-full-data

(Continued)

TABLE 11.1 (Continued)

Case	Location	Date	Year	Summary	Fatalities	Injured	Total victims	Prior signs of possible mental illness	Mental Health
IHOP shooting	Carson City, Nevada	9/6/2011	2011	Eduardo Sencion, 32, opened fire at an IHOP restaurant. He died from a self-inflicted gunshot wound.	5	7	12	Yes	Sencion was diagnosed with paranoid schizophrenia as a teenager and feared demons were stalking him.
Tucson shooting	Tucson, Arizona	1/8/2011	2011	Jared Loughner, 22, opened fire outside a Safeway during a congresswoman's constituent meeting. This continued until he was subdued by bystanders and arrested.	6	13	19	Yes	Though no diagnosis was offically made, Loughner was flagged for schizophrenia and delusional disorder.
Hartford Beer Distributor shooting	Manchester, Connecticut	8/3/2010	2010	Omar S. Thornton, 34, opened fire at his place of work, Hartford Beer Distributor, after he was disciplined by his boss. He then committed suicide.	9	2	11	No	Thornton claimed there was ongoing racist agitation against him at work, which led to the shooting.

Weapons obtained legally	Where obtained	Type of weapons	Weapon details	Race	Gender	Sources
Yes	Purchased from an individual	Two rifles (both assault), one revolver	AK-47 Norinco Arms variant, AK-47 Romarm Cugir variant automatic rifles; .38-caliber Colt revolver	Latino	Male	Chereb, S. (2011, October 3). Eduardo Sencion, IHOP shooter, was convinced demons were after him. *Huffingtonpost.com*. Available online at www.motherjones.com/politics/2012/12/mass-shootings-mother-jones-full-data Chereb, S. (2011, September 6). Sheriff: Gunman used AK-47 in Carson City IHOP shooting. *Lasvegassun.com*. Available online at www.motherjones.com/politics/2012/12/mass-shootings-mother-jones-full-data Associated Press. (2011, October 23). Carson City rampage prompts call for Nevada gun law review. *Lasvegassun.com*. Available online at www.motherjones.com/politics/2012/12/mass-shootings-mother-jones-full-data
Yes	Sportsmen's Warehouse in Tucson, Ariz.	One semiautomatic handgun	9mm Glock 19 semiautomatic handgun	white	Male	Cloud, J. (2011, January 15). The troubled life of Jared Loughner. *Content.time.com*. Available online at www.motherjones.com/politics/2012/12/mass-shootings-mother-jones-full-data Feldmann, L. (2011, January 10). Why Jared Loughner was allowed to buy a gun. *Csmonitor.com*. Available online at www.motherjones.com/politics/2012/12/mass-shootings-mother-jones-full-data Lacey, M., & Herszenhorn, D. M. (2011, January 8). In attack's wake, political repercussions. *The New York Times*. Available online at www.motherjones.com/politics/2012/12/mass-shootings-mother-jones-full-data
Yes	Gun dealer in East Windsor, Connecticut	Two semiautomatic handguns	Two 9mm Ruger SR9 semiautomatic handguns	African-American	Male	Haynes, K. (2010, August 4). Omar Thornton: "I killed the five racists". *Cbsnews.com*. Available online at www.motherjones.com/politics/2012/12/mass-shootings-mother-jones-full-data Associated Press. (2010, August 4). Nine dead in shooting at Conn. beer distributor. *nbcnews.com*. Available online at www.motherjones.com/politics/2012/12/mass-shootings-mother-jones-full-data Associated Press. (2010, August 04). Police: Conn. warehouse gunman targeted managers. *Foxnews.com*. Available online at www.motherjones.com/politics/2012/12/mass-shootings-mother-jones-full-data

guns, (2) the illegal drug market, (3) greater racial discrimination, (4) greater exposure to violence, and (5) greater economic inequality (Beeghley, 2003).

These contemporary explanations of murder, however, have been challenged by recent research that calculates murder rates over the centuries. Murder was much more common in the Middle Ages than it is today (Dean, 2007), but the rate dropped precipitously in the seventeenth, eighteenth, and nineteenth centuries. Most theories would predict that the opposite would have happened, that the murder rate would go up as family and community bonds in rural areas broke down and urbanization took hold. One of the more plausible explanations of the decrease in crime after the Middle-Ages can be found not in urbanization patterns or patterns of economic growth but in an internal, psychological shift in attitudes toward crime. In the Middle Ages most killings occurred in front of many witnesses and were carried out to settle disputes. Other means to resolve differences, such as civil suits, would come to replace violent actions (Johnson & Monkkenon, 1996).

Subculture of Violence: Jerry

Jerry was a white prison inmate serving time for murder and who was often visited by one of the authors of this text. Jerry's imprisonment was the outcome of a trivial altercation. He had been sharing a trailer with another man who was moving out. Both had been drinking and when they disagreed about the ownership of a small table, the victim-to-be threatened Jerry with a gun. Jerry convinced him to put away the weapon, and then proceeded to beat him to death, explaining that the man should have known better than to point a gun at him if he was not going to use it. When Jerry was released on bail, several relatives of the victim appeared at his trailer and commenced shooting. Jerry caught one of them after he had exhausted his ammunition. He held the man down with his foot and shot him to death. He expressed respect for this victim, concluding that those who initiated the attack against him were "doing what they had to," because he had killed a member of their family. Shortly after his admission to prison, Jerry killed an inmate he said had stolen his radio, proclaiming that "they wasn't going to make no girl of me. You let somebody steal your stuff and they will try anything."

By outward appearance, Jerry was a pleasant man. He often displayed qualities such as candor and humor that were admired by other inmates, prison staff, and visiting criminology students. Jerry expressed some regrets and felt some sorrow for the victims, but did not contend that he would do anything differently under similar circumstances. To the contrary, he clung to a subcultural definition of "manhood," often referencing "what a man's got to do." While he understood that the homicides were products of a trivial disagreement, he differed markedly from less violent people in his conception of honor and manhood. Wolfgang's (1958:188–9) observations fit very well:

> Quick to resort to physical combat as a measure of daring, courage,
> or defense of status appears to be a cultural expectation, especially

for lower socio-economic class males. . . . When such a cultural norm response is elicited from an individual engaged in social interplay with others who harbor the same response mechanism, physical assaults, altercations, and violent domestic quarrels that result in homicide are likely to be relatively common.

Subcultural theories such as Miller's (1958) focal concerns, Wolfgang and Ferracuti's (1967) subculture of violence and Anderson's (1999) code of the street are consistent with much of the data regarding homicide (see Chapter 8 for a review of these perspectives). But these theories are susceptible to charges of being a circular argument that at its core declares that violent people are people who commit violent acts (Brookman, 2005:109).

Structural explanations of homicide maintain that economic inequality leads to violence through a process of **relative deprivation**, a factor that Anderson incorporates in explaining the origin of the code. A person resents that his or her share of material resources is slight relative to others'. Violence triggered by relative deprivation typically is directed against those close at hand rather than at the real, but more distant, oppressors. Ramiro Martinez (1996) found that as there is an increase in the income gap in the Hispanic population (although not necessarily between Hispanics and the general population), the rate of killings increases, with low educational attainment being the strongest predictor of homicide.

A notable series of studies of the impact of immigration into the United States by minority groups found that the influx of newcomers into Miami and El Paso did not result in a higher rate of homicide. The existence of large welcoming minority populations eased the transition for the immigrants. So too did the fact that the new arrivals felt that they had better prospects in the United States than they did in their own countries (M. T. Lee, 2003; P. Lee, 2003; Martinez et al., 2004). The same finding of a nonsignificant impact of immigration on homicide was the result of a study that included blacks and whites as well as Latinos (Feldmeyer & Steffensmeier, 2009).

Despite "the stereotype of immigrants as more dangerous and violent than their U.S.-born counterparts . . . research has solidly demonstrated that immigrants are less likely than their U.S.-born counterparts to engage in crimes and violence" (Dipietro & McGloin, 2012:733). While it is generally thought that acculturation will cancel this conforming advantage, these researchers found that third- and later-generation immigrants were less influenced by peers to engage in violent behavior than their first- and second-generation counterparts. Newer immigrant youths were more influenced by peers than native-born youths, but the effect did not hold for third-generation or beyond. While this overall process of acculturation and attraction to violence is complex, a fundamental point is that immigrants, on average, are less violent than native-born Americans.

Lower rates of violence have been found to exist in urban neighborhoods that show a strong sense of community and shared values, neighborhoods in which most parents discipline children for missing school or scrawling graffiti and confront those who are creating disturbances in public space. The best predictor of the violent crime rate was labeled "**collective efficacy**," a term used to indicate a sense of trust, common values, and cohesion in neighborhoods (Sampson et al., 1997:918). The essential element of "collective efficacy" was a willingness by residents to intervene in the lives of their children to halt behaviors such as truancy and loitering on street corners. The study results were said to undercut theories that focus exclusively on poverty, unemployment, single-parent households, or racial discrimination, although such circumstances clearly can feed into the nature of neighborhood life. Some of the neighborhoods studied by Sampson and his coworkers were largely African-American and poverty-stricken but showed low rates of violence.

R. Maria Garcia and two colleagues sought to determine more exactly an element of efficacy as it relates to violent crime. Residents in 45 Philadelphia neighborhoods were asked if they agreed or disagreed with the statement: "Most people in my neighborhood can be trusted." Not unexpectedly, those neighborhoods showing the greatest level of such trust showed the lowest rates of violence (Garcia et al., 2007). It is not clear whether the absence of trust was brought about by the local violence or vice versa, but the results contradict the theme that street crime tends to unite a neighborhood against predators in its midst.

In terms of the risk of homicide, although they themselves do not use drugs, people are 11 times more likely to be killed if they live in homes where drugs are present. When alcoholism exists in a home, nondrinkers living there are 70 percent more likely to be killed than nondrinkers in a home without alcoholism present (Rivara et al., 1997).

Marital status is one of the stronger correlates with homicide. Kevin Breault and Augustine Kposowa (1997) found that divorced women are more likely to be homicide victims than married females, while single women do not differ from married women in their victimization rate. The major changes in female roles and status since the 1970s have had no discernible impact on female homicide victimization rates or on the number of women killed by partners (Marvell & Moody, 1999). For males, single men are 91 percent more likely to die from murder than married men. For divorced men the rate is 72 percent higher than for married men. Routine activities theorists maintain that the low rate for single women occurs because they are much less involved in domestic violence and because they less often engage in the kinds of risky behavior that gets men killed. Examining routine activities theory in terms of homicides, Terance Miethe and his coworkers faulted the theory because data showed no notable changes in homicide patterns despite significant alterations in activity patterns over time (Miethe et al., 2004).

All criminology theories attempt to provide an understanding of forms of violence, including homicide and the other behaviors considered in this chapter. Each has virtues; each has deficiencies. Looking at the full spectrum, Margaret Zahn and her colleagues concluded:

These theories are difficult to integrate into a parsimonious explanation because they define the phenomenon differently; use multiple
levels of analysis and multiple variables that frequently do not cross
over from one theory to another; the underlying assumptions differ; and evidentiary bases exist in various bodies of literature that are
not easily linked to each other or to existing theories (Zahn et al.,
2004:260).

They also point out that the theories fall short because they focus only on violence
that is illegal or deviant rather than on all forms of violence that inflict harm.
Finally, thinking back to a pie chart for violent behavior, it is clear that some theories will do a good job explaining some forms of violence, but not others.

Assault and Battery

Broadly defined, **assault** is a threat or an attempt to do bodily harm to another
while **battery** is the actual conduct, although in common usage the distinction
usually is between simple and aggravated assault, with battery being implied if the
act has been carried out. The Uniform Crime Reports (UCR) annually show about
one million aggravated assaults, which easily qualifies assault as the most frequent
violent crime. There are far more cases of simple assault, which do not involve the
use of dangerous weapons, such as guns, knives, and tire irons, but these are not
recorded in the UCR. Victim surveys indicate that about one-half million assault
cases are not reported to the authorities each year. The context for aggravated
assaults, the more serious variety that involve use of a weapon, is much the same
as with homicide. The difference lies in whether the attempt to injure someone
results in a loss of life. An aggravated assault can aptly be viewed as an incomplete
homicide, or conversely, a murder can be seen as an assault that has come to a
homicidal conclusion. That is not to say that every assaulter intends to kill his
or her victim or that every murderer so intended. Both kinds of events, however,
transpire under similar circumstances and the ultimate outcome is influenced by
numerous other circumstances such as the speed and quality of medical assistance.
As with homicide, there is considerable overlap between victims and offenders.

Terrorism

Terrorism has four significant elements. First, it involves an act of violence
intended to create fear in those exposed to it. It targets both active opponents
as well as innocent victims, and it has a political purpose. The U.S. Department
of State declares that terrorism is "premeditated, politically motivated violence
perpetrated against noncombatant targets by substantial groups or clandestine
agents, usually intended to influence an audience." Cindy Combs (2006:1)
offers another definition. Terrorism, she observes, is "a synthesis of war and
theater, a dramatization of the most proscribed kind of violence—that which
is perpetrated on innocent victims—typically played before an audience in the
hope of creating a mood of fear for political purposes."

Richard Rosenfeld (2002) observes that terrorism deserves a high priority in criminology research because it is qualitatively different from the common forms of violence and does not fit easily with many current criminological theories, such as the developmental and life-course perspective, social control theories, or those stressing self-control. (See also Savelsberg, 2006.)

Terrorism remains a particularly difficult concept to pin down. One writer notes: "This has never been, since the topic began to command serious attention, some golden age in which terrorism was easy to define, or, for that matter, to comprehend" (Cooper, 2001:881). Cooper points out that one person's terrorist will be another person's freedom fighter. He offers his own definition: "Terrorism is the intentional generation of massive fear by human beings for the purpose of securing or maintaining control over other human beings" (Cooper, 2001:883; for other definitions and a discussion titled "Why Is Terrorism So Difficult to Define?" see Whittaker, 2001; see also Young, 2006).

Victims of terrorism, as David Shichor points out, "might feel more helpless than victims of street crimes because they have less control over their own fate. They cannot identify anything that they have done wrong or could have done better to avoid victimization and they do not have clear guidelines for protecting themselves from further attacks" (Shichor, 2007:275).

The United States' war in Iraq had been pressed on the ground that Iraq's leader had accumulated a terrorist record of murderous genocide against the Kurdish minority in his country. Iraq was also said to be stockpiling nuclear armaments and lethal poisons which could be used against the United States or Israel, America's close ally, or sold to others who would so employ them. Iraq also was said to have aided the terrorists who attacked the World Trade Center. When the allegation of Iraqi involvement in the September 11, 2001, assaults and the possession of weapons of mass destruction proved to be inaccurate, the rationale for the war was redefined as an effort to bring peace and democracy to the Middle East by establishing Iraq as a model of what could be achieved.

In waging war against Iraq, the United States itself and its leaders were regarded by some people as launching a terrorist campaign (Falk, 2003; Pious, 2006). In a 2011 book, the one-time head of the nuclear inspection team at the United Nations accused former President Bush and members of his team of invading Iraq when there was "no imminent threat" and asked: "Should not the International Criminal Court investigate whether this constituted a 'war crime' and who is accountable?" (El Baradei, 2011:316).

There are several important criminological lessons here. The first is that often where you live and the values you have affect how you decide who the terrorists are. During World War II, Germany's leaders engaged in the cold-blooded slaughter of six million Jews, the most awful national act in the history of mankind (Friedrichs, 2000). Yet, Nazi sympathizers in France denounced the underground resistance against the Germans as "terrorism" (Kaplan, 2000:54).

In introducing a series of articles addressing lone-offender terrorists, Gary LaFree (2013) delineates challenges that have left criminological research on terrorism far behind all other categories of crime. Yet both national and international databases are evolving to facilitate understanding of these crimes. Conceptualization of terrorism was dramatically altered on September 11, 2001. The Islamic terrorists who flew hijacked airplanes into the World Trade Center and Pentagon redefined the topic from focusing almost exclusively on extreme right-wing terrorism in the U.S. (exemplified by earlier terrorist events such as the 1993 Branch Davidian cult shooting of four ATF agents in Waco, Texas; the 1995 bombing of Oklahoma City's federal building by Timothy McVeigh; and Eric Rudolph's 1996 bombing of the Olympic Games in Atlanta, Georgia). While it is certainly the case that criminologists know far less about most types of terrorists than other criminal offenders, it is clear that understanding is advancing and that this will be a growing topic for criminologists in the years ahead.

Rape

Common law defined rape as sexual knowledge of a female forcibly and against her will. This definition has given way to gender-neutral statutory definitions that embrace homosexual rape, sexual assault of females upon males, and non-consensual sexual activity other than penile–vaginal intercourse. All states now outlaw marital rape—sex between a woman and her husband induced by force or fear; none had criminalized this act 40 years ago (Martin et al., 2007). Ten to fourteen percent of married women are believed to have been victims of marital rape. They typically do not leave the marriage until they see an increase in the frequency and severity of the aggression they suffer (Bergen, 1996).

Reports from South Africa indicate a growing focus on the rape of males by males, a "hidden crime" which is said to occur beyond institutional settings and often in connection with car hijackings and burglaries (Davis & Klopper, 2002). South Africa manifests a notably high rape rate, with 52,417 cases reported in a recent year (Rumney & van der Bilj, 2010). Analysts claim that the rape rate is a function of a very violent society that manifests a general tolerance toward rape, typically blaming the offense not on the perpetrator but on the victim (Jewkes & Abrahams, 2002).

Virtually all criminologists now regard rape as a crime of violence rather than a sexual crime, although sexual degradation often is an essential component of the offense. Rape may have increased, paradoxically, because of the greater degree of sexual license now in evidence. Eugene Kanin (1985) found that in the past men were more likely to desist from aggressive sexual acts against women they deemed to be chaste or who otherwise desired to refrain from sexual intercourse. Today, some men assume that all women are "fair game," that all beyond a certain age are willing to engage voluntarily in sexual intercourse, and that the rejection of their overture represents a rejection of them and not of the behavior. This may produce anger and frustration that could have been diverted in earlier times by blaming social standards rather than personal rejection. Women emphasize, and the law clearly agrees, that they always retain the right to say "no," and that men must learn at their peril to heed such a response.

FIGURE 11.1
Rate of rape or sexual
assault for females, by age
and postsecondary
enrollment status,
1997–2013.

Source: Bureau of Justice
Statistics, *National Crime
Victimization Survey,
1995–2013*.

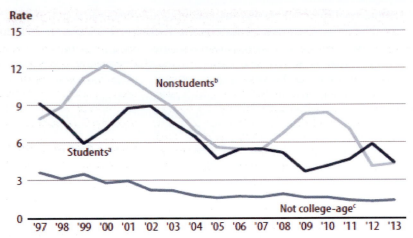

Note: Estimates based on 3-year rolling averages centered on the most recent year. See appendix table I for estimates and standard errors.

[a]Per 1,000 females ages 18 to 24 enrolled part time or full time in a post-secondary institution (i.e., college or University, trade school, or vocational school).
[b]Per 1,000 females ages 18 to 24 not enrolled in a post-secondary institution.
[c]Per 1,000 females ages 12 to 17 and age 25 or older.

The age group of women most victimized by rape is 18–24. Data for 1995–2013 from the NCVS (Sinozich & Langton, 2014) indicated an average annual rate of 7.6 rapes per thousand for nonstudent women, compared with 6.1 per thousand in college. Figure 11.1, however, illustrates that the rates were down but that the gap closed, with both groups of women showing 4.3 rapes per thousand. For the entire period, students were less likely to report the crime to police (20 percent of them) than were nonstudent women (32 percent). Both groups knew their assailant in 80 percent of the cases and both reported use of a weapon 10 percent of the time.

Catharine MacKinnon has pointed out that rape differs from other offenses in one notable aspect: When you are walking down the street and "somebody jumps you and takes your money, the law does not assume you were a walking philanthropist, nor do the police question how many times this has happened to you or whether you gave to United Charities last week," MacKinnon (1992:189) notes sarcastically. MacKinnon is absolutely correct in her analysis, but the difficulty with rape prosecutions is not notably with the "jumping out" cases of sexual assault but those involving circumstances in which it becomes difficult to prove beyond a reasonable doubt whether the sexual act was, in MacKinnon's term, "charitable" or whether it was forced. Another problem, however, resides in the estimate that from 2 to 10 percent of rape reports are false (Lonsway, 2010). The discussion of two controversial cases in Highlight 11.3 raises this matter.

Reports of rape have increased in recent years, something that may be a function of more sensitivity by law enforcement officials to the plight of the rape victim. Not many years ago (and to some extent today; Page, 2010), there was a

HIGHLIGHT 11.3 ARE RAPE ALLEGATIONS EVER FALSIFIED?

Rape is an offense that is grossly underreported because of numerous difficulties that legal processing poses to victims. Most rapes are perpetrated by acquaintances, and transpire in privacy, which raises the legal challenge of whether sexual contact was consensual or even whether it occurred in some cases. One notorious case of false rape allegations took place at Duke University in 2006. One of two black strippers who had performed at a party held by the lacrosse team accused three white players of rape. This prompted the Durham District Attorney, Mike Nifong, to file charges and take the case to trial, where DNA evidence exonerated the three. Unfortunately, this was after the lacrosse team had been banned, the coach fired, and the three accused suspended from school. Nifong was subsequently disbarred for withholding evidence and lying to the court. Their accuser was convicted in the 2011 stabbing death of her boyfriend.

As the ninth edition of *Criminology: Explaining Crime and Its Context* was going to press, revelations of "inconsistencies" in the rape claims of "Jackie," a female student at the University of Virginia were emerging. She had claimed being a victim of gang rape by eight members of the Phi Kappa Psi fraternity and to publish her story, *Rolling Stone* agreed not to question the accused. Their story wrought indignant outrage that the University of Virginia was enmeshed in a "rape culture." But in light of changes in Jackie's story, evidence that the fraternity had not sponsored a party on the 2012 night in question and other inconsistencies, *Rolling Stone* added that it "had misplaced its trust" in the accuser. Greek organization activities had already been suspended on the campus for the remainder of the semester. In retrospect, what lessons may the University of Virginia fraternity case have provided for considering rape allegations? How about the Duke lacrosse case?

Sources: Goldberg, J. (2014, 12–08). Using allegations of rape in a grab for power, *Los Angeles Times*.

Mantaldo, C. (2014, 6–13). Duke lacrosse team scandal. http://crime.about.com/od/current/a/duke_lacrosse.htm.

The Rakyat Post (2014, 12–09). U.S. school won't reinstate fraternity activities over rape allegation, http://www.bing.com/search?FORM=SOLTDF&PC=SUN1&q=The+Rakyat+Post+(2014,+12–09).+U.S.+school+won%E2%80%99t+reinstate+fraternity+activities+over+rape+allegation&src = IE-SearchBox.

Randazza, M. (2014, 12–07). Should we always believe the victim? *CNN Opinion*, http://www.cnn.com/2014/12/05/opinion/randazza-uva-rape-allegations/index.html.

Robertson, G. (2014, 12–09) University of Virginia president lays out plan to stop sexual assaults: 'there is a piece of our culture that is broken', *Business Insider*, http://townhall.com/news/politics-elections/2014/12/09/university-of-virginia-lays-out-student-safety-plan-n1929273#!

strong tendency by the criminal justice system to shift blame onto the victim and to subject her to further stress and embarrassment. Victims of rape were twice violated, first by the rapists and then by the justice system. The prospect of insensitive police questioning, courtroom attacks on their character and previous behavior, and innuendos regarding their consent to sexual relations deterred women from reporting rapes (see Highlight 11.4). A growing willingness to report has been brought about by a greater frankness about sexual matters as well as the establishment of rape crisis centers, the use of female officers to interview victims, and the passage of rape shield laws that bar inquiry in court into the sexual history of the complainant. Susan Caringella (2009), however, argues persuasively that these updated approaches are essentially symbolic band-aids in regard to what happens in reality in the handling of rape cases by the criminal justice system.

The one percent of women accused of rape almost invariably are accessories; they may, for instance, hold a gun on the victim while their male companion rapes her. Males in the 20-to 24-year-old group contribute the largest number of offenders. Overwhelmingly, victims and offenders share racial identification.

HIGHLIGHT 11.4 RAPE AND BLUE JEANS

Italy's Supreme Court overturned the conviction of a 45-year-old driving instructor who had allegedly raped his 18-year-old student. A lower court ruling had sentenced the man to two years and eight months in prison. The appellate ruling was based on the ground that the woman was wearing blue jeans. The court reasoned that "it is a fact of common experience" that tight blue jeans cannot be removed "without the active cooperation of the person who is wearing them" and that, therefore, the sexual intercourse must have been consensual. The court also made note of the fact that neither the accused nor the alleged victim showed bruising.

The decision met with indignation. One observer pointed out that the ruling had done something very rare in Italian life: it had united virtually all people, albeit in opposition to the court decision. The female members of the national legislature, all dressed in blue jeans, staged a protest, and talk show hosts and others sarcastically labeled blue jeans as the modern chastity belt (Calavita, 2001).

HIGHLIGHT 11.5 A CASE OF RAPE IN CHINA

Rape usually remains unreported in China because to bring forward a complaint may seriously damage the reputation of the accuser, however innocent. Gil and Anderson (1999) tell of the forcible rape of Alice, a young woman who secured a summer job in an ice-cream factory before beginning college. Her employer relied on her traditional Chinese respect for older persons and people in authority to rape her when other employees had gone home for the two-hour lunch break and she stayed behind rather than venture outside into a heavy rain.

The next day Alice visited a nurse she knew to ask if she might be pregnant. "You were right in not telling," the nurse said. "There is a law against rape, but it would be very difficult for you to prove that this man did it. And you would have been shamed and, too, your family. Forget it ever happened" (Gil & Anderson, 1999:1160).

Rape most certainly reflects attitudes toward women as Highlight 11.5, a report from China, illustrates.

Date rape concerns have increased with the growing involvement of several drugs, including gamma hydroxybutyrate (GHB) and Rohypnol (the trade name for flunitrazepam, sometimes called "roofies"), that can render the person who ingests them unconscious. In large or poorly synthesized doses, the drugs can be lethal (Adams, 2007). Girls and women have been advised to cap bottles between sips, never to leave their drink unattended, and not to accept a drink from someone they do not completely trust. Highlight 11.6 touches upon an extremely high-profile case that is relevant to many key issues involving the crime of rape.

Explaining Rape

Forcible rape is an offense typically interpreted in terms of the offenders' personal pathologies. Psychological profiles of rapists find them to be driven by a quest for power, by anger, or by sadism. A publication issued by the American Psychological Association notes that "rape is part of a general antisocial, aggressive, and risk-tolerant lifestyle" (Lalumiere et al., 2005:184).

The prevalence of psychological accounts notwithstanding, rape is perpetrated disproportionately by lower-class, minority urban males, who experience

HIGHLIGHT 11.6 BILL COSBY AND RAPE ALLEGATIONS

Drugging potential victims is an MO [*modus operandi*] deployed by some rapists, but it is also consistent with the belief of many that rape is more motivated by a desire for control than by sex. One of the top crime stories as this edition of the book was being finalized was the emergence of allegations by more than 20 women that comedian/actor Bill Cosby had drugged and sexually violated them many years ago. While some were suggesting conspiracies to gain pay-offs from a very wealthy man, most commentators appeared to believe that there was substance to the claims. While Cosby had never been charged with a crime and had settled only one prior civil case of this nature, he quickly lost many contracts and became *persona non grata*. One of the shocking features of the scenario was the huge gap between the accusations and Cosby's image. It was ripe for discussion of male power and privilege. In retrospect, what lessons may the Cosby case have provided for considering rape allegations?

an environment hospitable to crimes of violence. Some men learn to use violence to achieve goals, to see sexual contact as a test of virility, and to regard force to attain this goal as acceptable.

Studying rape in Sweden, a country known for its sex-role equality, Gilbert Geis and Robley Geis (1979) concluded that the high frequency of rape in Stockholm was an artifact of the greater number of "rape-enabling" situations characteristic of the lifestyles of Swedish women who are much less reluctant than American women to invite a person they barely know to their apartment. Culture conflict may account for part of the rape situation in Stockholm. A large proportion of rapes are perpetrated by foreign males who misread friendly acts by local women as sexual invitations.

Explanations for rape noted by Lee Ellis (1989) include feminist theory, social learning theory, and evolutionary theory. Feminist theory considers rape to be the result of long and deep-rooted traditions in which males have dominated political, social, and economic life. Women are viewed as little more than property and as such they have to depend upon particular men for protection against other men.

Social learning theory portrays rape as part of a pattern of aggressive behavior by men that is learned and reinforced through four interrelated processes: (1) by imitating rape scenes and other acts of violence toward women that are seen in person, conveyed by others, or depicted by the media; (2) by associating sexuality and violence; (3) by adopting "rape myths," such as "No means Yes" and "Women secretly desire to be raped"; and (4) by desensitizing men to the pain, fear, and humiliation of sexual aggression.

The evolutionary or sociobiological theory maintains that the lower degree of certainty of becoming a parent induces a tendency in men to evolve traits that increase their chances to have a large number of children rather than to take diligent care of a few. According to evolutionary theorists, the tension between different approaches to sex by males and females is responsible for much of the frustration, compromise, and deception that both sexes tend to exhibit during courtship and, in some ways, throughout life.

Still another way of viewing rape myths is through the lens of neutralization theory. Following this line of thought, some men may understand that rape is wrong, but be able to draw upon neutralizations to facilitate offending. Widespread perpetration of rape by soldiers during wartime may be consistent with this perspective. Likewise, the learning of rape myths in all-male environments might help explain some major pockets of rape perpetration.

LESS RECOGNIZED FORMS OF VIOLENCE

Family Violence

Sentimentalists typically think of the family as a bastion of love, support, and nurturing and, most assuredly, there are families that show an abundance of all of these characteristics. On the other hand, a person is most likely to be subjected to interpersonal violence within his or her own family. Because they transpire in private space, such offenses are substantially less likely than more public law-breaking to be reported to the criminal justice system.

Child Abuse

Child abuse usually takes one of four forms: physical abuse, sexual abuse, emotional abuse, or neglect (McCabe, 2003). Children are easy targets of violence because they are incapable of offering much resistance. All of us have heard stories from friends (if we have not had the experience ourselves) of how they were persistently beaten by their father (or, less often, their mother) until they realized that they were strong enough to fight back and either did so or said so. Thereafter, the beatings often stopped. Children can, at least at times, be a frustrating burden, emotionally and financially, and frustration often is a precursor to violence. Finally, of course, they are handy targets. The more parents and children are able to separate themselves during periods of tension—in houses with many rooms— the less likely parents are to take out their aggravations on a child.

A "**cycle of violence**" appears to be associated with child abuse. Cathy Widom and Michael Maxfield (2001), following 1,575 persons from childhood through young adulthood, discovered that children who had been abused or neglected had a 30 percent higher adult criminal record for violent offenses than those who had not been so treated.

For most parents in the United States, the traditional attitude was that they had the right (even the obligation) to use physical punishment to control and train their children, an attitude that is far from retired (see Highlight 11.7). In the 1960s, however, the social problem of violence toward children was "discovered." The climate was ripe for a greater focus on the care of children and affluence allowed more people to attend more closely to the quality of parent–child relationships. The publicity accorded the **battered-child syndrome** led to the passage of child abuse laws in all 50 states and produced a rapid rise in reports. There also was a striking increase in court cases in which, prodded by mental health workers, persons in treatment "recalled" (often unreliably) their abuse

HIGHLIGHT 11.7 CORPORAL PUNISHMENT AS CHILD ABUSE

Corporal punishment of children is legal in all 50 states and an estimated 65–70 percent of Americans believe it apropos. Is it? If not, why? If so, when should it be defined as having crossed the line into criminal violence? For (former) Minnesota Vikings running back Adrian Peterson, the line was crossed when he disciplined his four-year-old son with a tree limb, leaving visible bruises and cuts on his ankles, thighs, buttocks, back, and genitals. Peterson pleaded guilty to a misdemeanor assault charge, which resulted in a $4,000 fine and a requirement of 80 hours of community service. He was suspended by the NFL for the remainder of the season.

http://www.usatoday.com/story/sports/nfl/2014/10/08/adrian-peterson-in-court-for-child-abuse-case/16898015/

http://espn.go.com/nfl/story/_/id/11534340/adrian-peterson-minnesota-vikings-faced-previous-child-abuse-accusation

http://www.csmonitor.com/USA/Society/2014/1019/To-spank-or-not-to-spank-Corporal-punishment-in-the-US

as infants or youngsters and initiated criminal prosecution against a parent or sued for psychological damages (Loftus & Ketcham, 1996; Loftus & Geis, 2011).

The political battles that can be launched by criminological research are illustrated by the hullabaloo created when a published review of 59 studies of college students who had been sexually abused as youngsters concluded that the consequences of such incidents are not as severe as most people presume, with men reacting much less negatively than women (Rind et al., 1998). The finding produced a barrage of criticism, including a statement from a Congressional leader who said that it trivialized the impact of sexual abuse and was "pedophile propaganda masquerading as science" (Dallam, 2002:112). The American Psychological Association, which publishes the journal in which the article appeared, felt obliged to announce that they had "always condemned the sexual abuse of children" and that it was taking steps to see that "journal editors will fully consider the social policy implications of articles on controversial topics," although in the same breath it indicated that it did not endorse censorship of scholarly research. The authors of the article declared that "lack of harmfulness does not imply lack of wrongfulness."

Partner Battering

Violence against women perpetrated by husbands and live-in male companions for a long time was regarded by the male-dominated realm of law enforcement and the equally male-dominated realm of social science as a private affair, best left in the shadows. There was a myth that women enjoyed being hit, interpreting it as attention, and therefore a sign of caring. It is true that some women who are beaten do not see themselves as real victims, but merely as suffering the usual lot of females. The popular country song "Stand by Your Man" reflects that element of sex role socialization (Brown, 1986:280).

By capitalizing on the expansionist interests in the social work, mental health, and legal professions, and offering a good subject for the media, feminists were able to demonstrate that there was a problem demanding serious attention (Tierney, 1982). Hundreds of shelters for **battered women** that provide an alternative to remaining with abusive males soon were operating (Merry, 2009; Walker, 2009). At the same time research determined that there was no difference in recidivism rates if an assailant was assigned to a batterer program or put under judicial control with reporting requirements or involved in neither of these interventions (Labriola et al., 2008).

Police officers sometimes lament that battered wives get to the station house before the officers arrive with the husbands they have arrested, saying that they now forgive their mates and want them back home. The problem often is that the woman is unable to support herself and her children without the male income and that she fears even greater aggression if she pursues criminal charges. Deborah Sontag (2002:54) points out that the wife or live-in partner "oftentimes stays for the same reasons that people in other kinds of imperfect relationships do: because of the kids, because of her religion, because she doesn't want to be alone, or simply because she loves him." Linda Mills (2008) maintains that the mandatory arrest of batterers now required fails to take into account the dynamics of the particular marital relationship and can be more destructive than helpful. The title of an article by Drew Humphries (2002) sums up the situation in regard to domestic violence: "No Easy Answers: Public Policy, Criminal Justice, and Domestic Violence."

There are contradictory data about whether men or women act violently more often against their spouses or domestic partners (Miller, 2005). But men hit much harder and thereby wreak considerably greater damage (Felson, 2006). Indeed, 40 percent of all calls to the police come from women endangered by their husbands. Pregnant women seem to be particular targets: 37 percent of them are physically abused by their partners (Schneider, 2000). A partial explanation may lie in the fact that males have doubts about the paternity of the expected child (Waite & Gallagher, 2000).

Men's alcohol use and economic insecurity are particularly tied to their involvement in wife-battering. Ethnicity is only minimally related to the phenomenon. The greatest risk for women is posed by former partners after the couple has split up (Fleury et al., 2000). Research by Leona Bouffard and her colleagues learned that women who commit domestic violence "specialize" in that kind of behavior while wife-battering men are guilty of a variety of other violent acts. They point out that treatment programs for the men that focus exclusively on domestic violence fail to address more pervasive difficulties (Bouffard et al., 2008). In a study of 406 women who had taken their battering case to court, the authors found that the women were disappointed when they learned that incarceration was in order; they would have preferred mandated counseling, anger management treatment, or drug abuse treatment. They often faulted the court for failing to follow up on its judgment, such as an injunction against a man stalking them, but granted that the existence of a court order did inhibit some objectionable behaviors by the offender (Bell et al., 2011).

The "battered-wife syndrome" at times has been successfully introduced into criminal trials to excuse a woman who killed her husband after being subjected to physical abuse over a period of time. Many men take exception to such acquittals, insisting that lethal force is a disproportionate response; after all, they say, assault is not a capital offense. They also argue that the women could have departed rather than killed (Ammons, 2003). Many women take strong exception to this male position. They insist that the victims of violence had lost their self-respect, their judgment, and that they retaliate out of desperation (Hattery, 2009). A recent cartoon reflected the ever-growing use of victimization defenses in criminal cases. "I understand that he hit me because he had been abused as a child," a woman on the witness stand says. Then she adds: "And that was the same reason why I killed him."

Violence Toward Siblings

Sibling abuse is said to be "the most underresearched and underrecognized form of family violence" (Hines & Malley-Morrison, 2004:263). The largest number of domestic violence cases take place among siblings (Comstock, 2008), and the annals of such violence include biblical stories in which Cain slew his brother Abel and Joseph's brothers stripped him of his coat of many colors and threw him into a pit in the wilderness (Butler, 2006). Most parents accept squabbling and occasional hitting among their children as part of the growing-up process. Few would consider reporting even serious violence to the police, unless they concluded that one of the children was badly out of control.

Marjorie Hardy and her colleagues (2010) note that when an adult hits a child, the act is defined as abuse, and that when a child hits an unrelated peer, the behavior is typically considered bullying. However, when a sibling hits a brother or sister, the tendency is to regard the activity as a normal form of sibling rivalry. To test the responses to such behavior, the researchers presented a vignette to 506 students in a southern college, varying the gender of the vignette participants randomly. In the vignette, a 12-year-old and a nine-year-old contended for control of the television remote control. After some back and forth struggles, the older sibling responded to the younger one's attempt to retrieve the control by hitting him/her in the face with the instrument, causing a gash that would require stitches to close. The researchers found that males were more accepting than females of the grappling and its consequences. Participants with no siblings regarded the initial grabbing of the control and changing of the channel more seriously than did study participants who had siblings. Family size and age differences among siblings in the respondent group had no significant impact on the results. In the qualitative segment of the research, the respondents placed considerable blame on the parents for leaving the youngsters alone or, at least, unsupervised.

Violence Against the Elderly

Public and media attention has come to be focused on the mistreatment of the aged. Such abuse involves "intentional actions that cause harm or a serious risk of harm to a vulnerable elder by a caregiver or a person who stands in a trust relationship with the elder, or failure by a caregiver to satisfy the elder's basic needs or to protect the elder from harm" (Abbey, 2009:52). Demographic trends have fed into the problem: During the past half century, life expectancy has increased 50 percent. There also are fewer children to share the burden of care for elderly parents than there were in earlier times and families tend to be more geographically dispersed than they once were.

Most acts of elder abuse are committed by spouses, with sons rather than daughters being the most frequent offspring to abuse elderly parents. There is no difference in victimization rates by race. Old men are the more likely victims in terms of rate, but, because females live longer, in total numbers they are abused more often than males. Injuries inflicted on elderly women generally are considerably worse than those inflicted upon elderly men.

A recent study reinforced the conclusion that women were most likely to be the victims of severe abuse. Perpetrators were found to be the spouse or partner (32 per cent), a child of the victim (32 per cent), a friend or roommate (15 per cent), nephew or other relative (10 per cent), grandchild (7 per cent), or sibling (5 per cent) (Friedman et al., 2011).

Explaining Family Violence

Family violence is more prominent in lower-class homes than in the other social echelons of society. This does not mean that such crimes are unique to the lower classes, but only that family violence disproportionately plagues that social stratum. The stresses of poverty, welfare existence, poor housing and education, limited opportunities, and similar aspects of life on the bottom rungs of the social ladder undoubtedly contribute heavily to family violence (Barnett et al., 2005).

Conflict theory is useful for interpreting much family violence. The primary victims of such violence, women and children, usually possess little power in relation to that of their assailants. Classical theory (see Chapter 5) also has been utilized to explain family violence; the absence of serious threats of punishment may be a factor in some cases. Perhaps holding the most explanatory power are social learning theories (Chapter 8) as suggested by the intergenerational character of much family violence. In sum, a wide variety of theories seem to hold promise for understanding violence directed against family members.

CORPORATE, GOVERNMENT, AND PROFESSIONAL VIOLENCE

While homicide and other violent crimes and, increasingly, forms of family violence are occupying the limelight, other types of violence, equally fearsome and more widespread, are often overlooked. White-collar crimes perpetrated by businesses, governments, and professionals kill and injure, but they get much less public attention than more flamboyant incidents of death dealing. Notorious examples of white-collar violence include the release into public waters of the chemical pesticide Kepone, cancer-causing asbestos in homes and in the workplace, mines with inadequate safety precautions that cave in, high rates of brown-lung afflictions among cotton mill workers, and harmful levels of radiation exposure among factory workers.

In part because the victims of these forms of violence exceed those of street crimes by several-fold (Reiman, 2004), some criminologists have argued that violent crime should be conceptualized to include all forms of avoidable death and injury. Some violent white-collar crime episodes represent violation of existing criminal statutes, while others, equally serious, go unheeded because of successful lobbying on the part of powerful business interest groups to keep them out of penal codes. This arrangement brings us back to the centrality of the concept of the relativity of crime discussed in the opening chapters.

Each year, consumer products result in about 30,000 deaths and 20 million serious injuries, while about 14,000 lives are lost and two million persons are disabled on the job. Much of this harm is a form of violence rather than the consequence of accidental forces because the risk was unreasonable, avoidable, or associated with violation of existing regulatory or criminal law (Rosoff et al., 2007).

Corporate Violence

The following are illustrative episodes of corporate violence:

- Illegal dumping by the Veliscol Chemical Company into wells that resulted in chronic depression in several families for years until they learned that chloroform had seeped into their water, acting as a daily sedative. The truck driver who hauled Veliscol's leaking barrels of chemical waste lost his sight after continued exposure to corrosive fumes. His 24-year-old son, who worked with him, developed nerve damage. His legs began to have uncontrollable tremors; one summer, he drowned while swimming (Rosoff et al., 2007).
- There was continued exposure of workers and consumers to asbestos after conclusive scientific evidence of its lethal effects became known. Even relatively low levels of asbestos exposure can have fatal effects on some people and hundreds of thousands of people with higher levels of exposure have died from such diseases as lung cancer, mesothelioma (a rare cancer of the lining of the lungs and stomach), and asbestosis.

Government Violence

Governments commit violence upon their own citizens and those of foreign countries; witness the genocidal pulverizing that Muslims have undergone at the hands of Serbs in Kosovo in what formerly was Yugoslavia, and the slaughter of the Kurds by the former Iraqi government. Subtler forms of violence at home (although not legally defined as crimes) might be alleged in the failure of the United States to provide medical care for about 50 million Americans in the face of the fact that all other industrialized nations offer such care.

The Tuskegee Syphilis Experiment provides one of the ugliest illustrations of governmental violence. Between 1932 and 1972, the U.S. Public Health Service, working with local health officials, withheld treatment from more than 400 syphilitic men in an economically depressed, predominantly African-American county in rural Alabama. The aim was to compare the incidence of death and debilitation among untreated subjects with a treated sample of syphilitic men and a healthy control group.

Officials did not tell the subjects that their work involved syphilis, but only that tests were to determine "bad blood" (Jones, 1993). No therapeutic intervention was offered to the subjects, nor to wives who contracted the disease, nor to children who were born with congenital syphilis. Even when penicillin was determined in 1941 to be an effective cure for syphilis, treatment still was withheld. Stephen Rosoff and his co-authors (2007:377) note: "This is particularly troubling because the advent of penicillin seemingly obviated any rational purpose for the experiment." When details of the research finally were uncovered, an Alabama court awarded each of the 70 survivors $37,500, which worked out to $2.50 a day for the 40 years in which their medical need was flagrantly ignored. In 1997, President Clinton officially apologized for the government in a ceremony attended by a handful of survivors of the Tuskegee experiment. He told the audience:

> To the survivors, to the wives and family members, the children and grandchildren, I say what you know. No power on Earth can give you back the lives lost, the pain suffered, the years of internal torment and anguish. What was done cannot be undone. But we can end the silence. We can stop turning our heads away. We can look you in the eye and finally say on behalf of the American people, what the American government did was shameful, and I am sorry (Clinton, 1997).

Professional Violence: Physicians

Because of their power and position, some physicians are able to perpetrate more violence without interference than persons in other occupational areas. A report prepared by a component of the National Academy of Sciences estimates that between 44,000 and 98,000 Americans die each year due to preventable medical mistakes (Kohn et al., 2000). Paul Jesilow and his colleagues (1985:153) note that "unnecessary surgery, knowingly performed, is equivalent to assault." Such assaults occur more than two million times annually. This violence results in pain, suffering, maiming, and sometimes death, in addition to fleecing the victims, insurance companies, and taxpayers. A considerable proportion of malpractice cases fall into the category of criminal behavior, although the victims or their survivors almost invariably are more intent on compensation through civil remedy than punishment through

President Clinton and Vice President Al Gore with Herman Shaw, a Tuskegee Syphilis Study victim, during a 1997 news conference. Making amends for a shameful U.S. experiment, Clinton apologized to men whose syphilis went untreated by government doctors between 1932 and 1972.

CREDIT: AP Photo/Doug Mills.

criminal process. Also thoroughly documented are sexual assaults by doctors under the guise of examination and treatment. Such behavior can be more serious than street crimes because of the violation of trust (Jacobs, 1994).

Organized Crime

Organized crime is not a statutory offense such as murder, robbery, or similar forms of lawbreaking. Some of the work of members of organized crime syndicates is perfectly legal. Owning mortuaries, for instance, is particularly attractive to organized crime groups because they can be used as a cover for a murder (organized criminals do not like the word "murder"; "whacked" is the in term). Bodies of organized crime victims can be cremated or can be buried underneath the coffin of a person who died of natural causes.

The hallmark of organized crime is a willingness to resort to violence to gain an advantage. "Violence is a generic resource of organized crime that may well remain latent for long periods of time until it is dusted off for coercive action against those that threaten either the firm or the competitive integrity of its personnel," Dick Hobbs observes. He adds: "Violence is a feature of organized crime's power, characterizing its establishment in the market place, its dominance of a section of the market, and the method by which it resolves feuds and grievances" (Hobbs, 2003:683).

Asked what quality is most necessary for a good mob boss, author Jerry Capeci responded: "First and foremost is ruthlessness. He must have a well-earned reputation for violence that will inspire his men to do whatever he wishes" (Capeci, 2006:WK5).

Criminal syndicates got their start in the 1920s with the advent of national Prohibition when they were able to supply liquor to customers who thought the federal ban on alcoholic beverages was ill-advised (Critchley, 2009). From there the tentacles of organized crime were extended into prostitution, gambling, and, notoriously, into drug operations and labor racketeering (Jacobs, 2006). Organized crime activities also include lending money at exorbitant interest rates, and a number of **extortion** practices grouped generally under the heading of "rackets." **Money laundering** involves taking illegally gained funds and running the money through processes that make it appear to be legitimate income (and preferably nontaxable). It particularly exposes the failure of efforts to coordinate law enforcement on a global level (Kochan, 2005; Madsen, 2009).

Highlight 11.8 provides details about the way money laundering is done. Adaptability is a hallmark of organized crime activity. As Jay Albanese and his co-authors note, organized criminals are quick to respond to changes in supply, demand, law enforcement, and competition: "they move geographically, shift to another illicit product, find new partners, or take other methods to ensure profitability" (Albanese et al., 2003:6). In response, prosecutors now employ the Racketeer Influenced and Corrupt Organizations Act (RICO) to secure restraining orders, obtain injunctions and trusteeships, and to purge the ranks of organized crime.

HIGHLIGHT 11.8 MONEY LAUNDERING

Franklin Jurado, a Colombian economist and Harvard University graduate, was arrested in Luxembourg, where law enforcement agents seized computer disks with records of 115 bank accounts in 16 locations from Luxembourg to Budapest. Jurado's five-stage laundering scheme was designed to clean money derived from drug trafficking. Assets were moved in a series of steps from a higher-to a lower-risk condition:

1. The initial deposit, which is the riskiest stage because the money is still close to its origins and therefore still tainted, involved placement of funds in Panama banks.

2. The funds were then transferred from Panama to Europe and placed into corporate accounts. This involved moving U.S. dollars from Panama banks to more than 100 accounts in nine European countries. Deposits ranged from $50,000 to $1 million.

3. The money then was shifted to new individual accounts established under phony European names. This tactic sought to evade the heightened surveillance generally accorded Colombian and Hispanic-surnamed accounts.

4. The money was then transferred to European-front companies that would offer no reason for suspicion.

5. The funds were returned to Colombia through investments by the European-front companies in Colombian businesses such as restaurants, construction companies, pharmaceutical enterprises, and real estate (Blum et al., 1998:39–40).

The aim of organized crime typically is to secure a monopoly on some activity that will produce large profits. The reliance on organization offers the same advantages that underlie corporate activity: diversity and specialization (Federico, 2010). Organized criminals often have their own accountants and keep one or several lawyers on retainers. It becomes crucial that nobody tells tales, jeopardizing the others; thus, the traditional emphasis on silence and the lethal retaliation against members of the group who fail to adhere to this code.

The collapse of *omertà*, the code of silence, was manifest when Joseph (Big Joey) Massino, a Mafia leader, began to tell all to the government to avoid the death penalty after he was convicted in 2004 of racketeering, seven murders, arson, extortion, loan sharking, illegal gambling, conspiracy, and money laundering. Massino squealed on Vincent Bonano, a Mafia don, for ordering the murder of a faithless underling. "There isn't a hunk of cheese big enough for that rat," Massino quoted his former boss as saying about the man Bonano wanted eliminated (DeStefano, 2006).

Explaining Organized Crime

Organized crime can be interpreted most readily in terms of anomie theory. It represents recourse to illegal means to achieve ends (most notably, financial ends) that are heavily emphasized by our society. As Dick Hobbs (2000:157) puts it, organized crime offers "an alternative mode of advancement to ethnic groups who found legitimate routes blocked by the inflexibility of normative society." Organized criminals typically come from the lower echelons of society and are handicapped by poor education or other barriers to social mobility. Recruits to organized crime often are slum neighborhood youngsters who demonstrate useful talents, and who see that the people with the expensive cars, elegant clothes, and the most opulent lifestyles are not the honest and the hard-working but the kingpins in the organized crime syndicate.

The careers of organized criminals, aside from the element of illegality and the use of violence, correspond closely to mythical American stories of personal achievement. The racketeer reaches for success by breaking the windows of the mansion of American society rather than entering through the front door. Organized criminals often will send their children to prestigious schools and push them toward legitimate occupations. Not surprisingly perhaps, organized crime reflects the racial prejudices of those who work in it, and until recently there has been a notable absence of African Americans involved in crime syndicates.

SUMMARY

Conventional forms of homicide are a byproduct of social interaction; their incidence increases on weekends, holidays, and other times of more intense social activity. Although uncommon, mass and serial killers receive extensive media attention. The dynamics of aggravated assault are quite similar to homicide. A homicide often can be viewed as a completed assault and an aggravated assault as an unfinished murder.

Rape has undergone reconceptualization during the past two decades from a sex crime to a crime of violence, although it obviously has a strong sexual component. This component involves the use of sexual dominance as an indication of power and superiority.

The feminist movement is responsible for highlighting domestic violence that can result in serious harm to women and children. More recently, particularly with the graying of society, concern has been expressed about the abuse of the elderly. Sibling violence remains a subject that largely has gone unattended, although it may play a role in socialization into the use of violence.

Business, government, and professional violence form a very large, but often overlooked, part of the roster of serious harm-inflicting offenses. Injuries are often brought about by a failure to take proper precautions or by deceit in validating tests, as with new drugs.

Finally, organized crime is a term used to categorize groups of offenders, usually of similar ethnic identification, who will use force to get their way. Organized criminals engage in activities such as extortion, drug trafficking, money laundering, and protection rackets in which for a certain payoff they will "protect" a merchant from their own willingness to wreck his or her store and from predation by other mobsters.

KEY TERMS AND CONCEPTS

Assault and Battery	Manslaughter
Battered-Child Syndrome	Mass Murderers
Battered Women	Money Laundering
Collective Efficacy	Premeditation
Cycle of Violence	Relative Deprivation
Extortion	Serial Killers
Felony-Murder	Street Code
Homicide	Subculture of Violence
Lifetime Murder Risk	Terrorism
Malice Aforethought	Victim Precipitation

KEY CRIMINOLOGISTS

Elijah Anderson	Robert Sampson
Jack Katz	Marvin Wolfgang

CASES

Auman v. People, 109 P.3d 647 (Colo. 2005)

People v. Noel, 28 Cal. Rpt. 3d 369 (2005)

DISCUSSION QUESTIONS

1. Almost 1,000 prize fighters have been killed in boxing bouts in the United States since 1890. Do you believe that boxing should be outlawed as a crime of violence? And how about football?

2. Do you believe that adolescents should not be permitted access to violent video games?

3. What actions do you think the school you are attending should take to try to prevent the kinds of mass killings that have occurred on campuses in recent years?

4. Do you believe adult students (those 18 and over) should be allowed to carry weapons in order to have a chance to protect themselves and others against violence by a classmate intent on mass murder?

5. How do you differentiate between a terrorist group and a second group that in the name of counterterrorism kills a great number of innocent civilians and tortures captives?

6. Do you view rape primarily as a sexual or a violent crime?

7. How should allegations of sexual assault be dealt with on a college campus?

8. What policy would you favor for dealing with domestic violence between a married couple or partners sharing living quarters?

REFERENCES

Abbey, L. (2009). Elder abuse and neglect: When home is not safe. *Clinics in Geriatric Medicine, 25* (February), 47–60.

Adams, C. (2007). *Rohypnol: Roofies—The date rape drug.* New York, NY: Rosen.

Albanese, J. S., Das, D. K., & Verma, A. (2003). *Organized crime: World perspectives.* Upper Saddle River, NJ: Prentice Hall.

Anderson, E. (1999). *Code of the street: Decency, violence and the moral life of the inner city.* New York, NY: W.W. Norton.

Apel, R., Dugan, L., & Powers, R. (2013). Gender and injury risk in incidents of assaultive violence. *Justice Quarterly, 30,* 561–93.

Ammons, L. L. (2003). Why do you do the things you do? Clemency for battered incarcerated wives: A decade's review. *American University Journal of Gender, Social Policy and the Law, 11,* 533–65.

Baglivio, M. T., Jackowski, K. & Greenwald, M. A. (2014). Serious, violent, and chronic juvenile offenders: A statewide analysis of prevalence and prediction of subsequent recidivism using risk and protective factors. *American Society of Criminology, 13,* 83–116.

Barmash, P. (2005). *Homicide in the biblical world.* New York, NY: Cambridge University Press.

Barnett, O., Miller-Perrin, C. L., & Perrin, R. D. (2005). *Family violence across the lifespan: An introduction* (2nd ed.). Thousand Oaks, CA: Sage.

Beard, V., Hunter, S., Kern, L., & Kiley, B. (2014). Death-related crime: Applying Bryant's conceptual paradigm of thanatological crime to serial homicide. *Deviant Behavior, 35,* 959–72.

Beeghley, L. (2003). *Homicide: A sociological explanation.* New York, NY: Rowman & Littlefield.

Bell, M., Perez, S., Goodman, L., & Dutton, M. (2011). Battered women's perceptions of civil and criminal court helpfulness: The role of court outcome and process. *Violence against Women, 17,* 71–88.

Berg, M. T., Stewart, E. A., Schreck, C. J., & Simons, R. L. (2012). The victim-offender overlap in context: Examining the role of neighborhood street culture. *Criminology, 50,* 359–90.

Bergen, R. K. (1996). *Wife rape: Understanding the response of survivors and service providers.* Thousand Oaks, CA: Sage.

Binder, G. (2004). The origins of American felony-murder rules. *Stanford Law Review, 57,* 84–244.

Binder, G. (2008). The culpability of felony murder. *Notre Dame Law Review, 83,* 965–1060.

Black, D. (1993). *The social structure of right and wrong.* New York, NY: Academic Press.

Blum, J. A., Levi, M., Naylor, R. T., & Williams, P. (1998). *Financial havens: Banking secrecy and money laundering.* New York, NY: United Nations.

Blumstein, A. & Rosenfeld, R. (1999). Explaining recent trends in U.S. homicide rates. *Journal of Criminal Law and Criminology*, 88, 1175–1216.

Bouffard, L. A., Wright, K. A., Mufti, L. R., & Bouffard, J. A. (2008). Gender differences in specialization in intimate partner violence: Concerning the gender symmetry and violent resistance perspectives. *Justice Quarterly*, 25, 571–94.

Breault, K. D. & Kposowa, A. J. (1997). The effects of marital status on adult female homicides in the United States. *Journal of Quantitative Criminology*, 13, 217–30.

Brookman, F. (2005). *Understanding homicide*. London, UK: Sage.

Brown, S. (1986). Police response to wife beatings: Neglect of a crime of violence. *Journal of Criminal Justice*, 12, 277–88.

Burgason, K. A., Thomas, S. A., Berthelot, E. R., & Burkey, L. C. (2014). Gats and gashes: Street culture and distinctions in the nature of violence between youth and adult offenders. *Deviant Behavior*, 35, 534–54.

Butler, K. (2006). Beyond rivalry, a hidden world of sibling violence. *New York Times*, (February 28), D1, D6.

Calavita, K. (2001). Blue jeans, rape, and the deconstructive power of law. *Law & Society Review*, 35, 89–116.

Capeci, J. (2006). Will the real Mafia stand up. *New York Times*, (March 5), WK5.

Caringella, S. (2009). *Addressing rape: Reform in law and practice*. New York, NY: Columbia University Press.

Clinton, W. J. (1997). *Apology for study done in Tuskegee*. Washington, DC: Office of the Press Secretary, the White House (May 16).

Combs, C. C. (2006). *Terrorism in the twenty-first century* (4th ed.). Upper Saddle River, NJ: Pearson/Prentice Hall.

Comstock, G. (2008). A sociological perspective on television violence and aggression. *American Behavioral Scientist*, 51, 1184–1211.

Cooper, H. H. (2001). Terrorism: The problem of definition revisited. *American Behavioral Scientist*, 44, 881–93.

Critchley, D. (2009). *The origin of organized crime in America: The New York City Mafia, 1891–1931*. New York, NY: Routledge.

Dallam, S. J. (2002). Science or propaganda? An examination of Rind, Tromovitch, and Bauman (1998). *Journal of Child Sex Abuse*, 9, 109–34.

Davis, L. & Klopper, H. (2002). *Personal communication (May 22)*.

Dean, T. (2007). *Crime and justice in medieval Italy*. London, UK: Cambridge University Press.

DeFronzo, J., Ditta, A., Hannon, L., & Prochnow, J. (2007). Male serial homicide: The influence of cultural and structural variables. *Homicide Studies*, 11, 1–14.

DeStefano, A. (2006). *King of the Godfathers: Joseph Massino and the fall of the Bonano crime family*. New York, NY: Pinnacle Books.

Dipietro, S. M. & McGloin, J. M. (2012). Differential susceptibility? Immigrant youth and peer influence. *Criminology*, 50, 711–42.

Dugan, L., Nagin, D. S., & Rosenfeld, R. (1999). Explaining the decline in intimate partner homicide: The effect of changing domesticity, women's status, and domestic violence resources. *Homicide Studies*, 3, 187–214.

Duwe, G. (2007). *Mass murder in the United States: A history*. Jefferson, NC: McFarland.

Edwards, R. (2014). *Jack the Ripper unmasked: How amateur sleuth used DNA breakthrough to identify Britain's most notorious criminal 126 years after string of terrible murders.* www.dailymail.co.uk/news/article.

El Baradei, M. (2011). *The age of deception: Nuclear diplomacy in a treacherous time.* New York, NY: Henry Holt.

Ellis, L. (1989). *Theories of rape: Inquiries into the causes of sexual aggression.* New York, NY: Hemisphere.

Falk, R. (2003). *The great terror war.* New York, NY: Olive Branch Press.

Federico, V. (2010). *Organized crime.* New York, NY: Routledge.

Feldmeyer, B. & Steffensmeier, D. (2009). Immigration effects on homicide offending for total and race/ethnicity disaggregated populations (white, black, and Latino). *Homicide Studies, 13,* 211–26.

Felson, R. B. (2006). Is violence against women about women or about violence? *Context, 5,* 21–25.

Fessenden, F. (2000). They threaten, seethe, and unhinge. They kill in quantity. *New York Times,* (April 9), 1.

Fleury, R. E., Sullivan, C. M., & Bybee, D. I. (2000). When ending the relationship does not end the violence: Women's experience of violence by former partners. *Violence against Women, 6,* 1263–83.

Foakes, R. A. (2003). *Shakespeare and violence.* Princeton, NJ: Princeton University Press.

Fontaine, R. G. (2010). An attack on self-defense. *American Criminal Law Review, 47,* 57–89.

Friedman, L. S., Avila, S., Tanouye, K., & Joseph, K. (2011). A case control study of severe physical abuse of older adults. *Journal of the American Geriatrics Society, 59,* 417–22.

Friedrichs, D. (2000). The crime of the century? The case for the Holocaust. *Crime, Law and Social Change, 34,* 21–41.

Garcia, R. M., Taylor, R., & Lawton, B. A. (2007). Impacts of violent crime and neighborhood structure on trusting your neighbors. *Justice Quarterly, 24,* 679–704.

Geis, G. & Geis, R. (1979). Rape in Stockholm: Is permissiveness relevant? *Criminology, 17,* 311–22.

Gil, V. E., & Anderson, A. (1999). Case study of rape in contemporary China: A cultural-historical study of gender and power differentials. *Journal of Interpersonal Violence, 14,* 1151–71.

Gius, M. (2014). An examination of the effects of concealed weapons laws and assault weapons bans on state-level murder rates. *Applied Economics Letters, 21,* 265–7.

Godwin, M. & Rosen, F. (2005). *Tracker: Hunting down serial killers.* New York, NY: Thunder's Mouth Press.

Hardy, M., Beers, B., Burgees, C., & Taylor, A. (2010). Personal experience and perceived acceptability of sibling aggression. *Journal of Family Violence, 25,* 65–71.

Hattery, A. J. (2009). *Intimate partner violence.* Lanham, MD: Rowman Littlefield.

Henriques, D. (2011). *The wizard of lies: Bernie Madoff and the death of trust.* New York, NY: Henry Holt.

Hickey, E. W. (2009). *Serial murderers and their victims* (5th ed.). Belmont CA: Wadsworth.

Hines, D. A. & Malley-Morrison, K. (2004). *Family violence in the United States: Understanding and combating abuse.* Thousand Oaks, CA: Sage.

Hobbs, D. (2000). Researching serious crime. In R. D. King, & E. Wincup (Eds.), *Doing research on crime and justice* (pp. 153–83). New York. NY: Oxford University Press.

Hobbs, D. (2003). Organized crime and violence. In W. Heitmeyer, & J. Hagan (Eds.), *International handbook of violence research* (pp. 679–99). Dordrecht, The Netherlands: Kluwer.

Huff-Corzine, L., Corzine, J., & Moore, D.C. (1991). Deadly connections: Culture, poverty, and the direction of lethal violence. *Social Forces, 69*, 715–32.

Humphries, D. (2002). No easy answers: Public policy, criminal justice, and domestic violence. *Criminology & Public Policy, 2*, 91–96.

Jacobs, B. (2000). *Robbing drug dealers: Violence beyond the law*. New York, NY: Aldine de Gruyter.

Jacobs, J. (2006). *Mobsters, unions, and feds: The Mafia and the American labor movement*. New York, NY: N.Y.U. Press.

Jacobs, S. (1994). Social control of sexual assault by physicians and lawyers within the professional relationship. *American Journal of Criminal Law, 19*, 43–60.

Jesilow, P. D., Pontell, H. N., & Geis, G. (1985). Medical criminals: Physicians and white-collar offenses. *Justice Quarterly, 2*, 149–65.

Jewkes, R. & Abrahams, N. (2002). The epidemiology of rape and sexual coercion in South Africa: An overview. *Social Science and Medicine, 55*, 1231–44.

Johnson, E. A. & Monkkenon, E. H. (Eds.). (1996). *The civilization of crime: Violence in town and country since the Middle Ages*. Urbana, IL: University of Illinois Press.

Jones, J. H. (1993). *Bad blood: The Tuskegee Syphilis Experiment*. New York, NY: Free Press.

Kanin, E. J. (1985). Date rapists: Differential sexual socialization and relative deprivation. *Archives of Sexual Behavior, 14*, 219–31.

Kaplan, A. (2000). *The collaborator: The trial & execution of Robert Brasilach*. Chicago, IL: University of Chicago Press.

Katz, J. (1988). *The seduction of crime: Moral and sensual attractions of doing evil*. New York, NY: Basic Books.

Kirk, D. S. & Hardy, M. (2014). The acute and enduring consequences of exposure to violence on youth mental health and aggression. *Justice Quarterly, 31*, 539–67.

Kochan, N. (2005). *The washing machine*. Mason, OH: Thomson.

Kohn, L. T., Corrigan, J. M., & Donaldson, M. S. (Eds.). (2000). *To err is human: Building a safer health system*. Washington, DC: National Academy Press.

Kramer, S. & Ratels, K. (2012). Young black men's risk to firearm homicide in night time Johannesburg, South Africa: A retrospective analysis based on the national injury mortality surveillance system. *African Safety Promotion Journal, 10*, 16–28.

Labriola, M., Rempel, M., & Davis, R. C. (2008). Do batterer programs reduce recidivism? Results from a randomized trial in the Bronx. *Justice Quarterly, 25*, 252–87.

LaFree, G. (2013). Lone-offender terrorists. *Criminology & Public Policy, 12*, 59–62.

Lalumiere, M. L., Harris, G. T., Quinsey, V. L., & Rice, M. E. (2005). *The causes of rape: Understanding individual differences in male propensity for sexual aggression*. Washington, DC: American Psychological Association.

Lee, M. T. (2003). *Crime on the border: Immigration and homicide in urban communities*. New York, NY: LFB.

Lee, P. (2003). Reason, rape, and angst in behavioral studies. *Science*, (July 18), 301–13.

Levin, J. (2008). *Serial killers and mass murderers: Up close and personal.* Amherst, NY: Prometheus.

Loftus, E. F. & Geis, G. (2011). Collaborating to deter potential public enemies: Social science and the law. *UCI Law Review, 1,* 175–86.

Loftus, E. F. & Ketcham, K. (1996). *The myth of repressed memories: False memories and allegations of sexual abuse.* New York, NY: St. Martin's Griffin.

Lonsway, K. (2010). Trying to move the elephant in the living room: Regarding the challenge of false rape reports. *Violence against Women, 10,* 1356–71.

McCabe, K. A. (2003). *Child abuse and the criminal justice system.* New York, NY: Peter Lang.

MacKinnon, C. A. (1992). Feminist approaches to sexual assault in Canada and the United States: A brief retrospective. In C. Backhouse, & D. H. Flaherty (Eds.). *Challenging times: The women's movement in Canada and the United States* (pp. 186–92). Montreal, CN: McGill-Queen's University Press.

Madsen, F. G. (2009). *Transnational organized crime.* London, UK: Routledge.

Maimon, D., Antonaccio, O., & French, M. T. (2012). Severe sanctions, easy choice? Investigating the role of school sanctions in preventing adolescent violent offending. *Criminology, 50,* 495–524.

Martin, E. K., Taft, C., & Resick, P. A. (2007). A review of marital rape. *Aggression and Violent Behavior, 12,* 329–47.

Martinez, R., Jr. (1996). Latinos and lethal violence: The impact of poverty and inequality. *Social Problems, 34,* 131–45.

Martinez, R., Jr., Lee, M. T., & Nielsen, A. L. (2004). Segmented assimilation, local context and determinants of drug violence in Miami and San Diego: Does ethnicity and immigration matter? *International Migration Review, 38,* 131–57.

Marvell, T. B. & Moody, C. E. (1999). Female and male homicide victimization rates: Comparing trends and regressions. *Criminology, 37,* 879–900.

Merry, S. E. (2009). *Gender violence: A cultural perspective.* Malden, MA: Wiley-Blackwell.

Miethe, T. D., Regoeczi, W., & Drass, A. (2004). *Rethinking homicide: Exploring the structure and process underlying deadly situations.* New York, NY: Cambridge University Press.

Miller, S. L. (2005). *Victims as offenders: The paradox of women's violence in relationships.* New Brunswick, NJ: Rutgers University Press.

Miller, W. B. (1958). Lower-class culture as a generating milieu of gang delinquency. *Journal of Social Issues, 14,* 5–19.

Mills, L. G. (2008). *Violent partners: A breakthrough plan for ending the cycle of abuse.* New York, NY: Basic Books.

Newton, M. (2006). *The encyclopedia of serial killers* (2nd ed.). New York, NY: Facts On File, Inc.

Page, A. D. (2010). True colors: Peace officers and rape myth acceptance. *Feminist Criminology, 5,* 316–38.

Papachristos, A. V., Hureau, D. M., & Braga, A. A. (2013). The corner and the crew: The influence of geography and social networks on gang violence. *American Sociological Review, 78,* 417–47.

Pious, R. M. (2006). *The war on terrorism and the rule of law.* New York, NY: Oxford University Press.

Polk, K. (1993). *When men kill: Scenarios of masculine violence.* Melbourne, Australia: Oxford University Press.

Quinet, K. (2011). Prostitutes as victims of serial homicides: Trends and case characteristics. *Homicide Studies, 15,* 74–199.

Reichert, D. (2004). *Chasing the devil: My twenty-year quest to capture the Green River Killer.* New York, NY: Little Brown.

Reiman, J. H. (2004). *The rich get richer and the poor get prison: Ideology, class, and criminal justice* (7th ed.). Boston, MA: Pearson/Allyn & Bacon.

Rind, B., Bauserman, R., & Tromovitch, P. (1998). A meta analytic examination of assumed properties of child sexual abuse using college samples. *Psychological Bulletin, 124,* 22–43.

Rivara, F. P., Mueller, B. A., Spomes, G., Mendoza, C. T., Rushforth, N. B., & Kellerman, A. L. (1997). Alcohol and illicit drug use and the risk of violent death in the home. *Journal of the American Medical Association, 278,* 569–75.

Rosenfeld, R. (2002). Why criminologists should study terrorism. *The Criminologist, 27*(November-December), 1, 3–4.

Rosoff, S. M., Pontell, H. N., & Tillman, R. H. (2007). *Profit without honor: White-collar crime and the looting of America* (4th ed.). Upper Saddle River, NJ: Prentice Hall.

Roy, L. (2009). *No right to remain silent: The tragedy at Virginia Tech.* New York, NY: Harmony Books.

Rumney, P. N. S. & van der Bilj, C. (2010). Rape attitudes and law enforcement in South Africa. *New Criminal Law Review, 13,* 826–40.

Sampson, R. J., Raudenbush, S. W., & Earls, F. (1997). Neighborhoods and violent crime: A multi-level study of collective efficacy. *Science, 277,* 918–24.

Sander, P. (2009). *Madoff: Corruption, deceit, and the making of the world's most notorious Ponzi scheme.* Guilford, CT: The Lyons Press.

Savelsberg, J. (2006). Underused potentials for criminology: Applying the sociology of knowledge to terrorism. *Crime, Law and Social Change, 46,* 35–50.

Schlesinger, L. (Ed.). (2001). *Serial offenders: Current thought, recent findings.* Boca Raton, FL: CRC Press.

Schneider, E. (2000). *Battered women and feminist lawmaking.* New Haven, CT: Yale University Press.

Shattuck, R. (1996). *Forbidden knowledge: From Prometheus to pornography.* New York, NY: St. Martin's.

Shichor, D. (2007). Thinking about terrorism and its victims. *Victims and Offenders, 2,* 269–87.

Sinozich, S. & Langton, L. (2014). *Rape and sexual assault victimization among college-age females, 1995–2013.* Bureau of Justice Statistics. http://www.bjs.gov/index.cfm?ty=pbdetail&iid=5176

Skeem, J. L. & Monahan, J. (2011). Current directions in violence risk assessment. *Current Directions in Psychological Science, 20,* 38–42.

Sontag, D. (2002). Fatal entanglements. *New York Times Magazine,* (November 12), 52–62 84.

Tierney, K. J. (1982). The battered woman movement and the creation of the wife beating problem. *Social Problems, 29,* 207–20.

U.S. Department of Labor (2014). *News release: National census of fatal occupational injuries in 2013 (preliminary results).* Bureau of Labor Statistics. http://www.bls.gov/news.release/pdf/cfoi.pdf

Waite, L. & Gallagher, M. (2000). *The case for marriage: Why married people are happier, healthier, and better off financially.* New York, NY: Doubleday.

Walker, L. E. A. (2009). *The battered woman syndrome* (3rd ed.). New York, NY: Springer.

White, H. R., Lee, C., Mun, E. Y., & Loeber, R. (2012). Developmental patterns of alcohol use in relation to the persistence and desistance of serious violent offending among African American and Caucasian young men. *Criminology, 50*, 391–426.

Whittaker, D. J. (Ed.). (2001). *The terrorism reader*. London, UK: Routledge.

Widom, C. P. (2014). Varieties of violent behavior. *Criminology, 52*, 313–44.

Widom, C. P. & Maxfield, M. G. (2001). *An update on the "cycle of violence."* Washington, DC: Research in Brief, National Institute of Justice, U.S. Department of Justice.

Wolfgang, M. E. (1958). *Patterns in criminal homicide*. Philadelphia, PA: University of Pennsylvania Press.

Wolfgang, M. E. & Ferracuti, F. (1967). *The subculture of violence*. London, UK: Social Science Paperbacks.

Young, R. (2006). Defining terrorism: The evolution of terrorism as a legal concept in international law and its influence on definitions in domestic legislation. *Boston College International and Comparative Law Review, 29*, 23–103.

Zahn, M. A., Brownstein, H. H., & Jackson, S. L. (Eds.). (2004). *Violence: From theory to research*. Newark, NJ: LexisNexis/Matthew Bender.

Zeoli, A. M., Pizarro, J. M., Grady, S. C., & Melde, C. (2014). Homicide as infectious disease: Using public health methods to investigate the diffusion of homicide. *Justice Quarterly, 31*, 609–32.

Economic Crime

Jealousy of what other people have, lust for personal possessions, and competitive striving for material goods derive from cultural emphases. These conditions give rise to the crime of theft—the illegal taking of another's possessions by stealth or force. Americans typically say that what they want for themselves and for their children is "happiness." Happiness can be had in many forms, like watching a lovely sunset, enjoying the company of friends and fellow students, or reading a good book. But very often the pursuit of what we regard as happiness becomes related to money—how much we have and how much we'd like to have. This acquisitive pattern emerged in the United States in the beginning of the nineteenth century with the decline of a subsistence economy in which most Americans lived on what they produced. The shift was toward a market economy in which goods were produced and sold outside the home (Reynolds, 2008:12). The transition was fueled by the Industrial Revolution, about which an English writer aptly observed after poring over records of the development: "They left me with an acute awareness of how the delights of discovery and achievement led to tragic consequences as they became more oriented toward profit—how idealism capsized into greed and squalor" (Athill, 2008:137). When we place a heavy stress on material wealth, but limit legitimate opportunities for its acquisition, theft is a particularly likely outcome. Robert K. Merton (1964) maintains that the United States does just this: we encourage, almost demand, that people be financially successful if they are to be well regarded. As discussed in Chapter 7 of this text, Steven Messner and Richard Rosenfeld (2007) argue that the high levels of property crime in the United States are tied directly to the "**American Dream**"—the relentless push toward material acquisitions.

The gap between the rich and the poor in the United States is one of the most pronounced in the world and is gradually getting worse. Recent figures indicate that one percent of American households own 34 percent of all the country's privately held wealth, and that the next 19 percent hold 50 percent, leaving only 16 percent for the remaining 80 percent of the country's households (Domhoff, 2010). With respect to income, economic disparity has been increasing. While the top one percent of families received 11.3 percent of the pre-tax income in 1944, this amount had risen to 22.5 percent by the end of 2012. The wealth disparity presumably can only go so far before the situation becomes incendiary.

ACQUISITIVENESS AND THEFT

Almost all of us get somewhat caught up in the race to enhance our sense of self-worth by the acquisition of things. Those unable or unwilling to obtain material possessions in a legitimate manner may be impelled to resort to criminal behavior to acquire them. We call such crimes "economic crimes," but many other forms of criminal behavior also have financial considerations at their root. Murder may be committed to get an inheritance and arson may be committed to obtain an insurance payoff.

Honesty may be placed on a back burner when unemployment, under-employment, or addiction to drugs is involved. A cartoon makes fun of an attitude that can give rise to economic crime in the business world. "Honesty may be the best policy," a chief executive informs one of his middle managers. "But it is not our policy."

Theft also may be preferred to working routinely at a tedious job. Greed also can underlie economic crimes. Those who have much often desire much more. Somebody will have more than you do, a newer car, a bigger yacht. Merton noted that crime can be produced among those who are well off by the "anomia of success," which, he said, "arises when progressively heightened aspirations are fostered by each temporary success and by the enlarged expectations visited on [successful people] by associates" (Merton, 1964:225). Wants can be insatiable. Criminology students might ponder this point. What will satisfy them? At what point, if any, do they believe they might violate the law to obtain material goods? Are wants without limits?

Acquisitiveness Cross-culturally

We know of some people for whom, although murder is not uncommon, theft and cheating are unknown. The Dakota Indians had a strong code against placing value on goods. The prestige they attached to property was derived from giving it away. In the same manner, undue wealth was regarded by the Navajos as the product of a lack of generosity, perhaps even the result of malicious witchcraft.

In both ancient Jewish and German law, stealing was viewed as more serious than many crimes of violence. It was a Hebrew belief that thieves who committed their crimes in secrecy thought themselves not to be watched by God. The German tribes regarded stealing, because it was premeditated, as more serious than crimes against the person, which tended to be impulsive. They punished theft with death, while allowing fines to be paid for maiming and murder.

Historically, Christian societies have fought a constant battle to inhibit acquisitiveness. The Bible exhorts individuals to strip themselves of worldly possessions in order to prepare for a heavenly state. It asserts that it will be more difficult for a rich man to achieve divine indulgence than for a camel to pass through the eye of a needle (Matthew 19:14). Despite these dicta, few persons in nominally Christian societies appear to take this religious injunction against the accumulation of wealth very seriously.

Social Conditions and Theft

Although definitions of private property vary from culture to culture, there remains a nuclear agreement that some things must remain inviolable. It may be commendable in some societies to live modestly, but in no society is it considered desirable to allow everything that you possess to be stolen. A state of social chaos would result if persons dared not leave their home for fear that someone else might legally take possession of it, or if people dared not use their cars for fear of having them stopped and appropriated.

Automobile theft illustrates the relationship between possessions and property crime. Besides its obvious value as convenient transportation, having an automobile conveys status; the more expensive the car, the more important its owner appears to be. In the United States, over time different car models become the prime targets of thieves. While car thefts have declined in recent years, more than 1 million vehicles were stolen in 2010, which cost consumers and insurance companies more than $8 billion. According to the National Insurance Crime Bureau Hot Wheels Report, the models targeted most frequently in 2010 were the 1994 Honda Accord followed by the 1995 Honda Civic, and the 1991 Toyota Camry. Also in the top ten were a number of domestic cars including the Ford F-150 pickup truck, the Ford Explorer SUV, the Dodge Ram and Caravan, and pickups by Chevrolet and GMC (Elliott, 2011).

The Law of Theft

The law of theft is one of the most complex segments of criminal codes. **Larceny**, the broadest form of theft, involves the taking of property from a person without that person's consent and with the intent to deprive the person permanently of the use of the property. Larceny is often broken down into **grand larceny** and **petit (petty) larceny** (generally less than $50), depending on the value of the property stolen. It can be argued that the distinction between grand and petty larceny reflects a class bias. The theft of $10 from a person who has no more money is at least as serious as the theft of thousands of dollars from a person who possesses millions. Regardless, the $10 theft in many jurisdictions is regarded as petty larceny, a misdemeanor, while the second is defined as grand larceny, a felony.

Robbery is a form of theft in which goods or money are taken from a person through the use of violence or fear. The fear must be of such a nature as to arouse a reasonable apprehension of danger in a reasonable person. Robbery is a more serious crime than larceny, regardless of the amount of money or the value of the goods involved. About 3 percent of robbery victims suffer personal injuries serious enough to require hospitalization (Tunnell, 2000).

Burglary generally is defined as a crime against a dwelling. A burglar under the old common-law definition was a person who broke into and entered the house of another in the night with the intent to commit a felony. Statutes have greatly extended the common-law scope of burglary to include warehouses, storehouses, offices, and similar structures as "dwelling houses." "Night" in early English law, before the use of watches and clocks, was regarded as any time when there was insufficient light to make out a person's features. Contemporary statutes define the time limits more precisely. New York specifies the hours from sunset to sunrise. That state also divides burglary into three degrees: burglary three, which occurs by day and in an unoccupied site; burglary two, in which a human being is present in the dwelling; and burglary one, which is a nighttime

HIGHLIGHT 12.1   *TOMBAROLI*

There exists a specialized kind of theft in Italy carried out by *tombaroli*, or tomb raiders. One practitioner in the town of Ceveteri, west of Rome, scavenges for Etruscan ruins that lie buried in graves. He primarily seeks gold, bronzes, jewelry, and decorated vases.

Today, the Ceveteri graveyard thief mourns the decline in his business. "Nobody wants to do this work anymore," he complains. "Young people want money fast and without working. They don't want to go out at night, dig, work hard. They content themselves in an office job with a pittance for a salary. Our experience is being lost."

The graveyard thief argues that the goods are being wasted lying in coffins. Besides, the government would put what it found into museums, under glass, whereas his patrons can always enjoy the pleasure of personal possession (Lattanzi, 1998).

offense, or one in which the burglar is armed with a dangerous weapon, or an offense in which the burglar commits assault while on the premises.

Even with such precise definitions, the law of burglary can present perplexing questions. How, for instance, would you define theft from graves, as described in Highlight 12.1?

Robbery

Some criminals commit robberies and burglaries as well as other offenses when they find an opportunity too appealing to ignore. Nonetheless, different patterns of offending tend to go with different criminals. Robbery is "easier" than burglary in the sense that there is a direct confrontation that quickly garners a payoff and there is no need to dispose of stolen goods. On the other hand, some offenders shy away from face-to-face contact with their victim and are nervous that they later can be identified. They also fear that they may have to shoot a victim who resists, thereby escalating the robbery into murder; 10 percent of all homicides occur in the context of a robbery (about one robbery in 300 ends with a murder).

A common impulse for robbery, as it is for burglary, is to meet the requirements for success in a depressed neighborhood. An incarcerated robber, talking to a custodial officer in New York's Sing Sing prison, summarized the situation: "In the ghetto you get no respect if you don't look right, have a car, a Mercedes-Benz—those things. No women will go out with you. That's reality" (Conover, 2000:292).

Robbery requires very different skills than burglary, develops at a different pace, and provides its own kind of emotional rewards, most notably the opportunity to show "courage." For many offenders, burglary is seen as boring, too slow. As one robber notes:

Sticking up gave me a rush that I never got from B&Es [breaking and enterings]. There was an almost magical transformation in my world when I drew that gun on folks. I always marveled at how the toughest cats whimpered and begged for their lives when I stuck the barrel of a shotgun into their faces. Adults who ordinarily would have commanded my respect were forced to follow my orders like obedient kids (McCall, 1994:97)

Richard Wright and Scott Decker (1997) interviewed 86 robbers living in St. Louis. Thirty-one percent said that they had committed more than 49 robberies during their lifetime. One-third of the group had never been arrested for robbery, while another 26 percent had one or more arrests, but had never been convicted. Most (85 percent) usually committed street robberies; the remainder did their work in commercial establishments, most notably convenience and liquor stores, pawnshops, bars, and gas stations. Many preyed upon individuals who themselves were involved in lawbreaking; drug dealers were the likeliest victims. Dealers usually have a lot of money on them and they are unlikely to report the crime. As one robber said: "What they gonna tell the police? He robbed me for my dope?" (Wright & Decker, 1997:64; Jacobs & Wright, 2008). Robberies tend to be confined to specific sites. As Braga and his colleagues report: "Roughly one percent and 8 percent of street segments and intersections in Boston were responsible for nearly 50 percent of all commercial robberies and 66 percent of all street robberies between 1980 and 2008" (Braga et al., 2011:8).

A Chicago study found that robbers tend to select targets near where they live. They are wary of social barriers, that is, dissimilarities between the community where the crime is committed and their own community and themselves in regard to such matters as ethnic and racial demographics (Bernasco & Block, 2009). While some suburbanites fear the introduction of light rail systems as enabling urban criminals to invade their communities, research does not support such fears.

A study of robbers in England who target commercial establishments notes their puzzlement when employees refuse to hand over money peacefully. "It's not their money, why should they risk their lives?" the robbers wonder (Matthews, 2002:24–5).

The expanding use of credit cards has altered robbery patterns (see Highlight 12.2). Robbers no longer see well-dressed persons as necessarily prime targets because they often are short of cash and heavy with credit cards. Whites are preferred victims because they are likely to offer less resistance. This is especially true of white women, although some robbers shy away from such targets because they believe that some women will respond with strong emotions, perhaps screaming, and thus jeopardize the success of the encounter. One robber explained his victim preference this way:

Women are easy; they are so easy because they panic so quick [sic]. Women will throw their purse to you and you just snatch it in. But men, they will hesitate sometimes so that you got to show them you are serious, shoot them in the leg (Wright & Decker, 1997:85).

HIGHLIGHT 12.2 CASH AND CRIME

In a recent article, Richard Wright and colleagues reported on the changing nature of crime attributed to the transition from a cash-based economy to one based on electronic transfers (e.g., credit cards, debit cards, and electronic benefit transfers). Professor Wright offers this summary of his hypothesis. (For a more detailed account, consult Wright et al., 2014.)

> Cash has been criminogenic from its earliest days, initially being used mostly by "paupers and ne'er do wells so notoriously down on their luck that no one would extend credit to them" (Graeber 2011:327). Part of the appeal that cash holds for criminals is its transactional anonymity, which facilitates the exchange of illicit goods and services without leaving a trace. Criminologists have long recognized that most predatory street crimes are motivated by a

perceived need for cash, and that much of that cash is spent on hedonistic activities, especially illegal drug use (Wright & Decker, 1994; 1997). The neighborhood drug dealer does not accept checks, debit, or credit cards. Cash is king on the street corner. This raises an intriguing question: Could reducing the amount of cash in circulation lead to a drop in street crime?

In poor urban neighborhoods, where street crime is heavily concentrated, a major source of circulating cash traditionally came in the form of welfare payments. Initially, these payments were made to recipients using paper checks. Because many welfare beneficiaries do not have a bank account, they were forced to convert their checks to cash at local check-cashing facilities and keep the funds with them. In the early 1990s, however, the federal government

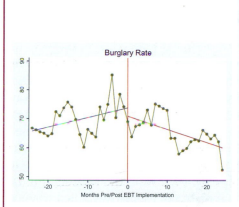

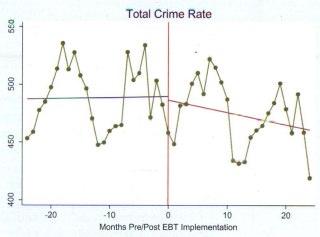

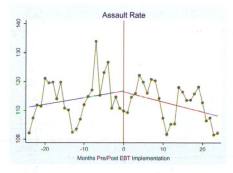

FIGURE 12.1

began to urge states to disburse welfare payments using Electronic Benefit Transfer (EBT) debit cards. In response, Missouri implemented a state-wide EBT program in eight geographically distinct phases between June 1997 and May 1998. The variation in implementation dates across Missouri counties over a 12-month period gave me and my co-authors a chance to examine how reducing the amount of cash on the street by moving from welfare checks to EBT affected crime rates.

To do that, we used Uniform Crime Report data (see Figure 12.1) to look not just at crime rates before and after the implementation of EBT, but also at how those rates compared to counties that had not yet adopted the new payment scheme. The results are striking and provide powerful testimony to the important role of cash in motivating street crime. Controlling for a wide range of alternative explanatory factors, the overall crime rate fell by nearly ten percent, and there also were substantial drops in specific crimes such as burglary and assault (Wright, Topalli & Tekin 2014).

These results are all the more remarkable when you consider that the introduction of EBT did not eliminate cash on the street, but simply reduced it. To this day, EBT recipients can use their cards to withdraw cash. The difference is that even those who are "unbanked" need not withdraw all of it at once as was usually the case with welfare checks.

What do the results of our research portend for the future of street crime? Cash continues to decline as a transactional medium across the world, which is bad news for those trying to bankroll a life of illicit action via predatory street crime. A recent article in the New York Times (Goldstein 2014) put it this way: "These are lean times for pickpockets. People carry more credit cards and less cash." Indeed, this may help to explain the dramatic drop in street crime that began in the 1990s and continues to the present day.

This is not to suggest, of course, that all forms of crime will decline. As more and more financial transactions are conducted electronically, we can expect to see a substantial rise in cybercrime committed by individuals with the expertise necessary to exploit these new criminal opportunities.

One consideration in robbery is how to relieve victims of money and valuables. To ask that these things be handed over is to run the risk that victims will pass along only a portion of what they have on them. To search them means that you have to get in close to the victim and may thereby further endanger yourself. For offenders who do not use guns this possibility increases dramatically. During the Wright and Decker (1997) study, one robber told them that he had to employ a knife to pull off his robberies because no one would lend him a gun. He said that he was fearful that someone would overpower him. The interview was held in the afternoon; that night the robber was killed when an intended victim grabbed his knife and stabbed him in the chest.

The major influence on the timing of commercial robberies is the robbers' idea of the amount of money that might be on hand. The robbery rate is higher in the winter because of the longer hours of darkness, a cover; this also means that stores that stay open later are more likely robbery targets. One interesting scheme involved a robber having two of his friends shopping in the store when he held it up so that they could provide the police with false identifications of the perpetrator.

Failure to distinguish statistically between different forms of robbery often results in misleading portraits of trends. In South Africa, robberies are classified into five major categories; bank robberies, robberies of cash in transit, truck hijacking, business robberies, carjacking, and house robberies. House robberies account for about one-third of the offenses (Berg & Kimnes, 2009).

Burglary

Burglars show varying degrees of skill, from those who carefully "case" (reconnoiter) a house from which they will steal to amateurs who carelessly intrude into the most convenient target. A typology based on 456 house burglars indicated four major types of career house-breakers: those who are (1) young and versatile, (2) vagrants, (3) drug-oriented burglars, and (4) sexual predators. The last group has the most serious criminal records (Vaughn et al., 2008).

Wright and Decker tell of the feeling of exaltation that comes over burglars when they find themselves inside a house: everything that they see is theirs for the taking, presuming they can carry it away without being observed. On the other hand, burglars tell of their terror when they first enter a dwelling. They know that they might be confronted by a resident with a gun who pumps bullets into their body. Convicted burglars interviewed by Darci Barry and Stephen Brown (1997:10) documented this fear:

> You don't really fear getting caught. It's the fear of having to do something you really don't want to do. You can't never [sic] tell when someone is going to walk into you and run a stick or gun in [your] face. I mean, are you going to let them shoot you or do you try and get away? I mean, can't never tell in situations like that what you're going to do. That's what scares me; what I might do if the people or police come in.

In England, researchers speculated that the increased use of security devices by the affluent may have been influential in a sharp drop in burglaries, but they noted too that burglars tend to avoid affluent neighborhoods because they are likely to be recognized as intruders (Tilley et al., 2011). Some safety devices diminish the opportunity for the resident to get out of the house in the event of a fire or earthquake. In one instance, an 11-year-old in California died of smoke inhalation when she was trapped because iron security bars covered the house windows. Her three-year-old brother had set the house ablaze while playing with a cigarette lighter.

Burglars have been known to drop identifying material, such as their wallets, in sites they enter illegally, probably out of nervousness, although professional and amateur psychiatrists are likely to say that such "mistakes" represent a desire to get caught. Folklore sometimes maintains that burglars, out of hostility toward those more affluent than they, will urinate or defecate in the houses they burglarize, but field studies report that almost never happens, except when the offenders are young kids stealing from those against whom they have a grudge. Burglary can impose considerably more serious emotional pain on its victims than robbery where the financial loss is usually more impersonal. One burglary victim poignantly depicted his feelings:

> They stole my memories—they removed a portion of my mind. The insurance people asked how much my things were worth. I told them truthfully they were priceless. I would never look on these objects again and remember. For a period of time, I ranted like a fanatic. Sentimental

> value, people said. But for me there is no other value. If all we were talking about was money, then these things could have been replaced and I would have had no problem (Theroux, 2000:32).

An English writer recalling a burglary of the countryside house in which she had been raised, similarly observed that the crime "felt to my parents as if the house had been raped" (Seymour, 2007:282).

Targets of Burglary

Virtually all burglaries are triggered by a need, real or perceived, for money. Burglars will enter a house that they know is occupied only in the rarest of circumstances. Burglars also are concerned about neighbors. Common tactics for determining occupancy include accumulated mail or newspapers, watching the house, calling on the telephone, or just knocking on the door (Rengert & Goff, 2011).

Paul Cromwell and his coworkers report that, in the Texas town where they did research, burglars look for lawns with signs proclaiming that a member of the high school football team lives there. The burglars presume that the occupants will be watching the team play and choose home game times to break into the residence (Cromwell et al., 1991:24). In Muslim neighborhoods, religious people will leave their shoes at the front door before entering a residence. If burglars see no footwear there, they presume that nobody is home. Other burglars like to drive slowly through residential neighborhoods on very hot days. Closed windows and air conditioners that are not running are taken as signs that nobody is home.

Time and Place in Burglary

A burglar's major enemies are time, noise, and light. Their working attitude has been well expressed by Malcolm X, who was a burglar before he became a highly respected leader in the civil rights movement:

> I had learned from some of the pros, and from my own experience, how important it was to be careful and plan. Burglary, properly executed, though it had its dangers, offered the maximum chances of success with the minimum risk. If you did your job so that you never met any of your victims, it lessened your chances of having to attack or perhaps kill someone. And if through some slip-up you were caught, later, by the police, there was never a positive eyewitness (1982:141–2).

Houses on the edge of an unoccupied area are much more likely targets than those in the interior of a residential section. A study of 96 burglaries of student housing found a considerably disproportionate number of them to be from first-floor and corner units. Only 27 percent of the residences had corner locations but 53 percent of the burglaries targeted these places (Robinson & Robinson, 1997). Police patrols are unlikely to observe a burglary in progress. Burglars minimize the amount of time they spend in a house. A usual rule for an experienced burglar is to remain within a dwelling no more than five minutes, preferably fewer. Even the fastest response to a silent alarm (unless the house is across the street or down the block from the police station) would not threaten them.

Burglars almost invariably search only places where they have learned that most people keep valuables, especially money, jewelry, electronic equipment, cameras, and weapons. Typically, burglars head first for the bedroom. Shrewd homeowners sometimes secrete their valuables in a child's room, an area rarely entered by burglars.

Big-time Burglary

The ingenuity of career burglars is shown by a big-time jewelry theft. It took place in a Boston hotel during a national jewelry exhibit. About 9:15 each evening, exhibitors would place their wares in trunks, which were hauled to a vault where a timing device kept the doors from being opened until the following morning. Phil Cresta, a professional thief, formed a plan with two crooked Chicago jewelers that involved placing Cresta's 5-foot, 2-inch lightweight accomplice in their trunk and providing him with an air tank for breathing. The trunk was carted to the vault by the guards. Its occupant spent the next few hours transferring jewels from other trucks into his. The haul later was sold for more than half a million dollars; in addition, the Chicago jewelers filed a fake claim with their insurance company for what they alleged was their own loss (Wallace & Crowley, 2000).

Burglary Statistics

About 8 percent of American households are burglarized each year. Two out of three burglaries are against residences. The average loss (both for resident and nonresident property) is about $1,200. Burglars sometimes derive an ironic satisfaction in comparing what they have stolen with media accounts of what they are said to have stolen, a matter that feeds their belief that they were not the only crooks involved in the episode, and that their victims are intent on cheating insurance companies.

Slightly more than 90 percent of the persons apprehended for burglary are males. In the Wright and Decker (1994) study, the few female offenders typically worked with men, and said that, if caught, they would try to shift blame onto their male associates.

Perspectives on Burglary

The major explanation employed for burglary is "rational choice" theory (see Chapter 5), which postulates that the decision to offend is the result of a deliberate weighing, however rudimentary, of potential costs and rewards. Wright and Decker (1994), however, concluded that rational choice explanations pay too little attention to the subjective influence of emotions on burglars' decision-making process.

Wright and Decker (1994) rely on a theoretical position formulated by John Lofland and Lyn Lofland (1969). Lofland and Lofland maintained that the decision to carry out most crimes involves a three-phase process, beginning with (1) a perceived threat, moving to (2) a state of "psychosocial encapsulation," and culminating in (3) the specific criminal act. Perceived threats involve such things as the possibility of physical harm or, more likely, the risk of social disapproval in the eyes of others who are important to the person. Often men will egg each other on by "collaboratively constructed conceptions of opportunity" (Hochstetler, 2001), so that they commit a crime together that none of them would have ventured on alone.

Psychosocial encapsulation is most likely to occur when the perceived threat is immediate, when it is experienced infrequently, and when the threat occurs in circumstances in which the individual feels socially isolated, that is, unable to seek help from others. Encapsulation, the Loflands (1969:53) maintain, encourages "simple, short-term, quick, and close-at-hand" solutions, many of which are illegal.

Most burglars spend the money they gather on alcohol or other drugs and status-enhancing consumer goods, such as fancy clothes, which suggests that the threat has most to do with their sense of self-worth. As Wright and Decker (1994:201) put the matter: "To be seen as hip on the street, one must be able to keep the party going." Burglary also has been interpreted as a rebellion against demands to behave like most other people, particularly to hold down a job. As Kenneth Tunnell (2000:92) observes, burglars "withdraw from participating in officially approved activities. Persistent thieves refuse to work and dislike others who do; they don't vote; they reject formal education; they don't curb their alcohol and drug use, and often maintain nomadic life styles."

Shoplifting and Employee Theft

Shoplifting is sometimes referred to as the "five-finger discount" or, during the late 60s and early 70s, some referred to it as "liberation." It involves theft from a retailer during the hours the store is open for business. The extent of shoplifting cannot be established accurately because many stores blend shoplifting losses into their *"inventory shrinkage"*—a figure that includes damaged merchandise that is sold at a reduced price, bookkeeping errors, breakage, and employee thefts. The best estimate is that about 80 percent of inventory shrinkage is due to theft, and that approximately three-quarters of that involves theft by store employees.

Stores prosecute only a relatively small percentage of the thieves they catch. This selection process is often based on factors such as the attitude of the person apprehended or the person's ethnic or racial background and financial standing. African Americans and poor persons are more likely to be prosecuted than upper- or middle-class whites. Persons who sign a confession are sometimes then released. Those who refuse to sign are more likely to be prosecuted so that the business will not be faced with a false arrest lawsuit.

Professional shoplifters can be differentiated from amateurs, who greatly outnumber them, by the fact that they steal merchandise in order to resell it, usually to a **"fence,"** who will pay the thief about one-third the retail value of the article (Klockars, 1974; Steffensmeier, 1986). Increasingly stolen goods are sold online: it is estimated that 70 percent of the gift cards marketed on e-bay have been stolen. Some shoplifters steal to order: customers specify their desire for certain goods and the shoplifter targets these (for a similar pattern in burglary, see Clare, 2011).

Amateur pilferers flourish in department stores and in supermarkets, where they take the invitation to "self-service" literally. The height of the shoplifting season comes right before Christmas when the pressures to purchase are most intense.

Mary Owen Cameron, in her classic study of shoplifters apprehended in Chicago's Marshall Field's department store, concluded that older amateur shoplifters are not compulsive uncontrolled thieves suffering from psychological disturbances, but rather respectable people who pilfer systematically. She found that they come to the store prepared to steal and continue to steal until apprehended. Cameron maintained that the damage to the arrested amateur thief's self-concept is usually sufficient to inhibit further stealing. She notes:

> Pilferers generally do not think of themselves as thieves, and they resist being pushed to conceive of themselves in these terms. It is often quite difficult for the store staff to convince the arrested person that he has actually been arrested. Again and again the store police explain to pilferers that they are under arrest as thieves, that they will, in the normal course of events, be taken in a police wagon to jail, held in jail and tried in court before a judge and sentenced. "Yes, I took the dress," one woman sobbed, "but that doesn't mean I'm a thief" (Cameron, 1964:161).

Shoplifters employ a variety of tactics from "grazing" in supermarkets (that is, consuming food while strolling about the store) to fraudulent returns to department stores. Professionals may use a **booster box**, a wrapped parcel with a hidden spring that allows the thief to reach inside and open the bottom while it is resting on merchandise to be stolen. Other techniques involve "crotching," in which goods are hidden beneath loose clothes and held between the thief's thighs, and the switching of labels from less to more expensive items. Some shoplifters plot to get arrested by stealing while in full view of a store detective, and then unloading the product surreptitiously before they are apprehended. Thereafter, they can file a suit for damages for slander, false arrest, or false imprisonment, a tactic that can be used only a limited number of times. Professionals sometimes resort to particularly blatant tactics. A couple of thieves

An anti-theft device on clothing. An electronic sensor sets off an alarm if the products are taken out through a store exit.

CREDIT: ©iStockphoto.com/©Tommounsey.

hoisted a canoe onto their shoulders in a crowded New York department store and, unmolested, marched out the front door. Then there was the shoplifter who would set fire to a clothing rack and make off with other merchandise during the ensuing panic (Newman, 2006). One shoplifter observed that customers complain that they can't find anyone to wait on them in the large department stores. "I say," he observed, "thank you. Let them keep it that way" (Trebay, 2000: A24).

Stores, for their part, now tag products with electronic sensors that set off an alarm if the products are taken out through a store exit. They secure some items to the racks, and use cameras to monitor sales areas and fitting rooms. Placing clothes on a rack with every other hanger pointing in a reverse direction forestalls shoplifters who might try to grab an armful of merchandise and flee from the store. Many stores now are built with fewer angles, so that they provide unobstructed sight lines for those on the lookout for shoplifters (Gregg & Kresevich, 2011). But as Highlight 12.3 indicates, dedicated shoplifters are not without counter-moves.

Employee Theft

A typical employee theft tactic is to "sell" an item to a friend, say a $150 pair of shoes, but to charge for a $2 container of shoe polish. Some employees paste a bar code for an inexpensive item on their wrist and use that when making a much more expensive "sale" to friends. Employees also often take merchandise out with them when they leave work.

Retailers have sought to control thefts by establishing a national database that lists all employees caught stealing. The blacklist now contains the names of about one million persons. Nobody can be placed on the list unless the store has a signed confession or the names of two persons who verify that there was an oral confession (Coleman, 2000).

Perspectives on Shoplifting

Many criminology students undoubtedly can offer their personal stories about the forces that underlie shoplifting expeditions. Lloyd Klemke (1992) found that 56 percent of the 165 college students he surveyed admitted that they had been involved in at least one shoplifting offense. Jack Katz (1988) analyzed shoplifting accounts obtained primarily from women criminology students at UCLA. He emphasizes the "seductive power of objects," the "cheap thrills," and the "profoundly moving experience." Katz believes that for the students

---

HIGHLIGHT 12.3 THE LEGO THIEF

An Oregon man specialized in shoplifting Lego equipment, the Danish building toys. Over three years, he stole more than $600,000 worth of them from dozens of stores in five western states. He counterfeited bar codes that altered the price of Lego sets from $100 to $15. Then he sold the loot to toy collectors on a Web site.

Source: Zimmerman (2006).

shoplifting is a tactic in a war against boredom rather than against poverty. While granting the accuracy of Katz's insight, Bill McCarthy (1995) insists that it focuses on only one of a considerable number of correlates of shoplifting at the expense of other variables.

The "thrills" of shoplifting are noted by a persistent practitioner who indicates that "if the store manager is standing here and I could take something right under his nose, that's what I'd get because it's more of an accomplishment." Asked if he had tried legitimate employment, the shoplifter replied: "Never looked for none [sic] because there wasn't anything that I enjoyed more than shoplifting" (Tunnell, 2000:100). Judith Wallerstein and her colleagues document the appeal of shoplifting with an interview report of a practitioner:

> We loved to shoplift. That was the best. We'd go in a group to a store and someone would make a disturbance and when the authorities went to see what happened we'd take expensive cosmetics and other things that look good. I remember the feeling—my stomach would be all knotted with fear and I'd be light-headed and almost dizzy because I felt so exhilarated. Getting out and running fast even made it better. I never needed or even wanted anything we stole. What was important was the excitement (Wallerstein et al., 2000:118).

Theories to explain shoplifting have been compiled by Klemke (1992). The list begins with psychiatric and psychological postulations that typically blame pathological sexual conditions, and often equate the items that are stolen, like fountain pens, to sexual organs. A national survey found that 11.3 percent of 43,000 respondents could be identified as lifetime shoplifters. These persons were said to be characterized by deficits in impulse control, antisocial personality disorders, substance abuse, pathological gambling, and bipolar disorders (Blanco, et al., 2008).

Increases in shoplifting during periods of economic recession and especially in times of inflation are employed to verify anomie and strain theory insights. In terms of social control theory, Klemke observes that "there is rather consistent support for the proposition that weak social bonds in the family are moderately related to shoplifting," while the research results on ties to school and shoplifting "are less consistent" (Klemke, 1992:97).

Sykes and Matza's (1957) idea that neutralization is an important element in the commission of crime finds support in the shoplifting literature. A 20-year-old justified her stealing from stores in terms of what Sykes and Matza would call "denial of the victim," in which the offender insists that nobody has been hurt who did not deserve that injury:

> I felt the whole system—who owns the stores, who makes the profit—is set up by the same people, the people who have everything. I thought it served them right[;] they have more than they know what to do with. Every time I stole something, I'd say, "They rip us off every time we buy something, so I'm just getting even" (Klemke, 1992:106–7).

In her historical survey of shoplifting, Rachel Shteir (2011) echoes this student's observation, noting that with the 1971 publication of radical Abbie Hoffman's *Steal This Book*, shoplifting took on an aura of an antiestablishment rebellious act, a resistance to the pressure to purchase (Hoffman, 1971).

Telemarketing Fraud

Telemarketing becomes illegal when the seller oversteps established limits of merchandising truthfulness. It is a crime to promise a person on the other end of the telephone line that he or she will receive a 33 percent annual return if they invest in your oil drilling company if you have no legitimate basis for specifying that level of profit. The offense is even more obvious if the oil well does not exist. Victims' active involvement distinguishes **telemarketing fraud** from burglary and robbery.

Telemarketing scammers purchase lists of possible customers ("smooches" is what they are called in the trade) and cold-call them. The salespeople, almost always men, often will adopt aliases so that they cannot be located if there is a later complaint. Sometimes complainers are told that while the person from whom they bought the original purchase is no longer employed there, the salesman now talking to them will get their money and more back if they invest in his product. About 10 percent of telemarketers are believed to engage in illegal activities, and Americans lose about $40 billion a year to fraudulent sales pitches, although only 1 in 10,000 victims will report their loss to the authorities, usually because they are embarrassed by their gullibility (Stevenson, 1998).

A successful telemarketing scammer (they are called "yaks" in the business) requires verbal skills and an ability to improvise, although the basic pitch and recommended responses usually are scripted. For instance, if a customer says that she does not like doing business over the phone, the following response is in order:

> If doing business over the phone is difficult for you, I certainly can empathize with you. It is difficult for me as well. However, business lives on the phone. I know for a fact that there are literally thousands of people much like yourself who are making $50,000 and $100,000 from business conducted over the phone. A $20,000 investment is not a lot of money and it won't hurt you financially. So I'm asking you to give me just one percent of your confidence and the opportunity to earn the other 99 percent. Let me prove to you what I can do for you and base all future activity on the results I get. Fair enough?

The story is told of a new telemarketing employee who pondered a customer's response that he never did business over the telephone, and then replied with perplexity: "Not even to buy a pizza?"

Improvisation tactics are exemplified by the following story of a telemarketer selling phony investments:

> When I was new in phone sales I closed an oil and gas deal, but the client asked me first, how long have you been working in oil and gas? I told him to hang on a minute, I had another call. My supervisor asked me,

how long have you been driving? I said for fifteen years. He said, "Then you've been working with oil and gas for fifteen years, haven't you?"

With women, especially elderly women, salespersons will employ a considerable number of "dears" in their pitch and will call customers "sir" and "ma'am." Older people generally are more reluctant, out of what they regard as politeness, to hang up abruptly on callers, although the scammers prefer rapid turndowns if the person is not a likely purchaser, because they operate on the premise that the more calls they make the more likely they are to hook a sucker. They generally cite a ratio of one buyer to about 100 calls.

Novelist Doris Lessing (1961:52) provides a clue to the dynamics that drive many telemarketing salespersons. She writes about a con man who sought to exploit her: "His strength was—and I could feel just how powerful that strength was—this terrible, compelling anxiety that he should be able to force someone under his will." Lessing observes further: "It was almost as if he were pleading silently, in the moment when he was tricking a victim: Please let me trick you; please let me cheat you; I've got to; it's essential for me."

The self-esteem of the trickster becomes involved with the zest of combat. One telemarketing fraud manager expressed the feeling in these words:

> When I make a sale, it's like woooo. It's like Yes! I got addicted to it. It's like more exciting than anything. To know that the money was on the table and it was a battle of wills and I won! Yeah! I backed the guy down. He woke up that day not expecting a call from me. The furthest thing in his mind was getting into oil and gas (Doocey et al., 2001).

Various forms of swindling such as telemarketing scams are pervasive throughout the world. Highlight 12.4 describes a scheme used in Ghana.

White-collar Economic Offenses

The complexity and awkwardness of the concept of **white-collar crime** inheres in the fact that there is no agreement on whether the category should be:

1. Restricted to the class position of people who commit certain kinds of offenses (Sutherland, 1949/1983), or whether it should be
2. Applied only to the offenses themselves, regardless of who the perpetrators are (Weisburd et al., 2001).

HIGHLIGHT 12.4 STREET SWINDLING BY FAST TALKERS

Swindling, also called *azah* in Ghana, is usually perpetrated by people who are versatile in twisting words to confuse unsuspecting victims. Some swindlers were alleged to have combined magic with rhetoric, and promised to either double victims' monies, give new or superior products, help victims win fortunes, or give them potions to entice and neutralize those in authority. Generally, swindlers are interested in money, but may be content with clothing, jewelry, wristwatches, or any readily available portable valuables. Females accounted for 68 percent of the swindling victims, but 98 percent of the perpetrators were males in their mid to late thirties.

(Appiahene-Gyamfi, 2003:9).

For those who favor definition (1), white-collar crimes are regarded as offenses committed by persons of high status in the course of their business, professional, or political lives. How high such status needs to be to qualify for the category is one of the definitional dilemmas. For those who favor definition (2), a white-collar crime is any offense involving violations of certain laws such as those that forbid conspiracies in restraint of trade, as well as statutes that outlaw false advertising, embezzlement, and laws that come under the general heading of fraud. With this definition it does not matter who violates the law; it is the nature of the law that counts. The difficulty here is that in some categories that come to be called white-collar crime, almost one-half of the violators can be unemployed, a matter that undercuts the original intent of the concept of white-collar crime to call attention to abuses of power by those in leadership positions.

This dilemma highlights the strong ideological element that has been part of the idea of white-collar crime. When restricted to persons of status and power, the category of white-collar crime serves to correct the tradition of tying the idea of crime to the activities of the poor, members of minority racial and ethnic groups, and other persons who do not share equally in the wealth of the society. Others regard such a focus as propaganda, rooted in a desire to bring about social reform by attending to the wrongs of the powerful. The usual response is that most definitions in criminology are ideological and that the study of crime is a reformist enterprise. Criminologists seek to understand crime and wrongdoing in order to reduce it, whether by reforming the social system or the individual.

Background of White-collar Crime

Reformers always have complained about the crimes of persons with power who used their offices and their wealth to exploit others. In the Bible, prophets hurled ferocious denunciations at usury—the lending of money at excessive interest rates much like contemporary payday loan operations—and against merchandising tricks, such as withholding commodities from the market until scarcity and near-starvation forced people to pay unconscionably high prices for the products.

Criminologists at first only glancingly attended to the phenomenon of white-collar crime. Thorstein Veblen, an iconoclastic social economist, was one of the earliest scholars to upbraid upperworld law breakers. In his *Theory of the Leisure Class*, Veblen noted that the ideal captain of industry was like the ideal delinquent in his "unscrupulous conversion of goods and persons to his own ends, and a callous disregard of the feelings and wishes of others, and of the remoter effects of his actions" (Veblen, 1912:237). Edward A. Ross, a pioneering sociologist, also unloosed some colorful invective against the crimes of the well-placed, whom he labeled *criminaloids*. Ross (1907:47) wrote: "They are not degenerates tormented by monstrous cravings. They want nothing more than what we all want—money, power, consideration—in a word, success; but they are in a hurry and they are not particular about the means."

Andrea Schoepfer and Stephen Tibbetts (2011) have traced concepts that labeled and deplored upper-class wrongdoing back to the 1890s and the early part of the following century. They point out, for instance, that H.J. Kenner in a 1926 article criticized what he called the "white-collar bandit," defined as the "gentleman who steals the savings of the uninformed and gullible by stock swindling and fraudulent brokerage practices" (Kenner, 1926:54). The term "white-collar crime" was introduced in 1939 when Edwin H. Sutherland of Indiana University employed it in the title of his presidential address to the American Sociological Society. Sutherland, who was Nebraska-born and a product of populist politics, berated his audiences for ignoring such behavior. This neglect, Sutherland maintained, had led them to adopt superficial theories of crime causation. Broken homes and poverty, Sutherland insisted, cannot be causes of crime because white-collar crime is committed by persons of affluence who typically come from intact homes (or, at least did so when Sutherland was writing). Nor do such psychiatric explanations as Oedipal fixations hold water, since corporate executives who violate the antitrust laws rarely can be found to suffer from such syndromes (Sutherland, 1940).

Concern with precise definition was not of much importance to Sutherland because he assumed that, whatever the definition, white-collar crime could adequately be explained by the theory of differential association (see Chapter 8). The definitional chaos established by Sutherland has continuously plagued the study of white-collar crime (Geis, 2007). Among proposed definitions, the one that most closely adheres to Sutherland's original concept is that by Albert J. Reiss Jr. and Albert Biderman (1980:4):

> White-collar violations are those violations of law in which penalties are attached that involve the use of a violator's position of economic power, influence, or trust in the legitimate economic or political institutional order for the purpose of illegal gain, or to commit an illegal act for personal or organizational gain.

The relative shortage of scholarly work on white-collar offenders can be traced to the complexity of the subject, which may involve matters of criminology, civil and criminal law, organizational theory, psychology, economics, accounting, and other specialties. Besides, the subject does not lend itself readily to quantitative analyses, which these days dominate the social sciences (Highlight 12.5 provides additional discussion of the difficulty of white-collar crime research). In addition, persons who commit white-collar crimes are much less accessible to research inquiries than, say, juvenile delinquents. Stephen Rosoff, who interviewed physicians convicted of defrauding Medicaid, tells of some of the issues involved in such work:

> White-collar criminals often have enjoyed great respect in the past, a respect they have unwillingly forfeited. My experience teaching in prison left me with a sense that while most convicts proclaim their "innocence," it is usually a pro forma ritual. My experience

HIGHLIGHT 12.5 RESEARCHING WHITE-COLLAR CRIME

While much criminological research is based on quantitative methods, there exists a rich tradition of qualitative research, including ethnographies and case studies. Most of these qualitative studies have focused on traditional "street" crime and not "suite" crime. There are studies of drug dealers (Adler, 1992), gang members (Campbell, 1991; Decker & Van Winkle, 1996; Miller 2001), professional fences (Klockars, 1974; Steffensmeier, 1986), a professional thief (Sutherland, 1937), a shoplifter (Cameron, 1964) as well as studies of robbers (Wright & Decker, 1997) and burglars (Wright & Decker, 1994). With respect to white-collar criminals, there are also case studies of unsuccessful swindlers such as Michael Milken, Bernie Madoff, and others. What is lacking is criminological explorations of white-collar offenders that are similar to those focused on street offenders.

Years ago, one of the authors of this textbook approached a representative from the National Institute of Justice (NIJ), the research branch of the U.S. Department of Justice, and proposed (somewhat jokingly) a different line of research from that which NIJ normally funds. While it is not uncommon for funding agencies to support ethnographic research investigating lower-class crimes, it is rare to find support for comparable investigations of upper-class crime. Research costs associated with, for example, a participant observation study of drug dealing such as that conducted by Adler is relatively low. Consider, however, the costs associated with infiltrating the social circles of Wall Street bankers in order to learn more about the inner workings of insider trading deals. For a researcher to adopt such a lifestyle would be cost-prohibitive. The relative lack of basic research on white-collar offenders leaves many questions unanswered for the next generation of criminological researchers.

with "peculating physicians" left me with a different sense. These guys not only proclaim their innocence, they believe it—or, at least, they desperately want you to believe it. They hunger for the respect they once had. The first challenge in interviewing an elite offender is to extract information without being too adversarial. If I were interviewing a convicted burglar, I would probably call him Charlie (or whatever his first name is), while he might call me Doc. There is a role reversal when the offender is an elite deviant. I respectfully called the Medicaid fraud subject Dr. So-and-so. And I might well be called Steve in return—or called nothing at all. No problem. When the interview ends, I'm still the one without a parole officer (Dodge & Geis, 2006:86).

Forms of White-collar Crime

The global economic meltdown that began in late 2008 involved white-collar crimes, greed, irresponsibility, and a not inconsiderable dosage of stupidity. The trigger was the out-of-control sale of home mortgages, often on the basis of false documentation or no documentation at all, to persons who could not afford what they were induced to purchase. Real estate agents assured buyers that the value of their house would increase dramatically and they could then refinance, using the dwelling as if it were an ATM machine. Teaser loans carrying one or two percent interest in a few years would reset at exorbitant rates, driving payments up from, say, $800 a month to $2,400. Defaults and foreclosures followed apace and Wall Street behemoths such as Bear Stearns (Bamber & Spencer, 2009; Kelly, 2009; Greenberg & Singer, 2010), Lehman Brothers

(McDonald & Robinson, 2009; Ward, 2010), American International Group (Cohan, 2009; Schelp & Ehbar, 2009), and Merrill Lynch (Farrell, 2011) found themselves over their heads in debt. These companies, whose balance sheets were saturated with so-called subprime mortgages, collapsed, were bought by competitors, or were bailed out by the federal government with huge infusions of taxpayer money. The unemployment rate soared and states were faced with staggering budget shortfalls.

Criminal charges were not common because it is not a criminal offense to be reckless with stockholders' money. Angelo R. Mozilo, CEO of Countryside Financial, was among the few malefactors formally charged. He had sold $129 million of his own stock in the company while at the same time telling investors that it was a marvelous investment when he well knew otherwise (Michaelson, 2009). Mozilo vowed that he would fight criminal charges vigorously, but agreed to a settlement in 2010 with the Securities and Exchange Commission of $65.5 million, $20 million of which would be paid by Countrywide as part of his employment contract. The settlement involved but a miniscule portion of Mozilo's estimated net worth of $600 million.

The most publicized offender was Bernie Madoff who had run a Ponzi scheme, paying old investors not out of profits but out of money secured from new investors. He was sentenced to 150 years in federal prison when the impossible mathematics of his situation caught up with him (Sander, 2009; Strober & Strober, 2009; Henriques, 2011).

In the 1980s and 1990s, there had been the looting of savings and loan institutions of billions of dollars. One estimate is that by the year 2021, the bailout costs for insolvent thrifts will reach $473 billion. The savings and loan scandals highlighted a form of white-collar crime in which officials within the corporations were not acting, as in antitrust and similar kinds of violations, to enhance company profits but rather were engaged in what has been called "collective embezzlement" in order to gain personally at the expense of the institution (Calavita et al., 1997:177; Pontell, 2005).

There also is a long roster of offenses committed by medical doctors against government benefit programs such as Medicare (for the elderly) and Medicaid (for the poor). The cost of such fraud is said to be somewhere between 10 to 25 percent of the total amount of money expended on the programs. Some of the cases are bizarre. In Illinois, a psychiatrist was found to have billed Medicaid for 4,800 hours of work during the year, or almost 24 hours each workday. Other physicians have been caught billing for visits from persons who were dead at the time of the alleged medical service. A psychiatrist billed Medicaid for sexual liaisons with a patient, claiming that he had submitted the bills for "professional services" so that his wife, who handled his accounts, would not become suspicious.

The category of white-collar crime also includes such matters as false advertising. Department stores often raise the price of a product one day and then the next day drop it back to where it had been, maintaining in their advertising that it now is "on sale" and "reduced by 70 percent." In bait-and-switch tactics, a store will advertise a specific product at a strikingly low price, but when the customer tries to buy the item, the store indicates either that it no longer is available, or a clerk demonstrates that the on-sale item is much inferior to the thing that the store really wants to sell (Blumberg, 1989).

Other Characteristics of White-collar Crime

If the category of white-collar crime is confined to persons with power who commit offenses in the course of their occupational work, the definition restricts the ranks of possible perpetrators. Anybody with strength, or a gun and decent aim, or access to poison, can commit murder, but only corporate executives are in a position to violate the Sherman Antitrust Act. You and I can canvass the neighborhood and try our hand at burglary, presuming we have the nerve and are not intimidated by the risk of prison or the restraints of conscience. But only a physician (or someone who pretends to be a physician) can overservice patients enrolled in government medical benefit programs by ordering unnecessary X-rays or performing unneeded surgery.

A characteristic of many kinds of white-collar crime is that its victims often are not aware that they have been harmed. Death from asbestos poisoning is likely to be slow and insidious, and victims will be hard pressed to relate their terminal illness to its precise cause, given other possible contributing factors. A factory worker with cancer cannot be certain whether it was the toxic chemicals that she handled for 15 years, the fact that she smoked too many cigarettes, poor genes, or bad luck that is shortening her life.

In many white-collar crimes, the harm tends to be widely diffused and, for each person, rather insignificant. If you purchase what you believe to be orange juice, but actually get an orange concentrate diluted with water, you probably will not know the difference and, even if you do, you are not likely to make a fuss about it. But companies can earn millions of "extra" dollars by charging higher prices for products that do not meet the standards they are alleged to attain. Exceedingly few people who pay for a package of 100 thumbtacks will take the time to count the contents; it would be an easy and safe venture to put 92 thumbtacks in each package, and some merchandisers find the temptation irresistible.

The Dog That Didn't Bark in the Night

In a famous Sherlock Holmes short story, Holmes is investigating the disappearance of the racehorse Silver Blaze, the favorite to win the prestigious Wessex Cup. Holmes has this interchange with Gregory, the Scotland Yard inspector assigned to the case:

> Gregory: "Are there any other points which you wish to draw my attention to?"
> Holmes: "The curious incident of the dog in the night-time:"
> Gregory: "The dog did nothing in the night-time."
> Holmes: "That was the curious incident."

We leave it to the reader, if interested, to locate the short story titled "Silver Blaze" to learn about the significance of the nonbarking dog. For present purposes we note that this theme was highlighted in an investigative report by Gretchen Morgenson and Louise Story, two *New York Times* staffers, who were intrigued by the failure of U.S. federal enforcement agents to bark at the culprits responsible for the country's economic meltdown. "Several years after the financial crisis which was caused in part by reckless lending and excessive risk taking by major financial institutions," they wrote, "no senior executives have been charged or imprisoned, and a collective government effort has not emerged" (Morgenson & Story, 2011:B10).

The reporters noted that in the wake of the savings and loan banking scandals there had been more than 1,000 criminal referrals by investigators and that some 800 persons received prison terms. It would be only after the *Times* report appeared that the first criminal conviction associated with the economic meltdown occurred.

Why was this so? Morgenson and Story conclude that the government had taken the attitude that to roil the waters by publicly exposing the self-interested and shameless behavior of some leading business executives would have further deleterious effects on an already fragile domestic economy. They noted that the Department of Justice had requested that the FBI devote additional resources to the business failures, but various U.S. attorney offices protested, and the order became optional rather than mandatory. The reporters offered no explanatory information, but noted that prosecutors are intent upon compiling an impressive numerical record of courtroom success. It looks good if you have triumphed during a particular time period in 12 of 14 cases involving such matters as drug trafficking and post office robberies rather than to have to report that you have succeeded in only one of four white-collar crime trials. White-collar crime cases are tedious, time- and resource-consuming, and difficult to win.

There was a lesson in the fact that an early prosecution of two Bear Stearns hedge fund operators who allegedly had gulled customers into stupid investments resulted in a "not guilty" verdict. Ralph R. Cioffi and Matthew M. Tannin were charged with persistently lying to customers about the true value of their holdings. They both were indicted on charges of wire fraud, security fraud, and conspiracy. Cioffi was also charged with insider trading for taking $2 million of his own money out of a hedge fund without informing his client investors in the fund about his action. For 18 months the pair had indicated in their monthly statements to investors that only 6 percent of their fund holdings were in subprime mortgages when the true figure was 60 percent. Both men were acquitted in late 2009 after a three-week trial. The jury based its verdict on a judgment that the accused pair had made poor investment decisions but that doing so was not a criminal offense.

These kinds of activities obviously were complicated situations from the standpoint of the law, with its essential requirement that the prosecutor has to prove criminal intent beyond a reasonable doubt. Besides, the defendants' attorneys, often former federal prosecutors who have left for the greener fields of private practice (green being the color of money), could prove to be very formidable courtroom opponents. In addition, there was a public relations dilemma. Suppose that a company was heavily fined and paid the fine with the federal government bail-out money. This would mean that taxpayers were being made to pay the penalties levied against malevolent corporations.

The inertia of federal regulation has been documented by the Syracuse University Transactional Records Clearinghouse, which found that in 1995 bank regulators referred 1,837 cases to the FBI for investigation and criminal prosecution. That number dropped steeply in the years between 2006 and 2010 to an average referral of only 72 cases a year.

Within days of the *Times* report, Lee Farkas, the former chairman of the Taylor, Beam, and Whittaker Mortgage Corporation in Ocala, Florida, was convicted of 14 counts of fraud. Over seven years, Farkas had bilked investors of $2.9 billion. He owned dozens of automobiles, several airplanes, and many homes. Critics pointed out that like the savings and loan miscreants, Farkas was not a big fish Wall Street financier, but rather a relatively small fry operating in a hinterland pond.

The Sokol Scandal

Lax enforcement activity constitutes a particular problem for criminologists who believe that white-collar crime is a much more serious threat to the vitality and integrity of a society than street crime because it destroys trust in the country's leaders. Part of the reason that so much white-collar wrongdoing goes unattended is that criminal laws are enacted by persons who share with white-collar offenders the same social backgrounds and similar beliefs. Lobbyists work assiduously and are handsomely paid to see that laws are not passed that might inconvenience their affluent clients in their pursuit of wealth. Indeed, it could be argued that the contributions of campaign funds and other perks by lobbyists to politicians could reasonably be regarded as a form of bribery, but it is the recipients of these endowments who have the power and privilege to decide what acts should be penalized as bribery.

The 2011 case involving David L. Sokol illustrates the kind of legal murkiness that characterizes much of the study of white-collar crime. Sokol had worked as the leader of several companies owned by the Berkshire Hathaway conglomerate, a company run by Warren Buffett, the second richest man in the United States (Bill Gates of Microsoft is the richest). Sokol was a very wealthy man; he had exercised stock options in MidAmerican Energy, a company he had run, for $96 million. Unlike Buffett, who lives in the house he bought in Omaha in 1959 for $31,500, Sokol not only owns an Omaha residence but also a house in the upscale ski site of Jackson Hole, Wyoming, and another house on the waterfront in Fort Lauderdale, Florida, where he keeps his yacht. Sokol had been seriously considered as the man likely to succeed the 80-year-old Buffett when he no longer ran Berkshire Hathaway.

Unbeknownst to Buffett, Sokol had arranged meetings with Citigroup about possible Berkshire takeovers. He was advised that an appealing purchase was Lubrizol, an English chemical company. Lubrizol executives had been contacted, again without Buffett's knowledge, and had agreed that they would be amenable to being bought. Sokol pitched the company to Buffett but only mentioned "in passing" that he owned some stock in Lubrizol, allowing Buffett apparently to think that he had invested some time ago and believed that the company's future looked promising. In truth, Sokol had purchased $10 million worth of stock in Lubrizol the week before and was defying Berkshire's in-house policy against any employee having a conflict of interest in his or her

David Sokol talks to shareholders of MidAmerican Energy prior to participating in the annual shareholders' meeting, in Omaha, Nebraska.

CREDIT: AP Photo/Nati Harnik.

dealings. Sokol made a $3 million profit when Berkshire Hathaway purchased Lubrizol for $9 billion. He resigned from Berkshire when his investment became public, issuing a statement saying that he was leaving the company in order to make some more money for his family. Buffett, who had earned a reputation for integrity and honesty, at first said only that what Sokol had done "wasn't in any way unlawful." Soon after, the audit committee at Berkshire declared that Sokol's "misleadingly incomplete disclosures to Berkshire Hathaway's senior management concerning these purchases had violated the duty of candor he owed to the company." At a stockholders' meeting not long after Buffett changed his line, declaring now that Sokol's action was "inexplicable and inexcusable." Puzzling to Buffett was the fact that a few years earlier Sokol had been offered $12.5 million as an incentive reward for his work. He insisted that the money instead be given to his assistant. It might be that Sokol was trying to demonstrate his virtue to his boss. In response to Buffett, Sokol's lawyer maintained that his client was "a man of uncommon probity and did nothing wrong (Ng & Holm, 2011)." The best key to Sokol's behavior may lie in the four words that form the title of his self-published book: *Pleased, but Not Satisfied* (Sokol, 2007).

The Securities and Exchange Commission was said to be looking into the matter. Legal experts were divided on the possibility of criminal charges, and criminologists pondered whether they were seeing a case of a brazen white-collar criminal or that of a shrewd businessman, although they appreciated that a gap in the law that failed to prohibit what Sokol had done was a big part of the issue.

Criminological Theory and White-collar Crime

Neil Shover (1998) believes that underlying white-collar crime are pressures to meet self-defined or externally imposed standards of successful performance. When medical scientists experience pressure to produce research breakthroughs, or when athletic coaches have a string of losing seasons, or when business owners see their profits decline, the odds are increased that they will resort to criminal resolutions.

When Sutherland first wrote of white-collar crime, he maintained that it was best explained by his theory of differential association (see Chapter 8). For Sutherland, the law-breaking behavior of businessmen, professionals, and politicians (as well as all other law violators) was the product of a learning process. White-collar offenders encountered examples of law-breaking among those with whom they worked, and they drifted or jumped into such patterns of behavior as part of their routine indoctrination into the requirements of their job. In time, they found that the definitions they encountered favorable to violation of the law overruled those encouraging law-abiding behavior.

The trouble with such an explanation, as we have seen, is that it is extremely difficult, if not impossible, to test. Controversy also exists regarding the ability of theoretical constructs to suitably interpret criminal charges against corporations rather than against individuals within them. Donald Cressey (1988) insisted that a corporation cannot form the requisite intent to allow satisfactory social psychological theorizing about its behavior. John Braithwaite and Brent Fisse (1990), rebutting Cressey, insisted that organizations possess a mind of their own (as represented, for instance, by corporate guidelines) that is distinct from the sum of the minds of those who contribute to its decisions, and that it is possible to offer theoretical interpretations of organizational acts.

The limited ability of strain theory to explain white-collar crime was recently demonstrated by Lynn Langton and Nicole Leeper Piquero (2007) who found the theory was applicable to a select group of white-collar offenders, but not likely to explain violations by corporate officers. They also noted that the strains involved differed for white-collar offenses from those of street criminals.

SUMMARY

This chapter began with an emphasis on the fundamental cause of economic offenses, the desire to acquire money and goods and the ability and willingness to use illegal means to achieve that end. Human beings vary considerably in their devotion to material goods, their needs (real or imagined), and the likelihood that they will break the law to achieve financial ends. Some societies do not emphasize wealth and material goods; instead they value gift giving and plain living. Most religions deplore an undue accumulation of wealth in the face of others' poverty.

Burglary was seen to be marked by a calculation of risks and a routine that included getting into and out of a house in short order. Burglars overwhelmingly invade houses that are not occupied. They particularly choose as targets dwellings that cannot readily be seen by neighbors or passersby. The three-phase theoretical outline by John Lofland and Lyn Lofland was put forward as providing a particularly helpful interpretative scheme in regard to burglary. They maintained that burglary ensues from a perceived threat (which often is to the offender's self-esteem) that escalates into a state of encapsulation (in which the offender can think of no other way out of the dilemma) and then results in the crime.

Shoplifting, once largely a female crime, now shows a higher percentage of male offenders, a reflection of changes in shopping habits. Shoplifting by students was interpreted in a theoretical framework that focused on excitement and the seductive power of objects. It was said to be motivated more by boredom than poverty. The dynamics of employee theft are much the same as those that propel persons to shoplift.

White-collar crime, defined commonly as offenses committed by persons of power and status in the course of their occupations, has challenged many of the commonplace explanations of crime, such as those that regard broken homes as important contributors to lawbreaking. The concept of white-collar crime nonetheless is suffused with definitional dilemmas.

KEY TERMS AND CONCEPTS

American Dream	Petit Larceny
Booster Box	Psychosocial Encapsulation
Burglary	Robbery
Fence	Shoplifting
Grand Larceny	Telemarketing Fraud
Larceny	White-Collar Crime

KEY CRIMINOLOGISTS

John Braithwaite	Lyn Lofland
Mary Owen Cameron	Edwin H. Sutherland
Donald Cressey	Thorstein Veblen
Gilbert Geis	Richard T. Wright
John Lofland	

DISCUSSION QUESTIONS

1. What are the two major definitions of white-collar crime, and what advantages and disadvantages does each possess?
2. Why do you believe that a corporate executive who has been given 40 million dollars in bonuses during the previous five years will thereafter risk his or her reputation and a possible prison term by establishing or endorsing an illegal hedge fund scheme?

3. If an acquaintance of yours was seriously contemplating committing a street economic crime and asked whether you would recommend burglary or robbery, which would you choose for him or her? Why?

4. Why, from your reading or your experience or that of friends, do you believe people shoplift merchandise they don't even want or will not use?

5. How would you explain the actions of the Berkshire Hathaway manager, and what do you believe should be done about such behavior?

REFERENCES

Adler, P. A. (1992). *Wheeling and dealing: An ethnography of an upper-level drug dealing and smuggling community* (2nd ed.). New York, NY: Columbia University Press.

Athill, D. (2008). *Somewhere towards the end: A memoir*. New York, NY: W. W. Norton.

Appiahene-Gyamfi, J. (2003). Urban crime trends and patterns in Ghana: The case of Accra. *Journal of Criminal Justice, 31,* 1–11.

Bamber, B. & Spencer, A. (2009). *Bear trap: The fall of Bear Stearns and the panic of 2008*. New York, NY: Black Tower Press.

Barry, D. & Brown, S. (1997). *Rational choice and environmental cues among residential burglars.* Paper presented at the annual meeting of the American Society of Criminology. November, San Diego, CA.

Berg, J. & Kimnes, I. (2009). An overview of crime in South Africa. *The Criminologist,* (May/June), 22–24.

Bernasco, W. & Block, R. (2009). Where offenders choose to attack: A different choice model of robberies in Chicago. *Criminology, 47,* 93–130.

Blanco, C., Grant, J., Petry, N. M., Simpson, H. B., Alegria, A., & Liu, S. M. (2008). Prevalence and correlates of shoplifting in the United States: Results from the National Epidemiological Survey on Alcohol and Related Conditions (NESARC). *American Journal of Psychiatry, 165,* 905–13.

Blumberg, P. (1989). *The predatory society: Deception in the American marketplace*. New York, NY: Oxford University Press.

Braga, A. A., Hureau, D. M., & Papachristos, A. V. (2011). The relevance of micro places to citywide robbery trends: A longitudinal analysis of robbery incidents at street corners and block faces in Boston. *Journal of Research in Crime and Delinquency, 48,* 7–22.

Braithwaite, J. & Fisse, B. (1990). On the plausibility of corporate crime theory. In W. S. Laufer, & F. Adler (Eds.), *Advances in criminological theory* (Vol. 2, pp. 15–38). New Brunswick, NJ: Transaction.

Calavita, K., Pontell, H., & Tillman, R. H. (1997). *Big money crime: Fraud and politics in the savings and loan crisis*. Berkeley, CA: University of California Press.

Cameron, M. O. (1964). *The booster and the snitch: Department store shoplifting*. New York, NY: Free Press.

Campbell, A. (1991). *The girls in the gang* (2nd ed.). New York, NY: Basil Blackwell.

Clare, J. (2011). Examination of systematic variation in burglars' domain-specific perceptual and procedural skills. *Psychology, Crime and Law, 17,* 199–214.

Cohan, W. D. (2009). *House of cards: A tale of hubris and wretched excess on Wall Street*. New York, NY: Doubleday.

Coleman, C. (2000). As thievery by insiders overtakes shoplifting, retailers crack down. *Wall Street Journal,* (October 4), A1, A16.

Conover, T. (2000). *Newjack: Guarding Sing Sing.* New York, NY: Random House.

Cressey, D.R. (1988). The poverty of theory in corporate crime research. In W.S. Laufer, & F. Adler (Eds.), *Advances in criminological theory* (Vol. 1, pp. 31–56). New Brunswick, NJ: Transaction.

Cromwell, P.F., Olson, J.N., & Avery, D.W. (1991). *Breaking and entering: An ethnographic approach to burglary.* Newbury Park, CA: Sage.

Decker, S.H. & Van Winkle, B. (1996). *Life in the gang: Family, friends, and violence.* New York, NY: Cambridge University Press.

Dodge, M. & Geis, G. (2006). Fieldwork with the elite: Interviews with white-collar criminals. In D. Hobbs, & R. Wright (Eds.), *The Sage handbook of fieldwork* (pp. 79–92). London, UK: Sage.

Domhoff, G.W. (2010). *Who rules America? Challenges to corporate and class dominance.* Boston, MA: McGraw Hill Higher Education.

Doocey, J.H., Shichor, D., Sechrest, D.K., & Geis, G. (2001). Telemarketing fraud: Who are the tricksters and what makes them trick? *Security Journal, 4,* 7–26.

Elliott, H. (2011). *The most stolen cars in the country.* Forbes.com. http://www.forbes.com/sites/hannahelliott/2011/08/02/the-most-stolen-cars-in-the-country/

Farrell, G. (2011). *Crash of the titans: Greed, hubris, the fall of Merrill Lynch, and the near collapse of Bank of America.* New York, NY: Crown.

Federal Bureau of Investigation (2010). *Crime in the United States, 2010.* http://www.fbi.gov/about-us/cjis/ucr/crime-in-the-u.s/2010/crime-in-the-u.s.-2010/property-crime/burglarymain.

Geis, G. (2007). *White-collar and corporate crime.* Upper Saddle River, NJ: Prentice Hall.

Goldstein, J. (2014) The pickpocket's tale, *New York Times,* July 18th.

Graeber, D. (2011) *Debt: The first 5,000 years.* Brooklyn, NY: Melville House

Greenberg, A.C. & Singer, M. (2010). *The rise and fall of Bear Stearns.* New York, NY: Simon and Schuster.

Gregg, A. & Kresevich, M. (2011). *Retail security and loss prevention solutions.* Boca Raton, FL: Auerbach.

Henriques, D. (2011). *The wizard of lies: Bernie Madoff and the death of trust.* New York, NY: Times Books.

Hochstetler, A. (2001). Opportunities and decisions: Interactional dynamics in robbery and burglar groups. *Criminology, 39,* 732–67.

Hoffman, A. (1971). *Steal this book.* New York, NY: Grove Press.

Jacobs, B.A. & Wright, R. (2008). Researching drug robbery. *Crime and Delinquency, 54,* 511–31.

Katz, J. (1988). *Seductions of crime: Moral and sensual attractions to doing evil.* New York, NY: Basic Books.

Kelly, K. (2009). *Street fighters: The last 72 hours of Bear Stearns, the toughest firm on Wall Street.* New York, NY: Portfolio.

Kenner, H.J. (1926). The fight on stock swindlers. *Annals of the American Academy of Political and Social Science, 125,* 54–58.

Klemke, L.W. (1992). *The sociology of shoplifting: Boosters and snitches today.* Westport, CT: Praeger.

Klockars, C. (1974). *The professional fence.* New York, NY: The Free Press.

Langton, L. & Piquero, N. L. (2007). Can general strain theory explain white-collar crime? A preliminary investigation of the relationship between strain and select white-collar offenses. *Journal of Criminal Justice*, *35*, 1–15.

Lattanzi, G. (1998). Raiders of the lost ark. *UTNE Reader*, (September 10), 36.

Lessing, D. (1961). *In pursuit of the English*. New York, NY: Simon and Schuster.

Lofland, J. & Lofland, L. H. (1969). *Deviance and identity*. Englewood Cliffs, NJ: Prentice Hall.

McCall, N. (1994). *Make me wanna holler*. New York, NY: Random House.

McCarthy, B. (1995). Not just "for the thrill of it": An instrumental elaboration of sneaky thrill property crimes. *Criminology*, *33*, 519–38.

McDonald, L. G. & Robinson, P. (2009). *A colossal failure of common sense: The inside story of the collapse of Lehman Brothers*. New York, NY: Crown.

Malcolm X. (1982). *The autobiography of Malcolm X*. New York, NY: Grove Press.

Matthews, R. (2002). *Armed robbery*. Cullompton, UK: Willan.

Merton, R. K. (1964). Anomie, anomia, and social integration: Contexts of deviant behavior. In M. Clinard (Ed.), *Anomie and deviant behavior: A discussion and critique* (pp. 213–42). New York, NY: The Free Press.

Messner, S. F. & Rosenfeld, R. (2007). *Crime and the American dream* (4th ed.). Belmont, CA: Thompson/Wadsworth.

Michaelson, A. (2009). *The foreclosure of America: The inside story of the rise and fall of Country-wide: Home loans, the mortgage crisis and the default of the American Dream*. New York, NY: Berkley Books.

Miller, J. (2001). *One of the guys: Girls, gangs, and gender*. New York, NY: Oxford University Press.

Morgenson, G. & Story, L. (2011). A financial crisis with little guilt: After widespread reckless banking, a dearth of prosecutions. *New York Times*, (April 14), A1, B10–B11.

Newman, A. (2006). A fire unset led to a thief's arrest. *New York Times*, (January28), B1.

Ng, S. & Holm, E. (2011). Berkshire says Sokol misled Buffett. *Wall Street Journal*, (April 28), A5.

Pontell, H. N. (2005). White-collar crime or just risky business? The role of fraud in major financial debacles. *Crime, Law & Social Change*, *42*, 309–24.

Reiss, A. J., Jr. & Biderman, A. D. (1980). *Data sources on white-collar lawbreaking*. Washington, DC: National Institute of Justice, U.S. Department of Justice.

Rengert, G. & Goff, E. (2011). *Residential burglary: How our environment and lifestyles play a contributing role*. Springfield, IL: Charles C. Thomas.

Reynolds, D. (2008). *Unlikely giant: America in the age of Jackson*. New York, NY: HarperCollins.

Robinson, M. B. & Robinson, C. E. (1997). Environmental characteristics associated with residential burglary of student apartment complexes. *Environment and Behavior*, *29*, 657–75.

Ross, E. A. (1907). The criminaloid. *The Atlantic Monthly*, *99*(January), 44–50.

Sander, P. (2009). *Madoff: Corruption, deceit, and the making of the world's most notorious Ponzi scheme*. Guilford, CT: Lyons Press.

Schelp, D. & Ehbar, A. (2009). *Fallen giant: The amazing story of Hank Greenberg and the history of AIG* (2nd ed.). Hoboken, NJ: John Wiley.

Schoepfer, A. & Tibbetts, S. G. (2011). From early white-collar bandits and robber barons to modern-day white collar criminals: A review of the conceptual and theoretical research. In D. Shichor, L. Gaines, & A. Schoepfer (Eds.), *Reflecting on white-collar and corporate crime* (pp. 63–83). Long Grove, IL: Waveland Press.

Seymour, M. (2007). *Trumpton Hall: A memoir of my father's house*. New York, NY: HarperCollins.

Shover, N. (1998). White collar crime. In M. J. Tonry (Ed.), *Handbook of crime and punishment* (pp. 133–58). New York, NY: Oxford University Press.

Shteir, R. (2011). *They steal: The cultural history of shoplifting*. New York, NY: Penguin.

Sokol, D. L. (2007). *Pleased, but not satisfied*. Omaha, NE: Author.

Steffensmeier, D. J. (1986). *The fence: In the shadow of two worlds*. Totowa, NJ: Rowman and Littlefield.

Stevenson, R. J. (1998). *The boiler room and other telephone sales scams*. Urbana, IL: University of Illinois Press.

Strober, D. & Strober, G. (2009). *Catastrophe: The story of Bernard L. Madoff, the man who swindled the world*. Beverly Hills, CA: Phoenix Books.

Sutherland, E. H. (1937). *The Professional Thief*. Chicago, IL: University of Chicago Press.

Sutherland, E. H. (1940). White-collar criminality. *American Sociological Review, 5*, 1–12.

Sutherland, E. H. (1949/1983). *White collar crime: The uncut version*. New Haven, CT: Yale University Press.

Sykes, G. M. & Matza, D. (1957). Techniques of neutralization: A theory of delinquency. *American Sociological Review, 22*, 664–70.

Theroux, P. (2000). *Fresh air fiend: Travel writings, 1985–2000*. Boston, MA: Houghton Mifflin.

Tilley, N., Tseloni, A., & Farrell, G. (2011). Income disparities of burglary risk: Security availability during the crime drop. *British Journal of Criminology, 51*, 296–313.

Trebay, G. (2000). Shoplifting on a grand scale: Luxury wear stolen to order. *New York Times*, (August 8), A24.

Tunnell, K. D. (2000). *Living off crime*. Chicago, IL: Burnham.

Vaughn, M. G., Delisi, M., Beaver, K. M., & Howard, M. O. (2008). Toward a quantitative typology of burglars: A latent profile analysis of career offenders. *Journal of Forensic Sciences, 53*, 1387–92.

Veblen, T. (1912). *The theory of the leisure class*. New York, NY: Macmillan.

Wallace, B. P. & Crowley, B. (2000). *Final confession: The unsolved crimes of Phil Cresta*. Boston, MA: Northeastern University Press.

Wallerstein, J., Lewis, J., & Blakeslee, S. (2000). *The unexpected legacy of divorces: A 25 year landmark study*. New York, NY: Hyperion.

Ward, V. (2010). *The devil's casino: Friendship, betrayal, and the high-stake games played inside Lehman Brothers*. Hoboken, NJ: John Wiley.

Weisburd, D., Waring, E., & Chayet, E. F. (2001). *White-collar crime and criminal careers*. New York, NY: Cambridge University Press.

Wright, R. T. & Decker, S. H. (1994). *Burglars on the job: Street life and residential break-ins*. Boston, MA: Northeastern University Press.

Wright, R. T. & Decker, S. H. (1997). *Armed robbers in action: Stickups and street culture*. Boston, MA: Northeastern University Press.

Wright, R. T., Topalli, V., & Tekin, E. (2014) Reducing crime by removing cash from the streets via EBT, *Mastercard Cashless Pioneers*, April. http://newsroom.mastercard.com/2014/04/02/reducing-crime-by-removing-cash-from-the-streets-through-ebt/

Zimmerman, A. (2006). As shoplifters use high-tech scams, retail losses rise. *Wall Street Journal*, (October 25), A1, A12.

Crimes without Victims and Victims without Crimes

LEARNING OBJECTIVES

After reading Chapter 13, you should be able to:

- Understand why driving under the influence of alcohol or other drugs (DUI) is a crime even though there are no victims.
- Define "crimes without victims."
- Explain the basis for the feminist campaign against pornography.
- Summarize Patrick Devlin's argument in support of victimless crimes.
- Explain the implications of the term "slippery slope" as it refers to physician-assisted suicide.
- Appreciate that prostitution in the United States is moving from the streets onto the Internet and to cell phones.
- Tell the story of the downfall of New York's Governor Eliot Spitzer.
- Know that methamphetamines are the most abused drug in the world.

Most crimes create a victim—a person or an entity that suffers physical or emotional harm or the deprivation of something to which the victim has a legal right. In some instances the tie between the criminal action and the harm is inferred. Driving while intoxicated may not produce victims, but it is presumed that drunk drivers will not be in control of their vehicle as well as sober drivers and that their erratic driving may sooner or later cause harm. Some inebriated motorists may drive more carefully than they ordinarily do because they know that they are incapacitated, but they will not be able to drive as well as they could if they were equally attentive but not under the influence of alcohol. At the same time, it has to be appreciated that five out of six drunk drivers who kill in alcohol-related accidents have no previous official record for driving under the influence (Ross, 1992). Driving under the influence (DUI) becomes a crime with a statistical likelihood of causing harm and possibly death. **Criminalization** (making an act into a criminal offense) and **decriminalization** (the abolition of criminal penalties in relation to certain acts) are reactions to the relativity of crime.

CRIMES WITHOUT VICTIMS

There is a group of offenses that come under the heading of crimes without victims (Schur, 1965). Their common characteristic is that they involve consensual participation, that is, the parties to the illegal event engage in the behavior voluntarily. No participant complains about what occurs. It is the state in the form of the criminal law that objects and penalizes those caught in such behavior, although there also are many persons who object to the behaviors, usually on moral grounds (Carpenter & Hayes, 2010).

Prostitutes, for example, enter into sexual relationships with customers who purchase a commodity, much as someone would purchase the services and skills of a plumber or a lawyer. Indeed, in contemporary lawyer bashing, the practice of law is sometimes equated to prostitution because many attorneys sell their wares to any party possessing the wherewithal to buy them, regardless of their own view about the guilt or innocence of the client or the rightness of the civil claims they are pursuing or defending against. Illegal drug transactions also typically have no involuntary participants. Someone sells a product, just like people sell food, clothing, or household items, and someone else pays the asking price, bargains for a lower one, takes his or her business elsewhere, or does without.

Should They Be Crimes?

Those who believe that the roster of victimless crimes ought to be thinned or eliminated argue that an essential trait of a democracy is that it extends freedom to all citizens so long as that freedom does not infringe upon the equivalent liberty of other people. Those holding this view assert that victimless offenses are outlawed primarily on religious grounds or moral grounds. Prostitution violates theological dictates condemning fornication and adultery. But most Western religions, they point out, also condemn a considerable variety of other acts that the criminal law ignores, such as taking the Lord's name in vain, usury, and cursing a parent (an offense for which the Bible dictates the death penalty). Suicide also is abhorred in Catholic theology. In earlier times, suicides were declared criminal offenders, their goods confiscated, and their bodies buried in unhallowed ground at crossroads, with stakes driven through their hearts. These views no longer influence secular law. Nor, it is argued, should other facets of any group's moral or religious beliefs be imposed by law on those who do not accept the group's principles, unless it can be shown that a particular action harms others. Nevertheless, most debates regarding the legal status of victimless crimes place religious interest groups at odds with the affairs of members of various subcultures, whom the religious collectivities often regard as engaging in immoral behavior. The religious groups often assume the role of moral entrepreneurs, holding that victimless crime is a faulty construct; that in actual fact there is no such thing. Prostitutes, for instance, are said to degrade women in general, transmit AIDS and venereal diseases, disrupt families, rob their customers, and support **pimps**—men who exploit them ruthlessly. Similarly, the moral entrepreneurs contend, drug addicts often are unable to engage in productive work and they steal from innocent victims in order to obtain money for their fix. Successes in the drive in the U.S. to legalize marijuana possession and use in recent years has been over the objection of many religious opponents.

Victimless crimes serve as the preeminent category illustrative of the relativity of crime that has been highlighted throughout this text. The continual debate between moralists and other interest groups keeps virtually every one of these behaviors, and there are many, in the limelight. Moreover, they tend to evolve rapidly, while also showing immense variation across space. Victimless crimes are best understood through the framework of interactionist theories, as the underlying disagreements regarding the appropriateness of the behaviors provide a fundamental lens for evaluation. Beyond that, it can always be asked what motivates persons to seek the pleasures or stimulation of such activities as pornography, prostitution, drugs, or the thrill of the wind in their hair as they ride a motorcycle free of the constraints of a helmet.

Pornography

There is intense debate about pornography, a purported "victimless crime." Many people maintain that pornography routinely depicts awful scenes of male brutalization of women and that it encourages acts of rape and sadism directed against women. Legislative bodies in Indianapolis and Minneapolis passed ordinances banning "sexually explicit" materials that "graphically sexually exploit subordination of women, whether in words or pictures" (MacKinnon & Dworkin, 1997). The failure to provide a satisfactory definition of the term "sexually explicit" and, more basically, the conflict between the ordinances and the First Amendment right to free speech led the Minneapolis mayor to veto the ordinance, and a court to rule that the Indianapolis law did not meet constitutional standards (*American Booksellers Assn. v. Hudnut*, 1985). Particularly disturbing has been the recent appearance of Webcam sites in which adults induce children to undress and perform various sexual acts that are transmitted live on computer portals (Note, 2009; Otis, 2009).

Those defending legal pornography, while they usually are hard-pressed to say much good about the product, believe that the First Amendment to the U.S. Constitution protects unpopular forms of expression, including pornography. Debate also centers on the actual consequences of exposure to pornography, and whether it reflects social values rather than introduces them. The fundamental questions are first, whether the publication and purchase of pornography is a crime without victims; second, whether innocent people suffer harmful consequences because of its legal status, and third, whether a free society is obligated to tolerate certain activities because they are part of the spectrum of constitutionally protected rights (Cothran, 2002).

Motorcycle Helmets

Ideological dispute often comes to rest on a prototypic victimless crime: riding a motorcycle without a helmet. In 1975, all but three states had laws mandating helmet use for motorcyclists. Failure to enact such a statute at the time would result in the loss of federal highway funds. However, lobbyists successfully sought repeal/modification of legislation, and today two states (Illinois and Iowa) have fully decriminalized riding without a helmet, while 28 states provide the option for riders meeting a minimum age as well as insurance requirements in some. Opponents of mandatory helmet requirements insist that it should be the motorcyclist's choice; if he or she elects not to wear a helmet, this should be nobody else's business. Those who advocate a law mandating the wearing of helmets say that the protection afforded the motorcyclist is also a social protection because it guards against outcomes such as might ensue if a rock strikes the unprotected head of the motorcyclist, who then loses control of the vehicle and crashes into a passing car, injuring or killing its occupants. This line of reasoning was offered early on when a federal court in Massachusetts upheld the constitutionality of the state's requirement of helmets for motorcyclists. The court decision stated:

> From the moment of injury, society picks the person up off the highway, drives him to a municipal hospital and municipal doctors, provides him with unemployment compensation, if, after recovery, he cannot replace his lost job, and, if the injury causes permanent disability, [society] may assume responsibility for his and his family's subsistence. We do not understand a state of mind that permits plaintiff to think that only he himself is concerned (Simon v. Sargent, 1972:279; see also Atwood, 2008).

The federal government estimates that fatalities for motorcyclists are about 35 times that for automobile drivers per miles traveled, primarily because motorcycles are less stable than automobiles in terms of braking maneuvers and less visible to other drivers. A person killed on a motorcycle is 2.5 times more likely to be under the influence of alcohol than a person killed in a car and three times more likely not to have a proper license (Wald, 2008). A national study of all admissions to hospitals from 2002 to 2007 focused on the 122,578 motorcyclists who had been involved in accidents, finding that helmeted patients demonstrated less severe injury patterns in all categories of brain and skull trauma. The researchers calculated that if all motorcyclist patients over the seven-year study period had worn helmets, the health care system would have saved $32.5 million solely in terms of intensive care unit costs (Croce et al., 2009).

The argument against a mandatory helmet requirement is that all human existence is filled with risks and that we cannot handcuff every exercise of human freedom in order to try to reduce hazards. After all, nobody would seriously suggest that we cut down the heavy toll of highway deaths by banning automobiles, although many more people are killed each year in automobile accidents than are victims of homicides. Several popular motorcycle helmet stickers bluntly express the philosophical objection that permeates the biker subculture: "Legalize Freedom," "Worn Under Protest," "Helmet Laws Suck." "DOT" (a humorously feigned stamp of approval by the U.S. Department of Transportation) is often decaled on the back of "novelty" helmets worn by many bikers. Such helmets are far lighter, more comfortable, and claimed by many riders to be safer because they allow them both to hear and to move their heads to see better than is the case with DOT-endorsed headgear. Similarly, the popular "Loud Pipes Save Lives" stickers denote the belief that bikers are best protected by (illegally) loud exhaust pipes that forewarn automobile drivers of their presence than by heavily padded DOT-approved helmets protecting their skulls after a collision.

The city of Myrtle Beach, South Carolina, engaged in an unusual effort to criminalize helmet-free riding, loud pipes, group motorcycle parking, accessory vending, and other elements of bike rally subcultures. Their efforts were not morally or religiously motivated but a reaction to lawsuits filed against the city alleging that individual business establishments closed during the Memorial Day Bikefest that draws a predominantly black crowd, but not during the predominantly white-attended Myrtle Beach Bike Week taking place the same month. Consequently, the city passed laws to discourage continuation of both activities and asserted that they were in the interest of public safety. The laws were passed with a unanimous vote of the city council in September 2008, but a lawsuit was filed by a group of local business owners.

Signs posted on Highway 17 in Myrtle Beach, South Carolina, warned motorcyclists to wear a helmet. A string of ordinances passed by Myrtle Beach City Council are part of an effort to discourage bike rallies.

CREDIT:
AP Photo/Mary Ann Chastain.

Subsequently, in June of 2010, the helmet law was overturned by the South Carolina Supreme Court. The court's conclusion was, "We find that the City Helmet Ordinance fails under implied field preemption due to the need for statewide uniformity and therefore issue a declaratory judgment invalidating the ordinance." A later appeal of the "loud pipes" law led to some modification as well.

Where helmet wearing is mandatory for motorcyclists, the rationale is that the inconvenience to the rider is hardly so burdensome as to constitute an intolerable deprivation of liberty. As a legal scholar put the matter: "Any new law at all is some restriction on liberty, but not all restrictions are threats to it" (Woozley, 1983:1300). Helmets (at least once a collision has occurred) assuredly save lives, although it is notable that 84 percent of those killed in motorcycle accidents in the states where helmets are mandated were helmeted.

PROS AND CONS OF VICTIMLESS CRIMES

Opponents of the libertarian position that calls for minimum interference with human choices believe that a civilized society has a right to enforce a "common morality." In a forceful argument for this position, Patrick Devlin (1965:13), then a British high court judge, maintained that social harm results if we fail to secure adherence to a general standard of morality:

> Societies disintegrate from within more frequently than they are broken up by external pressure. There is disintegration when no common morality is observed and history shows that the loosening of moral bonds is often the first stage of disintegration, so that society is justified in taking the same steps to preserve its moral code as it does to preserve its governmental and other institutions.

Devlin's position was seconded by Robert Bork, a Yale Law School professor: "Moral outrage is a sufficient ground for prohibitory legislation," Bork declared. "Knowledge that the activity is taking place is harm to those who find it profoundly immoral" (Bork, 1991:132).

A seventeenth-century English divine used a colorful analogy to express his opposition to allowing individuals to go their own way (or, in contemporary language, to do their own thing) if what they do detracts from social well-being. Well known, because it formed the basis for the title of a novel by Ernest Hemingway, is this dictum of John Donne (1624, No. 7):

> No man is an island entire of itself; every man is a piece of the continent, a part of the main. . . . Any man's death diminishes me, because I am involved in mankind. And therefore never send to know for whom the bell tolls: It tolls for thee.

Standing at the opposite end of this controversy is Friedrich Nietzsche, the German philosopher, who maintained that "morality is the best of all devices for leading mankind by the nose" (Nietzsche, 1844/1920:44). Debunkers note that Nietzsche ended his life in a mental hospital, which, while interesting, neither proves nor disproves the wisdom or lack or wisdom of his observation.

Other arguments insist that laws must balance outcomes. To prohibit the use of narcotics, it is sometimes maintained, creates many of the situations that are then used to defend the prohibitory law. If narcotics were readily and cheaply available, the argument goes, addicts would not have to steal to support their habits, and organized criminals would not be able to dominate the traffic in drugs. Similarly, prostitutes would not have to suffer the harassment of the police and their self-image might improve if they were engaged in a lawful occupation, perhaps one licensed in the same manner as other public services. In addition, the decriminalization forces argue that laws against prostitution have proven ineffective since the dawn of civilization, and that the United States now has sought to control narcotics without notable success for almost a century.

Those holding the opposite position argue that, while the statutes have not eliminated or perhaps even reduced the behaviors they deem undesirable, there is no way of knowing how much more often these behaviors would occur if they were not against the law. The empirical question is how many additional persons would seek the services of a prostitute (or employment), elect to ingest drugs, or go in search of pornographic materials given new-found opportunities of such services being legalized. Clearly the answer would vary across the variety of forms of behavior within the victimless crime realm. Because the behavior is readily observed by police, most persons riding a motorcycle who might long for more wind in their hair refrain from the helmetless ride (i.e. are deterred) by criminalization of the act, but would that hold for engaging in the sex trade or drug use? Or does the underground already satisfy most of the demand, albeit at higher prices and with certain risks, for sex and drug markets?

The Decriminalization Drift

What is notable is the dramatic change in the way the law has come to view some victimless crimes during our own lifetime and that of our parents, a manifestation of the relativity of law. Forty or so years ago, prostitution, gambling, drug use, homosexuality, and abortion were serious criminal behaviors. Today, abortion during the first trimester of pregnancy is a legal right, although fierce controversy rages about the propriety of this position. Gambling, once permitted only in Nevada, today is legal in virtually all American jurisdictions. Homosexuality now raises virtually no criminal liability issues. While certain drugs continue to be banned and our jails and prisons continue to overflow with inmates charged with drug law violations, marijuana possession and usage statutes have been eased, and there is growing sentiment to experiment with legal distribution of drugs. Of these, only prostitution remains under broad interdiction in the United States.

It has been suggested that, like much else in society, the possession of power is the key to understanding changes in the law's approach to victimless crimes. Legalizing abortion was supported by powerful women whose lives could be distressed by unwanted pregnancies. The ranks of homosexuals also included powerful persons—lawyers, legislators, and wealthy folk—who could make an impact on the law. Gambling, besides offering a large amount of money to hard-pressed state budgets, was engaged in by people with power, and marijuana was a drug sometimes used by their children. Only prostitutes, largely powerless, catering primarily to the marginal and dispossessed, remain condemned by the criminal law throughout virtually all of the United States.

Physician-assisted Suicide

Considerable controversy in the victimless crime realm has focused on the idea of **physician-assisted suicide** or, as some call it, "hastened death." Those in favor say that persons with debilitating illnesses, if they so desire, ought to be allowed to determine the time and the manner of their death. They should not have to suffer mercilessly from pain and invasive medical procedures while they move toward an inevitable demise. Their medical expenses when mortally ill can be inordinately high. Fifty percent of the total budget for Medicare is devoted to the costs for elderly people who are in their last six months of life. It is also argued that sanctioning physician-assisted suicide only makes overt the practice of many doctors who allow patients to die by giving them lethal doses of sedatives or withholding procedures that might keep them alive for a short time.

Those opposed to physician-assisted suicide say that it can be a "slippery slope" (see Wright, 2000), an entry point that will expand to allow physicians to kill persons suffering from transient bouts of depression and children who have disabilities (Lode, 1999). Laws permitting physician-induced suicide might encourage some people to give up rather than to fight to construct what could prove to be a happy and fulfilling continuing existence. Besides, to save money, pressure might be exerted to "clear the underbrush" (Nuland, 1994) by eliminating persons who are on a downward health spiral but who, if not encouraged otherwise, would prefer to remain alive. Such a measure, some say, would substitute a "duty to die" for a "right to die." That the law may be abused is illustrated by a case from Japan detailed in Highlight 13.1. This issue was highlighted in 2010 when an opponent of the federal health care program enacted by the Congress lambasted the measure by announcing, incorrectly, that it provided for "death panels" that would determine who among the ill elderly should be exterminated.

Oregon, with its Death with Dignity Act, enacted in 1994, was the first American jurisdiction to permit physician-assisted suicide, followed in 2009 by Washington and Montana (by judicial decree) (Mason, 2011). In both Oregon and Washington, the patient must be an adult and a state resident, initiate the request to die (or, more literally, to kill himself or herself), show no documented depression, and be diagnosed by two doctors as having no more than six months to live. Doctors must outline for the patient alternative paths, including hospice care and pain-control medications. The laws also establish a 15-day waiting period between the patient's verbal request and the signing of a consent form. They allow the doctor to prescribe a lethal dose of drugs that the patient must take by himself or herself. Opponents of the law declare that death from some drugs being employed could require as long as three hours and that patients sometimes vomit the drugs reflexively.

HIGHLIGHT 13.1 JAPAN—ASSISTED SUICIDE WITHOUT CONSENT

Public opinion polls conducted by Japanese newspapers revealed up to 70 percent of respondents in favor of legalizing assisted suicide. Around 10 percent did not object to the idea of terminally ill people being killed without their consent. Nearly half of doctors questioned said they had been asked by family members to end the life of patients without the patients' consent or, in many cases, since the typical Japanese cancer patients are never told the truth about their diagnosis, without the patient ever knowing that he or she was mortally ill (Editorial, 1997:18).

They also insist that the programs undercut what could be effective end-of-life palliative care: one set of writers believes this has been true in Oregon (Hendin & Foley, 2009; see also Jeffrey, 2009; an opposing conclusion is reported by Gill, 2009).

By the end of 2010, 525 persons had been killed (or allowed to kill themselves, depending on how you view the issue) under the Oregon law. Those who chose the option were overwhelmingly white and, by a slight margin, males, and a majority were suffering from terminal cancer and ended their life at home. Almost all declared that it was their loss of autonomy that led them to elect to die. Virtually all of the deaths were brought about by the use of fast-acting barbiturates combined with an antiemetic agent. Most patients became unconscious within five minutes and most died within an hour, although one person, while unconscious, lingered for 11.5 hours (Chin et al., 1999). A ten-year review of the Oregon program concluded that the "weight of evidence suggests that the predictions of dire consequences were incorrect" and that the program had not "caused physicians, patients, or Oregonians in general to value life less" (Lindsay, 2009:19).

A particularly interesting analysis of physician-assisted suicide by Tania Salem (1999) points out that the Oregon law has medicalized suicide, transforming what almost always is a private act into a medical event. Salem notes that the law does not, as its supporters maintain, increase human autonomy and freedom, since competent persons always have been able to leave this life when they desired: now they must involve medical assistance; or, in Salem's words, they must "request public endorsement and legitimization of the act of suicide" (Salem, 1999:33).

PROSTITUTION—SEX WORK

Female Prostitution

What can be said of an act of female *prostitution*? Is it:

- An ugly and intolerable consequence of the power of males over females and the sexual exploitation of girls and women?

Or is it:

- A sensible commercial enterprise engaged in by a seller who possesses a commodity that has a market value?

For American feminists, **prostitution,** that is, sex for money or other consideration, has been a difficult and divisive issue. Some favor the second interpretation of prostitution stated above, seeing prostitutes as sex-trade workers. Others adopt the first position. They regard prostitution as the outcome of a patriarchal society in which women are defined as sex objects. Child sexual abuse, incest, and similar female victimizations are said to often lie at the core of entry into prostitution. Many feminists equate prostitution to slavery, especially when pimps are involved (Holsopple, 1999). Andrea Dworkin (1997:145) took the position that "when men use women in prostitution, they are expressing a pure hatred of the female body."

South Korea's experience echoes the contravention between competing threads of feminism. Tracing changing responses to Korean sex workers, Sealing Cheng (2012) observes that passage of 2004 Anti-Prostitution Laws, ostensibly crafted to protect women from human trafficking, wrought considerable harm to the lives of women engaged in the trade. As Cheng notes, "the ideologically driven debates divert attention from the human beings whose lives they are trying to shape; but they also further reinforce the marginalization of 'the prostitute'" (2012: 35). While prostitution had been illegal in South Korea since 1961, in practice, the criminal justice system had tolerated, if not regulated, the business. The effect of the "anti-trafficking discourse" was to launch a crackdown on prostitution, including demolition of the Yongsun red-light district that was in the heart of Seoul. An urban renewal project, launched in 2004, in combination with police crackdowns, removed women from both work and home environments that had shaped lives for decades. Cheng (2012: 38) summarized it this way:

> Neoliberal initiative of urban renewal coincides with the clamor to 'Stop Trafficking,' making the replacement of the red-light district with tall shiny buildings appropriate for a cleaner city seem like an absolute good. In effect, the lives, communities, histories and futures of women who live in the red-light districts have no place in a city's modernization project.

The argument of conventional feminists is that patriarchal control of prostitution is said to be reflected in the fact that many prostitutes depend upon pimps, men who take most of their earnings, and, in return, offer them protection from violence by customers and from the police as well as real affection or a caricature of it. For middle-class persons, the dynamics of pimping often seem difficult to comprehend. The effective pimp typically persuades several women that the only way that they can gain his love is to work the streets, bars, and hotels, seeking out customers (johns) for a sexual encounter. The pimp–prostitute roles reverse the usual (but changing) gender courtship pattern in American society in which the male must persuade the female that he is a suitable partner. Today, however, the word "pimp" appears to have replaced "cool" in popular American slang. Lisa Richardson (2000) points out that middle-class college students, chat-room denizens, and others who have nothing to do with the sex trade now designate things such as birthday presents, bikes, and clothes as "pimp." The trend illustrates the tendency of outlaw language and styles to relocate in mainstream usage.

In response to feminist protests, some police departments now use sting campaigns to arrest men who visit prostitutes, although their general belief is that the results are more symbolic than effective in reducing the level of sex trade. Some jurisdictions also revoke driving licenses of men who solicit streetwalkers and/or put the johns' photographs in public places or on the Internet.

More drastic is the policy of asset forfeiture in which the vehicle that the customer used to solicit a prostitute is confiscated.

Mary Dodge and her coworkers' interviews with female police officers involved in sting operations found that they had ambivalent feelings about such work. One officer, who had played the part of a streetwalker at least once a month for six years, said: "Being a decoy does feel kind of slimy, but it's an ego trip to get the johns because they're the scum of the earth." Another officer, with ten years' experience, commented: "At first, I thought: What am I doing? You get out there and you don't want to fail. It's pride. What if nobody picks me up?" (Dodge et al., 2005:76–77).

The United States is "one of the few western nations in which all forms of prostitution are illegal almost everywhere" (Anderson, 2002:748). The exceptions to the "almost everywhere" is Nevada. Since 1971, Nevada law has permitted prostitution if a county with a population of less than 250,000 elects to do so. Prostitution now is legal in 14 of Nevada's 17 counties, although it actually occurs in only 11 counties where there are 28 brothels. Nevada's legal brothels (they call themselves "ranches") are said to "offer the safest environment available for women who sell consensual sex for money." They rely on panic buttons in the assignation rooms, listening devices, and management surveillance (Brents & Hausbeck, 2005:289). Legal prostitutes in Nevada have undergone testing for AIDS since 1988 and "none has tested HIV positive since testing was mandated" (Weitzer, 2005:217). Legalized prostitution, compared to unregulated illegal prostitution, results in a lower rate of AIDS because the women are in a better position than freelancers to insist that customers use condoms. Streetwalking prostitutes will not carry many condoms on their person for fear that the police will use them as evidence that they are practicing an illegal trade (Campbell, 1991).

The greatest AIDS danger for prostitutes is not from their work but from their sexual relations with men with whom they have formed a romantic attachment and with whom they do not insist on the use of condoms (Campbell, 1991). As an Australian prostitute noted: "I can't use a condom with my boyfriend. What'll he think—that I'm gonna charge him next?" (Waddell, 1996:81).

Women working in Nevada brothels usually are fingerprinted and must carry identification cards. Nevada requires that houses of prostitution not be located on a principal business street or within 400 yards of a schoolhouse or church. The women work as independent contractors. They typically turn over one-half of their receipts to the owners, and pay a daily fee for room and board. Generally, they work seven consecutive 12-hour days, then are off for two or three weeks. They average six customers daily and charge anywhere from $150 to $500, with the price varying with the time of day, the day of the week, the customer's attitude, and how drunk or high he is (Albert, 2001).

Prostitution offers a range of vocational advantages (depending, of course, on the alternative kinds of work available to the person), including flexible

A prostitute who works at the historic Chicken Ranch brothel in Nevada sits in the bedroom where she conducts business. Nevada requires that houses of prostitution not be located on a principal business street or within 400 yards of a school or church.

CREDIT:
AP Photo/ Ronda Churchill.

work hours, contact with diverse kinds of persons, a heightened sense of activity, and the opportunity to make substantial sums of money. Such benefits do not, however, accrue to all practitioners and may not endure for very long. For those women whose involvement is tawdry, prostitution represents a dangerous and dirty enterprise. They experience physical violence and earn little money (Dalla, 2007). The likely loss of self-esteem is in part a function of broader social attitudes, which in some degree are tied to the legal sanctions against the behavior.

On the other hand, for some prostitutes the social definition of immorality seems rather flexible. The novelist Doris Lessing reports living in a New York apartment among a number of women engaged in the sex trade. She asked one of them if she enjoyed sex. "If you're going to talk dirty," said the prostitute, "I'm not interested" (Klein, 2000:220).

For many male customers, a prostitute represents a commodity that can be purchased and used without emotional involvement or complications. Responses solicited from 700 johns found that 47 percent found the liaison "exciting," while 43 percent indicated that they wanted "a different experience than my partner provides," and 42 percent agreed with the statement: "I am shy and awkward when I am trying to meet a woman." Smaller but significant numbers said that they did not have the time for a conventional relationship or that they did not want the responsibilities of such a relationship (Monto, 2004). As one customer put it: "I don't care about the excitement of the chase one bit. What I would really like would be a brothel where you simply go in, pay your money, and go home at a reasonable hour without any understanding on either side" (Davenport-Hines, 1995:223). A different view is offered by the Nobel Prize winning author V.S. Naipaul: "When I was young, I was a greater frequenter of prostitutes. I found them intensely stimulating. But what happened was that by the time I was in my mid-thirties, I began to feel depressed by sex with a prostitute. I felt cheated and frustrated" (French, 2008:475).

Some prostitutes have taken to the Internet, cellular phones, and the camouflage of "escort services" to carry on their sex work. The yellow pages of New York City's telephone book has more than fifty pages of listings for escort services, some of them legal businesses, others camouflages for illegal prostitution. Failure to differentiate carefully what might be called "suite prostitution" from "street prostitution" can lead to erratic conclusions about the practice.

One study found that 75 percent of call girls, 19 percent of brothel workers, and none of the streetwalkers reported that they frequently had orgasms in their work. Almost all call girls indicated that they experienced an increase in self-esteem when they entered the trade; only eight percent of the streetwalkers gave the same response (Prince, 1986).

The Eliot Spitzer Scandal

The upper echelons of the practice of prostitution hit the headlines in 2008 when New York Governor Eliot Spitzer was detected after making arrangements with an escort agency for the sexual services of a high-priced ($2,000 an evening) call girl who would come from New York for a rendezvous in the Washington, DC, hotel in which he was staying after a business meeting. Spitzer, 48 years old, married to a Harvard Law School classmate, and with three teenage daughters, had arranged at least seven other liaisons with women employed by the Emperors Club VIP, which advertised itself in the following manner:

> Emperors Club VIP is the most preferred international social introduction service for those accustomed to excellence. Introducing the most impressive models to leading gentlemen of the world is our expertise. We specialize in introductions of fashion models, pageant winners and exquisite students, graduates and women of successful careers (finance, art, music, etc.) to gentlemen of exceptional standards. When seeking an evening date, a weekend travel companion or a friend to accompany you during your evening business/social function our models are the perfect preference.

The hook was baited with flattery: "We act for a selected group of educated and refined international clients who give their best in all they do and who, in return, only want to receive the best." The potential john is told that he will be matched with a "companion" who will seek to fulfill the Club's goal "to make life more peaceful, balanced, beautiful and meaningful."

A wiretap of the telephone conversations between the escort agency and the woman going under the name of Kristen who had been selected to liaise with Spitzer gives a hint of one of the possible risks of the trade—as well as the caution about not being specific. The agency representative on the telephone tells Kristen that Spitzer "would ask you do things that, like, you might not think were safe—you know—I mean that—very basic things." Kristen says she is up to the challenge: "I have a way of dealing with that—know what I mean."

Kristen, who avoided prosecution by turning state's evidence against the agency personnel, was living under the name of Ashley Alexandra Dupré, although her birth name was Ashley R. Youmans. She had legally changed her name in 2006 to Ashley Rae Maika DiPietro, using the last name of her stepfather, an oral surgeon, who introduced her to affluent living, including driving her to school in his Jaguar. She had been born in Bellflower, New Jersey, and her Web site announced that she left an abusive and broken family to move to Manhattan to record pop music and to "pursue my career." According to her aunt, however, rather than being abusive, her home life had been marked by privilege and indulgence. At age 17 she went to live with her father and his second wife in Kill Devil Hills in North Carolina. Then she relocated to New York after she finished high school and worked at a variety of jobs before signing up with the Emperors Club in 2004. At the time of her assignation with Spitzer, she was living in an apartment on West 25th Street in Manhattan and paying $4,000 a month rent.

"I'm all about music," Ashley had written on her Web site, "and my music is all about me. It flows from what I've been through and what I've seen and how I felt." She also noted: "I made it. I'm still here. I love what I am. If I never went through the hard times I would not be able to appreciate the good. Cliché, yes, but I know it's true." Observers marked the tattoos in Latin and Arabic on her body that were said to serve as her mantra. Her brother, Kyle Youmans, said that she was "the best sister you could have" and that he was sticking by her. For her part, Ashley's mother, Carolyn Capablo, indicated that her daughter was "a very bright girl who can handle someone like the governor. But she is a 22-year-old, not a 32- or 42-year-old, and she got involved in something much larger than her."

Ashley Dupré would tell media people that she had not slept for three days after the announcement of Spitzer's fall and hoped that the public would not consider her a "monster." For its part, the tabloid *New York Post* featured a front-page picture of Spitzer's sexual partner with her hands covering her bare breasts and the words "BAD GIRL" in large capital letters underneath the picture. An Internet posting of her picture drew more than seven million viewers in the three days after her name became public knowledge. She also allegedly had been offered a million dollars by *Hustler* to pose nude. And within two days after her identity was revealed there were more than three million hits on her MySpace rendition of a song titled, "What We Want." She reportedly earned more than $200,000 from downloads of the song. *People* took as the title of its interview with Ms. Dupré her insistence that "I am a Normal Girl." Whatever her attributes might be, few people would likely list normality as one of them (Elkind, 2010).

Decriminalizing Prostitution?

The possibility of decriminalizing prostitution in the United States (it is legal in many foreign countries: see Highlights 13.2 and 13.3) seems unlikely in the near future. The leading group advocating a change in the law is Call Off Your Old Tired Ethics (COYOTE), a San Francisco-based organization. It demands total removal of the criminal law's involvement with prostitution (see further Hayes-Smith & Shekarkhar, 2010). The movement, however, continues to meet strong resistance; overwhelmingly, Americans define prostitution as immoral and, as is often the case, they believe that if it is morally wrong it ought to be outlawed.

HIGHLIGHT 13.2 GERMANY—PROSTITUTION REFORM

The German government in 2000 inaugurated a sweeping revision of laws regulating prostitution. Sex work had not been illegal in Germany, but the old law did not regard it as equivalent to other kinds of occupations. The new law eliminated the word *sittenwidrig*—meaning immoral—from the prostitution statutes, thereby allowing prostitutes to apply for health insurance and social security benefits. There are an estimated 500,000 prostitutes at work in Germany. One survey found that every day 1.2 million Germans pay for commercial sex, a figure that annually comes to nearly $7 billion.

(Weitzer, 2012).

HIGHLIGHT 13.3 THE NETHERLANDS—A DIFFERENT APPROACH TO PROSTITUTION

Designated streetwalking zones have been established in major Dutch cities. They are said to function as safe sites in which women serve as sex workers. The zone is also said to offer the benefit of a shelter that affords prostitutes a place to meet with their colleagues, talk to health care professionals, and relax. Earlier, both the prostitutes and the police had concluded that frequent raids were only making matters worse. The women were frightened and often on the run. And the police believed that they were failing to make the streets any safer.

(Klinger, 2000:19).

Male Prostitution

A recent study of an escort service offering male partners found that two-thirds of the men hiring male escorts were involved in heterosexual marriages (Smith & Grov, 2011). Interviews with 30 of the 32 male sex workers (MSWs) employed by an Internet-based agency located in a mid-Atlantic city with a population of about 40,000, emphasized how the men established physical and psychological barriers between their work and their personal lives. The first was accomplished by defining areas of the escort service site where clients were not invited, and the second by imposing limitations on their relationships with clients, with other escorts, and with the agency manager. The average age of the MSWs was 22, they were all Caucasian, identified themselves as gay, and had at least a high-school education. Five of the MSWs lived in the agency headquarters; the usual length of such a stay tended to be four months. Two-thirds of the men held other jobs (Smith & Seal, 2007; Smith et al., 2008).

Jim Cates and Jeffrey Markley (1992) report that a major goal of male prostitutes is to form a liaison with an older man—a "sugar daddy"—who will support them. As with female prostitutes, virtually all of the American male prostitutes say that financial incentives motivate their involvement. Martin Weinberg and his colleagues (1999) found that male prostitutes report more satisfaction from their sexual encounters than females.

One form of male prostitution involves transgender dressers, men who dress as women and solicit male customers for oral copulation. They are involved in a risky business because some customers, if they learn of the bodied gender of the prostitute, may react with violence. A study in New York found that transgender male prostitutes dressed more scantily than female streetwalkers and were more aggressive in approaching potential customers (Cohen, 1980).

Sex Work in Scandinavia

In Sweden in 1999, the law was altered so that it no longer was a crime to engage in prostitution, but it is an offense to patronize a prostitute (Gould, 2001). Some women in the sex trade in Sweden insist that since the enactment of the new law they have been at greater risk of harm because the more genteel of their clients became apprehensive about arrest and were no longer patronizing them. Norway, in 2009, followed the Swedish model, as did Iceland in the same year. Finland in 2006 made it illegal for a customer to solicit a prostitute who had been the victim of human trafficking (Viuhko, 2010).

In a comprehensive Internet survey that tapped into the views on prostitution of 1,726 Norwegians and 1,815 Swedes in the age bracket between 15 and 65, Niklas Jakobsson and Andreas Kotsadam found that men and sexual liberals of both genders were more positive toward the practice of prostitution and that men and women who were conservative or supported gender equality were more negative on the issue. The survey results further indicated that persons who held anti-immigration views (many Scandinavian prostitutes come from former Soviet Union satellites) were more likely than pro-immigration respondents to find prostitution acceptable.

To a statistically significant degree, Norwegians were more likely than Swedes to favor legalized prostitution. The authors speculate that this finding might result from Sweden having had its law for a decade longer than Norway and that the existence of the legislation may have influenced attitudes in Sweden and might, in time, alter those in Norway (Jakobsson & Kotsadam, 2011).

Explaining Prostitution

In today's world, prostitution is interpreted most often in sociopolitical terms. Nanette Davis (1993:viii) summarizes the prevalent view:

> Legal, social, and political patterns both generate and sustain prostitution in its various societal forms. The international focus also demonstrates the selective, gender-based, hierarchal nature of control that often exploits and damages women. Prostitution is both a social problem, linked to existing social and political structures (and hence can change only as institutions change), and, given market economies, a social opportunity for women, their male managers, and local entrepreneurs.

Ronald Weitzer (2012) warns that attempts to explain prostitution cannot focus only on streetwalkers, who represent the lowest rung of the occupation. They typically are depicted as victims of sexual abuse at an early age and other forms of exploitation. Virtually no studies have attempted to characterize factors that convince escort service employees to adopt that calling, but the appeal of significant earnings and a more glamorous lifestyle than they otherwise might enjoy are undoubtedly among the prominent incentives.

DRUG OFFENSES

Illegal drug use is an activity in which a person inhales, swallows, or injects a banned pharmaceutical product that directly affects only that person, although the act can have far-reaching consequences in terms of crime, driving accidents, and illness, among other matters.

About 70 percent of the federal prison inmates now are drug offenders. In 1980, there were 41,000 persons in American prisons for drug offenses; in 2009, that figure had escalated to 500,000 prisoners. Drug sentences often exceed those for manslaughter, sexual abuse, assault, and arson, and cost taxpayers more than $20,000 annually for each inmate. At the same time, there has been a slight, but growing, movement to experiment with the decriminalization of drug transactions and usage. Since the use of alcohol and cigarettes is permitted, and both can produce devastating health consequences, people wonder why other drugs are singled out for illegal status. It also is argued that the campaign against cigarette smoking has enjoyed modest success. Some believe that a powerful anti-drug program could prove more effective than punitive laws.

Among concerns regarding decriminalization of drug use is that there is little agreement on how the procedure might operate. Most favor some form of "medicalization" by means of which drugs would be dispensed under controlled conditions, but it is uncertain whether a black market might not spring up for those who would want to avoid official channels or would want to obtain more or different drugs than what might be available to them from licensed sources (Mosher & Akins, 2007). Highlight 13.4 portrays the approach to drug use in the Netherlands today.

Internationally, the United Nations estimates that about 140 million people—about 2.5 percent of the world's population—smoke marijuana or hashish, a form of marijuana. At least 13 million people are believed to

---

HIGHLIGHT 13.4 THE NETHERLANDS—A FREE DRUG MARKET

In the Netherlands, where drugs that are illegal in the United States have been freely available since 1976, reports indicate that there has been a notable reduction in crime. The Dutch drug addiction rate is one of Europe's lowest, with an estimated 15,000 hard-core drug addicts and 600,000 marijuana users in a nation of 15 million persons. A needle-exchange program has given the Dutch one of the lowest AIDS rates in the world for intravenous drug users. But the cause-effect relationship is not that simple. Spain, which decriminalized "soft" drugs for personal use more than a decade ago and tolerates heroin and cocaine use, has the highest AIDS death rate in Europe, with 75 percent of the mortalities stemming from intravenous drug use. Obviously, other factors besides the stance of the law feed into these diverse outcomes.

(Zimmer & Morgan, 1997:175; see further Korf et al., 1999).

sniff, smoke, or inject forms of cocaine. Another 8 million use heroin. The international business in illegal drugs generates an estimated $400 billion a year, amounting to 8 percent of all international trade. Cultivation of opium poppies now covers more than 691,000 acres worldwide. About 300,000 million tons of coca leaves, from which cocaine is derived, are grown in Peru, Colombia, and Bolivia (Wren, 2000).

Opiate Drugs

Opiates include heroin, morphine, laudanum, and codeine, the last a less potent form than the others. The drugs are addictive in the sense that their continued use builds up a tolerance, requiring heavier dosages to obtain the same physiological response. In addition, cessation of opiate use brings on withdrawal symptoms that can involve intense physical distress. The drugs are depressants; they produce a feeling of euphoria. In this respect, addicts sometimes suffer from serious physical ailments that are masked by the effects of the drug. Opiates also blunt sexual feelings.

Before passage in 1914 of the Harrison Act, the initial federal statute outlawing opiates, the incorporation of opiates in patent medicines created addicts at all social levels. There were more female than male addicts because of the use of palliatives containing opiates for "female troubles." Narcotics could be purchased over the counter or ordered through the mail (Jonnes, 1999). Heroin was hailed as the new wonder drug, a treatment for respiratory ailments and a cough suppressant. It was produced cheaply with a high degree of purity and was usually taken orally. The name itself comes from "heroic," indicating the pharmaceutical value that the Bayer laboratories put upon it when they began marketing heroin in 1898 (Booth, 1999).

After 1914, addicts increasingly came to be concentrated in the lower socioeconomic classes, and the ratio of male to female addicts changed dramatically. Following World War II, narcotics began to be defined as a formidable public problem. The medical profession deserted the field of treatment, largely in response to threats by federal law enforcement agents based upon their agencies' arguable reading of several court decisions (Cartwright, 2001; Musto & Korsmeyer, 2002). Summarizing the situation, Paul Jesilow and his colleagues (1993:22) write:

> What is particularly notable about doctors and narcotics is the extraordinary and hasty retreat of U.S. medical practitioners from the field once the government began to regulate it. In England doctors refused to abdicate what they deemed as their responsibility for persons addicted to drugs. In the United States, there were a few prosecutions of doctors who defied or tried to evade the authority of the government, and the matter was settled. American doctors had found drug clients largely unsavory, the financial return uncertain, and the whole business not worth their trouble.

Heroin use, like most human behavior, is intended to provide the person with a satisfying outcome, at least in the short run. "It's like, the best way I can think of, sweet death," a life-long addict has said. "Because it is sweet, overpoweringly so in a lot of ways, but with an edge of real terrible danger, I guess that's why everyone has to play with it" (Hughes, 1961:124). Note that this addict presumes that "everyone" has or will flirt with heroin use, a wildly inaccurate premise. Pleasure, as the quotation suggests, has its costs and risks. It is one thing to use morphine to dull the awful pain of a terminal illness, but another to try to avoid unpleasantness in human existence. Ultimately, social values dictate the illegal status of heroin; the government will not tolerate people being lulled and dulled by a drug, but wants them to participate with as clear a mind as they can command in whatever course life lays out for them (Zimring & Hawkins, 1993).

A 33-year longitudinal study documents decades of despair associated with the lifestyle of heroin users. Of the 581 men in the original study, 284 had died, 29.6 percent from drug overdoses or from poisoning by adulterants added to the drug. An additional 38.6 percent died from cancer or from heart or liver disease, the last often associated with hepatitis C, a contagious condition transmitted by needles used for drug injections that are not sterile. Three died of AIDS, while homicides, suicides, or accidents killed another 9.4 percent. The death rates were dramatically higher than those for an equivalent population.

The men still living were struggling. About 40 percent reported using heroin within the past year, and abuse of other illegal drugs was also frequent. Those men who had abstained from heroin use for five years were less likely to return to use, but even in this group 25 percent resumed use, some after 15 years of abstinence. Use of alcohol and illegal drugs other than heroin was common among the heroin abstainers (Hser, et al., 2002; for a similar study in Australia, see Danke et al., 2009).

Perspectives on Heroin Use

There are a variety of explanations offered for heroin use, but none that has obtained a large measure of agreement within the criminological community. Since the behavior is usually done alone rather than as part of a group, psychological and psychiatric theories dominate the field. It is commonly believed that heroin addicts tend to be passive persons, prone to dependence upon a pharmacological agent that allows them to avoid confrontation with the imperatives of "reality." But in many regards the demands of a heroin addict's existence are a great deal more "real" than the demands of life lived in more routine ways. The addict must obtain money, often on a daily basis, to buy the drug. He or she also must locate a source and evade the police: it can be a frantic lifestyle (Caputo, 2008). One writer captures this view with the observation that "what appears to be a lack of will is in fact a serious commitment to the downward spiral" (Powers, 2000:145).

Suggested psychiatric explanations seem equally superficial. "Drugs are the instant mother, the instant mother they never had," psychiatrist Bruno Bettelheim (1969:125) maintained. This observation is based on the idea that there is a necessary quantity of "mothering" required to produce "normal" behavior, and that drug use is an "abnormal" substitute for a healthy upbringing. The postulation is riddled with questionable assumptions. For one thing, the dramatic shift of drug use from middle-class women to lower-class men was not accompanied by any notable change in patterns of mothering.

Sociologists sometimes claim that heroin use is a response to the misery of slum existence and poverty, a painkiller for the distress of unemployment and a bleak pattern of life, and that therefore the most effective means to reduce addiction is to eliminate economic and social inequality. Such conditions are abhorrent as matters of social injustice, but it is not readily demonstrable that they produce addiction. Again, the fact that opiate use formerly prevailed in the middle class tends to undermine this idea.

Cocaine

Cocaine, an alkaloid derived from coca plant leaves, is a central nervous system stimulant that results in bursts of energy and gregarious enthusiasm. Among the difficulties associated with cocaine use is that it is expensive, and after the brief initial flood of energy it at times sends users into mild to severe depression. More cocaine may be used to avoid such depression, continuing the process until, for many users, the habit becomes unmanageable. The drug is indigenous to South America, Mexico, and the West Indies, and the leaves are often chewed in these sites to help alleviate altitude sickness and to increase physical endurance.

While cocaine is not physically addictive, as heroin is, it usually creates a psychological dependency. Cocaine also can produce hyperstimulation, digestive disorders, nausea, loss of appetite, weight loss, convulsions, and sometimes delusions of persecution. Repeated inhalation can erode the mucous membranes and perforate the nasal septum. A chronic "runny nose" often is the hallmark of the regular cocaine user.

Crack Cocaine

Crack cocaine costs considerably less than regular cocaine and is smoked rather than snorted or sniffed. The smoking utensil can be a special glass pipe or a makeshift device fabricated from beer and soda cans, jars, bottles, and other containers known as "stems," "straight shooters," "skillets," "tools," or "ouzies" (Inciardi et al., 1993). Crack or freebase cocaine is a different chemical product than cocaine itself, but is derived from it. It produces a rapid, potent high, and, as Inciardi and his colleagues (1993:8) note, when it arrived on the drug scene in quantity, crack "became a popular fast-food analog of cocaine because of the ease with which it could be concocted."

Crack usage has been especially pronounced among women, and the media have been prone to highlight crack-addicted newborns on the pediatric wards of county hospitals. Such media portrayals of horrific damage inflicted on their babies by crack-using mothers are contradicted by a number of scientific studies that demonstrate that prenatal cocaine use has minimal effects on newborn infants, and that such effects are primarily limited to minor growth deficits. The researchers point out that the media stories fail to separate the mother's crack use from other factors such as recourse to additional illegal substances, poor nutrition, poverty, and failure to secure adequate medical attention (Day & Richardson, 1993).

What has been marked in the realm of crack usage is the emergence of "crack-houses" in which women, desperate for crack, exchange sex for the drug. After studying the phenomenon in Miami, Inciardi and his coworkers concluded:

> The sex-for-crack phenomenon and the incredible degradation of women surrounding much of its routine enactment is like nothing ever seen in the annals of drug use, street life, prostitution, or domestic woman-battering. It entails a variety of hypersexual behaviors—high-frequency sex, numerous anonymous partners, public as well as private sex, groups as well as couples, heterosexual or homosexual or both simultaneously (Inciardi et al., 1993:39).

Tanya Sharpe points out: "A woman who shares a man's crack supply is obliged to perform a sexual act in exchange for smoking. Men who smoke with other men are not required to do so." She notes that this represents "a clear example of gender bias and is exemplary of male primacy in the crack culture" (Sharpe, 2005:65).

The crack epidemic, as one writer observes, "behaved much like a fever. It came on strong, appearing to rise without hesitation, and then broke, just as the most dire warnings were being sounded" (Egan, 1999:A27). Crack users became defined as the biggest losers on the street, and a generational revulsion against the drug apparently developed.

Perspectives on Cocaine and Crack Cocaine

For Inciardi and his colleagues, the abuse of drugs, and most notably of cocaine and crack cocaine, is a reflection of other problems and not the cause of them. They note:

> Drug abuse is a disorder of the whole person; the problem is the person and not the drug, and addiction is but a symptom and not the essence of the disorder. In the vast majority of drug users, there are cognitive problems, psychological dysfunction is common, thinking may be unrealistic or disorganized, values misshapen, and frequently there are deficiencies in educational, employment, parenting, and other social skills (Inciardi et al., 1993:145).

They argue that what the crack-dependent person needs is not rehabilitation, which implies a return to a previously known way of life, but habilitation, which would involve the building of a positive self-image and socialization into a productive and responsible way of life (Inciardi et al., 1993).

There has been ongoing dispute that the much heavier penalties for amounts of crack cocaine compared to powder cocaine were racist, because it was African Americans who most often were convicted of crack offenses. A 1986 federal law decreed a mandatory five-year sentence for a first-time conviction for possession of five grams of crack cocaine. The same penalty applied for possession of 500 grams of powder cocaine. Eighty percent of the crack cocaine offenders were African Americans while most of the powder cocaine users were Caucasians. In 2010, Congress changed the statute so that it requires possession of 28 grams of crack to receive a penalty equal to possession of 500 grams of powder cocaine. As one cynic put it, the law now is "only one-fifth as racist as it used to be."

Methamphetamine

Methamphetamines (also known as "crank, "speed," "go fast," and "meth") is a central nervous system stimulant. The United Nations reports that methamphetamine is the most widely abused drug on earth, with almost as many addicts as for heroin and cocaine combined.

Methamphetamine is relatively easy to manufacture; other drugs required in the process, such as ephedrine, generally are smuggled into the United States from Mexico. Amphetamines are distinctive but related pharmacologically to methamphetamine. They have been widely used by persons seeking to lose weight and by students in all-night cramming sessions before exams or trying to finish a term paper on time. An occasional relationship has been found between acts of violence and meth usage, but the writers note that "violence is not an inevitable outcome of chronic methamphetamine use" (Baskin-Sommers & Sommers, 2006).

Arrest figures show slightly higher usage rates for methamphetamine among females than males. Perhaps this is because most buyers of the drug do not have to deal with organized criminals; methamphetamine often is available at neighborhood bars. In Montana, meth sales and use are reported to be responsible for 80 percent of the total prison population, and 90 percent of the female inmate total. A philanthropist in 2005 donated millions of dollars for an anti-meth media advertising campaign. The advertisements are grim:

> The camera follows the teenager as she showers for her night out and looks down to discover the drain swirling with blood. Her methamphetamine-addicted self is oozing from scabs she had picked all over her body because the drug made her think there were bugs crawling beneath her skin, and she lets out a scream worthy of [the movie] Psycho (Zernike, 2006:17).

The impact of the campaign in Montana has been impressive. In 2005, the state ranked fifth in the nation in the rate of methamphetamine usage; in 2010 it was thirty-ninth and in that year *Barron's*, a leading financial publication, rated the Montana anti-meth campaign, which has now been duplicated in several other states, as the world's third most impressive philanthropic effort.

In its pure form, methamphetamine is white, odorless, and bitter. Street meth is likely to have a yellowish hue and to come in capsules or chunks. Users today tend to be white, lower middle-class, high-school educated, and in the 20- to 35-year age bracket (Roll et al., 2009). In previous years methamphetamine was injected intravenously, but fear of HIV infection from contaminated needles has led to an upsurge in meth smoking. The effect of the drug will last for about ten to twelve hours, compared to the usual 45-minute effect of cocaine (Halkitis, 2009).

Marijuana

A major difficulty in the medical and criminological material regarding **marijuana** (or 9-THC, which stands for delta-9-trans-tetrahydrocannabinol, the drug's main ingredient) lies in the interweaving of fact and ideology. Much argument surrounds the question of the short- and long-term physical consequences of chronic marijuana usage. Some writers suggest that smoking of marijuana several times a day for a period of, say, a decade, is likely to produce deleterious organic conditions. At the moment about 0.8 percent of Americans smoke marijuana on a daily or near daily basis (Zimmer & Morgan, 1997). Marijuana smoke has been reported by the National Institute of Drug Abuse to have a higher carcinogenic content than that of cigarettes, but few marijuana users smoke the 20 or more cigarettes daily that often feed the habit of the tobacco addict.

The main physical risk from marijuana is damage to the lungs from smoking (Zimmer & Morgan, 1997:139; see generally Earlywine, 2002). There is some—but far from uniform—belief that marijuana use by pregnant women presents potential dangers for the fetus, and many point out that the better part of wisdom, given the uncertain consequences, is to be wary of the drug if pregnant. A middle-aged person's risk of heart attack increases nearly fivefold during the first hour after smoking marijuana, since ingestion of the drug increases the heart rate by about 40 beats per minute (Mittelman et al., 2001). Similarly, a quartet of doctors reviewing the effect of marijuana on cardiac responses title their article, "Keep off the Grass" (Caldicott et al., 2005). Donald Jasinski, a medical professor at Johns Hopkins University and director of the Center for Chemical Dependence, answered several rhetorical questions: "Does it destroy as many lives as alcohol? No. Does it kill as many people as cigarettes? No. Does it have as many deaths associated with it as aspirin overdoses? No" (Carroll, 2002:C24).

Marijuana at one time was used in medical practice as commonly as aspirin is today, and it was known to have a relaxing effect. In 1937, the federal Marijuana Tax Act made it illegal to possess marijuana unless you had purchased a tax stamp; but there were, for all practical purposes, no stamps to be bought. Use of marijuana then was largely confined to members of underprivileged or fringe groups. The early laws were made tougher during the immediate post–World War II period as marijuana came to be viewed in the public mind as a precursor to heroin addiction. By the late 1960s, use of marijuana (also commonly called "pot," "weed," or "grass") had spread dramatically into the mainstream of American society. Along with the Vietnam War and dissent on college campuses, marijuana had become a major topic of controversy. This development triggered medical research designed to pinpoint the effects of the drug. A recent comprehensive review of all the allegations about the possible harmful effects of marijuana conducted by Lynn Zimmer and John P. Morgan, the latter a medical doctor, found little or no support for them. They point out that in 1995, *Lancet*, the highly reputable British medical journal, stated that "the smoking of cannabis [marijuana], even long term, is not harmful to health" (Zimmer & Morgan, 1997:17). The simplest summary of the research would be that marijuana has been found to be neither as dangerous as its fiercest opponents claim, nor as innocuous as its fiercest proponents insist. Return to Chapter 2 for more discussion of the ebb and flow of marijuana laws. Also, Zimmer and Morgan's conclusions regarding the effect of the drug are delineated in Highlight 2.2.

Critics of the current laws against marijuana maintain that the penal code pointlessly turns those who use the drug into criminals and in some instances generates an overall hostility toward the law and the police. They also point out that great amounts of money that might be used for better purposes are employed to enforce the laws against marijuana. They argue that by keeping marijuana illegal, but failing to eliminate it, the society has turned over the marketing of the drug to organized crime groups that engage in a wide variety of other illegal and dangerous acts (Husak & de Marneffe, 2005).

Marijuana as Medicine

The debate regarding drug offenses as victimless crimes recently has taken another twist as persons who maintain that their medical condition could be helped and their pain alleviated if marijuana were made legally available to them joined the fray. A study of 2,400 oncologists (doctors specializing in treating cancer) found that 40 percent had recommended that their patients use marijuana. The drug also is believed to reduce eye pressure caused by glaucoma. In addition, marijuana has been claimed to lessen muscular spasms in persons with neurological disorders and to relieve migraine headaches and the pain from "phantom limb" conditions that often follow amputations. For some of these problems a synthetic capsule of THC is available by prescription, but it is not believed to be as effective for many patients as smoked marijuana, and it may produce more unpleasant side effects (Zimmer & Morgan, 1997). By 2015, 23 states had legalized some measure of medicinal marijuana use, with four of those states allowing its sale and use for recreational purposes.

The federal Food and Drug Administration has countered the medical marijuana movement by declaring that no sound scientific study supports the value of the medical use of marijuana and that the government would withdraw prescription-writing privileges from doctors who prescribed marijuana, bar them from being paid for treating Medicare and Medicaid patients, and would consider prosecuting them criminally. This threat grew much stronger when the U.S. Supreme Court in 2005 by a 6–3 margin ruled that the Controlled Substance Act gave the federal government the power to outlaw the growing of marijuana for medical purposes since such activity could substantially affect interstate commerce (*Gonzales v. McClary*, 2005).

In 2002, California Judge Mary Schroeder ruled that the first amendment protected the right of physicians to discuss the use of marijuana with patients they deemed might benefit from it. The rights of states, the judge declared, should prevail, "particularly in situations in which the citizens of a State have chosen to serve as a laboratory in the trial of novel social and economic experiments"(*Conant v. Walters*, 2002:639). In an editorial, the prestigious *New England Journal of Medicine* called the government's opposition "foolish," "hypocritical," and "inhumane" (Kassirer, 1997).

Opponents of medical use of marijuana challenge the view that marijuana is as effective as claimed and maintain that, even if it is, there are legal drugs that would do the job just as well or better. They also argue that the move to legalize marijuana for medical purposes is largely a camouflage for an entry point to totally decriminalize marijuana. The accuracy of this perspective is shown by a 2009 editorial in the *Washington Post* declaring that "California's medical dispensaries provide a good working example, warts and all, that legalized drug distribution does not cause the sky to fall" (Moskos & Franklin, 2009:A13). Opponents of medical marijuana also insist that once prescriptions can legally be written for marijuana there are doctors aplenty who would authorize persons with no medical need to obtain the drug. They further maintain that marijuana use by patients with ailments such as AIDS would further damage the users' immune system and make them more susceptible to bacterial and fungal infections (Wasserman, 2005).

Employees of a medical marijuana evaluation center advertise the process of legally obtaining pot by acquiring a physician's approval. Although it is federally illegal, many states continue to trump federal jurisdiction and apply state law instead.

CREDIT:
©iStockphoto.com/Joe Belanger.

Explaining Marijuana Use

For Ronald Akers and Gary Jensen (2003), the most productive theoretical approach to marijuana use is to see it as the outcome of a process of differential association. The interaction between young persons and their peers, parents, and other persons, Akers and Jensen maintain, provides them with a social environment in which they learn ways of behaving. The peer group, particularly close friends, is the most important association for the initiation and continuing use of marijuana. Both the frequency and quantity of use are related to the number and type of current users one has as friends (see also Esbensen &

Huizinga, 1993). Parents, other family members, church and religious groups, schoolteachers, authority figures, and others in the community also have an influence in determining whether marijuana will be used, and how much and for how long. Akers (1985:115) writes:

> When these [groups] act in harmony to move youngsters in the direction toward either using or not using, the chances of their behaving that way are maximized. When these sources are in conflict, adolescents will most often behave similarly to close peers. It is in peer groups that drugs typically are first made available and opportunities for use are provided.

An interesting research twist is a finding by Pamela Black and Lauren Joseph (2014) that marijuana use among "baby boomers," the 1946–64 birth cohorts, was also best explained by social learning theory. This is a generation of Americans who went through their formative years in the 1960s and 70s, a period when drug use was at its highest and affiliated with a politically active youth subculture that viewed marijuana in particular as symbolic of the movement. Learning theory suggests that the values of this "Woodstock generation" may have simply been imbedded in the group and played forward into the older leisure years. As Black and Joseph (2014:826) state, "Viewed through a social learning lens, members of the baby boom cohort adopted pro-marijuana norms and values that they are carrying into adulthood." As they note, older adults partaking of "grass" tend to generate more chuckles than concern, but their findings contribute to our theoretical understanding of substance use.

Trends in Drug Use

Most high school students find illegal drugs more common at their schools than in their neighborhoods. Forty-one percent of the students in one inquiry said that they had seen drugs sold at their school, while only 25 percent had seen them being sold in their neighborhood. Twenty-five percent of the students said that they could purchase marijuana within an hour at their school.

The survey also reported that 35 percent of the teenagers identified drugs as the most important problem they face. An overwhelming majority of the teachers favored expelling a student caught with drugs at school, conducting random searches of lockers, and testing athletes for drugs. But most teachers opposed testing all students for drugs (Wren, 1999).

The initiation and progress of drug usage has been studied by Finn-Aage Esbensen and Delbert Elliott (1994), who examined data in regard to 1,172 respondents aged 11 through 30. They found that once drug use is started, it tends to be maintained for an extended time and that social learning variables are more important in accounting for initiation than demographic variables such as age and gender. Marijuana use drops on the average by more than one-third when young adults get married or cohabit and cocaine use drops by one-half. The explanation seems to be that the drug usage is no longer private, but now involves the continuing awareness of someone else. If a divorce takes place, the "marriage effect" is reversed and usage returns to about the same level as when the person was single (Bachman et al., 1997).

VICTIMS WITHOUT CRIMES

Criminology most often involves the study of illegal behavior and criminology textbooks typically concentrate most of their attention on acts that are proscribed by the criminal law. Some criminologists, especially those falling within the interactionist paradigm, feel uneasy about the blinders that this approach puts upon criminological scholarship. They object that it restricts them to looking only at behavior that is defined as criminal by appointed and elected officials. Usually those who fashion the law condemn behaviors that virtually everybody regards as unacceptable—murder, robbery, car theft, and similar kinds of acts. But there are some things, such as the victimless crimes, that are outlawed for reasons that are at least arguable. And then there are other matters that involve self-evident social harms that never find their way into the criminal laws, **victims without crimes**. For instance, almost all continental European and South American countries have laws that mandate that persons who can aid others without risk to themselves can be criminally charged if they fail to do so. In the United States, except for five states, it is perfectly legal for a person to stand by and watch an infant drown yards away in shallow water, or for you to indifferently observe a blind man walk past and plunge over a cliff only a few feet away without making any attempt to stop or warn him (Schiff, 2005).

The Michigan Supreme Court spelled out the prevailing American doctrine when it overturned the conviction for manslaughter of a man who had left for dead a woman after he had observed her taking morphine and camphor tablets before she fell into a coma (*People v. Beardsley*, 1907). A leading criminal law scholar believed that the court decision, and many others like it, was abominable:

> To be temperate about such a decision is difficult. In its savage proclamation, it ignores any impulse of charity or compassion. It proclaims a morality that is smug, ignorant, and vindictive. In a civilized society, a man who finds himself with a helplessly ill person who has no other source of aid should be under a duty to summon help, whether the person is his wife, his mistress, a prostitute, or a Chief Justice. The Beardsley decision deserves emphatic repudiation (Hughes, 1955:624).

Cigarette Smoking

The manufacture and sale of cigarettes offers perhaps the best illustration of victims without crimes. As was demonstrated in Chapter 2, this is a remarkable example of relativity of law. The tobacco story is a tale of an industry that makes extraordinary amounts of money and uses these profits in part to protect itself from regulation (Parker-Pope, 2001). The tobacco industry contributes large sums to politicians, hoping to gain their support for legislation favorable to it. Cigarette manufacturers undoubtedly do not want to kill people, but by employing tactics of obfuscation, denial, and manipulation, they have fed their financial self-interest at the expense of the lives of millions of their customers. Cigarettes are said to "cause more deaths than any other recognized lethal agents, including all the known bacteria, known viruses, bullets, wild animals, chemical poisons, and even the American automobile" (Kluger, 1996:204). The campaign to reduce smoking as of 2011 had highly disproportionate success rates with different segments of the population. More men than women continue to smoke: 24 percent against 18 percent. The difference in rates is striking in terms of education, with only 6 percent of persons who have done graduate work using cigarettes; 11 percent for those with an undergraduate degree, compared to 34 percent for those with 9 to 11 years of education, and 49 percent of persons who have a high school equivalency (GED) diploma.

Before it yielded to lawsuits, the tobacco industry insisted that correlation was not causation: just because persons who smoked a great deal showed significantly higher rates of lung cancer did not prove that the smoking caused the cancer. Many persons who smoked as much or more than those who died of lung cancer lived to a ripe old age and died of something else. And some who did not smoke died of the same diseases that killed those who smoked. In addition, people who smoke might be distinctive in some ways that leads to their demise earlier than those who do not smoke. As one physician indicated when he argued that reports of a causative connection between smoking and lung cancer were "absolutely unwarranted": "Simply because one finds bullfrogs after a rain does not mean that it rained bullfrogs" (Kluger, 1996:166).

Cigarette manufacturers maintain, as those who seek decriminalization of narcotics use also argue, that how people choose to live their lives and contribute to their death is their own business, that life itself is a terminal disease. People have enough information to make a sensible decision, at least if we overlook that (1) strenuous advertising efforts were launched to get and keep people smoking and (2) the nicotine in cigarettes is addictive, in the sense that it is painful to give up.

The first significant development in the control of cigarette purveyance came when the government prohibited cigarette companies from advertising on television. This restriction was a considerable aid to the bigger cigarette manufacturers because, absent heavy advertising outlays, potential entrants into the market could not seriously challenge them. At the same time, the cigarette manufacturers turned to advertisements placed strategically in sports arenas so that their products would be clearly visible to television audiences.

The television ban was also welcomed by the manufacturers because the government had invoked the "fairness doctrine," which authorized rebuttal of controversial positions. The tobacco companies were being savaged during the free television time offered to those who scorned them. But notable in the decision to uphold the ban on cigarette advertising was the defense of free speech in a dissenting opinion. Judge Skelly Wright did not doubt that the attractive woman in Salem ads was in fact "a seductive merchant of death" and that the real "'Marlboro Country' is the graveyard." But the First Amendment, the jurist stated, "does not protect only free speech that is healthy or harmless" (*Capital Broadcasting Co. v. Mitchell*, 1971:582).

Subsequently, largely on the initiative of the Surgeon General, the government demanded that all cigarette packages (and, later, advertisements as well) carry a warning about the dangers of smoking. The manufacturers spent millions to get a message that was as innocuous as they could negotiate. They were not altogether displeased with the requirement of a warning because they believed that it might protect them from liability, since they could claim that they had informed people that they were engaging in risky behavior and therefore they could escape the imposition of financial damages (Brandt, 2007).

The shift to controlling public smoking demonstrates how law changes and offers some hope that the evolution of knowledge and consensus may lend protection to innocent persons, while not falling into the trap of criminalizing a vice that is in high demand. If as much progress could be made on other criminological fronts as has been made in the realm of tobacco, an infinite number of lives could be saved and human suffering avoided. Perhaps there is reason for optimism.

SUMMARY

By and large, law enforcement activities have proven ineffectual for controlling victimless crimes; for instance, long-standing statutes outlawing the behaviors seem to have made little impact on the extent of drug use and prostitution (Meier & Geis, 2006). The experiment in the prohibition of the sale of alcoholic beverages in the United States ended in shambles and resulted in the repeal of the ill-fated Volstead Act. Perhaps the most instructive lesson comes from the experience in America with cigarette smoking. Educational campaigns, appealing to medical findings and self-interest in personal health, supported by peer pressures, have made a notable indent into the extent that Americans smoke cigarettes today. On a per capita basis the number of smokers has declined to a level last seen in the late 1930s.

Philosophers often have inveighed against attempts to use the criminal law for purposes that it cannot adequately accomplish. Two of the more famous statements are those of Baruch de Spinoza (1632–77) and Jeremy Bentham (1748–1832). Spinoza advocated the removal from statute books of laws restricting activities that do not injure another party on the ground that "he who seeks to regulate everybody by law is more likely to arouse vices than to reform them. It is best to grant what cannot be abolished, even though it be itself harmful" (Spinoza, 1670/1937:141).

Bentham warned against "imaginary offenses," illustrating his position by reference to fornication and drunkenness, two acts that were outlawed in early American history. With what chance of success, Bentham asked, could a legislator seek to extirpate drunkenness and fornication by dint of legal punishment? "Not all the torture which ingenuity could invent would compass it; and before he had made any progress worth regarding, such a mass of evil would be produced by the punishment as would exceed, by a thousand fold, the utmost possible mischief of the offense" (Bentham 1798/1948:420).

A useful set of ground rules is offered by Herbert Packer regarding behaviors that ought to be scrutinized closely in terms of the proper attitude of the criminal law toward them. These are offenses that "do not result in anyone's feeling that he has been injured so as to impel him to bring the offenses to the attention of the authorities" (Packer, 1968:151). Packer identified a number of conditions that he believed should be present before criminal sanctions are invoked, including:

- The conduct must be regarded by most people as socially threatening, and must not be condoned by any significant segment of the society;
- It can be dealt with through evenhanded and nondiscriminatory law enforcement;
- Controlling it through the criminal process will not expose that process to severe qualitative or quantitative strain; and
- No reasonable alternatives to the criminal sanction exist for dealing with it.

The record shows that such considerations have led to the steady decrease in the number of "victimless" behaviors that come within the scope of the criminal law. But by no means is it certain that the process will continue or that it will proceed in the same direction. History clearly tells us that the use of the criminal law to enforce moral positions often takes a cyclical form. Today, for instance, the status of abortion under the law remains a matter of intense debate, while new aspects of the various behaviors categorized as "crimes without victims" are arousing considerable public controversy, including such matters as physician-assisted suicide and the right to use marijuana.

Finally, we can note two letters to a national newspaper that tell the story of the contradictory opinions held by thinking people regarding the preferred legal status of one of the major victimless crimes, drug use. First is an advocate of continuing to outlaw drug use:

> Legalization would be catastrophic. There are 15 million alcoholics in this country and 5 million drug addicts; do we want the 5 to become 15? Parents know that taking away the law would increase drug use and related car crashes, school dropouts and work absences. Hospital emergency rooms would be flooded, and crime would return to the crisis levels of the 1970s and '80s, when drug use was at its highest. Domestic violence and date rape would be substantially higher (Weiner, 2006:A12).

On the other side, the argument took the following form:

> Everybody knows the drug war is an abject failure. Its collateral damages is fostering anti-Americanism throughout the globe, particularly in South America, and at home it has trashed the Fourth Amendment [regarding searches and seizures] and is filling our jails with people whose only crime is to find pleasure in ways other people don't like (Padden, 2006:A12; for debates on drug legalization see Husak & de Marneffe, 2005 and Huggins, 2005).

KEY TERMS AND CONCEPTS

Cocaine

Crack Cocaine

Crimes without Victims

Criminalization

Decriminalization

Marijuana

Methamphetamines

Opiates

Physician-Assisted Suicide

Pimps

Prostitution

Victims without Crimes

KEY CRIMINOLOGISTS

Ronald Akers

Jeremy Bentham

Nanette Davis

Erich Goode

James Inciardi

Edwin Schur

Franklin Zimring

CASES

American Booksellers Assn. v. Hudnut, 771 F.2d 323 (7th Cir. 1985), affirmed 475 U.S. 1001

Capital Broadcasting Co. v. Mitchell, 333 F. Supp. 582 (D.C. Cir. 1971)

Conant v. Walters, 309 F.2d 693 (9th Cir. 2002)

Gonzales v. McClary, 541 U.S. 1 (2005)

People v. Beardsley, 113 N.W.2d 1128 (Mich. 1907)

Simon v. Sargent, 946 F. Supp. 277 (D. Mass. 1972), affirmed 400 U.S. 1020

DISCUSSION QUESTIONS

1. How would you defend or object to the fact that alcoholic beverages and cigarettes are marketed legally but the sale of drugs such as cocaine and marijuana is illegal?

2. Would you favor a law that required automobile drivers and their passengers to wear helmets? If so, why? If not, why not?

3. Defend or criticize laws that allow physician-assisted suicide.

4. Do you believe that prostitution should remain a criminal offense? If not, what conditions would you place on its operation?

5. Do you agree or disagree with the policy that customers of prostitutes should be charged with a crime? If you agree, would you feel the same way about women seeking an abortion if it were to become illegal, as it once was?

6. Describe and defend or disagree with the way Sweden has chosen to deal with prostitution. Do the same with the Nevada model.

7. Do you think that states should enact a law demanding Good Samaritan behavior (helping others, such as an injured motorist, if you are competent and there is no risk to yourself)? If so, why? If not, why not?

REFERENCES

Akers, R. L. (1985). *Deviant behavior*. Belmont, CA: Wadsworth.

Akers, R. L. & Jensen, G. F. (Eds.) (2003). *Social learning theory and the explanation of crime*. New Brunswick, NJ: Transaction.

Albert, A. E. (2001). *Brothel: Mustang Ranch and its women*. New York, NY: Random House.

Anderson, S. A. (2002). Prostitution and sexual autonomy: Making sense of the prohibition of prostitution. *Ethics, 112*, 748–82.

Atwood, D. A. (2008). Riding helmetless: Personal freedom or societal burden? *Phoenix Law Review, 1*, 269–97.

Bachman, J. G., Wadsworth, K. S., O'Malley, P.M., Johnson, L. D., & Schulenberg, J. F. (1997). *Smoking, drinking and drug use in young adulthood: The impacts of new freedoms and new responsibilities*. Mahwah, NJ: Earlbaum.

Baskin-Sommers, A. & Sommers, I. (2006). Methamphetamine use and violence among young adults. *Journal of Criminal Justice, 34*, 661–74.

Bentham, J. (1798/1948). *Theories of legislation* (2nd. ed.). London, UK: Trubner.

Bettelheim, B. (1969). *Children of the dream*. New York, NY: Macmillan.

Black, P. & Joseph, L. J. (2014). Still dazed and confused: Midlife marijuana use by the baby boomer generation. *Deviant Behavior, 35*, 822–41.

Booth, M. (1999). *Opium: A history*. New York, NY: St. Martin's.

Bork, R. (1991). *The tempting of America: The political seduction of the law*. New York, NY: Simon & Schuster.

Brandt, A.M. (2007). *The cigarette century: The rise, fall, and deadly persistence of the product that defined America*. New York, NY: Basic Books.

Brents, B. G. & Hausbeck, K. (2005). Violence and legalized brothel prostitution in Nevada. *Journal of Interpersonal Violence, 20*, 270–95.

Caldicott, D.G., Holmes, J., Robers-Thomson, K.C., & Mahar, L. (2005). Keep off the grass: Marijuana use and acute cardiovascular events. *European Journal of Emergency Medicine,12*, 23–64.

Campbell, C. A. (1991). Prostitution, AIDS, and preventive health behavior. *Social Science and Medicine, 32*, 1367–78.

Caputo, G. A. (2008). *Out in the storm: Drug-addicted women living as shoplifters and sex workers*. Hanover, NH: University Press of New England.

Carpenter, B. & Hayes, S. (2010). Crimes against morality. In H. Hayes & T. Prentzert (Eds.), *Introduction to crime and criminology* (pp. 149–65, 2nd ed.). French's Forest, NSW: Pearson Education Australia.

Carroll, L. (2002). Marijuana's effects: More than munchies. *New York Times,* (January 29), C24.

Cartwright, D. (2001). *Dark paradise: A history of opiate addiction in America.* Cambridge, MA: Harvard University Press.

Cates, J. A. & Markley, J. (1992). Demographic, clinical, and personality variables associated with male prostitution by choice. *Adolescence, 27,* 695–714.

Chen, S. (2012). Private lives of public women: Photos of sex workers (minus the sex) in South Korea. *Sexualities, 16,* 30–42.

Chin, E., Hedberg, K., Higginson, G. K., & Fleming, D. W. (1999). Legalized physician-assisted suicide in Oregon: The first year's experience. *New England Journal of Medicine, 340,* 577–83.

Cohen, B. (1980). *Deviant street networks: Prostitution in New York City.* Lexington, MA: Lexington Books.

Cothran, H. (2002). *Pornography: Opposing viewpoints.* San Diego, CA: Greenhaven.

Croce, M. A., Zarzaur, B. L., Magnotti, L. J., & Fabian, T. C. (2009). Impact of motorcycle helmet and state laws on society's burden. *Annals of Surgery, 250,* 390–4.

Dalla, R. L. (2007). *Exposing the "Pretty Woman" myth: A qualitative evaluation of street-level prostituted women.* Lanham, MD: Lexington Books.

Danke, S., Mills, K. L., Ross, J., Williamson, A., Harvard, A., & Teeson, M. (2009). The aging heroin user: Career length, clinical profile, an outcome across 36 months. *Drug and Alcohol Review, 28,* 243–9.

Davenport-Hines, R. (1995). *Auden.* London, UK: Heinemann.

Davis, N. J. (1993). Introduction: International perspectives on female prostitution. In N. J. Davis (Ed.), *Prostitution: An international handbook on trends, problems, and policies* (pp. 1–13). Westport, CT: Greenwood.

Day, N. L. & Richardson, G. (1993). Cocaine use and crack babies: Science, the media, and miscommunication. *Neurotoxicology and Teratology, 15,* 293–4.

Devlin P. (1965). *The enforcement of morals.* London, UK: Oxford University Press;

Dodge, M. J., Starr-Gimeno, D., & Williams, T. (2005). Puttin' on the sting: Women police officers' perspectives on reverse prostitution assignments. *International Journal of Police Science & Management, 7,* 71–85.

Donne, J. (1624). *Devotions upon emergent conditions and several steps in my sickness.* London, UK: Augustine Matthews.

Dworkin, A. (1997). *Life and death.* New York, NY: Free Press;

Earlywine, M. (2002). *Understanding marijuana: A new look at the scientific evidence.* New York, NY: Oxford University Press.

Editorial. (1997). The way we are. *Wall Street Journal* (January 10), A18.

Egan, T. (1999). A drug ran its course, then hid with its users. *New York Times* (September 19), A1, A27.

Elkind, P. (2010). *Rough justice: The rise and fall of Eliot Spitzer.* New York, NY: Portfolio.

Esbensen, F.-A. & Elliott, D. S. (1994). Continuity and discontinuity in illicit drug use patterns and antecedents. *Journal of Drug Use, 24,* 75–97.

Esbensen, F.-A. & Huizinga, D. (1993). Gangs, drugs, and delinquency in a survey of urban youth. *Criminology, 31,* 565–87.

French, P. (2008). *The world is what it is: The authorized biography of V. S. Naipaul.* New York, NY: Knopf.

Gill, M. B. (2009). Is the legalization of physician-assisted suicide compatible with good end-of-life care? *Journal of Applied Psychology, 26,* 27–45.

Gould, A. (2001). The criminalisation of buying sex: The politics of sex in Sweden. *Journal of Social Policy, 30,* 437–56.

Halkitis, P. N. (2009). *Methamphetamine addiction: Biological foundations, psychological factors, and social consequences.* Washington, DC: American Psychological Association.

Hayes-Smith, R. & Shekarkhar, Z. (2010). Why is prostitution criminalized? An alternative viewpoint on the construction of sex work. *Contemporary Justice Review, 13,* 43–55.

Hendin, H. & Foley, K. (2009). Physician-assisted suicide: A medical perspective. *Michigan Law Review, 106,* 1613–40.

Holsopple, K. (1999). Pimps, tricks and feminists. *Women's Studies Quarterly, 27,* 47–52.

Hser, V. I., Hoffman, V., Grella, C. E., & Anglin, M. D. (2002). A 33-year follow-up of narcotics addicts. *Archives of General Psychiatry, 58,* 503–8.

Huggins, L. E. (Ed.). (2005). *Drug war deadlock: The policy battle continues.* Stanford, CA: Hoover Institution.

Hughes, G. (1955). Criminal omissions. *Yale Law Journal, 67,* 590–637.

Hughes, H. M. (Ed.). (1961). *The fantastic lodge.* Boston, MA: Houghton Mifflin.

Husak, D. & de Marneffe, P. (2005). *The legalization of drugs.* New York, NY: Cambridge University Press.

Inciardi, J. A., Lockwood, D., & Pottieger, A. E. (1993). *Women and crack cocaine.* New York, NY: Macmillan.

Jakobsson, N. & Kotsadam, A. (2011). Gender equity and prostitution: An investigation of attitudes in Norway and Sweden. *Feminist Economics, 17,* 31–58.

Jeffrey, D. (2009). *Against physician assisted suicide: A palliative care perspective.* New York, NY: Radcliffe.

Jesilow, P., Pontell, H., & Geis, G. (1993). *Prescription for profit: How doctors defraud Medicaid.* Berkeley, CA: University of California Press.

Jonnes, J. (1999). *Hep-cats, narcs, and pipe dreams: A history of America's romance with illicit drugs.* Baltimore, MD: Johns Hopkins University Press.

Kassirer, J. P. (1997). Federal foolishness and marijuana. *New England Journal of Medicine, 336*(3), 366.

Klein, C. (2000). *Doris Lessing: A biography.* New York, NY: Carroll & Graf.

Klinger, K. (2000). Prostitution, humanism, and a woman's choice. *The Humanist, 63,* (January–February),16–20.

Kluger R. (1996). *Ashes to ashes: America's hundred-year cigarette war and the unabashed triumph of Philip Morris.* New York, NY: Knopf.

Korf, D. J., Bullington, B., & Riper, H. (Eds.). (1999). Symposium: Windmills in the minds? Drug policy and drug research in the Netherlands. *Journal of Drug Issues, 29,* 443–726.

Lindsay, R. A. (2009). Oregon's experience: Evaluating the record. *American Journal of Bioethics, 9,* 19–27.

Lode, E. (1999). Slippery slope arguments and legal reasoning. *California Law Review, 87,* 1469–1544.

MacKinnon, C. A. & Dworkin, A. (Eds.). (1997) *In harm's way: The pornography of civil rights hearings.* Cambridge, MA: Harvard University Press.

Mason, E. (2011). Ignoring it will not make it go away: Guidelines for regulation of physician-assisted suicide. *New England Law Journal, 45*, 139–66.

Meier, R. F. & Geis, G. (2006). *Criminal justice and moral issues.* New York, NY: Oxford University Press.

Mittelman, M. A., Lewis, R. A., Machre, M., Sherwood, J. B., & Miller, J. E. (2001). Triggering myocardial interactions by marijuana. *Circulation, 103*, 2805–9.

Monto, M. (2004). Female prostitution, customers, and violence. *Violence against Women, 10*, 160–68.

Mosher, C. J. & Akins, S. (2007). *Drugs and drug policy: The control of consciousness alteration.* Thousand Oaks, CA: Sage.

Moskos, P. & Franklin, S. (2009). It's time to legalize drugs. *Washington Post*, (August 17), A13.

Musto, D. F. & Korsmeyer, P. (2002). *One hundred years of heroin.* Westport, CT: Auburn House.

Nietzsche, F. W. (1844/1920). *The Antichrist.* (H. L. Mencken, Trans.) New York, NY: Knopf.

Note. (2009). Child pornography, the Internet, and the challenge of upholding statutory terms. *Harvard Law Review, 122*, 2206–27.

Nuland, S. B. (1994). *How we die: Reflections on life's final chapter.* New York, NY: Knopf.

Otis, S. (2009). *Child pornography and sexual grooming: Legal and social responses.* New York. NY: Cambridge University Press.

Packer, H. L. (1968). *The limits of the criminal sanction.* Stanford, CA: Stanford University Press.

Padden, D. H. (2006). Our unwinnable war—Against drugs. *Wall Street Journal*, (March 7), A12.

Parker-Pope, T. (2001). *Cigarettes: Anatomy of an industry.* New York, NY: Public Affairs.

Powers, A. (2000). *Weird like us: My Bohemian America.* New York, NY: DeCapo.

Prince, D. A. (1986). A psychological study of prostitutes in California and Nevada. Ph.D. dissertation. San Diego, CA: United States International University.

Richardson, L. (2000). The pimp phenomenon. *Los Angeles Times*, (December 3),E1, E3.

Roll, J. M., Rawson, R. A., Ling, W, & Shoptaw, S. (Eds.). (2009). *Methamphetamine addiction: From basic science to treatment.* New York, NY: Guilford.

Ross, H. L. (1992). *Confronting drunk driving: Social policy for saving lives.* New Haven, CT: Yale University Press.

Salem, T. (1999). Physician-assisted suicide. *Hastings Center Report, 20*, (May), 30–36.

Schiff, D. (2005). Samaritans, good, bad, ugly: A comparative analysis. *Roger Williams University Law Review, 11*, 77–141.

Schur, E. (1965). *Crimes without victims: Deviant behavior and public policy.* Englewood Cliffs, NJ: Prentice Hall.

Sharpe, T. T. (2005). *Behind the eight ball: Sex for crack cocaine exchange and poor black women.* New York, NY: Haworth.

Smith, M. D. & Grov, C. (2011). *In the company of men: Inside the lives of male prostitutes.* Santa Barbara, CA: Praeger.

Smith, M. D. & Seal, D. W. (2007) Sexual behavior, mental health, substance use, and HIV risk among agency-based male escorts in a small U.S. city. *International Journal of Sexual Health, 19*, 27–39.

Smith, M. D., Grov, C., & Seal, D. W. (2008). Agency-based male sex work: A descriptive focus on physical, personal, and social space. *Journal of Men's Studies, 16*, 193–210.

Spinoza, B. de (1670/1937). Tractatus theologico-politicus. In A.G.A. Balz (Ed.), *Writings on political philosophy* (Chap. XX). New York, NY: Appleton-Century-Crofts.

Viuhko, M. (2010). Human trafficking for sexual exploitation and organized crime in Finland. *European Journal of Criminology, 7,* 61–75.

Waddell, C. (1996). HIV and the social world of female commercial sex workers. *Medical Anthropological Quarterly, 10,* 75–82.

Wald, M. (2008). Death of motorcyclists rise again. *New York Times,*(August 15), A11.

Wasserman, S. (2005). *Medical marijuana.* Denver, CO: National Conference of State Legislatures.

Weinberg, M.S., Shaver, F.M., & Williams, C.J. (1999). Gendered sex work in the San Francisco Tenderloin. *Archives of Sexual Behavior, 28,* 503–21.

Weiner, R. (2006). Our unwinnable war—Against drugs. *Wall Street Journal,* (March 7), A12.

Weitzer, R. (2005). New directions in research on prostitution. *Crime, Law & Social Change, 43,* 211–35.

Weitzer, R. (2012). *Legalizing prostitution: From illicit vice to lawful business.* New York, NY: New York University Press.

Woozley, A.D. (1983). A duty to rescue: Some thoughts on criminal liability. *Virginia Law Review, 69,* 1273–1300.

Wren, C.S. (1999). Study sees little change in drug use. *New York Times,* (December 19), 51.

Wren, C.S. (2000). Widespread drug use. *New York Times,* (January 23), A9.

Wright, W. (2000). Historical analogies, slippery slopes, and the question of euthanasia. *Journal of Law, Medicine & Ethics, 28,* 176–93.

Zernike, K. (2006). With scenes of blood and pain: Ads battle methamphetamine in Montana. *New York Times,* (February 26), 17.

Zimmer, L. & Morgan, J.P. (1997). *Marijuana facts, marijuana myths: A review of the scientific evidence.* New York, NY: The Lindesmith Center.

Zimring, F.E. & Hawkins, G. (1993). *The search for rational drug control.* New York, NY: Cambridge University Press.

Youth Violence

Violence committed by and against youths, ranging from gang-related drive-by shootings to mass killings at schools, has attracted considerable public and scholarly attention since 1990 (e.g., Loeber & Farrington, 1998; Zimring, 1998; Office of the Surgeon General, 2001; Thornton, et al., 2002; Klein & Maxson, 2006; Howell, 2009; Loeber & Farrington, 2012). In fact, in the mid-1990s, at the height of concern about youth violence, several social commentators warned of an emerging class of youthful offenders—"**superpredators**"—who would create an epidemic of youth violence (DiIulio, 1995; Fox, 1996). Twenty years later, it is clear that these dire warnings were unfounded. This rebuttal of the superpredator notion is not to claim that youth violence is not a societal problem worthy of attention. Along with violent crime rates in general (see Chapter 4), youth violence did increase dramatically in the late 1980s and early 1990s, but since 1993, the rate of youth violence has fallen to historical lows. Throughout this text, we have maintained the importance of understanding the source of information about crime and that criminological theories and criminal justice policy need to be supported by data. Understanding youth crime and youth violence is no different; as such we provide an overview of data sources that help to shape our understanding of youth violence. In addition to the three main sources of data reviewed in Chapter 3 (the UCR, self-report studies, and the NCVS), there are several additional data sources of particular value in the study of youth crime and violence.

You will recall that the Federal Bureau of Investigation's Uniform Crime Reports (UCR) provide the most commonly cited information about crime, including juvenile crime, in the United States. These data, reported annually by law enforcement agencies throughout the United States, include crimes known to the police, arrests, and/or crimes cleared by arrest, and they provide one picture of who offends and how offending changes over time. With the focus of this chapter on youth violence specifically, it is necessary to rely on data for which the age of the offender is known; in other words, arrest data. Relying upon UCR arrest data places several limitations on our ability to understand youth violence. First, given the group nature of youthful offending (Snyder & Sickmund, 1999), clearance rates may overestimate the number of offenses committed by youths (although not the number of offenders) relative to adults. Second, youthful offenders tend to be less sophisticated and thus are more likely to be caught and/or arrested for their transgressions than are older offenders, which thereby inflates the number of youthful offenders relative to older offenders.

The National Crime Victimization Survey (NCVS), while providing another source of information regarding the prevalence and frequency of violent crime victimization in the United States, is dependent on the victim's perception of the offender's age for information about violent offenders. To date, the NCVS data remain underutilized as a source of information about youth violence.

A key source of data on youth violence is self-report research. Since their inception in the 1950s, self-report studies have become a staple in the criminologist's toolkit. While many of these studies have been cross-sectional (at just one point in time), they have nonetheless provided us with a wealth of information about the correlates of youth crime in general and youth violence in particular. For the past 30 years, a growing number of longitudinal studies (both panel and cohort) have allowed for examination of trends in youth violence as well as examination of causal relationships.

Trends in youth violence can be examined with data from several nationally representative projects. The annual **Monitoring the Future (MTF) survey**, for example, assesses self-reported drug use and delinquency, as well as a host of other issues, among high-school seniors (e.g., Johnston et al., 2006); the **National Longitudinal Survey of Youth**, conducted by the Bureau of Labor Statistics (U.S. Department of Labor) gathers information about such behaviors as sexual activity, status offending, drug use and sales, delinquency (but not serious violence), and gang involvement; and the Centers for Disease Control and Prevention's **Youth Risk Behavior Surveillance Survey** includes various weapon-carrying and fighting items (e.g., Centers for Disease Control and Prevention, 2004). These surveys, however, do not include measures of more serious violent behavior. Several longitudinal panel studies such as the Causes and Correlates studies (see Chapter 3 of this text as well as Huizinga, et al., 2003; Loeber et al., 2003; Thornberry et al., 2003), the Seattle Social Development Study (Hawkins et al., 2003), the Montreal Study (Tremblay et al., 2003), and the G.R.E.A.T. studies (Esbensen et al., 2002, 2013b) do tap serious violence, but they do not use nationally representative samples, so caution must be used in generalizing findings from these studies.

DATA ISSUES

It is important to remember that self-report data reflect youths' reports of their actual behavior, while law enforcement data reflect societal response to youths' alleged behavior and victim data reflect the victim's perception of the offender and the crime (Hawkins et al., 1998; Hawkins et al., 2000). These data sources have different implications for the picture of adolescent offending: law enforcement estimates may exaggerate sex and race/ethnic gaps in offending (e.g., Hawkins et al., 2000; Snyder, 2003; Walker, Spohn, & DeLone, 2003), while self-report data may underestimate these gaps, especially if certain youths are more likely than others to underreport their violence involvement (Huizinga, 1991; Farrington, Loeber, & Stouthamer-Loeber, 2003).

The different limitations associated with these data sources about youth crime are especially important to keep in mind when thinking about the relationship between sex and/or race/ethnicity and youth violence. Debate still exists as to whether minorities' overrepresentation in the juvenile and criminal justice systems results from discrimination or from a tendency among minorities to commit more crime than their white counterparts (e.g., Wilbanks, 1987; Gibbons, 1997; Walker et al., 2003;). Influencing this debate is the finding that while racial/ethnic differences in offending appear in official statistics, fewer differences emerge in self-report data (Elliott & Ageton, 1980; Huizinga & Elliott, 1986; Walker et al., 2003). A similar debate exists about whether violence among females is on the rise, especially in comparison with males' rates. UCR data tend to reflect drastic increases in females' violent offending and a narrowing of the sex gap in violence, but the NCVS and self-report data show stable trends in both females' offending and the sex gap in offending (Steffensmeier et al., 2005; Heimer, Lauritsen, & Lynch, 2009; Lauritsen, Heimer, & Lynch, 2009).

YOUTH VIOLENCE TRENDS

Since 1980, juvenile violent crime, measured by both arrests and victim reports, increased until reaching a peak in 1993–4 and then steadily declined through 2012 (Snyder & Sickmund, 2006; Puzzanchera, 2013). For instance, by 2002, arrest rates for murder, forcible rape, and robbery had declined to or near their 1980 levels (Snyder, 2003). For robbery, there were 167.5 arrests per 100,000 juveniles aged 10–17 in 1980; the rate climbed to a high of 198.9 in 1995, and then declined steadily to a rate of 75.8 in 2003. This decline has continued, dropping by 31 percent between 2007 and 2011. Rates of simple assault arrests have a similar pattern, increasing from 299.8 per 100,000 in 1980 to a peak of 768 in 1997, and then declining to a rate of 712.0 in 2003 (Snyder & Sickmund, 2006). Juvenile arrest rates for simple assault have continued to decline, decreasing 19 percent from 2002 until 2011 (Puzzanchera, 2013).

Although data available from various self-report surveys are not directly comparable with law enforcement data, we are able to examine trends in some types of youth violence. The Centers for Disease Control and Prevention's (CDC) Youth Risk Behavior Survey (YRBS), conducted every two years beginning in 1991, is consistent with law enforcement data indicating that youth violence-related behaviors are on the decline. In this nationally representative survey, the percentage of high-school students who reported having been in a physical fight in the past year decreased from 43 percent in 1991 to 33 percent in 2003 and continued to decline through 2013, dropping to 24.7 percent (Centers for Disease Control and Prevention, 2004; 2014).

Data from the annual Monitoring the Future (MTF) survey on past 12-month offending by high-school seniors reveal different trends from 1982 to 2003, depending upon the violent behavior in question. For some offenses, the trend mirrors that found in UCR data, but others are not consistent. Further, the peak year of offending prevalence varies by offense. The percentage of youths who reported getting into a serious fight in the past 12 months, for example, decreased overall from 17.3 in 1982 to 14.3 in 2003, peaking at 19.7 percent in 1989. Robbery prevalence, however, increased overall from 2.3 percent in 1982 to 3.9 percent in 2003, peaking at 4.8 percent in 1994 (Pastore & Maguire, 1996; 2006).

PREVALENCE OF YOUTH VIOLENCE

According to the UCR data, offenders under the age of 18 accounted for approximately 11.7 percent of all violent crime arrests in 2012. A total of 1,020,334 juveniles were arrested in 2012 and approximately one-fourth (278,040) of these arrests were for Index offenses. As is the case with crime data in general, the majority of Index crime arrests of juveniles were for property offenses (47,237 arrests for violent crimes and 230,803 for property crimes). While this may appear to be a large number of juvenile violent offenders, this percentage actually represents a small proportion of the total juvenile population. To put these crime figures in context, the 2010 U.S. Census reported there were approximately 33.6 million juveniles aged 10 to 17 living in the United States. This means that less than one percent of juveniles were arrested for an Index offense in 2012, and only 0.14 percent of youths were arrested for a violent crime.

When UCR data are disaggregated by sex, males continue to be arrested for crimes at a higher rate than females. Among juvenile arrestees, males account for approximately 71 percent of all arrests, but 81 percent of violent crime arrests. This gender gap is less pronounced for Index property offenses, for which females account for 35 percent of the juvenile arrests in 2012. NCVS and self-report data also suggest that the gender gap in violent offending is relatively stable, with males committing a disproportionate amount of violent crimes. With respect to racial/ethnic differences in offending, it appears that young minorities' arrest rates are consistently higher than are whites' but that the decreases in serious violent offending since 1993 have been greater for African-American juveniles than for white juveniles (that is, the racial gap is narrowing).

Prevalence rates of violence are generally higher in self-reported data. This is due not only to the fact that many youths are not arrested for illegal behaviors they have committed, but also to the different behaviors emphasized in the different data sources; that is, some self-reported violent behaviors may not be as serious as those that would result in arrest (e.g., Huizinga & Elliott, 1986). High school seniors who participated in the 1995 Monitoring the Future survey reported whether they had engaged in a variety of violent behaviors over the past 12 months (Pastore & Maguire, 2006). The percentage of students who had been violent ranged from three percent who had hit an instructor or supervisor and four percent who had robbed someone to nearly 20 percent who had engaged with a group in a fight with another group. About 12 percent reported having seriously hurt someone and 15 percent had been in a serious fight.

Although arrests for violence are not common in the youth population as a whole (less than 1 percent, as estimated from arrest data), engaging in violent behavior is not a rare occurrence; almost one in four respondents in one large school-based survey reported committing a violent offense (Esbensen et al., 2010). Findings from this study, as is the case with arrest data, reveal that prevalence rates vary by both sex and race/ethnicity, with females and white youths reporting the lowest levels of offending. One might reasonably conclude that the depiction of the "dark stranger" (i.e., male, minority youths) is indeed an accurate reflection of the serious violent juvenile offender. However, the picture is a bit blurred: while males and racial/ethnic minorities tend to be overrepresented among violent offenders (regardless of measurement), the differences in self-report studies are not as great as those reported in the UCR data.

SCHOOL VIOLENCE

School shootings have received considerable media attention since the Columbine massacre in 1999. Two students (Eric Harris and Dylan Klebold) entered the school the morning of April 20 and shot and killed indiscriminately. All told, 12 students and one teacher (plus the two offenders) were killed

Evidence markers are seen in a first-grade classroom inside Sandy Hook Elementary School in Newtown, Connecticut. In December of 2012, Adam Lanza gunned down 20 first graders and six educators with a semiautomatic rifle at the school.

CREDIT: AP Photo/ Connecticut State Police.

that day but the consequences of that shooting continue. Columbine marks the end of innocence with regard to school safety. Subsequent to that event, schools have engaged in practices of **target hardening** (installing metal detectors, hiring safety personnel, establishing active shooter drills) and adopted programs attempting to reduce school violence. Not long after Columbine, shootings (not all fatal and not all involving multiple victims) occurred at other schools in the United States as well as in other nations (including Germany, Finland, and Russia). As we finalize this chapter for publication (December 2014), one source identifies more than 150 shootings on school property in the U.S. since the Columbine massacre (http://en.wikipedia. org/wiki/List_of_school_shootings). According to the list of school shootings on the Wikipedia website, there were 20 shootings on school property between 2000 and 2005, 36 between 2006 and 2010, and 96 between 2011 and November, 2014. In December 2012, a particularly disturbing shooting occurred at an elementary school. Many people, including President Obama, thought that the massacre at Sandy Hook Elementary School (in which 20 children and six adult staff members were fatally shot) would serve as a rallying point that would produce changes in gun laws and make it more difficult for individuals to obtain semiautomatic and/or assault weapons. To date, no such effect has been witnessed.

How Safe are American Schools?

With an apparent increase in school shootings, how safe are American schools? This should be a relatively easy question to answer, but it is not. The answer depends in large part on the type of behavior in question. While public and political perceptions about school violence are driven by the types of school shootings detailed above, most school victimizations involve relatively minor property and personal offenses (e.g., theft and minor assault). It is the multi-victim school shootings, however, that, while statistically rare, remain newsworthy because students are indeed killed on school property. The question remains: How common an occurrence is this? While there has been an increase in the number of school shootings, most of these events do not result in deaths of students or adults. Since 1999, the number of homicides committed on school property has fluctuated from the low teens (14 in both 1999 and 2000 school years) to a high of 33 in 1998–9 (this includes the Columbine massacre) and 32 in 2006–7 (see Table 14.1).

TABLE 14.1 Homicides on School Property

	Homicides at school	Number of Youth Homicides
1998–9	33	1,777
1999–2000	14	1,567
2000–1	14	1,509
2001–2	16	1,498
2002–3	18	1,553
2003–4	23	1,474
2004–5	22	1,554
2005–6	21	1,697
2006–7	32	1,803
2007–8	21	1,744
2008–9	17	1,605
2009–10	19	1,410
2010–11 (Last year for which data were available)	11	1,336

Source: Robers et al. 2014.

While the thought of children being killed at school is disturbing, we can assess these data from at least two perspectives. On the one hand, when students are killed on school property we can consider the situation outlandish and an indication that society is failing its children by not providing a safe learning environment. Or, we can marvel at the fact that, relatively speaking, so few children are killed on school property in a given year. Let us consider these murders in relativistic terms. In 2008–9 school year, for instance, 17 students were murdered on school property. During the same period, 1,605 youths were killed away from school. In other words; for every child killed on school property, 94 were killed away from school!

Bullying

School shootings such as those at Columbine and Sandy Hook have received considerable media attention but the reality is that schools have become less violent places since the early 1990s. The rate of student-reported nonfatal crimes has declined during this period and the violent crime victimization rate in 2005 was less than half the rate reported in 1992 (Dinkes et al. 2007:16). In spite of the decline of more serious forms of in-school victimization, there does not appear to be a similar decline in bullying, as evidenced in part by the growing interest in bullying victimization and bullying prevention programs (Olweus, 1993; Baldry & Farrington, 1999; Olweus et al., 1999; Wong et al., 2008; Carbone-Lopez et al., 2010).

While victimization prevalence rates vary by type of school (i.e., public versus private, urban versus rural, middle versus high school), the most common forms of victimization in all schools are property offenses and nonserious forms of assault, including bullying (DeVoe et al., 2004). Given the prevalence of bullying victimization, it is important to assess the consequences of being victimized in this manner.

As you might expect, there is a lack of agreement as to what constitutes bullying. However, regardless of definitional issues, there appears to be consensus that preventing bullying is a desirable goal and that reducing these "minor" infractions may well have an impact on other, more serious forms of victimization. Olweus and colleagues (1999:19–20), for instance, reported that their bullying prevention program was associated with not only reductions in bullying behavior but other problem behaviors as well (e.g., fighting, vandalism, and truancy). While we refer to acts of bullying as "minor" infractions, this is not intended to minimize the magnitude or the effects of these experiences. In fact, some research suggests that there are serious consequences for victims of bullying; bullied students have been reported to suffer from a lowering of self-esteem, to be frequently absent from school (in order to avoid victimization), and to feel unsafe and insecure in the school setting (e.g., Andreou, 2000; Berthold & Hoover, 2000; Rigby, 2003; Smokowski & Kopasz, 2005; Esbensen & Carson, 2009; Lovegrove & Cornell, 2014).

Definition and Measurement of Bullying

It is virtually impossible to disentangle measurement from definition, and this is certainly the case with the topic of bullying (see Highlight 14.1). While there is general consensus that bullying refers to victimization that occurs within the school setting, there is a lack of agreement as to what constitutes bullying and how it should be measured. The definition introduced by the Norwegian researcher, Dan Olweus, in 1993 has gained considerable acceptance. That definition includes the following criteria: (1) physically harming a person (e.g., hitting, kicking, pushing) or making fun of, excluding, and/or spreading rumors about a person; (2) the victimization must occur repeatedly over time; and (3) the victims do not have equal strength or power to the bully (see also Olweus, 1996; Forero et al., 1999; Berthold & Hoover, 2000; Sourander et al., 2000; Eslea et al., 2003; Solberg et al., 2007).

A range of behaviors comprises bullying and researchers have adopted different strategies for measuring this form of behavior. One common approach has been to assume that students (and teachers) have a shared understanding of what bullying means. For researchers, this means asking a single generic question (i.e., Have you been bullied?) and allowing the respondents to provide their own definition. This notion that there is a shared understanding of what constitutes bullying appears to be ill-founded; a number of researchers have explored this very issue and have found a lack of consensus among students as to what it means to bully or to be bullied (e.g., Arora and Thompson, 1987; Swain, 1998; Boulton et al., 2002). A different approach provides students with a list of behaviorally specific questions that includes both direct and indirect forms of victimization (i.e., emotional and psychological forms of aggression in addition to physical aggression). A growing number of researchers rely upon this latter approach (e.g., Andreou, 2000; Bond et al., 2001; Boulton et al., 2002; Seals & Young, 2003; Unnever & Cornell, 2003; Mouttapa et al., 2004; Ttofi & Farrington, 2008; Esbensen & Carson, 2009; Carbone-Lopez et al., 2010). Highlight 14.1 serves as an example of the consequences of reliance on different definitions.

Another issue surrounding bullying is the notion of repeated victimization. Some researchers consider one bullying experience to be sufficient to consider the student a bullying victim (e.g., Forero et al., 1999; Andreou, 2000; Berthold & Hoover, 2000; Mouttapa et al., 2004; Solberg et al., 2007). Others, however, maintain that only students who are victims of multiple instances of bullying should be considered bullying victims (e.g., Baldry & Farrington, 1999; Bond et al., 2001; Eslea et al., 2003). To date, there are a limited number of studies in which the researchers have relied upon multiple measures of victimization across time to define and measure bully victimization (notable exceptions are Bond et al., 2001, Esbensen & Carson, 2009, and Carbone-Lopez et al., 2010). While Olweus (1993) maintains that repeated victimizations across time are necessary for a victim to be bullied, much of the bullying research has relied upon cross-sectional research designs and has thereby limited the ability to examine the issue of victimization across time.

These definitional and measurement issues are more than mere academic debate; of particular concern is the fact that these different criteria for defining and measuring bullying victimization lead to vastly different estimates regarding the magnitude and distribution of the problem. Of added interest is whether these definitional issues affect the consequences of this form of victimization.

The effect of definition on prevalence rates can be illustrated by the following two estimates. One group of researchers obtained prevalence estimates utilizing both a list of 16 specific behaviors and a single generic question (Stockdale et al., 2002). They reported that 76 percent of sampled students had experienced verbal bullying and 66 percent physical bullying at least once in a one-week time frame. In response to the generic question, only 34 percent indicated that they had been bullied. The checklist approach identified twice as many victims of bullying than did the single generic question. In general, reliance upon a single item tends to produce lower prevalence estimates of bullying victimization than does inclusion of behaviorally specific questions about bullying.

In addition to the actual question(s) used to measure bullying, consideration must also be given to the time frame during which the reported behavior occurred. Forero et al. (1999), for instance, provided students with a definition of bullying similar to that of Olweus and asked whether students had been

HIGHLIGHT 14.1 DEFINING BULLYING AND ITS CONSEQUENCES

One important issue confronting researchers and policy-makers is the need to reach consensus regarding what constitutes bullying and bullying victimization; to date, multiple definitions and associated measures permeate the literature. This lack of a common standard has produced confusion concerning the prevalence of bullying as well as disagreement about what constitutes bullying. In this highlight we provide a detailed summary of a study (Esbensen and Carson, 2009) that focused specifically on the issue of defining bullying and the consequences of using different definitional criteria.

The authors examined the prevalence and consequences of bullying using data from a three-wave longitudinal panel study consisting of slightly more than 1,100 American students attending 14 schools in nine cities across four states. The first wave of data was collected in the fall of 2004, the second wave in the spring of 2005 and the third wave in the fall of 2005. With three waves of data, they were able to assess the consequences of bullying victimization by temporally correcting for victimization and attitudinal measures. The study also included both a single-item question and behaviorally specific measures of bullying victimization. The authors sought to address three specific questions:

1. To what extent does a single, generic bullying item capture bullying victimization when contrasted with four behaviorally specific questions that tap both indirect and direct forms of victimization?

2. Do the consequences of bullying victimization vary by definition and/or the type of measurement (i.e., generic item versus specific items)?

3. To what extent does repeated victimization influence the consequences of bullying victimization?

Study participants were disproportionately female (54 percent) and the sample participants were ethnically diverse: 39 percent were Hispanic, 35 percent were white, and 12 percent were African American. The age of the sample at Wave 1 ranges from 10 to 15 (students were in grades 6 through 9 at Wave 1).

Bully Victimization and Victimization Typology

Bullying victimization was measured via four questions addressing both direct and indirect forms of bullying. Students were asked to indicate how my times they had experienced the following during the preceding three months:

1) been attacked or threatened at school; 2) had mean rumors or lies spread about you at school; 3) had sexual jokes, comments, or gestures made to you at school; and 4) been made fun of at school because of your looks or the way you talk. In addition to these behaviorally specific questions, students were also asked how many times during the prior three months they had been bullied at school.

Students were assigned to one of three groups on the basis of their responses to the behaviorally specific questions: 1) *nonvictims*—those who reported no instances of bullying victimization across all three waves; 2) *intermittent victims*—those who reported one or more instances of being bullied during one data collection period or those who were bullied once during at least two separate reporting periods; and 3) *repeat victims*—those who were bullied two or more times during two or three reporting periods. A similar process was used to group students using the single item about being bullied.

These groupings or typologies allow the researchers to assess the effect of different levels of bully victimization on the consequences of being bullied. In other words, does bullying that occurs on multiple occasions across multiple waves of data produce more negative consequences than does intermittent victimization? And, importantly, does a behaviorally specific composite measure of bullying victimization produce different results than a single item measure?

The authors found substantially different prevalence estimates depending upon the definition applied. While 71.9 percent of the sample reported no bullying victimization according to the single-item measure, only 18.4 percent of students reported no bullying victimization across all three waves when the behaviorally specific measure was used.

Consequences of Victimization

To assess the consequences of bullying victimization Esbensen and Carson examined psychological well-being (e.g., self-esteem, empathy, self-efficacy, and sense of powerlessness) and social adjustment (e.g., commitment to positive and negative peers, conflict resolution skills, school commitment, fear of school victimization, perceived risk of school victimization, and assessment of school safety).

They found a number of differences based on victimization status. With the single generic measure, there were no differences between the three types of victims (nonvictims,

HIGHLIGHT 14.1 *continued*

intermittent, and repeat victims) on mental health outcomes. Three of the school-related outcomes, however, reveal differences, with the repeat victims reporting more fear of victimization in school, higher perceived risk of victimization, and a less safe school environment. When they used the behavior-specific measure they found differences on two of the mental health indicators (self-esteem and empathy) and five of the social adjustment scales (the same three school-related measures for the single item plus negative peer commitment and conflict resolution). The repeat victims reported lower self-esteem, higher empathy, greater commitment to negative peers, less use of conflict resolution skills, higher fear and perceived risk of victimization, and lower levels of perceived school safety.

Summary

The authors found that use of a single generic item to measure bullying victimization produces considerably lower estimates of the magnitude of the problem than does the use of a composite measure of behaviorally specific questions. Given the ambiguity of the term "bullied", it appears that many students underreport their actual victimization by not considering some types of behaviors as forms of bullying. For whatever reason, only 28 percent of students in this sample reported that they had been bullied (using the single generic item) compared with 82 percent when the four behaviorally specific questions were used to define being bullied.

The authors highlight that there was a general pattern of negative consequences associated with being bullied regardless of how bullying was measured. The consequences of being bullied, however, were greater for those students who reported victimization across multiple time periods. To date, relatively little attention has been given to the effect of repeated victimization in spite of the fact that Olweus (1996) and others argue that to classify victimization as bullying, it must occur repeatedly. Esbensen and Carson suggest that this lack of attention may be due to a relative absence of panel data in prior studies of bullying. They further caution that given the reliance upon cross-sectional research designs, much of the prior research on bullying may have underestimated the effects of being bullied.

---

bullied and/or whether they had been bullied *within the last term.* Using a similar technique Kaltiala-Heino and colleagues (2000) found that only five percent of girls and six percent of boys reported being bullied *on a weekly basis.* Such differences in measurement can produce drastically different results.

Correlates of Bullying Victimization

Prior research has found that bullying victimization, as with victimization in general, is not distributed evenly across the general youth population; rather, it appears to vary by sex, race/ethnicity, and age/grade level. Males, members of racial/ethnic minority groups, and students in middle school tend to experience more victimization than females, whites, and students in higher grades. The general descriptive research indicates that racial/ethnic minorities experience higher rates of school victimization.

Research suggests that bullying is more likely to take place in the early grades and tends to decrease at higher grades. In 2003, for example, 14 percent of sixth graders, 7 percent of ninth graders, and 2 percent of twelfth graders reported that they had been bullied at school (DeVoe et al., 2004). The use of physical aggression also decreases at higher grades, changing from aggressive to more passive, verbal forms (Olweus, 1993). Stockdale and colleagues (2002) account for this change in forms of bullying by suggesting that children find other ways to deal with anger and frustration as they grow older.

One of the most widely studied correlates of bullying is sex; the majority of studies find that boys experience higher rates of involvement in bullying incidents than do girls (Rigby & Slee, 1991; Olweus, 1993; Baldry & Farrington, 1999; Smokowski & Kopasz, 2005), although Carbone-Lopez and her colleagues (2010) noted that boys and girls are likely to experience different forms of bullying victimizations. Boys were more likely to be victims of direct and physical forms of bullying, while girls were more likely to be victims of indirect forms of bullying such as spreading rumors and excluding others from activities and groups.

While sex and age have been widely studied, the role of race/ethnicity in bullying victimization has not received the same degree of attention and findings to date provide inconsistent patterns. Two studies, for example, reported no differences in bullying victimization between African-American and white students (Kaufman et al., 1998 and Seals & Young, 2003) while two other studies found race/ethnic differences. According to the School Crime and Safety report in 2003, white students (8 percent) were more likely than Hispanic students (6 percent) to report being bullied. Mouttapa and colleagues (2004) reported that Asians were the most frequently victimized ethnic group in their study. Clearly, one contributing factor to the inconsistency of findings related to race/ethnicity is the lack of representation of multiple racial/ethnic groups in the different studies.

Consequences of Bullying Victimization

Research suggests that being the victim of bullying can have serious consequences for the individual, including contributing to low self-esteem, depression and anxiety, and avoidance behavior (e.g., Olweus, 1993; Austin & Joseph, 1996; Rigby, 2003; Esbensen & Carson, 2009; Lovegrove & Cornell, 2014). O'Moore (2000), for example, reported that victims of bullying can experience feelings of rejection, loneliness, and, in extreme cases, are at increased risk for suicide. While a number of researchers have found that bullying victims report low self-esteem (e.g., Olweus, 1993; Salmon et al., 1998; Andreou, 2001), these findings have been based on cross-sectional research. The possibility, therefore, remains that it is equally likely that students with low self-esteem are targeted to be the victims of bullying. When students are victimized, it may negatively impact their feelings of safety at school, reduce their

Pallbearers wearing anti-bullying T-shirts carry the casket of Rebecca Sedwick, age 12, to a waiting hearse. Polk County (Florida) Sheriff's Office investigators said they believe Sedwick took her own life following months of bullying.

CREDIT: AP Photo/Brian Blanco.

willingness to attend school, and thereby lower their academic achievement. Even minor forms of victimization, such as minor theft and being bullied, have been linked to these consequences. As such, minor victimization, although not very newsworthy, should not be ignored.

In a review article, Rigby (2003) categorized the consequences of bullying victimization into four types: (1) low psychological well-being, (2) poor social adjustment, (3) psychological distress, and (4) physical unwellness (Rigby, 2003:584). Other research has found that victims of bullying tend to be vulnerable, insecure, feel socially isolated, and have difficulty asserting themselves among peers (Perry et al., 1988; Slee & Rigby, 1993; Schuster, 1996). In general, research has revealed negative effects of bullying on the victim, including depression, loneliness, difficulties with school, and low self-esteem (e.g., Olweus, 1993; Austin & Joseph, 1996; Salmon et al., 1998; O'Moore, 2000; Andreou, 2001; Rigby 2003).

Strategies to Reduce School Violence

Violence at school, be it bullying or more serious forms of interpersonal violence, negatively impacts the learning environment. Most of the crime that occurs at school is relatively minor, ranging from minor theft, petty assault, and indirect forms of bullying (i.e., name-calling, teasing, and intimidation). Serious offenses, including felony assault, murder, and assaults with firearms, are relatively rare occurrences. Given that most adolescents spend a considerable amount of time at school, it is important to create a safe environment that fosters intellectual and social growth. A number of programs and policies have been adopted in attempts to make schools safer. The question is whether some programs or strategies are more effective than others.

Schools have become a focal point for general prevention programming and according to a national survey conducted by Gottfredson and colleagues (2000), the average middle school provided 14 different and unique violence, drug, and other social problem prevention programs. School administrators are tasked with determining which programs or strategies to adopt. Fortunately, a number of evaluations have been conducted and there is a growing body of knowledge about what works, what is promising, and what does not work. School-based prevention programs can be grouped into two large categories: environmental change strategies and individual-level change strategies (for an excellent review, consult Gottfredson, 2001).

Environmental Change Strategies

Environmental change strategies attempt to reduce problem behaviors by addressing organizational characteristics of the school. By changing the environment, the argument is that individual behavior will be impacted. These types of strategies include a wide range of approaches. One approach is to *build school capacity* by altering the decision-making processes or authority structures in the school. Schools are often organized in a hierarchical manner with the principal making decisions. Building school capacity might include creation of a team to diagnose school problems, formulate goals and objectives, and then develop solutions. In this manner, the hierarchical decision-making process is replaced by a participatory management orientation in which administrators, teachers, staff, students, and parents all participate in goal setting and decision making.

Another approach may involve *setting norms* for behavior. This might include schoolwide efforts to redefine norms and promote positive behavior. Examples of this approach include "red ribbon week" and schoolwide anti-bullying campaigns. Another environmental change strategy is *class management*, that is, the use of instructional methods to increase student engagement in the learning process, including cooperative and experiential learning. Rather than a focus on information dissemination through lectures, teachers incorporate team/group learning strategies as well as active learning strategies that engage students in the learning process. Cooperative learning strategies, for instance, provide initial instruction by teachers after which students are divided into smaller workgroups of four or five students of mixed skill levels; students then help each other learn.

Some school districts have also explored the *regrouping of schools* to address school safety. For example, some schools have reorganized classes or grades to create smaller learning units or different mixes of students. Rather than organizing grade levels by age as is the norm in most schools, a teacher may have a classroom of 25 students that is a combination of fourth, fifth, and sixth graders. This allows the older students to become mentors to the younger students and simultaneously disrupts the traditional age segregation that occurs in many school settings.

Individual Change Strategies

Individual change strategies include programs or strategies that instruct students, strive to change behavior patterns, employ counselors to work with individual students, engage students as peer mentors, or introduce recreational after-school programs. Programs classified as individual change strategies are relatively common in schools, in part because they can be easily packaged, that is, the program developers promote these programs as affecting particular problems. While some of these packaged programs targeted drug use/abuse, notably DARE and Life Skills Training (LST), others targeted victimization (Teens, Crime and the Community) and gang involvement (G.R.E.A.T.). These stand-alone programs are usually delivered to classrooms of students with the goal of changing the students' attitudes and behaviors regarding the targeted outcome. Highlight 14.2 provides an overview of one of these types of individual change strategies (the Gang Resistance Education and Training—G.R.E.A.T. —program) and associated evaluations of that program.

HIGHLIGHT 14.2 EVALUATION OF THE GANG RESISTANCE EDUCATION AND TRAINING (G.R.E.A.T.) PROGRAM

The Gang Resistance Education and Training (G.R.E.A.T.) program is a gang and delinquency prevention program delivered by law enforcement officers within a school setting. Developed as a local program in 1991 by Phoenix-area law enforcement agencies, the program quickly spread throughout the United States. The original G.R.E.A.T. program operated as a nine-lesson lecture-based curriculum taught primarily in middle-school settings. Results from the National Evaluation of the G.R.E.A.T. program (1995–2001) found that the program had an effect on several mediating variables (factors commonly identified as risk factors) associated with gang membership and delinquency but found no differences between G.R.E.A.T. and non-G.R.E.A.T. youths in terms of these behaviors (i.e., gang membership and involvement in delinquent behavior).

On the basis, in part, of these findings, the G.R.E.A.T. program underwent a critical review that resulted in substantial program modifications. The revised curriculum consists of 13 lessons aimed at teaching youths the life skills (e.g., communication and refusal skills, as well as conflict resolution and anger management techniques) thought necessary to prevent involvement in gang behavior and delinquency. Currently, the program is taught in middle schools across the U.S. as well as in other countries. In school districts with school-resource officers, the G.R.E.A.T. program is generally taught by the SROs. In other jurisdictions, law enforcement officers deliver the program as part of their assignment in community relations divisions, while elsewhere officers teach the program on an overtime basis. Regardless of officers' assignments, all instructors must complete G.R.E.A.T. Officer Training and be certified prior to their assignment to teach in local schools. This training (one week for officers with prior teaching experience and two weeks for others), in addition to introducing the officers to the program, includes sections on gang trends, issues associated with the transition from an emphasis on enforcement to one of prevention, middle-school student developmental stages, and teaching and classroom management techniques. The program's two main goals are:

1. To help youths avoid gang membership, violence, and criminal activity.

2. To help youths develop a positive relationship with law enforcement.

In 2006, following a competitive peer review process, the National Institute of Justice awarded the University of Missouri-St. Louis funding to conduct the National Evaluation of the G.R.E.A.T. program. The evaluation consists of both process and outcome components that include student surveys, classroom observations in G.R.E.A.T. and non-G.R.E.A.T. classrooms, surveys of teachers, school administrators, and law enforcement officers, interviews with G.R.E.A.T. officers and G.R.E.A.T. supervisors, and observations of G.R.E.A.T. Officer Training.

The evaluation design can best be described as an experimental longitudinal panel design, that is, classrooms in each of the 31 participating schools in seven cities were randomly assigned to the treatment (i.e., G.R.E.A.T.) or control condition (i.e., no program exposure), and students in these classrooms were scheduled to complete six waves of questionnaires (pre- and post-tests followed by four annual surveys). Thus, the final sample of students would be followed through their school experiences from sixth or seventh grade through tenth or eleventh grade. Importantly, all students in the selected classrooms were eligible to participate in the evaluation. A total of 4,905 students were enrolled in the 195 participating classrooms (102 G.R.E.A.T. and 93 control classes) in the 31 middle schools at the beginning of the data collection process.

One year after program exposure, positive program effects were found; students completing the G.R.E.A.T. program had lower rates of gang affiliation than did students in the control group. Additionally, the G.R.E.A.T. students reported a number of more prosocial attitudes, including more positive attitudes to the police, than did the control students. There were, however, no statistically significant differences between the two groups of students on self-reported delinquency.

These results reflect only short-term program effects. An important question remains: Are these short-term program effects sustained across time? To address this question, the authors continued to survey this group of students for three more years (most of the students were in tenth or eleventh grade at the time of the last survey administration). Remarkably (in light of the rather small program dosage of 13 lessons that averaged 40 minutes per lesson), the analyses revealed results similar to the one-year post-program effects, albeit

HIGHLIGHT 14.2 *continued*

with smaller effect sizes. Across four years post program the following ten positive program effects were found:

1. More positive attitudes to police (ES = .058)

2. More positive attitudes about police in classrooms (ES = .144)

3. Less positive attitudes about gangs (ES = .094)

4. More use of refusal skills (ES = .049)

5. Higher collective efficacy (ES = .096)

6. Less use of hitting neutralizations (ES = .079)

7. Less anger (ES = .049)

8. Lower rates of gang membership (24 percent reduction in odds)

9. Higher levels of altruism (ES = .058)

10. Less risk seeking (ES = .053)

These effects are all in the direction of beneficial program effects, but again, the effect sizes are modest (some would say small). Importantly, although the other comparisons between the two groups were not statistically significant, all indicated more prosocial attitudes and behaviors among the G.R.E.A.T. students.

For more information about the evaluations of the GREAT program, consult following sources: Esbensen et al., (2013a) or Esbensen et al., (2013b).

What Works and How Do We Know

There are a number of clearinghouses that provide information about programs and their relative effectiveness. The U.S. Department of Justice, for instance, maintains a website (www.crimesolutions.gov) that provides information about "evidence-based" programs that are effective in preventing or reducing various forms of illegal activity. Evaluation research results are used to classify programs as effective, promising, or not effective (or some similar sort of ranking). The various clearinghouses rely on slightly different criteria, which contributes to some confusion because the same program may receive different assessments of effectiveness by the different ranking systems. As a general rule, however, the following criteria are included:

1. There should be a logic model or program theory that establishes a correlation between the program and the intended outcome;
2. The program should be delivered before the intended outcome has occurred (assuming the objective is prevention and not intervention);
3. There must be both treatment and comparison groups;
4. Preferably the comparison groups meet standards associated with quasi-experimental conditions that allow for the control of other factors that might affect the desired outcome; and
5. Random assignment is highly desired (but rarely attained).

Evaluation results tend to suggest that the environmental change strategies hold promise (deemed effective by some). For example, schools that have introduced participatory management practices have resulted in higher teacher morale and less disorder in the school. Likewise, schools that have instituted clear rules and reward structures and/or have incorporated cooperative learning strategies experience less disorder. Most of the individual-level change strategies, however, are rated as inconclusive or promising at best.

Summary of Bullying and School Violence

Students and teachers experience a considerable amount of "minor" victimization on school property. Most of this victimization is in the form of minor property crime and minor assault. Serious violence, including assault with weapons and murder, is more likely to occur away from school. All in all, schools continue to be relatively safe havens for students and school personnel. Contrary to popular perception, rates of school violence have been relatively stable for the past 20 years and bullying is a common form of victimization in schools. As is the case with most social problems, there is no "silver bullet" to address the problem of school crime, but environmental change strategies hold more promise than individual change strategies.

YOUTH GANGS

Commensurate with the increase in youth violence in the late 1980s and early 1990s was the growing presence of youth gangs. In addition to the violence associated with youth gangs, the 1990s also brought renewed interest to the topic of youth gangs as "gangsta rap" grew in popularity and mega-gangs such as the "Bloods" and "Crips" appeared in cities across the country. The media attention afforded youth gangs gave citizens the impression that the nation's cities were "gang-infested" and that "drive-bys" and gang-related drug sales and homicides occurred on a daily basis. While the level of concern may have been exaggerated, there was certainly reason for a healthy level of attention to the problem of youth gangs. The increase in gang violence was quite real; for instance, the annual number of gang-motivated homicides in Chicago increased from 51 to 240 between 1987 and 1994, while gang-related homicides more than doubled (387 to 803) in Los Angeles County from 1987 to 1992 (Howell, 1999).

As was the case with youth violence in general, there was also growing concern about a "new breed of female offenders" that was increasingly violent and involved in gang crime (e.g., Chesney-Lind 1993; Chesney-Lind, Shelden, & Joe, 1996). In part because of this concern with a new violent female offender, one positive outgrowth has been an increased focus on and interest in the role of girls in gangs and violence (e.g., Esbensen & Deschenes, 1998; Fleisher, 1998; Miller, 1998; Chesney-Lind & Hagedorn, 1999; Deschenes & Esbensen, 1999a, 1999b; Miller, 2001; Moore & Hagedorn, 2001; Peterson et al., 2001; Maxson & Whitlock, 2002; Peterson & Carson, 2012; Weerman, 2012). In addition to the "discovery" of female involvement in gangs, gangs were also "discovered" in rural and nonurban communities during the 1990s, which led to greater diversity of gang membership, including the emergence of racially heterogeneous gangs (e.g., Starbuck, Howell, & Lindquist, 2001; Howell, Moore, & Egley, 2002). With the link between gangs and violence (e.g., Klein, Maxson, & Cunningham, 1991; Battin-Pearson et al., 1998; Esbensen & Winfree, 1998; Howell & Decker, 1999; Decker, 2000; Esbensen, Peterson, Freng, & Taylor, 2002; Thornberry et al., 2003), youth gangs received considerable attention from researchers and law enforcement during the 1990s and into the twenty-first century.

It is important to remember, however, that collective youth violence is not a new phenomenon. If you recall Shakespeare's *Romeo and Juliet*, his description of the Montagues and Capulets resembles adolescent youth gangs of today. And, historical accounts are replete with mentions and descriptions of troublesome youth groups. Youth gangs captured the interest of criminologists, law enforcement, and the public in general during the 1950s and early 1960s as is evidenced by the wide popularity of the movie *West Side Story*. This focus on youth gangs in the 1950s and 1960s led to the production of some classic criminological work (e.g., Cohen, 1955; Miller, 1958; Cloward & Ohlin, 1960; Short & Strodbeck, 1966) prior to a decline in the youth gang problem. Interest in youth gangs and their associated behavior tends to wax and wane across time (Bookin-Weiner & Horowitz, 1983) and following a brief hiatus, gangs re-emerged as a social problem in the late 1980s and 1990s.

Since the early 1990s, there has been an explosion of research on gangs. In this section, we take a closer look at youths who are gang-affiliated and examine some of the common stereotypes associated with youth gangs. For instance, to what extent are gang youths different from nongang youths? Are gang members more violent than other youths who also engage in violence, but are not gang members? Are there identifiable differences that can predict who will become gang members, and thereby suggest strategies by which to prevent youths from joining gangs? We begin with a brief review of the history of youth gangs in the United States.

History of Gang Research in the United States

Prior to the 1990s, surprisingly little was known about the prevalence of youth gangs in society. While gang research had been conducted since the early twentieth century, there were no national surveys and there was no national clearinghouse to gather and distribute information about gangs. In 1975, Walter Miller addressed this lack of information and conducted a survey of law enforcement agencies in twelve cities. He found that six of these agencies reported gang problems in their locales and, on the basis of this survey, he estimated that there were between 28,500 and 81,500 gang members in 760 to 2,700 gangs in the United States. This rather imprecise estimate was somewhat refined when Miller conducted another study in 1982 in which he interviewed representatives of 173 police agencies in 26 sites and projected there were 97,940 gang members in 2,285 gangs in 286 cities. These early efforts by Miller laid the foundation for subsequent national surveys (W. Miller, 2001) that resulted in creation of the National Youth Gang Center (NYGC) in 1996, which was renamed the National Gang Center (NGC) a few years later. The NYGC was tasked with conducting annual surveys of law enforcement agencies across the United States. From 1996 through 2001, when there were an estimated 846,428 gang members in 30,818 gangs, the NYGC reported a steady decline in the prevalence of youth gangs (Egley, 2002; Egley et al.,

2004). Since 2001, however, the NYGC has reported an increase in the number of youth gangs and gang members, although not yet reaching the 1996 peak (Egley & O'Donnell, 2008).

The NYGC documented that gangs existed in every state in the United States and in a wide range of communities, including small towns and rural counties. Without historical data, however, it is not possible to conclude that the appearance of gangs in these areas is a new phenomenon rather than the discovery of a pre-existing problem. During the 1990s there was a concern that the Chicago and Los Angeles gangs were establishing "satellite gangs" throughout the United States. An important finding from a survey of law enforcement officers refuted this common belief (Maxson, 1998); gangs were not establishing satellite affiliates across the country; rather the proliferation of gangs was attributable mainly to social and familial movement (i.e., 57 percent of law enforcement respondents mentioned social reasons for gang member migration, compared with 32 percent who indicated that the gang members' mobility was attributed to illegal attractions in the new city). An important finding from this research was that gangs developed in response to local conditions, not as part of a national conspiracy to establish drug distribution networks. In a 2006 publication utilizing NYGC data, Egley and Ritz replicated these earlier findings reported by Maxson.

Some Methodological Concerns

Much gang research can be described as ethnographic examinations (in-depth interviews and/or observation) of particular gangs or gang members that provide invaluable information about youth gangs (e.g. Hagedorn, 1988; Vigil, 1988; Campbell, 1991; Moore, 1991; Decker & Van Winkle, 1996; Fleisher, 1998; J. Miller, 2001). Some commentators, however, have questioned the extent to which research conducted in particular cities and usually involving members of only one gang can be generalized to other gangs and other cities. Some concern has also been raised about the validity of data collected by white, middle-aged researchers attempting to understand gang members who are primarily young and members of racial/ethnic minorities. Similarly, Campbell (1986) and others suggest that male researchers have systematically excluded females. Others have expressed concern about the potential impact the presence of the researcher might have on the subjects' behavior. To address some of these questions, gang research today is characterized by multiple methodologies and reliance on multiple data sources to better understand youth gangs in a wide range of locations, not just in the USA but internationally.

Law enforcement statistics provide information about the nature and extent of youth gangs and associated violence for both local and national settings. However, as is the case with police data in general, definitional and measurement issues arise, including the not-so-simple task of identifying gang members and gang-related crime. The absence of uniform definitions makes it difficult to make comparisons across jurisdictions (Bursik & Grasmick, 1995b; Curry et al., 1996). While definitional differences can influence the estimates provided by police data, Maxson and Klein (1990, 1996) found that the characteristics of gang-related crime did not differ substantially with different definitions.

Beginning with the Causes and Correlates Program (see Chapter 3) in the late 1980s (e.g., Bjerregaard & Smith, 1993; Esbensen & Huizinga, 1993; Thornberry et al., 1993), an increasing number of large-scale surveys have included information about youth gangs and gang-involved youths. These and subsequent studies, while not specifically gang studies, include questions that allow researchers to examine a number of issues of interest to both policymakers and researchers. Of particular importance has been the ability to investigate similarities between gang and nongang-involved youths (e.g., Esbensen, Huizinga, & Weiher, 1993; Hill et al., 1999; Thornberry et al., 2003), factors associated with gang joining and length of gang membership (Esbensen & Huizinga, 1993; Thornberry et al., 1993), and also to highlight the role of girls in gangs (Esbensen & Deschenes, 1998; Esbensen, Deschenes, & Winfree, 1999; Peterson, et al., 2001).

Definitional Issues—What Is a Gang and Who Is a Gang Member?

We have all heard the dictum "if it walks like a duck, talks like a duck, it's a duck" used to indicate that we know a gang member when we see one. Alas, it is not quite so simple. For instance, on the basis of common stereotypes, gang members are minority males. Does that mean white females cannot be gang members? And, we have also learned that gang members wear specific colors and clothing to indicate their affiliation. Does that mean that someone cannot be a gang member if they do not look the part? A number of issues arise when trying to determine what constitutes gang membership. Law enforcement agencies rely upon multiple indicators, including clothing, tattoos, association with known gang members, and claiming gang membership. Survey researchers rely primarily on self-nomination (self-identification as a gang member). How valid and reliable is this method? And why does it matter?

We will address the last question first. It is important to know the size of the problem and also the characteristics of gang members. Depending upon definition and measurement, widely different estimates of the number of gang youth and their demographic composition are found. Law enforcement data paint a picture of inner-city, minority males (generally from single-parent households). Ethnographic and other qualitative studies of older and more homogeneous samples tend to confirm this picture (e.g., Campbell, 1984; Hagedorn, 1988; Vigil, 1988; Decker & Van Winkle, 1996). These images are reinforced in the mass media (Esbensen & Tusinski, 2007) and often influence policymakers' decisions (Decker & Kempf-Leonard, 1991). Surveys involving younger samples, however, call into question the extent to which these stereotypes accurately depict youth gang members (e.g., Bjerregaard & Smith, 1993; Esbensen & Huizinga, 1993; Esbensen & Carson, 2012).

So, what is a gang? In 1927, Thrasher, introduced the following definition: a gang has a sense of organization and solidarity that sets it apart from a mob, a tendency to respond to outside threats, the creation of a shared *esprit de corps*, and identification of some geographic area or territory which it will defend through force if necessary (Thrasher, 1927/1963). Nowhere in his definition, however, did Thrasher mention delinquent or law-violating behavior as a criterion for a gang. Certainly, he acknowledged that the criminal gang was one type, but he also stressed that among his 1,313 gangs, some were good and some were bad (Thrasher, 1927/1963).

Some 40 years after Thrasher, Klein (1971) argued persuasively for the self-definition of gang members and for the necessity of including illegal activity as a criterion for classification as a gang. He proposed the following definition, which has since received considerable support: a gang is:

> any denotable adolescent group of youngsters who (a) are generally perceived as a distinct aggregation by others in their neighborhood, (b) recognize themselves as a denotable group (almost invariably with a group name), and (c) have been involved in a sufficient number of delinquent incidents to call forth a consistent negative response from neighborhood residents and/or law enforcement agencies (Klein, 1971:13).

Bursik and Grasmick (1995a) stressed the importance of including criminal activity in the definitional criteria of gang membership; they noted that the first two criteria are easily met by a number of social groups, including Greek fraternities. However, inclusion of delinquent involvement introduces a possible circular relationship in examinations of the degree to which gangs are involved in violence. If one of the defining characteristics of a gang is its delinquent involvement, then can delinquency also be said to be a consequence of being in the gang?

The bulk of gang research tends to include a merger of Thrasher's and Klein's elements, including being a social group, using symbols, engaging in verbal and nonverbal communications to declare their "gang-ness," a sense of permanence, gang-identified territory or turf, and, lastly, crime. During the past few years, some degree of consensus appears to have emerged with regard to definitional issues. For instance, a group of researchers interested in studying gangs cross-nationally has adopted the following "Eurogang" definition to guide their research: "A gang (or a troublesome youth group corresponding to a street gang elsewhere) is any durable, street-oriented youth group whose involvement in illegal activity is part of its group identity" (Weerman et al., 2009).

Esbensen et al., (2001a) investigated the validity of the self-report technique. They created five types of gang members. The first two types were identified by use of single items: (1) "Have you ever been a gang member?" and (2) "Are you now in a gang?" Three increasingly more restrictive definitions of gang membership were then created. The third type, "delinquent gang" member, included respondents who indicated that *their gang* was involved in at least one of the following illegal activities: getting in fights with other gangs; stealing things; robbing other people; stealing cars; selling marijuana; selling other illegal drugs; or damaging property. The fourth type, "organized" gang member, included delinquent gang members who also indicated that their gang had some level of organization. Specifically, the survey respondents were asked whether the following described their gang: "there are initiation rites; the gang has established leaders; the gang has symbols or colors." The last characteristic used to determine gang membership was an indicator of whether individuals considered themselves a "core" member or a "peripheral" member.

Depending upon which of the five different definitions of gang member was used, the number of gang members varied considerably: almost 17 percent of the respondents indicated that they had ever belonged to a gang, but less than 9 percent said they were current gang members (a point to which we will return later). As the gang definition became more restrictive, the number of gang youths decreased: just less than 8 percent belonged to a "delinquent gang"; 5 percent were in "organized delinquent gangs"; and slightly more than 2 percent of all the survey participants indicated that they were current "core" members of an organized delinquent gang. Thus, the size of the gang problem certainly depends upon how gang member status is defined. Importantly, though, the demographic characteristics of gang members remained relatively constant. Approximately 40 percent of gang members were female, between 24 and 30 percent of gang members were white, and the percentage of gang members whose parents had less than a high-school education ranged from 16 to 18 percent. One important finding from this particular study, and one that has been confirmed in a number of longitudinal studies, is that gang membership is a temporary status. Recall that approximately one-half of the youths who reported they had been in a gang were no longer gang members. In fact, research suggests that most youths belong to a gang for less than one year (Esbensen & Huizinga, 1993; Thornberry et al., 2003; Peterson et al., 2004; Gatti et al., 2005; Melde & Esbensen, 2014).

Girls in Gangs

As we mentioned above, gang membership is generally assumed to be the domain of males and as such, girls in gangs were relatively understudied and, until relatively recently, little was known about girls in gangs (e.g., Campbell, 1991; Chesney-Lind, 1993). If we rely on law enforcement estimates, there would be little reason to be concerned about female involvement in gangs, as police data indicate that less than 10 percent of gang members are females (e.g., Curry, Ball, & Fox, 1994; Goldstein & Glick, 1994; Huff, 1998). A different picture, however, emerges from studies not dependent on the filtering of data by law enforcement. As early as 1967, Klein and Crawford (1995) reported that their caseworkers' "Daily Contact Reports" identified 600 male and 200 female gang members. In other words, 25 percent of the Los Angeles gang members identified by caseworkers in the 1960s were female. Findings from recent youth surveys conducted in a number of countries find that girls account for between 20 and 50 percent of gang members (Bjerregaard & Smith 1993; Esbensen & Huizinga, 1993; Battin-Pearson et al., 1998; Esbensen & Winfree, 1998; Haymoz & Gatti, 2010; Esbensen & Carson, 2012; Pedersen & Lindstadt, 2012; Weerman, 2012).

Why the Difference?

Two primary reasons help to explain the discrepancy between self-report and law enforcement estimates of female involvement in gangs: (1) the research methodology utilized to produce the data and (2) the age of the sample members studied. Case studies, observational studies, and those relying upon law enforcement data tend to produce lower estimates of female involvement, while general surveys tend to find a greater level of female gang involvement. This may well be an artifact of differential recording policies for males and females. For example, the Los Angeles Sheriff Department's operating manual indicates that a youth should be classified as a gang member when that individual "claims" gang affiliation. The same manual, however, questions the validity of female self-nomination: "These same females will say they are members of the local Crips gang; however, evidence has shown that this is not so" (Operation Safe Streets Street Gang Detail, 1995: 40).

The second methodological issue, age of sample, is important because there is some evidence to suggest that girls mature out of gangs at an earlier age than do males (Esbensen & Huizinga, 1993; Harris, 1994; Fishman, 1995; Moore & Hagedorn, 1996). In both the Denver Youth Survey (Esbensen & Huizinga, 1993) and the Rochester Youth Development Study (Thornberry et al., 2003), the authors reported a lower percentage of girl gang members as the sample aged. According to Harris (1994), girls are most active in gangs between 13 and 16 years of age. Harris (1994: 300) suggests that "by 17 or 18, interests and activities of individual members are directed toward the larger community rather than toward the gang, and girls begin to leave the active gang milieu." Thus, gang samples consisting of older adolescents or gang members in their twenties are apt to produce a substantially different picture than studies focusing on middle-school- and high-school-aged youths.

Race/Ethnicity and Gang Membership

A common stereotype is that gang members come from racial and/or ethnic minorities (e.g., Fagan, 1989; Spergel, 1990; Esbensen & Tusinski, 2007; Howell, 2007). Black gangs such as the Bloods and Crips and Latino gangs such as the Latin Kings reinforce this image. Ethnographic studies of gangs and gang members provide further support for this stereotypical view of gang members. Police-based studies also suggest that this is the case, often reporting that approximately 90 percent of gang members are African American or Hispanic (Curry et al., 1994). This stereotype, however, runs counter to the early gang research that described gang members by the nationality (i.e., German, Italian, Irish) of European (i.e., white) immigrants. With changes in immigration and mobility patterns in the mid–twentieth century (more immigrants from Mexico and the Caribbean and the movement of African Americans from rural to urban areas), the demographic composition of urban areas changed, especially those characterized as socially disorganized (see Chapter 7). With these changes in urban demographics came a change in those coming to the attention of the police, including gang members.

With the renewed interest in gangs in the late 1980s and 1990s came ethnographic studies of gangs and gang members (e.g., Hagedorn, 1988; Vigil, 1988; Campbell 1991; Moore, 1991; Decker & Van Winkle, 1996; J. Miller, 2001; Vigil, 2002). These studies focused on black and/or Hispanic populations in cities with acknowledged gang problems: New York City, Los Angeles, Milwaukee, and St. Louis. As research expanded to include more diverse settings, this picture of gangs as a minority problem was called into question. The 2002 National Youth Gang Center survey provides an example of how expanding the sample can affect the apparent parameters of the gang problem (Egley et al., 2004). With wider coverage of the American population (including suburban, small towns, and rural areas), the racial/ethnic composition of gangs became more racially/ethnically mixed.

In their 11-city study, Esbensen and Peterson Lynskey (2001) examined the racial and ethnic composition of gangs in diverse communities. They found that gang youths resemble the youths in the larger community. In predominantly white communities such as Pocatello, Idaho and Will County, Illinois, the majority of gang members were also white. In cities with a majority African-American (Kansas City, Milwaukee, and Philadelphia) or Hispanic (Las Cruces, New Mexico and Phoenix) population, the gang members reflected that community composition. The authors caution, however, that it is important to note that, while the gang youths tend to reflect the racial and ethnic composition of their communities, there is nonetheless an overrepresentation of minority youths in the gang samples.

Gang Violence

Gang violence, especially homicide, attracted considerable attention in the late 1980s and early 1990s. In 1994, for example, Los Angeles experienced 370 gang homicides—an average of one gang homicide each and every day—accounting for 44 percent of all homicides in that city that year (Maxson & Klein, 2001). Despite a decrease in gang violence at the end of the century, gang homicides still accounted for 1,061 deaths nationwide in 1998 (Curry, Maxson, & Howell, 2001) and have shown slight increases since 2002. While murder and violent crime tend to be synonymous with gangs, it is important to acknowledge that gangs and gang members are engaged in a number of activities other than violent crimes. In fact, throughout most of the day, gang members are like other adolescents—going to school, working, hanging out, and eating with family or friends (e.g., Esbensen et al., 1993; Klein, 1995; Decker & Van Winkle, 1996; Fleisher, 1998). Criminal activity and violence, when placed in the context of daily activities, are relatively rare events. Regardless, it is the violence and other illegal activity in which gangs are involved that draws police and researcher interest.

Researchers seek to understand better the role of gangs in crime generally and violence in particular. Research that has focused on gangs as the unit of analysis has determined that some gangs can be classified as drug gangs, others as violent gangs, and yet others as lacking specialization. In his review of the gang literature, James Howell (1998:9) wrote: "Levels of gang violence differ from one city to another . . ., from one community to another . . ., from one gang to another . . ., and even among cliques within the same gang." In their research based on law enforcement surveys, Maxson and Klein (1995) identi-fied five types of gangs (traditional, neo-traditional, collective, compressed, and specialty) based on a variety of organizational characteristics. The one constant is that gangs and gang members commit more violent crime than nongang youths in the same environment.

While some research has focused on the gang as the unit of analysis, most contemporary research examines the gang member. This focus on individuals is in large measure due to the reliance upon surveys which are not well-suited to study group dynamics. With the introduction of longitudinal panel surveys into gang research, it has become possible to trace gang members' attitudes, beliefs, and behaviors across time, including pre-gang, gang, and post-gang periods. As we mentioned above, one important contribution of this line of research is documentation of the fact that the vast majority of gang-involved youths belong to the gang for a relatively short period of time, less than one year. Dur-ing the period of gang membership, however, there are changes in attitudes and behaviors that have immediate and long-term consequences for the youths. During gang membership, the youths' involvement in delinquent activity of all kinds increases significantly (e.g., Esbensen & Huizinga, 1993; Thornberry et al., 1993; Thornberry & Burch, 1997; Battin-Pearson et al., 1998; Thornberry et al., 2003; Gatti et al., 2005; Melde & Esbensen, 2011; 2014). Comparisons of gang and nongang youths consistently and historically have produced sig-nificant differences in both the prevalence and frequency of offending between these two groups. This finding has been found to hold in European studies as well (e.g., Esbensen & Weerman, 2005; Bendixen, Endresen, & Olweus, 2006; Sharp, Aldridge, & Medina, 2006). According to self-report surveys, gang youths account for approximately 70 percent of all self-reported violent offending in adolescent samples (Huizinga et al., 2003; Thornberry et al., 2003).

Gang Girls' Involvement in Violence

While females were generally excluded from early gang research, when refer-ence was made to females, it was usually in relation to their sexual activities or to their categorization as tomboys; rarely was attention paid to their participa-tion in the violent activities of the gang. The image of female gang members as auxiliary members or simply as gun/drug holders has been challenged by ethnographic research which has documented girls' involvement in a variety of gang activities (Campbell, 1991; Fishman, 1995; J. Miller, 1998; J. Miller &

Decker, 2001). Survey research has contributed to the growing evidence that gang membership increases involvement in serious and violent crime for both males and females (Fagan, 1990; Esbensen & Huizinga, 1993; Thornberry et al., 1993; Esbensen & Winfree, 1998). In addition to the individual sex of gang members, Peterson and her colleagues (Peterson, J. Miller, & Esbensen, 2001; Peterson & Carson, 2012) found that the sex composition of the gang influences offending patterns, with mixed-sex gang members reporting more violence than single-sex gangs. Homicide, however, appears to be the domain of male gang members (e.g., Decker & Van Winkle, 1996; J. Miller & Decker, 2001). Because females are less likely than males to use firearms and more likely to use weapons such as knives or razors, however, the results of their violent behavior are often less lethal than are males'.

Gang Membership, Race/Ethnicity, and Violent Offending

In addition to the racial/ethnic composition of gangs, another important issue to explore is whether the extent of involvement in delinquent activity varies by race/ethnicity of gang members. That is, are minority gang youths more delinquent than white gang members? The majority of investigations of gang offending have been restricted to ethnically or racially homogeneous gangs. As such, the issue of racial/ethnic differences in offending has rarely been explored. Of the research that has examined differential rates of offending by race/ethnicity among adolescents (e.g., Elliott & Ageton, 1980; Huizinga & Elliott, 1987; Curry & Spergel, 1992; Sellers, Winfree, & Griffiths, 1993; Winfree, Mays, & Vigil-Backstrom, 1994; McNulty & Bellair, 2003), relatively little has explored whether differences in offending exist within the gang. In one recent publication, Esbensen and Carson (2012) examined race/ethnic differences in offending and found that among gang-involved youths, the rates of violent offending were similar for white, black, and Hispanic youths. They also compared offending rates of gang members with those of nongang members and found that, regardless of race or ethnicity, gang members committed from five to ten times more violent crimes than nongang members.

Risk Factors for Gang Membership

Gang research conducted in the 1950s and 1960s contributed substantively and significantly to criminological theory development. The works of Cohen (1955), W. B. Miller (1958), Cloward and Ohlin (1960), and Short and Strodbeck (1966) contributed to the development of social strain theory, subcultural theories of crime, and group process theories. Contemporary gang researchers continue to make theoretical contributions, including developmental and life-course criminology (Thornberry et al., 2003; Melde and Esbensen, 2011; 2014), integrated theories (Winfree et al., 1996; Esbensen et al., 2010), and subcultural perspectives (Vigil, 1988; 2002; Freng & Esbensen, 2007; Drake & Melde, 2014). A recent trend, however, has been to adopt a public health model of examining risk and protective factors associated with gang joining. This **risk factor approach** assumes that the presence of multiple risk factors places an individual at an elevated risk for gang joining. Just as an individual who is overweight, smokes, leads a sedentary lifestyle, has high blood pressure, and has a family history of heart ailments is at an elevated risk of suffering a heart attack, this risk factor approach would argue that an individual who has a number of friends who are gang members, has parents who do not monitor his/her activity, is not committed to doing well in school, and believes that it is OK to break the law is at an elevated risk of becoming gang-involved. Two relatively recent publications provide excellent reviews of this research (Howell & Egley, 2005; Klein & Maxson, 2006). The risk factor approach tends to group risk factors into the following five domains: community, individual, family, school, and peers.

Community Risk Factors

Numerous studies indicate that poverty, unemployment, the absence of meaningful jobs, and social disorganization contribute to the presence of gangs (Hagedorn, 1988; Vigil, 1988; Fagan, 1990; Huff, 1990; Curry & Thomas, 1992). There is little debate that gangs are more prominent in urban areas and that they are more likely to emerge in economically distressed neighborhoods. However, as we previously stated, surveys conducted by the National Youth Gang Center have identified youth gangs in rural and sub-urban communities (e.g., Egley et al., 2004; Starbuck et al., 2001). The traditional image of American youth gangs, however, is characterized by urban social disorganization and economic marginalization; the housing projects or barrios of Los Angeles, Chicago, and New York are viewed as the stereotypical homes of youth gang members. Vigil (1988; 2002), for instance, suggests that the multiple marginalization (that is, the combined disadvantages of low socioeconomic status, street socialization, and segregation) explains gang membership. In addition to the pressures of marginal economics, gang members experience the added burden of having marginal ethnic and personal identities. These juveniles look for identity and stability in the gang and adopt the *cholo* subculture—customs that are associated with an attachment to and identification with gangs—that includes alcohol and other drug use, conflict, and violence.

Countering the effect of community, Fagan (1990; 207) comments: "inner-city youths in this study live in areas where social controls have weakened and opportunities for success in legitimate activities are limited. Nevertheless, participation in gangs is selective, and most youths avoid gang life." In his insightful book on American youth gangs, Klein (1995; 75–6) echoes Fagan's statement (emphasis added):

> In regard to who joins street gangs, then, first, it is not sufficient to say that gang members come from lower-income areas, from minority populations, or from homes more often characterized by absent parents or reconstituted families. It is not sufficient because most youths from such areas, such groups, and such families do *not* join gangs.

Family Risk Factors

Family risk factors for gang membership include several of the factors above (i.e., family structure and social class). In addition to these family social characteristics, potential risk factors in this domain include lower parental attachment, less monitoring and supervision, inconsistent discipline practices, family violence, and having a family member who is gang involved (e.g. Bowker & Klein, 1983; Brewer et al., 1995; Thornberry et al., 1995; Decker & Van Winkle, 1996; Howell, 1998).

Individual Risk Factors

Are gang youths substantively different from nongang youths? Recent surveys comparing gang and nongang youths' attitudes report numerous differences between the two groups, although relatively few of these differences were consistent across studies (for an excellent review, consult Klein & Maxson, 2006). Comparisons between gang and nongang youths have been reported from Rochester (Bjerregaard & Smith, 1993), Denver (Esbensen et al., 1993), Seattle (Hill et al., 1999), and San Diego (Maxson et al., 1998), as well as in the multisite studies conducted by Esbensen and his colleagues (Esbensen & Winfree, 1998; Esbensen, Deschenes, & Winfree, 1999; Esbensen et al., 2010; 2013b). While these studies used different questions and different sampling methods, they found a number of similar risk factors associated with gang joining. For example, gang youths held more antisocial beliefs, gang members had more delinquent self-concepts, greater tendencies to resolve conflicts by threats, and had experienced more critical stressful events.

Peer Risk Factors

One consistent finding from research on gangs, as is the case for research on delinquency in general, is the overarching influence of peers on adolescent behavior (Curry & Spergel, 1992; Bjerregaard & Smith, 1993; Menard & Elliott, 1994; Thornberry et al., 1995; Battin-Pearson et al., 1998; Hill et al., 1999; Warr, 2002). For example, Battin-Pearson and colleagues (1998) reported that the strongest predictors of sustained gang affiliation were a high level of interaction with antisocial peers and a low level of interaction with prosocial peers. Researchers have examined the influence of peers through a variety of measures, including exposure to delinquent peers, attachment to delinquent peers, and commitment to delinquent peers. Regardless of how this peer affiliation is measured, the results are the same: association with delinquent peers is one of the strongest predictors (that is, risk factors) of gang membership.

School Risk Factors

School factors have received less attention from gang researchers than have the other risk factor domains. Researchers have, however, examined the role of academic success, commitment to school, attachment to teachers, and educational aspirations. For the most part, these school factors are not as salient with respect to predicting gang joining as are the individual and peer risk factors.

Summary of Risk Factors

Gang members report the following risk factors at levels statistically significantly greater than their nongang counterparts:

- Individual: impulsivity, risk seeking, perceptions of guilt, neutralizations, self-esteem, and social isolation;
- Family: low levels of parental monitoring, lower levels of paternal and maternal attachment;
- Peer: more negative peer commitment, less positive peer commitment, less association with prosocial peers, more association with delinquent peers, unsupervised unstructured activity with friends, and hanging out where alcohol or other drugs available; and
- School: low school commitment, perceived limited educational opportunities, and perceived negative school environment.

Youth Gang Summary

While gangs are more likely to be found in inner cities experiencing economic disadvantage, this fact supports neither the accuracy nor the validity of two commonly articulated beliefs: (1) that gangs are only found in such disadvantaged areas and (2) that all youths in such areas are gang-involved. Contrary to these stereotypes, gangs can be found in a wide range of communities, and it is only a small minority of youths, regardless of community characteristics, who join gangs. Those youths who join gangs also tend to resemble—in terms of demographics—the youths in the community in which they live. Gang members are male and female, reside in single-parent as well as two-parent households, and are not exclusively racial or ethnic minorities. Nonetheless, personal and family demographic characteristics are associated with elevated risks of gang affiliation.

There is little doubt about the belief that gang youths are more violent than nongang involved youths. It is important to note that gang girls also report high levels of involvement in violent offending. Furthermore, while the prevalence rates of violent offending do differ by race/ethnicity, gang membership eliminates such differences. Gang members, regardless of race/ethnicity, are high-rate offenders.

Risk factor research paints a picture of gang members as significantly different from nongang members. They are more impulsive, have less parental monitoring, are more committed to negative peers, and possess lower levels of school commitment. Importantly, gang youths also report experiencing less guilt associated with illegal activity, and they

Former Gangster Disciples gang leader Delvin Lane works with the Booker T. Washington High School football team, some of whom are gang members, in Memphis, Tennessee. In 2012, Lane was selected to head 901 BLOC Squad, part of the city's gang violence prevention program.

CREDIT: AP Photo/*The Commercial Appeal*, Mark Weber.

indicate greater tolerance for the use of physical force to resolve differences. Two recent publications provide current assessments of the extent to which risk factors differ or overlap by sex (Peterson & Morgan, 2014) and the extent to which the risk factor approach can be used to identify high-risk youths who might benefit from participation in gang-prevention programs (Hennigan et al., 2014).

SUMMARY

This chapter has explored three types of youth violence: school shootings, bullying, and gang involvement. Youth violence, as measured by both arrests and victim reports, increased from the 1970s, reaching a peak in 1993–4 and then steadily declining through 2012. According to the UCR data, offenders under the age of 18 accounted for approximately 11.7 percent of all violent crime arrests in 2012. Among juvenile arrestees, males account for approximately 71 percent of all arrests, but 81 percent of violent crime arrests. This gender gap is less pronounced for Index property offenses, for which females account for 35 percent of juvenile arrests in 2012.

While public and political perceptions about school violence are driven by school shootings such as those experienced by Columbine High School in 1999 and Sandy Hook Elementary School in 2012, most school victimizations involve relatively minor property and personal offenses. That is not to say that deaths do no occur on school property. In fact, since 1999, the number of homicides committed on school property has fluctuated from the low teens (14 in both 1999 and 2000 school years) to a high of 33 in 1998–9 (this includes the Columbine massacre) and 32 in 2006–7.

The most common form of victimization at school is bullying and while there is general consensus that bullying refers to victimization that occurs within the school setting, there is a lack of agreement as to what constitutes bullying and how it should be measured. Regardless of definition and measurement, however, research suggests that being the victim of bullying can have serious consequences for the individual, including contributing to low self-esteem, depression and anxiety, and avoidance behavior. As is the case with most social problems, there is no "silver bullet" to address the problem of school crime but environmental change strategies hold more promise than individual change strategies.

Since the early 1990s, there has been an explosion of research on gangs. The National Gang Center has documented that gangs exist in every state in the United States and in a wide range of communities, including small towns and rural counties. Without historical data, however, it is not possible to conclude that the appearance of gangs in these areas is a new phenomenon rather than one of discovery.

Gangs are of particular criminological interest because of the elevated criminal activity found among gang members. However, throughout most of the day, gang members are like other adolescents—going to school, working, hanging out, and eating with family or friends. Criminal activity and violence, when placed in the context of daily activities, are relatively rare events. Regardless, it is the violence and other illegal activity in which gangs are involved that draw police and researcher interest.

While early gang research contributed substantively to criminological theory development, a recent trend has been to adopt a public health model of examining risk and protective factors associated with gang joining. This risk factor approach assumes that the presence of a range of potential risks places an individual at an elevated risk for gang joining. Risk factor research paints a picture of gang members as significantly different from nongang members. They are more impulsive, have less parental monitoring, are more committed to negative peers, and possess lower levels of school commitment. Some gang researchers have recently begun to link this risk factor approach to several theoretical perspectives, most notably life-course and developmental criminology.

KEY TERMS AND CONCEPTS

Bullying

Environmental Change Strategies

Evidence-based Programs

Individual Change Strategies

Monitoring the Future survey

National Longitudinal Survey of Youth

Risk Factor Approach

School Violence

Superpredators

Target Hardening

Youth Gangs

Youth Risk Behavior Surveillance Survey

Youth Violence

KEY CRIMINOLOGISTS

Meda Chesney-Lind

G. David Curry

Scott Decker

Arlen Egley

Delbert S. Elliott

Finn-Aage Esbensen

David Farrington

James C. Howell

David Huizinga

Malcolm W. Klein

Cheryl Maxson

Chris Melde

Jody Miller

Dan Olweus

Dana Peterson

Terence Thornberry

DISCUSSION QUESTIONS

1. How common is youth violence and what are the characteristics of violent offenders?

2. Much of the media attention associated with school violence focuses on relatively rare school shootings. After reading this chapter, do you agree or disagree with the media's decision to focus on these events?

3. What are some of the issues associated with defining the term bullying and does it really matter how you define bullying?

4. Youth gang members are often depicted as being predominately male, inner-city, and racial/ethnic minorities. To what extent is this depiction accurate?

5. Are youth gangs different from other youth groups and is there a reason to be concerned about this adolescent phenomenon?

REFERENCES

Andreou, E. (2000). Bully/victim problems and their association with psychological constructs in 8- to 12-year-old Greek schoolchildren. *Aggressive Behavior, 26,* 49–56.

Andreou, E. (2001). Bully/victim problems and their association with coping behaviour in conflictual peer interactions among school-age children. *Educational Psychology, 21,* 59–66.

Arora, C. M. J. & Thompson, D. A. (1987). Defining bullying for a secondary school. *Educational and Child Psychology, 4,* 110–20.

Austin, S. & Joseph, S. (1996). Assessment of bully/victim problems in 8 to 11 year-olds. *British Journal of Educational Psychology, 66,* 447–56.

Baldry, A. C. & Farrington, D. P. (1999). Types of bullying among Italian school children. *Journal of Adolescence, 22,* 423–6.

Battin-Pearson, S. R., Thornberry, T. P., Hawkins, J. D., & Krohn, M. D. (1998). Gang membership, delinquent peers, and delinquent behavior. Washington, DC: Office of Juvenile Justice and Delinquency Prevention, *Juvenile Justice Bulletin* (October).

Bendixen, M., Endresen, I. M., & Olweus, D. (2006). Joining and leaving gangs: Selection and facilitation effects on self-reported antisocial behaviour in early adolescence. *European Journal of Criminology, 3,* 85–114.

Berthold, K. A. & Hoover, J. H. (2000). Correlates of bullying and victimization among intermediate students in the Midwestern USA. *School Psychology International, 21,* 65–78.

Bjerregaard, B. & Smith, C. A. (1993). Gender differences in gang participation, delinquency, and substance use. *Journal of Quantitative Criminology, 4,* 329–55.

Bond, L., Carlin, J. B., Thomas, L., Rubin, K., & Patton, G. (2001). Does bullying cause emotional problems? A prospective study of young teenagers. *British Medical Journal, 323,* 480–4.

Bookin-Weiner, H. & Horowitz, R. (1983). The end of the youth gang: Fad or fact? *Criminology, 21,* 585–602.

Boulton, M. J., Trueman, M., & Flemington, I. (2002). Associations between secondary school pupils' definitions of bullying, attitudes towards bullying, and tendencies to engage in bullying: Age and sex differences. *Educational Studies, 28,* 353–70.

Bowker, L., & Klein, M. W. (1983). Etiology of female juvenile delinquency gang membership: A test of psychological and social structural explanations. *Adolescence, 72,* 739–51.

Brewer, D., Hawkins, J. D., Catalano, R. F., & Neckerman, H. (1995). Preventing serious, violent, and chronic juvenile offending: A review of evaluations of selected strategies in childhood, adolescence, and the community. In J. C. Howell, B. Krisberg, J. D. Hawkins, & J. J. Wilson (Eds.), *Serious, violent, and chronic juvenile offenders* (pp. 61–141). Thousand Oaks, CA: Sage Publications.

Bursik, R. J., Jr. & Grasmick, H. G. (1995a). Defining gangs and gang behavior. In M. W. Klein, C. L. Maxson, & J. Miller (Eds.), *The modern gang reader*. 1st edition (pp. 8–13). Los Angeles, CA: Roxbury Publishing Company.

Bursik, R. J., Jr. & Grasmick, H. G. (1995b). The collection of data for gang research. In M. W. Klein, C. L. Maxson, & J. Miller (Eds.), *The modern gang reader*. 1st edition (pp. 154–7). Los Angeles, CA: Roxbury Publishing Company.

Campbell, A. (1984). *The girls in the gang*. 1st edition. New York, NY: Basil Blackwell.

Campbell, A. (1986). The streets and violence. In A. Campbell and J. J. Gibbs (Eds.), *Violent transactions: The limits of personality* (pp. 115–32). New York, NY: Basil Blackwell.

Campbell, A. (1991). *The girls in the gang*. 2nd edition. Cambridge, MA: Basil Blackwell.

Carbone-Lopez, K., Esbensen, F.-A., & Brick, B. T. (2010). Correlates and consequences of peer victimization: Gender differences in direct and indirect forms of bullying. *Youth Violence and Juvenile Justice, 8*, 332–50.

Centers for Disease Control and Prevention. (2004). Violence-related behaviors among high school students: United States, 1991–2003. *Morbidity & Mortality Weekly Report, 53*, 651–5.

Centers for Disease Control and Prevention. (2014). 1991–2013 High School Youth Risk Behavior Survey Data. Available at http://nccd.cdc.gov/youthonline/.

Chesney-Lind, M. (1993). Girls, gangs and violence: Anatomy of a backlash. *Humanity and Society, 17*, 321–44.

Chesney-Lind, M. & Hagedorn, J. M. (1999). *Female gangs in America: Essays on girls, gangs, and gender*. Chicago, IL: Lake View Press.

Chesney-Lind, M. & Shelden, R. G. (1998). *Girls, delinquency, and juvenile justice*. 2nd edition. Belmont, CA: West/Wadsworth.

Chesney-Lind, M., Shelden, R. G., & Joe, K. A. (1996). Girls, delinquency, and gang membership. In C. R. Huff (Ed.), *Gangs in America*. 2nd edition (pp. 185–204). Thousand Oaks, CA: Sage Publications.

Cloward, R. A. & Ohlin, L. E. (1960). *Delinquency and opportunity: A theory of delinquent gangs*. New York, NY: The Free Press.

Cohen, A. K. (1955). *Delinquent Boys: The culture of the gang*. New York, NY: Free Press.

Curry, G. D. & Spergel, I. A. (1992). Gang involvement and delinquency among Hispanic and African-American adolescent males. *Journal of Research in Crime and Delinquency, 29*, 273–91.

Curry, G. D. & Thomas, R. W. (1992). Community organization and gang policy response. *Journal of Quantitative Criminology, 8*, 357–74.

Curry, G. D., Ball, R. A., & Decker, S. H. (1996). *Estimating the national scope of gang crime from law enforcement data*. Washington, DC: Office of Justice Programs, National Institute of Justice, Research in Brief (August).

Curry, G. D., Ball, R. A., & Fox, R. J. (1994). *Gang crime and law enforcement record keeping*. Washington, DC: Office of Justice Programs, National Institute of Justice, Research in Brief (June).

Curry, G. D., Maxson, C. L., & Howell, J. C. (2001). *Youth gang homicides in the 1990s*. Washington, DC: Office of Juvenile Justice and Delinquency Prevention, OJJDP Fact Sheet (March).

Decker, S. H. 2000. Legitimizing drug use: A note on the impact of gang membership and drug sales on the use of illicit drugs. *Justice Quarterly, 17*, 393–410.

Decker, S. H., & Kempf-Leonard, K. (1991). Constructing gangs: The social definitions of youth activities. *Criminal Justice Policy Review, 5,* 271–91.

Decker, S. H. & Van Winkle, B. (1996). *Life in the gang: Family, friends, and violence.* New York, NY: Cambridge University Press.

DeVoe, J. F., Peter, K., Kaufman, P., Miller, A., Noonan, M., Snyder, T. D., & Baum, K. (2004). *Indicators of school crime and safety: 2004.* (NCES 2005–002/NCJ 205290). Washington, DC: US Department of Education.

Deschenes, E. P., & Esbensen, F.-A. (1999a). Violence among girls: Does gang membership make a difference? In M. Chesney-Lind, & J. M. Hagedorn (Eds.), *Female gangs in America* (pp. 277–94). Chicago, IL: Lake View Press.

Deschenes, E. P., & Esbensen, F.-A. (1999b). Violence and gangs: Gender differences in perceptions and behavior. *Journal of Quantitative Criminology, 15,* 63–96.

DiIulio, J. (1995). The coming of the superpredators. *Weekly Standard* (November 27):23.

Dinkes, R., Cataldi, E. F., & Lin-Kelly, W. (2007). *Indicators of school crime and safety: 2007.* (NCES 2008–21/NCJ 219553). Washington, DC: National Center for Education Statistics, Institute of Education Sciences, U.S. Department of Education and Bureau of Justice Statistics, Office of Justice Programs, U.S. Department of Justice.

Drake, G. & Melde, C. (2014). The problem of prediction: The efficacy of multiple marginality in a cross-sectional versus prospective models. *Journal of Crime & Justice, 37,* 61–78.

Egley, A., Jr. (2002). *National Youth Gang Survey trends from 1996–2000.* Washington, DC: Office of Juvenile Justice and Delinquency Prevention, OJJDP Fact Sheet (February).

Egley, A., Jr. & O'Donnell, C. E. (2008). *Highlights of the 2005 National Youth Gang Survey.* Washington, DC: Office of Juvenile Justice and Delinquency Prevention, OJJDP Fact Sheet (July).

Egley, A., Jr. & Ritz, C. E. (2006). *Highlights of the 2004 National Youth Gang Survey.* Washington, DC: Office of Juvenile Justice and Delinquency Prevention, OJJDP Fact Sheet (April).

Egley, A., Jr., Howell, J. C., & Major, A. K. (2004). Recent patterns of gang problems in the United States: Results from the 1996–2002 National Youth Gang Survey. In F.-A. Esbensen, S. G. Tibbetts, and L. Gaines (Eds.), *American youth gangs at the millennium* (pp. 90–108). Long Grove, IL: Waveland Press.

Elliott, D. S. & Ageton, S. S. (1980). Reconciling race and class differences in estimates of delinquency. *American Sociological Review, 45,* 95–110.

Esbensen, F.-A. & Carson, D. C. (2009). Consequences of being bullied: Results from a longitudinal assessment of bullying victimization in a multisite sample of American students. *Youth & Society, 41,* 209–33.

Esbensen, F.-A. & Carson, D. C. (2012). Who are the gangsters? An examination of the age, race/ethnicity, sex, and immigrant status of self-reported gang members in a seven-city study of American youth. *Journal of Contemporary Criminal Justice, 28,* 465–81.

Esbensen, F.-A. & Deschenes, E. P. (1998). A multisite examination of youth gang membership: Does gender matter? *Criminology, 36,* 799–828.

Esbensen, F.-A. & Huizinga, D. (1993). Gangs, drugs, and delinquency in a survey of urban youth. *Criminology, 31,* 565–89.

Esbensen, F.A. & Peterson Lynskey, D. (2001). Youth gang members in a school survey. In M. W. Klein, H.-J. Kerner, C. L. Maxson, & E. G. W. Weitekamp (Eds.), *The Eurogang paradox: Street gang and youth groups in the US and Europe* (pp. 93–114). Amsterdam, The Netherlands: Kluwer Press.

Esbensen, F.-A. & Tusinski, K. (2007). Youth gangs in the print media. *Criminal Justice and Popular Culture, 14*, 21–38.

Esbensen, F.-A. & Weerman, F. (2005). Youth gangs and troublesome youth groups in the United States and the Netherlands. *European Journal of Criminology, 2*, 5–37.

Esbensen, F.-A., & Winfree, Jr., L.T. (1998). Race and gender differences between gang and nongang youth: Results from a multisite survey. *Justice Quarterly, 15*, 505–26.

Esbensen, F.-A., Deschenes, E.P., & Winfree, Jr., L.T. (1999). "Differences between gang girls and gang boys: Results from a multisite survey." *Youth and Society, 31*, 27–53.

Esbensen, F.-A., Huizinga, D., & Weiher, A.W. (1993). Gang and non-gang youth: Differences in explanatory factors. *Journal of Contemporary Criminal Justice, 9*, 94–116.

Esbensen, F.-A., Peterson,. D., Freng, A., & Taylor, T.J. (2002). Initiation of drug use, drug sales, and violent offending among a sample of gang and non-gang youth. In. C.R. Huff (Ed.), *Gangs in America*. 3rd edition (pp. 37–50). Thousand Oaks, CA: Sage Publications.

Esbensen, F.-A., Peterson, D. Taylor, T.J., & Freng, A. (2010). *Youth Violence: Sex and Race Differences in Offending, Victimization, and Gang Membership*. Philadelphia, PA: Temple University Press.

Esbensen, F.-A., Peterson, D., Taylor, T.J., & Osgood, D.W. (2013a). Is G.R.E.A.T effective? Program implementation quality and results from the national evaluation of the Gang Resistance Education and Training (G.R.E.A.T.) Program. In C.L. Maxson, J. Miller, M.W. Klein, & A. Egley, Jr. (Eds.), *The Modern Gang Reader*. 4th edition. New York, NY: Oxford University Press.

Esbensen, F.-A., Winfree, Jr., L.T., He, N., & Taylor, T.J. (2001a). Youth gangs and definitional issues: When is a gang a gang and why does it matter? *Crime and Delinquency, 47*, 105–30.

Esbensen, F.-A., Osgood, D.W., Peterson, D. Taylor, T.J., & Carson, D.C. (2013b). Short- and long-term outcome results from a multisite evaluation of the G.R.E.A.T. Program. *Criminology and Public Policy, 12*, 375–411.

Eslea, M., Menesini, E., Morita, Y., O'Moore, M., Mora-Merchan, J.A., Pereira, B., & Smith, P.K. (2003). Friendship and loneliness among bullies and victims: Data from seven countries. *Aggressive Behavior, 30*, 71–83.

Fagan, J. (1989). The social organization of drug use and drug dealing among urban gangs. *Criminology, 27*, 633–67.

Fagan, J. (1990). Social processes of delinquency and drug use among urban gangs. In C.R. Huff (Ed.), *Gangs in America*. 1st edition (pp. 183–222). Newbury Park, CA: Sage Publications.

Farrington, D.P., Loeber, R., & Stouthamer-Loeber, M. (2003). How can the relationship between race and violence be explained? In D.F. Hawkins (Ed.), *Violent crime: Assessing race and ethnic differences* (pp. 213–37). New York, NY: Cambridge University Press.

Fishman, L.T. (1995). The vice queens: An ethnographic study of black female gang behavior. In M.W. Klein, C.L. Maxson, & J. Miller (Eds.), *The modern gang reader*. 1st edition (pp. 83–92). Los Angeles: Roxbury Publishing Company.

Fleisher, M. 1998. *Dead end kids*. Madison, WI: University of Wisconsin Press.

Forero, R., McLellan, L., Rissel, C., & Bauman, A. (1999). Bullying behaviour and psychosocial health among school students in New South Wales, Australia: Cross sectional survey. *British Medical Journal, 319*, 344–8.

Fox, J.A. (1996). *Trends in juvenile violence: A report to the United States Attorney General on current and future rates of juvenile offending*. Washington, DC: United States Department of Justice (March).

Freng, A. & Esbensen, F.-A. (2007). Race and gang affiliation: An examination of multiple marginality. *Justice Quarterly, 24*, 600–628.

Gatti, U., Tremblay, R.E., Vitaro, F., & McDuff, P. (2005). Youth gangs, delinquency and drug use: A test of the selection, facilitation and enhancement hypotheses. *Journal of Child Psychology and Psychiatry, 46*, 1178–90.

Gibbons, D.C. (1997). Review essay: Race, ethnicity, crime, and social policy. *Crime and Delinquency, 43*, 358–80.

Goldstein, A.P. & Glick, B. (1994). *The prosocial gang: Implementing aggression replacement training*. Thousand Oaks, CA: Sage Publications.

Gottfredson, D.C. (2001). *Schools and delinquency*. New York, NY: Cambridge University Press.

Gottfredson, G.D., Gottfredson, D.C., Czeh, E.R., Cantor, D., Crosse, S.B., & Hantman, I. (2000). *National study of delinquency prevention in schools: Final Report*. Ellicott City, MD: Gottfredson Associates, Inc.

Hagedorn, J.M. (1988). *People and folks: Gangs, crime, and the underclass in a rustbelt city*. Chicago, IL: Lakeview Press.

Harris, M.G. (1994). Cholas, Mexican-American girls, and gangs. *Sex Roles, 30*, 289–301.

Hawkins, D.F., Laub, J.H., & Lauritsen, J.L. (1998). Race, ethnicity, and serious juvenile offending. In R. Loeber & D.P. Farrington (Eds.), *Serious & violent juvenile offenders: Risk factors and successful interventions* (pp. 30–46). Thousand Oaks, CA: Sage Publications.

Hawkins, D.F., Laub, J.H., Lauritsen, J.L., & Cothern, L. (2000). *Race, ethnicity, and serious and violent juvenile offending*. Washington, DC: Office of Juvenile Justice and Delinquency Prevention, *Juvenile Justice Bulletin* (June).

Hawkins, J.D., Smith, B.H., Hill, K.G., Kosterman, R., Catalano, R.D., & Abbott, R.D. (2003). Understanding and preventing crime and violence: Findings from the Seattle Social Development Project. In T.P. Thornberry & M.D. Krohn (Eds.), *Taking stock of delinquency: An overview of findings from contemporary longitudinal studies* (pp. 225–312). New York, NY: Kluwer/Plenum Publishers.

Haymoz, S. & Gatti, U. (2010). Girl members of deviant youth groups, offending behavior and victimization: Results from ISRD-2 in Italy and Switzerland. *European Journal of Criminal Policy Research, 16*, 167–82.

Heimer, K., Lauritsen, J.L., & Lynch, J.P. (2009). The National Crime Victimization Survey and the gender gap in offending: Redux. *Criminology, 47*, 427–38.

Hennigan, K.M., Maxson, C.L., Sloane, D.C., Kolnick, K.A., & Vindel, F. (2014). Identifying high-risk youth for secondary gang prevention. *Journal of Crime and Justice, 37*(1), 104–28.

Hill, K.G., Howell, J.C., Hawkins, J.D., & Battin-Pearson, S. (1999). Childhood risk factors for adolescent gang membership: Results from the Seattle Social Development Project. *Journal of Research in Crime and Delinquency, 36*, 300–22.

Howell, J.C. (1998). *Youth gangs: An overview*. Washington, DC: Office of Juvenile Justice and Delinquency Prevention, *Juvenile Justice Bulletin* (August).

Howell, J.C. (1999). Youth gang homicides: A literature review. *Crime and Delinquency, 45*, 208–41.

Howell, J. C. (2007). Menacing or mimicking? Realities of youth gangs. *Juvenile and Family Court Journal, 58*, 39–50.

Howell, J. C. (2009). *Preventing and reducing juvenile delinquency: A comprehensive framework.* 2nd edition. Thousand Oaks, CA: Sage Publications.

Howell, J. C. & Decker, S. H. (1999). *The gangs, drugs, and violence connection.* Washington, DC: Office of Juvenile Justice and Delinquency Prevention, *Juvenile Justice Bulletin* (January).

Howell, J. C. & Egley, A., Jr. (2005). Moving risk factors into developmental theories of gang membership. *Youth Violence and Juvenile Justice, 3*, 334–54.

Howell, J. C., Moore, J. P., & Egley, A., Jr. (2002). The changing boundaries of youth gangs. In C. R. Huff (Ed.), *Gangs in America*. 3rd edition (pp. 3–18). Thousand Oaks, CA: Sage Publications.

Huff, C. R. (1990). Denial, overreaction, and misidentification: A postscript on public policy. In C. R. Huff (Ed.), *Gangs in America*. 1st edition (pp. 310–17). Newbury Park, CA: Sage Publications.

Huff, C. R. (1998). *Comparing the criminal behavior of youth gangs and at-risk youths.* Washington, DC: National Institute of Justice, Research in Brief (October).

Huizinga, D. (1991). Assessing violent behavior with self-reports. In J. S. Milner (Ed.), *Neuropsychology of Aggression* (pp. 47–66). Boston, MA: Kluwer Publishers.

Huizinga, D. & Elliott, D. S. (1986). Reassessing the reliability and validity of self-report delinquency measures. *Journal of Quantitative Criminology, 2*, 293–327.

Huizinga, D. & Elliott, D. S. (1987). Juvenile offenders: Prevalence, offender incidence, and arrest rates by race. *Crime and Delinquency, 33*, 206–23.

Huizinga, D., Weiher, A. W., Espiritu, R., & Esbensen, F.-A. (2003). Delinquency and crime: Some highlights from the Denver Youth Survey. In T. P. Thornberry and M. D. Krohn (Eds.), *Taking stock of delinquency: An overview of findings from contemporary longitudinal studies* (pp. 47–91). New York, NY: Kluwer/Plenum Publishers.

Johnston, L. D., O'Malley, P. M., Bachman, J. G., & Schulenberg, J. E. (2006). *Monitoring the future national results on adolescent drug use: Overview of key findings, 2005.* Bethesda, MD: National Institute on Drug Abuse.

Kaltiala-Heino, R., Rimpela, M., Rantanen, P., & Rimpela, A. (2000). Bullying at school: An indicator of adolescents at risk for mental disorders. *Journal of Adolescence, 23*, 661–74.

Kaufman, P., Chen, X., Chandler, S. P., Chapman, K. A., Rand, C. D., & Ringel, M. R. (1998). *Indicators of school crime and safety.* (NCES 98–251/NCJ-172215).Washington, DC: Government Printing Office, U.S. Departments of Education of Education and Justice.

Klein, M. W. (1971). *Street gangs and street workers.* Englewood Cliffs, NJ: Prentice-Hall.

Klein, M. W. (1995). *The American street gang: Its nature, prevalence, and control.* New York, NY: Oxford University Press.

Klein, M. W. & Crawford, L. Y. (1995). Groups, gangs, and cohesiveness. In M. W. Klein, C. L. Maxson, & J. Miller (Eds.), *The modern gang reader*. 1st edition (pp. 160–7). Los Angeles, CA: Roxbury Publishing Company.

Klein, M. W. & Maxson, C. L. (2006). *Street gang patterns and policies.* New York, NY: Oxford University Press.

Klein, M. W., Maxson, C. L., & Cunningham, L. C. (1991). "Crack," street gangs, and violence. *Criminology, 29*, 623–49.

Lauritsen, J. L., Heimer, K., & Lynch, J. P. (2009). Trends in the gender gap in violent offending: New evidence from the National Crime Victimization Survey. *Criminology, 47*, 361–400.

Loeber, R. & Farrington, D. P. (1998). Never too early, never too late: Risk factors and successful interventions with serious and violent juvenile offenders. *Studies on Crime and Crime Prevention, 7*, 7–30.

Loeber, R. & Farrington, D. P. (2012). *From juvenile delinquency to adult crime: Criminal careers, justice policy, and prevention*. New York, NY: Oxford University Press.

Loeber, R., Farrington, D. P., Stouthamer-Loeber, M., Moffitt, T. E., Caspi, A., White, H. R., Wei, E. H., & Beyers, J. M. (2003). The development of male offending: Key findings from fourteen years of the Pittsburgh Youth Study. In T. P. Thornberry, M. D. Krohn, A. J. Lizotte, C. A. Smith, & K. Tobin (Eds.), *Taking stock of delinquency: An overview of findings from contemporary longitudinal studies* (pp. 93–136). New York, NY: Cambridge University Press.

Long, J. D., & Pellegrini, A. D. (2003). Studying change in dominance and bullying with linear mixed models. *School Psychology Review, 32*, 401–17.

Lovegrove, P. J. & Cornell, D. G. (2014). Patterns of bullying and victimization associated with other problem behaviors among high school students: A conditional latent class approach. *Journal of Crime and Justice, 37*, 5–22.

McNulty, T. L. & Bellair, P. E. (2003). Explaining racial and ethnic differences in adolescent violence: Structural disadvantage, family well-being, and social capital. *Justice Quarterly, 20*, 1–31.

Maxson, C. L. (1998). *Gang members on the move*. Washington, DC: Office of Juvenile Justice and Delinquency Prevention, *Juvenile Justice Bulletin* (October).

Maxson, C. L. & Klein, M. W. (1990). Street gang violence: Twice as great, or half as great? In C. R. Huff (Ed.), *Gangs in America*. 1st edition (pp. 71–100). Newbury Park, CA: Sage Publications.

Maxson, C. L. & Klein, M. W. (1995). Investigating gang structures. *Journal of Gang Research, 3*, 33–40.

Maxson, C. L. & Klein, M. W. (1996). Defining gang homicide: An updated look at member and motive approaches. In C. R. Huff (Ed.), *Gangs in America*. 2nd edition (pp. 3–20). Thousand Oaks, CA: Sage Publications.

Maxson, C. L. & Klein, M. W. (2001). Defining gang homicide: An updated look at the member and motive approaches. In J. Miller, C. L. Maxson, and M. W. Klein (Eds.), *The modern gang reader*. 2nd edition (pp. 173–85). Los Angeles, CA: Roxbury Publishing Company.

Maxson, C. L. & Whitlock, M. L. (2002). Joining the gang: Gender differences in risk factors for gang membership. In C. R. Huff (Ed.), *Gangs in America*. 3rd edition (pp. 19–36). Thousand Oaks, CA: Sage Publications.

Maxson, C. L., Whitlock, M. L., & Klein, M. W. (1998). Vulnerability to street gang membership: Implications for practice. *Social Service Review*, March, 70–91.

Melde, C. & Esbensen, F.-A. (2011). Gang membership as a turning point in the life course. *Criminology, 49*, 513–52.

Melde, C. & Esbensen, F.-A. (2014). The relative impact of gang status transitions: Identifying the mechanisms of change in delinquency. *Journal of Research in Crime and Delinquency, 51*, 349–76.

Menard, S. & Elliott, D. S. (1994). Delinquent bonding, moral beliefs, and illegal behavior: A three-wave panel model. *Justice Quarterly, 11*, 173–88.

Miller, J. (1998). Gender and victimization risk among young women in gangs. *Journal of Research in Crime and Delinquency, 35*, 429–53.

Miller, J. (2001). *One of the guys: Girls, gangs, and gender*. New York, NY: Oxford University Press.

Miller, J. & Decker, S. H. (2001). Young women and gang violence: Gender, street offending, and violent victimization in gangs. *Justice Quarterly, 18*, 115–40.

Miller, W. B. (1958) Lower-class culture as a generating milieu for gang delinquency. *Journal of Social Issues, 14*, 5–19.

Miller, W. B. (2001). *The growth of youth gang problems in the United States:1970–1998*. Washington DC: Office of Juvenile Justice and Delinquency Prevention.

Moore, J. (1991). *Going down to the barrio: Homeboys and homegirls in change*. Philadelphia, IL: Temple University Press.

Moore, J. & Hagedorn, J. M. (1996). What happens to girls in the gang. In C. R. Huff (Ed.), *Gangs in America*. 2nd edition (pp. 205–20). Thousand Oaks, CA: Sage Publications.

Moore, J. & Hagedorn, J. M. (2001). *Female gangs: A focus on research*. Washington, DC: Office of Juvenile Justice and Delinquency Prevention, *Juvenile Justice Bulletin* (March).

Mouttapa, M., Valente, T., Gallaher, P., Rohrbach, L. A., & Unger, J. B. (2004). Social network predictors of bullying and victimization. *Adolescence, 39*, 315–35.

Office of the Surgeon General. (2001). *Youth violence: A report of the Surgeon General*. Washington, DC: U.S. Public Health Service, Department of Health and Human Services.

Olweus, D. (1993). *Bullying at school: What we know and what we can do*. Oxford, UK: Basil Blackwell.

Olweus, D. (1996). Bully/victim problems in school. *Prospects, 26*, 331–59.

Olweus, D., Limber, S., & Mihalic, S. (1999). *Bullying prevention program: Blueprints for violence prevention, book nine*. Blueprints for Violence Prevention Series, ed. D.S. Elliott. Boulder, CO: Center for the Study and Prevention of Violence, Institute of Behavioral Science, University of Colorado.

O'Moore, M. (2000). Critical issues for teacher training to counter bullying and victimisation in Ireland. *Aggressive Behavior, 26*, 99–111.

Operation Safe Streets Street Gang Detail. (1995). L.A. style: A street gang manual of the Los Angeles County Sheriff's Department. In M.W. Klein, C.L. Maxson, & J. Miller (Eds.), *The modern gang reader* (pp. 34–45). Los Angeles, CA: Roxbury Publishing Company.

Pastore, A. L. & Maguire, K. (1996). *Sourcebook of criminal justice statistics 1995*. Washington DC: U.S. Department of Justice, Bureau of Justice Statistics.

Pastore, A. L. & Maguire, K. (2006). *Sourcebook of criminal justice statistics 2005*. Washington DC: U.S. Department of Justice, Bureau of Justice Statistics.

Pedersen, M. L., & Lindstadt, J. M. (2012). The Danish gang-joining project: Methodological issues and preliminary results. In F.-A. Esbensen & C. L. Maxson (Eds.), *Youth gangs in international perspective: Results from the Eurogang Program of Research* (pp. 239–50). New York, NY: Springer.

Perry, D. G., Kusel, S. J., & Perry, L. C. (1988). Victims of peer aggression. *Developmental Psychology, 10*, 426–41.

Peterson, D. & Carson, D.C. (2012). The sex composition of groups and youths' delinquency: A comparison of gang and nongang peer groups. In F.-A. Esbensen & C. L. Maxson (Eds.), *Youth gangs in international perspective: Results from the Eurogang Program of Research* (pp. 189–210). New York, NY: Springer.

Peterson, D. & Morgan, K. A. (2014). Sex differences and the overlap in youths' risk factors for onset of violence and gang involvement. *Journal of Crime & Justice, 37*, 129–54.

Peterson, D., Miller, J. & Esbensen, F.-A. (2001). The impact of sex composition on gangs and gang member delinquency. *Criminology, 39*, 411–40.

Peterson, D., Taylor, T. J., & Esbensen, F.-A. (2004). Gang membership and violent victimization. *Justice Quarterly, 21*, 793–815.

Puzzanchera, C. (2013). *Juvenile arrests 2011*. Washington, DC: U.S. Department of Justice, Office of Juvenile Justice and Delinquency Prevention.

Rigby, K. (2003). Consequences of bullying in Schools. *Canadian Journal of Psychiatry, 48*, 583–90.

Rigby, K. & Slee, P. T. (1991). Bullying among Australian school children: Reported behavior and attitudes towards victims. *The Journal of Social Psychology, 131*, 615–27.

Robers, S., Kemp, J., Rathbun, A., & Morgan, R. E. (2014). *Indicators of school crime and safety*. (NCES 2014–42/NCJ243299). Washington, DC: National Center for Education Statistics, U.S. Department of Education, and Bureau of Justice Statistics, Office of Justice Programs, U.S. Department of Justice.

Salmon, G., James, A., Smith, D. M. (1998). Bullying in schools: Self-reported anxiety, depression, and self-esteem in secondary school children. *British Medical Journal, 317*, 924–25

Schuster, B. (1996). Rejection, exclusion, and harassment at work and in schools: An integration of results from research on mobbing, bullying, and peer rejection. *European Psychologist, 1*, 293–317.

Seals, D. & Young, J. (2003). Bullying and victimization: Prevalence and relationship to gender, grade level, ethnicity, self-esteem, and depression. *Adolescence, 38*, 735–47.

Sellers, C. S., Winfree, L. T., Jr., & Griffiths, C. T. (1993). Legal attitudes, permissive norm qualities, and substance use: A comparison of American Indian and non-Indian youth. *Journal of Drug Issues, 23*, 493–513.

Sharp, C., Aldridge, J., & Medina, J. (2006). *Delinquent youth groups and offending behaviour: Findings from the 2004 Offending, Crime and Justice Survey*. London, UK: Home Office Online Report 14/06.

Short, J. F., Jr. & Strodbeck, F. L. (1966). *Group processes and gang delinquency*. Chicago, IL: University of Chicago Press.

Slee, P. T. & Rigby, K. (1993). The relationship of Eysenck's personality factors and self-esteem to bully victim behaviour in Australian school boys. *Personality and Individual Differences, 14*, 371–3.

Smokowski, P. R. & Kopasz, K. H. (2005). Bullying in school: An overview of types, effects, family characteristics, and intervention strategies. *Children & Schools, 27*, 101–10.

Snyder, H. N. (2003). *Juvenile arrests 2001*. Washington, DC: Office of Juvenile Justice and Delinquency Prevention, Juvenile Justice Bulletin.

Snyder, H. N., & Sickmund, M. (1999). *Juvenile offenders and victims: 1999 National Report*. Washington, DC: Office of Juvenile Justice and Delinquency Prevention (September).

Snyder, H. N., & Sickmund, M. (2006). *Juvenile offenders and victims: 2006 National Report*. Washington, DC: Office of Justice Programs, Office of Juvenile Justice and Delinquency Prevention (March).

Solberg, M. E., Olweus, D., & Endresen, I. M. (2007). Bullies and victims at school: Are they the same pupils? *British Journal of Educational Psychology, 77*, 441–64.

Sourander, A., Helstela, L., Helenius, H., & Piha, J. (2000). Persistence of bullying from childhood to adolescence—a longitudinal 8-year follow-up study. *Child Abuse & Neglect, 24*, 873–81.

Spergel, I. A. (1990). Youth gangs: Continuity and change. In M. Tonry & N. Morris (Eds.), *Crime and justice: A review of research*, vol. 12 (pp. 171–275). Chicago, IL: University of Chicago Press.

Starbuck, D., Howell, J. C., & Lindquist, D. J. (2001). *Hybrid and other modern gangs*. Washington, DC: Office of Juvenile Justice and Delinquency Prevention, *Juvenile Justice Bulletin* (December).

Steffensmeier, D., Schwartz, J., Zhong, H., & Ackerman, J. (2005). An assessment of recent trends in girls' violence using diverse longitudinal sources: Is the gender gap closing? *Criminology, 43*, 355–405.

Stockdale, M. S., Hangaduambo, S., Duys, D., Larson, K., & Sarvela, P. D. (2002). Rural elementary students', parents', and teachers' perceptions of bullying. *American Journal of Health Behavior, 26*, 266–77.

Swain, J. (1998). What does bullying really mean? *Educational Research, 40*, 358–64.

Thornberry, T. P. & Burch, J., II. (1997). *Gang members and delinquent behavior*. Washington, DC: Office of Juvenile Justice and Delinquency Prevention, *Juvenile Justice Bulletin* (June).

Thornberry, T. P., Huizinga, D., & Loeber, R. (1995). The prevention of serious delinquency and violence: Implications from the programs of research on the causes and correlates of delinquency. In J. C. Howell, B. Krisberg, J. D. Hawkins, & J. J. Wilson (Eds.), *Serious, violent, and chronic juvenile offenders* (pp. 213–37). Thousand Oaks, CA: Sage Publications.

Thornberry, T. P., Krohn, M. D., Lizotte, A. J., & Chard-Wierschem, D. (1993). The role of juvenile gangs in facilitating delinquent behavior. *Journal of Research in Crime and Delinquency, 30*, 55–87.

Thornberry, T. P., Krohn, M. D., Lizotte, A. J., Smith, C. A., & Tobin, K. (2003). *Gangs and delinquency in developmental perspective*. New York, NY: Cambridge University Press.

Thornton, T. N., Craft, C. A., Dahlberg, L. L., Lynch, B. S., & Baer, K. (2002). *Best practices of youth violence prevention: A sourcebook for community action*. Atlanta, GA: Centers for Disease Control and Prevention and National Center for Injury Prevention and Control.

Thrasher, F. M. (1927/1963). *The gang: A study of one thousand three hundred thirteen gangs in Chicago*. Chicago: University of Chicago Press.

Ttofi, M. M., & Farrington, D. P. (2008). Bullying: Short-term and long-term effects, and the importance of defiance theory in explanation and prevention. *Victims and Offenders, 3*, 289–312.

Tremblay, R. E., Vitaro, F., Nagin, D., Pagani, L., & Séguin, J. R. (2003). The Montreal longitudinal and experimental study: Rediscovering the power of descriptions. In T. P. Thornberry and M. D. Krohn (Eds.), *Taking stock of delinquency: An overview of findings from contemporary longitudinal studies* (pp. 205–54). New York, NY: Kluwer/Plenum Publishers.

Unnever, J. D., Cornell, D. G. (2003). Bullying, self-control, and ADHD. *Journal of Interpersonal Violence, 18*, 129–47.

Vigil, J. D. (1988). *Barrio gangs: Street life and identity in southern California*. Austin, TX: University of Texas Press.

Vigil, J. D. (2002). *A rainbow of gangs: Street cultures in the mega-city*. Austin, TX: University of Texas Press.

Walker, S., Spohn, C., & DeLone, M. (2003). *The color of justice*. Belmont, CA:Wadsworth.

Warr, M. (2002). *Companions in crime: The social aspects of criminal conduct*. New York, NY: Cambridge University Press.

Weerman, F. M. (2012). Are the correlates and effects of gang membership sex-specific? Troublesome youth groups and delinquency among Dutch girls. In F.-A. Esbensen & C. L. Maxson (Eds.), *Youth gangs in international perspective: Results from the Eurogang program of research* (pp. 271–90). New York, NY: Springer.

Weerman, F. M., Maxson, C. L., Esbensen, F.-A., Aldridge, J., Medina, J., & van Gemert, F. (2009). *Eurogang program manual: Background, development, and use of the Eurogang instruments in multi-site, multi-method comparative research.* St. Louis, MO: University of Missouri-St. Louis.

Wilbanks, W. (1987). *The myth of a racist criminal justice system.* Monterey, CA: Brooks/Cole.

Winfree, L. T., Jr., Esbensen, F.-A., & Osgood, D.W. (1996). A school-based gang prevention program and evaluation: From a theoretical perspective. *Evaluation Review, 20,* 181–203

Winfree, L. T., Jr., Mays, G. L., & Vigil-Backstrom, T. (1994). Youth gangs and incarcerated delinquents: Exploring the ties between gang membership, delinquency, and social learning theory. *Justice Quarterly, 11,* 229–55.

Wong, D. S.W., Loc, D. P. P., Lo, T.W., & Ma, S.W. (2008). School bullying among Hong Kong Chinese primary schoolchildren. *Youth & Society, 40,* 35–54.

Zimring, F. E. (1998). *American youth violence.* New York, NY: Oxford University Press.

Author Index

Subject Index

Page numbers followed by *b* indicates box, *f* indicates figure, *gf* indicates gang feature, *h* indicates highlight, *i* indicates image, and *t* indicates table.